SOCIAL PROBLEMS

A CANADIAN PERSPECTIVE

Lorne Tepperman
James Curtis

With the assistance of
Albert Kwan and Amy Withers

OXFORD

UNIVERSITY PRESS

1904 ❖ 2004

100 YEARS OF
CANADIAN PUBLISHING

OXFORD
UNIVERSITY PRESS

70 Wynford Drive, Don Mills, Ontario M3C 1J9
www.oup.com/ca

Oxford University Press is a department of the University of Oxford.
It furthers the University's objective of excellence in research, scholarship,
and education by publishing worldwide in

Oxford New York
Auckland Bangkok Buenos Aires Cape Town Chennai
Dar es Salaam Delhi Hong Kong Istanbul Karachi Kolkata
Kuala Lumpur Madrid Melbourne Mexico City Mumbai Nairobi
São Paulo Shanghai Taipei Tokyo Toronto

Oxford is a trade mark of Oxford University Press
in the UK and in certain other countries

Published in Canada
by Oxford University Press

National Library of Canada Cataloguing in Publication

Tepperman, Lorne, 1943–
Social problems : a Canadian perspective / by Lorne Tepperman, James Curtis ;
with the assistance of Albert Kwan and Amy Withers.

Includes bibliographical references and index.
ISBN 0-19-541649-X

1. Social problems. 2. Canada—Social conditions.
I. Curtis, James E., 1943– II. Title.

HN103.5.T46 2003   361.1   C2003-903672-3

Cover Design: Brett Miller

1 2 3 4 - 07 06 05 04
This book is printed on permanent (acid-free) paper .
Printed in Canada

Contents

Each chapter ends with Questions for Critical Thought, Recommended Readings, Recommended Web Sites, References, and a Glossary.

Preface

At the beginning of a book as large and wide-ranging as this one, it is necessary to lay out some ground rules, or basic assumptions. These assumptions guide the work in the book and show why it is organized as it is.

First, we assume there is such a thing as a 'social problem'. A social problem is any circumstance that many people experience and that has both social consequences and social causes. The social problem in each case actually exists. We can verify that fact with our own eyes and with the measurement tools of social science. Yet the social problem is also socially constructed, in the sense that people *think* it exists and tend to agree on this. They *define* it as a social problem. The condition in question has become a problem for people, and if they did not think it was a problem, it would cease being one, at least at the level of consciousness, social definition, and social action.

As a result of this socially constructed aspect of social problems, we can trace historically the rise and fall of social problems over time. We can study when people came to share the understanding that it was a problem. To take a simple example, few people in Canada today consider the so-called promiscuity of young women to be a social problem, although this was not the case in the past. Or consider, as another example, that few Canadians today see miscegenation—couples from two different races having sexual relations—as a social problem, although in earlier times many people considered this a serious problem.

Sociologists study why certain behaviours come to occupy our concern and evoke the label of 'social problem' while others do not. This takes us into the areas of changing morality and moral panics—sudden, intense, widespread, and often fleeting concerns about the immorality of one particular group.

Also of interest to sociologists, though, are social problems that can be shown to do major harm to our quality of life but that only a few people see as a problem and that government and other powerful agencies are doing little to address.

The social problems that are longest lasting and that evoke concern among the largest numbers of people are problems that are not merely socially constructed and, in that sense, problems 'in people's minds'. They are also serious matters of health, and of life and death. Poverty, racial discrimination, bad working conditions, domestic violence—these are all serious social problems because, at the extremes, they hurt or kill people. In less extreme circumstances, they increase illness and reduce people's well-being and quality of life. Increasingly, we live in what Ulrich Beck (1992) has called a *risk society*, in which we are all, always, in danger of harm from sources that are often hidden from view and beyond human control. Often these risks are a result of human activity, especially the applications of science and technology to the natural environment. Often they are a result of what we are taught to regard fondly as 'progress'.

So apart from the perceived immorality, injustice, or unfairness of the problems we will discuss in this book, serious social problems cost our society many human lives and many days lost from work and family life, as well as shattered families, workplace conflict, and destroyed hopes. These problems are not merely 'in people's minds'. In fact, the job of the sociologist, in these cases, is to bring them to people's conscious attention.

Sometimes people are unaware of the risks surrounding them because they have been taught—indeed, disciplined—to view the harmful as safe, the inhumane and dangerous as normal. To some degree, we are all victims of techniques of management and moral regulation that some, following Michel Foucault (2000), have called *governmentality*. Our trained unawareness and secret but effective regulation ensure that we will usually abide by the rules of society, thus protecting the advantage of those who are in power.

Social science has a poor batting average in solving human problems. It has not done well at bringing about change, as we will see. The problem here is in part the complexity of the roots of social problems and in part the will and ability of society's agencies of power to address the problems. Yet we, the authors of this book, assume that the purpose of sociology today, just as two centuries ago when sociology began, is to use knowledge to improve social life. Thus our goal in a book like this is to aid the understanding of the roots of social problems, their health consequences for individuals and society as a whole, and how these can be addressed. For this task, it is important to explore facts and theories concerning the ways in which problems develop and are maintained, and how problems are connected, one with another. We believe that these theories help us organize our facts and help us work toward solving our problems.

We will see that sociologists, like other social scientists, have a variety of theories about society and its social problems. Throughout this book, we will return to three sociological theories: structural functionalism, conflict theory, and symbolic interactionism. Each contributes important elements to our understanding of society and social problems. None rules out the validity or contribution of any other. Each of the theories approaches social life from a different standpoint, asking different questions and looking at different kinds of evidence. Therefore, each pays off for our understanding of social problems, in different ways. These approaches compete for our attention and loyalty. Sociologists tend to prefer and attach themselves to one approach rather than another. At the same time, applied sociologists go about analyzing and solving real-life problems in families, workplaces, organizations, and societies at large by combining insights from all three approaches.

We also introduce an additional, fourth perspective—the population health perspective—and employ it in each chapter. This perspective focuses attention on the harm to individuals caused by social problems and, thereby, on the harm caused to society. This perspective also emphasizes the social sources and consequences of people's illness and health. The population health perspective complements the other three perspectives: it not so much contradicts them as it adds to and extends them. It simply has a more explicit focus on the issues of the health of individuals and societies. All four of the theoretical approaches will be discussed in further detail.

We have organized this book to reflect our assumptions about social problems. We begin each chapter with a brief general introduction to the problem at hand. We then follow with a section containing some facts about the problem, setting the stage for our understanding of it. This section is not meant to replace other information about the problem from, for example, academic reports, newspapers, magazines, or television reportage. Facts in books such as this one must be somewhat selective, and they tend to age quickly. We therefore urge the reader to seek additional facts about all of the problems discussed in this book from other sources.

Next in each chapter, we review a range of theoretical approaches to the problem under discussion. We show how these approaches ask different questions and come to different conclusions. These theories help us organize our understanding of the problem. Since the theory sections are invariably brief, we urge the reader to explore further the assumptions and implications of the different approaches, as with much else in this book. Critical-thinking questions at the end of each chapter will help the reader do this.

After the theoretical approaches follows, in each chapter, a section on the social consequences of the social problem in question. As we shall see throughout this book (often by way of mild repetition), most of the social problems we discuss are connected to one another, some more closely than others. For example, there is no way to adequately discuss homelessness without discussing poverty, no way to discuss racial conflict without discussing discrimination and exclusion, and no way to discuss ageism without discussing stereotypes. A few general principles having to do with social inequality and social exclusion return time and again to inform our discussion.

Many serious social problems share a similar range of consequences. Problems such as exploitation, discrimination, and exclusion tend to impoverish people, isolate them, and give them less stake in the future of the community. The results of some social problems also commonly include crime, violence, addiction, stress, mental illness (for example, depression), and physical illness. We view these consequences as problems in their own right, and our goal would be for societies to solve them or at least reduce their prevalence. We therefore need to deal with the root causes of the social problems. These root causes are very much social. As sociologists, we need to explain what occurs and why, and suggest how this situation might be improved. As citizens, we should try to understand the problems and their roots, and do what we can to improve the situation—for ourselves and for our families in the future.

We should say a few final words about the purpose of a book as general as this one. This book duplicates some of what students have learned in their first course, or Introduction to Sociology. The duplication is intentional. We want to refresh your memory of the basic principles of sociology before proceeding to a close discussion of social problems. Some instructors may even find that this book can substitute for a book that introduces first-time students to the field of sociology. Additionally, this book covers a variety of problems, each briefly. This brevity is also intentional. We want to get students thinking in a particular way so that they can study these same problems, new problems, or changed problems on their own. We do not offer the last word on any social problem presented here—only the beginnings of a discussion informed by sociological principles.

We do not offer sociology as a panacea, or cure-all. We emphasize how very difficult many social problems have been to solve and how little has been done about some of them. Like many of our colleagues in sociology, we understand the concerns of postmodernity. The 'project' of modernization that engaged thinkers and social practitioners for much of the last three centuries has taken a new turn. The horrors of the twentieth century shook our faith in reason and in the power of humans to build a better world using science and technology, social legislation, mass media, higher education, and secular values. No one who spends a few moments thinking about the Holocaust, the two world wars, the terrorism of September 2001 and the ensuing war in Afghanistan, environmental destruction, and practices of imperialist domination will readily indulge fantasies about the perfection, or even the perfectibility, of human societies. Part of the reason for this is that the solutions to social problems are often complex and costly. Another reason is that the solutions are political matters requiring strong commitment from society's elites.

In this respect, one of sociology's three founders was more prescient than the others. Sociologist Max Weber saw the nightmare of modern society coming. His eyes were open to the 'iron cage' of modernity, especially to how bureaucracies and governments can enslave and torment humans more effectively than had ever been known before. Weber believed that bureaucracies would become all-powerful in society, that their elites would end up largely serving their own interests, very often contrary to the interest of average people. Only those problems and solutions seen as important by powerful interests would be addressed in societies of the future (that is, in our time now). Another founder of sociology, Karl Marx, believed that communism would solve all problems of the human condition. He appears to have been wrong, although some still argue that his theories have never been put to a proper test in any society. Émile Durkheim was, of sociology's three founders, the most optimistic, and therefore the most wrong about the twentieth century. He believed that societies change in a progressive direction, solving social problems over time through the differentiation and specialization of tasks, with modest negative side effects of *anomie*, or alienation on the part of individuals because of the processes of social change.

Yet, as human beings shaken by the twentieth century and its horrors, we persist in our efforts. As long as we live, most of us strive to build a better world for ourselves, our children, our community. It is in the hopes of continuing this optimistic effort that we have written this book. We believe that social problems really do exist and really do do great harm. Furthermore, we believe that knowledge and purposeful informed action may still improve human life. This, then, is where we begin our study of social problems.

Pedagogical Features and Ancillaries

Pedagogical Features

A number of pedagogical features have been incorporated into the text in order to make it a more effective learning tool for students. Each chapter includes the following components:

- Chapter Objectives
- an introduction that sets the contents of the chapter in a wider context
- a conclusion that summarizes key points discussed in the chapter
- Questions for Critical Thought

- annotated Recommended Readings
- annotated Recommended Web Sites
- a glossary
- references

An appendix about research methods in sociology is included at the end of the text.

The text's well-developed art program is designed to make the book more accessible and engaging. Twenty-three photographs, 41 figures and charts, 19 tables, and 44 boxed inserts covering the full range of subject matter help clarify important concepts and make the subject come alive.

Ancillaries

Test Bank
A Test Bank is available to instructors adopting the text. Each chapter in the Test Bank contains the following: 20 multiple-choice questions, 10 true/false questions, 10 short-answer questions, and 10 discussion questions.

Instructor's Manual
An Instructor's Manual is also available to adopters. Each chapter in the Instructor's Manual contains the following: chapter table of contents, summary, 5–10 learning objectives, 10 key concepts, and 10 audiovisual materials and teaching aids.

Instructors should contact their Oxford University Press representative regarding ancillary materials.

References

Beck, Ulrich. 1992. *Risk Society: Towards a New Modernity*. Translated by Mark Ritter. London: Sage.

Foucault, Michel. 2000. *Power*. Translated by Robert Hurley et al. New York: New Press.

What Are Social Problems?

Chapter Objectives

After reading this chapter the student should understand:
- what a social problem is
- how sociologists conceptualize the sociological imagination
- how researchers conceive of social change
- the importance of the historical context of social problems
- the meaning of social structure and culture
- how information can be seen as a valuable resource
- the theories that sociologists employ as lenses to magnify and hide aspects of social problems

What Is a 'Social Problem'?

When you hear the words **social problem**, what do you think of? Juvenile delinquents? Drug addicts? Homeless people? Sex workers? Or do you think about insider trading, tax fraud, arms sales, and the mass marketing of junk food? How about witchcraft, devil worship and interplanetary abduction, celebrity sex scandals, and the secret lives of powerful people? The words *social problem* are often applied to each of these topics and more.

Sociologists sometimes differ in what they believe constitutes a social problem. Certainly the definition of *social problem* is neither static nor absolute, and it has changed according to social and historical context. Moreover, even within a specific context, the definition people accept is based on both objective and subjective factors.

Objective factors refer to the existence of a social condition. The condition is a reality; it exists, and we can see that it is hurting people. We can study its effects without necessarily making any moral judgment. Occurrences of sexual abuse, environmental pollution, and racially motivated hate crimes in society are examples, however sobering, of such problems. They hap-

pen. As sociologists, we study what changes in social life cause the numbers or rates of these occurrences to go up and down.

Subjective factors refers to people's *evaluations* of the situation. These factors include people's application of moral labels ('wrong', 'immoral', and so on) to particular acts or situations, as well as people's accounts of the reasons for these acts and situations. These definitions and accounts are generally accompanied by the **belief** that something should be done about the problems, that we should try to change these circumstances for the better. For example, most people in Canadian society today view rape, deforestation, and lynching as wrong and in need of eradication. This reflects their subjective valuation of these acts and situations as inappropriate in their society.

Thinking only of the subjective or evaluative process, one response to the question 'What is a social problem?' would be 'It depends'—on historical and cultural contexts, on people's **values** and beliefs. Taking this approach, although the specifics may vary from one group to the next, most sociologists would define a *social problem* as a social condition or behavioural pattern that a sizeable portion of society views as harmful and warranting collective action to remedy. Bringing together both the objective and subjective elements, we can define a social problem as both a condition—an empirically observed condition that threatens the well-being of a significant segment of society—and as a process—the process of identification and definition by which members of society come to see a condition as a social problem.

So, in response to the question 'Do social problems really exist?' there are two answers: Yes, and yes. Yes, many social conditions have observably harmful effects. And yes, people believe that the conditions they have singled out as social problems cause harm and ought not to occur frequently.

Why Study Social Problems?

To anyone concerned with the state of the society in which they live, the answer to this question should be obvious. If social problems harm our social environment, a sense of civic duty directs us to be at least aware of these conditions or, better yet, to be actively involved in their correction.

Beyond this, studying social problems from a sociological perspective helps people to understand the complex ways in which social structure interacts with and influences members of society. It allows people to move beyond a purely common-sense approach to understanding their social environment. It allows them to use more powerful methods of investigation that reveal the multi-layered, multi-faceted, and elaborate ways that the social world around them—local, national, and global—is interconnected.

The formal processes by which such sociological study is undertaken (discussed in detail in the appendix) allow researchers to generate hypotheses, carry out experiments in controlled conditions (as much as possible), gather objective evidence, and draw careful and sound conclusions. We can then formulate theories or explanations from which we can hope to derive practical solutions and policies. Further, at the bottom of this research is an approach we call the *sociological imagination*. This approach can be of great use to us in most aspects of our lives.

Social Problems and the Sociological Imagination

According to sociologist C. Wright Mills (1959), the **sociological imagination** is the ability to see connections between one's personal life and the social world in which one lives. This relationship between close-to-home aspects of social life and broad social trends, between private troubles and public issues, is the core subject matter of sociology. Further, this relationship is one of the most important things we need to know about if we want to understand how social problems affect our lives.

To use Mills's example, unemployed people may view their lack of employment as a private trouble that involves only them, their immediate family members, and their friends. They brought the problem on themselves, they may think. In fact, however, widespread unemployment—often the source of the individual's own private trouble, multiplied several-thousand-fold across other people's lives, too—is caused by factors such as economic recession, corporate downsizing, and advances in technology that replace people with machines. In fact, plant closings and the resulting unemployment are part of a workplace struggle between workers and the people who own and manage workplaces (Zipp and Lane, 1987).

The public aspect of the problem does not end there; it extends into later generations. Parental unemployment, along with a variety of family factors such as parental divorce, low parental affective involvement, and adolescent relationship problems, is more likely to lead to youth unemployment than are individual (personal) variables such as educational career and work commitment (de Goede et al., 2000).

Thus, unemployment is not merely a private trouble. It is also a public issue. The process is similar for other social problems—crime and victimization, family issues, poverty, drug abuse, pollution, racism. The sociological imagination means stepping back to consider one's own place in the big picture in order to make the connection between the conditions of one's own life and the larger social context in which one plays out that life.

Sociologists make these connections by considering two levels of analysis, that is, by looking closely at two kinds of things. **Microsociology**, or *micro-level analysis*, focuses on the interaction between individuals in small groups. This approach, which investigates people's understanding and experience of social problems at the local, personal level, is similar to that used by social psychologists. **Macrosociology**, or *macro-level analysis*, focuses on the societal level. It explores the ways in which the processes and social trends occurring within major bureaucratic organizations and social **institutions**, such as the economy or the government, affect the population as a whole. We need both levels of understanding for a proper understanding of social problems, and for seeing that many private troubles are essentially public issues.

Social Problems Research as a Moral Enterprise

Sociology is, for the most part, an engaged, progressive, and optimistic discipline founded on the notion that people can improve society through research and the application of research-based knowledge. Accordingly, many sociologists focus on research aimed at preventing genocide, fighting hunger, ending violence, reducing inequalities, and expanding democratic choices to create more freedom, pleasure, and power in individual lives ('Utopian Visions', 2000).

Paradoxically, people's efforts to improve society sometimes backfire. Modernization itself and its associated social systems and techniques, such as the economic market system and bureaucratic organization, not only leave fundamental problems unresolved, they lack adequate problem-solving mechanisms to ensure that we preserve life and quality of life. The cost may be mass deaths and even genocide—realities in the twentieth century (Wallimann, 1994). As others have remarked, modernization also carries harsh costs for the natural environment; we will discuss these costs in later chapters.

Five social innovations of the past millennium that people designed to solve problems have brought new problems that threaten all of our lives. These five innovations are the amoral state, the imperialistic corporation, the feudal crime organization, relativistic culture, and the self-interested individual (Montgomery, 1998). We will discuss each of these in the chapters that follow. As we will see, it will take more than a single unified policy of action to correct these five innovations and the problems they create.

Sociologists who study social problems often think of themselves as engaged in a moral enterprise whose goal is to improve human societies through social change (Alvarez, 2001). Much of the research that sociologists do on social problems is guided by seven value preferences:

- life over death
- health over sickness
- knowing over not knowing
- cooperation over conflict
- freedom of movement over physical restraint
- self-determination over direction by others
- freedom of expression over restraint of communication

As a result, much of the research on social problems criticizes the existing social order.

Criticizing the Social Order

Much of the social problems literature shows a desire to change society, protect the vulnerable, and redress injustices. So, for example, Jim MacLaughlin (1996) writes about the ideological roots of anti-Traveller (that is, anti-Gypsy) sentiment in Ireland and its consequences for the health and social exclusion of these people, and

Emery Castle (1995) writes about the hidden complexity and vulnerability of rural society in North America and the tendency to ignore rural problems because of stereotypes of and mythology about rural life.

Like much research in the field of social problems, these authors are often concerned with myths, ideologies, and stereotypes—for example, about Gypsies or rural people—that perpetuate harmful conditions for vulnerable peoples. A related concern is the frequently observed tendency for 'public issues' to be turned into 'private troubles'. The public and public officials often wrongly see a social problem as the personal responsibility of the sufferers, who are blamed for having these problems.

Consider depressive disorders, which are a major public health problem today. They occur frequently and produce severe suffering for the people affected and their families, leading to higher risks of death, disability, and secondary illness. For various reasons, including the aging of the population and the extended life expectancy of people suffering from chronic physical disorders, the frequency of depressive disorders will increase in years to come (Sartorius, 2001).

Chronic pain is another increasingly common condition, and one that is sending ever more people in search of complementary and alternative medical treatments. It may be related to childhood trauma (Bell, Schjødt, and Paulsberg, 2000). Chronic fatigue also appears to have complex social and psychological roots. Chronically fatigued people are often older and have worse health histories than people who are only occasionally fatigued. They also have a distinctive social profile: their educational level, occupational classification, and income are lower than those of people who are not chronically fatigued, and they are more often unemployed. As well, chronically fatigued women are more often divorced or widowed than non-chronically fatigued women (Van Mens-Verhulst and Bensing, 1998). There are social, and not only psychological and biological, roots to these conditions. That makes them public issues, not merely private troubles.

Social problems researchers often express concern that sufferers are dealing with their problems in idiosyncratic ways that may not work as wanted. Michael Montagne (1992), for example, notes that the medicalization of poorly defined health disorders—depression, chronic pain, and chronic fatigue, but also male pattern baldness, small women's breasts, and obesity—have led to increased self-medication. When biomedical explanations and remedies fail to help, consumers are prompted to self-medicate to achieve symptomatic relief. Self-medication may include the excessive use of drugs and alcohol, often with harmful outcomes. For example, alcoholism, birth defects, drunk driving, fighting, and rowdy behaviour, along with health problems such as liver disease, are all common results of drinking too much distilled spirits and beer. Even excessive wine consumption has these effects, though fewer people recognize it (Klein and Pittman, 1998).

The social costs of self-medication are huge, especially when they include the use of addictive drugs, such as opiates. Though most people view the regular use of opiates as a social and health problem, they rarely stop to estimate the cost. One survey aimed at estimating the social costs of untreated opiate addiction in Toronto (Wall et al., 2000) established that the annual social cost generated by a sample of 114 regular opiate users amounted to more than $5 million. The costs break down as follows: crime victimization (45 per cent), law enforcement (42 per cent), productivity losses (7 per cent), and health care use (6 per cent). Given roughly 8,000 to 13,000 opiate users in Toronto, the estimated social cost of this addiction is between $43 and $69 per Toronto resident per year.

Institutional Critique

Some social problems researchers criticize society's dominant institutions for their failure to recognize, fund, or deal adequately with important problems. They argue that these actions should be taken, and that the right actions at the right time can have enormous effects. As an example of the latter, consider workplace smoking bans. Where these have been implemented, they have succeeded in bringing about changes in the behaviour and attitudes of smokers. Moreover, smokers' levels of acceptance of these regulations increase following their adoption, and attitude changes follow changes in behaviour. Thus, large-scale patterns of constraints and opportunities that influence choices and actions *do* affect harmful behaviours and attitudes (Owen, Borland, and Hill, 1991).

However, dominant institutions often fail to act as effectively as they should. Often, they insufficiently fund useful programs. For example, Lisbeth Schorr (1991) notes that the kinds of programs that work best in reducing problems of teenagers—high rates of school dropout, pregnancy, violent crime, and the beginnings of long-term dependency on welfare—give access to a variety of services, emphasize trust and respect, are community based, and recognize the needs of those most at risk. However, such programs are at odds with the health, mental health, social service, and educational institutions that might provide such services and with the government institutions that fund them.

Evaluating Social Structure

Social problems researchers point out the social-structural conditions that make people vulnerable. Consider medical patients and their needs for social support. Some suffer from *social insufficiency*—inadequate networks of social support and the incapacity of their familiar surroundings to guarantee and satisfy all their needs (Carmona et al., 1999). Homeless people are another vulnerable population with an insufficiency of social supports. They typically suffer from a variety of problems, including unemployment, poverty, physical impairments, substance abuse, and

mental illness. Mental disorders are just one of several factors contributing to the process by which they become homeless, although, by one estimate, two-thirds suffer from mental illness. No less important is their social isolation and the insufficiency of assistance they receive as outpatients (Kellinghaus et al., 1999).

Social problems researchers point out social-structural factors that increase the likelihood of problem behaviours. For example, peer influences are highly associated with health-risk behaviours, including early and risky sexual activity, tobacco use, alcohol use, and marijuana use (Beal, Ausiello, and Perrin, 2001). Risky sexual behaviour may lead to teenage parenthood, which reduces the likelihood of school completion and economic independence (Hoffman, Foster, and Furstenburg, 1993). Dropping out of school early also substantially increases the risk of early parenthood (Gest, Mahoney, and Cairns, 1999), as do low socio-economic **status**, low academic achievement, and low popularity.

Identifying New Problems

Social problems researchers also point out new problems that, if left unattended, may become large problems in the future. Here are a few examples:

- *Genetic engineering.* Potential problems include the creation and subsequent escape from the laboratory of dangerous biological forms, uncontrollable experimentation, and the emergence of a new eugenics movement (McFalls et al., 1987).
- *Unregulated antibiotics.* The misuse of antibiotics by physicians, pharmacists, and the public, the emergence of poor-quality drugs, and conditions such as crowding, lack of hygiene, and poor hospital infection control lead to the evolution and global spread of new, resistant bacteria (Isturiz and Carbon, 2000).
- *Manufactured longevity.* Advances in biomedical sciences that add more years to life

expectancy in industrial countries result in unprecedented rates of survival into older ages and produce new issues of caregiving (including family organization) and quality of life (Hassan, 2000).

- *Global refugees.* More than 15 million refugees are scattered around the world, most of them in less developed countries. Suffering from a variety of social, economic, psychological, and health problems, they threaten to destabilize the countries that have granted them asylum (Clinton-Davis and Fassil, 1992), and refugee camps may serve as seedbeds for violent terrorism.

Warnings, Panics, and Claims

Warnings surround us—about cancer, HIV/AIDS, rape, and mental illness, among other things— and some think that these warnings increase stress and damage interpersonal relations. Public discussion of harm and harm prevention has increased for a variety of reasons: more emphasis on litigation in everyday life, more emphasis on medicine, the development of interest groups around illnesses and social problems, and a growing respect for science and technology (Reinharz, 1997).

Many issues that we are concerned about today are issues that people were less concerned about—or unconcerned about—50 years ago. For example, today we all consider family violence (Walker, 1990), child sexual abuse (Scott, 1995), and preoccupations with fatness and thinness (Sobal and Maurer, 1999) to be legitimate social problems that require public attention. They 'became' problems not because their occurrence increased, but because people became more concerned about them. In that sense, people constructed them as social problems in the last 50 years. These problems all required 'construction' to gain public attention. Today, other problems are currently under construction, including concerns about workplace violence (Mullen, 1997),

stalking (Emerson, Ferris, and Gardner, 1998; Morewitz, 2001), money laundering (Nichols, 1997), the failure to disclose homosexuality (Cain, 1989), and drowsiness, or sleep disorder (Kroll-Smith, 2000).

People construct social problems when they lead other people to feel concern about a given condition. A problem so constructed may not bear a close relationship with the concrete harm or damage that the condition causes. So, for example, workplace violence, child pornography, and school bullying are all issues that some people view as important problems in need of construction; however, many people believe these problems rarely occur or rarely do much harm.

Some perceived problems generate intense feelings of concern that, viewed from a distance, are more than one might expect from the actual harm posed by the threat. In some parts of the population, abortion and welfare fraud fall into that category. Another example is the recent concern over witchcraft, devil worship, and satanic rituals (see, for example, Lippert, 1990). Sociologists refer to short-lived, intense periods of concern as *moral panics*, and to the people held responsible for the perceived threats as *folk devils*. Though moral panics, like fads, are short-lived, they generally leave a legacy, whether as laws, stereotypes, cultural beliefs, or changed attitudes (Goode and Ben Yahuda, 1994).

The notion of *social construction* implies that we are building or inventing something. Sometimes, construction means making up 'types' of people with simplified composite features (Kroll-Smith, 2000), for example, 'welfare bums'. Often it involves stereotyping and classifying some people as deviants (Goode and Ben Yahuda, 1994). People whom sociologists call **moral entrepreneurs** do this construction work; they may be members of the grassroots community, elites, or interest groups. The process of constructing problems and folk devils involves *claims-making*, a process that describes, explains, and blames people who are involved with the problem.

Claims-making relies on common rhetorical idioms and claims-making styles that reflect and legitimize core cultural values (McMullan and Eyles, 1999). Often the rhetoric used invokes certain types of risk and risk avoidance as pre-eminent goals. For example, we often call upon people to take action to protect their country, their children's health, or their community. Particular images or icons may be used to sway public opinion. The media play a large part in shaping public opinion of a problem. In fact, popular perceptions and beliefs today are more often shaped by media depiction than by personal experience, so how the media depict a problem plays a crucial part in how the public will respond (Szasz, 1995). Part of the media's influence comes through putting 'problems' on the agenda for repeated discussion in news reports. Some comes through portraying the problem in particular ways, with heroes and villains in fictionalized stories. Some media portrayal is implicit, as in soap operas and talk shows. We learn community standards of behaviour—what is deviant and normal, praiseworthy and shocking—as members of the audience for as the 'shameless world' of TV talk shows (Abt, 1996). Here, the hosts are moral entrepreneurs and claims-makers, but the studio audience (and the home audience) is the court of public opinion.

Ordinary people make some of the claims. We all learn how to tell stories that describe or explain problems, and how to blame others for these problems; however, some people learn these skills particularly well. For example, high school debaters learn how to take both sides of an argument, express ideas with which they do not personally agree, and present powerful if sometimes questionable evidence. This teaches them how to engage in social problem discourse and trains them for moral entrepreneurship (Fine, 2000). They then hone these skills in law schools across the nation.

Interest groups that have a particular view of the problem and its solution make some of the claims. For example, COYOTE (Call Off Your Old Tired Ethics) has aided in redefining prostitution as a social problem, removing it from the arenas of sin and crime. COYOTE proposes that prostitution should be considered work, not crime; that prostitutes choose to work at their occupation; and that we should protect that occupation, as work that people have a right to choose, like any other respectable service occupation. This organization has achieved success by becoming a link between public health agencies and sex workers, connecting the problems of prostitutes to women's rights issues, and engaging law enforcement groups in debate over criminal laws (Jenness, 1990).

The organization FARM has been less successful in influencing public opinion. With the ultimate goal of eliminating the use of cows, pigs, and chickens as human food, FARM (Farm Animal Reform Movement) adopted the short-term goal of reducing the suffering of farm animals by eliminating factories that use modern intensive farming techniques. However, claims about the suffering of animals did not persuade the public, so FARM began, in the early 1990s, to focus attention on personal health, longevity, and environmental endangerment in their rationale for rejecting factory farming. These claims gained wider support for the organization, though it has not yet succeeded in its long-term goals (Kunkel, 1995).

In the past, religious leaders were heavily involved in moral claims-making. Today, they have an ever-diminishing influence in this regard, at least in Canada. People with professional and scientific expertise are much more often allowed to make claims. For example, increasingly since the 1980s, police elites (for example, chief constables) have gained the power to legitimately name, diagnose, and classify social problems (Loader and Mulcahy, 2001).

Medical doctors have continued to exercise control over the definition of many personal and social problems. Medical claims-makers concentrate on detecting, diagnosing, and treating problems of vulnerable people in terms of their own bodies and lives. In emergency homeless shelters, for example, they teach homeless people to look within themselves for the cause of their homelessness, and 'treatment' concentrates on reforming and governing the self (Lyon-Callo, 2000). Adolescent episodes of 'acting up' and 'acting out' have been medicalized under the rubric of *conduct disorder*, a psychiatric category with broad professional diagnostic criteria (Potter, 2000). Implicit in such a medical assessment is the notion that we can study and fix teen misbehaviour without reference to the social or interaction context within which it occurs.

Sometimes, organization insiders (for example, in nuclear power or tobacco)—called *whistle-blowers*—aid in claims-making. Whistle-blowers are unusual claims-makers in that they gain credibility for speaking out contrary to their own interests and those of their employer, but they lack the organizational power to promote their definitions of the social problem. A few prominent whistle-blowers, blacklisted in their industries, turn to social movement organizations for employment (Bernstein, 1991).

Since social problems arise out of claims-making, and since claims-making is a social activity that occurs within a historical context, we must understand the construction and spread of social problems within their historical context.

The Historical Context of Social Problems

Many issues that were considered social problems a century ago have changed considerably since then. This is most clear in areas of human activity that give pleasure (such as sex) or alter consciousness (such as drugs). The definition of *social problems* has changed dramatically over time in these battlegrounds.

In England during the early Industrial Revolution, for example, there was a surge in gin drinking that some called a 'gin epidemic'. The underlying problems were overcrowding and poverty, both of which led to social unrest. This unrest led to increased drunkenness when cheap

gin became available after Parliament did away with the distilling monopolies that had kept prices high. Reformers, ignoring the social causes of unrest, focused their attention on gin drinking by the poor. They feared it would endanger England's wealth by weakening its labour force and reducing its workforce. The response was to pass a Gin Act in 1743 and a Tippling Act in 1751 that raised gin prices and reduced consumption (Abel, 2001).

In the United States, the pattern was different, though it also varied over time. In the seventeenth and eighteenth centuries, almost everyone held alcohol in high regard and consumed it. Campaigns against alcohol began in the nineteenth century, with temperance supporters holding alcohol responsible for most major social problems. They were briefly successful in having alcohol prohibited in the 1920s, a topic we discuss in chapter 2, on alcohol and drug abuse.

Since the 1930s, the focus of national concern has been on the treatment of alcoholics. As in eighteenth-century England and the nineteenth-century United States, most people today continue to blame drinking and individual weaknesses for many problems that have broader political and economic causes (Levine, 1984).

In North America today, many people still fear epidemics of drug-induced misbehaviour. Two centuries ago in England, it was the gin epidemic. In the 1980s and 1990s, it was the 'crack attack', a supposed epidemic of drug abuse. Drug scares today are characterized by anti-drug extremism, by the association of a certain drug with various social problems, and by the linking of that same drug to a subordinate minority group. In the crack scare, between 1986 and 1992, drug use was used as a scapegoat to account for lower-class unemployment, poverty, violence, and crime. This served to explain away growing urban poverty without requiring politicians to address the real issues. The scare had secondary consequences, including increases in drug use resulting from exaggerated and dramatized media coverage, declines in health services aimed at helping addicts, and neglect of the social problems that inspire drug use (Reinarman and Levine, 1995).

Abortion is another area in which the definition of a social problem has changed over time. In the mid-nineteenth century, the United States criminalized a previously unregulated practice of abortion; in the early twentieth century, Sweden liberalized a previously harsh law against abortion. These diametrically opposed policies were based on different understandings of abortion. Today, Sweden remains one of the most liberal countries where abortion—and sexuality more generally—is concerned (Linders, 1998). The United States has decriminalized abortion, but abortion is still hard to obtain in some regions and the topic remains morally charged in many parts of the country.

Along similar lines, out-of-wedlock pregnancy (including illegitimacy, or 'bastardy') changed its public meaning in Canada and the United States in the last half of the twentieth century. Today, most people no longer view the pregnancy of single women as morally reprehensible; however, views and policies vary somewhat depending on the pregnant woman's race (Solinger, 1992). Poor black women are viewed somewhat more critically than poor white women, let alone middle-class white women, and teenage mothers are viewed most critically of all.

Rates of teenage pregnancy are high and increasing in the United States compared to other industrial nations. Americans, accordingly, are much more likely than Canadians or the Dutch to view unplanned pregnancy as a 'very big problem' (Delbanco et al., 1997). Two-thirds of Americans mistakenly believe that more women have unplanned pregnancies today than 10 years ago (Mauldon and Belbanco, 1997); in fact, it is only the teenage portion that is increasing. Researchers relate this latter trend to poverty, hopelessness, and an absence of sex education in the schools.

Considering these changes in sexual behaviour, social conservatives have called for a renewal of 'family values'. For example, David Popenoe (1993) states that American family decline since 1960 has been extraordinarily steep and its social consequences serious, especially for children. He argues that families have lost functions, power, and authority; that familism as a cultural value has diminished; and that people have become less willing to invest time, money, and energy in family life, turning instead to investment in themselves. Some commentators have responded by saying that such diagnoses of moral and social decline are wrong and have harmful consequences. These diagnoses divide people into righteous 'us' and wicked 'them', and when these lines are drawn, they throw progressive thinking and social justice out the window (Morone, 1996).

These brief examples illustrate the point that historical changes in the perception and treatment of social issues—changes in their problematization and normalization over time—are often connected to social and cultural conflicts in the society. Often these conflicts are over major changes in social inequality, whether in respect to social class inequality, ethnic and racial inequality, age inequality, or gender inequality. As groups conflict, people use moral rhetoric to exclude, punish, and blame one another. The most powerful often penalize the least powerful.

Often the rhetoric used is particular to the **culture** and period. So, for example, themes involving health and purity were common to many movements against alcohol, drugs, smoking, and sex in the last century or two (Wagner, 1995). Increasingly, with the rise to dominance of science and medicine, we have seen *medicalized social problems*: social problems are often cast in an individualistic medical model. The patient is blamed for his or her sickness, and then told to change. Occasionally, solutions to social problems are cast in the *public health mode*: the goal is to prevent the illness through social or personal action and, if necessary, reduce the harm associated with it.

The tendency to medicalize problems is also congruent with the individualistic tendency in our culture that holds people responsible for their own success and failure. For many, 'self-esteem' and 'self-help' are held to be the keys to overcoming both personal problems and social problems. In pop psychology, all social problems are thought to stem from relationships and from problems between individuals (Cravens, 1997). This approach emphasizes self-efficacy and self-esteem as personal attributes, independent of such aspects of social structure as control over and access to power and the social resources that individuals need to take certain actions (Franzblau and Moore, 2001).

In this book, we will see that to understand social problems and their history, we must understand the social structures within which they rise, flower, and fall.

Social Organization, Culture, and Social Problems

Sociology is the study of social organization and culture. **Social organization** is any enduring, predictable pattern of social relations among people in society. This is the basic organization of a society, and it takes form in social institutions, formal organizations, smaller **social groups**, and **roles**. *Social institutions*—stable, well-acknowledged large-scale social relationships that endure over time—include family, the economy, education, politics, religion, mass media, medicine, and science and technology. They provide the bedrock on which people base the rest of social life.

Social institutions are made up of *social groups*, two or more individuals who have a specific, common identity and who interact in a reciprocal *social relationship*. The associations between politician and constituent member, doctor and patient, teacher and student, and parent and child are examples of social relationships that characterize political, medical, educational, and familial social groups and organizations. In turn, these social groups and organizations sum across whole populations to form their respective social institutions.

Social organization refers to how society is organized, from a dyadic (two-person) relationship all the way up to a broad social institution. **Culture**, in contrast, refers to the meanings and lifestyles constructed by human populations. These include beliefs, values, **symbols**, and **norms**. Together, these elements differentiate human populations into unique societies.

Social organization and culture are double-edged swords with respect to social problems. They are centrally implicated in the development and maintenance of social problems, and they hold hope, in the form of socio-cultural change directed by human collective action, for solutions to social problems. Society and culture also define how we come to think about our own personal troubles and the social problems that they exemplify.

Four aspects of social organization and culture seem to limit people's opportunities to obtain what they want out of life, whether it is to get out of poverty and continue to avoid it or to escape other negative situations. These mechanisms that cause an individual's continued involvement with social problems are *exclusion*, *disability*, *decoupling*, and *scarcity*.

Exclusion

Power is often used to exclude people from desirable situations, and **exclusion** rewards people unequally for equal performances. Organizations practise exclusion against other organizations, ethnic groups practise it against other ethnic groups, social classes practise it against other classes, and individuals practise it against other individuals. Every type of exclusion, whether motivated by fear, stereotyping, or mere economic interest, is an exercise of power.

If power is nothing else, it is the ability to make rules about who will get the biggest share of social goods: wealth, authority, and prestige (Murphy, 1982). Every group has an elite; the top few per cent in a society, business, university, or political party is that group's elite. The idea of a fixed group of people dominating politics and economics goes against the view that Canadians are equal, but the first idea is the correct one. As John Porter (1965) and Wallace Clement (1975) have demonstrated, there is a socially cohesive Canadian ruling class. The corporate elite owns and controls the largest businesses. It contributes to political campaigns, lobbies elected officials, and influences the media—which it owns. The elite can also embarrass politicians by publicly questioning their competence or honesty.

Not only social classes but also ethnic and religious communities use exclusion to protect themselves and advance their own interests. Minority ethnic communities differ as much from one another as they do from the dominant white Anglo or francophone communities. However, some groups face serious discrimination on their arrival in Canada. Accordingly, they organize themselves differently, using **institutional completeness**, to retain their identity and maintain group survival (Breton et al., 1990). For some groups, residential or occupational segregation may be most important. However, retention and use of the ethnic language also plays a key part in keeping the community together.

The expectation that ethnic occupational inequality would diminish or disappear as ethnic groups acquired educational credentials and became culturally assimilated into Canadian society has proved illusory. Investing in human capital (for example, higher education) has not led to equality for racial minorities. Many, especially Native peoples, who have been the targets of aggressive policies intended to bring about their assimilation, have resisted and survived as distinct peoples. Most ethnic and racial minorities are still not represented among the economic elite. Again, this is particularly true of visible minorities.

This is not to deny that some ethnic communities and some individuals within those communities have prospered. The strategy that the most successful among them have employed, both to insulate their members and to promote their interests in the wider community, is the practice of exclusion. Aboriginal peoples, however, have

little opportunity to practice exclusion in their own interest. Although there has been considerable progress in educational achievement, employment, and income over time, the picture is not as positive as that of white Canadians. While the number of Aboriginal people completing high school has increased since the 1960s, racial differences at the postsecondary level remain large. Furthermore, education does not produce the same income returns for Aboriginal people as for whites. So although more Aboriginal men and women have moved into the middle class, economic opportunities for Aboriginal and white Canadians remain unequal.

We also find exclusion in the job market, where professional associations and unions use exclusionary practices to protect their members, their jobs, and their salaries. Degrees from medical schools are particularly valuable in this way since almost no doctors are unemployed or poorly paid. We see exclusion at work in the continuing battles over health care—the debates about who shall pay and who is entitled to receive how much, and the exclusion of such competitors as chiropractors, homeopaths, and midwives from public recognition and coverage under public health plans. Professional associations help middle-class people protect middle-class incomes; unions help working-class people protect working-class incomes. Professional associations use special means to protect their members. The example of medicine shows that successful professionalization gives restricted groups the power to exclude others and to control public and private spending on specialized services. The very notion of a 'career' is an idea tied to processes of exclusion. It has occurred because of the growth of a new middle class, the expansion of higher education, and the spread of a new demand for more credentials for selected people (Bledstein, 1976).

Disability

Socialization teaches us how and why to conform to cultural values and social norms. Some people receive socialization that teaches them not to compete for society's most valued goals. This crippling socialization is *social disability*—**disability** for short. For many people, disability means learning ways of thinking about themselves that make them less than what they might otherwise be. This kind of socialization leads to lower aspirations, a lack of assertiveness, even withdrawal from competition.

The common element is our society's *dominant ideology*—specifically, the ideas that our culture promotes about success and failure. When asked whether they think hard work or good luck or help from others accounts for success, about two-thirds of respondents in a national Canadian survey say 'hard work' (Curtis and Grabb, 1999). People's thinking is largely *ideological*, based on acquired beliefs that we keep insulated from reality and from everyday experience. Others have called these same beliefs the principles of 'laissez-faire capitalism', 'liberal democracy', and the 'liberal ideology'.

Liberal democracy rests on (supposedly) free choice, free competition, and a free market in labour, goods, and ideas (Macpherson, 1965). We find freedom of this kind in societies with a capitalist economy, universal suffrage, and two or more political parties. This is why a person who is unable to find work is likely to blame personal failings rather than the high unemployment rate, discrimination, business mismanagement, or poor handling of the economy by the government. It explains why a dual-income family that is struggling unsuccessfully to meet all its obligations may turn its aggression inward, one spouse against the other spouse, parent against child, child against parent. In this way, family members end up destroying their family rather than blaming exploitive employers or bad government— not easy targets to attack.

Michael Mann (1970) argues that false consciousness disables voters. The main political parties lead voters to believe in vague political philosophies that contradict voters' everyday experience and support the status quo; the politi-cians appeal to patriotism, tradition, harmony, and national unity to mask their failings to achieve greater economic opportunities for the broad base of citizens. Thus, voters are disabled by misdirection and by their own optimism and gullibility.

People are also disabled by failed attempts to change their circumstances. Below these types of false consciousness—a willingness to blame oneself, a readiness to reinvest in the status quo, a tendency to see public issues as personal problems—we find a more general set of illusory beliefs about social inequality. This 'split personality' defence gives many people temporary relief from the effects of a cruel social order. Defences they erect against feelings of worthlessness and powerlessness allow life to go on; however, these defences also keep people from fighting the system of inequality that is at the root of their troubles.

Marxists believe that people are also disabled by religion. Karl Marx ([1843] 1970) characterized religion as an 'opiate' of the people in that it deadened them to the pain of inequality and injustice. However, others see religion in a more positive light. For example, Mohammed Fazel and David Young (1988) found that Tibetan refugees in India display more life satisfaction than local Indian Hindus, despite language problems and fewer financial resources. Though both the Hindus and the Tibetans subscribe to a fatalistic attitude, called 'karma' by both, the Tibetans adopt a 'proactive' posture, compared with the 'reactive fatalism' of the Hindus (Fazel and Young, 1988: 229).

A much more effective (if self-deluding) strategy is illustrated by Bruce Headey and Alex Wearing (1988). They write that as a group, Australians report a high level of satisfaction, or subjective well-being. Headey and Wearing attribute this to the tendency of Australians to experience a sense of relative superiority in every area of their lives. For example, about 86 per cent of Australians report that they perform above average in their main job; only 1 per cent report performing below average. They achieve this feat of self-congratulation by giving particular weight (in their own minds) to things that really are going smoothly and by comparing themselves with reference groups that are, as the authors say, 'restricted'. This attitude deters them from perceiving actual problems with their own performance and taking corrective action.

Decoupling

A third limit on opportunity is **decoupling**. This word makes us think of a disconnected railway car that has been shunted onto a sidetrack. For example, the job vacancy created by a death or retirement may set off a chain reaction leading to the upward movement of dozens of others in an organization (White, 1970). For this reason, career advancement is as much the result of 'vacancy chains' as of the accomplishment of the individuals promoted. Depending on economic conditions, an initial change (such as retirement or death) may produce a longer or shorter chain of reactions.

Some people are decoupled by a lack of useful social contacts. Social contacts are important in every social setting. A survey of managers showed that people typically find the best white-collar jobs through their personal contacts (Granovetter, 1974). That is because employers know that hiring through networks of personal contact is the simplest, most trustworthy approach. Mark Granovetter found that the most valuable job information is passed on by acquaintances. Because we have a great many more acquaintances than close friends, we are more likely to get useful information from an acquaintance. Further, people who begin moving between organizations early in their careers and who have more social contacts than others benefit most. This process creates a 'snowballing' of career opportunities over time. By contrast, people who stay with the same organization for much of their working life have trouble finding a new job when forced to do so.

Research shows, however, that people seeking careers within ethnic communities might do better by maintaining contact with old friends and kin than by seeking new acquaintances. Working-class people may also need to rely on friends and kin. They are likely to find their first job through friends and relatives in a similar line of work. Later in life, they start finding jobs by answering advertisements and through other formal means. Middle-class people do the opposite: they use their educational credentials to find a first job, and then they find later jobs through acquaintances they have met at work.

As we shall see in chapter 6, the networking process works against groups who are underrepresented in the better jobs and socially decoupled from the dominant group. For example, whites tend to make the acquaintance of other whites, men the acquaintance of other men. When asked to recommend people for jobs, white men will tend to recommend other white men. Even without people intending to 'discriminate', the process has a discriminatory outcome in that the organization remains racially or sexually unbalanced.

A final point is that decoupling affects more than your chances of getting a better quality of life; it also directly affects your life satisfaction. Ronald Burt (1987) has shown that people with larger networks of acquaintances are happier than people with smaller networks, even after differences in socio-economic status, age, sex, race, and marital status are taken into account. Burt found that the presence of close relations has no positive effect on people's happiness, while the presence of strangers has a negative effect.

Scarcity

A fourth reason for limited opportunity is that often there are too few resources to go around—what people want is in short supply. **Scarcity** varies with the ratio of competitors to desired goods. Thus, eliminating competitors through the practice of exclusion, disability, and decoupling can reduce scarcity. Increasing the supply of goods to be shared out can also reduce it. As the rich get even richer, the rest get poorer, and even the traditional middle class declines in relative size.

Often scarcity is due to exclusion—the monopolization of desired goods by people powerful enough to control access to them. Capitalists want a large 'reserve army of the unemployed' (Marx, 1962) to keep down wages, and they want shortages to keep up prices. Moreover, with the technical improvements in capitalist production, certain jobs are bound to disappear. According to this theory, capitalism creates too few jobs—indeed ever fewer jobs than that. Prices rise, and inequality increases steadily. Typically, high rates of economic growth give most people more of the goods they want without breaking the existing monopolies.

Beyond material scarcity, we find 'social limits to growth' (Hirsch, 1978) expressed in a growing sense of scarcity. Increasingly, people value scarce items—the unique vacation, the unusual home, designer clothing—*because they are scarce*. This kind of scarcity can never be eliminated as long as those who control our consumer culture continually invent and distribute new objects of desire to signify that some people have more money, leisure, or taste than other people.

Diffusion of Information and Other Valuable Resources

The four types of structural and cultural constraints we have just discussed all grow out of problems with the easy diffusion of information and other forms of scarce resources to those who need them. Simply put, **diffusion** is the spread of information and other resources through a population. This includes the spread of cultural information from one society to another, the spread of investment information, the communication of safecracking techniques or informal rules in a prison, the telling of tall tales and nasty gossip among friends, the passing along of job information and the 'inside dope' on job candidates, advice about birth control or safe sex, the

distribution of income and wealth, and the distribution of all manner of goods and services.

In the chapters that follow, we will see different types of diffusion and constraints to diffusion, in different concrete settings. From a sociological point of view, we will be looking for answers to certain general questions about the ways societies work. These questions include but are not limited to the following: How does a thing we call 'social structure' influence how fast people get information and other resources, who gets the resources, and how many people in total get them? What kinds of socially harmful, irrational, or inefficient outcomes are caused by limited flows of resources? How can we overcome these limitations?

For example, we find in most universities a relative abundance of professors who are white, able-bodied males. What is there about the flow of job information and people with different types of job credentials that is likely to work against the hiring of women, visible minorities, Native people, or the physically disabled? What sorts of actions, besides the enactment of employment equity policies, are likely to change this situation? This topic and others will be discussed throughout this book.

In answering these and other questions about diffusion, we will look at the various conditions that influence diffusion. Specifically, we will consider these questions: (1) How do the social contacts that make resources flow (and that constrain flow) develop? (2) What kinds of resources are most likely to be transmitted, and why? (3) Under what conditions do recipients accept what is received? (4) How does what people receive affect their behaviour?

Broad Theories About Social Problems

Social problems are not the exclusive domain of sociologists. In fact, both the natural and the social sciences have contributed their own unique understandings and perspectives to the study of social problems. It is important for the student of sociology (and of any other academic field) to note that where truth-finding is concerned, disciplines are not in competition with each other. For example, the contributions made by psychologists are not 'right' and those by anthropologists 'wrong'; both are correct, according to their own designs and self-imposed limitations. Each approach furthers our understanding of the problems we are considering.

The study of social problems is best understood as a complementary, multi-levelled cooperative action in which the findings of one field or discipline corroborate or elaborate upon the research and theories of the others. This is not to suggest an absence of conflicting data or results in areas of study. The contradictory findings likely signify a flaw in one or another theory, calling for closer scrutiny and further refinement of theory.

With this mind, consider three of the more prominent contributors to the theories of social problems: biology, psychology, and sociology.

Biological Perspectives

Biologists who investigate social problems attempt to uncover the biological bases for socially harmful behaviour. To this end, their focus of study is centred on the individual and on the genetic, hormonal, neurological, and physiological processes that contribute to that individual's dysfunction in society.

An example is biology's contribution to understanding violence in society. A proponent of the biological approach might cite evidence showing that increases in hormonal levels (for example, of testosterone) or in neurotransmitter levels (for example, of serotonin) are associated with increased aggression in both human and animal subjects. Other biologists might add that there is a genetic component to violence, pointing out how many primate species, including humans and chimpanzees, our closest evolutionary relatives, typically 'go to war against one another' over limited resources or position on the social dominance hierarchy.

Psychological Perspectives

Like biological perspectives, psychological perspectives centre on individuals. Unlike biologists, though, psychologists are concerned mainly with cognitive and perceptual processes. However, despite different loci of study, there has been a growing convergence between biology and psychology in recent years. Many of the most illuminating and important discoveries in psychology, for instance, have been in the subfield of neuropsychology, an amalgam of neuroanatomy and modern behavioural psychology.

Much of the contribution made by psychology to the understanding of various social problems has come from social psychologists, who study the ways in which social and mental forces determine action. Social psychologists distinguish themselves conceptually from sociologists by limiting their research to the thought processes and personality characteristics of individuals as they are influenced by and represented in a social context. For example, a social-psychological approach to the Holocaust might focus on the ways in which a charismatic authority can create unwavering obedience among subordinates, as a way of explaining why Nazi soldiers would carry out the atrocities ordered by Adolf Hitler against the Jews in the concentration camps.

Notice how this perspective emphasizes the individual soldier and his cognitive processes rather than the entire National Socialist (Nazi) party as a social group or the political ideology of German society. In practice, however, social psychological and sociological approaches often overlap.

Sociological Perspectives

Unlike the explanations put forward by researchers working within a biological or psychological framework, sociological theories focus on group relations and culture rather than on individual person processes. Even so, within the field of sociology, different perspectives specialize in different aspects of group relations and culture, with some preferring macroanalysis at the societal level and others opting to concentrate on microanalysis at the small-group level. The two major macroanalytical approaches that have emerged in sociology are the structural-functional and conflict perspectives, while the major microanalytical paradigm is the symbolic interactionist perspective.

The Structural-Functionalist Perspective

The **structural-functionalist perspective** views society as a set of interconnected elements that operate together in equilibrium to maintain the overall stability and efficiency of the whole. The individual social institutions—families, the economy, government, education, and others—each make a vital contribution to the larger functioning of society. Families, for instance, operate to reproduce and nurture members of society, while the economy regulates the production, distribution, and consumption of goods and services.

Robert Merton (1968), a key figure in the development of this perspective, argued that social institutions perform both manifest and latent functions. **Manifest functions** are those that are intended and easily recognized; **latent functions** are unintended and often hidden from participants. Education, for example, is manifestly responsible for providing students with the knowledge, skills, and cultural values that will help them to operate effectively in society. Both the school system and its participants formally recognize these functions. At a latent level, however, education also functions as an institutional 'babysitter' for young children and teenagers not yet ready to work full-time or to roam the streets independently while their parents are at work, and as a 'matchmaker' where older high school and university students socialize with potential future lovers or marriage partners. These functions, though important to society and accomplished with equal success, are considered latent because they are not the intended consequences envisioned by designers of the educational system, nor

are they acknowledged in any official way by school administrators, students, or parents.

The functionalists' emphasis on the interconnectedness of society has also been useful in highlighting the ways in which one part of the overall social system influences other parts. For example, recent changes to the family, such as the rise in divorces and in single-parenting, have important consequences for work and education, particularly with respect to time constraints among those juggling the dual—and often conflicting—roles of employee and parent.

According to functionalists, the cause of most social problems is a failure of institutions to fulfill their functions during times of rapid change. This *social disorganization* view of social problems holds that sudden cultural shifts disrupt traditional values and common ways of doing things. For example, during the phases of industrialization and urbanization in Western Europe and North America in the late nineteenth and early twentieth centuries, crime, poverty, unsanitary living conditions, environmental pollution, and other forms of social disorganization increased sharply. French sociologist Émile Durkheim (see, for example, [1893] 1964, [1897] 1964, [1912] 1995) introduced the term *anomie*, or normlessness, to reflect this condition in which social norms are weak or in conflict with one another. As traditional forms of guidance break down, social control declines and people experience less cohesion and bonding with one another; they become more likely to participate in nonconforming, deviant types of behaviour (crime, drug use, and so on). The general solution to social problems, according to this perspective, is to strengthen social norms and slow the pace of social change.

Conflict Theory

Conflict theory has its roots in the basic division between the 'haves' and the 'have-nots'. Conflict theorists take exception to the structural-functionalist explanation of social problems, criticizing its assumption of consensus among members of society and its limited attention to power struggles and competing interests within the population. The conflict perspective instead views society as largely a collection of disparate groups struggling over a limited supply of resources and power.

Conflict theory has its origins in the works of German economic-political philosopher Karl Marx (see, for example, [1843] 1970, [1867] 1965) and others. Marx believed that as societies make the transition from an agricultural to an industrial economy, the predominant social concerns of the people shift from survival to earning a living wage. In an industrialized capitalist system, two broad groups emerge: the *bourgeoisie*, the elite owners of the means of production, and the *proletariat*, the working class who must sell their labour power in exchange for a liveable wage. As the social class with control over the economic system, the bourgeois minority holds a superior position to the proletariats within the society. Moreover, they use their considerable economic power and political influence to ensure that they remain in a position of dominance.

Marxist conflict theories argue that social problems stem from the economic inequalities that exist between these two groups. Obviously, to hold wealth and power is to be in an enviable position, since one reaps the financial, political, and social benefits of a system that works in favour of one's own group over others. However, in order for the capitalist class to maintain its wealthy, privileged status, it must also ensure that those below it in power do not have an opportunity—and if possible, even the desire— to encroach upon bourgeois power. Because the bourgeoisie reap so much economic gain from the system without giving much back in the form of social welfare support, there are often sizeable minorities who live in poverty. This poverty of the less fortunate working and lower classes is a social problem in itself since it is unjust and conflict-producing. It is also associated with many other social problems, including crime, drug use, underemployment and unemployment, homelessness, environmental pollution, gender issues, and racism, as well as physical and mental health problems.

Marxists also contend that labourers in a capitalist system often experience a feeling of alienation from the processes and products of their labour since these processes and products are highly fragmented and specialized; they have narrow job functions and are therefore powerless to control or change the conditions of their work. The plight of the working class as envisioned by Marx is illustrated in the opening vignette of the classic film *Modern Times* (1936), in which Charlie Chaplin plays a hapless and beleaguered factory worker who becomes so overwhelmed by the pace of the assembly line that he eventually goes insane and himself becomes a part of the machinery.

Besides exploiting their workers, boardroom executives—the post-industrial successors to the factory owners of the industrial era—sometimes maximize profits through the perpetration of **corporate violence**, actual and potential harm caused to workers, consumers, and the public for the sake of the company's efficiency or success. Examples of these corporate crimes include the failure to remedy unsafe working conditions, exposing employees to hazardous materials, knowingly marketing dangerous or inferior products, and releasing industrial pollution into the environment.

Given its emphasis on economic inequality, the Marxist solution to social problems calls, not surprisingly, for the abolition of class differences. As well, it advocates that work should be altered so that labourers have more control of their workplace and a wage scale on par with supervisors and executives.

Two main criticisms of the Marxian conflict theory approach are that, historically, communist societies founded on Marxism have failed either to prosper or to eliminate inequality and that the approach overemphasizes the importance of economic inequality at the expense of other types of inequality and social injustice. Non-Marxist conflict theories argue that many social conflicts are based on non-class-based interests, values, and beliefs. While they recognize the value people place on differences in income and social class, proponents of this perspective believe that other divergent interests and characteristics can also lead to conflict and oppression. Thus, conflict theorists have noted that women and men often have competing interests and that this is as much a cause of some social problems as is economic inequality. Others cite the conflicting interests of various ethnic groups, for example, Aboriginal and non-Aboriginal groups, blacks and whites, heterosexuals and homosexuals, the young and the old, liberals and conservatives, urbanites and rural-dwellers, environmentalists and industrialists. We will have more to say about all of these conflicts in the course of this book.

Symbolic Interactionism

Whereas the structural-functionalist and conflict perspectives focus on large elements of society, such as social institutions and major demographic groups, **symbolic interactionism** focuses on the opposite end of the sociological spectrum: on small-group interactions. Taking an approach that overlaps substantially with parts of social psychology, the interactionists look at society as constructed by people. Society is essentially made up of the shared meanings, definitions, and interpretations held by interacting individuals. In studying social problems, followers of this perspective analyze the ways that certain behaviours and conditions come to be defined or constructed as social problems and how people learn to engage in such activities.

One of the forerunners of the interactionist approach was German sociologist Georg Simmel ([1943] 1997), who investigated the effects of urbanization on group relations at the community level. He found the urban lifestyle to be relentless and ultimately alienating, with inhabitants numbing their emotional contacts with others in order to cope with the excessive stimulation that city life offered. The fragmentation of urban life leads to a reduction in shared experience. It is within such a framework of distinctive, isolated, and isolating experiences that urban people must work out their social lives.

Labelling theory, a major social theory originating in the symbolic interactionist tradition, rests on the premise that a given activity is viewed as a social problem simply because groups of people define it as such. Howard Becker (1963), for example, argued that *moral entrepreneurs*—usually those in positions of power and influence—extend their own beliefs about right and wrong into social rules and norms. Those who violate these guidelines are labelled as 'deviant', and their actions are defined as social problems. Among their concerns, symbolic interactionists are interested in why some people break the rules and others do not.

Consistent with the basic premise of labelling theory, Herbert Blumer (1971) proposed that social problems develop in stages. The first stage is *social recognition*, the point at which a given condition or behaviour—say, drug use—is first identified as a potential social concern. Second, *social legitimating* takes place, in that society and its various institutional elements formally recognize the social problem as a serious threat to social stability. In the case of drug use, this stage might occur, for example, when high-profile drug-related fatalities make news headlines or when public officials discover a connection between drug abuse and crime and violence. The third stage is termed *mobilization for action*; it marks the point at which various social organizations begin planning strategies for remedial action. The final stage is the *development and implementation of an official plan*, such as the government-sanctioned 'war on drugs'.

Critics of the symbolic interactionist perspective argue that social problems still exist even when they are not recognized as such. Date rape and spousal abuse, for example, were not considered problematic behaviours before a few decades ago, but the infliction of physical and emotional harm was still hurtful for the victims, regardless of the historical or social context. As well, symbolic interactionism is often criticized for not making detailed connections between microsociological-level activities and macrosociological forces.

Population Health Perspectives

Common sense tells us that many conditions in society are correctly identified as social problems. From an operational standpoint, few would dispute the claim that violent crime, say, or homelessness fits the necessary criteria for such a label. In each case, the issue in question (1) is a social condition or behaviour, (2) is harmful to society and its members, and (3) warrants and requires collective remedial action. Beyond that, there is a moral component to our perception and understanding of social problems. A vague feeling of indignation or distress upon hearing about single mothers living in poverty or the effects of industrial water pollution on a small residential community remind us that, at least according to the values and beliefs in our culture, gender inequality and corporate environmental negligence are indeed worthy of social concern.

Still, this common-sense approach to distinguishing legitimate social problems from private concerns or unsubstantiated and unchecked moral reactions becomes problematic for social scientists trying to study social problems systematically. The basis for proper scientific study is an operational definition of the topic (which was given at the start of this chapter) and a means for measuring it. The common-sense approach fails to offer any concrete, measurable criteria for labelling a given condition as a social problem beyond the claim that it violates some popularly held value.

Consider inequality, whether economic, racial, or gender-based. Many people would consider it a social problem because it benefits a privileged few at the expense of others. However, not everyone agrees that unfairness alone constitutes a sufficient criterion for defining a condition as a social problem. Many people—particularly those who benefit most from social inequality—might argue that discrepancies between social classes, racial groups, or genders occur because some people work harder or are more deserving than others. Therefore, without denying the subjective component of social problems, it would be useful to devise some form of objective criteria that could be used to determine what is and what is not a social problem.

Increasingly, social scientists have noted that many social problems are associated with health consequences. From these observations has emerged the **population health perspective**, a broad approach to health whose goals are to improve the health of the entire population and to reduce health inequalities between social groups. According to this perspective, health includes not only the traditional genetic or biological foundations, but also socio-economic, environmental, material, cultural, psychosocial, and health system characteristics (Starfield, 2001). As a Health Canada study says, 'These factors, referred to as "determinants of health", include income and social factors, social support networks, education, employment, working and living conditions, physical environments, social environments, biology and genetic endowment, personal health practices, coping skills, healthy child development, health services, gender and culture' (Health Canada, 2001). Further, the understanding is that 'these determinants do not act in isolation of each other. It is the complex interactions among these factors that have an even more profound impact on health' (Health Canada, 2001). In turn, health status indicators should be recast to go beyond the traditional measures of disease, disability, and death. Ideally, they would also include factors such as 'mental and social well-being, quality of life, life satisfaction, income, employment and working conditions, education and other factors known to influence health' (Health Canada, 2001).

Some researchers have also suggested changing the notion of disease commonly held by the medical establishment to acknowledge the fluidity and variability that exist in the concept depending on historical and cultural contexts. A new definition should recognize both biological and environmental factors (Brean, 2001). It has also been argued that the cultural and economic influences on health are so great that social gradients in health status are 'surprisingly independent of diagnostic categories of illness, tending to persist across shifts in disease pattern and in hazardous exposures over time, and across societies' (Frank, 1995: 162).

Because of complex interactions among the determinants of health, the population health perspective employs a multidisciplinary approach to theory and research, combining insights from a variety of government divisions, such as health, justice, education, social services, finance, agriculture, and environment, along with input from academic fields such as medicine, social work, psychology, cultural anthropology, and sociology.

This book takes as the proper criteria for the study of social problems the effects that social conditions have on the overall physical and mental health of the population. There are several advantages to this approach. The first is that health consequences can be more easily measured than some other criteria being used in the study of social problems. Because they are tangible and directly observable phenomena, physical and mental illness and death are easier to study. Second, many people take health seriously, as they should.

To show that certain family issues are a social problem because they disrupt familial relationships may spark interest and action in some, but not in all. Conversely, to show that those same family issues are a social problem because they can lead to suppressed immune functioning, cognitive impairment in children, or a significant three-year decline in life expectancy is both a more concrete argument and more likely to result in enthusiastic collective action to achieve a solution. Almost everyone wants good health and would agree that the spread of

preventable illnesses is a serious problem. For this reason, social conditions that have harmful health effects should be taken seriously.

Solutions to Social Problems

Each chapter in this book will contain a section on solutions to the social problems under discussion, solutions that have been tried with varying degrees of vigour and success in Canada. These are solutions that individuals, groups, and organizations are using to address the problems, or solutions that should be undertaken to address them. For the time being, let's note that we should be careful to attend to solutions of two broad types: *individual solutions* and *group-based or organization-based solutions*. We will see examples of many of each of these types of solutions as we move through the chapters that follow.

C. Wright Mills's point in describing 'the sociological imagination' in the way he did (1959) was that 'knowledge can be power'—if individuals choose to act upon it. That is to say, when we know what is going on in society then act accordingly and in our best interests, we stand some chance of maximizing our opportunities. Under individual-level solutions, we can act to 'work the system' to our benefit.

For example, if you learn that some sections of the workforce are shrinking while others are expanding, you can consider preparing yourself for a job you would like in one of the expanding sectors. We all have choices of this type to make. Your power to choose means that while society and culture may constrain your options, they do not entirely determine your life. What you choose to do at certain points in life can make a difference. Opportunities can be exploited or squandered, difficulties overcome or compounded. The trick is to know what is occurring and how to help your chances. Information and understanding can lead us to some solutions for some problems, as we will see in the remaining chapters.

You can also consider getting involved in groups or organizations—there are political parties and interest groups of all sorts. Some of them will have goals for social changes that you would like to see realized. Here, too, knowledge of your society and culture is a prerequisite for making good decisions about which groups and organizations are most appropriate to your interests. Your values and ideologies (which are socially derived, remember) will also determine your choices of goals and organizations.

People acting in groups and organizations make history. The chapters that follow will demonstrate this many times over for different areas, especially around social policy changes. Consider, for example, the changes in family law (discussed in chapter 7) that have been forced by reform groups, and the changes that are yet to come. Be warned, though, that this strategy of political action through groups and organizations can be a very slow road. And many of your journeys may be unsuccessful. The analyses to come will indicate that dominant groups often oppose certain solutions to certain social problems because they are not particularly in their interests. As Marx and Max Weber, along with other scholars, have emphasized, such groups will have considerable organizational and ideological power.

However, political struggles can be won. There are many examples in Canada and the United States alone of successful protest movements by subordinate groups: the civil rights movement in the United States, the Quiet Revolution in Quebec, the women's movement in both countries, to name only three. Another important example is the success of the labour movement in Canada and the United States, fighting over many decades to secure better wages and job conditions for the working class. We will have occasions to discuss many such group-based strategies for solving social problems, including many initiated by government agencies. Such developments should give us heart concerning the possibilities of political action to resolve social problems. Many problems are formidable, but there is room to effect change.

Concluding Remarks

The authors of this book assume that the purpose of sociology today, just like two centuries ago when sociology began, is to use knowledge to improve social life. We are concerned about all social problems that cause harm to people. However, we attend here particularly to social problems that can be shown to do major harm to our quality of life but that only a few people see as a problem and that government and other powerful agencies are doing little to address.

This book takes as the proper criteria for the study of social problems the effects that social conditions have on the overall physical and mental health of the population. Thus, our goal here is to aid our understanding of the roots of social problems, their health consequences for individuals and society as a whole, and how these can be addressed.

For this task, it is important to explore facts and theories concerning the ways that problems develop and are maintained, and how problems are connected, one with another. If social problems negatively affect our social environment, a sense of civic duty directs us to be at least aware of these harmful conditions, or, better yet, to be actively involved in their correction.

Beyond this, studying social problems from a sociological perspective helps people understand the complex ways in which culture and social structure influence individual members of society. Indeed, the relationships between close-to-home aspects of people's lives and broad social and cultural trends, between private troubles and public issues, are the core subject matter of sociology.

Accordingly, this book explores how processes and social trends occurring within major bureaucratic organizations and social institutions, such as the economy or the government, affect the population as a whole. As we have seen, sociology is the study of social structure and culture, roles and statuses, institutions, networks, and organizations. Social structure constrains people through a variety of mechanisms—exclusion, decoupling, disabling, and scarcity—and these processes are involved in many social problems.

The four types of structural and cultural constraints we have just listed are all problems in the easy diffusion of information and other forms of scarce resources to those who need those resources in order to avoid negative circumstances. Therefore, we will have repeated occasion to discuss flows and diffusion of information and other resources.

The two major macroanalytical approaches that have emerged in sociology are the structural-functional and conflict perspectives, while the major microanalytical paradigm is the symbolic interactionist perspective. The individual social institutions—families, the economy, government, education, and others—each make a vital contribution to the larger functioning of society, according to functionalists. In their view, the cause of most social problems is a failure of institutions to fulfill their functions during times of rapid change. As we shall note, sociologists who support competing explanatory approaches hotly debate this view. The contentious searches for the appropriate explanations and solutions for each problem make the sociology of social problems fascinating to newcomers and professional sociologists alike. The great harm caused by many social problems, their continuing threat to individuals and society, gives this area of study a pressing importance.

Questions for Critical Thought

1. Think of a problem that you are familiar with and that you consider to be a 'social problem'. Write point-form notes that could become a debate between people who think that the problem is actually a problem and those who think it is a pseudo-problem that we should not be concerned with changing. For example, you might consider criminal law regarding 'soft' drugs, gender inequality, or inequality in the workplace.
2. Briefly reread one of the theories or paradigms covered in this chapter. Choose a social problem that you think is going to be covered in this book (check the index if necessary) and apply one or two of the theories to this problem. Ask yourself, for example, how would a conflict theorist view unemployment?
3. Should researchers aim to promote social change? Can researchers objectively report data to policy makers, and should they try? This question requires an opinion from you.
4. The sociological imagination is not restricted to tenured sociology professors. Using the explanation of the sociological imagination provided in this chapter, consider a social problem that you have some personal experience with, whether through acquaintances or directly, and seek an explanation that employs the sociological imagination.
5. Using social structure and individual interaction as two reasons for people's actions, explain a social problem such as drug abuse, petty crime, racism, or the caregiver burden.

Recommended Readings

Sheila L. Croucher, 'Constructing the Image of Ethnic Harmony in Toronto, Canada: The Politics of Problem Definition and Non-definition', *Urban Affairs Review*, 32 (1997), 319–47.

Toronto's reputation for harmonious ethnic relations is analyzed in this paper using a social constructionist approach. The question dealt with is how Torontonians construct this identity by defining which social issues are problems and which are not.

John Hagan and Bill McCarthy, *Mean Streets: Youth Crime and Homelessness* (Cambridge: Cambridge University Press, 1997).

After 10 years of research on homeless youth in Toronto and Vancouver, the authors wrote this award-winning book comparing the delinquent and criminal behaviour of homeless youth and youth who live at home.

Ann Hartman, *Reflection and Controversy: Essays on Social Work* (Washington, DC: NASW Press, 1994).

The book addresses three critical social problems facing society: poverty, racism, and limited access to the middle class. The courses of action advocated are changes in the national and local leadership, preparing the excluded class to enter the opportunity structure, and a renewed emphasis on stopping racism wherever it appears.

E. Nick Larsen, 'Urban Politics and Prostitution Control: A Qualitative Analysis of a Controversial Urban Problem', *Canadian Journal of Urban Research*, 8, no. 1 (1999), 28–46.

This qualitative analysis of prostitution in Toronto from 1975 to 1995 identifies the causal factors that led to the 1985 changes in the Criminal Code that problematized prostitution. The actors in the study include the police, the municipal government, and interest groups.

Duncan Lindsey, *The Welfare of Children* (New York: Oxford University Press, 1994).

Lindsey describes the US and Canadian child welfare systems, and examines the effects of poverty on children. He also recommends a detailed reconfiguration of the child welfare system.

A.H. Thompson, A.W. Howard, and Y. Jin, 'A Social Problem Index for Canada', *Canadian Journal of Psychiatry*, 46, no. 1 (2001), 45–51.

The authors construct an index of social problems using statistics across the provinces and territories of Canada. The social problems included are various violent and non-violent crimes, addictions, and divorce. The index aims to find correlations among the problems across provinces. Thompson, Howard, and Jin conclude that their index is useful because most provinces with high rates of one problem also have high rates of the other social problems.

Margaret Weir, Ann Shola Orloff, and Theda Skocpol, eds, *The Politics of Social Policy in the United States* (Princeton: Princeton University Press, 1988).

This is a book of compiled essays that examine why the United States lagged behind European countries in mounting social insurance programs and national health insurance. It presents case studies that analyze the evolution and impact of US social provisions since the New Deal.

Recommended Web Sites

The following Web sites are an absolute foundation for research on the topics covered in this text. Alas, one site that is missing is <www.insert-the-name-of-your-local-research-library-here.ca>.

Canadian Social Research Links
www.canadiansocialresearch.net/research.htm

This site provides links to a variety of useful topics regarding social science research in Canada. The site provides annotations of the links that it recommends.

Statistics Canada
www.statscan.ca

This site is easy to use: either search by subject or search using keywords. Remember to ask only for free information and that searching by word means that you must use the terms Statistics Canada uses. For example, on some tables gender is 'sex'.

Health Canada
www.hc-sc.gc.ca
    Health Canada is a federal government department. The research reports you find here are geared toward the health focus of this text.

Parliament of Canada
www.parl.gc.ca
    This is the home page of the two houses of the federal government, the Senate and the House of Commons. Using keywords, you can search reports to Parliament and transcriptions of the speeches made in Parliament. This is most useful for tracing the way federal policy is being created regarding specific social problems.

References

Abel, E.L. 2001. 'The Gin Epidemic: Much Ado About What?' *Alcohol and Alcoholism*, 36: 401–5.

Abt, Vicki. 1996. 'Coming After Oprah: The Shameless World of TV Talk Shows Revisited'. Paper presented at the annual conference of the Society for the Study of Social Problems.

Alvarez, Rodolfo. 2001. 'The Social Problem as an Enterprise: Values as a Defining Factor'. *Social Problems*, 48, no. 1: 3–10.

Beal, A.C., J. Ausiello, and J.M. Perrin. 2001. 'Social Influences on Health-Risk Behaviors Among Minority Middle School Students'. *Journal of Adolescent Health*, 28: 474–80.

Becker, Howard. 1963. *Outsiders: Studies in the Sociology of Deviance*. New York: Free Press.

Bell, R.F., B. Schjødt, and A.G. Paulsberg. 2000. 'Childhood Trauma and Chronic Pain'. *Tidsskr Nor Laegerforen*, 120: 2759–60.

Bernstein, Mary. 1991. 'Whistle Blowing as Claims-Making in Technological Controversies'. Paper presented at the annual meeting of the American Sociological Association.

Bledstein, Burton J. 1976. *The Culture of Professionalism: The Middle Class and the Development of Higher Education in America*. New York: Norton.

Blumer, Herbert. 1971. 'Social Problems as Collective Behavior'. *Social Problems*, 8: 298–306.

Brean, Joseph. 2001. 'Semantics of Disease'. *National Post*, 3 August, A16.

Breton, Raymond, Wsevolod Isajiw, Warren Kalbach, and Jeffrey Reitz. 1990. *Ethnic Identity and Equality: Varieties of Experience in a Canadian City*. Toronto: University of Toronto Press.

Burt, Ronald S. 1987. 'A Note on Strangers, Friends and Happiness'. *Social Networks*, 9: 311–32.

Cain, Roy. 1989. 'Disclosure and Secrecy Among Gay Men: A Shift in Views'. Paper presented at the annual meeting of the Society for the Study of Social Problems.

Carmona, Saez T., F. Garcia, Mayoral P. Romero, C. Roman Fernandez, A.J. Jimenez Alvarez, and I. Rodrigo Santos. 1999. 'Social Failure: The Concept and a Method for Its Clinical Assessment'. *Medicina Interna*, 16: 442–6.

Castle, Emery N. 1995. 'The Forgotten Hinterlands'. In *The Changing American Countryside: Rural People and Places*, edited by Emery N. Castle, 3–9. Lawrence: University Press of Kansas.

Clement, Wallace. 1975. *The Canadian Corporate Elite: An Analysis of Economic Power*. Toronto: McClelland and Stewart.

Clinton-Davis, Stanley, and Yohannes Fassil. 1992. 'Health and Social Problems of Refugees'. *Social Science and Medicine*, 35: 507–13.

Cravens, Hamilton. 1997. 'Postmodernist Psychobabble: The Recovery Movement for Individual Self-Esteem in Mental Health Since World War II'. *Journal of Policy History*, 9, no. 1: 141–54.

Curtis, James, and Edward Grabb. 1999. 'Social Status and Beliefs About What's Important for Getting Ahead'. In *Social Inequality in Canada*, 3rd edn, edited by James Curtis, Edward Grabb, and Neil Guppy, 330–46. Scarborough, ON: Prentice-Hall.

de Goede, M., E. Spruijt, C. Maas, and V. Duindam. 2000. 'Family Problems and Youth Unemployment'. *Adolescence*, 35: 587–601.

Delbanco, Suzanne, Janet Lundy, Tina Hoff, Molly Parker, and Mark D. Smith. 1997. 'Public Knowledge and Perceptions About Unplanned Pregnancy and Contraception in Three Countries'. *Family Planning Perspectives*, 29, no. 2: 70–5.

Durkheim, Émile. [1893] 1964. *The Division of Labor in Society*. Translated by George Simpson. Glencoe, IL: Free Press.

————. [1897] 1964. *Suicide*. Translated by John A. Spaulding and George Simpson. Glencoe, IL: Free Press.

————. [1912] 1995. *The Elementary Forms of Religious Life*. Translated by Karen E. Fields. New York: Free Press.

Emerson, Robert M., Kerry O. Ferris, and Carol Brooks Gardner. 1998. 'On Being Stalked'. *Social Problems*, 45: 289–314.

Fazel, Mohammed K., and David M. Young. 1988. 'Life Quality of Tibetans and Hindus: A Function of Religion'. *Journal for the Scientific Study of Religion*, 27: 229–42.

Fine, Gary Alan. 2000. 'Games and Truths: Learning to Construct Social Problems in High School Debate'. *Sociological Quarterly*, 41: 103–23.

Frank, John W. 1995. 'Why "Population Health"?' *Canadian Journal of Public Health*, 86, no. 3: 162–4.

Franzblau, Susan H., and Michael Moore. 2001. 'Socializing Efficacy: A Reconstruction of Self-Efficacy Theory Within the Context of Inequality'. *Journal of Community and Applied Social Psychology*, 11, no. 2: 83–96.

Gest, S.D., J.L. Mahoney, and R.B. Cairns. 1999. 'A Developmental Approach to Prevention Research: Configural Antecedents of Early Parenthood'. *American Journal of Community Psychology*, 27: 453–65.

Goode, Erich, and Nachman Ben Yehuda. 1994. 'Moral Panics: Culture, Politics, and Social Construction'. *Annual Review of Sociology*, 20: 149–71.

Granovetter, Mark. 1974. *Getting a Job: A Study of Contacts and Careers*. Cambridge, MA: Harvard University Press.

Hassan, R. 2000. 'Social Consequences of Manufactured Longevity'. *Medical Journal of Australia*, 173: 601–3.

Headey, Bruce, and Alex Wearing. 1988. 'The Sense of Relative Superiority—Central to Well-Being'. *Social Indicators Research*, 20: 497–516.

Health Canada. 2001. *Population Health Approach*. Available at <www.hc-sc.gc.ca/hppb/phdd/index.html>, accessed 10 January 2003.

Hirsch, Fred. 1978. *The Social Limits to Growth*. Cambridge, MA: Harvard University Press.

Hoffman, Saul D., E. Michael Foster, and Frank F. Furstenberg. 1993. 'Reevaluating the Costs of Teenage Childbearing'. *Demography*, 30, no. 1: 1–13.

Isturiz, R.E., and C. Carbon. 2000. 'Antibiotic Use in Developing Countries'. *Infection Control and Hospital Epidemiology*, 21: 394–7.

Jenness, Valerie. 1990. 'From Sex as Sin to Sex as Work: COYOTE and the Reorganization of Prostitution as a Social Problem'. *Social Problems*, 37: 403–20.

Kellinghaus, C., B. Eikelmann, P. Ohrmann, and T. Reker. 1999. 'Homeless and Mentally Ill: Review of Recent Research and Results on a Doubly Disadvantaged Minority'. *Fortschritte der Neurologie-Psychiatrie*, 67, no. 3: 108–21.

Klein, Hugh A. and David J. Pittman. 1998. 'Perceived Consequences Associated with the Use of Beer, Wine, Distilled Spirits, and Wine Coolers'. Paper presented at the annual meeting of the Society for the Study of Social Problems.

Kroll-Smith, Steve. 2000. 'The Social Production of the "Drowsy Person"'. *Perspective on Social Problems*, 12: 89–109.

Kunkel, Karl R. 1995. 'Down on the Farm: Rationale Expansion in the Construction of Factory Farming as a Social Problem'. In *Images of Issues: Typifying Contemporary Social Problems*, 2nd edn, edited by Joel Best, 239–56. Hawthorne, NY: Aldine de Gruyter.

Levine, Harry Gene. 1984. 'The Alcohol Problem in America: From Temperance to Alcoholism'. *British Journal of Addiction*, 79: 109–19.

Linders, Annulla. 1998. 'Abortion as a Social Problem: The Construction of "Opposite" Solutions in Sweden and the United States'. *Social Problems*, 45: 488–509.

Lippert, Randy. 1990. 'The Construction of Satanism as a Social Problem in Canada'. *Canadian Journal of Sociology*, 15: 417–40.

Loader, Ian, and Aogan Mulcahy. 2001. 'The Power of Legitimate Naming: Part I—Chief Constables as Social Commentators in Post-War England'. *British Journal of Criminology*, 41, no. 1: 41–55.

Lyon-Callo, Vincent. 2000. 'Medicalizing Homelessness: The Production of Self-Blame and Self-Governing Within Homeless Shelters'. *Medical Anthropology Quarterly*, 14: 328–45.

McFalls, Joseph A., Jr, Marguerite Harvey McFalls, Brian Jones, and Bernard J. Gallagher III. 1987. 'Genetic Engineering: Social Problems and Social Policy'. *Sociological Viewpoints*, 3, no. 1: 1–22.

MacLaughlin, Jim. 1996. 'The Evolution of Anti-Traveller Racism in Ireland'. *Race and Class*, 37, no. 3: 47–63.

McMullan, Colin, and John Eyles. 1999. 'Risky Business: An Analysis of Claims-Making in the Development of an Ontario Drinking Water Objective for Tritium'. *Social Problems*, 46: 294–311.

Macpherson, C.B. 1965. *The Real World of Democracy*. The Massey Lectures. Toronto: Canadian Broadcasting Corporation.

Mann, Michael. 1970. 'The Social Cohesion of Liberal Democracy'. *American Sociological Review*, 35: 423–39.

Marx, Karl. [1843] 1970. *Critique of Hegel's 'Philosophy of Right'*. Translated by Annette Jolin and Joseph O'Malley. Cambridge: Harvard University Press.

———. [1867] 1965. *Capital: A Critical Analysis of Capitalist Production*, Vol. 1. New York: International.

———. 1962. *Capital*. Translated from the 4th German edn by Eden Paul and Cedar Paul. London: Dent.

———. 1978. *Karl Marx: Selected Writings*. Edited by David McLellan. Oxford: Oxford University Press.

Mauldon, Jane, and Suzanne Delbanco. 1997. 'Public Perceptions About Unplanned Pregnancy'. *Family Planning Perspectives*, 29, no. 1: 25–9.

Merton, Robert K. 1968. *Social Theory and Social Structure*. New York: Free Press.

Mills, C. Wright. 1959. *The Sociological Imagination*. London: Oxford University Press.

Montagne, Michael. 1992. 'The Promotion of Medications for Personal and Social Problems'. *Journal of Drug Issues*, 22: 389–405.

Montgomery, John, D. 1998. 'The Next Thousand Years'. *World Policy Journal*, 15, no. 2: 77–81.

Morewitz, Stephen J. 2001. 'The Psychosocial Effects of Stalking: A Social Problem'. Paper presented at the annual meeting of the Society for the Study of Social Problems.

Morone, James A. 1996. 'The Corrosive Politics of Virtue'. *American Prospect*, no. 26 (May/June): 30–9.

Mullen, Elizabeth A. 1997. 'Workplace Violence: Cause for Concern or the Construction of a New Category of Fear?' *Journal of Industrial Relations*, 39, no. 1: 21–32.

Murphy, Raymond. 1982. 'The Structure of Closure: A Critique and Development of the Theories of Weber, Collins and Parkin'. *British Journal of Sociology*, 35: 547–67.

Nichols, Lawrence T. 1997. 'Social Problems as Landmark Narratives: Bank of Boston, Mass Media, and "Money Laundering"'. *Social Problems*, 44: 324–41.

Owen, Neville, Ron Borland, and David Hill. 1991. 'Regulatory Influences on Health-Related Behaviours: The Case of Workplace Smoking-Bans'. *Australian Psychologist*, 26, no. 3: 188–91.

Popenoe, David. 1993. 'American Family Decline, 1960–1990: A Review and Appraisal'. *Journal of Marriage and the Family*, 55: 527–55.

Porter, John. 1965. *The Vertical Mosaic: An Analysis of Social Class and Power in Canada*. Toronto: University of Toronto Press.

Potter, Deborah Anne. 2000. '"Acting Up" and "Acting Out": "Conduct Disorder" and the Medicalization of Adolescent Aggressive Behaviours'. Paper presented at the annual meeting of the Society for the Study of Social Problems.

Reinarman, Craig, and Harry G. Levine. 1995. 'The Crack Attack: America's Latest Drug Scare, 1986–1992'. In *Images of Issues: Typifying Contemporary Social Problems*, 2nd edn, edited by Joel Best, 147–86. Hawthorne, NY: Aldine de Gruyter.

Reinharz, Shulamit. 1997. 'Enough Already! The Pervasiveness of Warnings in Everyday Life'. *Qualitative Sociology*, 20: 477–85.

Sartorius, N. 2001. 'The Economic and Social Burden of Depression'. *Journal of Clinical Psychiatry*, 62, Suppl. 15: 8–11.

Schorr, Lisbeth B. 1991. 'Children, Families, and the Cycle of Disadvantage'. *Canadian Journal of Psychiatry*, 36: 437–41.

Scott, Dorothy. 1995. 'The Social Construction of Child Sexual Abuse: Debates About Definitions and the Politics of Prevalence'. *Psychiatry, Psychology, and Law*, 2, no. 2: 117–26.

Simmel, Georg. [1943] 1997. 'The Metropolis and Mental Life'. In *On Individuality and Social Forms: Selected Writings*, edited by Donald N. Levine, 324–39. Chicago: University of Chicago Press.

Sobal, Jeffrey, and Donna Maurer, eds. 1999. *Weighty Issues: Fatness and Thinness as Social Problems*. New York: Aldine de Gruyter.

Solinger, Rickie. 1992. *Wake Up Little Susie: Single Pregnancy and Race Before Roe v. Wade*. New York: Routledge.

Starfield, Barbara. 2001. 'Basic Concepts in Population Health and Health Care'. *Journal of Epidemiology and Community Health*, 55: 452–4.

Szasz, Andrew. 1995. 'The Iconography of Hazardous Waste'. In *Cultural Politics and Social Movements*, edited by Marcy Darnovsky, Barbara Epstein, and Richard Flacks, 197–222. Philadelphia, PA: Temple University Press.

'Utopian Visions: Sociologies for the 21st Century'. 2000. *Contemporary Sociology*, 29, no. 1: 1–241.

Van Mens-Verhulst, J., and J. Bensing. 1998. 'Distinguishing Between Chronic and Nonchronic Fatigue: The Role of Gender and Age'. *Social Science and Medicine*, 47: 621–34.

Wagner, David. 1995. 'Historicizing Social Constructionist Perspectives: The Example of Temperance Movements'. Paper presented at the annual meeting of the Society for the Study of Social Problems.

Walker, Gillian A. 1990. *Family Violence and the Women's Movement: The Conceptual Politics of Struggle*. Toronto: University of Toronto Press.

Wall, R., J. Rehm, B. Fischer, B. Brands, L. Gliksman, J. Stewart, W. Medved, and J. Blake. 2000. 'Social Costs of Untreated Opioid Dependence'. *Journal of Urban Health*, 77: 688–722.

Wallimann, Isidor. 1994. 'Can Modernity Be Sustained? Prevention of Mass Death and Genocide'. *Population Review*, 38, nos 1–2: 36–45.

White, Harrison C. 1970. *Chains of Opportunity: System Models of Mobility in Organizations*. Cambridge, MA: Harvard University Press.

Zipp, John F., and Katherine E. Lane. 1987. 'Plant Closing and Control over the Workplace'. *Work and Occupations*, 14, no. 1: 62–87.

Glossary

Belief Any statement or part of a statement that describes an aspect of collective reality. Beliefs are ideas and explanations of what is commonly accepted as the truth.

Conflict theory A theoretical paradigm that emphasizes conflict and change as the regular and permanent features of society, because society is made up of various groups who wield varying amounts of power.

Corporate violence Actual and potential harm caused to workers, consumers, and the public for the sake of a company's efficiency or successful corporate crimes.

Culture The objects, artifacts, institutions, organizations, ideas, and beliefs that make up the symbolic and learned aspects of human society.

Decoupling A way of controlling access to rewards and opportunities. It disconnects certain groups from rewards by keeping them uninformed about good opportunities and about ways of taking advantage of them. It also keeps people from knowing others who could help them gain rewards.

Diffusion The spread of information through a population. This includes the spread of cultural information from one society to another, the spread of investment information, and the transmission of rumours in a community.

Disability A label attached to certain categories of people, discouraging them from competing for the rewards everyone desires. Some people simply think of themselves as unable to compete.

Exclusion One way of controlling access to rewards and opportunities. It prevents people from entering contests they might win and it rewards people unequally for equal performances.

Institution An enduring set of ideas about how to accomplish goals generally recognized as important in a society. Institutions are the stable, well-acknowledged social relationships that endure over time, including the family, the economy, education, politics, religion, mass media, medicine, and science and technology. They provide the bedrock upon which the rest of social life is based.

Institutional completeness Usually the characteristic of ethnic enclaves where all the necessary institutions and services are present, allowing the area to be self-sufficient without aid from the host culture.

Latent functions   Unintended outcomes, often hidden from participants.

Macrosociology   Focuses on the societal level. It explores the ways in which the processes occurring within major social institutions and organization, such as the economy or the government, affect the population as a whole. Marxism, functionalism, and systems theory are regarded as macrosociological.

Manifest functions   Intended outcomes, easily recognized.

Microsociology   Focuses on the face-to-face world of social interaction. This approach, which investigates the understanding and experience of social problems at the local, personal level, is similar to that used by social psychologists. Theoretical tools include symbolic interactionism, exchange theory, and ethnomethodology.

Moral entrepreneurs   Usually those in positions of power and influence, they extend their own beliefs about right and wrong into social rules and norms.

Norms   The rules and expectations of appropriate behaviour under various social circumstances. Norms create social consequences that have the effect of regulating appearance and behaviour.

Objective factors   Refers to the existence of a social condition that is factual and based solely on the circumstances present, without any judgment of value or morality. Many sociological methods are designed to protect the investigator from bias in collection and interpretation.

Population health perspective   A broad approach to health whose goals are to improve the health of the entire population and to reduce health inequalities between social groups. It deals with the socio-economic, environmental, material, cultural, psychosocial, and health system characteristics of a population.

Role   A set of ideas associated with social status that defines its relationship with another position. The role of the teacher, for example, is built around a set of ideas about teachers in relation to students. It is through roles that individuals are connected to social systems.

Scarcity   A shortage of opportunities to be shared out. True scarcity (as opposed to unequal distribution of goods) can be reduced by producing more of the desired goods.

Social group   A number of individuals, defined by formal or informal criteria of membership, who share a feeling of unity or are bound together in stable patterns of interaction; two or more individuals who have a specific, common identity and interact in a reciprocal social relationship.

Social organization   Any enduring, predictable pattern of relations between people in groups, communities, or societies; used by some to refer specifically to formal organization (such as bureaucracies).

Social problem   A generic term applied to the range of conditions and aberrant behaviours that are held to be manifestations of social disorganization. A sizeable portion of society usually views social problems as having both social consequences and social causes, changing according to social and historical context.

Sociological imagination   A term coined by C. Wright Mills for the faculty that allows one to see connections between one's personal life and the social world in which one lives.

Status   A socially defined position that a person holds in a given social group (for example, nurse or student). Note that *status* is a purely relational term, as each status only exists through its relation to one or more other statuses.

Structural-functionalist perspective   Also called *functionalism*, this is a theoretical paradigm that emphasizes the way each part of a society functions to fulfil the needs of society as a whole.

Subjective factors   Refers to an evaluation of objective reality in people's perceptions. It includes the application of labels ('wrong', 'immoral', and so on) to particular acts or situation, and systematic accounts of the reasons for these acts and situations.

Symbolic interactionism   A theoretical paradigm that studies the process by which individuals interpret and respond to the actions of others and that conceives of society as the product of this continuous face-to-face interaction.

Symbols   The heart of cultural systems, for with them we construct thought, ideas, and other ways of representing reality to others and to ourselves; gestures, artifacts, or language that represents something else and evokes an emotion or that represents a value.

Values   Shared ideas about how something is ranked in terms of its relative social desirability, worth, or goodness; what a society views as right and wrong, good and bad, desirable and undesirable.

Chapter 1

Poverty and Economic Inequality

Chapter Objectives

After reading this chapter the student should understand:
- the difference between 'relative' and 'absolute' poverty
- the different theoretical perspectives on economic inequality
- the solutions and policies that Canada and other countries have used to try to rectify inequalities
- different definitions of poverty, with the added ability to comment on LICOs and poverty lines
- the concentration of wealth that exists in capitalist societies today
- how poverty is related to work, crime, violence, drug and alcohol abuse, discrimination, and ethnicity
- the effects of poverty on youth and the elderly
- the problem of homelessness
- the health consequences of poverty and the significance of the Whitehall studies

Poverty Is a Social Problem and a Cause of Problems

This chapter is about rich and poor people, individuals and families, households, communities, and nations. It is about being absolutely poor, being only relatively poor, and suffering not from poverty at all but from inequality. Finally, it is about the harsher results of poverty and inequality. These results include crime, bad living conditions, and poor health. As we will see throughout this book, the major social problems are in one way or another all related to **economic inequality**, and most of them have vital health consequences. Economic inequality includes large differences in income and wealth across individuals and groups, and large differences in the economic power of nations.

As early as 1759, Adam Smith—the father of modern economics—recognized that poverty is a thorny problem. He, and many scholars since, saw that poverty is not merely poor living conditions and an absence of money, but also a cause

of social isolation, illness, and mental unease (Gilbert, 1997). Research shows that these personal experiences of need are the strongest influences of poverty on psychosocial health (Piko and Fitzpatrick, 2000; Sennett and Cobb, 1993). Yet societies and their governments have not found a way to sever the link between poverty and health.

These issues may sound simple, but they are not. One complexity is that we must subdivide poverty itself into **absolute** and **relative poverty**. People suffer from relative poverty when they can survive but live far below the common standards of the society. Though less harsh than starvation, relative poverty affects people's lives in important ways, too, because it affects their aspirations and self-esteem.

We will see that sociologists study social problems from a variety of perspectives. We will discuss three main sociological outlooks on, or theories of, poverty and economic inequality: structural-functional theories, conflict theories, and symbolic interactionist theories. We will also discuss a theory that has kinship with a symbolic interactionist approach, the 'culture of poverty' theory. Each theoretical approach points to important aspects of economic inequality. Each provides an understanding of how people become rich or poor. Each yields a different recipe for action—what to do about economic inequality—and each deserves criticism for failing to address certain issues, as we will show.

As sociologists, we have to help conquer ignorance and narrow-mindedness about poverty. People often stereotype recipients of welfare, for example, as lazy and careless, more interested in seeking pleasure than in working hard and becoming financially self-reliant. Many believe that people who are well educated almost never wind up on welfare. Such beliefs are misguided. After the last recession (1990–7) ended, welfare caseloads in most areas of Canada continued climbing because of continued high rates of joblessness. Education offers no absolute protection from welfare. For example, fully 11 per cent of the heads of Canadian families on welfare in March 1997 had received some type of postsecondary education (National Council of Welfare, 1998).

BOX 1.1
Poverty and Health

Statistics for southwestern Quebec tend to bear out something health professionals have said for centuries: poor people are more likely to be sick. The statistics are part of a report by staff of the Monteregie health board. The report says areas of the Monteregie with the lowest average incomes tend to have the highest mortality rates over all, the highest mortality rates from heart disease and the largest rates of babies with low birth weights.

In the Longueuil area, 17 per cent of families live below the poverty line, compared with 15.8 per cent for the Monteregie as a whole. But Longueuil had a somewhat worse performance for the three health indicators:

- The mortality rate was 648 per 100,000 population, compared with 613 for the Monteregie as a whole.
- The heart-disease mortality rate was 279, compared with 258.
- And 6.3 out of every 100 newborns weighed less than 2.5 kilograms, compared with 6.2 in the Monteregie as a whole.

The study notes that the Longueuil area is home to about 40 per cent of low-income families in the Monteregie. The study is based on data from around 1986.

The study notes that experts have pointed to various links that might exist between low income and poor health.

- Poor health could contribute to low income. The chronically ill, for example, will find it hard to get good jobs.
- More of the poor might live in polluted, high-traffic neighborhoods.
- The poor often have worse health habits. They smoke more, they are more likely to be obese and, although fewer of the poor than the better off drink alcohol, those who do drink are more likely to overdo it.
- The poor are less likely to visit health-care services, whether because of lack of knowledge or because of costs like bus tickets.
- Studies also have linked levels of education and physical health.

SOURCE: Harvey Shepherd, 'Study Shows Link Between Poor Areas and Poor Health in Monteregie', *The Gazette* (Montreal), 12 April 1995, G2. Reprinted by permission of *The Gazette*.

Some have called poverty the world's leading health problem. According to the *absolute income hypothesis*, with all other things being constant, higher income should mean better health. Going beyond this issue, economic inequality can be argued to be the most basic social problem that Canada and the world face. We say this because, as you will see throughout this book, many if not all of the social problems we discuss are in one way or another related to economic inequality.

As we have said, economic inequality includes both differences in income and wealth across individuals and groups and differences in the economic power of nations. Both inequality and poverty cause social problems. Social problems are also a result of the division of power and authority, as we will see in later chapters. In the end, most social problems are due to unequal sharing of power and wealth and to the lack of action by powerful elites to vigorously address the problems inequality produces.

Definitions and Measurements of Poverty and Economic Inequality

Some think that poverty has always been with us. Others think that capitalism and the class relationships it produces give poverty a unique historical and social context (Novak, 1996). Certainly, we cannot discuss, or even define, poverty without understanding its social and historical background (Pritchard, 1993). With so complicated an idea as poverty, we are bound to have problems of meaning and measurement. Let us consider, first, some of these issues of types of poverty and how to measure them.

Relative and Absolute Poverty

Sociologists agree that people who live in poverty have much less than the average standard of living. However, we can view poverty in two ways: as absolute and as relative. People who live in **absolute poverty** do not have enough of the basic requirements—food, shelter, and medicine,

for example—for physical survival. By contrast, people who live in **relative poverty** can survive, but their living standards are far below the general living standards of the society or social group to which they belong.

Researchers disagree about how to measure poverty. Although you may think that deciding whether a particular lifestyle qualifies as 'poor' is easy, in practice it is difficult. In fact, cross-national evidence from the United States, Great Britain, Canada, and Australia shows that the **poverty line** is elastic, responding both to changes in the real income in a given country and to the success of advocates fighting to increase social welfare by redefining or remeasuring poverty (Fisher, 1998).

Two Methods of Measurement

Until recently, Statistics Canada, the primary data-gathering agency for all of Canada, has relied on two different measurement strategies when compiling statistical data on poverty: LICOs and LIMs. The first method uses low-income cut-offs (LICOs), which are based on the percentage of income devoted to daily necessities such as food, shelter, and clothing (see Figure 1.1). Although some consider LICOs to be equivalent to poverty lines, Statistics Canada stresses that they are not.

LICO varies with the size of the family and the size of the community of residence because of geographic differences in the cost of living for families of different sizes (see Figure 1.2). Thus, LICO is higher in a large city than a rural area, and higher for a large family than for a small one. In a community with a population of 500,000 or more, if 'the average family' of four spends 35 per cent of its income on food, shelter, and clothing, then any four-person household that spends 55 per cent or more of its income on these necessities is considered 'low-income'. Using this method, one first calculates an income that covers the basic needs of one adult, and then assumes that need increases in proportion to family size. Each added adult requires 40 per cent more,

FIGURE 1.1
Calculation of a Low-Income Cut-off (LICO)

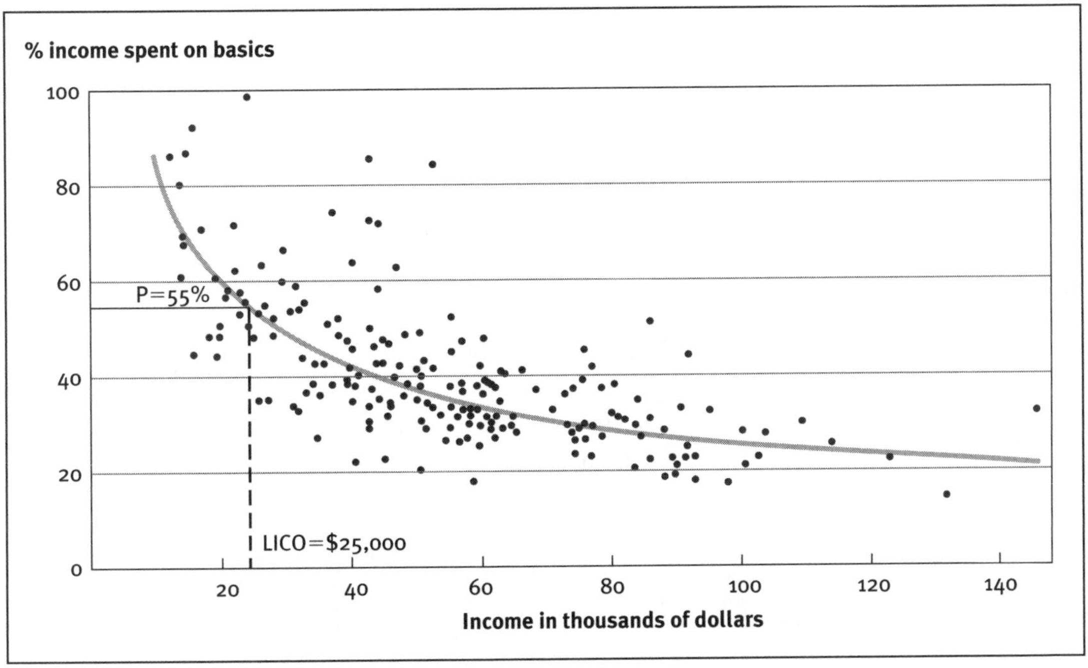

% income spent on basics

P=55%

LICO=$25,000

Income in thousands of dollars

SOURCE: Cathy Cotton, Yves St-Pierre, and Maryanne Webber, *Should the Low Income Cutoffs Be Updated? A Discussion Paper* (Income Research Paper Series, Cat. no. 75F0002MIE1999009) (Ottawa: Statistics Canada, 2000).

each added child 30 per cent more of the resources required by the first adult.

The second methodology used by Statistic Canada has been the low-income measures (LIMs)—a set of figures representing 50 per cent of the median 'adjusted family income'. Actual incomes are compared with LIMs to determine whether or not a family can be considered 'low-income'.

A third, alternative measure, the 'market basket measure', has been years in the making—a result of work by the Federal/Provincial/Territorial Working Group on Social Development Research and Information—and is designed to define and measure poverty in absolute, not relative, terms. This working group has proposed a preliminary market basket measure (MBM) of poverty based on an imaginary basket of market-priced goods and services. The new poverty line, then, is based on the income needed to purchase the items in the basket (Pellegi, 1997).

This MBM measure signals a change in our perceived obligations to the poor because it replaces a relative measure of poverty—the LICO—with a market basket measure. HRDC officials have been instructed by politicians to create a measure 'related to changes in the cost of consumption rather changes in income' (HRDC, March 1998, cited in Shillington, 1999). Implicit in the market basket approach is the idea that our obligations to low-income people consist of a particular basket of goods, not a share of Canada's wealth. In doing so, HRDC officials acknowledge that many children will be socially excluded and isolated but not, by their measure, poor (Shillington, 1999).

FIGURE 1.2
Family Type by Income Below the Poverty Line[a]

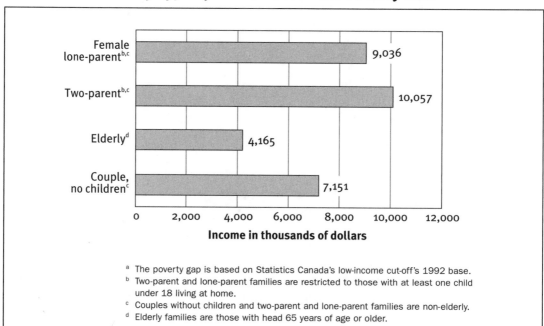

a The poverty gap is based on Statistics Canada's low-income cut-off's 1992 base.
b Two-parent and lone-parent families are restricted to those with at least one child under 18 living at home.
c Couples without children and two-parent and lone-parent families are non-elderly.
d Elderly families are those with head 65 years of age or older.

SOURCE: Vanier Institute of the Family, 'Depth of Poverty Shown as $ Below the "Poverty Line" by Family Type', in *Profiling Canadian Families*, vol. 2 (Ottawa: Vanier Institute of the Family, 1997), citing Statistics Canada, *Low Income Persons 1980–1997* (Cat. no. 19-569-XIB), Table 49.

While the topic of measurement is specialized and may seem dry to the beginner, we need to emphasize that the measurement of poverty is complicated and politically contentious. Moreover, as in any area of social science, if you cannot measure something, you cannot make good theories about how it varies.

Wealth

At the wealthy end of the income scale, we find a concentration of economic resources in the hands of very few people. This is because private wealth is usually derived from corporate wealth, which is also concentrated. Michael Parenti points out that more than 80 per cent of the output of the US private sector originates from fewer than 1 per cent of all corporate businesses (1995: 10). According to an Institute for Policy Studies report on the rise of global corporate dominance, the total sales recorded by each of the top five global corporations—General Motors, Wal-Mart, Exxon Mobil, Ford Motor, and DaimlerChrysler—were larger than the gross domestic products of at least 182 countries (Anderson and Cavanagh, 2000: 3, 6).

The fastest-growing segment of millionaires is made up of baby boomers, who stand to inherit roughly $20 trillion (US) within the next two decades (Davidson, 1997). Currently, the richest man in the world, Sam Robson Walton, the chair of Wal-Mart, is worth approximately $65.4 billion (US), followed by Microsoft mogul Bill Gates, whose holdings declined from $76.5 billion in 2000 to a meager $54 billion in 2001 following a worldwide drop in the value of high-technology stocks. The richest man in Canada is currently Kenneth Thomson, chair of Thomson Corporation, with $15.6 billion (US) in holdings (Woods, 2001).

Global Poverty

Despite economic growth, with a growing concentration of wealth in fewer hands it is inevitable that more people will have less. Global inequality is widespread and growing. The World Health Organization, for instance, observes that 'the number of urban poor is growing rapidly and it is estimated that in the year 2000 at least 1000 million people in urban areas will be counted among the poor'. This report goes on to show that 'on the average, 50% of the urban population in developing countries live in conditions of extreme deprivation and the figure may be higher in some cities' (1997: 55, 56).

What people consider 'poor' varies from one society to another and, within a given society, from one group to another. As well, definitions of poverty vary from one location to another, as we have seen. Some countries calculate a poverty line so that it represents a minimal standard of living. For example, the World Bank (Doraid, 1997) has calculated its 'poverty threshold' to be $1 (US) per day in developing nations, while $2 per day is often used in Latin America, $4 per day in Eastern Europe, and $14.40 per day in industrialized countries. These estimates are based on an absolute notion of poverty. However, even calculated this way, the poverty line is generally higher in cities, reflecting the higher cost of living in urban areas. This may produce paradoxical results: in India, a country people consider poor by Western standards, only 19 per cent of the population lives below the official poverty line. This proportion is low because a large fraction of the Indian population lives in (less expensive) rural areas.

A different estimate, by the Canadian Council on Social Development, shows that 22.4 per cent of households were poor using LICO to classify them as 'low-income' individuals or households in 1997. The child poverty rate was 19.9 per cent, which translates into 1.4 million poor children (CCSD, 2000: Tables 3.1 and 4.6). It is difficult to say how much higher or lower this figure is than figures on poverty for the United States or other Western nations. In North America, strategies of measurement vary, though most communities use a combination of relative and absolute definitions of poverty. By the United States's own measurement, the US poverty rate decreased recently, only to rise again (CCSD, 2000: 30). In 2000, it was calculated as 11.3 per cent, and it rose in 2001 to 11.7 per cent—a total of 32.9 million poor (US Bureau of the Census, 2002). This figure is lower than the figure cited above for Canada because the income cut-off for the United States is lower.

It should be evident by now that estimates of poverty and of the number of the poor are likely to vary widely. Comparing poverty across societies should be undertaken with the greatest caution. However, using most measures, the same 'kinds' of people tend to be poor in different societies.

Those Most Likely to Be Poor

In the United States, as in Canada, some people are more likely to be poor than others. Poor families are disproportionately found among African Americans, among Native Americans, or headed by female single parents. Thus, 22.7 per cent of African American families live in poverty, compared to 21.4 per cent of Hispanic Americans, 10.2 per cent of Asian Americans and Pacific Islanders, and 7.8 per cent of white non-Hispanic Americans (US Bureau of the Census, 2002: 4). Poverty rates also vary by sex. In Canada, for example, one in five women is poor (up from one in six in 1988), and in 1991, households headed by single-parent mothers made up only 6 per cent of all families but 30 per cent of poor families (National Council of

FIGURE 1.3

Percentage of Women in Poverty in Canada, 1988–1998

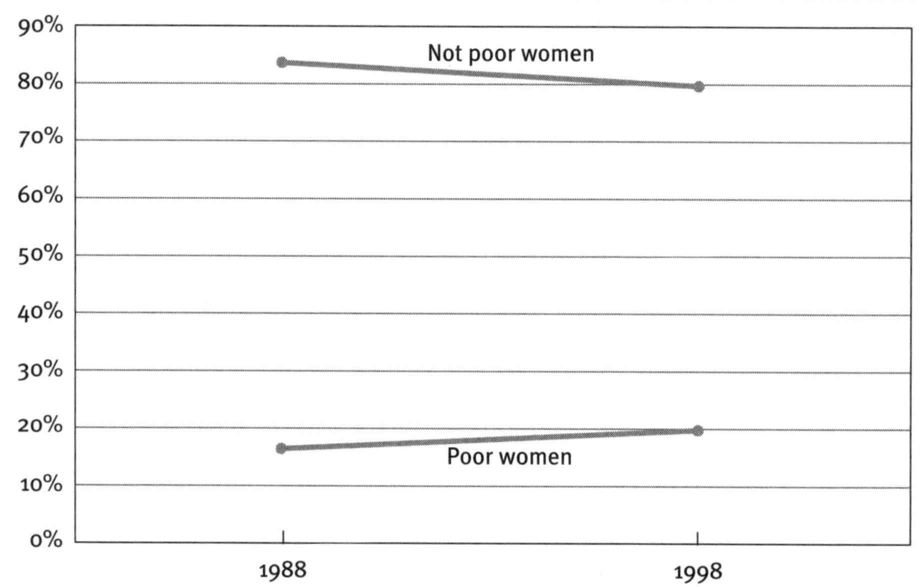

SOURCE: National Council of Welfare, *Profiles of Welfare: Myths and Realities* (1998); available at <www.ncwcnbes.net/ htmdocument/reportprowelfare/repprowelfare.htm>, accessed 10 January 2003. Reproduced with permission of the Minister of Public Works and Government Services Canada, 2003.

Welfare, 1998). (See Figure 1.3.) Generally, women, racial minorities, rural people, and people with less education are more likely to be poor, whatever society you might examine.

Social Problems Associated with Poverty and Economic Inequality

As we said, most social problems are related to poverty and economic power. We will introduce, briefly, in this section several of the social problems associated with poverty and income inequality. Each of these topics will be addressed more fully in later chapters. We begin with reminders that poverty and inequality are associated with all of the following: work and unemployment, crime and violence, drug and alcohol abuse, gender, ethnicity, age discrimination, homelessness, and relative social isolation.

Work and Unemployment

No matter how we measure them, poverty is about having too little money and wealth is about having plenty of it. Thus, poverty and wealth are closely related to employment, the main source of income for most people. More and better jobs mean more money. Today in Canada, most families have trouble living comfortably on a single income. To avoid poverty, many households need two or more incomes, so two or more adult household members have jobs. Yet even this is no guarantee of prosperity. Often even the gainfully employed live on the edge of poverty.

Many work lives, particularly those of people working in the secondary sector of the dual-labour market, are characterized by periods of employment followed by stretches of unwanted idleness. (Poor pay, low status, low security, high turnover, and easy entry mark jobs in the *secondary work sector*, such as unskilled labourer, cab driver, and salesperson.) Moreover, low wages prevent many people from putting away part of their income to serve as a safety net during times of unemployment. The result is that many must rely on social assistance programs, such as unemployment insurance, welfare, and workfare. These programs, though helpful and well intentioned, do little to help the people for whom they were devised. They help the poor survive but rarely help them change their lives for the better.

As well, unemployment and poverty are often related to health status. In countries with high levels of unemployment, employed workers tend to be healthy while unemployed people are not (Lahelma et al., 2000). People with jobs and people without them lead different lives. Often unemployment gives rise to psychological distress, fatalistic attitudes, feelings of lack of control, and feelings of personal inefficacy. Even in the short term, unemployment can be devastating. Unemployment and poverty harm people's health by diminishing their access to health care, for example.

Some unemployed people become demoralized and fall apart. Others do not, however. For example, one study found that young Irish workers who continued living an essentially normal life while unemployed quickly recovered their psychological well-being when they regained employment (Hannan, Ó Riain, and Whelan, 1997). It is important to recognize this variation, because where the effects of a social variable (such as unemployment) vary, it may be possible to create social programs that reduce or prevent the worst effects from occurring.

Not only does unemployment often lead to poor health, but poor health can also lead to unemployment—to job loss, early retirement, or unemployability—and thus to economic dependence and poverty. Health limitations make it harder to get a job, keep a job, work normal hours, or demand normal wages (Figueroa, 1996), especially for workers in the secondary labour market—for example, minority-group, less educated women.

Crime and Violence

According to a recent Statistics Canada study (2002), income distribution patterns in Canada and the United States have diverged during the past 10 years despite free trade and increased economic integration between the two nations. This result suggests a widespread difference in overall income distributions between Canada and the United States. Since 1974, Canada has not seen the substantial increase in income inequality that has occurred in the United States. At the bottom of the income spectrum, Canadian families are better off in terms of purchasing power than are their American counterparts. The income gap between rich and poor families in Canada has remained roughly stable since the mid-1970s, while it has increased in the United States, especially since the mid-1980s. This change has apparently increased criminal behaviour in the United States.

Researchers have noted a parallel increase in crimes of violence such as robbery, assault, rape, and murder (Braun, 1995). Part of this growth in crime and violence was due to a connection between poverty and racial inequality; part was due to the erosion of community cohesion and social supports in poor neighbourhoods. Bruce Kennedy and colleagues (1998) show that neighbourhood income inequality and lack of social capital (as measured by social trust and membership in voluntary associations) are strongly correlated with homicides and violent crimes using firearms. We will discuss this relationship further in chapter 3, on crime and violence.

Many believe that the poor, desperate to improve their financial state, are more likely than other people to commit opportunistic crimes, such as petty theft, muggings, or burglary. Research bears out this belief, at least in part. (Braun, 1995; Hagan, 1994; Kennedy et al., 1998). The poor have fewer legitimate opportunities to achieve the economic and social goals that our culture teaches us to value. The rise in crime may be due to greater desperation, or even to an increase in self-destructive attitudes among those who are poor; or it may reflect a decrease in community social cohesion in conditions of poverty.

Still, this is only half of the story. The poor do not commit all of society's crimes. As chapter 3 will point out, violations of the law committed wholly by the wealthy—so-called corporate crimes and white-collar crimes—are equally challenging and may harm many more people's lives. However, because these crimes are often hidden, the wrong-doers powerful, and the legal code more tolerant, white-collar infractions remain low on most law enforcement agencies' list of priorities. By contrast, the police target certain high-profile crimes—homicides, robberies, drug trafficking, and so on—that receive much more media attention and, therefore, cause much more public concern.

Drug and Alcohol Abuse

Another consequence of poverty and inequality is the excessive use of alcohol and drugs, whether for pleasure or to dull pain. This type of behaviour, like crime, is found in all social classes and is not restricted to the poor. Nor is it caused only by social inequality. However, the desperately poor, deprived of legitimate opportunities to achieve wealth and success, are more likely to use alcohol and drugs to deal with what Robert Merton (1957b) called *anomie*, the gap between what they have been taught to want and what they are able to get.

Is there a 'drug problem' in North America today? Part of the so-called drug problem is due to labelling and to prejudice in the enforcement of drug laws. As we will see in the next chapter, on drug and alcohol abuse, the justice system tends to unduly condemn drug and alcohol use by poor and marginalized people. Crack cocaine users, who are often poor and non-white, are punished more severely by the law than powder cocaine users, who are more often middle- or upper-class and white.

Having said that, there is little doubt that people turn to alcohol and drugs to help them deal with pain and depression—conditions

increased, if not caused, by poverty and economic inequality. Though far from all, some people who live in poverty abuse drugs and alcohol. Rhonda Jones-Webb and colleagues (1997), for instance, found that people living in poor neighbourhoods are more likely to suffer from alcoholism. Not only does poverty affect the occurrence of drug and alcohol use, it also increases the influence of drug and alcohol use on people's lives. One study found that poverty accounts for 69 per cent of the variance in the cocaine and opiate overdose mortality rates in New York City (Marzuk et al., 1997). Said another way, by far the single best predictor of death from a drug is the poverty of the drug user. Drugs do their worst harm when people are already leading lives stressed by low income, poor health, bad nutrition, and inadequate housing. All of these conditions reduce the immunity to disease that helps us survive.

Children and Their Development

Poverty is also age-related in most societies. People without an income (for example, children) or with a fixed income (for example, elderly people) are more vulnerable to the risks of poverty and inequality than other members of society. For children, longer durations of poverty produce a greater number of more harmful outcomes. Children who grow up continuously poor develop higher rates of anti-social behaviour than children who are poor only briefly or not at all (McLeod and Shanahan, 1993, 1996). Timing also matters: poverty during the earlier years of life (that is, preschool, elementary school) is most harmful, causing lower school-completion rates (Brooks-Gunn and Duncan, 1997). Poverty is particularly important for the cognitive development of preschoolers, who need a rich learning environment to reach their potential (Duncan and Brooks-Gunn, 1997).

An Ontario study found that children in families with lower socio-economic status—for example, with poorly educated mothers—are

Child poverty is a huge social problem in Canada, as it is in many developed nations. In 1989, one in seven Canadian children was living in poverty. Now we're at almost one in five. (Chris Schwarz)

more likely to have trouble with school, and even more psychiatric difficulties. The change to living in a female-headed household, after separation or divorce, is a strong predictor of poor academic performance and of emotional and behavioural problems, particularly if the change occurs later in a child's life. However, the associations between poverty, family status, and child morbidity are lower in Ontario than in the United States, suggesting the possibility of US–Canadian differences with respect to poverty, social safety nets, and other contextual factors (Lipman and Offord, 1997).

Poor conditions in childhood, especially low socio-economic status, are often related to poor health behaviours and mental states in adulthood (Lynch, Kaplan, and Shema, 1997). However, this is not certain or always enduring (see, for example, Hauser and Sweeney, 1997). Good parenting, for example, can limit the effects of child-

hood poverty on adult self-esteem, depression, and loneliness (De Haan and MacDermid, 1998; Jones et al., 2002). Finally, poverty is not the only important influence on childhood development. Peers are important, as are mass media and the schools. Some even find that the childhood experience of divorce is a stronger predictor of behavioural problems than is low income during childhood, probably because of the correlation between divorce and family conflict (Pagani, Boulerice, and Tremblay, 1997).

Poverty is rarely the main or the only condition that drives children onto the streets in Canada (see Hagan and McCarthy, 1997). More often, the cause is parental violence, abuse, or neglect. These problems, however, are often a result of combined poverty, addiction, unemployment, and psychological disorder. The long-run consequences are serious. Street children run the risks of worse health, reduced safety, and poorer prospects that

they will, in time, gain the education and economic independence they will need as adults.

Research on children who grow up poor
leads to three conclusions about poverty: (1) raising the income level of families in poverty, even
just barely above the poverty-line level, will
improve the learning ability and performance of
young children; (2) raising the educational status
of parents will have a similar effect; and (3) raising *both* the income and the education level of
parents will have more effect than targeting only
one or the other (Smith et al., 1999). However, it
may be easier to raise family incomes than to raise
parental education levels.

The Elderly

At the other end of the age distribution, the fight
against poverty among elderly people was one of
Canada's biggest success stories in the latter part
of the twentieth century. Poverty rates for people
65 and older have fallen noticeably over the years
and continue to fall. In 1998, the poverty rate for
women 65 and older fell to an all-time low of
21.7 per cent. That pushed the overall poverty
rate for seniors down to a near-record low of
17.5 per cent. The explanation for these changes
is probably improved pensions for men and
women who have been in the workforce.

Researchers have proposed two hypotheses
to connect age and poverty. One, the **affluence-
trajectory hypothesis**, argues that as people get
older, they typically earn higher incomes, until
late middle age, when most people reach their
maximum earning potential. After that point,
economic hardship will begin to rise through the
combination of inflation and a fixed income.
Another, the **adequacy-gradient hypothesis**,
argues that as people get older, they accumulate
wealth and other resources; simultaneously, their
needs decline, especially after children leave the
household. As a result, economic hardships will
consistently decrease as age increases. And either
way, people will become healthier, and more
equally healthy, as they age.

Studies testing these two theories for the
United Stated has found support for the latter
theory (Cairney and Avison, 1999; Mirowsky
and Ross, 1999). The health gap between rich
and poor people does not appear to increase as
people age, perhaps because older people enjoy
more similar levels of income adequacy. As well,
rich and poor people suffer equally from many of
the same infirmities of old age. However, poor
health in old age reflects a lifetime of vulnerabilities, often related to lifelong experiences of low
income. Compared with the more economically
advantaged, the less advantaged on each post-
retirement measure have high lifetime exposure
scores on a variety of environmental health hazards (Berney et al., 2000).

The Homeless

One of the most pressing social problems today
is homelessness, a growing problem in Canada's
urban centres. Although the exact number of
homeless people in Canada is unknown, some
estimates illustrate the size of the problem.
Toronto's Homelessness Action Task Force noted
that 26,000 people used the city's shelter system
in 1996 (1999: iv). The fastest-growing groups
were youth under 18 and families with children,
with the latter group accounting for 46 per cent
of all shelter users (ibid., 1999).

Other frequent shelter users include
Aboriginal people and people with severe mental
illnesses or other serious health problems (such
as AIDS). More than 100,000 people, or 37,000
households, were on the Toronto Social Housing
Connections waiting list in 1996. Of this group,
more than one-third had incomes of less than
$800 per month per household. The shrinking
availability of affordable housing has exacerbated
the problem of homelessness.

Most low-income families are renters, not
homeowners. As a result, when rent prices
increase or owners change rental units into
owner-occupied condominiums, many families
are forced on the streets and into shelters. In

1996, more than 4 in every 10 tenant-households in Toronto paid over 30 per cent of their income for rent. Between 1991 and 1996, almost 60,000 rental units in the city changed from the low-rent category to the middle range of prices. Moreover, middle-income families (who earn $30,000 or more per year) take roughly half of the low-rent units. Many landlords give them special treatment because of their stable income and ability to always pay the rent. Besides the 37,000 homes currently needed by people already on the waiting list, the task force estimated in 1999 that Toronto would need another 2,000 homes each year for the future to house the expected increase in homeless individuals and families (Toronto, Homelessness Action Task Force, 1999: 137–40).

Social Involvement and Social Support

Research has shown that people who are poor or have lower incomes have less social contact with

---

BOX 1.2
Affordable Housing

The growing lack of affordable housing is a pressing problem in Hamilton-Wentworth, Halton and much of Ontario, and it shouldn't be that way in an affluent province like ours. Chronic shortages can be eased with creative, public-private partnerships that won't stress governments and taxpayers. What's missing is a determination to take action and a recognition that affordable housing pays for itself.

As shown in this week's Spectator series, most politicians and builders aren't tackling the issue with appropriate urgency. For too many of us, affordable housing is someone else's problem. In reality, we all have a stake. The future of our cities, especially downtown areas and inner-city neighbourhoods, depends to a large extent on how we respond to the need to supply decent housing to lower-income families.

An obvious quick-fix—a massive government building program—isn't practical. On balance, that's probably good, considering what happens when large-scale public housing projects deteriorate, isolated from the community. Many high-density projects built in the 60s and 70s testify to the failure of that approach. The problem is compounded by the unwillingness of private developers to supply affordable housing, especially rental apartments, because the cost involved doesn't match the revenue potential.

Neither the public nor private sectors can meet the challenge on their own, but together they can make a big difference. Governments can help by giving tax credits to those who invest in affordable housing and making concessions such as lifting the GST on building materials; eliminating or reducing development charges; releasing surplus lands and offering more generous housing allowances.

All of these ideas involve some expense for governments, but the cost of not acting is greater. In Ontario, thousands of lower-income families and individuals can afford only cramped, run-down apartments that many people wouldn't dream of living in. It's a moral and economic imperative that they get help. Substandard housing and even worse, homelessness, are a recipe for inner-city decay and increasing costs for welfare, shelters and social assistance of all kinds. Measured against that, affordable housing is a bargain.

SOURCE: 'Collective Solutions to the Affordable Housing Crisis' (Editorial), *Hamilton Spectator*, 21 July 1999, A10. Reproduced courtesy of The Hamilton Spectator.

others in the community—whether friends, acquaintances, or relatives. We only need to think about poor elderly people and the homeless, the two social categories just discussed, to know that this is correct, at least at these extremes of poverty. Poverty means more limited contact with others—indeed, sometimes it means social near-isolation. There is ample research evidence, though, that the relationship between income and social involvement is a general one, extending beyond just the low-income extremes. It appears that the higher one's income, the greater one's level of social contact with others. If social contact means greater opportunity to receive social support when one needs it, those with greater income have more opportunity for social support.

Data from a recent large national survey of the social involvement patterns of adult Canadians support the above conclusions. Using data gathered by Statistics Canada, M. Hall and colleagues (1998) showed that people with lower incomes and lower education levels did less informal and formal volunteering of their time, and gave less assistance to others, in the past year than did those with higher income and education. Informal volunteering was defined as help given to relatives, neighbours, friends, and others on an ad hoc, personal basis. Formal volunteering was defined as help given under the auspices of some group or organization. Both forms of help increased as the income and education of the respondent increased. Further data from this study showed that the frequency of visiting with friends outside the neighbourhood was also positively related to how much money the respondent or his or her household earned.

James Curtis, Douglas Baer, and Edward Grabb (2001) have also shown that people's income and education predict how many affiliations they have with voluntary community organizations, and how active they are in organizations. The results are for Canada and over 30 other countries (see also Curtis, Grabb, and Chui, 1999, for further results for Canada).

Robert Putnam drew a similar conclusion based on US studies: 'People with lower incomes and those who feel financially strapped are much less engaged in all forms of social and community life than those who are better off' (2000: 193).

Part of the explanation for these patterns may lie with (1) the amount of financial resources available for use in social involvement, (2) the amount of free, flexible time available for this purpose, and (3) available opportunities (all versus social exclusion from such organizations).

Nan Lin (2000) has emphasized, from his review of previous research, that similar patterns hold for gender, racial, and ethnic differences in social involvement. Evidence shows that (with some exceptions for specific ethnic groups) men and the majority ethnic group have more extensive and varied social contacts with others than do women and minority groups. Here, again, differences in financial resources, available time, and opportunities for participation probably play a part in the explanations of these patterns of social involvement.

Theories of Poverty

We noted earlier that sociologists differ in the ways they explain poverty and inequality, and in the ways they explain the correlation of other social problems with social inequality. The basic theories can be distinguished as follows.

The Structural-Functionalist Perspective

The sociological perspective or theory called *structural functionalism* was the dominant sociological approach through most of the twentieth century, especially in North American universities. This approach argues that society consists of a connected network of groups, organizations, and institutions that work together to maintain the well-being of a society. In the eyes of a structural-functionalist, everything in a society has a purpose or function. For example, families produce and train the next generation of people; in that sense, the 'function' of a family is to reproduce society and its workforce. Workplaces produce incomes for individuals and prosperity for society; crime allows the disadvantaged to gain socially desirable goals (such as money); religion gives people a moral compass and a definition of culturally acceptable behaviour; and schools prepare young people to participate in the economic system. All of these are *functions* that, when fulfilled, permit society to continue, or 'survive', in its present form. Everything has a function, or else it would not exist.

Accordingly, the structural-functionalist perspective argues that poverty and inequality also serve important functions in society. Inequality comes to be defined as a graded ladder of people with different occupational roles and income levels. Poverty motivates people to work harder to move up the ladder. The jobs at the top of this ladder require much more investment in education and effort, and they therefore carry greater rewards. They are also, according to this theory, the most socially useful and socially valued jobs.

Consider, as an example, the job of physician. Doctoring requires a great deal of skill and expertise. Physicians need many years of education to develop their skills. After obtaining a medical degree, physicians then face a highly stressful career filled with long shifts and hard, challenging work. Noble intentions alone are not enough to inspire people to become physicians. Few people would likely subject themselves to such a tiring life were it not for the rewards society attaches to doctoring, this theory says. These rewards suit the social importance of the job and the study and sacrifice required to prepare for the job.

By contrast, consider the job of serving person at a doughnut counter. The training required to do this job is virtually zero. The job complexity and associated stress and responsibility are virtually zero. Almost anyone could do this job on five minutes' notice. So there is little need for the doughnut store to pay high salaries to induce people to take the job or stay in it. As a result, the pay for this work is low. Again, the rewards suit the

social importance of the occupation and the study and sacrifice required to prepare for the job.

When skill and effort are consistent with compensation, as with doctors and doughnut servers, the functional theory of inequality works well. However, structural-functionalists are hard pressed to explain the inflated salaries received by professional athletes, entertainers, and criminals, or the much lower salaries of nurses, teachers, and child care workers. In these cases, the rewards do not obviously suit the social importance of the job and the study and sacrifice required to prepare for it.

Conflict Theory

The conflict theory of poverty and inequality relies heavily on ideas first developed by Karl Marx and Max Weber. This sociological approach, which concerns class conflict and social stratification in industrial economies and which has always been popular outside North America, enjoyed a surge of popularity everywhere in the late twentieth century.

According to Marxist theory, the *bourgeoisie* is the social class comprising the owners of the means of production. As the controllers of factories and business establishments, the bourgeoisie can decide the nature of the work for the second, lower class of society, the *proletariat*. This latter group, lacking the means to produce merchandise on their own, must resort to selling the only remaining commodity they have: their labour power. The bourgeoisie, recognizing the proletariat's dependence on the wages earned from work, are free to exploit the labour of the working class and to amass more wealth for themselves. They keep wages low to ensure that their workers remain dependent on them for economic survival. By manipulating the schools and mass media, they ensure that popular thinking continues to support the unequal distribution of wealth and power in society.

This practice continues in the present era, the theory argues. Those who control the means

Many Canadians find themselves dropping in and out of poverty. We will see later that periods of low income have serious outcome effects. (Harry Cutting Photography)

of production continue to control the market system, although in a post-industrial economy the controllers are no longer just local factory owners. Today, multinational corporations—or, more precisely, the powerful executives who run them—continue to amass huge annual profits that are grossly inconsistent with the payment offered to their employees. In developed nations, employers are more likely pay workers a reasonable wage for work done under safe conditions, owing to the influence of unions and labour legislation. In developing nations, employers are less constrained. Transnational corporations enjoy great freedom to maximize their profits by reducing costs and exploiting workers almost without limit, thanks to their influence on the global political and economic systems.

Conflict theorists also recognize the biased nature of laws and policies that favour the rich, such as low-interest government loans to bail out failing business ventures and give tax breaks to corporations. As might be expected, conflict theories are more likely to discuss the types of social structural and cultural constraints on extracting oneself from poverty that we discussed in the introductory chapter. Conflict theorists see many mechanisms of exclusion, disability, decoupling, and scarcity at work in creating and maintaining poverty for some groups, and in maintaining economic inequality per se.

Symbolic Interactionism

The symbolic interactionist approach developed out of a combination of European and American philosophical approaches and took its current form at the University of Chicago in the mid-twentieth century. It is particularly concerned with the ways people work together to 'make sense' of social reality.

In relation to poverty, symbolic interactionists focus on the ways in which people construct the labels 'wealthy' and 'poor' through social interaction and on the costs of being identified by such labels. The typical though unspoken stereotype of a poor person in North American society runs as follows: a lazy, irresponsible, undeserving, freeloading ethnic minority (probably black, Latino, or Aboriginal) who would rely on welfare and social assistance instead of finding a steady job to support himself or herself; a person who probably dabbles in petty crime and spends much of his or her money on alcohol and drugs; possibly a violent and dangerous threat, and a nuisance to society. On the other hand, the stereotyped depiction of a rich person is this: greedy, shallow, snobbish, egotistical, callous, extravagant, wasteful, and probably white; has no qualms about stepping on others for personal gain; born with a silver spoon in his or her mouth and has always lived a life of sheltered privilege; inherited the already sizeable wealth of mommy or daddy, and therefore, without expending any personal effort in building or increasing the family fortune, has only succeeded in taking advantage of an unjust economic and social system skewed toward the privileged few at the expense of the disadvantaged many.

Like all stereotypes, these ones are exaggerations. To be sure, some poor people are lazy and irresponsible, but so are some rich people. Similarly, both the poor and the rich can be greedy and shallow. Still, even if such labels may be arbitrary and unfounded, their consequences are real enough. Being labelled as 'poor' creates many problems that extend beyond, and contribute further to, poverty. Employers mindful of these stereotypes are less likely to offer poor people well-paying, stable jobs. Poor people are more likely to be the targets of unwarranted police scrutiny and harassment. Members of the public will see any reliance on government assistance by the poor as confirming the validity of the applied stereotype. These are some ways in which the poor become excluded and decoupled from normal social and economic activity.

Culture versus Economic Inequality as Explanations of Poverty

Oscar Lewis's well-known 'culture of poverty' theory (1966) is consistent with the interactionist approach to studying culture and stereotyping. However, it is the subject of considerable scholarly debate. Does Lewis fairly depict the urban poor in their struggle for survival and dignity? Or is he lending scholarly support to a coarse stereotype that bigoted people are glad to endorse?

The 'Culture of Poverty' Theory

The result of years of studying urban ghettos in Mexico, Puerto Rico, the continental United States, and elsewhere, Lewis's theory characterizes the urban poor as having a distinct set of values and norms. These include a shortsighted view of the future, an impulsive and hedonistic attitude that lacks discipline and restraint, a failure or unwillingness to participate in mainstream culture, and a tendency to accept their marginalized status in society. These urban poor, many of them from an alien rural background, cobble together a meaningful understanding of an otherwise chaotic and punishing social world. Some of these groups remain poor because they pass on their fatalistic values and belief systems to future generations. Most group members lack the skills to escape to better lives and better communities. In these ways, they remain decoupled and disabled.

This summary is too brief to capture the full richness of Lewis's analysis. However, it highlights the reasons why this theory polarizes opinion. Some say it portrays the poor as deserving their poverty because they do not make the effort to escape it. Indeed, some people still hold this view today, and it appears in stereotypical characterizations of poor people as 'naturally' lazy or incapable. This idea has long since fallen out of favour as a sociological or anthropological explanation. However, the idea that certain types of culture restrict people, prevent them from achieving their potential, and therefore act to keep their members—groups, or even whole societies—in poverty still enjoys a considerable currency in popular thinking. Indeed, we can relate this idea to our idea that culture and social structure can disable people by hurting their self-esteem and lowering their aspirations.

Economic Inequality as a Cause of Poverty

What if we view poverty not as a personal failure or commitment to a flawed value system, but instead as a result of the uneven distribution of resources within society? If we do, we come to see the urban or rural poor in our own country, and elsewhere, in a different light.

The sheer physical fact of poverty has implications for the people who deal with it on a daily basis. When money is scarce and not guaranteed in the future, it makes little sense to speak of 'improvidence'. Daily survival is more important. Rather than saying that children from poor families have internalized norms of laziness, we can point out that they have to deal with conditions that their wealthier peers do not face: underequipped classrooms, crowded home conditions, the lack of a place to study, even hunger during the day, which prevents children from giving full attention to their classwork.

Saying that a culture of poverty and the people who share it are responsible for this uneven distribution of physical resources is blaming the victim (Ryan, 1976). Victim blaming sometimes occurs because people believe that work is a duty and that not working is sinful. These views are supported, in part, by that set of beliefs Max Weber labelled the *Protestant Ethic*; the idea that people who are not at work are sinful or immoral is a complement to the idea of worldly success marking out those who are 'God's elect'. So the notion that a culture of poverty is responsible for

keeping people poor fits with part of our society's dominant ideology. This dominant ideology says that poor people deserve to be poor because they have bad values. Yet, though it may fit society's preconceptions, this way of thinking does not explain the facts of poverty very well.

For example, the 'culture of poverty' theory implies that people in poverty will remain there and that even the children of poor families will themselves stay poor. However, the theory cannot explain many people's poverty. For example, among the many who are poor today in North America, some are unemployed and some of these are not seeking employment—the stereotypical 'people on welfare' (but see Table 1.1 on welfare levels). Most others, however, are in the workforce, and recent Canadian and US figures show a rise in the numbers of the working poor. The majority of poor people move in and out of poverty over years, decades, and generations.

In fact, in modern industrial societies most families move up and down the job and income hierarchy over generations (see Figure 1.4). The mechanisms for this mobility are talent, effort, luck, social connections, and formal education. There is very little evidence that occupational aspirations are immutable, that educational aspirations are restricted to the rich, or that religious and cultural values (for example, Catholicism versus Protestantism) affect mobility. Mainly, it is opportunities for good jobs that affect mobility. In fact, the central finding of a generation's worth of research on social mobility is this: children who get the same amount of education get the same kinds of jobs and incomes regardless of the class they start out in. The trick for society, then, is ensuring equal access to higher education and stimulating the creation of good jobs.

For poor people not seeking work, asking why may be instructive. Some live in areas where there is little work to seek. Moving out may not be an option that makes much sense, particularly if people can add to their family economies in ways other than by directly earning a wage (such as by taking care of other family members—children or

TABLE 1.1

Welfare Incomes as Percentage of Average Incomes and Welfare Benefits in Constant Dollars, 2001[a]

	Single, Employable	Person with a Disability	Single Parent, One Child	Couple, Two Children
Welfare incomes as percentage of average incomes				
Newfoundland and Labrador	17	**46**	**58**	30
Prince Edward Island	**28**	42	42	**34**
Nova Scotia	21	36	48	28
New Brunswick	**15**	30	52	**15**
Quebec	26	37	45	25
Ontario	22	37	39	21
Manitoba	21	35	46	27
Saskatchewan	24	35	45	27
Alberta	18	**26**	**31**	24
British Columbia	20	30	45	24
Mean across provinces	19.2	35.4	45.1	23.5
Welfare benefits in constant dollars				
Newfoundland and Labrador	**3,070**	8,656	11,704	12,596
Prince Edward Island	5,604	8,532	9,564	14,521
Nova Scotia	4,611	8,067	9,284	13,474
New Brunswick	3,168	6,696	9,922	**11,328**
Quebec	6,209	9,062	10,351	12,041
Ontario	6,623	11,466	10,861	13,452
Manitoba	5,352	8,117	9,363	12,847
Saskatchewan	5,772	8,424	9,401	13,332
Alberta	4,824	**7,380**	**8,741**	13,425
British Columbia	6,251	9,522	11,103	13,534
Yukon	**12,045**	**13,545**	16,449	22,786
Northwest Territories	8,731	11,091	17,824	23,021
Nunavut	10,188	12,288	**25,290**	**29,567**

[a]Highest and lowest figures are shown in boldface.

SOURCE: National Council on Welfare, *Welfare Incomes Report 2000–2001* (2002), Tables 4 and 5a; available at <www.ncwcnbes.net/index.htm>, accessed 1 March 2003. Reproduced with the permission of The Minister of Public Works and Government Services.

elderly relatives). Moving may merely mean that the expenses for another household have to be found, somehow, with no guarantee of a job. As we will see in chapter 4, migration is a high-risk activity, and migrants seek to minimize their risks as well as maximize their gains.

If the only jobs to be found pay a minimum wage, earnings may fall below the poverty line

FIGURE 1.4
University Graduates by Parental Education, by Gender, 1982–1995

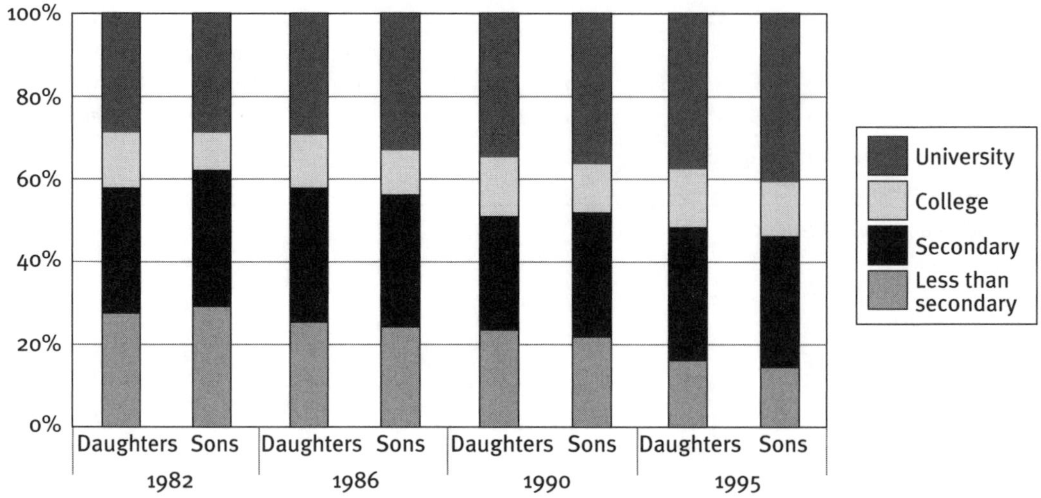

Question: How does the culture of poverty theory explain upward mobility?

SOURCE: Statistics Canada, *Are the Kids All Right? Intergenerational Mobility and Child Well-Being in Canada* (Analytical Studies Branch research paper series, Cat. no. 11F0019MIE2001171, National Graduates Survey, various years).

for a household with one or more children to support, especially in an expensive city. Some may have sought work so often already that they are burnt out, dispirited, injured by the experience. Rather than seeing this as a cultural fact, we may better regard this as a reaction to the material situation of their lives and to the ways in which others treat them.

What of the other parts of the 'culture of poverty' theory, the idea that the poor are frivolous spenders, concerned only with instant satisfaction? This idea betrays ignorance about the hardship and sheer banality of poverty. For many poor people, being poor means not having enough money to pay the rent or power bills regularly. 'Budgeting' means going to each company to whom the household is in debt and explaining, yet again, how much they can pay this month so that no one cuts off the power or evicts them. Going into debt to feed and house oneself or one's

family means that any money earned is already spoken for. Debt and the interest on it accumulate fast. These are some of the common, banal, and far from gratifying experiences of poverty.

Rather than blaming the victim, it makes sense for sociologists to ask how labelling comes about and how society is involved in it, how society constructs dependency in people so labelled, and how some groups manage to break free of it.

Health Consequences of Poverty and Economic Inequality

Poverty is not only hard and depressing, it also harms your health. What is more, poor health is sometimes a cause of poverty, not vice versa. For chronically ill people, for example, poverty and inequality are continuing problems they cannot handle on their own. Their lives force us to evaluate ideas such as 'responsibility', 'justice', 'brother's keeper', and 'citizenship'. However, changes in health do not appear to influence changes in income as much as changes in income influence changes in health (Thiede and Traub, 1997). Poor people are often caught in a poverty cycle of low food quality, low income, poor health, malnutrition, poor environmental sanitation, and infectious disease.

Poverty and Health

Studies show that, everywhere, poverty directly hinders the access to food of high quality (that is, food as a source of essential nutrients, vitamins, minerals, and so on), which then leads to poorer health (Akinyele, 1997; Bakken, Jezewska-Zychowicz, and Winter, 1999; Dowler, 1998; Kusumayati and Gross, 1998). For example, iodine deficiency among pregnant mothers can result in cretinism and other forms of mental retardation in the child. Iron deficiency—which affects 2 billion people globally—in youth can cause problems with coordination and balance. It has been estimated that because of poor nutrition, 226 million children are shorter than they should be for their age, while another 183 million are underweight (United Nations Children's Fund, 1998: 15). Chronic hunger leads to serious health problems, including rickets, scurvy, intestinal infections or damage, a depressed immune system, and impaired cognitive development. As well, hungry children are more likely to be hyperactive, to have problems concentrating in school, and to have other serious behavioural problems (Akinyele, 1997; Bakken, Jezewska-Zychowicz, and Winter, 1999; Dowler, 1998; Kusumayati and Gross, 1998).

Poverty is also likely to worsen health problems through the social problems to which it is related, such as crime (see Figure 1.5) and substance abuse. These other problems can also lead to poverty and the health problems that poverty entails. We discuss the specific health consequences of these other social problems in their respective chapters.

It is a sobering fact that in many countries, income inequalities are also correlated with the chances of dying early (see, for example, Kawashi and Kennedy, 1997). For Canada, for almost every cause of death we can examine in national statistics, the rate of early mortality is higher for people of lower socio-economic status or is lower for people of the higher socio-economic classes (see, for example, Health Canada, 1999). This *mortality gradient* is most notable in deaths from hypertensive heart disease, tuberculosis, asthma, pneumonia, and bronchitis. Early mortality is also much higher for Aboriginal people than for other Canadians (Health Canada, 1999).

Effects of Inequality

In short, inequality is bad for our health. There is evidence that being at the bottom end of a hierarchy—no matter how affluent that hierarchy may be—leads to health problems. Much of the relevant research has revolved around the *relative income hypothesis*, which proposes that income inequality alone (as opposed to absolute levels of deprivation) is enough to bring on various health differences, including differences in mortality, within a population. This theory argues that the fact of inequality in a society has real and measurable health consequences for those at the lower end of the hierarchy. An influential study (Wilkinson, 1994, 1996) found a correlation between life expectancy and the proportion of income received by the poorest 70 per cent of the population. Richard Wilkinson showed that the greater the difference in income distribution between the least well off 70 per cent and the most well off 30 per cent, the greater the levels of early mortality in a society or community.

Further evidence in support of relative (versus absolute) income inequality comes from the finding that GNP (gross national product) per capita is correlated with health only up to a boundary of $5,000 GNP per capita per year. Beyond this threshold, increases in standard of living have little effect on people's health. Thus,

FIGURE 1.5
Household Income in Relation to Violent Victimization
(Rate per 1,000 Population)[a]

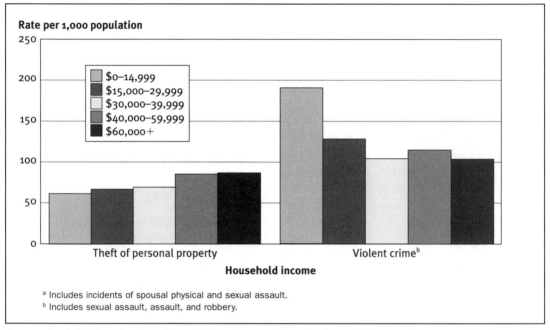

a Includes incidents of spousal physical and sexual assault.
b Includes sexual assault, assault, and robbery.

SOURCE: Statistics Canada, *Canadians with Low Incomes* (Canadian Centre for Justice Statistics Profile Series, cat. no. 85F0033MIE2001004) (Ottawa: Statistics Canada, 2001).

in developed countries, people's disadvantage in relation to others, rather than their absolute deprivation, leads to health inequalities. As Norman Daniels, Bruce Kennedy, and Ichiro Kawachi note, 'the health of a population depends not just on the size of the economic pie but on how the pie is shared. . . . Differences in health outcomes among developed nations cannot be explained by the absolute deprivation associated with low economic development' (2000: 9).

George Kaplan and colleagues (1999) found that income inequality is also related to various health-related measures, including increased homicide and violent crime rates, expenditure per capita on health care and prevention, low-birthweight children, sedentary behaviour, and smoking. Thus, social inequality produces poor health and social problems; the question is how and why?

Two Explanations

Researchers have offered two complementary avenues of interpretation to explain how income inequality causes poor health. First, according to one macro-level sociological explanation, *income inequality breaks down social cohesion*. Also, as we have said, within societies, people's levels of income predict the extent of their social involvement and types of contact with others. The final part of this explanation is evidence that social integration and social support networks are vital resources supporting good health. The latter may be due to a mix of factors, including a buffering effect on stress, reduction of high-risk behaviours, more sources of financial and social assistance, greater emotional and spiritual support, and increased access to health-related information.

Robert Putnam (2000) cites the results of numerous studies that indicate a link between social cohesion and social connectedness on the one hand and health and longevity on the other. Individuals with higher levels of social involvement are healthier and live longer; also, areas of the United States that show higher social integration have better health and mortality records. Further comparisons across countries varying in levels of social integration show better health experiences and longer longevity in the countries with higher social integration (OECD, 2001; Putnam, 2000; Wilkinson, 1996).

Furthermore, a breakdown in social cohesion is associated with increased levels of crime and violence, which, in turn, has both direct consequences for health status (for example, exposure to drugs, physical injury) and indirect (for example, lowered social capital and property values within the community, greater unemployment, lower quality or absence of health care services). As David Coburn (2000) points out, neo-liberal economic policies are often at the root of this problem, by producing both higher income inequality and lower social cohesion while undermining social supports historically provided by the welfare state.

According to a second, micro-level sociobiological analysis, income inequality may have physiological consequences for people. *Income inequality may create dangerous stress* and other dangerous environmental or psychological factors. Bruce McEwan (1999) calls the problem one of 'allostatic load'. He defines *allostasis* as 'the ability to achieve stability through change' (interview with Norman Swan, 13 April 1998, *The Health Report*, Radio National). According to this theory, health decline under stressful conditions is the result of overuse of natural bodily processes. In an indirect way, the famous Whitehall studies support this theory.

The Whitehall Studies

The best-known and most often cited investigations of economic status and health are the Whitehall studies. Researchers have published hundreds of research reports based on the data derived from the original study of roughly 18,000 male British civil servants in the late 1960s and the 1970s. A major finding was that mortality rates, particularly from coronary heart disease (CHD), were three times higher among workers in the lowest civil service positions (messengers, door keepers, and so on) than among those in the highest positions (such as top administrators), even after accounting for risk factors such as obesity, smoking habits, amount of leisure time and physical activity, other illnesses, baseline blood pressure, and height (Marmot, Shipley, and Rose, 1984).

One explanation of the variance in CHD mortality is the difference in control and support experienced by workers along the job hierarchy (Marmot, Kogevinas, and Elston, 1987). In short, people with less control over their job and its performance are more likely to suffer heart conditions. Moreover, blood pressure at work is linked to various forms of job stress, including lack of skill use, tension, and lack of clarity in tasks. So the line of argument is as follows: *people in low-status jobs have less control over their work*; this lack of control produces more stress; and more stress produces higher blood pressure and higher risks of heart disease (for example, strokes and heart attacks).

To further test the hypothesis that inequality in occupational settings contributes directly to heath problems and increased mortality, researchers undertook a second Whitehall study, involving more than 10,000 male and female British civil servants, in 1985. Findings from that research have confirmed that, indeed, low work control—characteristic of low-status occupations such as clerical and office support workers—increases the risk of developing CHD (Bosma et al., 1997). Not surprisingly, low levels of work control are associated with more frequent absence from work (North et al., 1996).

These correlational findings, gained through longitudinal studies of the British civil service, have gained support from laboratory and field research on the chemistry of higher primates.

Explanations from Biology and Chemistry

Several studies have used primate subjects in laboratory and field settings to show that inferior status (which is presumably a stressful experience) is associated with coronary artery atherosclerosis (Shively and Clarkson, 1999), depression (Shively, Laber-Larid, and Anton, 1999), and raised levels of the stress hormone cortisol (Sapolsky, Alberts, and Altmann, 1999).

Also, the effects of cortisol levels have been investigated in humans by M. Kristenson and colleagues (1998). These researchers found cortisol levels to be related to differential rates of CHD among men in Lithuania (high rates of occurrence) and Sweden (low rates of occurrence). Cortisol, a glucocorticoid hormone, is the body's major chronic stress response agent. Our bodies often release it during situations characterized by a sense of helplessness or lack of control, and it prepares the individual for vigilance and long-term action or change. We also know that it induces measurable physiological responses, including raised blood pressure, disrupted circadian rhythms (sleep patterns), increased blood sugar and fatty-acid levels, and the suppression of the immune system. Cortisol is also involved in healing cuts, bruises, and swelling resulting from physical injury.

These bodily reactions are all evolutionarily important, as they in one way or another assign the body's resources and allow for greater levels of physical action. However, researchers are coming to believe that the bodily responses to raised cortisol levels, if repeated often, will do more harm than good, leading to problems such as heart ailments (resulting from high blood pressure and cholesterol levels) and increased susceptibility to various diseases (particularly in HIV/AIDS patients, whose immune systems are already compromised).

In short, we now have evidence that social inequality has not only social and psychological but also biological and health consequences. Experiencing social inequality over extended periods can be harmful to your health if you are toward the bottom of the hierarchy. Relative deprivation, as well as absolute deprivation, seems to affect people's life chances. Income and status affect health and longevity.

Solving the Problems of Poverty and Inequality

Solutions to the problems of poverty and inequality have been debated for centuries, if not millennia. They fall into two main categories—individual and collective—and we will discuss both types of solution. Individuals, usually in their own interest, undertake *individual solutions. Collective solutions* require the cooperation of many individuals for their mutual benefit. Let us begin by considering some of the ways in which individuals deal with their own personal experience of poverty and/or inequality in North American society.

Individual Solutions

Throughout this book we will use four concepts—exclusion, disability, decoupling, and scarcity—to explain the limits on people's opportunity. Remedies for these problems fall into two categories, individual and group, as we have said.

As an individual, you may best solve the problem of exclusion by getting whatever credentials allow you to enter the group you hope to spend your life in. Higher education is the single best investment you can make if your goals are material, and perhaps even if they are creative. However, racial and ethnic discrimination continue to limit people's opportunities to enter many lines of activity. For example, members of groups that suffer discrimination may not do as well in work settings controlled by other ethnic groups as they would by remaining within their own ethnic community, even with less education. The decision you have to make here, a complex one, depends on several factors: the actual extent of discrimination against your ethnic or racial group, the chance of a significant reduction in that discrimination during your lifetime, the range of attractive occupational opportunities within your own racial or ethnic community, and the chance of a significant increase in these opportunities during your lifetime.

BOX 1.3
Bread for All

The 'community development' project described in this article is an example of the important role that individuals can and do play in their neighbourhoods.

Jutta Mason shows up early one morning at Dufferin Grove Park, leans her bike against the fence, opens the door of the rec centre with a key—she has her own. She roots in a bin for some sticks of wood and a bundle of kindling, loads the wood into a wheelbarrow, and pushes the wheelbarrow out the door and over to a brick oven in the park. Isn't this how everyone makes bread? She dumps a yeast starter into the bowl of a Hobart mixer, turns on the machine, adds water and flour, sugar and salt. There's a story behind the mixer, just like there's a story behind the wood and the oven.

Not so long ago, Jutta saw a documentary about a village in which life seemed centred around a communal outdoor oven. Hmm. Then she met an Australian blacksmith who lives in California; he just happened to design brick ovens; hmm. The next thing you know . . . It's as simple as that. A guy who recycles wooden shipping pallets for a living heard about the oven; he decided to donate enough wood so the people who use the park could have fuel to bake bread. As simple as that. The Hobart mixer was sitting around, unused—I can't say where; somebody—I can't say who—decided Jutta could put it to better use. It's on permanent loan. Simple, huh?

In summer, neighbourhood tough guys hang out at night, playing basketball and cooking jerk chicken over open fires. One more story: Jutta was riding by the park one night and saw a gang of vandals trampling the garden. She called the cops and said she'd meet them at the park, which meant they had to come right away, if for no other reason than to protect her. They caught one kid. Jutta lobbied to have him do his community service in the very park he tried to wreck—he's the one who built the oven door. By the time she finishes telling stories, it's time to turn the dough into pans. Meanwhile, a dozen Portuguese and a dozen Italian men have drifted into the rec centre and are sitting around playing cards. Jutta rakes the ashes from the oven, loads it with risen bread, and seals the door tightly. While the bread bakes, she makes a batch of cookies in the rec centre kitchen. Dufferin Grove Park is a model of sorts, although you can't analyze these things too closely—the thing about community development is that it sometimes happens without the benefit of community developers.

Jutta? She's just a woman who lives in the neighbourhood, likes the park, and knows how to get things done without getting tangled up in red tape. Now, all of a sudden, the city's in the hole $305-million, and our councillors are looking for corners to cut. But Dufferin Grove Park is already a bare bones operation. It's also a little urban miracle. Leave it alone. The bread's too good.

SOURCE: Joe Fiorito, 'Outdoor Brick Oven Helps Bake Sense of Community: Dufferin Grove Park an Urban Miracle, So Leave It Alone', *National Post*, Toronto edition, 16 March 2001, A17.

Alone, you can do little to influence any of these factors. As an individual you can only choose between getting a higher education (and possibly cutting yourself off from your ethnic community) and getting less education (and building contacts within your ethnic community). The first choice risks discrimination outside the community; the second limits opportunities for selecting a career and advancing within the community. Your contribution to a group solution, to be discussed shortly, will be much more important.

You can solve the problem of personal disability by changing the way you think about yourself—not an easy task, but one that a great many people manage to accomplish. This is partly what the major social movements of our time—for example, feminism, Native rights, and gay rights—are all about. Learn more about the history of your disability as a member of a despised or belittled group. Discuss this problem with others; find mentors and role models in your group who have done what others want you to think you cannot do. Most important of all, reject the victim-blaming ideology that you use to whip yourself. You have enough problems without being your own worst enemy.

Again, individual remedies are less likely to succeed than group remedies. Women, for example, will only be able to demonstrate that they can succeed in activities previously thought to be outside their competence if they are given a chance. Opening up new opportunities often requires that an excluded group mobilize. Your personal contribution, therefore, might best be made toward a group remedy. Even still, results might be a long time in coming.

You can solve the problem of decoupling by building and making use of social networks. That is how people find good jobs and, sometimes, mates. Improve the size and variety of your network by getting to know people who have larger and 'better' networks: people who are themselves mobile and widely acquainted, who are (typically) higher in status, or who operate within institutions that encourage interpersonal contact. As we have seen, this social connectedness seems to be related to later health and the ability to deal with illness.

Social institutions that break down traditional gender, class, and ethnic barriers to interpersonal contact include colleges, universities, and government. Thus, higher education and involvement in civic affairs are doubly beneficial: they allow self-improvement and they encourage contact with others. However, both activities leave less time for participation in your own community. Here, wrong choices are potentially most costly. So try to become a 'cosmopolitan' member of your community, with feet in both camps (Merton, 1957a). This connects you and your community into the larger networks of influence and opportunity beyond.

Finally, you can cope with real scarcity as an individual by producing more of what people need, by adjusting your thinking downward from the imaginary to the possible, and by seeking creative alternatives to scarce goods. It is the human ability to do this that has kept our species alive for a million years.

The danger here lies in confusing scarcity with inequality, considering scarcity beyond remedy, or lowering our heads rather than raising the bridge. French demographer Alfred Sauvy has called this approach the 'Malthusian Spirit . . . a state of mind characterised by the fear of excess—faced with two quantities that need adjusting, it tends to lower the highest instead of boosting the lowest. It is the opposite of courage and generosity' (1969: 391). The Malthusian is the person who, facing a dinner party with too little food for the guests, tries to turn away guests rather than find more food.

When what appears to be scarcity is really a result of inequality or of a temporary shortage that could be remedied through innovation and higher productivity, group remedies are called for. But group remedies depend on the personal commitment of individuals who are willing to accept the effects that these remedies will have on their lives along with the solutions that they offer.

Collective Solutions

Social life today is increasingly group life. The chief actors in a large, modern society—even those who suffer anomie—are organized groups, not individuals. That is why we must look elsewhere for adequate solutions to inequality.

Reducing Material Inequality

Karl Marx and Friedrich Engels ([1848] 1955) contended that a revolution that would eliminate ruling and subordinate classes forever by eliminating private property—by placing the means of production in the hands of the state—would bring better conditions for all. With the eventual 'withering away' of the state, communism would end history as we have known it, for it would end social classes and class conflict.

There are two problems with this formulation. First, a reading of history shows that every society of any size has had a class structure and a ruling class. This would not lead sociologists to the confident conclusion that a society with no class structure and no ruling class is truly possible. Rather, it would lead in the opposite direction—in the direction most often associated with the name of Robert Michels (1916, 1962), who stated the 'iron law of oligarchy'. Michels's principle, based on a socialist's study of the German socialist party—a sympathetic observer studying a radically democratic organization—holds that in every social grouping a dominant group will struggle to perpetuate its power, whatever its original ideology. That is, inequality is inevitable in human groupings, whatever their size or their members' ideology.

Michels's 'iron law' has not proven completely unbreakable. For example, a sociological study of the International Typographical Union, a democratic printers' union in the United States and Canada, reports finding some of the conditions that prevent or minimize oligarchy (Lipset, Coleman, and Trow, 1963). So not every organization must be oligarchic. Yet oligarchic organizations in our own society and elsewhere far outnumber the democratic ones. There is no evidence of a society that has broken the hold of oligarchy. At best, there is only a slim chance that Marx was right about the possibility of a fully democratic society.

Second, the premise that history can end with a democratic, class-free society is far from supported by empirical evidence. History does not show that communist revolutions have actually succeeded in bringing about equality. In the century and a half since Marx and Engels's *Communist Manifesto*, a number of groups in different countries have experimented with communism. Some attempts have been utopian or anarchistic, based in a small community or region (see Hobsbawm, 1959; Kanter, 1972). But, except for Cuba, the Israeli kibbutzim, and Hutterite communities, these have all failed, for a variety of reasons. Some have been forcibly overturned; others have lacked a sufficient material base; still others still have suffered from demographic pressures from within and attack from without. Even the relatively successful kibbutzim and Hutterite communities have suffered serious losses of population, as native-born members deserted. For its part, Cuba's revolution has produced neither prosperity nor democracy.

Other attempts at communism have lasted longer. But contrary to Marx's expectation, they have produced new kinds of inequality. In every instance—in Russia, China, Albania, Cuba, Vietnam, Nicaragua, and so on—rule based on ownership of the means of production has merely been replaced by political and bureaucratic control. So inequality has lived on in a new form. In many places, communism has greatly reduced material inequality and the worst effects of this inequality. But the inequality that remained—rule by a political elite, or 'vanguard of the proletariat', as Lenin called it—never disappeared.

Many believe that the excesses of control under communism were not just temporary but were due to an inherent overcentralization of planning and political power. That is why throughout Eastern Europe and the former Soviet Union, people have rejected communism as unworkable. Communism has collapsed as a system of organization. In the end, citizens' behaviour in rejecting communism suggests that Marx's remedy does not work as he thought it would.

The communist alternative has proven more attractive in less developed parts of the world. In fact, the benefits of capitalism and liberalism have meant little to many twentieth-century Third World peoples. They consider European nations unsuitable models to imitate, since they carry the stigma of colonialism. Further, 'free enterprise' seems less likely to succeed in the Third World than large-scale economic planning. As Geoffrey Barraclough writes, 'one of the outstanding attractions of communism to Asian and African eyes [is] that it [offers] the underdeveloped peoples a blueprint for development' (1967: 223).

On the other hand, material inequality can be significantly reduced without communism, as it has been in the democratic socialist countries of Scandinavia and, to a smaller degree, in certain other countries. Moreover, many people in the industrial capitalist countries—and not simply the very rich and powerful—do not want to give up private property in favour of communism. Values justifying acquisitiveness and free enterprise arise whenever personal acquisition becomes possible. People offered the chance to improve their wealth and status seize that opportunity almost without fail. They do not easily give it up.

As we will see throughout this book, liberal democracy does not give people an equal chance to get what they want out of life. So it would be satisfying to believe that some alternative (such as communism) could do so. However, we have been unable to demonstrate that Marx's proposed remedies lie within the realm of the possible, or that they satisfactorily link the advancement of group and individual interests. That is not to say that more modest socialist remedies would also fail to meet our needs. Indeed, any remedies that equalize income and power will benefit the majority. So let us turn to some truly possible remedies and see whether they meet our requirements.

Other Group Remedies

Wherever opportunity is limited, any wholly individual remedies are no more than quick fixes with temporary effects. In the long run, your chance of getting more opportunity is greater as part of a group. But if we rule out the revolutionary option, what remains? Again, what follows is merely schematic. It would be impossible to encompass all remaining scenarios within the scope of this book.

Two group remedies to exclusion are truly possible. One is legislation and other group action that would make discrimination against people like you more difficult. To bring this about requires banding together with others who suffer discrimination, joining forces across ethnic, class, gender, and regional boundaries where necessary. It also means electing sympathetic legislators to push for changes. If successful, the result will be a more assimilated, less discriminatory society. A second remedy is to mobilize within your own group—whether class, ethnic, religious, or regional—to increase community organization. This has the effect of discriminating in your own favour to counter the discrimination against you. Many groups use this tactic today, notably class-based political parties, unions, lobbies, and associations.

Group mobilization carries the risks of increasing inter-group conflict without eliminating the underlying conditions that gave rise to it. By pitting one group against another—women against men, blacks against whites, gays against heterosexuals—this tactic increases the risk of misunderstanding and injustice. A society torn by such disputes is no further ahead than a society marked by smouldering resentment. Events in the Balkans, Somalia, Israel, Northern Ireland, and the former Soviet Union show that civil war is considerably worse than smouldering resentment.

Group mobilization also narrows people's field of vision. People become less available for solving problems that cut across groups: international problems of peace and scarcity, national problems of cultural unity and political or economic independence, problems of class and gender inequality, and others. The first solution—a frontal group assault on privilege—is the only one that will benefit everyone in the long run.

Social education and re-education can reduce disability; the schools and the mass media are key vehicles for such a change. As already noted, the strengthening of individual identities is best done collectively, since nothing changes people's minds more readily than the evidence that change is possible.

The benefits of slow, incremental individual change are much more limited (Kanter, 1977). For example, a sole woman given the opportunity to 'model' executive abilities in a large organization is under unusual pressures to succeed 'on behalf of all women' and is judged by criteria quite unlike those applied to men. Confusion will arise between the unique characteristics of the individual and the 'type' she represents. Consequently, we really do not learn what excluded groups can do until we see many group members performing in common, emotionally neutral situations. Achieving this requires legislation that ensures inclusion for as many representatives of a social 'type' as may seek it. Laws against discrimination not only break down traditional patterns of exclusion, they also reduce disability and decoupling. Again, governments will not pass and enforce such laws without group mobilization.

Groups can remedy decoupling by building bridges to other groups—for example, to other racial, ethnic, regional, and occupational groups. Typically, increased communication among the leaders of these groups is the key to success. But everyone can play a part in this process by participating in broadly based activities and organizations.

Finally, material scarcity can be reduced if more of what people want and need is produced. This requires an international commitment to economic growth and redistribution and the breaking up of monopolies that restrict productivity as well as sharing.

These solutions to inequality are group remedies, not individual remedies. All are truly possible. However, they do not systematically address the question of how people might link their own advancement with that of society as a whole. C. Wright Mills (1959) maintained that personal lives are linked with public issues; another way of putting it is that personal troubles are shared and socially structured. This implies that personal and social problems must be solved at the same time.

Concluding Remarks

We have learned from this chapter that poverty has many definitions. Typically, the government decides the poverty line, so the meaning of poverty varies by society and, within societies, varies over time. Some think that poverty is caused by the continuation of economically damaging cultural habits (this is the 'culture of poverty' approach), while others believe it is simply caused by an unfair distribution of resources (the conflict approach). Functionalists believe that economic rewards are merit-based and inequality and poverty are mostly inevitable. It is not clear, however, from this standpoint, why women and ethnic minorities have the most poverty.

The 'culture of poverty' argument, which has close kinship with functional theory, ends up blaming poor people for their problems. It fails to adequately explain poverty for various reasons. In particular, it completely ignores the structural elements—laws, social policies, institutionalized discrimination, and so on—that contribute to the maintenance of a marginalized subset of the population, the presence of which ultimately benefits the powerful ruling class. Further, this theory ignores the fact that people's ability to 'get ahead' depends less on their values and motivation than it does on the job structure: the opportunities for good jobs in the community where a person lives and the non-discriminatory willingness of employers to hire into these jobs.

Widespread poverty is evident in Canada and throughout the world. For this country, we could classify nearly 18 per cent of the population (5.3 million people) as 'low-income' individuals or households. Yet many people move in and out of poverty. Longer durations of poverty produce more harmful outcomes, and children who are continuously poor have higher rates of anti-social behaviour than transiently poor or non-poor children. Sometimes, poor health is a cause of poverty, not vice versa. However, for most people, the reverse is true. Poverty and inequality will be continuing problems they cannot handle on their own.

As we have seen, both inequality and poverty are thorny ideas—not merely conditions of economic deficiency, but also causes of physical and mental health problems. Further, lower income means a greater probability of dying relatively young than does higher income. These patterns make it especially important—for both individuals and for society—that we attempt to lessen economic inequality and try to discover ways of unlinking health and death from income level. Much of the research discussed in the remainder of this book is directed to these two ends.

Questions for Critical Thought

1. Draw upon structural functionalism, conflict theory, and symbolic interactionism to help offer insight into the source of poverty. How would each theory approach this problem?
2. Is poverty unique to capitalism? Why or why not? Consider information on communal societies such as Hutterite colonies and Israeli kibbutzim, and offer insight into whether or not experiences of economic inequality occur there.
3. This text emphasizes that poverty and inequality are matters of life and death. Discuss this statement, drawing upon articles in the newspaper that show how mortality rates are often related to income distribution and social class.
4. In your opinion, what is the government's proper role in dealing with the health problems associated with economic inequality? Should policies focus more on dealing with poverty on the individual level, or should efforts be focused more on redistribution issues? If neither, what is your proposed solution?
5. Consider the very high salaries that top athletes and movie stars make and the lower incomes of teachers and social workers. Do you agree with the structural-functional explanation of the discrepancy, or do you prefer alternative interpretations? Discuss.

Recommended Readings

Jeffrey M. Berry, Kent E. Portney, and Ken Thomson, *The Rebirth of Urban Democracy* (Washington, DC: Brookings Institute, 1993).

This book looks at five mid-size US cities that promoted citizen participation in order to redevelop poor neighbourhoods and compares them with cities that did not. The findings are mixed, but the lowest levels of participation come from lower-income residents.

Naomi Dachner and Valerie Tarasuk, 'Homeless "Squeegee Kids": Food Insecurity and Daily Survival', *Social Science and Medicine*, 54 (2002), 1039–49.

What is the food experience of homeless people? In developed nations such as Canada few people go hungry. This study uses ethnographic data from a drop-in centre in downtown Toronto to address this question. Food access was found to be insecure and dependent on sources such as charity and the more desirable option: squeegeeing for money to buy their own food.

Linda Gordon, *Pitied but Not Entitled: Single Mothers and the History of Welfare* (Cambridge, MA: Harvard University Press, 1994).

Gordon looks at responses to poverty in the twentieth-century United States and contrasts New Deal anti-poverty values with existing policies. The book is written from the standpoint of the single mother and focuses on the cultural meanings of the welfare system.

Joan Kendall, 'Circles of Disadvantage: Aboriginal Poverty and Underdevelopment in Canada', *American Review of Canadian Studies*, 31, nos. 1–2 (2001), 43–59.

This article connects the lower living standard of Aboriginal Canadians to social problems such as family violence, educational failure, poverty, ill health, and violence. Policy suggestions are made, along with warnings that emphasize the importance of self-determination.

Gwendolyn Mink, *The Wages of Motherhood: Inequality in the Welfare State, 1917–1942* (Ithaca, NY: Cornell University Press, 1995).

Mink addresses late-twentieth-century welfare reform, linking it to a central value in the execution of New Deal programs. Despite attention to the mother-child relationship and to homemaker mothers, this value and approach served to exclude blacks and many poor white women.

James T. Patterson, *America's Struggle Against Poverty, 1900–1994.* (Cambridge, MA: Harvard University Press, 1994).

This book looks at welfare in the twentieth century and highlights the long-standing general disinclination to spend sizeable tax dollars on the 'undeserving poor'.

Roxanne Rimstead, *Remnants of Nation: On Poverty Narratives by Women* (Toronto: University of Toronto Press, 2001).

This book is compiled from narratives regarding poverty by women. It could be used as case examples, as exploratory research, or as mini-ethnographies. Rimstead suggests that there is a 'poverty narrative' that informs national, cultural, and community identity.

Harrell R. Rodgers, Jr, *Poor Women, Poor Families: The Economic Plight of America's Female-Headed Households* (Armonk, NY: Sharpe, 1986).

Rodgers's work looks at the relationship between the feminization of poverty and social policies that may well stop or reverse this situation. He stresses the failure of the social services arena in adapting to the changing roles of women.

Benedetto Saraceno and Corrado Barbui, 'Poverty and Mental Illness', *Canadian Journal of Psychiatry*, 42 (1997), 285–90.

This is a literature review of studies that use poverty, cultural poverty, and service delivery inadequacy as risk factors in the development of mental illness. Saraceno and Barbui compare poverty and mental health rates in developing countries to those in developed countries.

D.L. Williamson, 'The Role of the Health Sector in Addressing Poverty', *Canadian Journal of Public Health*, 92, no. 3 (2001), 178–83.

The Canadian health care system has undertaken various initiatives, varying regionally, regarding poverty. These initiatives have included awareness of poverty, prevention of poverty, skills development and education, awareness of the consequences of poverty, and policy changes to alter economic and social conditions that contribute to poverty. These strategies are evaluated, and it is found that they do little to alleviate poverty.

Recommended Web Sites

National Council of Welfare
www.ncwcnbes.net

The National Council of Welfare oversees this Web site, which contains reports on poverty and on related social issues as well as statistical information and policy materials.

National Anti-Poverty Organization
www.napo-onap.ca

NAPO, the National Anti-Poverty Organization, represents the interests of low-income Canadians. This Web site provides information on key issues, statistics, and lists of publications with the goal of educating and informing the public on the plight of low-income Canadians.

References

Akinyele, Isaac O. 1997. 'Household Food Security in Africa'. *Development*, 40, no. 2: 71–3.

Anderson, Sarah, and John Cavanagh. 2000. *Top 200: The Rise of Corporate Global Power*. Washington, DC: Institute for Policy Studies. Available at <www.ipsdc.org/downloads/Top_200.pdf>, accessed 10 January 2003.

Bakken, Rosalie, Marzena Jezewska-Zychowicz, and Mary Winter. 1999. 'Household Nutrition and Health in Poland'. *Social Science and Medicine*, 49: 1677–87.

Barraclough, Geoffrey. 1967. *An Introduction to Contemporary History*. Harmondsworth, UK: Penguin.

Berney, Lee, David Blane, George Davey Smith, David J. Gunnell, Paula Holland, and Scott M. Montgomery. 2000. 'Socioeconomic Measures in Early Old Age as Indicators of Previous Lifetime Exposure to Environmental Health Hazards'. *Sociology of Health and Illness*, 22: 415–30.

Bosma, Hans, Michael G. Marmot, Harry Hemingway, Amanda C. Nicholson, Eric Brunner, and Stephen A. Stansfeld. 1997. 'Low Job Control and Risk of Coronary Heart Disease in Whitehall II (Prospective Cohort) Study'. *British Medical Journal*, 314: 558–65.

Braun, Denny. 1995. 'Negative Consequences to the Rise of Income Inequality'. *Research in Politics and Society*, 5: 3–31.

Brooks-Gunn, Jeanne, and Greg J. Duncan. 1997. 'The Effects of Poverty on Children'. *Future of Children*, 7, no. 2: 55–70.

Cairney, John, and William R. Avison. 1999. 'Age, Social Structure and Perceived Health'. Paper presented at the annual meeting of the American Sociological Association.

Canadian Council on Social Development (CCSD). 2000. *Canadian Fact Book on Poverty*. Ottawa: CCSD.

Coburn, David. 2000. 'Income Inequality, Social Cohesion and the Health Status of Populations: The Role of Neo-Liberalism', *Social Science and Medicine* 51, no. 1: 135–46.

Curtis, James, Douglas Baer, and Edward Grabb. 2001. 'Nations of Joiners: Explaining Voluntary Association Membership in Democratic Societies'. *American Sociological Review*, 66: 783–805.

Curtis, James, Edward Grabb, and Tina Chui. 1999. 'Public Participation, Protest and Social Inequality.' In *Social Inequality in Canada: Patterns, Problems, and Policies*, edited by James Curtis, Edward Grabb, and Neil Guppy, 371–86. Scarborough, ON: Prentice-Hall.

Daniels, Norman, Bruce Kennedy, and Ichiro Kawachi. 2000. 'Justice Is Good for Our Health.' In *Is Inequality Bad for Our Health?* edited by Norman Daniels, Bruce Kennedy, and Ichiro Kawachi, 3–33. Boston: Beacon Press.

Davidson, Paul. 1997. 'So, How Much Money Does It Takes to Be Rich?' *USA Today*, 20 June, A1.

De Haan, Laura G., and Shelley MacDermid. 1998. 'The Relationship of Individual and Family Factors to the Psychological Well-Being of Junior High School Students Living in Urban Poverty'. *Adolescence*, 33: 73–89.

Doraid, Moez. 1997. *Analytical Tools for Human Development*. Prepared for the United Nations Development Programme, Human Development Report Office. Available at <www.peoplefirst.net.sb/SIHDR/AnalyticalToolsforHD.doc>, accessed 10 January 2003.

Dowler, Elizabeth. 1998. 'Food Poverty and Food Policy'. *IDS Bulletin*, 29, no. 1: 58–65.

Duncan, Greg G., and Jeanne Brooks-Gunn. 1997. 'Income Effects Across the Life Span: Integration and Interpretation'. In *Consequences of Growing Up Poor*, edited by Greg J. Duncan and Jeanne Brooks-Gunn, 596–610. New York: Russell Sage Foundation.

Figueroa, Janis Barry. 1996. 'The Health Status and Lost Earnings of Hispanic and Non-Hispanic Women'. *New England Journal of Public Policy*, 11, no. 2: 155–68.

Fisher, Gordon M. 1998. 'Using a Little-Known Body of Historical Knowledge: What Can the History of U.S. Poverty Lines Contribute to Present-Day Comparative Poverty Research?' Paper presented at the annual meeting of the International Sociological Association (ISA).

Gilbert, Geoffrey. 1997. 'Adam Smith on the Nature and Causes of Poverty'. *Review of Social Economy*, 55: 273–91.

Hagan, John. 1994. *Crime and Disrepute*. Thousand Oaks, CA: Pine Forge Press.

Hagan, John, and Bill McCarthy, with Patricia Parker and Jo-Ann Climenhage. 1997. *Mean Streets: Youth Crime and Homelessness*. Cambridge: Cambridge University Press.

Hall, Michael, Tamara Knighton, Paul Reed, Patrick Bussiere, D. McRae, and Paddy Bowen. 1998. *Caring Canadians, Involved Canadians: Highlights from the 1997 National Survey of Giving Volunteering and Participation.* (Cat. no. 71-542-XIE). Ottawa: Statistics Canada.

Hannan, Damian F., Sean Ó Riain, and Christopher T. Whelan. 1997. 'Youth Unemployment and Psychological Distress in the Republic of Ireland'. *Journal of Adolescence*, 20: 307–20.

Hauser, Robert M., and Megan M. Sweeney. 1997. 'Does Poverty in Adolescence Affect the Life Chances of High School Graduates?' In *Consequences of Growing Up Poor*, edited by Greg J. Duncan and Jeanne Brooks-Gunn, 541–95. New York: Russell Sage Foundation.

Health Canada. 1999. 'Toward a Healthy Future: Second Report on the Health of Canadians'. Ottawa: Government Services.

Hobsbawm, E.J. 1959. *Primitive Rebels: Studies in Archaic Forms of Social Movement in the 19th and 20th Centuries.* New York: Norton.

Jones, Charles, Linn Clark, Joan Grusec, Randle Hart, Gabriele Plickert, and Lorne Tepperman. 2002. *Poverty, Social Capital, Parenting and Child Outcomes in Canada.* Ottawa: Applied Research Branch, Strategic Policy, Human Resources Development Canada.

Jones-Webb, Rhonda, Lonnie Snowden, Denise Herd, Brian Short, and Peter Hannan. 1997. 'Alcohol-Related Problems Among Black, Hispanic and White Men: The Contribution of Neighborhood Poverty'. *Journal of Studies on Alcohol*, 58: 539–45.

Kanter, R.M. 1972. *Commitment and Community: Communes and Utopias in Sociological Perspective.* Cambridge, MA: Harvard University Press.

———. 1977. *Men and Women of the Corporation.* New York: Basic Books.

Kaplan, George A., Elsie R. Pamuk, John W. Lynch, Richard D. Cohen, and Jennifer L. Balfour. 1999. 'Inequality in Income and Mortality in the United States: Analysis of Mortality and Potential Pathways'. In *The Society and Population Health Reader*, Vol. 1, *Income Inequality and Health*, edited by Ichiro Kawachi, Bruce P. Kennedy, and Richard G. Wilkinson, 50–9. New York: New Press.

Kawachi, Ichiro, and Bruce P. Kennedy. 1997. 'The Relationship of Income Inequality to Mortality: Does the Choice of Indicator Matter?' *Social Science and Medicine*, 45: 1121–7.

Kennedy, Bruce P., Ichiro Kiwachi, Deborah Prothrow-Stith, Kimberly Lochner, and Vanita Gupta. 1998. 'Social Capital, Income Inequality, and Firearm Violent Crime'. *Social Science and Medicine*, 47, no. 1: 7–17.

Kristenson, M., Z. Kucinskiene, B. Bergdahl, H. Calkauskas, V. Urmonas, and K. Orth-Gomer. 1998. 'Increased Psychosocial Strain in Lithuanian Versus Swedish Men: The LiVicordia Study'. *Psychosomatic Medicine*, 60, no. 3: 277–82.

Kusumayati, Agustin, and Rainer Gross. 1998. 'Ecological and Geographic Characteristics Predict Nutritional Status of Communities: Rapid Assessment for Poor Villages'. *Health Policy and Planning*, 13: 408–16.

Lahelma, Eero, Sara Arber, Ossi Rahkonen, and Karri Silventoinen. 2000. 'Widening or Narrowing Inequalities in Health? Comparing Britain and Finland from the 1980s to the 1990s'. *Sociology of Health and Illness*, 22, no. 1: 110–36.

Lewis, Oscar. 1966. 'The Culture of Poverty'. *Scientific American*, 2, no. 5: 19–25.

Lin, Nan. 2000. 'Inequality in Social Capital'. *Contemporary Sociology*, 29: 785–95.

Lipman, Ellen L., and David R. Offord. 1997. 'Psychosocial Morbidity Among Poor Children in Ontario'. In *Consequences of Growing Up Poor*, edited by Greg J. Duncan and Jeanne Brooks-Gunn, 239–87. New York: Russell Sage Foundation.

Lipset, Seymour Martin, James S. Coleman, and Martin A. Trow. 1963. *Union Democracy: The Internal Politics of the International Typographical Union.* New York: Simon and Schuster.

Lynch, John W., George A. Kaplan, and Sarah J. Shema. 1997. 'Cumulative Impact of Sustained Economic Hardship on Physical, Cognitive, Psychological, and Social Functioning'. *New England Journal of Medicine*, 337: 1889–95.

McEwan, Bruce S. 1999. 'Protective and Damaging Effects of Stress Mediators'. In *The Society and Population Health Reader*, Vol. 1, *Income Inequality and Health*, edited by Ichiro Kawachi, Bruce P. Kennedy, and Richard G. Wilkinson, 379–92. New York: New Press.

McLeod, Jane D. and Michael J. Shanahan. 1993. 'Poverty, Parenting, and Children's Mental Health'. *American Sociological Review*, 58: 351–66.

————. 1996. 'Trajectories of Poverty and Children's Mental Health'. *Journal of Health and Social Behavior*, 37: 207–20.

Marmot, M.G., M. Kogevinas, and M.A. Elston. 1987. 'Social/Economic Status and Disease'. *Annual Review of Public Health*, 8: 111–35.

Marmot, M.G., M.J. Shipley, and G. Rose. 1984. 'Inequalities in Death—Specific Explanations of a General Pattern?' *Lancet*, no. 1: 1003–6.

Marx, Karl, and Friedrich Engels. [1848] 1955. *The Communist Manifesto*. Translated by Samuel Moore. New York: Appleton Century Crofts.

Marzuk, Peter M., Kenneth Tardiff, Andrew C. Leon, Charles S. Hirsch, Marina Stajic, Laura Portera, and Nancy Hartwell. 1997. 'Poverty and Fatal Accidental Drug Overdoses of Cocaine and Opiates in New York City: An Ecological Study'. *American Journal of Drug and Alcohol Abuse*, 23: 221–8.

Merton, Robert K. 1957a. 'Patterns of Influence: Local and Cosmopolitan Influentials'. In *Social Theory and Social Structure*, rev. edn, 387–420. New York: Free Press.

————. 1957b. 'Social Structure and Anomie'. In *Social Theory and Social Structure*, rev. edn, 131–60. New York: Free Press.

Michels, Robert. [1916] 1962. *Political Parties: A Sociological Study of the Oligarchical Tendencies of Modern Democracy*. Translated by Eden Paul and Cedar Paul. New York: Free Press.

Mills, C. Wright. 1959. *The Sociological Imagination*. New York: Oxford University Press.

Mirowsky, John, and Catherine E. Ross. 1999. 'Economic Hardship Across the Life Course'. *American Sociological Review*, 64: 548–69.

National Council of Welfare. 1998. *Profiles of Welfare: Myths and Realities*. Available at <www.ncwcnbes.net/htmdocument/reportprowelfare/repprowelfare.htm>, accessed 10 January 2003.

North, F.M., L.S. Syme, A. Feeney, M. Shipley, and M. Marmot. 1996. 'Psychosocial Work Environment and Sickness Absence Among British Civil Servants: The Whitehall II Study'. *American Journal of Public Health*, 86: 332–40.

Novak, Tony. 1996. 'The Class Analysis of Poverty: A Response to Erik Olin Wright'. *International Journal of Health Services*, 26, no. 1, 187–95.

Organisation for Economic Co-operation and Development (OECD). 2001. *The Well-Being of Nations: The Role of Human and Social Capital*. Paris: OECD.

Pagani, Linda, Bernard Boulerice, and Richard E. Tremblay. 1997. 'The Influence of Poverty on Children's Classroom Placement and Behavior Problems'. In *Consequences of Growing Up Poor*, edited by Greg J. Duncan and Jeanne Brooks-Gunn, 311–39. New York: Russell Sage Foundation.

Parenti, Michael. 1995. *Democracy for the Few*, 6th edn. New York: St. Michael's Press.

Pellegi, Ivan P. 1997. 'On Poverty and Low Income'. Statistics Canada. Available at <www.statcan.ca/english/concepts/pauv.htm>, accessed 17 March 2003.

Piko, Bettina, and Kevin M. Fitzpatrick. 2001. 'Does Class Matter? SES and Psychosocial Health Among Hungarian Adolescents'. *Social Science and Medicine*, 53: 817–30.

Pritchard, Alice M. 1993. 'A Common Format for Poverty: A Content Analysis of Social Problems Textbooks'. *Teaching Sociology*, 21, no. 1: 42–9.

Putnam, Robert D. 2000. *Bowling Alone: The Collapse and Revival of American Community*. New York: Simon and Schuster.

Ryan, William. 1976. *Blaming the Victim*. New York: Vintage Books.

Sapolsky, Robert M., Susan C. Alberts, and Jeanne Altmann. 1999. 'Hypercortisolism Associated with Social Subordinance or Social Isolation Among Wild Baboons'. In *The Society and Population Health Reader*, Vol. 1, *Income Inequality and Health*, edited by Ichiro Kawachi, Bruce P. Kennedy, and Richard G. Wilkinson, 421–32. New York: New Press.

Sauvy, Alfred. 1969. *General Theory of Population*. Translated by Christopher Campos. New York: Basic Books.

Sennett, Richard, and Jonathan Cobb. 1993. *The Hidden Injuries of Class*. New York: Norton.

Shillington, Richard. 1999. 'What Do We Mean by Poverty? Or HRDC Reduces Our Obligations to Poor Children'. Available at <www.shillington.ca/poverty/mbm.htm>, accessed 17 March 2003.

Shively, Carol A., and Thomas B. Clarkson. 1999. 'Social Status and Coronary Artery Atherosclerosis in Female Monkeys'. In *The Society and Population Health Reader*, Vol. 1, *Income Inequality and Health*, edited by Ichiro Kawachi, Bruce P. Kennedy, and Richard G. Wilkinson, 393–404. New York: New Press.

Shively, Carol A., Kathy Laber-Larid, and Raymond F. Anton. 1999. 'Behavior and Physiology of Social Stress and Depression in Female Cynomolgus Monkeys'. In *The Society and Population Health*

Reader, Vol. 1, *Income Inequality and Health*, edited by Ichiro Kawachi, Bruce P. Kennedy, and Richard G. Wilkinson, 405–20. New York: New Press.

Smith, George Davey, Danny Dorling, David Gordon, and Mary Shaw. 1999. 'The Widening Health Gap: What Are the Solutions?' *Critical Public Health*, 9, no. 2: 151–70.

Statistics Canada. 2002. 'Income Inequality in North America: Does the 49th Parallel Still Matter?' Available at <www.statcan.ca/Daily/English/000728/d000728a.htm>,accessed 3 May 2003.

Thiede, Michael, and Stefan Traub. 1997. 'Mutual Influences of Health and Poverty: Evidence from German Panel Data'. *Social Science and Medicine*, 45: 867–77.

Toronto. Homelessness Action Task Force. 1999. *Taking Responsibility for Homelessness: An Action Plan for Toronto*. Toronto: City of Toronto.

United Nations Children's Fund. 1998. *The State of the World's Children 1998*. New York: Oxford University Press.

United States. Bureau of the Census. 2002. *Current Population Survey as of September 24, 2002*. Available at <www.whitehouse.gov/fsbr/demography.html>, Accessed 1 March 2003.

Wilkinson, Richard G. 1994. 'Income Distribution and Life Expectancy'. *British Medical Journal*, 304: 165–8.

———. 1996. *Unhealthy Societies: The Afflictions of Inequality*. London: Routledge.

Woods, Richard. 2001. 'Gates Ousted as World's Richest Man'. *The Sunday Times*, 22 April. Available at <www.sunday-times.co.uk>, accessed 11 June 2001.

World Health Organization (WHO). 1997. *Fact Sheet No. 170: Health and Environment in Sustainable Development*. Available at <www.who.int/inf-fs/en/fact170.html>, accessed 12 June 2001.

Glossary

Absolute poverty Lack of the basic necessities (food, shelter, medicine) for easy basic survival. Starvation is an example of absolute poverty.

Adequacy-gradient hypothesis The hypothesis that economic hardship consistently decreases as age increases.

Affluence-trajectory hypothesis The hypothesis that economic difficulties should decline as age increases up until late middle age, after which economic hardship should begin to rise.

Culture of poverty This theory, developed by Oscar Lewis, characterizes the urban poor as having a distinct set of values and norms, including shortsightedness, impulsiveness, and a tendency to accept their marginalized status in society, and as remaining poor because they pass on these values to future generations.

Economic inequality Large differences in income and wealth across individuals and groups; differences in the economic power of nations.

Low-income cut-off (LICO) A formal definition for measuring poverty based on the percentage of income devoted to daily necessities (food, shelter, clothing).

Poverty line Also called the *human poverty index*. It represents a usual standard of living and differs between countries. The definition of poverty varies by society, within societies, and also over time.

Relative poverty Survival, but far below the general living standards of the society or social group in which the poor live; affects people's lives in dramatic ways.

Chapter 2

Drugs and Alcohol Abuse

Chapter Objectives

After reading this chapter the student should understand:
- the health risks of drug and alcohol addiction
- the change in attitude over time toward drug use
- the definition of *drug*
- what is meant by 'abuse'
- arguments about whether or not abuse should be considered a social problem
- the difference between legal and illicit drugs
- theories explaining, and giving insight on, the topic
- health consequences of drug and alcohol abuse
- possible solutions, and what is meant by a 'war on drugs'

Are Alcohol and Drugs Social Problems?

In this chapter we discuss a variety of drugs: substances like tobacco, alcohol, marijuana, cocaine, and heroin that change a person's mental state. Taken to extremes, drugs can harm a person, and drug use is then considered *substance abuse*. Substance abuse can lead to serious health risks for the user, and for others. As we will see, there are close connections between drug use and a variety of public safety issues that include traffic safety and crime. Poverty and inequality, which we discussed in the previous chapter, are also related to **drug abuse**.

Drug and alcohol use do not always look like social problems. After all, many people use drugs or alcohol in one way or another, whether a beer with dinner or a Tylenol capsule for a headache. However, drug use is more than a personal choice. By changing our consciousness chemically, we change the risks to which we are subjecting other people. Alcohol and drug use inevitably affect other members of society. An obvious example of one person's drug use affecting others is drunk driving, which results in accidents, a common occurrence we will discuss

later in this chapter. Usually, however, the effects of drug use are less dramatic and less visible.

We begin with discussions of the changing definitions of *drugs* and *alcohol* and with the characteristics of the two types of substances.

Changing Social Definitions of *Drugs*

We can define a *drug*, generally, as any substance that causes a biochemical reaction in the body. However, some biochemical reactions inside your body are against the law. What people define as a legal drug or an illegal drug usually depends less on its chemical properties and more on surrounding economic, social, and political factors.

In Canada, the use of legal drugs, such as alcohol, tobacco, and prescription medicine, is much more common than the use of illegal drugs, such as heroin, cocaine, and marijuana. Many members of society treat the use of illegal drugs as a major problem while ignoring the harm done by legal drugs. Society's response to drug use is, therefore, irrational. Some substances that harm public health, such as alcohol and tobacco, are welcome almost everywhere in society, while others that may not be as danger-ous, such as marijuana, are often condemned and excluded. Our attitudes toward specific drugs also vary over time. When social and cul-tural sensibilities shift, people start to reject what they once accepted. So we cannot understand drug attitudes and drug laws without a historical account that explains why the attitudes changed as they did.

Examples of such attitude change abound. Consider opium, from which morphine and heroin are derived. Opium was a commonly used painkiller until the early 1900s. Cocaine, cur-rently the object of a 'war on drugs' in the United States, was an active ingredient in Coca-Cola until 1906, when caffeine replaced it (Witters, Venturelli, and Hanson, 1992). Somewhere along the line, opium and cocaine were deemed dangerous and subjected to strict regulation, if not banned outright. The reason is sociological, not pharmacological. We will say more about this later.

Likewise, in the 1950s people considered anabolic steroids 'wonder drugs'. They believed that steroids could cure the sick, build up the scrawny, speed up weight gain in cattle, even cure cancer. However, in 1988 Olympic officials stripped Canadian 100-metre sprinter Ben Johnson of his gold medal for using banned steroids to enhance his performance. Why this change in views about steroids? One researcher speculates that people were led to define the non-medical use of anabolic-androgenic steroids as a social problem to hide and protect dominant

---

BOX 2.1
Drugs, Labelling, and Politics

Earlier this month Julian Fantino, Toronto's police chief, sent a letter to the prime minister inviting him to a rave—an all-night dance party frequented by young people. According to Chief Fantino, raves are 'threatening the very fabric of Canadian society'. In the three-page letter, he offers to escort Jean Chrétien to a Toronto rave so he can witness 'kids, most of them under 16, high on drugs'. Chief Fantino believes 80% of those who attend these events are on drugs and insists this represents 'a health and safety emergency that could easily become an epidemic'. Since Mr. Chrétien's schedule has yet to accommodate a visit to a rave, I decided to attend my first one this past weekend.

Shops distribute dozens of postcard-sized glossy ads for upcoming raves. Chief Fantino has complained such promotional material incorporates drug imagery, thus sending young people the message that drug use is 'cool, safe and a must-do'. But that's not what I saw.

Indeed, two of the 50 or so ads I examined explicitly condemn drug use: 'Zero tolerance. No drugs!' reads one. 'Strict Searches. NO drugs, markers, weapons' warns the other.

Only once, at an establishment that served strictly non-alcoholic beverages, did I see a child definitely too young to be out partying at 2 a.m. The boy, well dressed and a cigarette smoker, told us he was 14 but looked 12. He said he'd come with friends, a 15- and 16-year-old, and that his parents thought he was sleep-ing over at their house. Is Chief Fantino right that the parents of such children need to be more vigilant? Absolutely. Should the promoters themselves be turning these kids away? Yes (many liquor-licensed events already do). But it's quite an exaggeration to say that the major-ity of ravers are under 16.

The only readily detectable illicit drugs were marijuana and hashish. But one doesn't need to attend a rave to find these.

SOURCE: Donna Laframboise, 'The Sky Isn't Falling', *National Post*, national edition, 16 May 2000, A18.

economic interests: by declaring steroids a 'problem', we declared their use in sports anomalous even though, in fact, the use of steroids and other dangerous drugs remains commonplace and fundamental to the sports establishment (Mekolichick, 1996).

In these instances, a commonly used drug was restricted or criminalized when prevailing attitudes changed. The new restrictions were rarely due to new medical research findings or even new discoveries that the drugs caused social problems. Often, as with cocaine and marijuana, the changes were due to new attitudes toward immigrants or racial minorities who were in some way associated with the drug. These attitudinal changes, in turn, often reflected new economic and social concerns. Typically, these changes penalized the least powerful members of society.

This tendency to penalize the powerless is nothing new. The same thing happened a century ago with alcohol—a drug that most people use today without giving it a second thought. In the late nineteenth century, the English medical profession labelled habitual drunkenness *dipsomania*, portraying it as a disease of the will and moral sense. They stressed the social effects of drunkenness, particularly among poorer members of society who were unable to support their families. Note that this shift from a moral to a medical definition of alcoholism, from vice to disease, most affected the poorest, least powerful members of society (Johnstone, 1996). Then, as now, shifting conceptions of deviant behaviour had little effect on the rich and powerful.

The drunkenness reform movement in England between 1860 and 1908 was driven largely by a growth in the power of the medical establishment. *Medicalization* is the process through which deviant behaviours formerly defined as sinful or immoral are changed into instances of illness—that is, deemed no longer sinful since they are outside personal control. This process has become increasingly important in the definition of social problems with the triumph of science over religion in the past century

and a half. Where alcohol abusers were once deemed sinners or moral weaklings and subjected to scorn or criticism, with medicalization they became sick people in need of treatment. However, this was merely a new way of controlling deviance. As sociologist Talcott Parsons (1951) wrote, sick people are expected to play the 'sick role' or 'patient role'. In return for an exemption from scorn and moral criticism, the sick person must accept the fact of his or her illness and comply with medical treatment. In time, the sick person is 'cured' and allowed to return to normal social roles. Thus, in the end, medicalization is a means of permitting medical doctors to declare people fit for society.

Alcohol abuse is one of many conditions that have evolved into diseases in this way. However, alcohol abuse does not conform perfectly to the processes of medicalization since organizations outside conventional medicine—for example, faith healers, social workers, politicians, and leaders of social movements—have also had a say in the redefinition of this behaviour previously regarded as deviant (Appleton, 1995).

Moreover, the redefinition of alcohol abuse as a disease is not merely a process of medicalization. The temperance and prohibition movements of the last two centuries were also connected with deeper cultural themes. This is evident when we compare a variety of historical temperance movements, all of which fought for purity, hygiene, and health. The specific targets of these temperance movements varied over time, and included alcohol, drugs, smoking, prostitution, and homosexuality (Wagner, 1995). The common element was an obsession with cleanliness (also purity, virtue, and hygiene) versus dirt (also sin, wickedness, and filth). Below the surface of this cultural dichotomy raged classic struggles between clean and dirty classes (middle and upper classes versus working class), clean and dirty communities (native-born versus immigrant), clean and dirty subcultures (rural versus urban), clean and dirty sexes (female versus male). These struggles provide excellent examples of the processes of exclusion and decoupling that we discussed in the introductory chapter.

A century later, groups and professions still fight over the right to define drug use. Currently, alcohol users are considered 'clean' but drug users are considered 'dirty'. Consider current views about crack cocaine, spread mainly by the police and religious-moral leaders in their 'war on drugs'. Three prevailing views are that crack is instantly addictive, that it leads people to binge on drugs, and that it inevitably ruins their lives (Reinarman et al., 1997). Poor people are said to be more likely than others to use crack cocaine, while middle- and upper-class people are more likely to use powder cocaine (Alden and Maggard, 2000). Because of its class connotation, the label 'crackhead' is intensely stigmatizing (Furst et al., 1999).

No corresponding class stigma attaches to the use of cigarettes. Cigarettes are considered neither 'clean' nor 'dirty', neither moral nor immoral, by most people. As a result, despite repeated warnings from health officials and medical researchers, millions of Canadians continue to smoke cigarettes every day. More than three million Canadians over the age of 12 even continue to think that environmental tobacco (second-hand smoke) does not affect non-smokers (Health Canada, 1999: 154). Cigarette smoke is a legal drug that our society has decided to regulate rather than ban, despite the known and widespread harm that it does to Canadians every year. There is no 'war on drugs' aimed at cigarettes because cigarette smoking, for generations a mainstream cultural habit, supports a legal billion-dollar industry.

Definitions of *Abuse*

Ideas about drug abuse change over time with changes in common use patterns. Overall, trends in alcohol, cigarette, and cannabis (marijuana) use are similar in the United States and Canada. A study of adolescents comparing Ontario with the United States finds that, in both places, alcohol use has steadily decreased since the late 1970s, while both cigarette and cannabis use peaked in the late 1970s, decreased throughout the 1980s, and then began to increase dramatically in the early 1990s. Cocaine use was consistently higher in the United States and LSD use consistently higher in Ontario over the period 1975–95. The similar trends in use of alcohol and cigarettes in the United States and Ontario suggests similar shifts in basic attitudes over time. Different trends in the use of less common drugs—cocaine and LSD—may reflect deeper cultural differences or national differences in drug policy or availability (Ivis and Adlaf, 1999).

The ideas of alcohol *abuse* and drug *abuse* begin with a notion of extreme or unsuitable use that results in social, psychological, and physiological harm. There are two aspects to this idea of abuse: objective and subjective. The objective aspect relies on physical, mental, or social evidence that drug use harms the individual and society. For example, drug abuse may lead to drug *dependency*, the routine need for a drug for physical reasons (such as to avoid withdrawal symptoms) and/or for psychological reasons (such as to maintain a sense of well-being). Related to drug dependency is the notion of tolerance. Drug-dependent people experience increases in drug tolerance, meaning they need larger and larger doses of the drug to get the same physical and psychological effects that a smaller dose originally produced. Drug abuse can also lead to domestic violence, marriage breakdown, job loss, and bankruptcy; all of these are objectively visible and verifiable aspects of drug use.

The subjective aspect of drug use reflects society's beliefs about the effects of overuse and about the courses of action that we should take to tackle the problem. People vary widely in their views about drinking and drugs. Some believe in total self-denial, often for religious reasons. They do not permit alcohol use under any conditions. In the past, such abstainers were more common than they are today. The early-twentieth-century temperance movement claimed that restrictions on alcohol use were for the benefit of society's health and cohesion. Members of the movement expressed concerns about the harmful, disorderly effects of drunkenness on family life and work. They had enough influence to bring about a prohibition on the sale of alcohol in the United States and in parts of Canada. This brief prohibition had little effect on drinking but enriched the organized criminals who supplied illegal alcohol.

Today we are repeating the same mistake. Some people want to totally ban recreational drugs. This goal is impossible, and attempting it serves mainly to enrich organized crime. What is more, a large amount of medical and social research confirms that the use of unlawful drugs carries far fewer physical and social costs than nicotine or alcohol abuse. However, our government is unable to legalize recreational drugs because a vocal minority opposes it. This minority thinks that drug use is sinful, wrong, or dirty, and opposes publicly funded care for substance abusers, which may be the only practical way to deal with drug problems in our society. The majority is simply uninformed but fearful. In practice, the laws against drug use in Canada are largely unenforced, though they remain on the books, and Canadian courts have begun to declare government penalties for cannabis use and possession to be unconstitutional. Further, majorities appear to be finding their voice on drug issues: Vancouver's population chose in 2002 to elect a mayor who ran on a much-publicized platform supporting liberalized care programs for substance abusers.

In short, ignorance and stereotypes have historically shaped people's attitudes to drugs and alcohol, and they continue to do so. These attitudes complicate the process of finding ways to solve the objective problems associated with alcohol and drug abuse. Emotion-charged beliefs continue to shape our understanding of drugs and drug users, and limit our ability to deal with drug problems in a sensible way.

Characteristics of Alcohol and Drugs

Alcohol

Like most other drugs, alcohol is a tame drug when used moderately and responsibly. However, it is one of the most destructive substances when abused. In 1994, for example, 6,504 Canadians (72 per cent of whom were men) died because of alcohol use, most often from a motor vehicle accident while intoxicated, from liver cirrhosis (excessive scarring of the liver tissue), or from suicide. In 1995/96, 80,946 people (64 per cent of whom were men) were hospitalized with an alcohol-related problem, such as an accidental fall or injuries from a motor vehicle crash (Canadian Centre on Substance Abuse and Centre for Addiction and Mental Health, 1999).

People drink alcohol to achieve its chemical effects: to relax, smooth social events, reduce tension, and slow down perceptual, cognitive, and motor functioning. The goal of drinking, then, is to escape from the speed, boredom, stress, or frustration of everyday life and, often, to do so in the company of others, as part of a shared, sociable haze. Impaired judgment usually accompanies these chemical changes.

Many people drink responsibly, remaining below their tolerance limit, practising restraint around minors, and giving up their driving duties to a chosen individual. However, some drinkers are not so responsible. Men are much more likely than women to drink heavily and to suffer the physical consequences (for example, injury or death). Women drink much more responsibly, as do university graduates: 'Canadians with university degrees are the least likely of all education groups to report regular heavy drinking. One-fifth (21%) of Canadians with less than a high school education regularly drank heavily, compared with just 12% of current drinkers with a university education' (Health Canada, 1999: 177). Thus, university graduates are more likely to be regular light drinkers but not heavy drinkers or abstainers, while the opposite is true for Canadians with only primary-school education.

Aside from sex, age is the most important determinant of drinking and drug use. Young people are the most extreme, and the most variable, in their drinking. In a 1994 survey of 1,236 Toronto high school students, 24 per cent reported never having tasted alcohol, 22 per cent had tasted alcohol but did not currently drink, 39 per cent were current moderate drinkers, 11 per cent were current heavy drinkers, and 5 per cent did not answer the question. Most said they drank for 'enjoyment' and to be 'in a party mood'. Students who reported drinking heavily were more likely to drink and drive, smoke daily, and have friends and parents who drank alcohol (Feldman et al., 1999: 48). (See also Figure 2.1.)

Tobacco

Tobacco is Canada's other major legal drug. Like alcohol, nicotine is a psychoactive drug that is to blame for many health problems, a highly addic-tive substance, and a costly habit, both for the individual and for society. Tobacco is also hugely popular. Nearly seven million Canadians, or approximately 28 per cent of the population over 12 years of age, smoked in 1996/97, a figure that has not noticeably changed in the past several years (Health Canada, 1999: 164).

Most adult smokers develop their habit of smoking before the age of 20. As with alcohol use, men are more likely than women to use tobacco, although the gender gap has been nar-rowing for the past quarter century. Health Canada (1999) has found that girls are more likely to smoke than boys until age 18, when boys begin to outpace girls. Unlike alcohol use, there is a simple linear relationship between edu-cation and cigarette smoking: 'People with less than a high school education are almost three times more likely than university graduates to be current smokers' (Health Canada, 1999: 165).

Banned Drugs

Since the middle of the twentieth century, banned or unlawful drug use has increased among Canada's youth population (Centre for Addiction and Mental Health, 1999; see also Table 2.1). Among youths, drug use declined throughout the 1980s, but the 1990s witnessed a revival. Since 1993, marijuana, MDMA (ecstasy, or E), and hallu-cinogens, along with alcohol and cigarettes, have all showed steady increases in rates of use. In turn, as the rates of use have risen, fewer secondary and postsecondary students have reported a complete avoidance of drugs. In 1997, 34.3 per cent claimed to be completely drug-free; in 1999, only 26.8 per cent could say the same. Researchers have blamed the increased rates of use on a weak-ened sense that drug use is harmful or immoral, and an increased availability of drugs.

FIGURE 2.1
Drug Use Among Manitoba High School Students in the Past Year

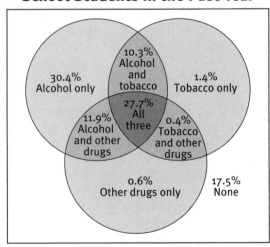

SOURCE: Brian Broszeit and Jastej Dhaliwal, *Substance Abuse Among Manitoba High School Students* (Winnipeg: Addictions Foundation of Manitoba, 2001). Available at <www.afm.mb.caHSSU.pdf>, accessed 15 March 2003. Reprinted by permission of The Vanier Institute of the Family.

Cannabis

Marijuana, or *cannabis*, is the most widely used drug in the world (UN Office on Drugs and Crime, 2000). Ninety-six per cent of all countries

TABLE 2.1
Primary Drugs of Abuse Among Persons Treated for Drug Problems

	Cocaine-type[a] %	Cannabis %	Amphetamines %	Heroin %
Canada (1995/96)	63.3	18.3	5.3	45.3
Mexico (1998)	32.3	24.3	0.4	7.2
United States (1999)	26.9	26.3	8.5	27.7

[a] Includes powder cocaine, crack cocaine, and basuco.

SOURCE: UNODCCP, *Global Illicit Drug Trends 2000*, UN, Vienna, 2000, 213.

reporting a drug abuse problem report the use of cannabis in either its leaf form (marijuana) or its resin form (hashish). It is also the most widely used unlawful drug in Canada, among youth in particular. In 1999, cannabis was used by 29.3 per cent of Ontario students in grades 7–13. During the 1990s, cannabis use ballooned, from 12.7 per cent of students in 1993 to almost 30 per cent in 1999. Cannabis use may not have reached its peak yet; between 1997 and 1999, it rose from 24.9 per cent to 29.3 per cent (Centre on Substance Abuse and Centre for Addiction and Mental Health, 1999: 1, 3). Many health care officials are worried about marijuana's possible role as a **gateway drug**, that is, as a drug that leads to the use of other banned drugs, such as cocaine or heroin (see, for example, Kane and Yacoubian, 1999). However, others have pointed out that, for social and psychological reasons, people who are willing to try one type of drug may already be likely to try another drug, with no particular 'gateway' process involved. That is, some people are disposed to trying many drugs and they merely start with marijuana. Research finds that the most popular combination for so-called **polydrug users** is alcohol, nicotine, and marijuana.

The active ingredient in marijuana is tetrahydrocannibinol (THC), which acts as a sedative or tranquillizer in small doses and as a hallucinogen in larger ones. Although its cancer-causing effects are similar to those of cigarettes, its other long-term effects remain unknown.

Cocaine
Cocaine is an inhaled stimulant; its effects include joy, excitement, self-confidence, and feelings of great well-being. It has been used for centuries, mainly for religious, social, and medicinal purposes. Anti-cocaine sentiment emerged in the United States and Canada only at the start of the twentieth century. At that time, the impetus for an attack on the use of the drug was more political and social than pharmacological. Urban blacks were the primary users of the drug, and the demonization of cocaine coincided 'with a wave of repressive measures defined to ensure the subordination of blacks' (Giffen, Endicott, and Lambert, 1991: 14). A negative view of the drug has persisted, fuelling the worldwide 'war on drugs', despite reports that have questioned cocaine's addictive properties (Van Dyck and Byck, 1982). Less than 1 per cent of the population in Canada uses cocaine regularly, and, like most other drugs, Canadian men are more likely than Canadian women to be users (Health Canada, 1999: 184).

Crack cocaine is a crystallized derivative produced by boiling baking soda, water, and cocaine together. Its effect is more intense than powder cocaine, in part because people inhale it directly into the lungs. There, it can be more readily

The dangers of injected drugs are a result not only of the high and of the risk of overdose but also of the method of transmission. Lack of clean-needle exchanges contributes to the spread of HIV. (CP, Nick Procaylo)

absorbed into the bloodstream than it can if taken through the mucous membrane in the nose. Research has not demonstrated that crack is more addictive than powder cocaine (Morgan and Zimmer, 1997).

Heroin

Heroin is a modified form of morphine that delivers an intense and addictive effect. It is the most commonly injected drug in Canada for recreational use, although, again, only about 1 per cent of the population reports having used it in the past year. The RCMP estimates that regular users of heroin number between 28,000 and 50,000 in Canada (Lafranire and Spicer 2002: 21). Still, because the preferred method of its delivery is injection, heroin poses particular risks to its users. Besides physiological hazards, which include collapsed veins, unplanned abortions, comas, and fatal overdoses, many heroin addicts are at risk of contracting HIV/AIDS, hepatitis B, and other diseases transmitted through the sharing of dirty needles. For example, Vancouver's downtown East Side, home to many intravenous drug users, has the highest rate of HIV infection in the Western world, according to one estimate by the members of the Killing Fields Campaign (Cernetig, 1997).

Hallucinogens

Hallucinogens (psychedelics) include many natural and manufactured substances, the most famous of which are mescaline, LSD, and ecstasy (E). The effects of hallucinogens include psychedelic illusions and altered perceptual and thought patterns. Less pleasurable effects include paranoia, loss of bodily control, delusions, and slurred speech.

The family of hallucinogens includes both natural forms (for example, mescaline) and synthetic forms (for example, PCP, or phencyclidine). LSD (lysergic acid diethylamide) has been the most commonly used hallucinogenic drug since the 1960s, although in recent decades, synthetic designer drugs have gained in popularity. MDMA (ecstasy), in particular, first became popular in underground rave parties and then spread among other groups in the wider society. Although the medical establishment is still debating its health effects, ecstasy made headlines—and was the target of an extensive police crackdown—in the late 1990s after a series of overdoses and overdose-related deaths occurred among teenage party-goers during all-night rave parties (NIDA, 2001).

Ecstasy's content varies widely, and it frequently includes substances entirely different from MDMA, ranging from caffeine to dextromethorphan (used in cough medicines) (NIDA, 2001). The 1998 National Household Survey on Drug Abuse (NHSDA) reports that an estimated 1.5 per cent of Americans (3.4 million) had used MDMA at least once during their lifetime. By age group, they reported the heaviest use among those between 18 and 25 years of age (5 per cent, or 1.4 million people) (NIDA, 2001).

Social Influences on Alcohol and Drug Abuse

As we have already seen, drug use is socially structured, in the sense that some groups are more likely than others to use and abuse drugs and alcohol. Thus, drug use and abuse are not merely biological or psychological issues, to be studied case by case. Trends in use vary across nations, communities, classes, and groups. Research on this topic is quite highly developed because of the relevance of social factors to issues of prevention and treatment.

Social Influences on Alcohol Abuse

Social factors influence alcohol abuse in at least three ways. First, they influence the odds that a person will learn to use alcohol to cope with stress. People under more stress and with more experience in the use of alcohol as a stress manager are at the most risk of doing this. Second, social factors influence the opportunities a person has to use alcohol for any reason. People with less access to alcohol, more access to other forms of activity, or friends who reject drinking are safer from the risks of alcohol abuse. Interestingly, these are instances in which forms of decoupling and scarcity have positive consequences for the individual; they work to the individual's advantage in staying off alcohol. As we have seen, many forms of decoupling and scarcity yield negative outcomes for those affected by them.

Perceptions and values affect the abuse of alcohol. Among adolescents, for example, both risk factors (such as low expectations of success, peer models for substance abuse, and poor school performance) and protective factors (such as intolerance of deviance, peer models for conventional behaviour, and participation in prosocial activities) affect the chances of drinking to excess. More risk and less protection are associated with more problematic use of alcohol (Costa, Jessor, and Turbin, 1999).

Learning to Use Alcohol

According to primary socialization theory, children learn societal norms within the family, the school, and the peer group (Nurco and Lerner, 1999). Children often learn to drink by watching their parents. Alcohol-abuse patterns pass from one generation to the next because, in part, people learn to behave in the ways they see around them as children. They imitate their parents and siblings. Children of parents with a drinking problem are more likely than other children to develop a problem themselves. Thinking back to the four structured constraints we discussed in the introductory chapter, the above are examples of disabling.

Using twins, researchers find lifetime alcohol use to have a heritability of 71–4 per cent. This level of heritability is lower than for cigarette smoking but higher than for use of other drugs, especially marijuana, whose use is mainly due to environmental influences (Maes et al., 1999). There is likely some genetic component to the inheritance of drinking patterns, but also a strong influence of imitation and learning within the family.

Thus, children of alcoholic parents are more likely than other children to develop alcohol-related problems, even in their adolescent years (Johnson, 1999). In part, this is due to the effects of alcohol abuse on family functioning. Marriages of alcoholic parents are more likely to be conflictual and to end in divorce—conditions that also increase drinking. Children of alcoholic parents are particularly likely to become alcohol abusers themselves if they have an alcoholic sibling. On the other hand, the children of alcoholic parents can lower the risk of alcohol abuse in adulthood by making a good marriage, one based on good marital communication (Jennison and Johnson, 1998).

A family history of alcohol abuse increases the learning of norms favourable to excess drinking. It also reduces educational attainment, particularly among men, which increases the likelihood of excess drinking (Curran et al., 1999). Further, an alcoholic, abusive, or otherwise dysfunctional family increases the likelihood that an adolescent will connect with deviant peers and learn deviant norms from them (Whitbeck, 1999). Street youths in Edmonton, Alberta, who use alcohol and hard drugs, for example, are more likely than average to come from families in which they witnessed parental substance abuse; long-term homelessness and peers who use drugs and alcohol also increase the risks of drug abuse among these street youth (Baron, 1999).

Parents who abuse or neglect their children increase the odds that their children will have higher-than-average rates of substance abuse and arrests for crimes (Widom and White, 1997). Abuse and neglect also increase the likelihood that a young person will end up living on the street, learning deviant norms from his or her peers.

The norms one learns from peers may be either prosocial or deviant, tending to discourage or encourage heavy drinking. Adolescents looking for thrills, for example, often seek out others with similar desires. Groups and subcultures form, made up of young people who drink and behave in similar ways. Persistent alcohol abusers in young adulthood (18–31) are mostly male and exhibit many problem behaviours (Bennett et al., 1999), as we said in the discussion of traffic accidents and problem driving. The norms of peer culture may condone drinking to excess—for example, binge drinking (see, for example, Bennett, Miller, and Woodall, 1999, who discuss binge drinking on a college campus).

Drinking patterns are heavily gendered; men and women use, and abuse, alcohol differently. They also often deal with their problems in different ways; for example, under stress, men with a drinking problem are more likely to drink, while women with a drinking problem are more likely to suffer from depression. Additionally, friends play a more important part in women's lives, as sources of social support, than they do in men's lives (Skaff, Finney, and Moos, 1999). Finally, women also develop alcohol abuse in a 'telescoped' way, with a faster progression through the landmark events in the development of alcohol abuse after first getting drunk regularly and first encountering drinking problems (Randall et al., 1999). Stress-related drinking is more common among women, and it becomes more prominent and problematic as the women age (Perkins, 1999).

Alcohol Use Opportunities

Social factors structure drinking interactions by encouraging or discouraging drinking occasions. Drinking norms vary from one society to another and from one ethnic group to another. For example, binge drinking is a cultural tradition in Russia (Bobak et al., 1999). Drinking norms even vary from one workplace to another, with drinking subcultures existing within certain workplaces. Under the best circumstances, the norms regulate drinking on the job (Macdonald, Wells, and Wild, 1999). Under the worst circumstances, a lax 'drinking climate', combined with

low worker cohesion, increases the risk of job stress, job withdrawal, health problems, work accidents, and absences. In one study, 40 per cent of employees reported at least one negative consequence of co-worker substance abuse (alcohol or drugs). Teamwork and cohesion are needed to buffer the harmful effects of a pro-drinking climate on co-workers (Bennett and Lehman, 1998).

The same is true in homes and schools. We have already noted that the children of heavy drinkers are much more likely to become heavy drinkers themselves. In addition to this, the odds of alcohol abuse are much greater than average among primary-school children who perceive no parental monitoring at all of their

---

BOX 2.2
Gender and Addiction

Sarah, 26, . . . took her first drink when she was five. 'A sip from a bottle of beer here, a sip there. I'd see adults drinking. . . . I thought it was a normal way of celebrating'.

Sarah suffered from the stigma peculiar to female alcoholics and drug users—she couldn't divorce her addiction from her own remorse at being a bad mother, or how her addiction had made her feel less (and this is an anachronistic but appropriate word) ladylike. Men can drink to excess, and be seen as tormented, solitary, even heroic figures in their addictions. Literature is full of the macho stereotype. But a woman brought low by addiction is not just a failure—she is fallen.

'There's a sort of double standard', said Gail Malmo, program director for the Aurora Centre, the women's-only drug and alcohol treatment clinic. 'When guys go out and get drunk, it would be considered manly, blowing off steam. The other problem for women seek-

ing help from their addictions is that there is more pressure for her not to leave home. They're very hesitant to leave for help if they think they're the only stable influence in the family. They also fear that their kids will be taken from them. And that does happen'.

It was to the Aurora Centre that Sarah finally turned. The centre's resident patient program offered six weeks of intensive psychotherapy and consultation. A remaining addiction, she admits, is tobacco. To which Malmo remarked: 'I find it interesting that in this province you can smoke your brains out, and wind up in the hospital and be treated free of charge. But there's a moral stigma to drinking that there isn't with smoking. You can drink yourself to death, and still have to pay to get treatment'. The daily fee at the centre is $40. Last year, it was $36. The raise, Malmo said, was precipitated by a provincial government beset with budgetary problems.

SOURCE: Pete McMartin, 'Women Walk Hard Road Back from Alcoholism', *Vancouver Sun*, final edition, 27 April 2000, A3. Reprinted by permission of Pacific Newspaper Group Inc.

alcohol use, whose parents allow them to drink alcohol at home, and who perceive high levels of parental permissiveness. Efforts to forbid drinking, by contrast, have no apparent effect on children (Jackson, Henriksen, and Dickinson, 1999). This tells us that the best parenting is authoritative, not lax or repressive.

Marriage also influences drinking opportunities. Overall, people drink less after they marry. People who never marry are more likely to drink heavily, in a way that contributes to their higher mortality. After divorce, people begin to drink more heavily than they did when they were married (Leonard and Rothbard, 1999). The heavy drinking of single, separated, and divorced adults is not due to selection effects (Power, Rodgers, and Hope, 1994). Rather, as Émile Durkheim showed in his classic work *Suicide* (1951), marriage sets limits to people's activities and in that way limits the damage they do to themselves.

Heavy drinking within marriage tends to harm marital quality and stability. At the same time, wives and husbands who are happily married tend to drink similarly, especially if they belong to higher socio-economic levels (Demers, Bisson, and Palluy, 1999). Happily married couples who are highly educated (and who therefore have higher income levels) likely do more of their drinking together, rather than with friends or alone. It is not clear whether heavy drinking harms a marriage when it is done in the company of a spouse.

Religiosity also affects opportunities for drinking, with more devout people drinking less and reporting fewer alcohol-related problems (Mason and Windle, 2000). Punjabi Canadians interviewed in Peel Region, Ontario, for example, have a lower-than-average prevalence of drinking than the general Ontario population, especially among women. Despite this, and because of their high standards, most Punjabi respondents believe that alcohol problems are widespread in their community. The most devout Punjabi Canadians drink even less alcohol than other Punjabi Canadians (Kunz and Giesbrecht, 1999). Again, this is likely for the reasons Durkheim outlined: like marriage, religion puts limits on people's lives and gives them meaning. It also integrates people into social groups that impose norms on drinking and other escapist behaviours. Similar tendencies are evident among the Straight Edge subculture, youths who advocate the avoidance of drug use; this subculture is also characterized by vegetarianism, avoidance of promiscuous and casual sex, and a preference for hardcore punk music (Irwin, 1999).

Social Influences on Drug Abuse

Much of what we have said about alcohol abuse applies equally to drug abuse. Factors that reduce the likelihood of drug use and abuse include strong family bonds, which reduce the use of all illegal drugs except marijuana (Ellickson, Collins, and Bell, 1999); a strong religious commitment (Yarnold, 1999); and normative boundaries that separate adolescents who use drugs socially, on an occasional basis, from those who use it often or in isolation (Warner, Room, and Adlaf, 1999). Marriage and parenthood are also important influences (Liu and Kaplan, 1999). Married people and parents who adhere to conventional values may use illegal drugs when they come under stress, for the reasons Robert Merton (1957) has suggested: the control of stress (and, more generally, of anomie) with drugs allows them to continue to conform to dominant values. The drugs reduce stress in a private and non-disruptive fashion (Liu and Kaplan, 1999). People committed to conventional values may find their own failure in valued social roles more distressing than people less committed to these values.

Factors that increase the likelihood of drug use include friends who use the drug, and parents who use tobacco or alcohol (Colson, 2000); early initiation into drug use (Dishion, Capaldi, and Yoerger, 1999); and a history of parental abuse (Bensley et al., 1999). Working conditions also make a difference. Workers with low cognitive ability make more use of cigarettes, alcohol, and marijuana the more complex their jobs are; workers with high cognitive ability, on the other hand, make less use of these substances the more complex their jobs are (Oldham and Gordon, 1999).

Even more than alcohol use, drug use is a learned behaviour that depends on social opportunities and on inclusion in social occasions where drugs are being used. Opportunities to use drugs, and actual drug use, are more common as youths get older. The probability of trying drugs, given the opportunity, also increases with age. Ethnic and gender differences in adolescent drug use correspond to differences in opportunities to try drugs with acquaintances, dating partners, and even parents (Moon et al., 1999).

Males tend to have more opportunities to use marijuana, crack cocaine, and other forms of cocaine, and at a younger age. However, they are no more likely than females to begin using drugs once an opportunity has arisen (Delva et al., 1999; Van Etten, Neumark, and Anthony, 1999). Normative boundaries restricting girls' access to and use of drugs are largely due to traditional gender roles that limit girls' access to certain types of leisure and sociability. Male peers enforce these norms in their capacity as drug dealers and distributors (Warner, Weber, and Albanes, 1999). While males are more likely to receive offers of drugs from other males and even parents, often in public settings, drug offers to females are more likely to come from other females or dating partners, often in private settings (Moon et al., 1999)

Theories of Drug and Alcohol Abuse

Several theories have been put forward by scholars concerning why drug and alcohol abuse occur. The sociological theories are variants of the three broad theories we have discussed in other chapters, and there are also biographical and psychological theories.

The Structural-Functionalist Perspective

Structural-functionalists hold that alcohol and drug abuse, like all social problems, result from the way the social structure influences the individual. Some theories, such as social disorganization theory, argue that institutions that have traditionally acted to discourage deviant behaviours become less effective during times of rapid social change. Because of rapid changes, norms and values become unclear. Other theories, such as **anomie theory**, argue that institutions and values remain strong but that they are often in conflict and that it is this conflict that causes drug and alcohol use.

Social Disorganization Theory

We can usefully apply this perspective, for example, to Canada's Aboriginal population and its problem with addictive substances, especially alcohol. For centuries after arriving in North America, Aboriginal peoples lived in many small communities or bands that varied widely but that had certain features in common. Despite differences in language and culture, the Native communities were all highly cohesive. A strong sense of community and moral custodians who stood guard over the group's traditions promoted the sharing and defence of moral values.

Forced off their traditional hunting lands and onto reserves by the arrival of whites, Aboriginal peoples came to depend on trade and foreign markets. Community norms and traditions broke down, speeded by the imposition of residential schooling. Alcohol abuse and suicide spread among Aboriginal peoples throughout the nineteenth and twentieth centuries. Few methods worked to stem this problem because they did not address the issue of social disorganization: the loss of traditional controls and values. In short, interaction with white society broke down traditional tribal societies, deprived Aboriginal peoples and individuals of a sense of meaning, and destroyed the ability of family, community, and religion to control people's actions. According to this theory, alcohol abuse was a result of all these factors.

The method of treatment that has worked best to control alcohol abuse has included addiction counselling by other Native people, sharing Aboriginal experiences, relearning the traditional culture, and practising Aboriginal rituals. Shuswap people on the Alkali Lake Reserve in British Columbia went from 100 per cent addiction to 95 per cent sobriety in 15 years (Hodgson, 1987). With the reversal of social disorganization, alcohol abuse has begun to subside.

Merton's Anomie Theory

According to Merton (1957), the cause of excessive drinking and other substance abuse lies not in an absence of values and institutions but in the conflict between them. According to this theory, excessive drinking is driven by a basic conflict or paradox—a gap between culturally defined goals and socially approved means for attaining those goals. Merton, using American society as his example, argues that one of the primary goals of that society is success, especially in obtaining money, material goods, and 'the good life'. Most people have been taught to value success. Yet social inequality ensures that most people will *not* succeed because they will not have access to the socially approved (that is, legal) means and resources that allow them to attain success—for example, higher education and good jobs.

Merton has called this gap between goals and means *anomie*. This state of anomie allows for a variety of solutions, which Merton called possible *adaptations*. They include what he called ritualism, retreatism, rebellion, and innovation. People try one or more of these solutions to bridge the gap between goals and means. Most people are *conformists*, recognizing that they will probably never 'strike it rich' and simply living out their lives as best they can. Others seem to conform, but they have given up all hope of personal success; they are *ritualists*, merely going through the paces. Still others *rebel* against inequality and reject the norms and values upon

which success is based. They may try to change the political order. As Merton described it, *innovation* occurs when a person has internalized the cultural goals but has not internalized a duty to the institutional norms, the legitimate 'ways and means' of attaining these goals. In its simplest form, innovation is crime, the use of dishonest means to attain wealth and success. We will discuss this at length in the next chapter. Finally, other people, realizing that they will never achieve their goals, just give up; they become *retreatists*—among other things, alcoholics, drug addicts, or suicides. Thus, according to Merton's anomie theory, alcohol and drug abuse are adaptations to anomie. Either increasing opportunities for success or reducing our culture's stress on achieving success could reduce these deviant adaptations.

However, the use of drugs and alcohol is not merely an individual adaptation; it is socially organized. Groups of individuals with different amounts of social capital, especially social network connections that offer them access to valued jobs, vary widely in their use of drugs and alcohol. As result, marijuana use varies widely among racial minority youth arrayed in ecological patterns that follow community, institutional, and personal network patterns (Brunswick, 1999). Chinese American youths (regardless of their length of residence) are least likely to use the drug, for example, because their ethnic group has the most human and social capital, while Pacific Island and Filipino youths are most likely to do so (Nagasawa, Qian, and Wong, 1999).

Anomie or underclass theory is primarily useful in explaining drug abuse as an adaptation to aggregate community-level conditions—for example, poverty, unemployment, and other measures of social breakdown—among minority-group people. It has less to say about majority-group people who live in stable or affluent communities. To account for their drug use, researchers more often distinguish between casual users and abusers, and focus on micro-level explanations such as family conflict (Covington, 1997).

Functionalists also argue that drug and alcohol use are common because these substances serve an important social function. Drinking and drug-using rituals, for example, are the basis of deviant communities that provide people with a powerful sense of belonging (see, for example, Becker, 1958). People use drugs to gain and retain membership in tightly cohesive social groups of deviants. As well, drug and alcohol use are almost mandatory on certain occasions—for example, Mardi Gras in New Orleans or Carnival in Rio de Janeiro, or New Year's Eve anywhere.

Conflict Theory

Alcohol and drug use affect different socioeconomic groups differently. The poor tend to suffer more harmful consequences more than the rich, in this as in other health conditions (see, for example, Makela, 1999). However, conflict theorists focus largely on the **labelling** and criminalization processes. They note that in a capitalist economic system that perpetuates inequality, the powerful members of society are in a position to define whether a substance is legal or illegal. The powerful are able to criminalize drug use by the powerless. Moreover, they are in a position to benefit from drug use at the same time as they may disavow it.

Alcohol and tobacco, for example, are drugs that are produced and sold by the powerful. The alcohol industry in Canada reaped $11.38 billion in sales, employed more than 14,000 people, and generated more than $3.34 billion in revenue for provincial governments in 1996/97 (see Figure 2.2). The tobacco industry took in another $3.94 billion in revenue during that same period. Both these industries are regulated but not considered illegal. Both profit the rich stockholders of alcohol and cigarette companies while harming the heavy users, who tend to be poor.

Ironically, of the $18.4 billion that it cost Canada to deal with substance abuse in 1992, over 50 per cent went to harm produced by tobacco ($9.5 billion) and alcohol ($7.5 billion), both legal drugs. In contrast, banned substances resulted in only $1.37 billion in economic costs (Canadian Centre on Substance Abuse and Centre for Addiction and Mental Health, 1999). Enforcing the laws on alcohol cost Canadians $1.36 billion, whereas law enforcement regarding illegal drugs cost only $400 million (Canadian Centre on Substance Abuse and Centre for Addiction and Mental Health, 1999). Thus, Canadian taxpayers indirectly subsidized the vacation homes of cigarette and alcohol magnates (such as the Bronfman family) while directly paying for lung cancer and heart treatments in working-class communities.

Banned substances are often forbidden not only because of their harmful pharmacological properties, but also for social and political reasons. Such cases generally provide good illustrations of principles of conflict theory. Let's consider two examples here: opium in Canada and marijuana in the United States.

Opium was brought to Canada by the Chinese, who themselves were brought over as a source of cheap labour to build the railroads. At the time, as long as the Chinese provided a useful service to the ruling white population, opium smoking was considered nothing more than 'an individual medical misfortune or personal vice, free of severe moral opprobrium' (Green, 1986: 25). The law offered no objections to either producing or possessing opium. However, as the economic situation began to decline and jobs became scarce, the Chinese came to be viewed as unwanted competitors for the limited positions that remained. Canadians demanded that Chinese immigration be limited or stopped, and they stigmatized the Chinese who already lived in Canada. Opium use provided a handy excuse.

In the same way, marijuana, which was initially brought over legally to the United States by Mexican factory and field workers during the 1920s, was suddenly criminalized during the Great Depression of the 1930s, when it was

FIGURE 2.2
Youth, Marketing, and Future Addiction: Internet Use by Age in Canada

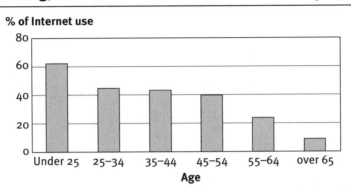

The Center for Media Education's 1998 research report *Alcohol and Tobacco on the Web: New Threats to Youth* has found that
* Major alcohol beverage companies are a growing presence on the Web, with more than 35 brands represented.
* The many websites and home pages dedicated to smoking are helping to foster an online Smoking-is-Cool culture.
* Web sites promoting alcohol and tobacco employ a number of techniques that appeal to children and youth, including:
  * themes and icons of youth popular culture such as interviews with rock stars
  * interactive games and contests
  * branded merchandise and free give-aways, including clothing, rock music clips and e-mail postcards with company logos
  * chat rooms in the form of clubs, graffiti walls and virtual bars
  * online magazines and marketing surveys

SOURCE: 'Contemporary Family Trends: Electronic Media and the Family' (1998), available at <www.vifamily.ca/cft/media/media.htm>, accessed 13 January 2003. Reprinted by permission of The Vanier Institute of Family.

determined that the foreigners needed to be driven out of the country so that their jobs could be given to US-born labourers.

Conflict theorists always ask who benefits from one or another social behaviour. The laws against opium and marijuana use were clearly biased against racial minorities and poor people while indirectly benefiting white people. When these laws threatened to penalize the college-aged children of the middle class, enforcement of the laws was markedly weakened.

Symbolic Interactionism

Symbolic interactionists focus on the social meanings and values associated with alcohol and drug use and on the labels people attach to others when they use drugs. This process of defining and treating others as deviant is what sociologists refer to as *labelling*. Often, alcohol abuse is related to other problems, of which labelling is one of the least important. These issues of labelling and its consequences are of prime importance to symbolic interactionists.

A person perceived by society as deviant and guilty of excessive drinking is labelled 'alcoholic'. It is clear that an 'alcoholic' is a person who, in the eyes of the community, cannot control the harmful effects of alcohol use. There is a sharp division between the 'social drinker' and the 'alcoholic'. Yet unlike attitudes toward other illnesses (such as heart disease and cancer), attitudes toward alcoholism and alcoholics are exclusionary and stigmatizing.

Paradoxically, friendly social drinking is the drinking code of the modern, advanced capitalist society. The links between alcohol use and leisure have been omnipresent in our society as individuals not only typically drink in their free time, but often do so to have a good time

(Carruthers, 1992). Yet alcoholics and heavy drinkers are stigmatized and stereotyped in our society. Many still believe that alcoholics have less education than other people, are seldom to be found in important business positions, are usually unemployed, and come from the lower socio-economic strata of the society, not from all walks of life. Some still identify various prior emotional difficulties—for example, an unhappy marriage—as precipitating factors that result in alcoholism.

The disease concept of alcoholism seems to be largely unrelated to other beliefs about alcoholism. Humanitarian or sympathetic attitudes toward alcoholics are largely independent of endorsement of the disease concept, for example (Crawford and Heather, 1987). Alan Marcus reports 'that one's evaluation of the seriousness of alcoholism does not seem to be primarily dependent upon one's objective judgment of the impact of alcoholism on the community, but may be more closely related to one's conception of the alcoholic' (1963: 22).

Attitudes toward alcoholism and alcoholics seem to be connected to the general processes of stigmatization, labelling, social distance, and exclusion, which are studied so well by symbolic interactionists. For example, Joseph Gusfield's study of the symbolic crusade that led to Prohibition in the United States (1963) provides a good example of the social construction of deviant behaviour that benefits one group more than another. Prohibition consisted of a ban, from 1920 to 1933, on the sale and public use of alcohol in the United States. The successful lobbying effort organized by the American temperance movement that led to Prohibition was an example of what Gusfield calls 'status politics'. *Status politics* is 'a struggle between groups for prestige and social position' (Gusfield, 1963: 3). Defending their position in the status order is as important to people as protecting or expanding their economic power; indeed, the two are often related.

Social Consequences of Substance Abuse

We will show, later, that alcohol and drug abuse can have serious health consequences. First, in this section, we will show that adverse social consequences of drinking, especially frequency of drunkenness, may be the best single indicator of problem drinking, especially among young adults. Adverse consequences may indicate a more serious form of problem drinking than do symptoms of dependency or other medical consequences (Bailey, 1999).

Crime and Violence

The 'war on drugs' has increased racial and class injustice by targeting the poor and racial minorities disproportionately. It has focused on drug users and street traffickers, not others (such as money launderers) in the drug economy, and has attributed their drug abuse and criminal activity to moral weakness rather than to a reduction in manufacturing jobs (Duster, 1997).

Having said that, drug and alcohol abuse are important social problems to study not only because of their direct effects on people and society, but also because they are linked indirectly to other social problems, including crime and violence, poverty, and racism. That substance abuse is linked to other deviant behaviour is not surprising, since most drugs influence both behaviour and inhibition mechanisms. The intake of too much of any substance results in unpredictable, and often deviant, activity.

The link between alcohol use and crime is well known. Alcohol use has been estimated to be involved in at least 40 per cent of all murders in the United States, and 50 per cent of all violent assaults. Of the 5.3 million offenders imprisoned in the United States in 1996, nearly 2 million had been drinking alcohol before committing their crimes. Nearly two-thirds of all convicted inmates reported having previously been in an alcohol-dependency treatment program

(Greenfield, 1998: 20–1). Further, driving while drunk is, of course, a criminal offence in itself, and drunk drivers are involved in over one-third of all traffic accident–related deaths in North America.

Criminal offences can also be committed to get drugs. According to the US Department of Justice, 19 per cent of state prisoners and 16 per cent of federal inmates in 1997 reportedly committed their current offence in order to obtain money for drugs (US Bureau of Justice Statistics, 1999: 5).

In a study of young men in prison, no particular incident of violence can be related to the use of a particular drug at a specific time. However, men who said they used drugs during their last year of freedom prior to their imprisonment—particularly those who used a combination of drugs, alcohol, and tobacco—were likely to have ever participated in violent offending, and to have done so that same year (Brownstein et al., 1999). Another study in Florida found that chronic drug users were significantly more likely than non-drug users to have assaulted, shot, stabbed, or robbed someone, and were also significantly more likely to have been both victims and observers of all violent acts (McCoy, Messiah, et al., 2000). (See also Figure 2.3.)

Alcohol use is more strongly and more consistently associated with both violent and non-violent offences than are marijuana and heroin use (Dawkins, 1997). Alcohol use and abuse are clearly implicated in the perpetration of physical assault, as well as in victimization (Scott, Schafer, and Greenfield, 1999). The literature supports the view that alcohol produces biochemical changes that produce behaviours that would not have occurred otherwise; it also provides a convenient excuse to engage in violent behaviours (Patton and Baird, 2000). A review of the literature also reveals that 50 per cent of all homicide offenders and victims are intoxicated from drug

FIGURE 2.3
Persons Charged with Offences
Related to Impaired Driving, 1998, by Province

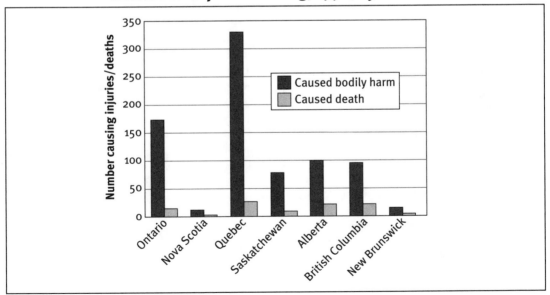

SOURCE: Statistics Canada, <http://dsp-psd.communication.gc.ca/Collection-R/Statscan/85-002-XIE/0119958-002-XIE.pdf>, accessed 1 March 2003.

or alcohol use at the time of the crime (Auerhahn and Parker, 1999).

Domestic Violence

Alcohol abuse is also unduly common among misfunctioning families and broken homes. First, alcohol has been implicated in roughly 75 per cent of all incidents of spousal violence (Greenfield, 1998: v), suggesting that alcohol use can act as the catalyst that ignites violence in an already explosive domestic environment. Such violence can also lead to other forms of family disruption and displacement, including divorce and child custody battles. (See also Figure 2.4 on alcohol, drugs, and violence in the lives of youth.)

Female victims of domestic violence are disproportionately likely to be married to extremely heavy drinkers. Drunkenness, not drinking per se, is the main predictor for threatening and physical-battering behaviour by husbands (Hutchison, 1999). Even among newlyweds, heavy drinking by the husband can degenerate into physical (versus verbal) aggression. Violent episodes are largely unrelated to the wife's drinking (Leonard and Quigley, 1999). Among male alcoholics, returns to drinking predict returns to domestic violence, even among men who have received treatment in a marital-therapy alcoholism treatment program (O'Farrell, Van Hutton, and Murphy, 1999).

Poverty and Income

Although alcohol use rates are higher among well-educated, high-income people than among poorly educated, low-income people, alcohol abuse and problem drinking are reported more often among the latter group. Whether poverty causes drug abuse or drug abuse causes poverty is difficult to distinguish. A vicious circle may occur as well, with poverty leading to abuse and abuse, in turn, reinforcing joblessness and poverty.

Alcohol and drugs such as heroin and cocaine provide their users with a temporary feeling of well-being and contentment while at the same time relieving feelings of loneliness, depression, and pain. The appeal of drugs to the disadvantaged, desperate, and marginalized is therefore considerable. However, because of the addictive properties of banned substances, the buildup of physical and psychological tolerance, and the desire to avoid painful withdrawal symptoms, many drug users soon require larger and larger quantities of the drug. This translates into a costly habit, and many addicts—unless they are gainfully employed—resort to prostitution, theft, and robbery to continue their drug use. As addicts begin to gather together in a single area, other social consequences of banned drug use arise, including poverty, social disorganization, homelessness, gang activities, and invasive drug trafficking and distribution systems.

FIGURE 2.4
Factors Keeping Young People on the Street

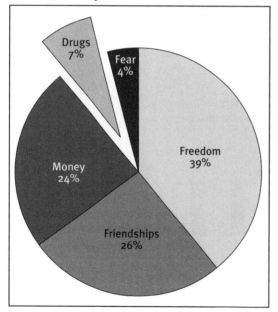

SOURCE: T. Caputo, R. Reiler, and J. Anderson, *The Street Lifestyle Study* (Ottawa: Health Canada, 1997).

At the other end of the income spectrum, laundered drug funds have been used to subsidize the world economy, including war-making by the major powers, since the economic crisis of the 1980s. The interdependence of the legal economy, state interests, and drug interests makes it almost impossible to distinguish between formal, informal, and criminal economies (Laniel, 1999).

Racism

The criminal justice system writes laws to govern behaviour in society and seeks to punish people who violate these laws. However, the system undermines its own authority when it fails to follow the 'blind justice' doctrine upon which it is founded. Several lines of evidence suggest that justice is *not* blind, at least in relation to drug enforcement and prosecution.

Within each ethno-cultural group, drug use is fairly similar. The US Substance Abuse and Mental Health Services Administration estimates that 10.4 per cent of American whites reported that they had used drugs in the past year; among African Americans, 13.0 per cent reported that they had used drugs in the past year, as did 10.5 per cent of Hispanic Americans (1999: 20–1). However, African Americans were 4 times more likely to be arrested for drug abuse violations, and as much as 10 times more likely to be arrested in some major cities (Meddis, 1993: 2A). Even though the majority of crack cocaine users were white, about 96 per cent of the crack defendants in federal court were non-white.

Other Social Consequences

Because of the high rate of alcohol and drug use, both legal and illegal, many aspects of social life have been affected. The Canadian Centre on Substance Abuse and the Centre for Addiction and Mental Health estimate that substance abuse costs more than $18.4 billion to the Canadian economy in 1992, or about 2.7 per cent of the GDP in that year (1999). Losses in productivity and premature death accounted for over 55 per cent of the costs of alcohol use, while law enforcement and health care accounted for most of the remainder. Other economic costs of drug and alcohol abuse are associated with homelessness, educational and rehabilitation treatment programs, and the medical treatment of drug addicts and of substance abuse–related injuries and fatalities.

Health Consequences of Substance Abuse

Because alcohol and other drugs are chemicals that have direct physiological effects on the human body, the health consequences arising from substance abuse are both widespread and severe.

Health Consequences of Alcohol and Drug Abuse

Alcohol abuse is probably the most dangerous form of drug abuse from a health standpoint. The physical consequences are tremendously complex and varied. To gain an appreciation for the scope of its effects, consider the results of a report by the United Kingdom's Royal College of Physicians (1987) that found that alcohol abuse was linked to disorders of the nervous system, strokes, paralysis and other nerve damage, liver damage, high blood pressure, heart failure, and many other health problems. However, the unique effects of alcohol on health are hard to parcel out since heavy drinkers tend to show other health-destroying characteristics as well: smoking, depression, unemployment, and so on (Fillmore et al., 1998).

Some evidence suggests that the volume of alcohol consumption per occasion has more harmful effects than the overall drinking volume; that is, binge drinking is more harmful in its social consequences than drinking or drunkenness per se (Rehm and Gmel, 1999). Overall, chronic drug users show greater health care needs than drug non-users, and are less likely to receive appropriate health care services (McCoy,

Metsch, et al., 2000). Poor eating habits and malnutrition are positively related to heavy drinking, as are social and family disorganization (Santolaria et al., 2000). Even among youth aged 12–18, the regular use of alcoholic beverages (beer, wine, and distilled spirits) contributes significantly to longitudinal decreases in physical health with no evidence that alcohol helps to cope with pre-existing psychological distress and physical symptoms (Hansell, White, and Vali, 1999). Adolescent substance use, in turn, predicts poor physical health in adulthood (Spohn and Kaplan, 2000).

The risk of suicidal thinking is increased by a family history of alcohol abuse among men, though not among women (Grant and Hasin, 1999). In particular, an alcoholic father in the home places the child at high risk for later problems, including suicide, mortality, drug abuse, and social maladjustment (Mutzell, 1994). Cannabis abuse or dependence is significantly associated with serious suicide attempts, even after controlling for other factors that predict dependence and suicide (Beautrais, Joyce, and Mulder, 1999). A longitudinal (17-year) study found that narcotic addicts are generally at high risk for mortality (including violent death) compared with the general population (Mutzell, 1996).

Early initiation into alcohol and marijuana use was found to predict earlier initiation of sexual activity and subsequent risky sexual behaviour among US adolescents and young adults, with males taking the greater risks (Staton et al., 1999). Parental monitoring mitigated later levels of alcohol misuse and sexual risk-taking (Thomas et al., 2000). The use of illicit drugs and alcohol appear to increase the likelihood that women will engage in sexual behaviour in which they would not have engaged if they had not been under the influence. The greater use of drugs and alcohol might be part of a wider pattern of sexual behaviour, including a higher number of sexual partners, although it does not result in unsafe or undesired sexual behaviour

(Taylor, Fulop, and Green, 1999). Some women who have worked in prostitution found that the use of crack cocaine undermined their safety at work and in other relationships, including greater risk of ill health, loss of earning, and violence through their drug use (Green, Day, and Ward, 2000).

Drug users run a higher risk of HIV infection, in part from unprotected sex with multiple partners (Inciardi et al., 1999). This practice is common in prisons, as well as outside. Women drug offenders are found to engage in numerous high-risk drug and sexual behaviours while in prison; on release, they represent a major public health risk. Criminal justice policies, grounded in deterrence and based on imprisonment, may be contributing to the spread of HIV infection in the wider society (Marquart et al., 1999). Crack cocaine injectors are at the greatest potential risk for exposure to heterosexually transmitted HIV, followed by other injecting drug users, crack smokers, and then other drug users (Cotton Oldenburg et al., 1999). The connection between drug use and the spread of HIV/AIDS is found throughout the world (see, for example, Bastos et al., 1999, on South America and the Caribbean).

Health consequences are not limited to the individual, however. Pregnant women who drink may also be placing their unborn child at risk. Fetal alcohol syndrome (FAS) occurs during prenatal exposure to alcohol, and can result in facial abnormalities and stunted growth after birth. In addition, damage to the central nervous system can lead to attention deficits and to intellectual, memory, and learning disabilities. FAS occurs in approximately 1 to 3 live births per 1,000, which is unfortunate as it is considered one of the most preventable forms of birth defect in Canada (see Williams and Gloster, 1999).

Health consequences faced by illicit drug users include shortened lifespans, dietary irregularities, severe weight loss, vomiting, mucous membrane damage, and brain lesions. Among injection drug users, the risk of contracting

HIV/AIDS from sharing contaminated needles is severe. A conservative estimate by the Canadian Centre on Substance Abuse and the Centre for Addiction and Mental Health (1999) indicates that one in every five AIDS cases in Canada was related in some way to intravenous drug use.

Alcohol and drug abuse can also lead to mental health problems. White and Labouvie (1994), for example, have demonstrated that drug users are more likely to develop anxiety disorders, phobias, depression, and anti-social personalities. Suicide is also more common among drug users, particularly adolescents. Marijuana, the illicit drug of choice among teenagers, has been associated with short-term memory loss, impaired learning, amotivational syndrome, and emotional deficits. Further, of all students in Ontario who reported alcohol problems in 1998, 40 per cent reported impaired mental health as a direct result.

Health Consequences of Tobacco Smoking

Tobacco smoking is the primary cause of lung cancer, which is the leading cause of cancer death. In 2001, over 18,000 Canadians were expected to die from lung cancer, and 21,000 expected to develop the disease. Another 11,000 were expected to die from cancer to the mouth, larynx, esophagus, stomach, bladder, kidney, and pancreas, all of which have been linked to cigarette and cigar smoking. Further, smoking can lead to elevated risk of asthma, pulmonary disease, emphysema, heart disease, stroke and other cardiovascular diseases, spontaneous abortions, and premature births. (For detailed information on these and other smoking-related health problems, see the Action on Smoking and Health Web site at <http://ash.org/>.)

Smoking near infants and children can also increase the child's susceptibility to sudden

Tobacco smoking is the primary cause of lung cancer, which is the leading form of cancer. Peer pressure among teens is particularly acute. More and more teenage women are now smoking. (Dick Hemingway)

infant death syndrome (SIDS), asthma, respiratory infection, and mental retardation. On an annual basis, smoking kills more people than alcohol, AIDS, car collisions, illegal drugs, murders, and suicides combined. In the United States, the yearly number of tobacco-related deaths is equivalent to three 747 jumbo jets crashing every day for an entire year, with no survivors. Not surprisingly, then, smoking is the leading cause of preventable disease and death in Canada and elsewhere.

Withdrawal Symptoms

Contrary to popular belief, the most deadly form of withdrawal symptoms are those associated with long-term alcohol abuse, and not—despite what the movie *Trainspotting* would have one believe—heroin addiction. Sudden withdrawal by chronic alcoholics can result in nausea, vomiting, intense seizures, and delirium tremens, a state of disorientation and confusion with a 2–10 per cent fatality rate.

Addiction to the other main legal drug, nicotine, is also extremely difficult to beat. Anyone who has tried—or has been around someone who has tried—to quit smoking knows that irritability, frustration, depression, insomnia, and lack of concentration are common experiences. Typically, ex-smokers require several months before they can report feeling comfortable with their new lives.

Attempting to withdraw from heroin addiction is also a harrowing experience. Symptoms can appear as early as a few hours after the last injection; they include drug craving, restlessness, muscle and bone pain, insomnia, diarrhea and vomiting, cold sweats and goosebumps (hence the term 'quitting cold turkey'), kicking motions (hence 'kicking the habit'), tremors, cramps, and panic attacks. Symptoms peak at around 48 hours and subside after approximately one week.

Withdrawal from other illicit drugs varies in severity. Any attempt to end addiction to barbiturates, or 'downers', results in roughly the same withdrawal symptoms as from alcohol, and is

therefore notoriously difficult and dangerous to accomplish.

Dangers of Recreational Drug Use

Some of the dangers associated with recreational drug use are illustrated by the findings of research on ecstasy (MDMA). Even seemingly harmless recreational drugs like ecstasy can have health costs, such as decreased levels of serotonin, a substance found in the brain that controls mood, pain perception, sleep, appetite, and emotions (Kish et al., 2000). Low levels of this chemical can result in slow speech, lethargy, and sluggish movement.

Many of the risks people face with MDMA use are similar to those found with the use of cocaine and amphetamines—psychological difficulties, including confusion, depression, sleep problems, drug craving, severe anxiety, and paranoia—while and sometimes weeks after taking MDMA. Physical symptoms such as muscle tension, involuntary teeth clenching, nausea, blurred vision, rapid eye movement, faintness, and chills or sweating also occur. Increases in heart rate and blood pressure pose a special risk for people with circulatory or heart disease.

Research links MDMA use to long-term damage to those parts of the brain critical to thought and memory. One study, in primates, showed that exposure to MDMA for four days caused brain damage that was evident six to seven years later.

MDA, the parent drug of MDMA, is an amphetamine-like drug that has also been abused and is similar in chemical structure to MDMA. Research shows that MDA destroys serotonin-producing neurons in the brain. MDMA is also related in its structure and effects to methamphetamine, which has been shown to cause degeneration of neurons containing the neurotransmitter dopamine. Damage to these neurons is the underlying cause of the motor disturbances seen in Parkinson's disease. Symptoms of this disease begin with lack of coordination and tremors and can eventually result in a form of paralysis.

Solutions for Alcohol and Drug Abuse

The 'War on Drugs'

Several approaches—some complementary, others conflicting—have been promoted in attempts to deal with substance abuse problems in society. The first approach, which has been the status quo for much of the past and which is also the most punitive way of handling the drug problem, is summarized by Charles McCaghy: 'Pass a law; if that does not work make the sentences harsher, get more policemen, get better detection devices, loosen up the law to make arrests easier and so on. Whatever you do, refuse to recognize that making some behaviors criminal does not prevent them' (1976: 300).

This perspective forms the basis of the so-called *war on drugs*, which follows the belief that drugs pose an immediate threat to the safety and well-being of society and that every effort should therefore be expended to prevent them from permeating people's lives. Strange to say, since 1960, gambling has been legalized and arrests on gambling charges decreased, virtually without comment, while arrests on drug charges have increased (Chilton, 1997). Arguing primarily from a moral standpoint, advocates of this approach call for severe laws intended to punish the producers, pushers, and users of illicit drugs. However, these strict regulations have largely failed for several reasons.

The seemingly capricious designation of legal and illegal status for various substances further undermines the legitimacy of drug laws, making it easier for people to ignore them whenever it suits them to. In the United States, the main victims of the 'war on drugs' have been black males. Many young people have trouble understanding why tobacco is legal and marijuana is not, for example. They are unlikely to take laws against marijuana use seriously if they disrespect the law (especially if young people do not expect strict enforcement). Further, as labelling theorists would point out, placing labels such as 'drug dealer', 'drug user', 'drug abuser', or 'criminal' on a person only serves to increase

---

BOX 2.3
Tackling Drugs

Some of these costs are found in medicine and public health. No one doubts that illegality makes drug use more hazardous than it need be (Miron and Zweibel 1995). In clandestine markets, the nature and purity of drugs are unknown. An undetected increase in the purity of heroin has been responsible for a spate of overdoses, most recently in Glasgow during July 1998. Users are reluctant to seek medical advice, except in emergencies.

Illegality drives users towards the more dangerous methods of ingestion and unhygienic settings. Harm reduction techniques introduced in the 1980s and changes in behaviour are held responsible for the decline in the HIV prevalence rate but hepatitis, variants B and C, remain a serious risk to public health. The cost of drug law also spills over in all manner of ways to innocent third parties—not least the taxpayer. Costs are found in burglary, sometimes aggravated, the fear of theft and violence, and the costs of averting theft.

Note: Miron, Jeffrey A., and Jeffrey Zweibel. 1995. 'The Economic Case Against Drug Prohibition'. *Journal of Economic Perspectives*, 9, no. 4: 175–92.

SOURCE: Richard Stevenson, 'Costs of the War on Drugs', in *Sensible Solutions to the Urban Drug Problem*, edited by Patrick Basham (Vancouver: Fraser Institute, 2001), 3, 4; available at <http://oldfraser.lexi.net/publications/books/drug_papers/UDStevenson.pdf>, accessed 20 February 2003. Reprinted by permission of The Fraser Institute.

the chance that a person will internalize that identity and behave accordingly. As well, the threat of judicial action for drug use does not get rid of the demand. Instead, it pushes the supply underground, where a well-paid black market, typically run by organized crime rings, quickly develops. Users looking for an illicit substance will go to where the source is, that is, to the criminal underworld. As Clayton Hartjen (1977) explains, the congregation of drug peddlers and addicts, away from the prying eyes of law enforcement, only serves to create a deviant subculture. Moreover, placing the international drug trade in the hands of criminals translates into a lack of quality control, resulting in impure drugs that are often more dangerous than they would be in their pure form.

To return to a historic example, as we have noted earlier, the US Prohibition era of the 1920s resulted not in a decrease in alcohol use, as was hoped by the Prohibitionists (indeed, the opposite occurred—drinking rates actually went up during this time), but in an increase in organized crime activity and the proliferation of illegal speakeasies and bootlegging operations.

Legalizing Drugs

Just like alcohol prohibition in the 1920s, drug prohibition has produced a large criminalized and lucrative industry. Research shows that decriminalization of the possession of marijuana since the early 1970s has resulted in decreased costs of enforcement and prosecution of marijuana-related offences (for a detailed account of this, see Haans, n.d.). So long as drug use is illegal, we can do little to monitor the quality of drugs available to users or the conditions under which people use these drugs.

Where alcohol and caffeine are concerned, food and drug regulations ensure that we do not consume dangerous or poor-quality substances. (The same cannot be said of cigarettes, which contain known carcinogens as well as nicotine.) Similarly, health protection rules would apply to recreational drugs if they were legalized.

One reason for repealing Prohibition was the realization that when quality-controlled alcoholic beverages are not in stock, people will drink just about anything. In the 1920s and 1930s, people died or went blind from drinking beverages that contained dangerous impurities or the wrong kind of alcohol (that is, methanol instead of ethanol). Similarly, some drug users have died from drug overdoses because they had no way of knowing the strength of the drug. Legalization could prevent this by regulating strength and quality so the user would be always aware of how much is a safe amount to use.

When drugs are illegal, users also take fewer health precautions. Needles shared among heroin users spread HIV/AIDS, for example. By driving the drug-user culture underground, the law works against safety, good hygiene, and disease prevention. Programs in other countries have reduced the sharing of contaminated equipment without increasing drug use.

An Alternative Solution?

Survey evidence shows that many people still oppose drug use and sales, and some oppose legalization. However, most Canadians are indifferent to legalizing non-addictive recreational drugs: they just do not care. They oppose efforts to construct a 'war on drugs', which they consider unnecessary. Some strongly favour legalization, for the reasons given in the previous section. Others actively support the use of marijuana for the treatment of people suffering from terminal illness such as AIDS or chronic illnesses such as epilepsy. Many medical researchers claim the drug has medicinal properties in certain situations.

The Canadian effort toward prevention and reduction of harm related to the use and distribution of psychoactive substances has gone through important changes in the last 35 years. It builds on public health lessons learned from a variety of infectious diseases and pushes for an integrated approach to both legal and illegal drugs

(Erickson, 1999). Methadone maintenance programs are good examples of harm-reduction efforts; heroin addicts stabilized on methadone can reduce illicit drug use and criminality and improve their life conditions even though they have not achieved abstinence (Cheung and Ch'ien, 1999). Prevention and harm reduction, with minimal application of criminal law, may be the most effective public health policy on drugs. The government can license the production and sales of soft drugs to regulate their quality, explore the potential of access mechanisms for drugs (free market versus government monopoly versus medical control), and tax the profits on legalized drug sales, then use the taxes for drug education. From a legal standpoint, one can reduce the penalties for using hard drugs, treat unlicensed drug-selling as a regulatory or tax offence that is punishable by huge fines, develop a full public health approach to addressing illegal drug problems, and educate the public against too much drug use and against the use of harmful drugs.

The Netherlands continue to be the model for a rational harm-reduction strategy. The Dutch policy on drugs is pragmatic, not ideological. It aims for prevention and harm reduction. Three principles serve as the cornerstones for the Dutch approach:

- a separation of the markets for hard and soft drugs
- treating drug users as ordinary citizens entitled to government assistance but also required to assume responsibility for their actions
- harm-reduction efforts directed at minimizing the damage done by drugs to users, communities, and the society as a whole (Korf, Riper, and Bullington, 1999)

Though this approach may have increased both lifetime and last-month prevalence of cannabis use by young people since 1984, only a minority of students report using cannabis on a regular basis (Kuipers and De Zwart, 1999). The two main threats to Dutch society posed by drug users are petty crime and drug trafficking (Partanen, 1997). Even crack cocaine use poses no threat to Dutch society, given the more rational Dutch drug policy: effective social policy is effective drug policy (Cohen, 1997). For that matter, crack cocaine use poses no major problem in Canada either (Cheung and Erickson, 1997).

In the Netherlands, as in North America, drugs—even powder and crack cocaine—are used differently according to socio-economic background. Middle-class 'party youth' make experimental use of the drugs in clubs and discotheques for recreational purposes. Deprived 'problem youth', from minority backgrounds, add the drugs to already troubled multi-problem behaviour in the context of their marginalized lifestyles (Nabben and Korf, 1999). This demonstrates that the problem to be solved is not drug use but deprivation.

Imagine the benefits if these policies were implemented in Canada and the United States instead of the 'war on drugs'. Currently, 47 US states make it illegal for injection drug users to possess syringes, a prohibition some say can lead to syringe sharing. Research finds that injection drug users concerned about being arrested are significantly more likely to share syringes and injection supplies. Thus, decriminalizing syringes and needles would likely result in reduction of behaviours that expose injection drug users to blood-borne viruses such as HIV (Blumenthal et al., 1999). A needle exchange would do more than reduce risks of infection; participants would also experience significant emotional benefits from the contact with needle-exchange workers (Larkins, 1999).

In Canada, despite a long history of empirical research pointing away from aggressive criminalization, the most recent law (the Controlled Drugs and Substances Act, May 1997) affirms both the seriously deviant status of illicit drug users and the primacy of the criminal justice model over the public health and social justice alternatives (Erickson, 1998).

Individual Responses

In terms of individual-level strategies, people should arm themselves and those around them with the facts on the health and social consequences of substance abuse, from both illegal and legal drug use (particularly tobacco and alcohol). The evidence, such as we have discussed here, gives more than sufficient reason for people to try to do whatever they can to guard against addiction, and, if addicted, to seek treatment. As we have seen, peers and family have a much greater effect on drinking behaviour than do schools, with the result that growing exposure to school prevention programs over the 1980s and 1990s had little influence on adolescent alcohol and other substance use (Welte et al., 1999). Networks of informal support for sobriety will play a large part in preventing and remedying individual addiction problems.

At the same time, people find it easier to avoid, control, and give up drug use if they have peers and friends with whom they do not use drugs. As we saw earlier, initiation into drug use depends on contacts with friends and family who use drugs. Cessation of drug use is also associated with having a lower proportion of your personal network who use drugs (Latkin et al., 1999). So controlling your drug use means making a judicious selection of friends. Membership in support groups, self-help programs, or grass-roots movements is also likely to help (Gundelach, 1994).

Concluding Remarks

Substances that are considered 'drugs' are not always defined as such by any absolute criteria. Instead, their definition depends in part on politics and culture. In this sense, drugs are social constructions. Laws that specify which drugs are legal and which are not are also socially constructed and influenced largely by politics. Laws are not consistently based on a drug's potential for harm. Many legal drugs, including nicotine and alcohol, may be more harmful to health than illegal drugs such as marijuana or even heroin.

The criminalization of drugs may cause more harm than good. Criminalization creates a black market, encourages organized crime, prevents quality control, and puts heroin drug users at higher risk of HIV/AIDS. People with a high socio-economic status are most likely to be heavy drinkers, yet they are safe from the law. How we view a drug, use it, and regulate it can have a large effect on how the person experiences and uses the drug. These perceptions tend to be influenced by one's peers and social milieu.

Substance abuse has many negative consequences for users and for individuals around them. These consequences involve other social problems and, often, severe health problems for users and their associates. For these reasons, substance abuse must be viewed, and pursued, as a social problem.

Questions for Critical Thought

1. The text outlines how attitudes to drugs changed historically in England and the United States. Search through microfilms of old newspapers and try to find evidence showing policy and/or attitude change regarding drug and alcohol use in Canada. Describe the patterns.
2. Do you agree that attitudes toward drugs and alcohol have been shaped as much by ignorance and stereotypes as by facts and first-hand experience? Is there a way to escape the social stigmatization of substance abusers and their lifestyles while addressing the social problems?

3. Merton argues that drug and alcohol abuse represent the individual retreating to 'alternate means'. Other scholars emphasize different macro-socio-cultural explanations. Based on your readings, what is (or are) the best explanation(s) of drug abuse? Why?

4. A major controversy surrounds the topic of whether the legalization of drugs may be beneficial or harmful to society. Go onto the Internet to the Marijuana Party of Canada's Web site (www.marijuanaparty.org) and look over their platform. What, in their view, are the major advantages of legalization? Differentiate between responsible and irresponsible drug use. What, if anything, is wrong with their platform?

5. There has been a significant rise in use of party drugs such as ecstasy among teens and young adults. Research the rave culture and analyze the role the drug plays in their activities.

Recommended Readings

James B. Bakalar and Lester Grinspoon, *Drug Control in a Free Society* (New York: Cambridge University Press, 1984).

This book describes some of the legal and ethical issues around drugs in North America and the United Kingdom. Using a historical analysis of drug policies, this book explains how factors such as a segregated youth culture have contributed to the problems discussed in this chapter.

Nils Christie, *Crime Control as Industry: Towards Gulags, Western Style?* (London: Routledge, 1993).

The failure of politicians to use alternatives to incarceration is sharply criticized in this book. The impact of the justice system on racial minorities is also addressed. The history of prison reforms in North America is examined, including the tendency of fixed sentences to lead to prison overcrowding and increased discretion for prosecutors.

Jon Elster, *Strong Feelings: Emotion, Addiction, and Human Behavior* (Cambridge, MA: MIT Press, 1999).

This recent text examines the relationship between emotion and addiction with a focus on the possibility of choice within compulsive behaviour. Chapter 3 includes a phenomenological analysis.

Patricia G. Erickson, 'Neglected and Rejected: A Case Study of the Impact of Social Research on Canadian Drug Policy', *Canadian Journal of Sociology*, 23 (1998), 263–80.

How does Canada create new drug laws? This article looks at the long-awaited creation of the Controlled Drugs and Substances Act, which was instated in May 1997. Erickson asks how the act responded to empirical and theoretical research on drugs and drug use. The author argues that the act opted for a criminal justice model rather than a public health lens through which to view drug users.

M. Haden, 'Illicit IV Drugs: A Public Health Approach', *Canadian Journal of Public Health*, 93 (2002), 431–4.

Within the polarized views of legalization versus criminalization of intravenous drugs, one question is forgotten: how do Canadian drug laws harm individuals and society? This article takes a public health perspective toward the dichotomy, arguing for a middle ground in policy.

James A. Inciardi, *Handbook of Drug Control in the United States* (New York: Greenwood Press, 1990).

This book looks at the intended and unintended consequences of drug laws, the history of drugs and drug policy, some constitutional issues in drug testing, links between drugs and crime, and the legalization of drugs. The text attacks current drug policy as ineffective, expensive, and intrusive but also presents arguments against legalization.

Jimmie Lynn Reeves and Richard Campbell, *Cracked Coverage: Television News, the Anti-Cocaine Crusade, and the Reagan Legacy* (Durham, NC: Duke University Press, 1994).

Reeves and Campbell examine the role of major American TV news programs in promoting the war against drugs by analyzing 270 news stories aired between 1981 and 1988. Their analysis reveals that drugs were not a genuine grassroots concern of the public initially but that concern developed after a relentless sensationalist torrent of media news coverage.

Thomas Szasz, *Our Right to Drugs: The Case for a Free Market* (New York: Praeger, 1992).

This book offers an alternative to the traditional arguments on drug policy. Szasz takes a rights-based approach that drug policies must maximize the responsibility of the individual rather than criminalize individual choice.

Franklin E. Zimring and Gordon Hawkins, *The Search for Rational Drug Control* (Cambridge: Cambridge University Press, 1992).

Zimring and Hawkins outline three ideal-type perspectives on the war on drugs. They clearly articulate their view that the government's strategy regarding drugs serves only to hide a political agenda.

Recommended Web Sites

Centre for Addiction and Mental Health
www.camh.net

The Centre for Addiction and Mental Health (CAMH) provides information regarding both addiction and mental health. There are several resources aimed at educating both the general public and those with health problems. Electronic resources are available for viewing, as well as a number of links to community events, volunteer opportunities, and current and future research.

Canadian Centre on Substance Abuse
www.ccsa.ca

The Canadian Centre on Substance Abuse is a non-profit organization working to minimize the harm

of tobacco, alcohol, and other drugs. Its Web site includes a resource database, statistics on substance abuse, and a network listing. Of considerable importance is the Topics/Issues link, which contains information on topics such as cannabis, gambling, seniors, the law, and policy and research.

MADD Canada
www.madd.ca

MADD Canada, or Mothers Against Drunk Driving, provides facts regarding activities around and incidents of drunk driving. The site has up-to-date news about drunk driving as well as a listing of programs that the organization administers solely or in conjunction with other organizations.

References

Alden, Helena, and Scott R. Maggard. 2000. 'Perceptions of Social Class and Drug Use'. Paper presented at the annual conference of the Southern Sociological Society.

Appleton, Lynn M. 1995. 'Rethinking Medicalization: Alcoholism and Anomalies'. In *Images of Issues: Typifying Contemporary Social Problems*, 2nd edn, edited by Joel Best, 59–80. Hawthorne, NY: Aldine de Gruyter,.

Auerhahn, Kathleen, and Robert Nash Parker. 1999. 'Drugs, Alcohol and Homicide'. In *Studying and Preventing Homicide: Issues and Challenges*, edited by M. Dwayne Smith and Margaret A. Zahn, 99–114. Thousand Oaks, CA: Sage.

Bailey, Susan L. 1999. 'The Measurement of Problem Drinking in Young Adulthood'. *Journal of Studies on Alcohol*, 60: 234–44.

Baron, Stephen W. 1999. 'Street Youths and Substance Use: The Role of Background, Street Lifestyle, and Economic Factors'. *Youth and Society*, 31, no. 1: 3–26.

Bastos, Francisco Imacio, Steffanie A. Strathdee, Monica Derrico, and Maria de Fatima Pina. 1999. 'Drug Use and the Spread of HIV/AIDS in South America and the Caribbean'. *Drugs, Education, Prevention and Policy*, 6, no. 1: 29–49.

Beautrais, Annette L., Peter R. Joyce, and Roger T. Mulder. 1999. 'Cannabis Abuse and Serious Suicide Attempts'. *Addiction*, 94: 1155–64.

Becker, Howard S. 1958. *Outsiders: Studies in the Sociology of Deviance*. New York: Free Press.

Bennett, Joel B., and Wayne E.K. Lehman. 1998. 'Workplace Drinking Climate, Stress, and Problem Indicators: Assessing the Influence of Teamwork (Group Cohesion)'. *Journal of Studies on Alcohol*, 59: 608–18.

Bennett, Melanie E., Barbara S. McCrady, Valerie Johnson, and Robert J. Pandina. 1999. 'Problem Drinking from Young Adulthood to Adulthood: Patterns, Predictors and Outcomes'. *Journal of Studies on Alcohol*, 60: 605–14.

Bennett, Melanie E., Joseph H. Miller, and W. Gill Woodall. 1999. 'Drinking, Binge Drinking, and Other Drug Use Among Southwestern Undergraduates: Three-Year Trends'. *American Journal of Drug and Alcohol Abuse*, 25: 331–50.

Bensley, Lillian Southwick, Susan J. Spieker, Juliet van Eenwyk, and Judy Schoder. 1999. 'Self-reported Abuse History and Adolescent Problem Behaviors, II: Alcohol and Drug Use'. *Journal of Adolescent Health*, 24, no. 3: 173–80.

Blumenthal, Ricky N., Alex H. Kral, Elizabeth A. Erringer, and Brian R. Edlin. 1999. 'Drug Paraphernalia Laws and Injection-Related Infectious Disease Risk Among Drug Injectors'. *Journal of Drug Issues*, 29, no. 1: 1–16.

Bobak, Martin, Martin McKee, Richard Rose, and Michael Marmot. 1999. 'Alcohol Consumption in a National Sample of the Russian Population'. *Addiction*, 94: 857–66.

Brownstein, Henry H., Sean D. Cleary, Susan M. Crimmins, Judith Ryder, Raquel Warley, and Barry Spunt. 1999. 'The Relationship Between Violent Offending and Drug Use in the Pre-prison Experience of a Sample of Incarcerated Young Men'. Paper presented at the annual meeting of the American Sociological Association.

Brunswick, Ann F. 1999. 'Structural Strain: An Ecological Paradigm for Studying African American Drug Use'. *Drugs and Society*, 14, nos 1–2: 5–19.

Canadian Centre on Substance Abuse and Centre for Addiction and Mental Health. 1999. *Canadian Profile 1999: Alcohol, Tobacco and Other Drugs*. Ottawa: Canadian Centre on Substance Abuse and Centre for Addiction and Mental Health.

Carruthers, Cynthia P. 1992. 'The Relationship of Alcohol Consumption Practices to Leisure Patterns and Leisure-Related Alcohol Expectancies'. *Dissertation Abstracts International*, 52, 7–A: 2700–1.

Centre for Addiction and Mental Health. 1999. 'Ontario Student Drug Use Survey: Executive Summary'. Available at <www.camh.net/addiction/ont_study_drug_use.html>, accessed 12 January 2003.

Cernetig, M. 1997. 'The HIV Epidemic in Vancouver's Lower East Side'. *Globe and Mail*, 8 October.

Cheung, Yuet W., and James M.N. Ch'ien. 1999. 'Previous Participation in Outpatient Methadone Program and Residential Treatment Outcome: A Research Note from Hong Kong'. *Substance Use and Abuse*, 34: 103–18.

Cheung, Yuet W., and Patricia G. Erickson. 1997. 'Crack Use in Canada: A Distant American Cousin'. In *Crack in America: Demon Drugs and Social Justice*, edited by Craig Reinarman and Harry G. Levine, 175–93. Berkeley: University of California Press.

Chilton, Roland. 1997. 'Victimless Crime in the Twentieth Century: Drug Prohibition as the Folly of Our Time'. Paper presented at the annual meeting of the Society for the Study of Social Problems.

Cohen, Peter D.A. 1997. 'Crack in the Netherlands: Effective Social Policy is Effective Drug Policy'. In *Crack in America: Demon Drugs and Social Justice*, edited by Craig Reinarman and Harry G. Levine, 214–24. Berkeley: University of California Press.

Colson, Tara A. 2000. 'Study of Marijuana Use Among Young Adults'. Paper presented at the annual meeting of the Southern Sociological Society.

Costa, Frances, M., Richard Jessor, and Mark Turbin. 1999. 'Transition into Adolescent Problem Drinking: The Role of Psychosocial Risk and Protective Factors'. *Journal of Studies on Alcohol*, 60: 480–90.

Cotton Oldenburg, Niki U., Kathleen B. Jordan, Sandra L. Martin, and Lawrence Kupper. 1999. 'Women Inmates' Risky Sex and Drug Behaviors: Are They Related?' *American Journal of Drug and Alcohol Abuse*, 25: 129–49.

Covington, Jeanette. 1997. 'The Social Construction of the Minority Drug Problem'. Paper presented at the annual meeting of the American Sociological Association.

Crawford, John, and Nick Heather. 1987. 'Public Attitudes to the Disease Concept of Alcoholism'. *International Journal of the Addictions*, 22: 1129–38.

Curran, Geoffrey M., Scott F. Stoltenberg, Elizabeth M. Hill, Sharon A. Mudd, Frederic C. Blow, and Robert

A. Zucker. 1999. 'Gender Differences in the Relationships Among SES, Family History of Alcohol Disorders and Alcohol Dependence'. *Journal of Studies on Alcohol*, 60: 825–32.

Dawkins, Marvin P. 1997. 'Drug Use and Violent Crime Among Adolescents'. *Adolescence*, 32: 395–405.

Delva, Jorge, Michelle L. Van Etten, Gonzalo B. Gonzalez, Miguel A. Cedeno, Marcel Penna, Luis H. Caris, and James C. Anthony. 1999. 'First Opportunities to Try Drugs and the Transition to First Drug Use: Evidence from a National School Survey in Panama'. *Substance Use and Misuse*, 34: 1451–67.

Demers, Andree, Jocelyne Bisson, and Jezabelle Palluy. 1999. 'Wives' Convergence with Their Husbands' Alcohol Use: Social Conditions as Mediators'. *Journal of Studies on Alcohol*, 60: 368–77.

Dishion, Thomas J., Deborah M. Capaldi, and Karen Yoerger. 1999. 'Middle Childhood Antecedents to Progressions in Male Adolescent Substance Abuse: An Ecological Analysis of Risk and Protection'. *Journal of Adolescent Research*, 14: 175–205.

Durkheim, Émile. 1951. *Suicide: A Study in Sociology*. Translated by John A. Spaulding and George Simpson. New York: Free Press..

Duster, Troy. 1997. 'Pattern, Purpose, and Race in the Drug War: The Crisis of Credibility in Criminal Justice'. In *Crack in America: Demon Drugs and Social Justice*, edited by Craig Reinarman and Harry G. Levine, 260–87. Berkeley: University of California Press.

Ellickson, Phyllis L., Rebecca L. Collins, and Robert M. Bell. 1999. 'Adolescent Use of Illicit Drugs Other Than Marijuana: How Important Is Social Bonding and for Which Ethnic Groups?' *Substance Use and Misuse*, 34: 317–46.

Erickson, Patricia G. 1998. 'Neglected and Rejected: A Case Study of the Impact of Social Research on Canadian Drug Policy'. *Canadian Journal of Sociology*, 23: 263–80.

———. 1999. 'Introduction: The Three Phases of Harm Reduction: An Examination of Emerging Concepts, Methodologies, and Critiques'. *Substance Use and Misuse*, 32: 1–7.

Feldman, Linda, Bart Harvey, Philippa Holowaty, and Linda Shortt. 1999. 'Alcohol Use Beliefs and Behaviors Among High School Students'. *Journal of Adolescent Health*, 24: 48–58.

Fillmore, Kaye Middleton, Jacqueline M. Golding, Karen L. Graves, Steven Kniep, E. Victor Leino, Anders Romelsjo, Carlisle Shoemaker, Catherine R. Ager,

Peter Allebeck, and Heidi P. Ferrer. 1998. 'Alcohol Consumption and Mortality. I. Characteristics of Drinking Groups'. *Addiction*, 93: 183–203.

Furst, R. Terry, Bruce D. Johnson, Eloise Dunlap, and Richard Curtis. 1999. 'The Stigmatized Image of the "Crack Head": A Sociocultural Exploration of a Barrier to Cocaine Smoking Among a Cohort of Youth in New York City'. *Deviant Behavior*, 20: 153–81.

Giffen, P.J., Shirley Endicott, and Sylvia Lambert. 1991. *Panic and Indifference: The Politics of Canada's Drug Laws*. Ottawa: Canadian Centre on Substance Abuse.

Grant, Bridget F., and Deborah S. Hasin. 1999. 'Suicidal Ideation Among the United States Drinking Population: Results from the National Longitudinal Alcohol Epidemiological Survey'. *Journal of Studies on Alcohol*, 60: 422–9.

Green, Anna, Sophie Day, and Helen Ward. 2000. 'Crack Cocaine and Prostitution in London in the 1990s'. *Sociology of Health and Illness*, 22: 27–39.

Green, Melvyn. 1986. 'The History of Canadian Narcotics Control: The Formative Years'. In *The Social Dimensions of Law*, edited by Neil Boyd, 24–40. Scarborough, ON: Prentice-Hall.

Greenfield, Lawrence A. 1998. *Alcohol and Crime: An Analysis of National Data on the Prevalence of Alcohol Involvement in Crime*. Washington, DC: US Department of Justice.

Gundelach, Peter. 1994. 'Communities, Grass-roots Movements, and Substance Abuse Problems: New Strategies'. *Nordisk Alkohol Tidskrift*, 11: 5–12.

Gusfield, Joseph. 1963. *Symbolic Crusade: Status Politics and the American Temperance Movement*. Urbana: University of Illinois Press.

Haans, Dave. n.d. 'The Effects of Decriminalization of Marijuana'. Available at <www.chass.utoronto.ca/~haans/misc/mjdcrim.html>, accessed 17 March 2003.

Hansell, Stephen, Helene Raskin White, and Firoozeh Molaparast Vali. 1999. 'Specific Alcoholic Beverages and Physical and Mental Health Among Adolescents'. *Journal of Studies on Alcohol*, 60: 209–18.

Hartjen, Clayton A. 1977. *Possible Trouble: An Analysis of Social Problems*. New York: Praeger.

Health Canada. 1999. *Statistical Report on the Health of Canadians*. Available at <www.statcan.ca/english/freepub/82-570-XIE/free.htm>, accessed 20 February 2003.

Hodgson, Maggie. 1987. *Indian Communities Develop Futuristic Addictions Treatment and Health Approach*.

Edmonton, AB: Nechi Institute on Alcohol and Drug Education.

Hutchison, Ira W. 1999. 'Alcohol, Fear, and Woman Abuse'. *Sex Roles*, 40: 893–920.

Inciardi, James A., Hilary L. Suratt, Hector M. Colon, Dale D. Chitwood, and James E. Rivers. 1999. 'Drug Use and HIV Risks Among Migrant Workers on the DelMarVa Peninsula'. *Substance Use and Misuse*, 34: 653–66.

Irwin, Darrell D. 1999. 'The Straight Edge Subculture: Examining the Youths' Drug-free Way'. *Journal of Drug Issues*, 29: 365–80.

Ivis, Frank J., and Eward M. Adlaf. 1999. 'A Comparison of Trends in Drug Use Among Students in the USA and Ontario, Canada: 1975–1997'. *Drugs, Education, Prevention, and Policy*, 6: 17–27.

Jackson, Christine, Lisa Henriksen, and Denise Dickinson. 1999. 'Alcohol-Specific Socialization, Parenting Behaviors, and Alcohol Use by Children'. *Journal of Studies on Alcohol*, 60: 362–7.

Jennison, Karen M., and Kenneth A. Johnson. 1998. 'Alcohol Dependence in Adult Children of Alcoholics: Longitudinal Evidence of Early Risk'. *Journal of Drug Education*, 28: 19–37.

Johnson, Valerie. 1999. 'Alcohol Problems, Deviance and Negative Affect Among Children from Alcoholic, Depressed and Comorbid Families'. Paper presented at the annual meeting of the Society for the Study of Social Problems.

Johnstone, Gerry. 1996. 'From Vice to Disease? The Concepts of Dipsomania and Inebriety, 1860–1908'. *Social and Legal Studies*, 5, no. 1: 37–56.

Kane, Robert J., and George S. Yacoubian, Jr. 1999. 'Pattern of Drug Escalation Among Philadelphia Arrestees: An Assessment of the Gateway Theory'. *Journal of Drug Issues*, 29: 107–20.

Kish, S.J., Y. Furukawa, L. Ang, S.P. Vorce, and K.S. Kalasinsky. 2000. 'Striatal Serotonin Is Depleted in Brain of a Human MDMA (Ecstasy) User'. *Neurology*, 55: 294–6.

Korf, Dirk J., Helene Riper, and Bruce Bullington. 1999. 'Windmills in Their Minds? Policy and Drug Research in the Netherlands'. *Journal of Drug Issues*, 29: 451–71.

Kuipers, S.B.M., and W.M. De Zwart. 1999. 'Trends and Patterns in Illicit Drug Use Among Students aged 12 to 18 in the Netherlands'. *Journal of Drug Issues*, 29: 549–63.

Kunz, Jean Lock, and Norman Giesbrecht. 1999. 'Gender, Perceptions of Harm, and Other Social Predictors of Alcohol Use in a Punjabi Community in the Toronto Area'. *Substance Use and Misuse*, 34: 403–19.

Lafranire, Gerald, and Leah Spicer. 2002. *Illicit Drug Trends in Canada 1998–2001: A Review and Analysis of Enforcement: Data Prepared for the Special Senate Committee on Illegal Drugs*. Ottawa: Law and Government Division, Parliamentary Research Branch of the Library of Parliament.

Laniel, Laurent. 1999. 'Drugs and Globalization: An Equivocal Relationship'. *International Social Science Journal*, 51: 239–40.

Larkins, Sherry. 1999. 'The Emotional Health Benefits of Needle-Exchange Contact'. Paper presented at the annual meeting of the American Sociological Association.

Latkin, Carl A., Amy R. Knowlton, Donald Hoover, and Wallace Mandell. 1999. 'Drug Network Characteristics as a Predictor of Cessation of Drug Use Among Adult Injection Drug Users: A Prospective Study'. *American Journal of Drug and Alcohol Abuse*, 25: 463–73.

Leonard, Kenneth E., and Brian M. Quigley. 1999. 'Drinking and Marital Aggression in Newlyweds: An Event-Based Analysis of Drinking and the Occurrence of Husband Marital Aggression'. *Journal of Studies on Alcohol*, 60: 537–45.

Leonard, Kenneth E., and Julie C. Rothbard. 1999. 'Alcohol and the Marriage Effect'. *Journal of Studies on Alcohol*, 60, suppl. 13: 139–46.

Liu, Xiaoru, and Howard Kaplan. 1999. 'Role Strain and Illicit Drug Use: The Moderating Influence of Commitment to Conventional Values'. Paper presented at the annual meeting of the American Sociological Association.

McCaghy, Charles H., ed. 1976, *Deviant Behavior: Crime, Conflict, and Interest Groups*. Boston: Allyn & Bacon.

McCoy, Clyde B., Lisa R. Metsch, Dale D. Chitwood, James E. Rivers, H. Virginia McCoy, and Sarah Messiah. 2000. 'Health Services for Chronic Drug Users in an Era of Managed Care: The University of Miami Community-Based Health Services Research Centre'. *Advances in Medical Sociology*, 7: 151–74.

McCoy, H. Virginia, Sarah E. Messiah, Zhinuan Yu, Kerry Anne McGeary, and Janvier Gasana. 2000. 'Drug Users as Perpetrators, Victims and Observers of Violence: Implications for Intervention'. Paper presented at the annual meeting of the Southern Sociological Society.

Macdonald, Scott, Samantha Wells, and T. Cameron Wild. 1999. 'Occupation Risk Factors Associated with Alcohol and Drug Problems'. *American Journal of Drug and Alcohol Abuse*, 25: 351–69.

Maes, Hermine H., Charlene E. Woodard, Lenn Murrelle, Joanne M. Meyer, Judy L. Silberg, John K. Hewitt, Michael Rutter, Emily Simonoff, Andrew Pickles, Rene Carbonneau, Michael C. Neale, and Lindon J. Eaves. 1999. 'Tobacco, Alcohol, and Drug Use in Eight- to Sixteen-Year-Old Twins: The Virginia Twin Study of Adolescent Behavioral Development'. *Journal of Studies on Alcohol*, 60: 293–305.

Makela, Pia. 1999. 'Alcohol-Related Mortality as a Function of Socio-economic Status'. *Addiction*, 94: 867–86.

Marcus, Alan M. 1963. *The Structure of Popular Beliefs About Alcoholism*. Toronto: Addiction Research Foundation.

Marquart, James W., Victoria E. Brewer, Janet Mullings, and Ben M. Crouch. 1999. 'The Implications of Crime Control Policy on HIV/AIDS-Related Risk Among Women Prisoners'. *Crime and Delinquency*, 45: 82–98.

Mason, W. Alex, and Michael Windle. 2000. 'A Longitudinal Study of the Effects of Religiosity on Adolescent Alcohol Use and Alcohol-Related Problems'. Paper presented at the annual meeting of the Southern Sociological Society.

Meddis, Sam V. 1993. 'Is the Drug War Racist? Disparities Suggest the Answer Is Yes'. *USA Today*, 23 July, 2A.

Mekolichick, Jeanne T. 1996. 'Anabolic-Androgenic Steroids: The Construction of a Social Problem'. Paper presented at the annual meeting of the Society for the Study of Social Problems.

Merton, Robert K. 1957. 'Social Structure and Anomie'. In *Social Theory and Social Structure*, rev. edn, chapter 3. New York: Free Press.

Moon, Dreama G., Michael L. Hecht, Kristina M. Jackson, and Regina E. Spellers. 1999. 'Ethnic and Gender Differences and Similarities in Adolescent Drug Use and Refusals of Drug Offers'. *Substance Use and Misuse*, 34: 1059–183.

Morgan, John P., and Lynn Zimmer. 1997. 'The Social Pharmacology of Smokeable Cocaine: Not All It's Cracked Up to Be'. In *Crack in America: Demon Drugs and Social Justice*, edited by Craig Reinarman

and Harry G. Levine, 131–70. Berkeley: University of California Press.

Mutzell, Sture. 1994. 'Mortality, Suicide, Social Maladjustment and Criminality Among Male Alcoholic Parents and Men from the General Population and Their Offspring'. *International Journal of Adolescence and Youth*, 4: 305–28.

———. 1996. 'The Use of Narcotic Drugs in Stockholm County, Sweden: A Follow-up After 17 Years'. *International Journal of Adolescence and Youth*, 6: 245–59.

Nabben, Tom, and Dirk J. Korf. 1999. 'Cocaine and Crack in Amsterdam: Diverging Subcultures'. *Journal of Drug Issues*, 29: 627–51.

Nagasawa, Richard, Zhenchao Qian, and Paul Wong. 1999. 'Theory of Segmented Assimilation and Patterns of Drug and Alcohol Use Among Asian Pacific Youths'. Paper presented at the annual meeting of the American Sociological Association.

National Institute On Drug Abuse (NIDA). 2001. 'MMDA (Ecstasy)'. Available at <www.nida.nih.gov/Infofax/ecstasy.html>, accessed 14 February 2003.

Nurco, David N., and Monroe Lerner. 1999. 'A Complementary Perspective to Primary Socialization Theory'. *Substance Use and Misuse*, 34: 993–1003.

O'Farrell, Timothy J., Valerie Van Hutten, and Christopher M. Murphy. 1999. 'Domestic Violence Before and After Alcoholism Treatment: A Two-Year Longitudinal Study'. *Journal of Studies on Alcohol*, 60: 317–21.

Oldham, Greg R., and Benjamin I. Gordon. 1999. 'Job Complexity and Employee Substance Use: The Moderating Effects of Cognitive Ability'. *Journal of Health and Social Behavior*, 40: 290–306.

Parsons, Talcott. 1951. 'Social Structure and Dynamic Process: The Case of Modern Medical Practice'. In *The Social System*, chapter 10. New York: Free Press.

Partanen, Juha. 1997. 'The Merchant, the Priest, and the Humble Engineer: Observations on the Drug Scene in Rotterdam'. *Nordisk Alkohol and Narkotikatidskrift*, 14, no. 3: 167–83.

Patton, Travis, and Anne Baird. 2000. 'Alcohol and Interpersonal Violence: Methodological Considerations'. Paper presented at the annual meeting of the Southern Sociological Society.

Perkins, H. Wesley. 1999. 'Stress-Motivated Drinking in Collegiate and Postcollegiate Young Adulthood: Life Course and Gender Patterns'. *Journal of Studies on Alcohol*, 60: 219–27.

Power, Chris, Bryan Rodgers, and Steven Hope. 1994. 'Heavy Alcohol Consumption and Marital Status: Disentangling the Relationship in a National Study of Young Adults'. *Addiction*, 94: 1477–87.

Randall, Carrie L., James S. Roberts, Frances K. Del Boca, Kathleen M. Carroll, Gerard J. Connors, and Margaret E. Mattson. 1999. 'Telescoping of Landmark Events Associated with Drinking: A Gender Comparison'. *Journal of Studies on Alcohol*, 60: 252–60.

Rehm, Jurgen, and Gerhard Gmel. 1999. 'Patterns of Alcohol Consumption and Social Consequences: Results from an 8–Year Follow-up Study in Switzerland'. *Addiction*, 94: 899–912.

Reinarman, Craig, Dan Waldorf, Sheila B. Murphy, and Harry G. Levine. 1997. 'The Contingent Call of the Pipe: Bingeing and Addiction Among Heavy Cocaine Smokers'. In *Crack in America: Demon Drugs and Social Justice*, edited by Craig Reinarman and Harry G. Levine, 77–97. Berkeley: University of California Press.

Royal College of Physicians. 1987. *Great and Growing Evil: The Medical Consequences of Alcohol Abuse* [working party report]. Cited by the Institute of Alcohol Studies, *The Nature of Alcohol Problems*, 2000, available at <www.ias.org.uk/factsheets/medsoc3.htm>, accessed 12 January 2003.

Santolaria, Francisco, Jose Luis Perez Manzano, Antonio Milena, Emilio Gonzalez Reimers, Maria Angeles Gomez Rodriguez, Antonio Martinez Riera, Maria Remedios Aleman Valls, and Maria Joe de la Vega Prieto. 2000. 'Nutritional Assessment in Alcoholic Patients: Its Relationship with Alcoholic Intake, Feeding Habits, Organic Complications and Social Problems'. *Drug and Alcohol Dependence*, 59: 295–304.

Scott, Kathryn D., John Schafer, and Thomas K. Greenfield. 1999. 'The Role of Alcohol in Physical Assault Perpetration and Victimization'. *Journal of Studies on Alcohol*, 60: 528–36.

Skaff, Marilyn McKean, John W. Finney, and Rudolf H. Moos. 1999. 'Gender Differences in Problem Drinking and Depression: Different "Vulnerabilities"?' *American Journal of Community Psychology*, 27: 25–54.

Spohn, Ryan E., and Howard B. Kaplan. 2000. 'Adolescent Substance Use and Adult Health Status: A Critical Analysis of a Problematic Relationship'. *Advances in Medical Sociology*, 7: 45–65.

Staton, Michele, Carl Leukefeld, T.K. Logan, Rick Zimmerman, Don Lyman, Rich Milich, Cathy

Martin, Karen McClanah, and Richard Clayton. 1999. 'Gender Differences in Substance Use and Initiation of Sexual Activity'. *Population Research and Policy Review*, 18, nos 1–2: 89–100.

Taylor, Jenny, Naomi Fulop, and John Green. 1999. 'Drink, Illicit Drugs and Unsafe Sex in Women'. *Addiction*, 94: 1209–18.

Thomas, George, Alan Reifman, Grace M. Barnes, and Michael P. Farrell. 2000. 'Delayed Onset of Drunkenness as a Protective Factor for Adolescent Alcohol Misuse and Sexual Risk Taking: A Longitudinal Study'. *Deviant Behavior*, 21: 181–210.

United Nations Office on Drugs and Crime. 2000. *World Drug Report 2000*. Available at <www.undcp.org/world_drug_report.html>, accessed 13 January 2003.

United States. Bureau of Justice Statistics. 1999. *Substance Abuse and Treatment, State and Federal Prisoners, 1997*. (NCJ 172871). Washington, DC: US Department of Justice.

United States. Substance Abuse and Mental Health Services Administration. 1999. *National Household Survey on Drug Abuse: Population Estimates 1998*. Washington, DC: US Department of Health and Human Services.

Van Dyke, Craig, and Robert Byck. 1982. 'Cocaine'. *Scientific American*, 246: 128–141.

Van Etten, Michelle, Yehuda D. Neumark, and James C. Anthony. 1999. 'Male-Female Differences in the Earliest Stages of Drug Involvement'. *Addiction*, 94: 1413–19.

Wagner, David. 1995. 'Historicizing Social Constructionist Perspectives: The Example of Temperance Movements'. Paper presented at the annual meeting of the Society for the Study of Social Problems.

Warner, Jessica, Robin Room, and Edward M. Adlaf. 1999. 'Rules and Limits in the Use of Marijuana Among High-School Students: The Results of a Qualitative Study in Ontario'. *Journal of Youth Studies*, 2: 59–76.

Warner, Jessica, Timothy R. Weber, and Ricardo Albanes. 1999. '"Girls Are Retarded When They're Stoned": Marijuana and the Construction of Gender Roles Among Adolescent Females'. *Sex Roles*, 40: 25–43.

Welte, John, Grace M. Barnes, Joseph H. Hoffman, and Barbara A. Dintcheff. 1999. 'Trends in Adolescent Alcohol and Other Substance Use: Relationships to Trends in Peer, Parent, and School Influences'. *Substance Use and Misuse*, 34: 1427–49.

Whitbeck, Les B. 1999. 'Primary Socialization Theory: It All Begins with the Family'. *Substance Use and Misuse*, 34: 1025–32.

White, Helene R., and Erich W. Labouvie. 1994. 'Generality Versus Specificity of Problem Behaviour: Psychological and Functional Differences'. *Journal of Drug Issues*, 24: 55–74.

Widom, Cathy Spatz, and Helene Raskin White. 1997. 'Problem Behaviours in Abused and Neglected Children Grown Up: Prevalence and Co-occurrence of Substance Abuse, Crime and Violence'. *Criminal Behaviour and Mental Health*, 7, no. 4: 287–310.

Williams, Robert, and Susan P. Gloster. 1999. 'Knowledge of Fetal Alcohol Syndrome (FAS) Among Natives in Northern Manitoba'. *Journal of Studies on Alcohol*, 60: 833–6.

Witters, Weldon, Peter Venturelli, and Glen Hanson. 1992. *Drugs and Society*, 3rd edn. Boston: Jones and Bartlett.

Yarnold, Barbara. 1999. 'Cocaine Use Among Miami's Public School Students, 1992: Religion Versus Peers and Availability'. *Journal of Health and Social Policy*, 11, no. 2, 69–84.

Glossary

Anomie theory According to Merton (1957), *anomie* is the gap between culturally defined goals and socially approved means for attaining those goals. This state of anomie allows for a variety of solutions, which Merton called *adaptations*, including ritualism, retreatism, rebellion, and innovation. Anomie may be a source of social innovation as well as a locus of social problems.

Drug abuse This concept begins with the notion of excessive or inappropriate drug use resulting in social, psychological, and/or physiological impairments. It stems from a chronic physical and psychological compulsion to continue taking a drug in order to avoid unpleasant withdrawal symptoms.

Gateway drug Proponents of this concept suggest that, for example, marijuana is a substance that paves the way for the use of other illicit drugs, such as cocaine or heroin. Others point out that someone who is willing to try one type of drug may be more likely to try any drug, with no particular 'gateway' process involved.

Labelling The process of defining and treating others as deviant. Labelling theory explores the effects of negative labels on individuals' self-conceptions and is interested in the development of a 'deviant identity'. Social reactions of condemnation and criminalization can lead actors to alter their individual characteristics and to adopt the values of their labelled identity.

Polydrug use Using drugs in combination, with the most popular combination being alcohol, nicotine, and marijuana. This concept is a cousin to the concept of gateway drugs.

Chapter 3

Crime and Violence

Chapter Objectives

After reading this chapter the student should understand:
- the definitions of *crime*, *laws*, and *social order*
- how to measure crime, and the problems associated with these measures
- different types of crime
- the demography of crime
- theories explaining criminal activities
- economic, social, and psychological consequences of crime
- the impact of crime on health
- possible solutions to the problem of crime, and the debate surrounding capital punishment

Introduction

This chapter is about crime and its victims. It discusses violence, murder, assault, homicide, and robbery, and also the more common and less dramatic criminal acts. Finally, it is about offenders and the reasons they commit their offences. Therefore, it is also about responsibility, socialization, guilt, and economic payoffs to crime.

Crime is a social problem for several reasons. First, as we will see, crime has real consequences for people's health, safety, and sense of well-being. Victimization can be traumatic. It can cause people to withdraw from normal social life. Second, and as a result, victimization on a large scale can reduce people's trust in social institutions and their willingness to take part in community life. Thus, fear of crime can diminish a community's vitality and cohesion. Third, crime and its repercussions can damage the central institutions of society—families, workplaces, and schools, for example—and in this way hinder our ability to carry out the most basic social activities of learning, earning, and raising children.

As we shall see, crime is a social activity, with social causes and consequences. Men are more likely to be involved in violent crimes than women, both as victims and as offenders—more likely than women to commit acts of murder, forcible rape, armed robbery, aggravated assault, and arson, for example (see Figure 3.1). Many scholars believe that **differential socialization** provides the best explanation for this pattern.

Theorists vary in their views on criminal causation and responsibility. Some argue that criminal behaviour, particularly where property crimes are concerned, is a result of rational calculation that takes into account the profitability and risk of a crime. Others argue that crime will result whenever groups possess different amounts of power and influence. As a result, criminal activity will increase whenever social inequality increases. Some argue that strict law enforcement and harsh prisons will solve the 'crime problem'. Others argue that prisons cause as many problems as they solve—in fact, they teach crime and harden criminals. Let us now look more closely at these beliefs and at the relevant evidence.

FIGURE 3.1
Adults and Youths Charged, by Offence Category and Gender, Canada, 2001

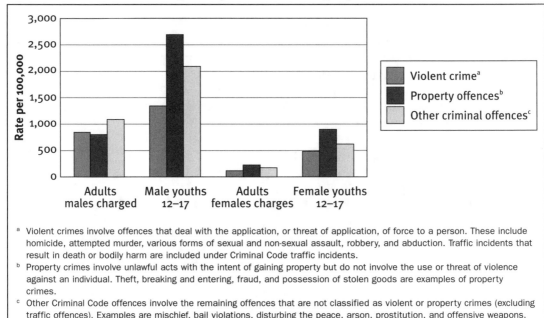

^a Violent crimes involve offences that deal with the application, or threat of application, of force to a person. These include homicide, attempted murder, various forms of sexual and non-sexual assault, robbery, and abduction. Traffic incidents that result in death or bodily harm are included under Criminal Code traffic incidents.

^b Property crimes involve unlawful acts with the intent of gaining property but do not involve the use or threat of violence against an individual. Theft, breaking and entering, fraud, and possession of stolen goods are examples of property crimes.

^c Other Criminal Code offences involve the remaining offences that are not classified as violent or property crimes (excluding traffic offences). Examples are mischief, bail violations, disturbing the peace, arson, prostitution, and offensive weapons.

SOURCE: Statistics Canada, *Health Indicators* (Ottawa: Statistics Canada, 2002), 11.

Defining *Crime, Laws,* and *Social Order*

All industrial societies make formal rules about what their members can and cannot do, and Canadian society is no exception. We know these formal rules as **laws**, and when someone violates a law, we say that they have committed a **crime**. Such laws, as we all know from personal experience, are important tools for promoting good behaviour—if people know that the police and courts will enforce these rules. The regularity of enforcement and the harshness of the punishment applied to rule breakers depend, in turn, on how seriously a society takes the offending behaviour.

Rule breaking itself makes crime a social problem because of the symbolic meaning of social order and disorder. **Social order** exists when people obey rules. Social order is better

than **social disorder**: with social order, life is predictable and 'safe'. The rules in place not only serve to show which behaviours are acceptable, they also allow people to foresee the behaviour of others. Social order does not emerge automatically out of kindly impulses and spontaneous cooperation—there are simply too many people and too many competing interests. Order must be manufactured and protected. Under the best circumstances, the social order is fair and accepted.

In other words, laws and other rules help create an orderly society that is safe for participants. They limit the risk of harm from others, and they influence how comfortable people will feel in public situations. When rules are broken routinely, disorder reigns. Because disorder is ill-defined and unpredictable, it is unsafe. It proves that control has been lost, that the rule system that once defined the boundaries of acceptable behaviour has broken down. Then people no longer restrain their actions. They are free to pursue their own interests without considering the costs for other members of society. They do so not because people are innately anti-social or vicious, but because they are protecting themselves. Under conditions of total uncertainty, nothing is more rational than pre-emptive self-interest.

Law and order signal to people that there is some certainty in the society. As we have said, social order is important because it symbolizes safe predictability and, by symbolizing it, maintains it. Once this safe predictability starts to break down, it is liable to break down more rapidly and seriously. If a broken window in a building is left unrepaired, all the rest of the windows will soon be broken. Window breaking blossoms because an unrepaired broken window signals that no one cares. Since no one cares and since breaking more windows costs them nothing, people are likely to break them (Wilson and Kelling, 1982; Zimbardo, 1969).

Crime in Canada and Elsewhere

A few crimes that are common, easily investigated, and cheaply prosecuted make up the bulk of our criminal statistics at any given time. As a result, the recorded rates of crime reflect mainly the reporting and prosecution of *particular* crimes. Changes in the overall crime rate also reflect changes in victims' willingness to report crimes and the willingness of police to investigate them. Measuring the total rate of crime is difficult, since **self-reporting measures**—records of crimes admitted by criminals—may not be accurate. **Victimization surveys** may yield a truer account. In these surveys, samples of people report how often, within a give amount of time, they have been victims of particular crimes. However, these surveys too are subject to distortion. Most often, we rely for our information on official statistics on arrest, conviction, and imprisonment, knowing that this information is incomplete and potentially biased.

BOX 3.1
Population per Police Officer in Canada

Most politicians would like to see the crime rate drop to zero—well, the quickest way to lower the rates of crime would be to reduce the number of police officers to zero. These bullet points describe the number of police officers in Canada over the past 40-odd years:

- In 1997, there were 54,699 police officers in Canada, an increase of less than 1 per cent (376) from the previous year. 1997 marked the first increase since 1992.

- Between 1962 and 1975, the number of Canadians per police officer showed consistent decreases from 711 to 486. However, from 1975 to 1985, this ratio increased slightly, reaching 515 people per police officer in 1985.

- In 1997, there were 554 persons for each police officer, the highest ratio since 1970.

- The population per police officer has been steadily increasing since 1991.

SOURCE: Adapted from Police Administration Survey, Canadian Centre for Justice Statistics, *A Graphical Overview of Crime and the Administration of Justice In Canada* (Cat. no. 85F0018XIE) (Ottawa: Statistics Canada, 1997).

In 1999, nearly 2.4 million Criminal Code offences were recorded across Canada. These offences ranged from illegal gambling to theft to murder (Statistics Canada, 2001). Of the 2.4 million violations in 1999, 55 per cent were property crimes, making them the most often occurring offences, a trend that has held for many years. We know a great deal more, however, about the prevalence of certain crimes such as murder, robbery, and kidnapping. That is because people are more likely to report occurrences of these crimes to the police and because such reports are more likely to lead to investigations, arrests, and convictions.

People are much less willing to report other crimes. Sexual assault is an example. Many women (who constitute most of the victims) fear the psychological, legal, and public humiliations that have often accompanied such reporting in the past. Besides, of the sexual assaults reported, only a small fraction result in convictions—judges and juries are often unwilling to believe the victim—and convictions often result in less than the top sentence. The victim may also fear retribution by the criminal or, if the offender is an intimate, may want to spare him a criminal record. Some victims may even feel they are to blame in some way.

Other crimes that are likely to go unreported are committed for gain by professional criminals. They include robbery, arson, selling drugs, and assault with a deadly weapon. Professionals are better able than amateurs to cover their tracks and avoid arrest and conviction.

Non-violent Crimes

Vice crimes include the use of illegal drugs, illegal gambling, communication for prostitution, and the possession, distribution, or sale of child pornography. These crimes provide the greatest opening for organized crime. That is because most societies prohibit legal access to these goods and services, yet sizeable minorities of people are willing to pay for them nonetheless. We will discuss organized crime shortly.

White-collar crimes are carried out as part of normal work, often within otherwise respectable organizations. Most often, they are crimes of fraud, embezzlement, or theft, and they can amount to anywhere from hundreds to millions of dollars. Fraud and other kinds of white-collar crime played an important role in the bankruptcy of once-prosperous Orange County, California, in 1994, for example. The financial downfall of that county was due to a political atmosphere that permitted ignorance on the part of officials who feared they would lose their positions of power (Will, Pontell, and Cheung, 1998). The same general recipe—ignorance, self-interest, and possible fraud—produced seven deaths and hundreds of hospitalizations in Walkerton, Ontario, in 2000. It is likely that the finances of a great many governments and private organizations are jeopardized by hidden fraud and embezzlement practices. However, these rarely come to light because powerful, respectable people have the ability to prevent this.

Fraudulent practices rely on the ignorance, fear, or greed of others. Typically, the unscrupulous take advantage of gaps in the social structure—for example, loopholes or uncertainties about new laws or economic conditions (Tillman and Indergaard, 1999). They thrive wherever governments have decided they have no important role to play in overseeing and safeguarding the economic marketplace. Governments generally accord white-collar crime a lower priority than **conventional crime**, despite considerable evidence that white-collar crime does vast economic and physical harm (Friedrichs, 1995).

Respectable people in large, respectable organizations can commit crimes of life and death, too. For example, evidence offered during a lawsuit against General Motors revealed that an internal study by the company had uncovered a gas-tank defect in one of its cars. The GM study noted that it would be cheaper to settle the lawsuits that might result from accidents in which the victim burned to death because of the defect (estimated to cost $2.40 [US] per car produced) than to recall and correct the design flaw (estimated to cost $8.59 per car produced). So although the company knew that the gas tanks on some of their vehicles were unsafe, likely to cause accidental deaths, and, in turn, likely to produce lawsuits, they chose to ignore the problem. A cost-benefit analysis convinced them it would be too expensive to correct the defect (White, 1999).

Offences against occupational health-and-safety laws are acts of workplace deviance—typically, regulatory offences rather than crimes—that are widespread and potentially harmful, though not always well monitored (Hutter, 1999). Employee safety and health are often sacrificed for the sake of corporate profit, as in the case of the Westray coal mine in Pictou County, Nova Scotia. There, 26 workers were killed when the mine exploded in 1992. A study found that the explosion resulted directly from the carelessness of those responsible for the workers' safety. Justice Peter Richard, during an official inquiry into the Westray accident, stated that the managers at the site 'displayed a certain distain for safety and appeared to regard safety-conscious workers as the wimps in the organization' (Hamilton, 1997).

Other types of corporate crime include price-fixing, antitrust violations, and tax fraud. Others still, discussed in chapter 10 on the environment and technology, include toxic waste disposal, pollution violations, and wilful destruction of the environment. As is evident from this list, corporate and white-collar crime, like organized crime, are widespread, costly, and dangerous. They are also well hidden, owing to the power and respectability of the criminals and their high degree of organization and influence.

Crimes of Violence

Contrary to the picture presented by the news media, which give violent crime far greater airtime than it deserves numerically, violent crimes in 2000 accounted for only about 12 per cent of total crimes reported. Taking into account the large number of 'hidden', unreported crimes committed by white-collar and organized criminals, they are probably a smaller fraction than that. Yet criminologists give these types of offences the term 'conventional crimes' because they are the traditional illegal behaviours that most people think of as crime. Additionally, they are crimes that people generally agree are serious and deserving of harsh punishment.

Homicide refers to the killing of one person by another; it can be subdivided into two categories, murder and manslaughter, depending on whether the homicide involves malicious intent. Typically, men are more likely to be involved in homicides than women, both as victims (67 per cent of all victims are men) and as offenders (88 per cent of those charged with homicide are men). Victims of homicide are more likely to be killed by a family member or acquaintance than by a stranger.

Sexual assault, most seriously rape but also sexual harassment, is another form of violent crime. Social science and law enforcement experts agree that most sexual assault victims probably do not report their experience to the police.

Stalking has recently emerged as a new social problem. This crime has gained a great deal of attention in recent years because it is common and is associated with gendered harassment, abuse, and violence. Repeated stalking is reported by up to 62 per cent of young adults, depending on the sample and on the precise definition of 'stalking' used. In a study of US college students, for example, 25 per cent of the women and 11 per cent of the men had been stalked at some point in their lives, and 6 per cent were currently being stalked (Bjerregaard, 2000: 401). The majority of legally defined stalking incidents, in which victim fear is a key component, involve men stalking women (Davis and Frieze, 2000).

Stalking is a type of relationship abuse that may evolve into other physical, psychological, and sexual forms, including violence against women. It has a variety of determinants—sociocultural, interpersonal, dyadic, situational, and

Crime is a serious social problem. Victimization can reduce people's trust in social institutions and their willingness to take part in community life. Thus, fear of crime can diminish a community's vitality and cohesion. (Bill and Peggy Wittman)

intrapersonal (White et al., 2000), often with deep roots in the history of the stalker. For example, men who experienced parental divorce or separation display more extreme stalking behaviours than men who did not experience parental divorce or separation (Langhinrichsen-Rohling and Rohling, 2000). Often, stalking follows a relationship breakup. The recipient of the breakup (that is, the person dumped) feels anger and jealousy, anxious attachment, and a need for control, and may express these feelings by intensified courtship and stalking (Davis, Ace, and Andra, 2000).

Most stalkers are former, rather than current, intimates. Typically, stalking involves efforts to re-

establish a relationship in the face of the other's resistance. Usually, the victim recognizes that she is being followed and learns that someone is seeking detailed information about her life and routines. She may have to deal with persistent relational proposals and efforts to escalate the relationship. Sometimes the pursuer's attentions may turn hostile and even violent (Emerson, Ferris, and Gardner, 1998). Stalked women often seek a restraining order so that police can charge the stalker with violating the restraining order (Tjaden and Thoennes, 2000).

As we will see in a later chapter, violence between intimates is common, with men particularly likely to carry out the most extreme types of violence, up to and including intimate-partner homicide (Browne, Williams, and Dutton, 1999). The combination of violence with stalking is lethal. Battered women who are relentlessly stalked report more severe concurrent physical violence, sexual assault, and emotional abuse than those who are infrequently stalked; increased post-separation assault and stalking; and increased rates of depression and post-traumatic stress disorder (Mechanic et al., 2000).

Patterns of Victimization

Crime produces victims, and some people are more likely than others to become victims. To some degree, this has to do with involvement in criminal activities: people who commit crimes are more likely to have crimes committed against them. *Routine activities theory* predicts that victimization requires the convergence in space and

time of likely offenders, suitable targets, and the absence of capable guardians. Generally, victimization reflects our routine activities—criminal and otherwise—and the increased opportunities for victimization in modern urban life.

Automobiles, vacations, college enrollment, female labour-force participation, and new consumer goods all improve our lives, but they also provide new occasions for criminal behaviour. For victimization to occur, an 'offender' and 'suitable target' must converge in a 'hot spot', or suitable locale, where 'effective guardians' are absent (Felson and Cohen, 1980). Hot spots where the risks of crime are particularly great include downtown entertainment districts (Cochran, Bromley, and Branch, 2000) and tourist attractions abroad (Mawby, Brunt, and Hambly, 2000). (See Figure 3.2 for the range of crime rates by province.)

FIGURE 3.2
Crime Rate per 100,000 Population, Canadian Provinces and Territories, 1997

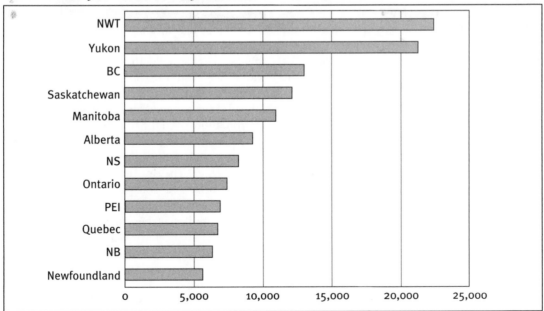

SOURCE: *A Graphical Overview of Crime and the Administration of Justice in Canada 1997* (Cat. no. 85F0018XIE) (Ottawa: Statistics Canada, 1997), 11.

Suitable Targets

Suitable targets are people who are routinely exposed to criminal activity or who for other reasons have heightened vulnerability. Taxi drivers have a greater than average risk of victimization because of their frequent interaction with strangers at night (Elzinga, 1996). Gay men and lesbians have a greater than average risk because of hostile public attitudes toward them in some quarters (Tiby, 2001). Overall, people who are powerless or vulnerable run higher risks of crime and violence. Thus, tourists are highly likely to experience crime while on holiday in a strange place (Mawby, Brunt, and Hambly, 1999). The risk of victimization is actually 8 to 10 times higher for foreign visitors to the Netherlands, for example, than for inhabitants there (Hauber and Zandbergen, 1996).

Three characteristics that put youth at risk of victimization probably apply to other types of people as well. They are the victim's target vulnerability (for example, physical weakness or psychological distress), target gratifiability (for example, female gender for the crime of sexual assault), and target antagonism (for example, ethnic or group identities that may spark hostility or resentment) (Finkelhor and Asdigian, 1996). Repeat victimization and situations involving the same victim should be considered over time (Gallagher, 2000) because they may identify people who are particularly susceptible to targeting.

Socio-demographic factors (such as age, race, and sex) and economic factors (such as income) predict victimization in a wide variety of situations, including homicide (Caywood, 1988). With some exceptions, poor and powerless people are more vulnerable than rich and powerful people, with one exception: people with more and better property—larger apartments, newer cars—are more likely to have their property stolen (Mesch, 1997).

As we have noted several times, women risk certain kinds of victimization more than men. Female homicide victims, for example, tend to be killed by a spouse, another family member, or an intimate partner as a result of domestic violence; men are more likely to be killed by a stranger in a public place (Pratt and Deosaransingh, 1997). Thus, 'home' and the routine activities associated with home have a different meaning for women and men. Men and women have different risks of victimization at home than they do in school and at places of public leisure (Mustaine and Tewksbury, 1997). However, public places carry their own risks for women. Women run higher than usual risks, for example, when using public transportation, living near a park, or drinking alcohol. Women are 46 per cent more likely to be victims than men, especially if they eat out often and spend time socializing. Risk of victimization is due, in these and other cases, to increased exposure to offenders and lack of capable guardianship (Mustaine and Tewksbury, 1998).

Elderly people run higher risks than middle-aged people, especially for crimes of robbery, intimidation, vandalism, and forgery or fraud (McCabe and Gregory, 1998). Robbery is the most serious offence committed against elderly victims of a violent incident, and men and women are equally likely to experience it (Bachman, Dillaway, and Lachs, 1998). Most such robberies take place outside the home during routine activities. Elderly people robbed in this way run higher risks of serious physical injury and even death than younger people who are robbed (Faggiani and Owens, 1999). Elderly people run a low overall risk due to their often private lifestyles and routine activity patterns. However, their risk of theft-related homicide is relatively high. They are more likely than younger persons to lack capable guardianship and to be perceived as suitable targets. This risk increases with age, and is higher among socially distant (that is, unconnected) victims and offenders (Nelsen and Huff-Corzine, 1998).

At the other end of the age distribution, juveniles aged 12 to 17 are more likely than adults to be victims of violent crimes and to suffer from a crime-related injury. Juvenile victims are also more likely than adult victims to know their offenders (Hashima and Finkelhor, 1999). A Canadian study of high school students in Calgary found that, except for sexual victimization, males reported higher victimization rates, in and out of school, than did females. Younger students reported higher rates of victimization at school than older students. Finally, students who reported moderate to high levels of victimization were more likely to report moderate to high levels of delinquency (Paetsch and Bertrand, 1999), confirming the link between criminal activity and criminal victimization.

Immigrants and ethnic minorities are also at greater than average risk of victimization, especially in respect to crimes against persons. We often refer to these as *hate crimes*. In Sweden, immigrants with a non-European appearance are more often victims of personal crimes than are other immigrants (Martens, 2001). The victimization of minority persons is higher than average in the Netherlands, too; their risk depends on their age and length of residence there (Junger-Tas, 1997). In North America, blacks are also the victims of hate crimes by whites, and there is some evidence that the number of hate crimes has risen in the last decade (Torres, 1999; but compare Cohen, 1999; Miller and Myers, 2000).

Gay men and lesbian women are sometimes victims of hate crimes. Recent debates about the cultural and legal status of sexual-orientation minorities have increased the visibility and awareness of violence against gays and lesbians (Tewksbury et al., 1999). It is not clear whether this form of violence itself has increased. Our information about the extent of hate crimes against these groups is hindered by low rates at which gays and lesbians report violent crimes because of concerns about police homophobia (Peel, 1999).

Inmates of 'total institutions' are also liable to suffer victimization on a day-to-day basis. Offences against prisoners include assault, robbery, threats of violence, theft from cells, verbal abuse, and exclusion (O'Donnell and Edgar, 1998). Prisoners are at particular risk of physical assaults by other inmates, as well as of theft of personal property (Wooldredge, 1998).

Hot Spots

Targets of crime and violence are at greater risk in some places than others. As we have just mentioned, prisons are very risky places for prisoners. Public places increase the risk of rape for women, and women who are highly mobile (working women, students, and younger women in general) are at a much greater risk of rape than women who are less mobile (Ploughman and Stensrud, 1986). Situational context—the where and when of a sexually violent crime—is an even better predictor of the outcome of rape attempts than victim or offender characteristics (Clay-Warner, 2000).

Crime on college campuses is a relatively unstudied phenomenon. We can be certain that crimes are going on there as everywhere else in society. However, colleges often use alternative strategies to resolve disputes and internal regulatory procedures to deal with, or hide, the offences that are taking place (Konradi, 1999). As a result, we know little about who is victimized, or how (Fernandez-Lanier, 1999).

Organized Crime: A Window on Our Culture?

North Americans are fascinated by the glamour and excitement of organized crime, as witnessed by the many books, movies, television programs, and music videos that feature organized crime figures such as drug dealers. Organized crime rings that currently exist in Canada include the Hong Kong Triad, the Colombian Mafia, the Russian Mafia, and some motorcycle gangs. These groups have been variously implicated in drug trafficking, prostitution, extortion, bribery, money laundering, assaults, and homicides. The stereotypical image of organized crime, however, is the Italian Mafia, as headed by a patriarchal,

---

BOX 3.2
Cops Play Chaperone

Some might argue that shows like COPS *and* The Sopranos *fail to perform a beneficial role for society by portraying criminals as slick, sexy, enviable. The article below reads like a 'society page' or 'who's who' in an entertainment newspaper—perhaps* TV *shows aren't the only perpetrators of the slick-criminal image.*

Flashing red and blue lights from police cruisers could be seen along the road that connects the town of Lennoxville to the city of Sherbrooke as police kept a close eye on the chapter's 15th-anniversary party. Officers from the Sûreté du Quebec and Sherbrooke regional police pulled over Hells Angels gang members suspected of having violated bail or having outstanding arrest warrants.

As of 8 p.m., only one man had been arrested, a member of the Ontario-based Death Riders, a gang the Hells Angels are on friendly terms with. A Sherbrooke police spokesman said the man had outstanding tickets to pay, took care of the problem immediately, then was released.

SQ Sgt. Guy Ouellette said Hells Angels from as far away as British Columbia and Manitoba attended the huge party, held at a reception hall called La Toque Rouge in Sherbrooke. The president of the gang's Vancouver chapter was in attendance, as was Maurice (Mom) Boucher, head of the Hells Angels' elite Nomads chapter in Quebec.

Ouellette said police were also watching for members of the Hells Angels' New York and Rochester chapters but tough immigration laws permit law enforcement agencies to turn back known members of crime gangs who enter Canada.

Early yesterday, Boucher could be seen having breakfast at a local restaurant. Boucher, who was acquitted last year of the murders of two provincial prison guards, appeared to be heavily guarded as he dined among the other patrons. Four members of the Rockers, an outlaw motorcycle gang that is an affiliate of the Hells, sat near him.

Law-enforcement agencies consider Sherbrooke one of the most influential Hells Angels chapters in Canada. With 25 full-patch members, it is the biggest in the country—and includes some members who have been there all 15 years.

SOURCE: Paul Cherry and Rita Legault, 'Cops Play Chaperone as Hells Angels Party', *The Gazette* (Montreal), final edition, 5 December 1999, A5. Reprinted by permission of The Gazette.

---

raspy-voiced Don Corleone figure making various 'offers that we cannot refuse'. Other portrayals of the organized criminal put him—it is always a 'him'—in the role of a modern-day Robin Hood, crazed psychopath, or ambitious and creative manager. We have many images of organized crime today, some more positive than others.

Early sociologists believed that crime resulted from poverty and that crime in poor neighbourhoods of the United States resulted from social disorganization: the more disorganization, the more crime. After roughly 1940, however, with the publication of William Whyte's classic work *Street Corner Society* ([1943] 1981), sociologists changed their views. They came to recognize that crime—especially crime in poor neighbourhoods—was highly organized. It was also intimately connected with the social, political, and economic life of the people in the community. It was an intrinsic part of city life—indeed, of national corporate and political life.

Research shows that modern organized crime operates at the intersection of legitimate and illegitimate business, family, and formal organization (see, for example, Ianni, 1972). It has as strong connections to white-collar crime as it does to vice crimes (such as drug trafficking, pornography, and prostitution). Organized crime draws on the talents of professional and amateur, older and younger criminals. What organized crime shows us dramatically is that crime is a learned, organized social activity with historical cultural roots. It is infused with traditional notions of kinship and friendship, honour and duty. Organized crime is a social form, not the mere result of a biological genetic peculiarity, as early criminologists such as Cesar Lombroso (in, for example, Lombroso-Ferrero, [1911] 1972) believed. Organized crime is not a deviation from mainstream society; it is fully a part of it, and it plays a vital role in the world's economic and political activities.

However, the need for secrecy means criminal organizations cannot be structured quite like other large formal organizations, such as the Catholic Church, the Canadian Forces, or IBM. Every secret organization depends, to an unusual degree, on friendship and kinship relations, which facilitate the maintenance of order and conformity (on this, see Erickson, 1981, and Simmel, [1906] 1950, on secret societies).

At the base of organized crime is an organizing principle that sociologists have variously called *patronage* or **clientelism**. Tony Soprano, the current 'Godfather' figure on a regular television series, might be surprised to learn that his 'boss' role in the cities and suburbs of modern New Jersey goes back many millennia to the agricultural organization of Mediterranean Europe. There, Tony would have been called the 'patron', and his henchmen and collaborators would have been called 'clients'. Our law-abiding society creates and maintains crime because there are things that crime can do for 'legitimate' society— whether break union strikes, steal elections, or provide drugs and prostitutes—that legitimate society cannot do for itself. The traditional forms of organized crime nicely suit the requirements of modern business and politics.

Organized crime in urban North America prospers wherever a community meets four key conditions. First, organized crime is associated with conditions of scarcity and inequality. It is most common in poor communities with a wide range of economic inequality and, often, strong family traditions. Second, it is common where poverty and prejudice keep people from moving easily to another community to find work elsewhere. Third, organized crime provides protection in a society that lacks equal legal or human rights or equal access to welfare, health care, and good-quality education. Finally, organized crime flourishes among people who lack human capital and cultural capital. North American capitalism is one type of economic and social system that

Crime is genderized—that is, men and women do not commit the same types of crimes, generally speaking. (David Glick/Getty Images)

produces these conditions, though it is not the only one.

The Demography of Crime

Gender

Organized crime is a 'guy thing'. So, to a large degree, are amateur and non-organized crime. The gender gap in crime is universal: women seem to always and everywhere commit fewer criminal acts than men (Steffensmeier and Allan, 1996).

As a result, gender is probably the single most important factor in any study of crime, violent or otherwise. In the United States, males account for 85 per cent of all murders and non-negligent manslaughters (US Bureau of Justice, 1991). There are few exceptions to this rule. One exception is the rate of females killing intimate partners, which is almost as high as that of men killing intimate partners (0.75:1), at least in North America (Wilson and Daly, 1992: 208). As well, teenage girls are more often arrested for running away from home and women are twice as likely to be arrested for prostitution (Wrangham and Peterson, 1997: 114).

Otherwise, the statistics for crimes are mainly about men: men are 9 times more likely than women to commit murder, 78 times more likely to commit forcible rape, 10 times more likely to commit armed robbery, 6.5 times more likely to commit aggravated assault, and 7 times more likely to commit arson (Wrangham and Peterson, 1997: 113–14). For example, in 1998 in Canada, the ratio of males to females charged with violent crimes in general was 5.5:1 (Canadian Centre for Justice Statistics, 1995: 19). A similar gender pattern emerges for non-violent offences as well, with men committing property crimes at a ratio of 4:1 to women (Canadian Centre for Justice Statistics, 1995: 19).

In the United States, men are 3.5 times more likely to commit fraud, 13 times more likely to be arrested for carrying or possessing a weapon, 10 more likely to break and enter, 9 time more likely to steal a car, 8.5 more likely to be arrested for drunkenness, 8 times more likely to vandalize, 7.5 times more likely to illegally sell stolen property, 6.5 more likely to be arrested for engaging in illegal gambling or drunk driving, and 5.5 times more likely to be arrested for sex offences (Wrangham and Peterson, 1997: 113–14).

The explanations for these gender differences vary. Some say that biology is the answer, that men's higher levels of testosterone incline them toward aggression and hostile actions. Others say that differential socialization is the answer, that males are raised in a more violent subculture and are taught to be ready to use aggressive and violent behaviours. These theories will be discussed in detail in the section in this chapter on theories of crime and violence.

Age

Stated simply, young people are more likely to commit criminal acts than old people. This is above all true for property crimes, where there is a large drop in the number of people accused after the age of 18. Those under the age of 25 committed 37 per cent of all violent crimes in 1997. Rebecca Kong (1999) notes that as the Canadian population has become older, the crime rate in recent years has also declined.

One explanation is that young people are more likely to be unemployed or to work in low-wage jobs. Thus, as Merton's anomie theory might propose, they are more likely to use innovations to achieve their culturally desired goals (that is, money and material goods). They have less investment in the old, conventional ways of doing things. As a result, wherever social events or occasions bring together large numbers of young men—especially unemployed or under-employed young men—there will be high rates of crime. This will be particularly true of cities with high unemployment rates and high rates of recent immigration from less developed countries. Moreover, juveniles are protected from many of the legal penalties of criminal activity;

BOX 3.3
Who Commits Crimes?

What the elderly are not doing with their time:

- Persons charged with non-violent crimes like break and enter, mischief, have a median age of 24, whereas those accused of violent crimes have a median age 29.
- Non-violent crimes are usually committed by persons aged 14–20 years old.

- Persons who are 16 years old are the single largest age group of persons charged with a non-violent crime.
- The involvement of persons in violent crime over the age of 32 decreases continually with age.

SOURCE: Statistics Canada, 'Age of Persons Accused, Violent and Non-Violent Incidents, 1997', available at <www.statcan.ca/english/kits/justic/2-21.pdf>, accessed 1 March 2003.

---

they may be arrested and convicted without any lasting legal consequence.

Theories of Crime

Let's turn now to sociological theories of why people get involved in deviant and criminal behaviour. There are several, which, again, can be grouped under the three broad sociological perspectives.

The Structural-Functionalist Perspective

The functionalist approach to deviance includes a variety of theories that converge on a few central tenets: namely, that crime is normal, universal, and inevitable, and that it is to be expected in any society. This view grows directly out of Émile Durkheim's classic notion of the 'normality of crime', discussed in his *Rules of the Sociological Method* (1938). It gives rise to one theory about the relationship between crime and social disorganization and three competing interpretations of the 'functions' served by crime: social bond theory, anomie theory, and subculture theory.

Social Disorganization Theory
Durkheim's early work in *Suicide* (1951) provides the basis for a theory that crime and other social

pathologies (including suicide) result from a breakdown in social norms and social integration. This breakdown, in turn, typically results from rapid social change and from organizational problems associated with rapid change—for example, the increased size, cultural diversity, and social mobility associated with urban industrial society. As the theory would predict, international data show that people in developing and transitional countries have higher victimization rates, express less satisfaction with law enforcement, and support a more punitive approach to controlling crime than people in fully industrial societies (Zwekic, 1996).

Social disorganization leads to a loss of social cohesion—a central concern of functionalist theory. Other things being equal, a loss of social cohesion increases the likelihood of robbery and assault near the home and of robbery and assault by strangers (Lee, 2000). Areas with high crime rates also have higher mortality rates from all causes, suggesting that crime rates mirror the quality of the social environment (Kawachi, Kennedy, and Wilkinson, 1999). High crime rates also desensitize residents to disorganization. Exposure to chronic use of guns, knives, and random violence in the community, for example, produces children who are more likely to act violently themselves (Scott, 1999). This is just one among several examples of disabling processes discussed in this chapter.

Supporting the validity of social disorganization theory is evidence that increased cohesion reduces crime. Consider this example: during the late 1970s, pre-Halloween pranks in Detroit, Michigan, had turned destructive. Hundreds of fires were set deliberately throughout the city. From 1985 to 1996, a citywide anti-arson campaign began to mobilize and train thousands of community volunteers, who participated in every aspect of this program. This effort to reduce delinquency through increased organization paid off: the number of annual Halloween fires declined dramatically (Maciak et al., 1998).

Social Bond Theory

Some members of society are constantly being exposed to external factors (such as poverty, lack of educational opportunities, and poor living conditions) and internal factors (such as feelings of aggression or jealousy) that tempt them to break society's rules of conduct. However, not every member of a disorganized community becomes a delinquent or a criminal. Moreover, some people's lives are socially disorganized even if they do not reside in socially disorganized communities, and such people run a risk of delinquent or criminal behaviour.

Travis Hirschi's social bond theory (1969) is relevant to this perspective. Social bond theory argues that developing a strong social bond can prevent people from giving in to the temptation to commit criminal acts. Four elements are involved in a strong social bond: an attachment to other people, a commitment to conventional goals, an involvement in conventional activities, and a belief in the legitimacy of conventional values, norms, and moral standards encouraged by society. When such a bond is weak and the individual is exposed to anti-social values and activities, the chance of participating in criminal behaviour increases.

Social bond theory can be viewed as an extension of social disorganization theory on the microsociological level. The theory directs our attention to the socialization we receive in childhood and the relationships we establish with family members. Though later peer influences and social opportunities will have an effect on our attachments and commitments as adults, early bonding experiences with parents and siblings are critical. Disorganized families hinder the formation of early attachments and commitments and reduce the likelihood that young people will embrace conventional norms and values. As a result, children from conflictual families— families marked by neglect, abuse, violence, separation, or divorce—are at a higher than average risk of delinquent behaviour (on this, see, for example, Cox, 1996; Ruchkin et al., 1998; Simons and Chao, 1996).

Anomie Theory

One perspective growing out of Durkheim's early book *The Division of Labor in Society* ([1893] 1964), on the pathologies of an industrial division of labour, is Merton's anomie theory. As we saw in the previous chapter, Merton theorizes that anomie and strain arise whenever unequal social opportunities prevent some people from achieving the culturally defined goals (such as money) by using legitimate means (such as a job). Merton characterized drug abuse as a retreatist adaptation to such anomie.

Anomie also leads some people to commit crimes. One of the five ways in which people confronted with a gap between culturally approved ends and the culturally approved means to achieve them can deal with the problem is *innovation*. They accept the goals but pursue them through socially disapproved means. This adaptation is most commonly associated with criminal activities, including theft, robbery, tax fraud, embezzlement, and organized crime. From Merton's standpoint, crime is a creative way to get what our society values. Crime, in that sense, supports social order: it allows us to continue believing in our traditional values and institutions. To solve the crime problem, according to this theory, one would give young people better opportunities to make the transition into conventional adult work and family roles; gun control would also help (Skolnick, 1994).

Implicit in anomie theory is the idea that criminals hold the same values and goals as everyone else; they just use alternative means to pursue those goals and values. Both legal and illegal work generate income. Choosing between them means rationally assessing likely returns and risks, punishment costs, and personal preferences. Crime rates rise where the expected wages from legal work are low, particularly among young men with limited job prospects. Crime can be a rational choice of work for people with few prospects of earning an income by legal means. Moreover, many criminals participate in both legal and illegal work, sequentially or at the same time. One kind of work does not rule out the other (Fagan and Freeman, 1999). This approach works well to explain crimes against property—shoplifting, theft, robbery, fraud, and embezzlement, for example. However, it does not work as well to explain crimes against persons (such as assault, rape, or murder of an intimate) or crimes against property that yield no gain (such as vandalism). For this, we must turn to subculture theory.

Subculture Theory

Subculture theory is another variant of the functionalist perspective. It has been applied to delinquents and criminals to explain how their values and belief systems contribute to unlawful behaviour. Personal experience tells us that, contrary to Merton's anomie theory, not everyone wants to get a college degree, land a responsible 9-to-5 job in some large organization, spend his or her life paying off the mortgage on a suburban home, and retire to a condominium in Florida. That is not everyone's idea of success or the good life. Some people want to maximize their fun, fame, relaxation, sex life, drinking—even the respect with which they are treated or the service they render their families or community.

Arguments between young males make up the most common pattern of homicide (Zahn and McCall, 1999). That fact needs explaining, and it can best be explained in the context of subculture theory. To a large degree, youth establish their identities and subcultures by opposing the middle-class social order (Le Moigne, 1998). As we said in the previous chapter, our culture's masculine identity is fashioned around toughness and respect, money and risk-taking (Collison, 1996). Crime and violence are parts of that package.

Inner-city youth often live according to a street code that justifies violence to gain respect from others through violence. Guns symbolize respect, power, identity, and manhood; they play a central role in initiating, sustaining, and escalating youth violence (Fagan and Wilkinson, 1998). Violence becomes appropriate behaviour for youth who are regularly exposed to violence, are gang members (see also Figure 3.3), have family or friends who are gang members, and have peer support for violence (Katz and Marquette, 1996; Powell, 1997). In these subcultures, men who behave fearfully are likely to be threatened (Vander Ven, 1998).

In poor urban areas, as in peasant societies and tribal societies, all goods—including honour—are scarce. Honour is the only good that everybody, without exception, can own (Cottino, 1983). So honour is an appropriate metric for measuring social worth, and it can be gained, in this subculture, by violence. People who live in more prosperous neighbourhoods can earn respect through their educational and career achievements. However, people who live in poorer areas, such as the inner city, may have to rely on physical strength, threats or violent acts, and tough anti-social rebellion to gain their peers' respect. Gangs provide minority youth with an alternative community for achieving social status, friendship, and economic mobility (Gibbs, 2000).

Violent subcultures are nothing new, not merely a result of social disorganization caused by industrialism. Many cultures in the past valued heroic violence, self-assertion, and elitism

FIGURE 3.3
Homicide Rate, Canada, 1961–2000, and Gang Violence

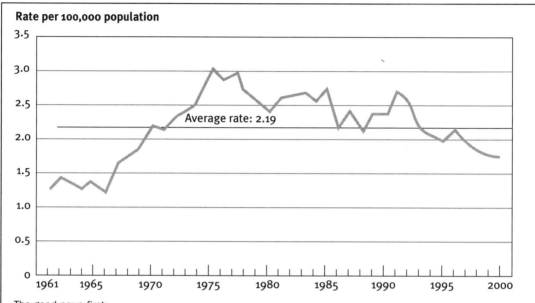

Rate per 100,000 population

Average rate: 2.19

The good news first:
- While family-related homicides declined in 2000, gang-related murders are increasing; four more homicides related to gangs occurred in 2000 than in 1999.
- Canada's rate was less than one-third that of the United States, and similar to those of France and Australia.
- Gang-related slayings accounted for one out of every eight homicides in 2000.
- There were 71 victims of gang-related homicides, up from 45 in 1999 and more than triple the 21 in 1995.
- Just over one-half of 2000's incidents occurred in the province of Quebec.
- Firearms continued to account for 34 per cent of all homicides; handguns accounted for almost 60 per cent of shootings in 2000.

SOURCE: Statistics Canada, 'Homicide Statistics, 2000', *The Daily*, 31 October 2001.

and emphasized honour and obedience to the communal code. The Vikings did (Jonassen 1983). So did the Greeks of Homeric legend. More recently, the American South did, too, and it continues to embrace violence in connection with such values as honour, courage, and manliness. Using violence to right a wrong or defend one's honour is still considered justifiable (Weaver et al., 2001). The culture of honour, which underwrote Southern slavery, continues to support high US homicide rates (Lane, 1999), as well as extreme militarism and patriotism.

However, the subculture of honour and violence is not universal. Therefore, it is not genetic,

biological, or otherwise inevitable, even among young men, peasants, or embattled ethnic minorities. The Semai of Malaysia are an aboriginal group in which violent crime is completely absent. The Semai have socialized their young to react to frustrating stimuli in a way that prevents them from committing violent criminal acts: they become fearful when frustrated, not violent (Moss, 1997).

Conflict Theory

Conflict theories of crime and violence point to inequalities in society as the cause of such deviant behaviour. Crime is believed to be inevitable whenever groups possess different levels of power and influence. One consequence is that as inequality increases in a society, criminal activity will also increase. People who are economically disadvantaged may react to inequality by getting money through unlawful means, such as robbery or embezzlement. Declining wages are related to increased rates of 'quick cash' crimes, particularly in societies lacking a safety net of unemployment benefits, universal health insurance, and income security provisions (Gaylord and Lang, 1997).

Additionally, people who are disadvantaged are also more likely to embrace violent subcultures of honour and respect, leading to higher rates of crimes against persons. Deprived areas marked by poverty and inequality spawn social exclusion, alienation, and violence in pursuit of respect (Wilkinson, Kawachi, and Kennedy, 1998). Subcultures of violence emerge in poor neighbourhoods, not rich ones: poverty and inequality are injurious to self-esteem—results of the 'hidden injuries of social class', to use the words of historians Richard Sennett and Jonathan Cobb (1973). This is why economic deprivation and a lack of local opportunities significantly increase the rates of intraracial (black-on-black) homicide in black urban communities (Parker and McCall, 1999). Violence inflicted on African American males through chattel slavery, as well as institutional racism and poverty, has led to the development of self-destructive attitudes, perceptions, and psychological states, which have caused the high rates of violence among young African American men (King, 1997).

As a result, locations in deprived areas are more likely to be repeatedly burglarized than are those in affluent areas (Ratcliffe and McCullagh, 1999). The homicide rates are highest in communities marked by low welfare-payment levels, a high percentage of female-headed families, and a high dropout rate from schools (Hannon, 1997). Mentally ill people discharged from psychiatric hospitals are more violent if they live in deprived areas (Silver, 1999).

However, socio-economic status (SES) has both negative and positive effects on delinquency, which, taken together, result in little overall correlation between SES and delinquency. Low SES promotes delinquency by increasing individuals' alienation, financial strain, and aggression and by decreasing educational and occupational aspirations. High SES promotes individuals' delinquency by increasing risk-taking and social power and by decreasing conventional values (Wright et al., 1999). High-SES delinquents are less likely to pay heavily for their delinquent episodes.

The conflict perspective also notes that people in privileged positions work to maintain their privileged status. One way of doing this is by defining what is considered a 'serious' criminal offence. Both dominant ideology and formal laws are social constructs shaped and maintained by the ruling class. They ensure, for example, that most people in society view drug use and vagrancy—some responses of the disadvantaged—as deviant and undesirable behaviours. By extension, then, drug users and the homeless come to be viewed through this dominant cultural lens as deviant and undesirable people. This ensures that they remain in their disadvantaged position, no threat to the advantaged power elite. Meanwhile, corporate crimes that benefit the upper class but harm the environment and place the public in needless danger continue to be largely ignored or undetected by the mass media, the general public, and policy makers.

Conflict theory also focuses on power differentials between men and women in a male-dominated society that disadvantages the latter group. One example of such inequality is the upholding of 'rape myths', which portray women as responsible for their own victimization. The beliefs that 'no' means 'yes', that a revealing style of dress is equivalent to 'asking for' sex, and that 'good girls' do not get raped are all examples of sexist myths that sometimes help acquit men of criminal and moral wrongdoing.

Symbolic Interactionism

Social Constructionism

Social constructionism looks at how deviant behaviours come to be defined as 'deviant' in the first place. This perspective stresses that behaviours are not innately right or wrong: they only become wrong, deviant, or criminal when someone in power ascribes a moral value to them. So, for example, we can study the concept of hate-motivated violence, or *hate crime*, as a social construct. Some deny that hate crimes are different from, or require different treatment than, comparable crimes of violence. The concept of hate crime was originally developed in terms of racial, ethnic, and religious prejudice. In recent years, gays, lesbians, children, and women have also been depicted as potential victims of hate crimes. The expansion of this concept results from claims-making activities by special interest groups that have documented instances of such crimes and called for legal remedies (Jenness, 1995). The packaging and presentation of news in the media plays a crucial role in the making of claims about crime and victimization (Sacco, 2000). In this way it contributes to the process of social construction of crimes and crime waves.

Computer hacking, joyriding, and raving are activities in postmodern youth culture that have been socially constructed as deviance, if not crime; that is, they have been subjected to criminal sanction, regulation, and government surveillance. They have in common mechanisms of dissent, inversion, and appropriation of economic forces. Because they celebrate excess, movement, and excitement, these activities pose problems for adult society and have, as a result, been construed as deviance and as social problems (Stanley, 1995).

Labelling Theory

The second symbolic interactionist approach is *labelling theory*. From the labelling point of view, deviance is not a quality of the act a person commits, but rather a consequence of the application by others of rules and sanctions to an 'offender'. Labelling theorists who study criminal behaviour distinguish between *primary deviance*—the initial acts of deviant behaviour committed by people

---

BOX 3.4
Who Are the Real Criminals?

The Ontario government tabled legislation yesterday that would significantly expand the powers of Canada's largest securities regulator and make it easier for investors to sue firms that issue false or misleading financial statements.

David Young, the province's Attorney General, said he will also urge the federal government to toughen its stance against corporate crime by increasing prison terms for fraud and improving procedures for conducting police investigations. Mr. Young said he will make a number of recommendations to the federal justice minister at a meeting in Calgary next week, including requests that Ottawa deploy more resources to the RCMP and eliminate the need for jury trials in certain cases.

The legislation introduced yesterday by Janet Ecker, the provincial Minister of Finance, would enable the Ontario Securities Commission to enforce certain rules outlined by Sarbanes Oxley, including a requirement that chief executives and chief financial officers personally vouch for the accuracy of their financial statements.

'There has certainly been a consensus that while we haven't had Enron here we can't assume that that will not happen, and there are more steps we need to take to prevent that',

continued

Ms. Ecker said. The proposed laws, first outlined by Ms. Ecker at a regulatory conference last month, would empower the OSC to levy fines of up to $1-million for securities violations and force offenders to give up any profits they made through illegal activities such as insider trading.

The new rules would also give investors broader rights to sue companies and their executives for making false disclosures to the public. The government said it is holding consultations on changes to the Ontario Business Corporations Act to offer investors added legal support in disputes with corporate malfeasance.

Ontario's securities laws would also be beefed up. Maximum civil court fines would be raised to $5-million from $1-million, while prison sentences would be lengthened to five years less a day, more than double the current ceiling of two years.

The new rules would also give investors broader rights to sue companies and their executives for making false disclosures to the public. The government said it is holding consultations on changes to the Ontario Business Corporations Act to offer investors added legal support in disputes with corporate malfeasance.

SOURCE: Sinclair Stewart, 'Ontario Targets Corporate Wrongdoers: Makes It Easier to Sue', *National Post*, national edition, 31 October 2002, FP1.

before they are labelled as a deviant individuals—and *secondary deviance*—further deviant activity that results from having been given the label of 'deviant' or 'criminal'.

Being labelled as deviant or criminal may promote further deviancy because the labelled person is unable to escape stigmatization. This results in a narrower field of legitimate opportunities and a subsequent reliance on illegitimate means for survival. Also, the labelled person begins to internalize and live out the identity of 'deviant'. It is often through this labelling and identification that the 'career criminal' is born (Hartjen, 1978).

Differential Association Theory

A third theory that is congruent with the symbolic interactionist perspective is *differential association theory*. This theory, first proposed by Edwin Sutherland (1939), states that deviancy and criminality are behaviours learned from frequent and extended interaction with people who live an anti-social lifestyle. Living in a high-crime neighbourhood or merely witnessing others benefiting from a criminal lifestyle are enough to raise the probability of engaging in the same illegitimate activities. The exposure to criminal influences, without effective condemnation of such elements by mainstream society, can teach a person not only the techniques of deviance, but also the motives for, rationalizations of, and attitudes of such a lifestyle.

Crime and Violence, and Other Social Problems

Poverty and Inequality

Of all the people arrested for violent street crimes, most are undereducated, poor, unemployed, or working in low-wage, low-status jobs. Other kinds of crimes and criminals receive less attention.

The police less vigorously pursue white-collar crimes, which are unduly committed by the middle and upper classes. Yet white-collar crimes affect many more people than street crimes. Moreover, the police and the public in general tend to assume that lower-class people are more likely to indulge in criminal activities. As such, they assign more personnel to watch low-income neighbourhoods, and pay greater

---

BOX 3.5
Women Who Fight Back

The author suggests that 'showing the whole picture' by publishing stories of women who 'fight back' will be a solution to sexual violence. Do you buy this? Who has access to these services? Who benefits from this solution?

The facts and destruction of an assault by young men are vividly described on the Jan. 9 cover of The Sun (Gang rape victim reveals she is HIV positive). Inside, a full page on rape shows Katie Koestner on the cover of Time beside a concise description of how she was raped. After reading descriptions of violence against women, it's reasonable to feel angry, captivated and helpless. The Sun reports news, but where is the whole picture? Why do the headlines deny Koestner's voice and that she is an extremely strong victim who has something to say about rape, men and violence? The media mute her ambassador and counseling work that fights violence against women, by mentioning them at the end of the article.

Coverage of the gang attack leaves the community with no sense of what women are doing about these problems, their thoughts, in effect, their voice. Tell readers about self-defense and how, or if, education and preventative plans to teach men respect and self-worth are being put into action. Give readers tools to help. We don't need another description of violence or pictures of complacent victims. Save it. Show the whole picture, including women's and communities' ideas about the anger, frustration, confusion and actions of men. You make it sound like there is no answer.

SOURCE: Anita Neufeld, 'Let Us Hear Rape Victims' Voice' (letter to the editor), *Vancouver Sun*, final edition, 15 January 2001, A11. Reprinted by permission of Pacific Newspaper Group Inc.

---

attention to lower-class individuals, resulting in higher arrest rates for street crimes. Laws against crimes that are mainly committed by the disadvantaged—drug-related crimes, assault, and robbery, for example—are also more rigorously enforced and severely punished (for example, with prison time) than corporate and occupational crimes, which often result only in fines.

Conflict theories have a lot to say about the way lower-class crimes are targeted by the police and policy makers while upper-class crimes are often overlooked. They suggest that if police investigated corporate, occupational, and political crimes nearly as vigorously, they would find equally high rates of crime among the affluent and, as a result, 'the wealthy might even be convicted and punished more than the poor' (Pepinsky and Jesilow, 1984: 81). Indeed, we know that white-collar crimes, both corporate

and occupational, are occurring with high frequency, as we have already mentioned above.

However, the arrest and conviction of poor people is not merely a result of bias in the police and courts. The existing social order serves the poor less well than it serves the rich and well educated. Accordingly, John Braithwaite (1993) provides a useful distinction between what he calls *crimes of poverty*, which are largely motivated by need and perpetrated to obtain goods for personal use, and *crimes of wealth*, which are motivated by greed and perpetrated to obtain goods for exchange (that is, goods that are surplus to those required for personal use). Both types of crimes are made possible by social and economic inequality.

The fact of living in poverty also provides significant pressures to commit crimes. As Merton's **strain (or anomie) theory** argues, people living in poverty may still desire socially approved goals, such as money, but because of their economic position, are unable to obtain the means of achieving their objectives. This temptation is further exacerbated by the fact that North American culture is highly materialistic, often measuring success in terms of the size of one's income, the prestige of one's job, and the amount and quality of one's material possessions. When faced with such tremendous pressure, many of those living in deprived conditions may choose to commit criminal acts they see as being profitable—a fast, easy way to escape their life of poverty.

The Racial Dimension

Because Canadian authorities do not tabulate crime statistics by the race of the offender, the connection between race and crime is murkier than in the United States. There, of all Americans arrested in 1992 for all crimes, 30 per cent were black; yet African Americans make up only 13 per cent of the population of the United States. Are blacks more motivated than whites to commit crimes? Or are the police and courts more motivated to prosecute and convict blacks than they are whites? These questions are being asked increasingly in Canada too.

Some see such high arrest and prosecution rates as indicating that law enforcement officers, prosecutors, judges, and the criminal justice system in general are racially prejudiced. Others even suggest that police target blacks, along with Latinos and Native Americans, because they are often poor, and that law enforcement agencies focus on crimes committed by all lower-class people rather than by blacks alone (Walker, 1989).

The media, as well, typically rely on stereotypes when portraying criminals in television dramas and movies, including the inner-city black or Latino gang member, the Arab terrorist, the Italian or Russian mafioso, and the Chinese Triad member. These images are distributed to wide audiences, perpetuating inaccurate and prejudicial notions about entire ethnic groups.

In Canada, attention has been paid in the last several decades to the excessive number of Aboriginal people arrested and convicted of violations of the law (see Figure 3.4). Although Aboriginal adults make up only 2 per cent of the Canadian population according to the 1996 census, they represented 19 per cent of those sentenced to provincial custody and 17 per cent of those sent to federal penitentiaries in 2000/2001 (Reed and Roberts, 1999: 10).

The discrepancy between Aboriginal and non-Aboriginal inmates is particularly striking in the Prairie provinces of Manitoba and Saskatchewan, where the ratios are 6:1 and 7.5:1, respectively. In Manitoba, for example, Aboriginal people make up only 9 per cent of the population but 61 per cent of the prison population. One study found that Aboriginal inmates are younger, more likely to come from dysfunctional backgrounds, and likely to have had more run-ins with the criminal justice system (for example, more previous arrests) than non-Aboriginal inmates (LaPrairie et al., 1996).

One common explanation is that, like some other ethnic groups, Aboriginal people are mostly poor, and it is poverty that drives them to criminal activity. Other explanations include a racially prejudiced law enforcement and correctional system, a conflict between the values of Aboriginal culture and mainstream Canadian culture, social and economic consequences of colonization and oppression by European settlers, and a breakdown in the traditional social fabric of Aboriginal communities.

Drug Abuse

Another social problem that is closely linked with crime is drug abuse. As we said in the previous chapter, some criminal offences are drug-related. The possession, cultivation, production, and sale of controlled substances are all against the law. Public intoxication, drunken and disorderly conduct, and driving while intoxicated are all behaviours that are explicitly prohibited by the Criminal Code. Besides that, drug use may

FIGURE 3.4
Aboriginal Adults as Percentage of General and Prison Populations by Provinces and Territories, 1999

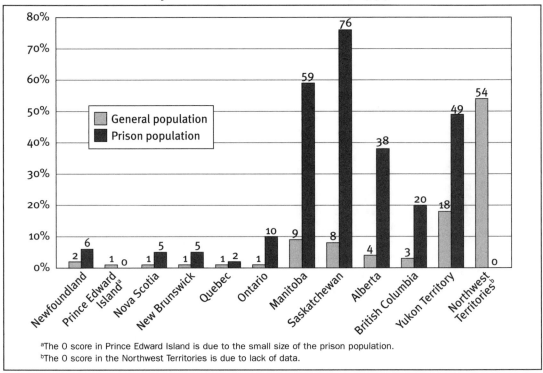

aThe 0 score in Prince Edward Island is due to the small size of the prison population.
bThe 0 score in the Northwest Territories is due to lack of data.

SOURCE: Statistics Canada, Canadian Centre for Justice Statistics, *Aboriginal Peoples in Canada* (Ottawa: Statistics Canada, 2001), page 10.

loosen inhibitions and lead to aggressive and violent behaviour; there is a well-established link between alcohol abuse and domestic violence, for example. Finally, as noted in the previous chapter, alcohol and drug addiction may lead to criminal activities aimed at raising money to feed the addiction.

Economic Consequences of Crime

Many financial costs are associated with crime. These include costs associated with the transfer of property, as is the case in bank robberies, carjackings, breaking and entering, embezzlement schemes, and copyright violations. In 1995, for example, $250 million worth of compact disks

and cassette tapes were illegally copied in China, according to one reported estimate (Faison, 1996). Other costs of crime are associated with criminal violence, including loss of productivity due to worker injury and the medical costs of treating victims of violent crime. Additionally, illegal expenditures of cash on gambling, drugs, prostitution, and other underground economies divert cash away from legitimate businesses.

Social and Psychological Consequences of Crime

Victims of violent crime, including rape, have been traumatized by the crime. Because of the extremely traumatic nature of rape, fear of retaliation by the rapist, and fear of social stigmatization, victims of rape in particular have often been unwilling to report the incidents to the police.

Other consequences of violent crime include the physical pain and suffering resulting from any injuries that are sustained by the victim, lowered self-esteem resulting from victimization, and the emotional loss experienced by the family and friends of victims of homicide. Fear of crime is not a problem only for individuals, it is also a social concern: 'If frightened citizens remain locked in their homes instead of enjoying public spaces, there is a loss of public and community life, as well as a loss of "social capital"—the family and neighbourhood channels that transmit positive social values from one generation to the next' (National Research Council, 1994: 5–6).

Even when crimes are not violent or personally invasive, they can cause harm and distress. White-collar crimes often lead to cynicism, for example. Such crimes, according to Elizabeth Moore and Michael Mills, may create '(a) diminished faith in a free economy and in business leaders, (b) loss of confidence in political institutions, processes and leaders, and (c) erosion of public morality' (2001: 54).

There are consequences for the criminal as well, particularly the psychological and social issues that must be dealt with after one is labelled a 'criminal'. Crimes, as we have seen, are committed for a variety of reasons, including boredom (for example, automobile theft for the sake of joyriding), psychopathological disorders (for example, serial killers such as David 'Son of Sam' Berkowitz), and desperation (for example, robbery for the sake of economic need). Not all criminals are necessarily destined to be repeat offenders once they are initially prosecuted, punished, and released.

However, being labelled as a criminal and having a criminal record means losing many opportunities. Convicts returning to the public community are sometimes greeted with uneasiness and fear. Many are denied employment; if they do find a job, it is often degrading and menial work. At the least, an ex-convict must carry the social stigma of having once been a criminal. Returning to the criminal lifestyle is sometimes the only available means for survival. This results in a vicious circle in which an initial act of (primary) deviance results in the expectation by society of further acts of (secondary) deviance, and in which the fulfillment of such expectations is nonetheless the only means of survival.

Health Consequences of Crime and Violence

Crimes have consequences, and criminal victimization harms people's health. Victims of crime consistently report lower than average levels of well-being, and victims of violent crimes suffer more psychological distress than victims of property crimes (Denkers and Winkel, 1998). Victims of violent crime report lower levels of perceived health and physical well-being, controlling for measures of injury and for socio-demographic characteristics. Younger victims of violent crime report greater decreases in their health than do older victims of violent crime. Victims of property crime also report lower levels of health and physical well-being, with older victims of crime suffering the most negative effects (Britt, 2001).

Victims of violent crimes suffer more distress symptoms and stressful life events than do non-victims and victims of non-violent crimes (Johnson, 1997). However, criminal victimization affects different people in different ways, even when the crime is identical. Resources such as social support, time, money, education, and the presence of other life stressors can affect one's resistance or vulnerability to stress (Gifford, 2001). In terms of both physical and emotional trauma, the health effect of a crime also depends on the social context of violence (Gilbert, 1996). For example, lesbians, gay men, and bisexuals who have been victimized by hate crimes report higher than average levels of depression, anxiety and anger, and symptoms of post-traumatic stress.

Victims of crimes are more likely than non-victims to suffer from post-traumatic stress disorder, major depressive episodes, and a variety of phobias. The reaction depends largely on the crime. Completed rape is strongly related to almost every disorder assessed, while robbery and burglary are not related to any disorder (Boudreaux et al., 1998).

Though victims are affected most, everyone in the community is affected by a high risk of homicide or assault. As Catherine Ross (2000)

reports, merely living in a poor, high-crime neighbourhood can create a level of stress, including depression. Research on homeless adults finds a significant relationship between witnessing violence and reporting mental-health symptoms (Fitzpatrick, LaGory, and Ritchey, 1999).

The Health of Criminals

Some forms of crime are more readily associated with health problems than others. For example,

---

BOX 3.6
Drug Tests for Inmates

Jail inmates would face random drug tests and no longer be freed automatically after two-thirds of their term under the Ontario government's latest attempt to crack the whip on criminals. Corrections Minister Rob Sampson billed the changes as another step in his campaign to craft a 'no-frills', more punitive jail system. Critics called it a politically motivated smokescreen that will keep offenders behind bars longer, but won't increase public safety one whit.

'Criminals will soon learn that if you want to leave prison early in this province, you must earn it . . . or get used to spending more time behind bars', said Sampson. 'We will establish the toughest standards for jails in this country.' The news conference had echoes of last week's announcement by Social Services Minister John Baird that the province would force some welfare recipients to submit to drug tests and drug treatment. Sampson's bill deals with inmates and went further, attacking a pet peeve of small-c conservatives across Canada: the so-called discount law that in almost all cases allows offenders to get out of jail after serving two-thirds of their sentence. In

Ontario's jails inmates are released after two-thirds of their time has been served—without any supervision or rehabilitation once they get out. In the federal system, released prisoners are put under the control of a parole officer and often have to take part in programs.

Ontario has tried to convince Ottawa to abolish the two-thirds rule, also known as earned remission. As a fallback, the new legislation would instead require inmates in provincial jails, those sentenced to less than two years, to comply with a series of conditions to qualify for early freedom. Those requirements include being drug-free, actively participating in rehabilitation and other programs and abiding by jail rules, Sampson said.

The new plan ignores studies which show criminals are less likely to re-offend if they are eased back into society with an early release and supervision outside of jail, said Bill Sparks of the John Howard Society. Sampson's bill would only keep criminals in jail longer, then free them cold turkey, with no parole officer to oversee them, he said. 'Keeping a person in jail longer because they don't have earned remission isn't going to make the community safer.'

SOURCE: Tom Blackwell, 'Ontario Inmates Face More Time, Random Drug Tests', *Edmonton Journal*, final edition, 21 November 2000, A16.

the health status of the drug abuser who resorts to criminal activities to support his or her habit is likely to be considerably lower than that of others in the general population. Alcohol is another often-abused drug that is associated with criminal behaviour. Whether health problems originate from the criminal behaviour or from the drug or alcohol use, however, is hard to determine.

Except for the most sociopathic offenders, a life of crime is stressful. Constantly looking over one's shoulder, being always on guard against the authorities, likely leads to an unhealthy level of stress that may negatively affect a person's health over time. It seems likely that stress, although felt by all criminals to some degree, is more acute among those who break the most consistently enforced laws (for example, rape or murder).

The health of prisoners has been widely studied by sociologists and health practitioners, who, not surprisingly, have concluded that prisons are harmful to health. The criminal justice system, with its increased reliance on punishment and coercive social control of the lower classes, produces self-defeating effects, including violence, human rights violations, drug abuse, the spread of HIV/AIDS, and racism (Welch, 1999). Violent assaults, rapes, unsanitary and overcrowded conditions, and staff brutality harm the prisoner's health. The overburdened mental health systems in prisons often ignore all but the most severe illnesses, such as schizophrenia or psychotic disorders. Post-traumatic stress disorder, often from rape and violent assaults, frequently goes undiagnosed or untreated because of lack of mental health resources, the stigma attached for the inmates, and lack of anonymity and safety (Kupers, 1996).

Other aspects of prison life also pose health risks to inmates. For example, Michael Vaughn and Linda Smith (1999) list six forms of ill treatment in prison facilities: (1) the use of medical care to humiliate prisoners; (2) the withholding of medical care from prisoners with HIV and AIDS; (3) the withholding of medical care from other prisoners; (4) the subjection of inmates to sleep deprivation and extreme temperature changes;

(5) the use of dental care as a means of torture; and (6) the falsification of prisoners' medical records. The authors argue that since prisons are run with efficiency in mind, rather than prisoners' health, some health care providers in the penal system forego their professional ethics.

These problems are only going to worsen as prison populations, like the rest of society, age. Already, aging prisoners require medical and hospice care at an increased rate. A growing number are displaying the typical symptoms of ill health associated with aging: disorientation, heart disease, diabetes, asthma, emphysema, and terminal illnesses such as cancer. Unlike the general population, however, inmates have neither the resources nor, in many cases, the desire to maintain their health or diet and to seek the special medical care that they need. Moreover, many have a history of alcohol and drug abuse, while others have suffered from mental disorders. The task of treating these illnesses belongs to the prison system officials and, ultimately, to the taxpayers.

Solutions to the Crime and Violence Problem

Reducing Crime

Other things being equal, a community is better off preventing crime than punishing it. Investment in improving education, creating jobs, supplying daycare, improving low-income housing, increasing access to health care, and otherwise supporting poor families—all of these front-end strategies to prevent crime are likely to work better, in the long run, than trying to contain or correct crime in prisons after a criminal has been produced by a harsh, unequal society. Other useful strategies include more use of probation, better gun control, and expansion of drug treatment (Anderson, 1994). As John Irwin and James Austin argue,

reducing crime means addressing those factors that are more directly related to crime.

This means reducing teenage pregnancies, high school dropout rates, unemployment, drug abuse, and lack of meaningful job opportunities. Although many will differ on how best to address these factors, the first step is to acknowledge that these factors have more to do with reducing crime than escalating the use of imprisonment. (1994: 167)

The Criminal Justice System

Part of the crime problem is that, in most societies, many people feel dissatisfied with and distrustful of public institutions—politicians, police, judges, lawyers, and the like. Though they dislike crime and criminals, they also dislike and distrust people in authority, too. This distrust may cause them to avoid reporting crimes or giving information to the police and courts, even to use violence—taking action into their own hands—to settle disputes. Such problems can be seen in Brazil (Noronha et al., 1999) and the former Yugoslavia (Nikolic-Ristanovic, 1998), for example. Means of preventing crime, in these as well as newly industrializing societies, might include focusing on controlled migration, planned urbanization, and more citizen participation in criminal justice matters (Seetahal, 1997).

Biases intrude into the criminal justice system, even in Canada, where Aboriginal and black minorities are overrepresented in the prison population. Research has found discrimination against blacks in denying bail and in sentencing, especially for drugs, sexual assault, and bail violations. The discrimination against Aboriginal and black people is strongest at the policing point (Roberts and Doob, 1997). Likewise, in the United Kingdom, Afro-Caribbeans are seven times more highly represented in the prison population than other groups, given their number in the general population; blacks tend to be the targets of proactive policing and are at a disadvantage when neutral criteria are applied in judgment, though these biases do not fully account for the high rates of arrest and conviction (Smith, 1997).

As we have seen, criminal behaviour is not fully rational. Yet the criminal justice system is based on the principle of **deterrence**. This notion assumes that most crimes are rational acts in which the offender weighs the perceived benefits of committing the crime against the probability of being caught and the severity of the punishment.

The 'get tough on crime' approach often discussed in recent years in North America calls for maximizing punishment to increase deterrent effects and thereby lower crime rates. However, a criminal justice system based on deterrence assumes that the probability of being punished is high, that is, that the law enforcement agencies are competent and efficient in apprehending offenders. Finally, a deterrence-based approach to criminal justice fails to acknowledge and address societal, economic, and political factors that promote the occurrence of crime in the first place: unemployment, racial inequality, poverty, and the unequal distribution of resources and opportunities.

The Capital Punishment Debate

The state-sanctioned taking of the life of a person as punishment for a crime is the extreme end point for a punitive justice system's quest for suitable forms of punishment. Some argue that it is the most crucial deterrent, believing that all but the most reckless individuals would pause to reconsider their participation in a crime when faced with the possibility of their own death. Supporters of the death penalty argue that even if the sentence has no practical value in preventing capital crimes like murder, it may at least have symbolic value in expressing the public's intolerance and disapproval of such violent acts. Moreover, in the wake of a shocking crime, knowing that the murderer has been put to death can be a source of comfort because it ensures that he or she cannot, through a legal technicality or a breakdown in prison security, escape and repeat the offence.

The debate over capital punishment is related to a larger discussion about the role of the criminal justice system. Is its purpose, as some believe, the healing of offenders to make them productive, law-abiding members of society? Are criminals the malleable product of social and psychological influences? If the answer to these questions is yes, then the criminal justice system should focus on identifying the specific circumstances that led to the criminal behaviour so that authorities can make changes to prevent recidivism (repeat offending).

The conflict theory of crime and deviance has already shown us that crimes are prosecuted differently according to the socio-economic class of the offender. The proper course of future action for the criminal justice system is to correct this type of inequality in order to prevent further crimes from being committed, and to ensure that reformed offenders are supported so that they need not return to the environment that led them to crime in the first place. Programs based on this notion of treatment include job training and education classes, individual and group therapy, and substance abuse counselling.

In contrast, others feel that the primary concern of the justice system should be to protect law-abiding citizens from criminals and to punish people who break the law for their own personal gain. The most common means of achieving these goals is by increasing the length of imprisonment so that the experience of prison life is enough to reduce the risk of recidivism. Supporters of this view believe that crime is ultimately a matter of free choice. While they may admit the influence that poverty and hardship have in luring people into crime, they believe that, ultimately, offenders commit crimes because they fail to take proper responsibility for their own lives. They note that many people grow up in impoverished conditions yet choose not to break the law, and instead work themselves out of the cycle of poverty.

Individual Strategies

Victims cope with crime in a variety of ways consistent with their gender role, their experience, and the nature of the crime. Some withdraw, practise denial, or reduce risks, while others cope more actively. Women are more likely to do the former and men the latter (Yee, Greenberg, and Beach, 1998).

Friends and family are the most frequent sources of victim assistance. Victim services programs help a substantial number of victims with counselling-related needs, but they are of little help in dealing with crime prevention, household needs, or property replacement (Davis, Lurigio, and Skogan, 1999). Partners are the most important suppliers of support. Victims whose partners give insufficient support suffer further reduced well-being (Denkers, 1999).

Much of what we have learned about crime we can do little about on our own (for example, organized crime, the poverty basis of crime, or the criminal justice system). Only a small number of university or college students or of university-educated people commit serious crimes, violent or otherwise. Therefore, readers of this book will seldom have reason to be especially wary of the risk factors for recruitment to crime. As individuals we may have acquaintances that would benefit from instruction on such risks, however.

Victimization risks are another matter. We know that many of us—particularly women, but men, too—bear a reasonably strong risk of being victimized on one or more occasions in our lifetimes. There is, thus, good reason for us to attend to the facts of the social and geographic distribution of victimization, and to act accordingly to lessen our risk wherever possible. This means, in part, that we should try to avoid being alone in those circumstances in which violent attacks and robberies are common. As we have seen, women are particularly at risk of some forms of crime. We can worry too much about these issues, and adversely affect our health, but we should be wary.

It only makes good sense, as well as good sociology, for us to try to lessen the risk of thefts against us by making the costs or obstructions high for possible perpetrators. For example, locks (on doors, windows, desk drawers, and so on), alarms, and the like are useful deterrents to attacks on our possessions, and we should use them. Also, we can join lobby groups calling for improvements in our criminal justice system, law enforcement, prisons, and the organization and safety of public places (see also Figure 3.5). Still other organizations are attempting to improve the economic circumstances of those groups highly at risk of recruitment to crime. There are various such organizations in our communities. Most will welcome any of us who want to pitch in with volunteer hours and financial support.

Some individuals are more likely than others to practise violent-crime-preventive behaviours. Not surprisingly, women, people who have experienced violent victimization and people who see benefits to preventive measures are most likely to practise them (Hammig and Moranetz, 2000). Awareness of the facts of crime and victimization as a social problem not only reduces the danger and risk, it may also be personally empowering and contribute to a growth of community cohesion.

Concluding Remarks

Along with the state of the economy, crime has been among Canadians' top five concerns for most of the last 20 years. Considered the most serious form of deviance, a crime is any act formally banned by law, specifically by the Criminal Code of Canada. Defining certain acts as 'crimes' gives the state the authority to seek, arrest, try, convict, and punish offenders, and the Criminal Code specifies a allowable range of punishments for each crime.

Within the bounds of the Criminal Code, we find many different kinds of crime. Some are

FIGURE 3.5

Percentages of National Populations Who Believe That the Police Are Doing a Good Job at Controlling Crime, 1996

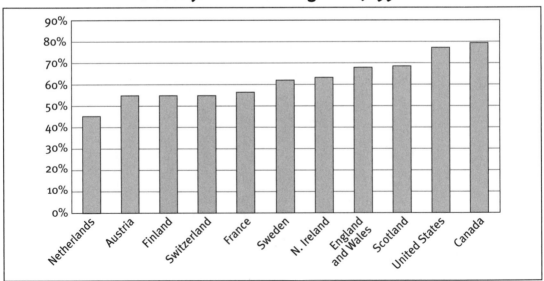

SOURCE: Statistics Canada, 'Criminal victimization: An International Perspective 2000', *The Daily*, 30 May 2002.

crimes considered extremely harmful by most people, such as murder, armed robbery, extortion, arson, sexual assault, and kidnapping. In general, there is widespread consensus in Canadian society—and in most other societies—that these behaviours are wrong and should be harshly punished. In contrast, there are crimes such as the possession of marijuana over which people disagree so much that the law has, in effect, lost control. Then there are the more standard crimes. Most people consider them wrong but do not wish to debate or increase the severity of punishment. These include offences against property such as breaking and entering, automobile theft, and shoplifting; minor assaults and drunk driving; and 'white-collar' offences such as embezzlement and fraud. All of these offences have a victim or (as in the case of drunk driving) run a serious risk of harming someone.

Despite biases in reporting, criminologists know enough about crime to permit several inferences. First is the issue of crime trends: crimes against property have increased over the last 20 years, but the rates of homicide and other crimes of violence have changed little. Second, crimes of violence, most of which are not committed for gain, often result from fights between spouses or friends. This is especially true when women are the victims. Men are more likely than women to be attacked by mere acquaintances or even strangers. Third, crimes that are committed for gain—for example, drug peddling, solicitation for prostitution, illegal gambling, and extortion—are often tied (however indirectly) to organized crime.

Crime, as we have seen, tends to be more characteristic of certain kinds of people—young, poor men, for example—though it is difficult to know precisely why. The exact relationship between these demographic variables and the criminal are complex and not entirely known. As we have suggested, the connection is probably a result of the interaction of economic and social variables. In many instances, criminals are more likely to be victimized than non-criminals, largely because of factors discussed in connection with routine activities theory.

Questions for Critical Thought

1. 'Laws, as well as their means of enforcement, maintain social order based on the illusion of order.' Discuss this statement. Do you agree with this? Why, or why not?

2. The figures and statistics on where crimes occur but are not reported are often termed the 'dark side' of crime. Seen most often with regard to sexual harassment and rape cases, the victim is often too afraid or traumatized to file a report. After reading about how crimes are (or aren't) reported, do you now question the authority and legitimacy of crime statistics? If so, when are they useful and valid pieces of evidence, and when should they be taken with a large grain of salt?

3. Canada, like other industrialized countries, is beginning to see a significant trend toward an older population. What are some of the major health consequences that prison and correctional facilities will experience as the Canadian population continues to grey?

4. Don Corleone, the notorious mafioso of the *Godfather* movies, provides popular culture with a prototype by which to envision mobster activities. Then there is the recent Soprano family of prime-time television. What are the effects of such movies and shows with regards to stereotypes? Also include in your discussion how other inner-

city ethnic 'gangs' (black, Latino, Italian, Russian, Arab) are portrayed either positively or negatively in the media.

5. Most introductory texts on social problems, social issues, and the sociology of law highlight the ongoing controversy surrounding capital punishment. Divide a blank piece of paper in two and discuss the different arguments for and against capital punishment as a deterrent for crime. Try to make an exhaustive list arguing for both the advantages and the disadvantages of such a practice.

Recommended Readings

Elijah Anderson, *Streetwise: Race, Class and Change in an Urban Community* (Chicago: University of Chicago Press, 1990).

Anderson looks at the factors that force young black people into lives of crime and violence primarily through case study analysis of Northton, a low-income community in a large northeastern US industrial city. Racial oppression and resulting poverty, abandonment of the community by the highly educated, lack of employment and opportunity, drugs, alienation, and disrespect are cited as primary determinants.

David Bayley, *Police for the Future* (New York: Oxford University Press, 1994).

The sociology of policing is discussed with a focus on why police have not been capable of preventing crime and what might make them more effective. The book may be criticized for its focus on policy to the exclusion of analysis and theories of crime.

Jane Caputi, *The Age of Sex Crime* (Bowling Green, OH: Bowling Green State University Popular Press, 1987).

Caputi analyzes serial sex crimes from 1888 to the present as well as mass-mediated myths to reveal a political quality of the crimes that is founded in patriarchal creation myths.

Peter J. Carrington, 'Group Crime in Canada', *Canadian Journal of Criminology*, 44 (2002): 277–315.

Participation in 'group crime', according to this study, is predicted by the age and gender of the offender as well as by the type of crime. The article uses both a functional and a developmental theoretical model to explain its findings.

Peter J. Carrington, 'Population Aging and Crime in Canada, 2000–2041', *Canadian Journal of Criminology*, 43 (2001): 331–56.

How will the rapidly aging Canadian population alter crime rates and criminal victimization rates? Generally, crime will continue to decline based on present demographics. Drinking and driving and sexual assault—crimes committed by older adults—will not change.

Peter J. Carrington, 'Trends in Youth Crime in Canada, 1977–1996', *Canadian Journal of Criminology*, 41 (1999): 1–32.

Youth crime in Canada between 1977 and 1996 is examined using the UCR (Uniform Crime Reports). Generally, youth crime has not changed, although there was a short peak in the early 1990s. Interestingly, the Young Offenders Act has given police less discretion, which has resulted in increased rates of youth crime.

Paul Chevigny, *Edge of the Knife: Police Violence in the Americas* (New York: New Press, 1995).

Chevigny presents a comparative investigation of police violence in several major cities in the United States, Latin America, and the Caribbean. He documents the prevalence of official violence in police work, explains the factors leading to the persistence or decline of police abuses, and suggests strategies to control police violence.

Francis T. Cullen, William J. Maakestad, and Gray Cavender, *Corporate Crime Under Attack: The Ford Pinto Case and Beyond* (Cincinnati, OH: Anderson, 1987).

This work examines corporate crime and damage caused by corporate irresponsibility. Also discussed are social movements opposed to corporate wrongdoing. Cullen, Maakestad, and Cavendar show that criminologists have played a large role in the social movement against white-collar crime.

John Graham and Ben Bowling, *Young People and Crime* (London: Home Office, 1995).

Graham and Bowling examine the extent, frequency, and nature of juvenile offending in Great Britain based on a Home Office study of approximately 2,500 youths aged 14–25. Persistent offenders were characterized by family poverty, lack of family supervision, parental divorce or separation, less attachment to families, low school performance, and friends involved in criminal activities.

Stuart L. Hills, ed., *Corporate Violence: Injury and Death for Profit* (Totowa, NJ: Rowman & Littlefield, 1987).

This book addresses corporate crime. The various authors also describe the range of corporate offences and heighten our awareness of the harm caused by the illegal actions of business executives.

N. Chabanyi Manganyi and André du Toit, eds, *Political Violence and the Struggle in South Africa* (London: Macmillan, 1990).

This book discusses ways in which prevailing discourses underscore the authority of the State and legitimize state repression and power. This collection shows the rich contribution that sociologists, psychologists, lawyers, criminologists, and political theorists have made to the study of such topics as policing, the operation of state judicial structures, social control, violence, gangsterism, and crowd behaviour.

Marc Ouimet, 'Crime in Canada and in the United States: A Comparative Analysis', *Canadian Review of Sociology and Anthropology*, 36 (1999): 389–408.

Although Canadians often proudly reflect on their relative crimelessness compared to their southern neighbours, this article examines this notion by controlling for mediating factors. The author finds that US crime rates appear higher than Canada's because of a few 'outliers', cities with extremely high crime rates. Crime in these cities is explained by residential segregation and ease of acquiring firearms.

Elizabeth Pleck, *Domestic Tyranny: The Making of American Social Policy Against Family Violence from Colonial Times to the Present* (New York: Oxford University Press, 1987).

Pleck's history of law and policy problematizes the role of the State in controlling violence. The book provides historic, methodological, semiotic, and policy analyses toward a theory of male violence in the family.

Vincenzo Ruggerio, Mick Ryan, and Joe Sim, eds, *Western European Penal Systems: A Critical Anatomy* (London: Sage, 1995).

This text analyzes the criminal justice systems of European Union member states. A trend toward convergence is observed, characterized by heightened imprisonment, longer sentences, the evolution of alternatives to imprisonment, the eating away of welfare and education within the penal system, and privatization.

Gresham M. Sykes, *The Society of Captives: A Study of Maximum Security Prison* (Princeton, NJ: Princeton University Press, 1958).

This classic study of prisons deserves to be revisited in the changed prison context of the current period. Sykes's main idea was that maximum-security prisons are unstable institutional settings and should be avoided. The prison population in the United States is now close to triple the size it was in 1958; the United States is a relatively violent country and relies more on imprisonment than other Western countries.

Recommended Web Sites

National Crime Prevention Strategy
www.crime-prevention.org

The National Crime Prevention Strategy is an agency within the federal Department of Justice. It provides information regarding the implementation of the National Crime Prevention Strategy along with a number of publications. The NCPS Web site also provides information regarding programs and services, and related links.

CAVEAT
www.caveat.org

Canadians Against Violence (CAVEAT) is a non-profit charitable organization working for safety, peace, and justice. It provides news, publications, educational kits, and information regarding submissions made to government on legislation. Related resources and links are also supplied.

Department of Justice Canada
www.canada.justice.gc.ca

The Department of Justice Web site provides information regarding the justice system in general, programs and services, consultation, news, and pertinent events. Also presented is information on departmental priorities in terms of youth justice, victims of crime, and crime prevention.

References

Anderson, Elijah. 1994. 'The Code of the Streets: Sociology of Urban Violence'. *Atlantic Monthly*, May, 80–91.

Bachman, Ronet, Heather Dillaway, and Mark S. Lachs. 1998. 'Violence Against the Elderly: A Comparative Analysis of Robbery and Assault Across Age and Gender Groups'. *Research on Aging*, 20: 183–98.

Bjerregaard, Beth. 2000. 'An Empirical Study of Stalking Victimization'. *Violence and Victims*, 15: 389–406.

Boudreaux, Edwin, Dean G. Kilpatrick, Heidi S. Resnick, Connie L. Best, and Benjamin E. Saunders. 1998. 'Criminal Victimization, Posttraumatic Stress Disorder, and Comorbid Psychopathology Among a Community Sample of Women'. *Journal of Traumatic Stress*, 11: 665–78.

Braithwaite, John. 1993. 'Crime and the Average American'. *Law and Society Review*, 27: 215–32.

Britt, Chester L. 2001. 'Health Consequences of Criminal Victimization'. *International Review of Victimology*, 8, no. 1: 63–73.

Browne, Angela, Kirk R. Williams, and Donald G. Dutton. 1999. 'Homicide Between Intimate Partners'. In *Studying and Preventing Homicide: Issues and Challenges*, edited by M. Dwayne Smith and Margaret A. Zahn, 55–78. Thousand Oaks, CA: Sage.

Canadian Centre for Justice Statistics. 1995. *Uniform Crime Reporting Survey*, 39.

Caywood, Tom. 1988. 'Routine Activities and Urban Homicides: A Tale of Two Cities'. *Homicide Studies*, 2, no. 1: 64–82.

Clay-Warner, Jody. 2000. 'Situational Characteristics of Sexually Violent Crime'. Paper presented at the annual meeting of the Southern Sociological Society.

Cochran, John K., Max L. Bromley, and Kathryn A. Branch. 2000. 'Victimization and Fear of Crime in an Entertainment District Crime "Hot Spot": A Test of Structural-Choice Theory'. *American Journal of Criminal Justice*, 24: 189–201.

Cohen, Howard. 1999. 'The Significance and Future of Racially Motivate Crime'. *International Journal of the Sociology of Law*, 27, no. 1: 103–18.

Collison, Mike. 1996. 'In Search of the High Life: Drugs, Crime, Masculinities and Consumption'. *British Journal of Criminology*, 36: 428–44.

Cottino, Amedeo. 1983. 'Criminalita contadina e giustizia borghese: Una ricerca sull'amminstrazione della diustizia nelle campagne del Cuneese all'inizio del secolo'. *Sociologia del Diritto*, 10, no. 3, 97–131.

Cox, Ruth P. 1996. 'An Exploration of the Demographic and Social Correlates of Criminal Behavior Among Adolescent Males'. *Journal of Adolescent Health*, 19: 17–24.

Davis, Keith E., April Ace, and Michelle Andra. 2000. 'Stalking Perpetrators and Psychological Maltreatment of Partners: Anger-Jealousy, Attachment Insecurity,

Need for Control, and Break-up Context'. *Violence and Victims*, 15: 417–25.

Davis, Keith E., and Irene Hanson Frieze. 2000. 'Research on Stalking: What Do We Know and Where Do We Go?' *Violence and Victims*, 15: 473–87.

Davis, Robert C., Arthur J. Lurigio, and Wesley G. Skogan. 1999. 'Services for Victims: A Market Research Study'. *International Review of Victimology*, 6, no. 2: 101–15.

Denkers, Adriaan. 1999. 'Factors Affecting Support After Criminal Victimization: Needed and Received Support from the Partner, the Social Network, and Distant Support Providers'. *Journal of Social Psychology*, 139: 191–201.

Denkers, Adriaan J.M., and Frans Willem Winkel. 1998. 'Crime Victims' Well-Being and Fear in a Prospective and Longitudinal Study'. *International Review of Criminology*, 5, no. 2: 141–62.

Durkheim, Émile. [1893] 1964. *The Division of Labor in Society*. Translated by George Simpson. New York: Free Press.

———. 1938. *The Rules of Sociological Method*. Translated by Sarah A. Solovay and John H. Mueller. Chicago: University of Chicago Press.

———. 1951. *Suicide*. Translated by John A. Spaulding and George Simpson. New York: Free Press.

Elzinga, Anne. 1996. 'Security of Taxi Drivers in the Netherlands: Fear of Crime, Actual Victimization and Recommended Security Measures'. *Security Journal*, 7, no. 3: 205, 210.

Emerson, Robert M., Kerry O. Ferris, and Carol Brooks Gardner. 1998. 'On Being Stalked'. *Social Problems*, 45, no. 5: 289–314.

Erickson, Bonnie H. 1981. 'Secret Societies and Social Structure'. *Social Forces*, 60: 188–210.

Fagan, Jeffrey, and Richard B. Freeman. 1999. 'Crime and Work'. *Crime and Justice*, 25: 225–90.

Fagan, Jeffrey, and Deanna L. Wilkinson. 1998. 'Guns, Youth Violence, and Social Identity in Inner Cities'. *Crime and Justice*, 24: 105–88.

Faggiani, Donald, and Myra G. Owens. 1999. 'Robbery of Older Adults: A Descriptive Analysis Using the National Incident-Based Reporting System'. *Justice Research and Policy*, 1, no. 1: 97–117.

Faison, Seth. 1996. 'Copyright Pirates Prosper in China Despite Promises'. *New York Times*, 20 February, A1, A6.

Felson, Marcus, and Lawrence E. Cohen. 1980. 'Human Ecology and Crime: A Routine Activity Approach'. *Human Ecology*, 8: 389–406.

Fernandez-Lanier, Adriana. 1999. *Crime in the Ivory Tower (College Campuses, Medieval Universities, Colonial Colleges)*. Unpublished doctoral dissertation, State University of New York–Albany.

Finklehor, David, and Nancy L. Asdigian. 1996. 'Risk Factors for Youth Victimization: Beyond a Lifestyles/Routine Activities Theory Approach'. *Violence and Victims*, 11, no. 1: 3–19.

Fitzpatrick, Kevin M., Mark E. LaGory, and Ferris J. Ritchey. 1999. 'Dangerous Places: Exposure to Violence and Its Mental Health Consequences for the Homeless'. *American Journal of Orthopsychiatry*, 69: 438–47.

Friedrichs, David O. 1995. 'Responding to the Challenge of White-Collar Crime as a Social Problem'. Paper presented at the annual conference of the Society for the Study of Social Problems.

Gallagher, Catherine A. 2000. *The Role of Victim Experience in Violent Situations: A Longitudinal Analysis of the National Crime Victimization Survey Data, 1992–1995*. Unpublished doctoral dissertation, University of Maryland–College Park.

Gaylord, Mark S., and Graeme Lang. 1997. 'Robbery, Recession and Real Wages in Hong Kong'. *Crime, Law and Social Change*, 27, no. 1: 49–71.

Gibbs, Jewelle Taylor. 2000. 'Gangs as Alternative Transitional Structures: Adaptations to Racial and Social Marginality in Los Angeles and London'. *Journal of Multicultural Social Work*, 8, nos 1/2: 71–99.

Gifford, Diane M. 2001. 'A Model for Analyzing the Effects of Neighbourhood Characteristics on Adolescent Depression'. Paper presented at the annual conference of the Southern Sociological Society.

Gilbert, Leah. 1996. 'Urban Violence and Health: South Africa 1995'. *Social Science and Medicine*, 43: 873–86.

Hagan, John. 1985. 'Toward a Structural Theory of Crime, Race and Gender: The Canadian Case'. *Crime and Delinquency*, 31: 129–46.

Hammig, Bart J., and Christine A. Moranetz. 2000. 'Violent Victimization: Perceptions and Preventive Behaviors Among Young Adults'. *American Journal of Health Behavior*, 24, no. 2: 143–50.

Hamilton, Graeme. 1997. 'Westray "Deceit" Deadly Mine Blast Preventable'. *Montreal Gazette*, 2 December, A1.

Hannon, Lance. 1997. 'AFDC and Homicide'. *Journal of Sociology and Social Welfare*, 24, no. 4: 125–36.

Hartjen, Clayton A. 1978. *Crime and Criminalization*, 2nd edn. New York: Praeger.

Hashima, Patricia Y., and David Finkelhor. 1999. 'Violent Victimization of Youth Versus Adults in the National Crime Victimization Survey'. *Journal of Interpersonal Violence*, 14: 799–820.

Hauber, Albert R., and Anke G.A. Zandbergen. 1996. 'Foreign Visitors as Targets of Crime in the Netherlands: Perceptions and Actual Victimization over the Years 1989, 1990, and 1993'. *Security Journal*, 7, no. 3: 211–18.

Hirschi, Travis. 1969. *Causes of Delinquency*. Berkeley: University of California Press.

Hutter, Bridget M. 1999. 'Controlling Workplace Deviance: State Regulation of Occupational Health and Safety'. *Research in the Sociology of Work*, 8: 191–209.

Ianni, Francis A.J., with Elizabeth Reuss-Ianni. 1972. *A Family Business: Kinship and Social Control in Organized Crime*. New York: Russell Sage Foundation.

Irwin, John, and James Austin. 1994. *It's About Time: America's Imprisonment Binge*. Belmont, CA: Sage.

Jenness, Valerie. 1995. 'Hate Crimes in the United States: The Transformation of Injured Persons into Victims and the Extension of Victim Status to Multiple Constituencies'. In *Images of Issues: Typifying Contemporary Social Problems*, 2nd edn, edited by Joel Best, 213–37. Hawthorne, NY: Aldine de Gruyter.

Johnson, Knowlton W. 1997. 'Professional Help and Crime Victims'. *Social Service Review*, 71, no. 1: 89–109.

Jonassen, Christen T. 1983. *Value systems and Personality in a Western Civilization: Norwegians in Europe and America*. Columbus: Ohio State University Press.

Junger-Tas, Josine. 1997. 'Ethnic Minorities and Criminal Justice in the Netherlands'. In 'Ethnicity, Crime and Immigration: Comparative and Cross-National Perspectives', special issue of *Crime and Justice* 21: 257–310.

Katz, Roger C., and Joe Marquette. 1996. 'Psychosocial Characteristics of Young Violent Offenders: A Comparative Study'. *Criminal Behaviour and Mental Health*, 6: 339–48.

Kawachi, Ichiro, Bruce P. Kennedy, and Richard G. Wilkinson. 1999. 'Crime, Social Disorganization, and Relative Deprivation'. *Social Science and Medicine*, 48: 719–31.

King, Anthony E.O. 1997. 'Understanding Violence Among Young African American Males: An Afrocentric Perspective'. *Journal of Black Studies*, 28, no. 1: 79–96.

Kong, Rebecca. 1999. 'Canadian Crime Statistics, 1997'. In Canadian Centre for Justice Statistics, *The Juristat Reader: A Statistical Overview of the Canadian Justice System*, 117–37. Toronto: Thompson Educational.

Konradi, Amanda. 1999. 'Campus Judiciaries and Sociological Inquiry'. Paper presented at the annual meeting of the Society for the Study of Social Problems.

Kupers, Terry A. 1996. 'Trauma and Its Sequelae in Male Prisoners: Effects of Confinement, Over-crowding and Diminished Services'. *American Journal of Orthopsychiatry*, 66: 189–96.

Lane, Roger. 1999. 'Murder in America: A Historian's Perspective'. *Crime and Justice*, 25: 191–224.

Langhinrichsen-Rohling, Jennifer, and Martin Rohling. 2000. 'Negative Family-of-Origin Experiences: Are They Associated with Perpetrating Unwanted Pursuit Behaviors?' *Violence and Victims*, 15: 459–71.

LaPrairie, Carol, et al. 1996. *Examining Aboriginal Correction in Canada*. Ottawa: Solicitor General of Canada.

Lee, Matthew R. 2000. 'Community Cohesion and Violent Predatory Victimization: A Theoretical Extension and Cross-National Test of Opportunity Theory'. *Social Forces*, 79: 683–706.

Le Moigne, Philippe. 1998. 'Sanction, Individuation and Deviance: The Social Organization of Recidivism Among the Young'. *Revue Suisse de Sociologie*, 24: 405–29.

Lombroso-Ferrero, Gina. [1911] 1972. *Criminal Man, According to the Classification of Cesare Lombroso*. Montclair, NJ: Patterson-Smith.

McCabe, Kimberly, and Sharon S. Gregory. 1998. 'Elderly Victimization'. *Research on Aging*, 20: 363–72.

Maciak, Barbara J., Madison T. Moore, Laura C. Leviton, and Mary E. Guinan. 1998. 'Preventing Hallowe'en Arson in an Urban Setting: A Model for Multisectoral Planning and Community Participation'. *Health Education and Behavior*, 25: 194–211.

Martens, Peter L. 2001. 'Immigrants as Victims of Crime'. *International Review of Victimology*, 8: 199–216.

Mawby, R.I., P. Brunt, and Z. Hambly. 1999. 'Victimisation on Holiday: A British Survey'. *International Review of Victimology*, 6: 201–11

———. 2000. 'Fear of Crime Among British Holidaymakers'. *British Journal of Criminology*, 40: 468–79.

Mechanic, Mindy B., Mary H. Uhlmansiek, Terri L. Weaver, and Patricia A. Resick. 2000. 'The Impact of Severe Stalking Experienced by Acutely Battered Women: An Examination of Violence, Psychological Symptoms and Strategic Responding'. *Violence and Victims*, 15: 443–58.

Mesch, Gustavo S. 1997. 'Victims and Property Victimization in Israel'. *Journal of Quantitative Criminology*, 13: 57–71.

Miller, J. Kirk, and Kristen A. Myers. 2000. 'Are All Hate Crimes Created Equal?' Paper presented at the annual meeting of the Southern Sociological Society.

Moore, Elizabeth, and Michael Mills. 2001. 'The Neglected Victims and Unexamined Costs of White-Collar Crime'. In *Crimes of Privilege: Readings in White-Collar Crime*, edited by Neal Shover and John P. Wright, 51–7. New York: Oxford University Press.

Moss, Geoffrey. 1997. 'Explaining the Absence of Violent Crime Among the Semai of Malaysia: Is Criminological Theory up to the Task?' *Journal of Criminal Justice*, 25: 177–94.

Mustaine, Elizabeth Ehrhardt, and Richard Tewksbury. 1997. 'Obstacles in the Assessment of Routine Activity Theory'. *Social Pathology*, 3: 177–94.

———. 1998. 'Victimization Risks at Leisure: A Gender-Specific Analysis'. *Violence and Victims*, 13: 231–49.

National Research Council. 1994. *Violence in Urban America: Mobilizing a Response*. Washington, DC: National Academy Press.

Nelsen, Candice, and Lin Huff-Corzine. 1998. 'Strangers in the Night: An Application of the Lifestyle-Routine Activities Approach to Elderly Homicide Victimization'. *Homicide Studies*, 2, no. 2: 130–59.

Nikolic-Ristanovic, Vesna. 1998. 'Victims and Police in Belgrade'. *International Review of Victimology*, 6, no. 1: 49–62.

Noronha, Ceci Vilar, Eduardo Paes Machado, Gino Tapparelli, Tania Tegina F. Cordeiro, Denise Helena P. Laranjeira, and Carlos Antonio Telles Santos. 1999. 'Violence, Ethnic Group and Color: A Study of Differences in the Metropolitan Region of Salvador, Bahia, Brazil'. *Pan American Journal of Public Health*, 5: 268–77.

O'Donnell, Ian, and Kimmet Edgar. 1998. 'Routine Victimization in Prisons'. *Howard Journal of Criminal Justice*, 37: 266–79.

Paetsch, Joanne J., and Lorne D. Bertrand. 1999. 'Victimization and Delinquency Among Canadian Youth'. *Adolescence*, 34: 351–67.

Parker, Karen, and Patricia L. McCall. 1999. 'Structural Conditions and Racial Homicide Patterns: A Look at the Multiple Disadvantages in Urban Areas'. *Criminology*, 37: 447–77.

Peel, Elizabeth. 1999. 'Violence Against Lesbians and Gay Men: Decision-Making in Reporting and Not Reporting Crime'. *Feminism and Psychology*, 9, no. 2: 161–7.

Pepinsky, Harold E., and Paul Jesilow. 1984. *Myths That Cause Crime*. Cabin John, MD: Seven Locks Press.

Ploughman, Penelope, and John Stensrud. 1986. 'The Ecology of Rape Victimization: A Case Study of Buffalo, New York'. *Genetic, Social, and General Psychology Monographs*, 112: 303–24.

Powell, Kathleen B. 1997. 'Correlated of Violent and Nonviolent Behavior Among Vulnerable Inner-City Youths'. *Family and Community Health*, 20, no. 2: 38–47.

Pratt, Carter, and Kamala Deosaransingh. 1997. 'Gender Differences in Homicide in Contra Costa County, California, 1982–1993'. *American Journal of Preventive Medicine*, 13, Suppl.: 19–24.

Ratcliffe, Jerry, and Michael McCullagh. 1999. 'Burglary, Victimization and Social Deprivation'. *Crime, Prevention and Community Safety*, 1, no. 2: 37–46.

Reed, Micheline, and Julian Roberts. 1999. 'Adult Correctional Services in Canada, 1997–98'. In Canadian Centre for Justice Statistics, *The Juristat Reader: A Statistical Overview of the Canadian Justice System*, 39–51. Toronto: Thompson Educational.

Roberts, Julian V., and Anthony N. Doob. 1997. 'Race, Ethnicity, and Criminal Justice in Canada'. *In Ethnicity, Crime, and Immigration: Comparative and Cross-national Perspectives*, edited by Michael Tonry, 469–522. Chicago: University of Chicago Press.

Ross, Catherine E. 2000. 'Neighborhood Disadvantage and Adult Depression'. *Journal of Health and Social Behavior*, 41: 177–87.

Ruchkin, Vladislav V., Martin Eisenmann, Bruno Hagglof, and C. Robert Cloninger. 1998. 'Aggression in Delinquent Adolescents vs Controls in Northern Russia: Relations with Hereditary and Environmental Factors'. *Criminal Behaviour and Mental Health*, 8, no. 2: 115–26.

Sacco, Vincent F. 2000. 'News That Counts: Newspaper Images of Crime and Victimization'. *Criminologie*, 33: 203–23.

Scott, Bridget T. 1999. 'Chronic Community Violence and the Children Who Are Exposed to It'. *Journal of Emotional Abuse*, 1, no. 3: 23–37.

Seetahal, Dana. 1997. 'Urbanisation and Industrialization on Crime: The Commonwealth Caribbean in the 1990s'. *Caribbean Journal of Criminology and Social Psychology*, 2, no. 2: 115–45.

Sennett, Richard, and Jonathan Cobb. 1973. *The Hidden Injuries of Class*. New York: Vintage.

Silver, Eric. 1999. *Violence and Mental Illness from a Social Disorganization Perspective: An Analysis of Individual and Community Risk Factors*. Unpublished doctoral dissertation, State University of New York–Albany.

Simmel, Georg. [1906] 1950. 'The Sociology of Secrecy and of Secret Societies'. In *The Sociology of Georg Simmel*, edited by Kurt H. Wolff, 305–76. Glencoe, IL: Free Press.

Simons, Ronald L., and Wei Chao. 1996. 'Conduct Problems'. In *Understanding Differences Between Divorced and Intact Families: Stress, Interaction, and Child Outcome*, edited by Ronald L. Simons and Associates, 125–43. Thousand Oaks, CA: Sage.

Skolnick, Jerome H. 1994. '"Three Strikes, You're Out" and Other Bad Calls on Crime'. *American Prospect*, 17, Spring: 30–7.

Smith, David J. 1997. 'Ethnic Origins, Crime, and Criminal Justice in England and Wales'. In *Ethnicity, Crime, and Immigration: Comparative and Cross-National Perspectives*, edited by Michael Tonry, 101–82. Chicago: University of Chicago Press.

Stanley, Christopher. 1995. 'Teenage Kicks: Urban Narratives of Dissent Not Deviance'. *Crime, Law and Social Change*, 23, no. 2: 91–119.

Statistics Canada. 2001. 'Crimes by Type of Offence'. Available at <www.statcan.ca/english/Pgdb/Pgdb/legal02.htm>, accessed 20 February 2003.

Steffensmeier, Darrell, and Emilie Allan. 1996. 'Gender and Crime: A Gendered Theory of Female Offending'. *Annual Review of Sociology*, 22: 459–87.

Sutherland, Edwin H. 1939. *Principles of Criminology*. Philadelphia: Lippincott.

Tewksbury, Richard, Elizabeth L. Grossi, Geetha Suresh, and Jeff Helms. 1999. 'Hate Crimes Against Gay Men and Lesbian Women: A Routine Activity Approach for Predicting Victimization Risk'. *Humanity and Society*, 23, no. 2: 125–42.

Tiby, Eva. 2001. 'Victimization and Fear Among Lesbians and Gay Men in Stockholm'. *International Review of Victimology*, 8: 217–43.

Tillman, Robert, and Michael Indergaard. 1999. 'Field of Schemes: Health Insurance Fraud in the Small Business Sector'. *Social Problems*, 46: 572–90.

Tjaden, Patricia, and Nancy Thoennes. 2000. 'The Role of Stalking in Domestic Violence Crime Reports Generated by the Colorado Springs Police Department'. *Violence and Victims*, 15: 427–41.

Torres, Sam. 1999. 'Hate Crimes Against African Americans: The Extent of the Problem'. *Journal of Contemporary Criminal Justice*, 15, no. 1: 48–63.

United States. Bureau of Justice. 1991. *Statistics Sourcebook*. Washington, DC: US Government Printing Office.

Vander Ven, Thomas M. 1998. 'Fear of Victimization and the Interactional Construction of Harassment in a Latino Neighbourhood'. *Journal of Contemporary Ethnography*, 27: 374–98.

Vaughn, Michael S., and Linda G. Smith. 1999. 'Practicing Penal Harm Medicine in the United States: Prisoners' Voices from Jail'. *Justice Quarterly*, 16, no. 1: 175–231.

Walker, Samuel. 1989. *Sense and Nonsense About Crime: A Policy Guide*, 2nd edn. Pacific Grove, CA: Brooks/Cole.

Weaver, Greg S., Thomas A. Peete, Jay Corzine, Janice E. Clifford Wittekind, Lin Huff-Corzine, and Gregory S. Kowalski. 2001. 'Race, Gender, Context, and the Subcultures of Violence'. Paper presented at the annual meeting of the Southern Sociological Society.

Welch, Michael. 1999. *Punishment in America: Social Control and the Ironies of Imprisonment*. Thousand Oaks, CA: Sage.

White, Jacqueline, Robin M. Kowalski, Amy Lyndon, and Sherri Valentine. 2000. 'An Integrative Contextual Developmental Model of Male Stalking'. *Violence and Victims*, 15: 373–88.

White, Michael. 1999. 'GM Ordered to Pay Accident Victims $49 B'. *National Post*, 10 July, A1.

Whyte, William Foote. [1943] 1981. *Street Corner Society: Social Structure of an Italian Slum*, 3rd edn. Chicago: University of Chicago Press.

Wilkinson, Richard G., Ichiro Kawachi, and Bruce P. Kennedy. 1998. 'Mortality, the Social Environment, Crime and Violence'. In *The Sociology of Health Inequalities*, edited by Mel Bartley, David Blane, and George Davey Smith, 19–37. Oxford: Blackwell.

Will, Susan, Henry N. Pontell, and Richard Cheung. 1998. 'Risky Business Revisited: White-Collar Crime and the Orange County Bankruptcy'. *Crime and Delinquency*, 44: 367–87.

Wilson, James Q., and George L. Kelling. 1982. 'Broken Windows'. *Atlantic Monthly*, March, 29–38.

Wilson, Margo, and Martin Daly. 1992. 'Who Kills Whom in Spouse Killings? On the Exceptional Sex Ratio of Spousal Homicides in the U.S.' *Criminology*, 30: 189–215.

Wooldredge, John D. 1998. 'Inmate Lifestyles and Opportunities for Victimization'. *Journal of Research in Crime and Delinquency*, 35: 480–502.

Wrangham, Richard, and Dale Peterson. 1997. *Demonic Males: Apes and the Origins of Human Violence*. Boston: Houghton Mifflin.

Wright, Bradley R. Entner, Avshalom Caspi, Terri E. Moffitt, Richard A. Miech, and Phil A. Silva. 1999. 'Reconsidering the Relationship between SES and Delinquency: Causation but Not Correlation'. *Criminology*, 37: 175–94.

Yee, Jennifer, Martin S. Greenberg, and Scott R. Beach. 1998. 'Attitudes Toward Various Modes of Coping with Criminal Victimization: The Effects of Gender and Type of Crime'. *Journal of Social and Clinical Psychology*, 17: 273–94.

Zahn, Margaret A., and Patricia L. McCall. 1999. 'Homicide in the 20th-Century United States: Trends and Patterns'. *In Studying and Preventing Homicide: Issues and Challenges*, edited by M. Dwayne Smith and Margaret A. Zahn, 10–30. Thousand Oaks, CA: Sage.

Zimbardo, Philip G. 1969. 'The Human Choice: Individuation, Reason, and Order Versus Deindividuation, Impulse, and Chaos'. *Nebraska Symposium on Motivation*, 17: 237–307.

Zvekic, Ugliesa. 1996. 'The International Crime (Victim) Survey: Issues of Comparative Advantages and Disadvantages'. *International Criminal Justice Review*, 6: 1–21.

Glossary

Anomie According to Durkheim, a condition characterized by a breakdown of norms and personal disorganization, which may lead to crime.

Clientelism A special relationship in which someone of influence or wealth continues to protect a subordinate client; seen traditionally as a single wealthy family or individual hiring socially or economically vulnerable wage-labourers. In a more modern sense, though, clientelism can be seen when new immigrants are protected by individuals of wealth or influence from potentially hostile environments.

Conventional crimes The traditional illegal behaviours that most people think of as 'crime'. For example, homicide and sexual assault are given the most media coverage but account for only 12 per cent of all crimes.

Crime Any behaviour that, in a given time and place, is prohibited by applicable statutory law. When a law is violated, a crime is said to have been committed.

Deterrence A justice system based on deterrence assumes that crimes are rational acts in which the offender weighs the perceived benefits of committing the crime against the probability of being caught and the severity of the punishment. It assumes that the probability of being punished is high and that the law enforcement agencies are competent and efficient in apprehending offenders.

Differential socialization The processes whereby individuals learn to behave in accordance with prevailing standards of culture or gender. For example, boys and men learn to be less inhibited in using aggressive and violent actions, and this may account for the disproportionate number of males involved in criminal activity.

Homicide The killing of a human being by another, directly or indirectly, by any means; includes *murder*, the unlawful killing of another human being with malicious intent, and *manslaughter*, the unlawful killing of another person without sufficient intent to constitute murder.

Law An orderly and dependable sequence of events, or a rule of conduct that may provide for the punishment of violators. In other words, the formal rules about what a society's members can and cannot do.

Self-reporting The victim reports to authorities that a crime has occurred. This is the most direct method of measuring crime rates. However, it is not the most accurate, as changes in the crime rate reflect changes in victims' willingness to report.

Social bond theory A type of control theory. A strong social bond prevents most people from succumbing to the temptation to engage in criminal activities.

Social disorder The uncertain and unpredictable condition in which rules are not obeyed. It is generally unsafe, and the boundaries of acceptable behaviour have been broken down.

Social order The prevalence of generally harmonious relationships; used synonymously with *social organization*. This condition exists when rules are obeyed and social situations are controlled and predictable. Rules serve not only to indicate which behaviours are acceptable, but also to allow participants to anticipate the behaviour of others.

Strain theory Merton holds that strain is produced when social structure prevents people from achieving culturally defined goals through legitimate means. He outlines various adaptive strategies: conformity, ritualism, retreatism, rebellion, and innovation. Innovation is most commonly associated with criminal activities, which include theft, robbery, tax fraud, embezzlement, and organized crime. Also known as *anomie theory*.

Subculture theory Investigates the norms that set a group apart from mainstream society. Specifically, this approach gives special insight into the subculture of the criminal, looking into the values and belief systems that may be conducive to delinquent and criminal action.

Vice crimes Deviant behaviour that may defined as immoral (for example, gambling, prostitution, public drunkenness). These crimes provide the greatest opportunity for organized crime.

Victimization surveys Samples of people are asked how many times within a given time period they have been the victim of particular crimes.

White-collar crimes The crimes that are committed by upper-status people in the course of their occupations. They are always distinguished from conventional criminal offences such as robbery or murder. White-collar crimes are performed as part of normal work and usually occur in reputable organizations.

Chapter 4

Race and Ethnic Relations

Chapter Objectives

After reading this chapter the student should understand:
- that social distance is maintained between different ethnic and racial groups
- how race and ethnic conflict occurs in Canada
- the varying intensities of prejudice
- selected other basic facts of race and ethnicity
- the process of chain migration
- what is meant by the 'vertical mosaic'
- what is meant by 'diaspora'
- different theoretical perspectives on ethnic and racial inequality
- social and health consequences of racial and ethnic inequality
- possible solutions to problems of race and ethnic relations

Introduction

This chapter is about minority groups and the social relations between them and majority groups—about problems of exclusion and discrimination, racism, prejudice, and conflict. The minority groups in question are racial and ethnic minorities.

Prejudice against minority groups is a social problem, for a variety of reasons. First, most people view prejudice as unjust and unfair; Canadians tend to hate unfairness and look for remedies to it. Second, because it is unfair, prejudice creates conflicts in our society—between minorities and the majority, and between people who are prejudiced and people who are not. Third, prejudice and its outcomes—discrimination, conflict, exclusion, hatred, distrust—are politically and economically wasteful. They make our society far less prosperous than it might be. A prejudiced society does not make the best possible use of its human resources.

One way to measure the quality of relations between two or more groups is to measure the **social distance** between them. That is exactly what E.S. Bogardus did in 1928. He asked respondents whether they would be willing to accept members of various ethnic groups into close kinship by marriage, their club as friends, their street as neighbours, employment in their occupation, their country as citizens, and their country as visitors. This approach to social distance showed that people feel varying comfort levels when interacting with members of other **cultures** under different conditions. People are more willing to have close relations with people whom they judge to be culturally and racially similar to themselves, and to have distant relations—if any at all—with people they view as different.

In studying race and ethnic relations, we still use this Bogardus measurement procedure today, along with others. Sociologists have learned that people who place other groups at a distance from themselves often hold prejudices about those other groups. They also sometimes act upon those prejudices and practise discrimination against the other groups, at work and in the wider community. This creates hardship for members of minority groups, so named not because they are few but because they are relatively powerless.

Discrimination against racial and ethnic minority groups, in Canada and elsewhere, is evident in a wide variety of settings. For example, even when members of minority groups find suitable work, they still often face bias when competing for promotions. We will see throughout this chapter examples of exclusion, decoupling, disabling, and scarcity because of discrimination against minority groups and the limiting of their opportunities for economic advancement. Discrimination has health consequences, too. The most dramatic and immediate health consequences are injuries and fatalities that arise from hate crimes. However, injuries to self-esteem and feelings of stress and low self-worth also carry health consequences for victims of racism. These facts make discrimination and prejudice important health problems, as well as social and moral problems.

BOX 4.1
Hate Legislation

A couple of sadistic killers pistol-whipped a 21-year-old Wyoming student named Matthew Shepard, then left him lashed to a fence to die. The thugs were heterosexual but accosted their victim, or were accosted by him, in a gay bar, which lent their brutal crime a socio-political dimension. In the words of the Globe and Mail: 'The codicil to virtually every news story about Mr. Shepard's death has been a call for the passage of new hate-crimes legislation.'

Wyoming has no hate laws, but it has an admirable law against robbery-murder. It makes Shepard's two accused killers eligible for the death penalty. 'Now, imagine the trouble they would be in,' commented George F. Will in the Washington Post, 'if Wyoming were one of the 21 states with laws against "hate crimes" based on sexual orientation.'

Hate laws can be extended to cover expressions of opinion, and used to silence anyone who questions any aspect of a society's dominant philosophy. Minimally, hate legislation can bring about a system of two-tiered justice. In Canada, for instance, the 'hate' section of the Criminal Code may result in the same crime drawing a more severe penalty upon evidence that the victim belonged to a protected group (not all groups are protected, of course) that the perpetrator hated. Luckily the climate is changing. The media that have played a major role in ushering in these trends are no longer at ease with them.

In the words of a recent Globe and Mail editorial: 'We're simply not comfortable with the idea that beating up someone because you don't like their religion or race or sexual orientation is "worse" than beating up someone because you don't like them.' Perhaps we're slowly coming to terms with liberty. Freedom may be a bargain, but it has a price. We pay for it in the coin of tolerance, not once but twice. First, tolerance entitles us do as we choose, and second, it entitles other people to have their own opinions about our choices.

Crimes are illegitimate acts, regardless of what motivates them. They should be neither mitigated nor aggravated by the perpetrators' feelings about their victims' looks, race, class, gender, or sexual preference. The young sadists who murdered Shepard should die, if convicted—but for murder, not for their sexual politics.

SOURCE: George Jonas, 'Hate Legislation Brings About Two-Tiered Justice', *The Province* (Vancouver), final edition, 22 October 1998, A42. Reprinted by permission of The Canadian Press.

Canada Is Multicultural—and Conflictual

Canada began as an outpost of the French and British empires. Missionary work, an early form of colonial governance, was used to convert the traditional identities of the Native people to 'civilized' Christians. This process subdued the Native peoples, destroyed their cultures, and simplified the theft of their land (Peikoff, 2001). It was aided by the myth of a 'frontier' made up of vast, empty spaces (Furniss, 1999). Gradually, immigrants from France, Britain, and elsewhere filled up this supposedly empty country with newcomers. Liberal capitalism, far from being a neutral doctrine of rights and citizenship, has served as a genocidal instrument of colonial domination and land usurpation (Samson, 1999).

Today, Canada prides itself on its multicultural makeup, and it is internationally recognized for its ethnic diversity. Yet multiculturalism is a complicated notion. Increasingly, Canadians have found it useful to distinguish between traditional, or liberal, multiculturalism and modern multiculturalism. *Traditional multiculturalism*, or *pluralism*, is concerned with the rights of individuals. It protects the rights of minority people through, for example, provincial human rights codes. By contrast, *modern multiculturalism* is concerned with the survival of cultural groups. In this case, it is the group, not the individual, that is protected by law. Modern multiculturalism treats each of us as the member of an ethnic or racial group—we are a proxy for the groups we belong to.

The difference between these two approaches is important. By its nature, traditional multiculturalism focuses on civil liberties. But where the traditional form protects individual job seekers against bias, modern multiculturalism supports blanket preferences, such as employment equity, to promote the hiring of disadvantaged groups.

Some criticize the federal policy of multiculturalism for emphasizing group differences, encouraging different value systems, and building isolated communities rather than promoting common interests and objectives. So long as Canada maintains diverse cultures within its borders, the argument goes, it will never have a clear national identity. The promotion of cultural differences splits the population into separate, hostile ethnic groups; racism is only one result. Without the social differences promoted by multiculturalism, there would be no exclusion, prejudice, or discrimination.

Few (if any) critics of multiculturalism would deny citizens an equal right to political and legal life. A liberal democracy such as Canada is supposed to treat all citizens in an equal way, and for the most part we do. We promise people certain rights—freedoms of conscience, speech, press, assembly, and association; due process; the rights to vote and to hold public office; and so on—whatever their race, ethnicity, religious practices, gender, or sexual orientation. The state refrains from telling people how they ought to live (criminal activity being the exception) and, instead, encourages citizens to pursue their own ideas of the good life. These rights are basic to all citizens of Canada, and few challenge them.

What is sometimes challenged is the provision of special treatment for minority groups, which seems to violate the rule of equal treatment. In a modern multicultural society, the state does not treat people exactly the same. Different groups have different rights. Because multiculturalism, by definition, celebrates diversity and difference, some groups enjoy certain advantages.

This situation, which has grown out of multiculturalism since the 1960s, has its roots in four social revolutions: the Quiet Revolution in Quebec; the acceleration of Aboriginal demands to settle Native land claims, which coincided with francophone demands for increased sovereignty; the impact of higher rates of immigration from developing countries with different cultures; and the cross-border influence of the US civil rights revolution (Duffy Hutcheon, 1998).

We can find other roots of modern multiculturalism in Canada's founding document, the British North America (BNA) Act. That document promotes regionalism: small provinces have proportionally more political representation and therefore clout per capita than do large provinces. Additionally, some religions receive special treatment under law. For example, we support Catholic schools out of public funds, while we do not support Jewish or Islamic schools in the same way. We require that French be available in all federal institutions, even when Chinese or other languages are spoken more often within the community. These differences and others arise out of the BNA Act.

This highly regionalized and fragmented structure provides a weak basis for national identity and claims to national sovereignty. No wonder that assertions of Canadian nationhood within the global economic and political system are, today, as fragile as the assertions of Quebec nationhood within the Canadian federation and the assertions of Aboriginal nationhood—specifically, claims of land and sovereignty—within the province of Quebec (Barsh, 1997).

The Aboriginal peoples also pose a big problem for Canadian multiculturalism. Some people believe that the political concerns of Canada's Aboriginal peoples will not be satisfied unless the Canadian public supports political autonomy for Native peoples (Warburton, 1997). Will Kymlicka (1995) argues that we should view Canadian Aboriginal peoples as 'national minorities'. He believes that their rights should bridge

Residential schools across Canada explicitly set out to eliminate Aboriginal identity. Today, fostering self-government and maintaining traditional culture and spiritual teachings are ways to retain culture in everyday life, to address injustice, and to move forward. (CP, Tom Hanson)

individual equality and collective self-determination, all this within the framework of liberal democratic principles (see also Spaulding, 1997). So far, however, movement in that direction has been slow.

In the struggle to gain sovereignty over their natural habitat, the Aboriginal people of Quebec mounted a campaign to stop a major hydroelectric development. Ironically, provincial administrators declared the right to self-determination for the people of Quebec as a whole but not for the Aboriginal peoples within Quebec. Thus, the problems in Quebec reflect the province's own difficulties within Canada. Quebec claims to be a melting pot where minorities are assimilated into the francophone culture; however, Aboriginal and other ethnic voters helped prevent a separatist victory in the 1980 and 1995 referenda on Quebec's secession from Canada (Hunt, 1996).

Aboriginal efforts to achieve self-government have not been entirely without effect. Canada's alternative Native justice systems, for example, emphasize collective, as opposed to individual, rights and accord different priorities to Native principles and practices of justice. In each community, a panel of fellow Native community residents incorporates and expresses Native values, though final authority rests with the State. Participation is voluntary but limited to minor offences (Clairmont, 1996). Such power-sharing between judges and Native communities seems to be more acceptable to the federal government than does the relevance of Aboriginal values in the matter of jury selection, trial location, and criminal liability (Melancon, 1997).

Can different groups coexist as a unified nation without promoting divisiveness and conflict? These were questions that sociologist Émile Durkheim asked a century ago, in his classic work *The Division of Labor in Society* ([1895] 1965). He answered that in a modern society, people will learn to value one another and live together peacefully. To do this, they will have to realize that, though they are not all the same, they are all interdependent. In Canada, we have

not fully learned how to do that yet. Canadians are generally happy with their citizenship in a multicultural society, and a distinct Canadian national identity does exist (Howard, 1998). However, prejudice, discrimination, and conflict persist too.

Social Exclusion of Minority Groups

At bottom, the problem of social distance between groups involves the social **exclusion** of minorities. This exclusion is due to selective ethnic and racial inclusion by the majority group. Inclusion always implies exclusion, because all inclusion means the creation and defence of group boundaries by one group against another.

We are all familiar with processes of exclusion and inclusion from our school days as children, when we had personal experience with **cliques**. Few escape childhood without becoming a member of a clique or feeling left out of—excluded from—a clique. And few forget the people who led the cliques that included or excluded them.

Exclusion is common in social life, but it is not something that people do all the time, since people are often sociable and cooperative. On the contrary, exclusion usually develops in situations in which one group wants to defend its social status or resources against others. Leaders play a key role in this process. In any clique, the leader is the most powerful or popular member and rules the other members through strategies of information control, threat, and shame. Leaders prey on the weaknesses of clique members and their need for belonging and admiration.

According to Georg Simmel ([1905] 1964), a *stranger* is a person who lives within a community and, therefore, often affects the life of the group but who is not given status by 'natives' as one of the **in-group**. Insiders decide that the stranger is 'not one of us', a notion that may be justified in terms of different nationality, race, or culture. Such a person enjoys certain freedoms denied to natives yet is denied the right to participate that other community members enjoy. Strangers, for better or worse, are rootless and free to come and go. Because of their marginality, social distance, and mobility, strangers are free to accept or reject local values and conventions. As outsiders, strangers can be agents of change. For these reasons, they often meet with surprising openness and confidences.

Often, however, strangers are also feared. People tend to fear strangers more than is warranted. That is because strangers are less well known, therefore less predictable, and because they are less connected to friends and relatives, therefore less controllable. By Simmel's definition, the 'stranger' or 'outsider' occupies a structural position in a community that arises from social marginality and lack of information sharing.

The rhetoric of inclusion and exclusion emphasizes the distinctiveness of insiders and strangers. Differences in cultural identity, traditions, and heritage provoke anxieties (Stolcke, 1999). Fears grow particularly under conditions of illegal immigration, increasing unemployment and crime, feelings of xenophobia and insecurity, and depleted state resources for social services (Fontana, 1997). We see people as 'others' and build barriers against them when we feel we are in competition with them. Through much of Canada's history, immigrants were shunned, tolerated only because we needed their labour. In times of distress, it was common to attack and exclude immigrants.

Of course, even the appearance of competition and scarcity because of immigration, race, or ethnicity can be a social construction. A question of interest to sociologists, then, is, What are the social conditions that make race or ethnicity a basis for isolating and excluding others? How (and when and why) do people define some people as 'others', by definition unlike themselves in significant ways? Answering this question brings us to a discussion of nationalism, which is to ethnicity as self-congratulation is to cliques.

Ethnic Nationalism

Nationalism—a sense of national peoplehood and a strong love of one's nation or ethnic group—grows out of the sense of a boundary or conflict between 'us' and 'them'. Some believe that nationalism is a good thing because national unity is a good thing. To the extent that Canada lacks such a national sentiment, Canadians have little knowledge of their own history and few symbols or rituals that bind them together. They do not feel or act like 'a people'.

Others believe that this lack of 'peoplehood' is a good thing. They deplore nationalism as a mindless, dangerous force in history. Along similar lines, they deplore the possibility that multiculturalism, by fostering ethnic cultural identities *within* Canada, will foster feelings of nationalism and group identity for some Canadians and not others. They believe that nationalism has done more harm than good in human history, and that encouraging pride in people's ethnicity will engulf us in wars and genocidal acts. In the days since 11 September 2001, this question has been on more and more people's minds.

The phrase 'ethnic nationalism' conjures up images of the horrors of war in the former Yugoslavia, of 'ethnic cleansing', of the struggle between the Hutu and Tutsi peoples in some central African countries, of the 'jihad' by Islamic terrorists against the United States and its way of life. *Ethnic nationalism* can also refer to the long-standing attempts of the Basques to maintain the boundary between France and Spain, or of the Kurdish people of the Middle East to achieve international recognition. Michael Ignatieff, in his book *Blood and Belonging: Journeys into the New Nationalism* (1994), outlines two kinds of nationalism: civic and ethnic. In his view, a community of citizens who as equals express loyalty and patriotic attachment to a shared set of values, both social and political, constitutes *civic nationalism*. For some groups, this is a simple statement of identity, reflecting family ties, language, religion, tradition, and culture. It can coexist with membership in a larger, multi-ethnic society and state.

Ethnic nationalism, by contrast, is a search for identity, a tracing of roots to a shared cultural past, together with a search for political recognition. It is a declaration of resistance against being treated as an 'other', outside the bounds of society, by those who are considered the 'mainstream'. Ethnic nationalism is particularly marked among peoples who do not have their own nation-state. All over Europe there have been movements seeking national autonomy. Basque, Scottish, and Welsh nationalism are only three of many possible examples.

In many parts of the world, people are calling for the right to govern themselves as they see fit. They claim that this right is based on their concept of nationhood, rooted in their culture and history. In making their claims, they speak not only of the traditions and customs they share, but also of legal, educational, and political systems and institutions that they consider uniquely their own. Within North America, there are also groups that claim nationhood rather than ethnic group status, most notably the people of Quebec, many of whom feel that they constitute a distinct society, and the many Aboriginal nations who point out that they were governed by their own political and legal systems long before Europeans landed on North American soil.

Not all Québécois seek independence from Canada. (Just over half of those who voted in the Quebec referendum of 1995 voted to remain part of Canada.) Many, however, including many of those who voted against separation, define themselves as Québécois rather than Canadian. However, where people with a geographical land base consider themselves as forming a nation, feel strongly loyal to that nation, and form or maintain their own institutions, such as political, legal, and educational systems, there seems little reason to insist that they are not a nation.

At its worst, ethnic nationalism denies basic humanity to others. The rhetoric of nationalism is full of contradictions and feeds the fantasies of power, particularly for those who wield their power by wielding weapons. This kind of ethnic nationalism, however it arises, is inherently destructive and cannot fit inside the context of a liberal-democratic multicultural society like Canada. The only real defence against such destructiveness is a political system that prevents the buildup of nationalism by denying the demagogues a platform while at the same time recognizing people's universal desire—even need—to reclaim their ancestry and build communities around it.

The Social Psychology of Prejudice

The social problems associated with race and ethnic conflict include prejudice and discrimination. We can define **prejudice** as 'an aversive or hostile attitude toward a person who belongs to a group . . . and is therefore presumed to have the objectionable qualities ascribed to the group' (Allport, [1958] 2000: 22).

As we noted earlier, Bogardus (1928) devised one useful way of measuring levels of prejudiced attitudes. He asked respondents whether they would be willing to accept members of various ethnic groups into close or more distant relationships. This measure of social distance shows that people experience varying comfort levels when interacting with members of other cultures in different circumstances. Responses on the social distance scale can range from a non-prejudiced score of 1 (willing to accept ethnic groups into close kinships by marriage) to a highly prejudiced score of 6 (willing to accept ethnic groups only as visitors). Generally, people who are willing to accept close or informal relations with members of a group are also willing to have more distant or formal relations with them.

As Gordon Allport ([1958] 2000) notes, people act out their prejudices with varying degrees of intensity. At the most benign level is **antilocution**, occurring when people share prejudiced beliefs only among like-minded friends. Prejudice that is more intense may show itself in the avoidance of a disliked group. Even stronger prejudice produces **discrimination**, which involves active attempts to dominate the minority. Discriminatory actions can involve the exclusion of the group in question from jobs, education, housing, and even political rights. Even more intense expressions of prejudice include hate crimes, acts of violence and destruction motivated by racial or ethnic prejudice that involve physical attacks—the desecration of religious buildings and graveyards, lynchings, mass executions.

Hate crimes are one of the most shocking signs of racism in society. The Department of Justice notes that Canada has consistently experienced a relatively low annual level of hate-motivated violence, averaging approximately 5.3 incidents per year, the majority of these incidents (96.9 per cent) occurring in Ontario, Quebec, and British Columbia, which, not coincidentally, are the provinces in which the largest proportion of minority group members and new immigrant populations lives (Gilmour, 1994).

These statistics likely underestimate the extent of the problem, since hate crimes have not been systematically collected and reported on a national Canadian scale. Moreover, hate crimes are often underreported by victims to the police; instead, the physical and psychological costs are often dealt with alone. The psychological costs to those victimized include fear, anger, and feelings of inferiority.

Researchers find that racial attitudes in Canada (and in North America generally) have become more tolerant in recent decades. However, although we have eliminated, or at least suppressed, many overt expressions of racism, subtle racial ambivalence persists among the majority of people (Gaertner and Dovidio, 2000; Reitz and Breton, 1999).

Some people are hard to classify because they hold contradictory views. For example, so-called **aversive racists** sympathize with the victims of past injustice; support public policies that, in principle, promote racial equality and reduce the harm of racism; identify more generally with a liberal political agenda; and view themselves as non-prejudiced and non-discriminatory. However, they still harbour negative feelings about the members of other races: 'The negative affect that aversive racists have for blacks is not hostility or hate. Instead, this negativity involves discomfort, uneasiness, disgust, and sometimes fear, which tend to motivate avoidance rather than intentionally destructive behaviours' (Gaertner and Dovidio, 2000: 289–90).

Canadians who have the greatest difficulty in accepting other races believe that race is a biological—and therefore immutable—fact. They see each 'race' as possessing unique physiological characteristics, based in genetic differences that are absent in the other races. Further, they are likely to believe that certain cultural or personality dispositions are genetically based as well. People taking this approach generally believe that there are at least three general categories of people in the present human species—Negroid ('black'), Caucasoid ('white'), and Mongoloid ('yellow')—from which all racial groups are derived. However, scientists increasingly reject this view of race in light of growing genetic evidence that shows that the human 'races' are more alike than they are different (Anderson, 1991). Further, research growing out of the Human Genome Project finds that groups belonging to different races are virtually identical on genetic grounds.

Race, then, should be understood not as an objective biological fact, but as a socially constructed idea about differences between groups. The job of the sociologist is to understand why people invent and preserve such exclusionary ideas as 'race' and endow them with such powerful, comprehensive, and emotion-laden ideas. Before examining the social problems that flow from false and dangerous ideas like race, let us first examine some basic facts about race and ethnicity.

BOX 4.2
Struggles of the Spirit

My grandfather used to lighten his skin with lemon juice, hoping he would pass for an Italian or a Greek. My grandmother never spoke her language, never attended a powwow or a sweat lodge. My mother has been spit on and called everything from a dirty squaw to a wagon burner. My brother and sisters have been taunted and jeered at. My youngest sister phoned a few weeks ago to say she had overheard white customers calling her 'an incompetent Indian'. The women avoided her checkout line.

Aboriginal peoples across the country have been subjected to cultural genocide through decades of government oppression and policies of assimilation, but native pride and traditions have never been completely stamped out.

Even when native languages and ceremonies were outlawed and sacred objects confiscated, when it was illegal for Indians to gather in significant numbers or leave their reserves, when Indian children were stolen from their families and put in residential schools or white foster homes to speed assimilation, there were always people keeping the flame of tradition alive—secretly passing on their knowledge to subsequent generations.

Sadly, their numbers were small compared with the vast majority who were stripped of their identities and taught to be ashamed of their Indian-ness. In Toronto, the city dubbed Canada's largest reservation because more Indian people live here than anywhere else in the country, there is no First Nation equivalent to Little Italy or Chinatown. There is no city politician championing aboriginal rights. Native-owned businesses are rare, and only a handful of aboriginal people can even be considered middle class.

Every year for the past 10 years, the Canadian Human Rights Commission has identified the plight of native people as a national tragedy. Mass unemployment, high suicide rates and inadequate housing were cited in a December report by the United Nations blasting Canada for the 'gross disparity' that continues to exist between aboriginal peoples and other Canadians.

SOURCE: Sara Jean Green, 'Struggles of the Spirit: Toronto's Aboriginal Community Finds a Connection to Traditional Culture Is a Talisman Against Despair', *Toronto Star*, 4 September 1999, B4, B5. Reprinted with permission Torstar Syndication Services.

Facts About Race and Ethnicity

Race

Some people believe that 'race' and 'ethnicity' are, if not the same, closely related: 'One race, one ethnicity—biologically Negroid, so therefore culturally African', for example. To be sure, a broad and generalized understanding of ethnicity has some value. Cultural differences undoubtedly exist between groups of people, sharpened by superficial differences in skin colour, height, facial structure, and other physical characteristics.

Differences in physical appearance are likely to make cultural differences seem more salient and meaningful.

Typically, the physical attributes supposedly shared solely by members of a 'race' are a result of collective evolutionary adaptation to specific environmental influences (for example, temperature, weather patterns, and geographic characteristics). However, race and ethnicity are not necessarily connected. People who look different may have the same cultural values. Conversely, people who look the same may think in vastly different ways.

Ethnicity

The cultural attributes people share as members of an ethnic group are usually the result of a collective history of experiences with a particular historical and regional background. Differences do exist between members of different ethnic groups, and there are good historical reasons for these differences. The divisive effects of ethnicity, however, result from the ways we interpret these differences.

The most valid way of defining *ethnic groups* is to see them as created by people through social interactions. We form ethnic groups relationally through processes of exclusion and inclusion around symbols of actual or perceived common descent, such as language, behavioural practices, and religion. For example, the internal criteria of group identification for people of English ethnicity in Canada have included white skin colour, English language, and Protestant or Catholic cultural traditions. Despite these criteria, however, people can join in the activities of an ethnic group by adopting its language, manners, and ideas. A person of Argentinian, Polish, or Australian descent can easily join the English ethnic group by speaking English in a particular way and by adopting local customs (ways of celebrating Christmas, preparing meals, raising children, and so on).

Social scientists used to define *culture* as an objective inventory of characteristics. Today, they understand it as a framework of values and practices that forms a context for people's lives that they adapt in changing historical and regional circumstances. Culture is not something constant or permanent. Most anthropologists would deny that there is a fixed pattern of 'Chineseness', for example, that is learned and enacted uniformly across generations and contexts by Chinese-looking people in Hong Kong, Malaysia, Trinidad, South Africa, and Vancouver. We cannot deduce people's ethnic group affiliations from their skin colour, language, religion, or other markers people use to place themselves and each other in groups.

Canadians should be familiar with such ideas by now. Of Canada's roughly 30 million citizens, over 11 per cent were classed as visible minorities in 1996, while another 3 per cent possessed an Aboriginal background (Statistics Canada, 2001). (See also Figure 4.1.) We often describe Canada as a *cultural mosaic*, reflecting the country's encouragement of difference and pluralistic cultural expression. In contrast, we often refer to the United States as a *melting pot*, since children there are raised to hold strong nationalistic beliefs and to identify themselves as Americans first and ethnic group members second.

Canada has been multicultural almost by necessity. It is a country of immigrants, with one of the highest rates of immigration in the world throughout the last century. In 1999, for example, Canada received 189,816 immigrants, including refugees (Citizenship and Immigration Canada, 2000). The vast majority settled in major metropolitan areas, with 44 per cent choosing to live in Toronto. That city contains many ethnic communities, including Little Italy, Little India, Little Jamaica, Little Portugal, Little Vietnam, Greektown, Koreatown, and at least three Chinatowns. This pattern of settlement has led the United Nations to call Toronto 'the most multicultural city in the world'. Vancouver and Montreal are other Canadian cities with large numbers of ethnic communities.

The Vertical Mosaic

Still, Canada has not always been as warm toward immigrants as one would imagine. Exclusion and devaluation of immigrant groups by majority groups has occurred repeatedly, with minority newcomers experiencing less access to better occupations and higher income. These facts led John Porter (1965) to describe Canadian society as a **vertical mosaic** in which English and French Canadians exist at the top of the hierarchy and other ethnic minorities are positioned below them on the economic ladder.

Porter traces this stratification to Canada's historical reliance on selective immigration as a means of satisfying specific labour-force needs during the process of industrialization. Gradually, as Canada industrialized, a reciprocal relationship between ethnicity and social class developed. Ethnic groups took particular roles in society and left the less preferred roles for other ethnic groups. With economic growth and immigration, the less preferred ethnic groups assumed an 'entrance status' and stayed in it. By **entrance status**, Porter meant lower-level occupation roles and subjection to processes of assimilation laid down and judged by the **charter groups**—specifically, the English and French Canadians.

Most of Canada's minority groups have at some time held this entrance status. Some, but not all, have moved out of it. Discrimination and a lack of educational opportunities sometimes made it difficult for the native-born children of ethnic minority immigrants to climb the economic ladder. This left a stable base of labourers upon which the dominant group could establish itself. 'Ethnic differences', Porter concludes, 'have been important in building up the bottom layer of the stratification system in both agricultural and industrial settings' (1965: 73). In this way, a low-paid reserve army of labour was always available.

The vertical mosaic persisted not only because of exclusionary practices by the dominant

FIGURE 4.1
Visible Minorities in the Total Population, Canada, 1996

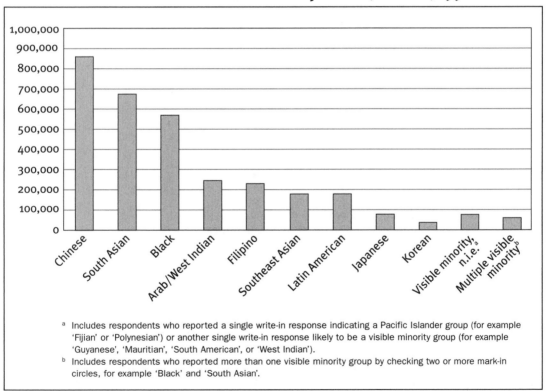

a Includes respondents who reported a single write-in response indicating a Pacific Islander group (for example 'Fijian' or 'Polynesian') or another single write-in response likely to be a visible minority group (for example 'Guyanese', 'Mauritian', 'South American', or 'West Indian').
b Includes respondents who reported more than one visible minority group by checking two or more mark-in circles, for example 'Black' and 'South Asian'.

SOURCE: Statistics Canada, 'Total Population by Visible Minority Population (1), for Canada, 1996 Census (20% Sample Data)', available at <www.statcan.ca/english/census96/feb17/vmcan.htm>, accessed 21 January 2003.

majority, but also because of migration and self-organization practices by the ethnic groups. The practice of *chain migration* maintained a link between Canada and the immigrants' countries of origin. The practice of *institutional completeness* maintained a link with the ancestral culture across generations. The practice of *diaspora* maintained a link with other comparable ethnic cultures around the world. Let us examine each of these briefly.

Chain Migration

The process of migration to Canada has been gradual for most ethnic groups. Some immigrants came to escape war, bad living conditions, or the infringement of human rights. Others came in hope of finding better jobs and education for their children. Typically, immigrants arrived, generation after generation, as part of a **chain migration** process that increased the likelihood that they would keep their ties to the homeland and their historic culture. Family members came, one or two at a time, established a home, got work, and sent for other family members, gradually creating a chain of linked migrations.

People generally migrate to nearby places they know about, usually through people they knew at home. Like many other social processes, migration relies on processes of information flow. The amount of migration between two countries is determined not only by distance and economic factors, as researchers originally thought, but also by the social networks of potential migrants. Social networks channel migrants into particular areas, and they link people to particular distant communities.

Institutional Completeness

Most chain migrants receive help from either relatives or co-villagers. With each arrival, the immigrant community becomes larger and more differentiated, containing a wider variety of communal institutions. As Raymond Breton has written (1964, 1978; Breton, Reitz, and Valentine, 1980), the communities gain in **institutional**

completeness: they build schools, churches, newspapers, lending societies, shops, and so on. In turn, the community's degree of completeness increases community solidarity and cohesion. It does this by increasing the number of members who carry out most of their activities within the ethnic group and retain ethnic culture and ethnic social ties. By retaining its ancestral language, religion, and culture, an immigrant community remains cohesive.

Because members of the host society view immigrants according to their ethnicity rather than their class, new immigrants are often forced to use their ethnic membership and assert their ethnic pride as a matter of economic and cultural survival. People who attempt to assimilate socially may find themselves marginalized—that is, members of neither the ethnic community nor the host culture. This is a particular problem for the children of immigrants, as sociologists W.I. Thomas and Florien Znaniecki ([1919] 1971) first pointed out in their classic work *The Polish Peasant in Europe and America*. Often, intergenerational value conflicts arise in immigrant families. Immigrants' grandchildren find themselves fully accepted into the society; immigrants' children—their parents— are only partly accepted; and the immigrants themselves, often limited in education, language skills, and social capital, are least accepted of all. Members of the same extended family have very different experiences of the same society.

Diasporas

Viewed from within our own society, immigrant groups are either included or excluded. Viewed internationally, immigrant groups such as the Arabs of Montreal or the Sikhs of Edmonton are often the members of a much larger community: the global Arab or Sikh community to which they belong.

Today, we use **diaspora** to mean the global spread of migrants and spread of cultures by means of these migrants. Until recently, the word was used only to describe the Jews outside of

---

BOX 4.3
Parents' Groups

Chinese-only parent groups have been formed in several B.C. school districts, sparking a debate about whether they will slow the process of assimilation or speed it up.

In Richmond, where a rush of Asian immigrants has boosted the English-as-a-second-language student population to 40 per cent of the total, a Chinese-only parents' group has raised the ire of Karen McNulty, chair of the Richmond District Parents' Association.

'It's ridiculous', she says of the existence of the Richmond Chinese Parents' Association, which formed two years ago and now has 50 members. 'They are parents, just as we are parents in the system. They should be represented in the same way as other parents are represented.'

Cham-Wah Yuen, chair of the Richmond Chinese parents' group, says 'Sometimes there is a language problem and parents may not be fully able to communicate their concerns to the appropriate authority.'

Philip Yung, who heads a similar Chinese parents' association in Vancouver, says: 'I made it very clear to the school trustees that the Chinese parents' association in Vancouver was actually a helping arm for them, and we haven't had the same kind of reaction as there has been in Richmond.'

'It should be the trustees' responsibility to be inclusive of all parents, but in reality, they have not been able to translate materials or even communicate with a lot of the Chinese parents in their own language.'

Mary Kambas, chair of the Vancouver district parent representatives, says she's neither surprised nor offended by immigrant parents forming splinter groups.

'When you don't speak English as a first language, you tend to think of saying something in your native tongue and then translating it. A lot of people don't feel comfortable with that delay.'

'I would never say my game is the only game in town. I'm thrilled that they're interested enough to find a way they can contribute to their children's education.'

SOURCE: Susan Balcom, 'Chinese-Only Parent Groups Stir Debate in Schools', *Vancouver Sun*, 1 December 1994, B1. Reprinted by permission of Pacific Newspaper Group Inc.

Palestine or Israel. Now it is used to describe the global dispersion of any historically victimized minority (for example, Gypsies or Armenians, or blacks in the Americas) or visible and potentially victimized minorities (for example, Arabs in Africa, Sikhs in the West Indies, and Chinese people in Indonesia). Almost any migrant community—especially a community made up mainly of refugees, deportees, or former slaves—is now referred to as 'diasporic'.

Traditionally, sociologists viewed immigration and ethnicity in terms of social disorganization. They assumed that immigrants suffered from the breakdown of their traditional culture and social organization in the adopted homeland. As we said earlier, breakdowns of traditional family authority led to intergenerational conflict in many communities. At the same time, however, immigrant groups in North America have usually organized themselves effectively for a new life in a new country. Often, immigrants have managed to both maintain a foothold in their homeland of origin and exercise influence over their new homeland.

The diasporic Jews illustrate this combination: a mixture of strong connections with their European, Asian, and African origin countries,

Kensington Market in downtown Toronto has changed over the years. Jamaican, Chinese, Portuguese, Mexican, Arab, and Jewish/Eastern European stores now line the streets that were once almost entirely Jewish. (Dick Hemingway)

with Israel—the historic 'homeland' of Jewry in Zionist thinking—and yet strong assimilation into all of the countries in which they are resident, especially Canada and the United States. Many Jewish families have links to other Jewish communities in South Africa, South America, and Europe as well as in North America as a result of migration over generations.

The diasporic Chinese illustrate another, different pattern. The Chinese in Canada originally did heavy labour, helping to build the railways. Unlike the African migration, overseas Chinese migration was mainly voluntary and took place in three stages: migration from inland China to coastal areas in ancient times, migration to Southeast Asian regions in more modern times, and migration to places all over the world after World War II. Despite a continuing identification

with Chinese culture in many diasporic communities, few but the most recent immigrants express a desire to return to China, Hong Kong, or Taiwan. However, like the Jews, the diasporic Chinese are likely to have family connections in many cities throughout the world.

In short, members of major diasporic groups are simultaneously members of the countries in which they live, which is often where they were born and grew up, and members of an international ethnic network that may span dozens of communities throughout the world. The resulting pattern, **transnationalism** among immigrant peoples, reflects the twentieth-century revolutions in communication and travel, the global expansion of human rights, and the maintenance of social networks that ease transnational migration patterns. Today, to think meaningfully about race and ethnic relations, we can begin with the nation-state, but we must eventually think about the world as a whole.

Theories of Race and Ethnic Relations

The Structural-Functionalist Perspective

As you will recall, the core of the structural-functionalist perspective is that universal, long-lasting social forms fulfill a social purpose and that the job of the sociologist is to understand this purpose. According to functionalists, even inequality between groups has a functional purpose. As we noted in chapter 1, they emphasize that social inequality provides incentives in the form of status and material rewards that prompt people to take on the most important social roles. Also, functionalists see exclusion, prejudice, and discrimination as providing functions for in-groups in particular. These practices, of course, can have hurtful, even devastating, consequences for **out-groups**.

Functionalists point out the value of maintaining distinct ethnic identities in a pluralistic society such as Canada for the purposes of socially integrating members of the groups. Ethnic identity provides roots and social connectedness in an otherwise individualistic, fragmented society. Many people value their ethnic heritage as part of their identity. It serves them as a link both to a rich cultural past and to current members of their ethnic group. Although the complete dissolution of ethnic boundaries might reduce inter-group conflict, it would also mean the end of an ethnic basis for group identity and cohesion. As well, racial diversity benefits society as a whole, functionalists argue, since it allows for the discussion of a wider range of opinions, perspectives, and values and for the development of a wider range of skills than might be available in a uni-ethnic society.

Even social conflict has value (see, for example, Coser, 1965). By drawing and enforcing boundaries, conflict intensifies people's sense of identity and belonging and gives groups more cohesion and sense of purpose. As we saw from our discussion of cliques, differentiation and conflict are as natural as cooperation; they are with us from childhood on. They allow us to simplify the universe, parcelling out reality into 'good guys' and 'bad guys' for easier understanding. Thus, cognitively, socially, psychologically, and culturally, ethnic and racial differentiation—even conflict—fulfill a social purpose.

Conflict Theory

Conflict theorists, unlike functionalists, do not focus on the social functions of conflict. Instead, they focus on how one group benefits more than another from differentiation, exclusion, and institutional racism. Ethnic discrimination most benefits those doing the discriminating at the expense of those being discriminated against.

To explain why such prejudice occurs in the first place, conflict theorists focus on social-structural explanations. They explore, for instance, how economic competition results in the creation and upholding of racial stereotypes and institutionalized racism. Conflict theory proposes that majority groups seek to dominate minorities because this is rewarding or makes them feel superior, or because the minority threatens the majority's economic superiority.

So, for example, as we mentioned earlier in this chapter, Chinese workers were brought over to Canada in the nineteenth century to be used as cheap labourers in constructing the nation's railroads. Once the transportation network was built, however, a surplus of Asian workers—initially recognized and admired for their hard work and discipline—came to be seen as a threat to the economic stability of the dominant white majority. A head tax was put into place in the hope of stemming further immigrant flow. A stereotype of the Chinese as corrupt and base opium fiends was popularized to discourage and marginalize the Chinese already present.

Conflict theorists also assert that corporate leaders construct and perpetuate racial stereotypes to increase personal profits. First, discrimination against a minority ensures that the oppressed group remains unemployed or underemployed. This surplus labour force, in turn, keeps wages low, production costs down, and worker unrest at a minimum. Discontented labourers who demand higher wages and more benefits can easily be replaced with workers more willing to accept existing working conditions. Second, racial tension diverts and divides workers, setting up competition along racial and ethnic lines. This division of the working class hinders collective mobilization and reduces the bargaining power that comes from shouting in a single voice. As long as labourers fight with one another, their anger is diverted from the exploitative capitalist elite, who continue to profit excessively from their work.

Symbolic Interactionism

Symbolic interactionists focus on microsociological aspects of race and discrimination, such as how people construct ethnic differentiation and how racial labels help to subordinate minority groups.

'Nigger', 'dago', 'wop', 'chink', 'kike', 'jap', 'gook', 'spic'—these are but a few of the numerous racial slurs and terms passed around in society. Sometimes they are used in a hateful manner, uttered specifically to hurt. Often they are tossed out casually within a group of friends to add emphasis in a racist joke or as a playful insult. However, these terms call attention to the continued inferior status in society of the minority groups in question. Not only are such slurs hurtful, they can also create a self-fulfilling prophecy. If people come to believe the slurs against their group—thinking that they themselves really are stupid, lazy, cheap, underhanded, and so on—they may come to behave as though the beliefs are true. They may come to hate themselves, reject their own group, or give in to impulses to fulfill others' worst expectations.

Interactionists study the origins and consequences of such labelling processes. They also point to racial socialization as another factor that contributes to the ongoing racial conflicts in society. **Racial socialization** is the process of social interaction that exposes people to their own and other people's racial or ethnic identity: to beliefs, values, cultural history, language, and social and economic implications of membership in different racial groups. A constant awareness of race in

---

BOX 4.4
Race in the News

Toronto newspaper coverage of the 1994 Just Desserts shooting went far beyond the death of Georgina 'Vivi' Leimonis, an innocent white woman whose alleged killers are black and of Jamaican descent. The coverage led to public discussions that linked social problems to race, according to The Racialization of Crime in Toronto's Print Media, a study released yesterday by Ryerson Polytechnic University. 'More than half of all the articles written about the Just Desserts shooting linked the case to wider social problems and each stage represents a

step in the racialization of the crime by the media', said Dr Frances Henry, chair of diversity at Ryerson.

After the shooting, newspaper reports were cited by politicians in Ottawa to make changes to the Immigration Act, which made it easier to deport landed immigrants with criminal records, Dr Henry said. Of the 355 deportation cases between 1996 and 1998, 39% were exiled to Jamaica, the study said. The study analyzed nearly 6,000 articles published between 1994 and 1997 by the Toronto Star,

continued

The Globe and Mail and the Toronto Sun. (The National Post was not included because it only started publishing last October.)

'We're trying to open up debate between researchers, journalism schools and practising journalists [by saying], 'Here are some of the things you do that inadvertently marginalizes people', said Dr Henry. Stepping outside the Just Desserts case, the study also looked at how the Jamaican and Vietnamese communities were portrayed in newspapers in general, said Dr Henry. When you monitor media fairly carefully, you see that almost all the stories about Vietnamese either had to do with crime or with restaurants', she said.

Of the 2,622 articles that mentioned Jamaicans, 45% of them fell into the categories of sports and entertainment. Social issues such as crime/justice, immigration and deportation made up 39% of the coverage on Jamaicans and of those only 2% of the stories were positive, the report said. The study showed The Globe and Mail used racial or ethnic identifiers involving blacks or persons of Caribbean heritage in 46% of crime articles. In The Toronto Star it was 38.5% and in the Toronto Sun 25.6%. Dr Henry said that journalists rely too heavily on police reports that use racial descriptors. In the descriptions of accused criminals, blacks are mentioned twice as often as whites in news stories, she said.

Dr Henry also stated newsrooms in Toronto should reflect the ethnic makeup of the population. A 1994 survey of 41 newspapers by the Canadian Daily Newspaper Association showed that only 67 of 2,620 of newsroom employees—just 2.6%—were visible minorities. In five years, the numbers haven't changed much and can be traced back to the few visible minorities enrolled in journalism schools across the country. John Miller, professor at Ryerson's School of Journalism, says journalism schools have to work harder to attract visible minorities. 'In my diversity class, there wasn't much diversity', he said.

SOURCE: Desmond Brown, 'News Coverage of Minorities a Crime: Study', *National Post*, Toronto edition, 31 August 1999, B3.

daily social interaction increases the likelihood of racial conflict. Whenever there is a conflict between people of different races or ethnicities—particularly where there is a troubled and volatile history (such as between blacks and whites in the United States, or Aboriginal people and whites in Canada)—the question of race and racism is never far from people's minds.

Racial identification still surrounds us. Today, for example, North American newspapers still characterize Asians as perpetrators and victims of crimes, as segregated in distinct neighbourhoods, as imposing a tax burden on white Americans, and as overpopulating the United States (Kim, 1997). Symbolic interactionists are interested in how and why such imagery survives.

Why, for example, are Chinese people depicted in that way, but not Jews or Norwegians?

Structural Theory

Another perspective, structural theory, helps us understand the experiences of racial and ethnic minorities in job markets. What happens to minorities, and particularly to immigrants, is as much a result of the nature of job markets as it is a result of the attitudes and behaviours of the host society or the majority culture. Generally, people who are most similar—racially, culturally, and educationally—to members of the host society will enjoy the easiest, most rapid assimilation into the labour market. They will be able to compete more successfully for the better jobs, and get them faster. This will be particularly true in times of economic growth. In recessionary times, everyone's assimilation will be slower and more conflictual. People's experiences will reflect the characteristics of the economy more than anything they do or believe.

The sorting of people into jobs in Canada usually begins in schools. By means of subtle and complex procedures, grade weighting belittles the achievements of lower-track students, reducing their postgraduate opportunities. In college, the sorting of students into different programs with different curricula also influences later opportunities by sending prospective employers different messages about the abilities of job candidates. Different schools have different kinds of linkages with employers. Such institutional linkages are valuable to employers and employees alike. However, some people, and some groups, are more likely to benefit from these linkages than others.

Once out of school and in the economy, people are streamed into certain types of jobs and away from others. For example, far more women and visible minorities are streamed into the secondary labour market, and far more white men into the primary labour market, than could have occurred by chance. However, there are differences among jobs even within these markets. The big difference between primary and secondary markets tends to blur important differences among jobs within the same market. For example, though both teachers and doctors are in the primary labour market, few teachers feel they have the sort of benefits and opportunities that doctors do.

Job markets will sometimes exclude people on the grounds of race, ethnicity, or gender. Think of the process of job-based racial inequality (or race-based employment) as a hiring queue in which racial minorities usually occupy the lower positions among workers ranked according to their desirability to employers. This is what Porter meant by 'entrance status'.

Throughout the United States, the larger the number of black men in the workforce, the higher the wages for whites (male and female) and black women. In Canada, new immigrants have held a similar position in the labour market, occupying the lowest entrance statuses. Even when they earn good wages, they earn relatively less than native-born Canadians with equivalent education and experience (see Figure 4.2).

Sometimes more educated, higher-status workers—for example, young, educated white people—work in *stop-gap* jobs. These are jobs that will not form part of their occupational life cycle or career. Taking such jobs places less educated youth, minority and white, at a competitive disadvantage (Oppenheimer and Kalmijn, 1995).

The continuing availability of new ethnic immigrants to fill the lowest-paying jobs has made race and ethnicity the crucial mechanism for ordering groups of people into distinct sets of jobs. There is a general bias against hiring nonwhites. That is why many immigrants—especially visible minorities—become 'middlemen'. Important middleman minorities around the world include the Chinese in Southeast Asia, the Jews, Greeks, and Armenians in Europe, the East Indians and Arabs in East Africa, and the Koreans in North America. All of these groups display a high degree of ethnic cohesion, and their members tend to achieve more than usual economic success in societies where they have been, at least at first, unwelcome. Typically, these are also diasporic peoples with connections in many different communities.

Research on middleman minorities finds that the following historical pattern is typical: a culturally or racially distinct group immigrates and suffers discrimination. Members of the group come to see themselves as 'strangers' in the country and, to protect themselves, settle in the larger towns and cities. There, they become self-employed as merchants or professionals. As a result, they come into competition with local capitalists of the dominant ethnic group. Their economic success depends on thrift, a high degree of education and organization,

FIGURE 4.2
Mean and Median Employment Income by Immigration Status, 1996

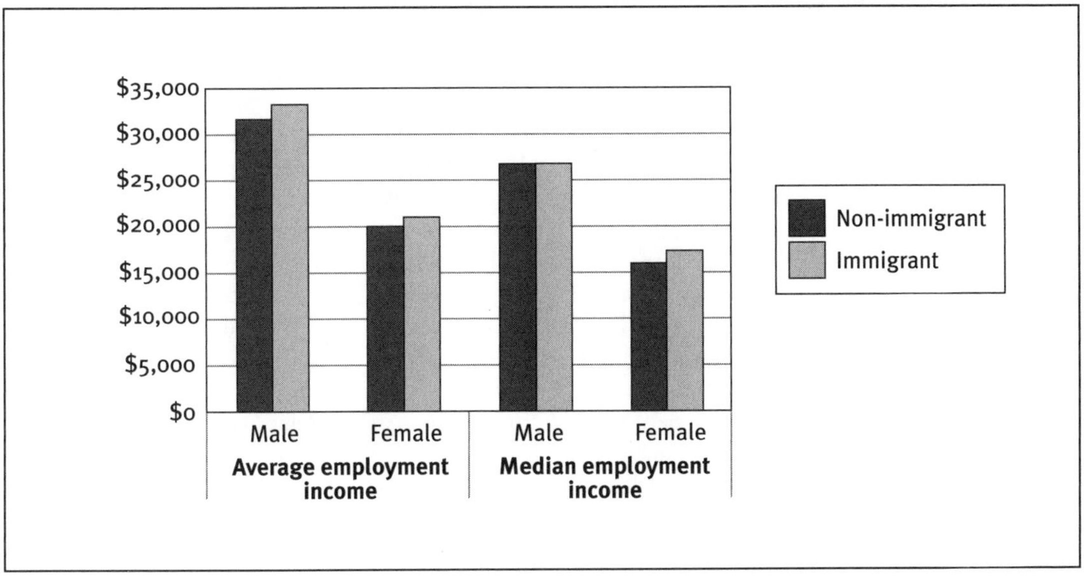

SOURCE: Statistics Canada, 1996 census data, cat. no. 94F0009xDB96066.

and the use of family and community ties in business. By these means the group achieves a middle-class standard of living.

Given the value of such self-protective behaviour, both for the minority group and (through innovation) for society as a whole, one might wonder why all minority groups do not become middleman minorities. The answer is that some—for example, Northern and Eastern European immigrant groups—lack visible distinctiveness and are less subject to discrimination. Others—for example black or Aboriginal Canadians—are both visibly distinct and socially vulnerable but may lack enough members or group assets to found a self-reliant community. Further, intra-community conflicts (for example, between American blacks and West Indian blacks) may limit cooperation.

Using the structuralist approach, the task of the sociologist is to understand the latent or hidden rules of the job market, and to understand what factors govern the development of the job market. This approach is similar to the conflict approach, but it has a specific focus on how the labour market is organized and it makes fewer assumptions about the role of ideologies, classes, and class relations.

Social Consequences of Race and Ethnic Relations

Gender

The interaction of gender and racism leads to unique problems for women of some minority groups. Women continue to be consigned to a lesser status in almost all immigrant groups. However, women in some cultures face a higher degree of oppression than in others. Not only is this oppression a problem in itself, but it also creates further conflict when new immigrants find their notions of proper gender relations clashing with the more progressive gender concepts in North America.

In some groups in which men dominate, for example, women are more exposed to health risks such as HIV/AIDS. The failure of current preventive programs that target Latinas is underscored by a continued rise of HIV infection in that population. Merely teaching sexual assertiveness is not enough. The spread of HIV is driven by a subcultural dynamic that limits a Latina's ability to demand safer (that is, contraceptive) sex from her partner (Gil, 1998–9).

Having to deal with unconcealed racism in the workplace and in society on a daily basis is hard enough. Having to deal with the constant sexism of a patriarchal social structure may be too hard an obstacle for many ethnic minority women to overcome. In particular, new immigrant women who belong to paternalistic cultures may find themselves isolated socially and linguistically at the same time as they are economically dependent on their husbands. These issues will be further detailed in the next chapter, on gender and sexism.

Work and Unemployment

As we have already noted, discrimination in the workplace is often directed along racial and ethnic lines (see Figures 4.3 and 4.4). Aboriginal people, members of visible minority groups, and recent immigrants to Canada all experience lower employment and pay rates in almost every region of Canada. Aboriginal people in Canada are less likely than other Canadians to attend college or to finish a college degree (Johnson and Boehm, 1995). Differences in income between various immigrant and ethnic minorities also result from differences in human capital, such as education, experience, credentials, and scarce expertise (Rodlandt, 1996).

According to the Canadian Council on Social Development (CCSD, 2000), visible minorities continue to fall behind in employment and income levels despite their high educational attainment when compared to non-racialized groups. Foreign-born visible minorities experience even greater discrepancies between their education levels and their occupations than do other groups. Less than half of foreign-born visible minorities with a university degree work in jobs with a high skill level, particularly during difficult economic times. Since the passage of the Employment Equity Act (1989 through 1993), the minority wage gap has decreased most rapidly for women but has widened for visible minorities and Aboriginal people (Leck, St. Onge, and Lalancette, 1995).

Many recent immigrants find that their educational and work credentials are not recognized in the Canadian employment system. They are forced into jobs that are below their level of training and expertise. Reitz (1998) shows that four institutions affect the entry-level job status of immigrants: (1) the specificity of skills required by the nation's immigration policy, (2) the educational competition experienced between immigrants and the native-born, (3) the labour market structure, and (4) the welfare state.

Race continues to play a role in people's work experiences. As one survey participant mentioned in an interview conducted by the CCSD,

> I've called about jobs and had people say 'come down for an interview', yet when I get there, I get the feeling they are surprised to see that I'm black because I sound like the average guy on the telephone. They've said 'Oh, the job has just been filled', or during the interview they'll say that I'm overqualified or ask me questions like 'Are you sure you want to work at this type of job?' (2000)

Frances Henry (1999; Henry and Ginzberg, 1985) graphically showed such processes in operation in Toronto. In field experiments, she sent two job applicants, matched with respect to age, sex, education, experience, style of dress, and personality, to apply for the same advertised job. The applicants differed in only one respect: race—one was white and the other black. Teams

FIGURE 4.3

Proportion in Occupational Category Who Belong to a Visible Minority, Canada, 1996

SOURCE: Statistics Canada, <www.statcan.ca/english/ads/11-008-XIE/vismin.html>, accessed 23 March 2003.

of applicants sought a total of 201 jobs in all in this way. Some applicants were young male or female students applying for semi-skilled or unskilled jobs—waitress, gas station attendant, busboy, or store clerk—that people might expect them to seek. Other applicants were middle-aged professional actors. Armed with fake résumés, they applied for positions in retail management, sales jobs in prestigious stores, and serving and hosting jobs in fancy restaurants.

In a second set of experiments, researchers called 237 telephone numbers published in the classified job section of the newspaper and presented themselves as applicants. The jobs they were seeking ranged widely from unskilled to highly skilled, well-paying jobs. Frances Henry and Effie Ginzberg (1985) report that callers phoned each number four times, using different voices. One voice had no discernible accent (it sounded like a white-majority Canadian), the

FIGURE 4.4
Number of Canadians by Income Level, Visible Minority Status and Sex

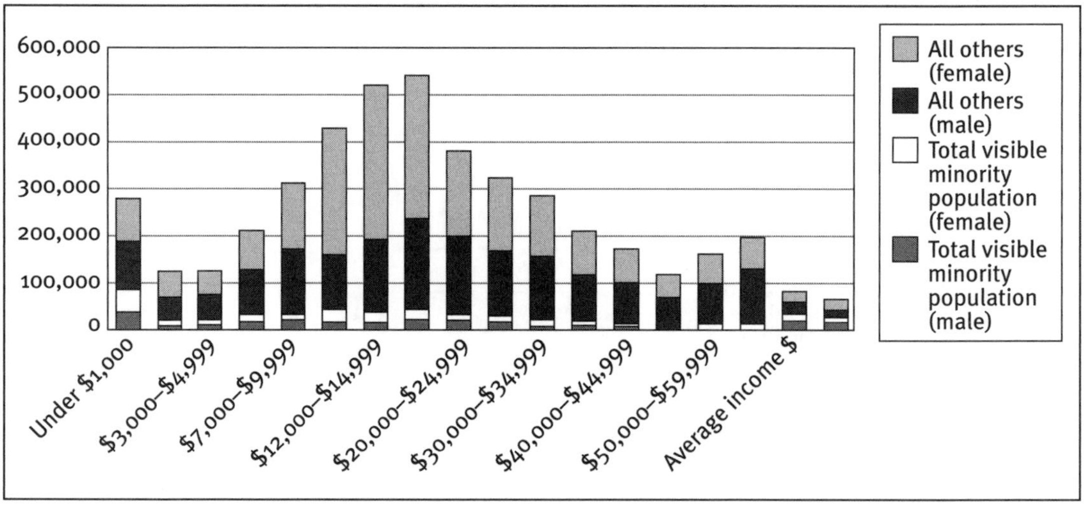

SOURCE: Statistics Canada, Census of Canada, 1996: Dimensions Series; cat. no. 94F0009XDB96095.

second had a Slavic or Italian accent, the third had a Jamaican accent, and the fourth had a Pakistani accent. Men who did the calling (no women took part in this study) presented themselves as having the same characteristics: the same age, education, years of job experience, and so on. As before, the applicants were suited in age and (imaginary) experience for the jobs they were seeking.

With data collected in this way, the researchers created an Index of Discrimination that combined the results of in-person and telephone testing. They found that in 20 calls, black applicants would be offered 13 interviews yielding 1 job. By contrast, in 20 calls, white applicants would be offered 17 interviews yielding 3 jobs. 'The overall Index of Discrimination is therefore three to one. Whites have three job prospects to every one that blacks have' (Henry and Ginzberg, 1985: 308).

This study and others like it prove that racial discrimination is not the result of the behaviour of a very few bigoted employers. Also, even after members of minority groups find suitable employment, they are sometimes faced with discrimination when competing for promotions. Compared to non-visible minorities, members of visible racial groups and Aboriginal people with a university degree are less likely to enter managerial or professional positions. For those who do, more than half are self-employed, compared to only one-third in non-minority groups.

Poverty and Wealth

Although the largest number of people living in poverty in Canada and the United States are white, the proportion of black, Latino, and Asian populations that is impoverished are greater in both countries. As discussed in chapter 1, immigrants and visible minorities are overrepresented in low-income groups, earning thousands of dollars below the average income. In Canada, Aboriginal people and foreign-born visible minorities are overrepresented at the bottom of the income scale, while other Canadian-born non-racialized groups are underrepresented (compare Gee and Prus, 2000; Hou and

Balakrishnan, 1996). Among the top 20 per cent of income earners, the positions are reversed: Aboriginal people and visible minorities are underrepresented, and non-visible (ethnic) minorities are overrepresented. It has been estimated that foreign-born visible minorities aged 35 to 44 earned only 79 cents for every dollar that a Canadian-born white individual earned. Similarly, the wealthy are disproportionately members of non-visible minorities.

Unlike Third World nations, Fourth World communities—indigenous peoples residing in developed nations—cannot separate from imperial power because of their location within the boundaries of the imperialist nation. Therefore, indigenous people must either obtain equal access to the political and economic opportunities of the democratic society or continue to struggle for political autonomy (Russell, 1996). As in many Third World societies, income disparity has increased and polarized among Aboriginal people in recent years, compared to the non-Aboriginal population. In terms of intra-Aboriginal inequality, Aboriginal groups rank from Inuit at the high end through Status Indians to non-Status Indians and, finally, to Métis (Maxim et al., 2001).

Crime and Violence

As we saw in the previous chapter, blacks and Aboriginal people are overrepresented in the criminal justice system, as both perpetrators and victims. A look at prison populations reveals racial discrepancies in the criminal justice system. In Canada, attention has been paid in the last several decades to the excessive numbers of Aboriginal people and blacks arrested and convicted of violations of the law. Explanations of this include unemployment, poverty, and substance abuse. There is also evidence of discrimination at the bail and sentencing stages (Roberts and Doob, 1997). Further, law enforcement officers tend to racialize, typify, and stereotype ethnic minorities, particularly when dealing with street gangs (Symons, 1999).

Although Aboriginal adults constitute only 2 per cent of the Canadian population, they represented 15 per cent of those sentenced to provincial custody and 17 per cent of those sent to federal penitentiaries in 1997/98 (Reed and Roberts, 1999; see also Frideres and Robertson, 1994). (See also Figure 4.5). In the United States, although blacks account for only 13 per cent of the population, they represent 30 per cent of

FIGURE 4.5
Federal Offender Population, Aboriginal and Non-Aboriginal, Percentages, 1999

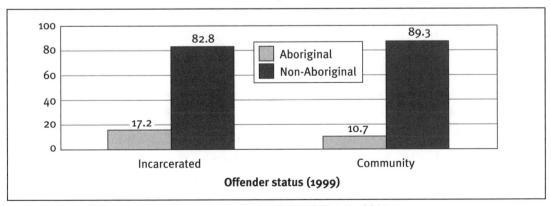

SOURCE: Solicitor General of Canada, <www.sgc.gc.ca/epub/Corr/eStatsNov99.htm>.

those arrested and approximately half of those incarcerated in a state or federal penitentiary. Aboriginal rates of violent victimization are higher than those for non-Aboriginal people because of their disadvantaged status (Weinrath, 1999). A study carried out in Australia, on Aborigine deaths in custody, likewise concludes that unemployment, poverty, poor health, homelessness, and disenfranchisement are the causes of overrepresentation at all stages of the criminal process (Broadhurst, 1996).

In short, disadvantage and poverty increase the likelihood of law-breaking by racial and ethnic minorities, while prejudice and discrimination increase the likelihood of arrest, conviction, and imprisonment.

Other Problems

Nowhere in North America are the problems resulting from exclusion, discrimination, and prejudice more evident than among the Aboriginal peoples. Severe socio-economic distress experienced by many Aboriginal families has led to serious social problems among adolescents, including substance abuse, school dropout, psychological problems, and violence (Beauvais, 2000).

Substance abuse is a significant problem among Canada's Aboriginal people. Gasoline is the most common inhalant used, often accompanied by alcohol and drug abuse (Coleman, Charles, and Collins, 2001). Similar problems are found among the indigenous peoples of the North in the former Soviet Union; even under Soviet rule, poverty, unemployment, and health problems, including alcoholism, suicide, high infant mortality, and shortened life expectancy were common (Ruttkay-Miklián, 2001).

Homeless Aboriginal people are all too common. They come from a variety of locales and are varied in their ages and genders. They are sometimes victims of discrimination in the housing market and may feel culturally isolated from mainstream services for the homeless. Additionally, they may have some distinctive special needs, such as traditional healing techniques (Klos, 1997).

One analyst characterizes this as the *historical trauma response*—a constellation of characteristics associated with massive cumulative group trauma across generations, similar to those found among Jewish Holocaust survivors and their descendants. Trauma response features include elevated mortality rates and health problems emanating from heart disease, hypertension, alcohol abuse, and suicidal behaviour. An analysis of the Lakota (Teton Sioux) finds evidence of men reporting more lifespan trauma over the life course (Brave Heart, 1999).

Health Consequences

The examples just discussed are only a very few illustrations of the health consequences of minority ethnic and racial status. Unfortunately, there are many others as well. We turn to some further details in this section.

Effects of Disadvantage

Disadvantaged groups lead different lives from the rest of the population. So, for example, among Asian Americans, longer life is associated with fewer years lived in poor health. By contrast, Native Americans' relatively longer lives are accompanied by extended periods of chronic health problems. Of all racial groups, American blacks live the fewest years, and they live a higher proportion of those years with a chronic health problem (Hayward and Heron, 1999). In Canada, though regional inequalities in health status are diminishing, the life expectancy of Aboriginal Canadians is still substantially shorter than that of other groups (D'Arcy, 1998; see also Waldram, Herring, and Young, 1996).

Studies of race and ethnicity as determinants of health have led to three different types of explanations: biological explanations that attribute differences in disease prevalence to gene-pool differences; cultural explanations that link cultural factors (such as diet) with disease susceptibility; and socio-economic explanations that focus on the association between minority status, economic disadvantage, and poor health (Spencer, 1996). Many differences in health between ethnic minorities are correlated with socio-economic differences; thus, the link between poor health and material advantage is clear (Farmer and Ferraro, 1999; Fenton, Hughes, and Hine, 1995). Accordingly, racial and ethnic differences in physical and mental health diminish significantly when we control for education and other factors related to income (Williams et al., 1997).

The current mortality conditions of Canadian Aboriginal people, American Indians, and New Zealand Maori reflect, in varying degrees, all of the problems associated with poverty, marginalization, and social disorganization. Of these three minority groups, Canadian Aboriginal people seem to suffer most from these types of conditions and the Maori the least (Trovato, 2001). In varying degrees, we see the same factors influencing the health of other Canadian minority groups.

Effects of Immigration

Institutional racism creates economic hardships with adverse health consequences. Chiefly, racial and ethnic discrimination in the workplace forces many visible minority members into low-paying jobs, unemployment, and poverty. Poverty and inequality both have health consequences, as we saw in chapter 1. Though Canadian research has found that neither the health status of immigrants nor their utilization rates of health services differ significantly from those of the Canadian-born population (Laroche, 2000), immigration can have harmful health effects over and above the effects of poverty and discrimination.

Immigrants often find employment in manual labour or unskilled work, as we noted earlier. In low-paying jobs, they are likely to be exposed to higher than average health risks. Second, immigrants often experience a lack of access to health care information and services. Sometimes they hesitate to use health services because of low levels of English-language literacy (for example, an elderly immigrant who does not speak English finds it difficult to communicate with English-speaking doctors).

Problems with their personal lives may also have health consequences for immigrants. For example, 80 per cent of refugees to Quebec from Africa and Latin America had experienced or were experiencing separations (averaging three years) from their partners and/or children (Moreau, Rousseau, and Berrada, 1999). Such separations, often associated with traumatic events, can lead to psychological distress and impede the process of adaptation to a new country. Additionally, immigrants may suffer from post-migration anxieties about discrimination, loneliness, and boredom. Asylum seekers may also suffer from pre-migration trauma, immigration difficulties, and racial discrimination, which give rise to post-traumatic stress disorder (Allotey, 1998; Silove et al., 1997). People who have been displaced by war are similar in some ways to people who are impoverished. However, they suffer over and above their material disadvantage. The individual and collective trauma of displacement often results in fear, disorientation, and distrust that are not easily alleviated (Segura Escobar, 2000).

Cultural Variations in Health

Cultural factors also influence group differences in health. Dietary and exercise habits and alcohol and cigarette use vary between ethnic groups. Groups vary in their exposure to health risk behaviours such as heavy drinking and smoking (Lee, Markides, and Ray, 1997). Bad eating patterns that result in obesity also vary from one group to another and cause health problems among minority groups (Arfken and Houston, 1996). For example, in Canada we often hear about the desirability of thinness, of watching

intake of fat, starches, and junk food, and of minimizing disease risk. However, Filipino immigrant
beliefs tend to value fatness, eating lots of fat and
rice, and maximizing disease resistance (Farrales
and Chapman, 1999). These health behaviours
are affected by a variety of other influences
besides ethnic culture (Rogers, Adamson, and
McCarthy, 1997). For whatever reason (probably
media influences in part), Canadians are eating
more and more junk food over time.

Some groups lack knowledge about different
diseases and how they might be prevented. In a
study of Cambodian American and Vietnamese
American women, more knowledge about cancer
and the identification of preventive measures were
associated with employment outside the home,
more years of education, and age, though not with
length of time in the United States (Phipps et al.,
1999). Groups also vary in their knowledge about
sex. Latino and African American magazines contain little information about sexual and reproductive health; least mentioned are abortion and
sexually transmitted diseases, including HIV/AIDS,
despite rates of pregnancy and HIV/AIDS that are
much higher than for Anglo-Americans (Johnson,
Gotthofer, and Lauffer, 1999).

After controlling for socio-economic and
demographic factors, some ethnic groups make
more use of medical and hospital services than
other groups (Cooper, Smaje, and Arber, 1999).
For example, South Asian children make more
use of GP services than any other ethnic group.
Asian Islamic women make less use of breast
cancer screening services. Socio-cultural barriers
include patient-physician communication and
beliefs about cancer and cancer prevention,
modesty considerations, and patriarchal marital
beliefs (Rajaram and Rashidi, 1999).

Access to Health Care

Immigrants and ethnic minorities often experience difficulties in accessing the health care system. A survey of Seattle, Washington, area
residents found that 20 per cent of all adult

respondents believe they have experienced some
form of racial or ethnic discrimination in the
health care system. One-sixth of the African
American interviewees and nearly 10 per cent of
all people of colour reportedly experienced discrimination in a medical care setting sometime
within the past year ('Study Reveals Disturbing
Trends in Care of Minorities', 2000). Another
study found that 40 per cent of all black respondents who felt they were discriminated against
by the medical establishment believed it was
because of their race, while white respondents
were more likely to believe that discrimination
was based on income level.

Racist attitudes have direct impact on the
availability and quality of the medical care
received by minorities. The behaviour and attitudes of white clinicians toward black patients
can lead to differences by race in treatment and
outcomes, despite lower levels of self-reported
prejudice among individuals (Whaley, 1998).
Racist attitudes also play a big role in the making
of public policies. Discriminatory legislation can
further worsen the physical and mental health of
ethnic minorities.

In some instances, stigmatized groups (such
as Haitians) are denied access to medical knowledge, testing, and treatment that could save their
lives (for example, from HIV/AIDS; on this, see
St. Jean, 1996). Haitians continue to suffer from
racist stereotypes that they embrace voodoo religion, and this increases their likelihood of acquiring and spreading serious diseases (Dubois,
1996). In a British study of psychiatric-service
users, ethnicity proved to be the most significant
factor in access to proper care, with Asians facing
impediments to primary health care after consultation and blacks receiving comparatively poor
levels of case recognition (Commander et al.,
1997). After an incident of discrimination occurs,
the victim is less likely to seek out subsequent aid
from what he or she perceives to be a biased and
hostile health care system.

The cultural truths or beliefs that constitute
'health truths' are often different from the main-

stream medical truths of the dominant Western-trained medical profession and society. Cultural factors can be causal, contributory, or protective in their relation to health and wellness, and they are numerous. Different cultures have different beliefs about such things as diet, personal hygiene, body alterations (body piercing, cosmetic surgery, tattooing, obesity, slimness), use of drugs (tea, coffee, alcohol, hallucinogens), and the use of non-traditional medical practitioners (Nakamura, 1999). As a result, each culture provides a culturally relevant diagnosis or cause and a framework for appropriate intervention. Ethnic group members living in a Western culture often find that non-Western health care alternatives are scarce or lacking. Thus, when forced to seek help from the only available option, the modern hospital, they approach the experience with a degree of apprehension and skepticism that can only aggravate the effects of the illness.

The Importance of Communication

Good communication plays an important role in ensuring good access to treatment. Independent of economic factors, minority patients are significantly more likely to report having a minority physician as their regular doctor, especially when they speak a language other than English (Gray and Stoddard, 1997; see also Callan and Littlewood, 1998; LaVeist, Diala, and Jarrett, 2000). The results of matching for cultural similarity are impressive. In one study, ethnically matched therapists judged their clients to have higher mental health functioning than did mismatched therapists (Russell et al., 1996). In another study, when clients were matched with an ethnically similar clinician who was also proficient in the client's preferred language, they had fewer emergency service visits than did unmatched clients (Snowden, Hu, and Jerrell, 1995).

Some minority populations are particularly vulnerable. For example, Canada's ethnic elderly who speak neither English nor French are iso-lated from the mainstream of North American society. Serious communication problems with this group in the delivery of social and health services can lead to poor treatment, extended hospital stays, unnecessary testing, premature discharge, and problematic follow-up. Added to the language barrier are, often, differences in cultural concepts about health and illness (Saldov, 1991). Ethnic elders from some cultures also patronize healers or herbalists from their native culture as well as Western health providers, illustrating the need to integrate Western and non-Western treatments for the elderly (Yeo, 1991).

The Health Effects of Racism

Racial discrimination, as well as socio-economic discrimination, contributes to the poor health of minorities. Some of the effects are obvious: discrimination, by increasing stress, increases the likelihood of psychiatric symptoms and cigarette smoking, for example (Landrine and Klonoff, 1996). To these, one must add the stress-related health consequences of discrimination itself (Krieger et al., 1993). The experiences of racial discrimination and resulting family stress also decrease the well-being of minority people. Other factors, such as alienation, poverty, inequality at work, and worries about unemployment, also contribute to the poor health of minority people. Shelly Harrell has identified six sources of racism-related stress:

- acute, intense, but relatively infrequent 'racism-related life events', such as being harassed by the police or discriminated against in the workplace;
- 'vicarious racism experiences', including the transmission of specific incidences of prejudice and discrimination experienced by family members and friends, or through the news media;
- 'daily racism micro stressors', which are subtle and frequent reminders of one's racially and/or ethnically linked subordinate status in

society, such as being ignored or overly scrutinized by sales staff;

- 'chronic-contextual stress', which arises from the need to adapt to the broad racial and ethnic inequalities in social structure, institutions, political systems, and resource distribution;
- 'collective experiences', which reflect 'the idea that cultural-symbolic and sociopolitical manifestations of racism can be observed and felt by individuals' and which include the 'economic conditions of members of one's racial/ethnic group, the lack of political representation, or stereotypic portrayals in the media'; and
- 'transgenerational transmission', or the historical context in which modern racial and ethnic discrimination has been bred and maintained, such as the removal of indigenous peoples from their land throughout North America, African slavery in the United States, the internment of Japanese Canadians during World War II, and the experiences of current refugees. (2000: 45–6)

The health outcomes of racism-related stress can be severe indeed. Several researchers have found, for instance, that the hostility and cynicism bred by racial victimization can give rise to stress-associated cardiovascular sensitivity and high blood pressure (Franklin, 1998; Williams, 1999). David Rollock and Edmund Gordon have further shown that 'racism can erode the mental health status of individual victims and dominate the institutional and cultural mechanisms through which it operates' (2000: 6). Merridy Malin also cites several studies of how 'racism that is internalized by the victim can negatively impact on an individual's sense of ambition, self-assertion, [and] erosion of sense of self and can lead to depression, anxiety, substance abuse, and chronic physical health problems' (2000: 5).

Racialization

Racism is the everyday outcome of a historic process called 'racialization', the tendency in a community to introduce racial distinctions into situations that can be understood and managed without such distinctions. Thus, race becomes a substitute for distinctions that would be otherwise based on class, education, age, or job experience, for example. In this way, race sometimes becomes the basis for decisions about hiring, purchasing, renting, befriending, and respecting others. Such changes of practice in the direction of racialization can happen easily, unless people take pains to avoid them.

In the police and judicial systems, *racial profiling*—a tendency to anticipate and interpret the acts of individuals differently on the basis of their race—can easily replace fair treatment. Police may pull over cars driven by young black or Aboriginal men but not by young white men in the expectation of finding alcohol, drugs, weapons, or other grounds for arrest there. Some evidence of this practice is reported by the Commission on Systemic Racism in the Ontario Criminal Justice System (1995). Evidence also indicates that the US government practises racial profiling against dark-skinned men at its borders in the expectation of finding Islamic terrorists in transit.

The Human Genome Project has demonstrated that only a tiny fraction of our genetic makeup as human beings varies by race. Yet many continue to believe that people can be usefully distinguished on the basis of race and that important human differences are biologically determined. As a result, though many people repudiate racism in principle, many also continue to behave as though the concept of race is meaningful. Most societies, our own included, continue to operate as though race really does make a difference. As a result, race continues to exercise considerable importance as a basis of social order and social inequality. As sociologist W.I. Thomas stated nearly a century ago, what people believe to be true is true in its consequences.

We can imagine a variety of reasons why race, racism, and racialization have persisted. Ignorance and childhood learning are important

---

BOX 4.5
Racial Profiling

Toronto has long prided itself on being a safe, clean, multicultural city. When a local newspaper analyzed data from police records, their findings dropped a bomb on the Toronto police. Citizens expressed outrage and resolve, and the police union filed a lawsuit against the newspaper, as well as encouraging a boycott.

Toronto doesn't need another review of police practices, say black community leaders. They want governments to act on what they say is systemic discrimination. A coalition of more than 20 groups has written to Ontario Premier Ernie Eves, asking him to hold police accountable for their actions. 'The African Canadian community is calling on Ernie Eves to show stronger leadership and foresight on this issue as we do not have faith in police Chief [Julian] Fantino or Mayor Mel Lastman', said Margaret Parsons of the African Canadian Legal Clinic during a news conference Thursday at Queen's Park.

A recent series of articles in *The Toronto Star* suggested that police in Toronto treat black people more harshly than whites. Using the police force's own arrest data, the paper said racial profiling might be behind some of the patterns it found.

Liberal provincial politician Alvin Curling says there is a crisis involving racism in not only the Toronto police, but in other institutions as well.

'It's not a police problem by itself', he said. 'It's a wider problem that impacts on not only black people, but all the people of Ontario.'

Ontario Minister of Public Safety and Security Bob Runciman said he would be willing to meet with Toronto's mayor, chief of police and leaders of the city's black community, in a summit called for by Lincoln Alexander. Alexander, the first black man to be appointed lieutenant-governor of Ontario, called for the summit after the *Toronto Star* began running a series of articles on police relations with the city's black population. Police chief Julian Fantino didn't comment on Monday, but issued a written statement that says he rejects the *Star*'s argument and will meet with black community leaders.

The defensive reaction on the part of the police chief is regrettable, said Allan Borovoy, of the Canadian Civil Liberties Association. He says no one believes Toronto police have an official policy of discrimination, but he wants the province to audit arrest records, to monitor how officers deal with different racial groups. 'It would help identify patterns', he said. 'It might even help identify certain people whose behaviour ought to be addressed.'

SOURCE: CBC, 'Stop Talking About Racism, Do Something: Toronto Coalition', 31 Oct. 2002, available at <www.cbc.ca/news>, accessed 31 October 2002.

SOURCE: CBC, 'Allegations of Profiling Rock Toronto Police', 21 October 2002, available at <www.cbc.ca/news>, accessed 21 October 2002.

---

reasons, for example. Structured social inequality that pits one racial community against another is another reason—especially when two or more communities are in active conflict. A third possible reason is the absence of class consciousness and class organization in most modern capitalist societies, and particularly in North America. What might have been understood and explained in terms of class categories a century ago in Europe would, in North America today, be more likely explained in terms of race (or, secondarily, in terms of personal attributes such as ambition and talent). In this sense, a racial system of distinctions is invented to make up for the absence of a contending class-based system.

A fourth, related reason is the absence of clearly understood national and ethnic distinctions. Americans in particular are poorly informed about other societies and cultures. They tend, therefore, to have trouble distinguishing between different kinds of Latin Americans, Africans, Asians, or Europeans. They have little understanding of the traditional rivalries, for example, between blacks from Jamaica and those from Barbados, or between blacks from the West Indies and those from the United States, or between blacks from Africa and blacks from the United Kingdom—though the differences and rivalries between these groups are real enough to blacks themselves.

In this sense, racialization is a tendency to blur national, ethnic, or cultural— not to mention class, educational, or other—distinctions that exist *within* racial groups, and to exaggerate the magnitude of distinctiveness—of difference—*between* racial groups. This kind of racialization is based on ignorance as much as on fear and indifference to the consequences for those who are treated in this way. Finally, racialization is often convenient and beneficial to people at the bottom end of the class and status hierarchy—people who, because they have the least, jealously guard what they have to maintain their own self-esteem. For those at the upper end of the class and status system, racialization is a good way of keeping down the price of labour.

Solutions to Problems

Multicultural Education

One of the keys to overcoming racial discrimination in society is the education system. Schools are, after all, sources of formal socialization and are effective in providing their students with socially sanctioned belief, value, and ideological systems. Moreover, informal means of socialization also occur during the school years, since they represent for most students the first opportunity for substantial interaction with other people who share similar ages and interests.

The increasingly diverse yet acculturated composition of Canada's younger generations has led to more interracial friendships and relationships, has provided greater exposure to and acceptance of other cultural practices, and has made skin colour less of an issue in social life. However, the educational curriculum being taught in schools continues to place an undue emphasis on Western European concepts, events, and ideas. Though valid as part of a complete education, they no longer wholly represent the racial and ethnic diversity that characterizes North American society.

Governmental and Organizational Intervention

The Employment Equity Act has been a part of Canadian federal policy since it was passed in 1986. It applies to the federal public service, Crown corporations and agencies, and private companies employing 100 employees or more, and is intended to ensure that the proportion of visible minorities, Aboriginal people, women, and people with disabilities hired in the workplace reflects the proportion of these groups applying for work in society. To ensure that equitable hiring practices are being undertaken, employers are required to submit annual reports to the federal government, which are then summarized and made available to the public.

As well, employers are required to identify and attempt to eliminate the barriers faced by members of underrepresented groups and to plan initiatives to increase their representation. Employment equity is intended to tackle what many sociologists—and, certainly, most conflict theorists—believe to be the cause of racial and ethnic inequality, namely, structural barriers erected by the dominant majority to bolster their privileged status. Other forms of government intervention have also been directed at institutional and interpersonal discrimination.

The Multiculturalism Act of 1988 made Canada the world's first officially multicultural nation. It also made it necessary for all federal institutions and employers to act in accordance with the country's stated fundamental belief in the importance and value of racial and ethnic diversity when constructing and implementing economic, social, cultural, and political policies. Canada has been a global leader in promoting and celebrating diversity, so much so that UNESCO (the United Nations Educational, Scientific and Cultural Organization) cited Canada's approach to multiculturalism as the ideal model to be followed by other countries.

Hate crimes are already condemned by Canada's Charter of Rights and Freedoms, which declares that 'every individual is equal before and under the law and has the right to the equal protection and equal benefit of the law without discrimination and, in particular, without discrimination based on race, national or ethnic origin, colour, religion, sex, age or mental or physical disability'. However, this will be meaningless rhetoric unless it is supported by sustained genuine efforts to protect and ensure the rights in practice of all ethnic groups.

Some argue that hate crimes should be punished more severely, reflecting society's particular revulsion from and condemnation of racially motivated violence. Supporters of this view lobby for, among other things, the lengthening of jail sentences for hate crimes. Critics, however, are concerned that the implementation of more severe hate-crime laws will only intensify the level of social hatred felt by racists. Rather than extinguish discriminatory attitudes in society, it is feared that anti-hate legislation may serve the opposite and unintended function of confirming the suspicions and maintaining the intolerance of extremist groups already partial to conspiracy theories and anti-government sentiments.

Individual Solutions

Again, as in other chapters, many of the problems of race and ethnic relations are beyond the efforts of given individuals to solve. The problems are structural in nature and require the concerted efforts of government, schools, the courts, and other organizations if they are to be adequately addressed. What is needed is the emergence of a widespread recognition that differences between people—physical, cultural, and so on—are problematic only insofar as these differences are used to justify prejudice, other xenophobic sentiments, and discriminatory behaviour. Laws, strongly enforced, will go a long way toward promoting equality. However, they must be accompanied by a corresponding desire on the part of most individuals to see them through in the course of daily interaction.

If members of minority and non-minority groups alike strive to follow principles of equal treatment, it will take us toward fully addressing the prejudice and exclusion associated with race and ethnicity. Whether we are members of a minority group or a majority group, we should recognize that there is no reasonable rationale for structural inequality and discrimination in the workplace or the wider community. Further, we do not have to stand for inequality or discrimination directed at ourselves or at others around us. This does not have support in Canadian values or in Canadian law. Indeed, there are laws and regulations against discrimination. There are investigative bodies (such as the courts, grievance committees in the workplace, and human rights commissions in different provinces) that will pursue cases of injustices when brought to their attention. The latter—calling attention to them—is our right and responsibility as citizens.

Concluding Remarks

People often try to justify racist beliefs by relaying misinformed assumptions about a minority group's innate physical, psychological, and cultural inferiority. Commonly, *racial groups* are defined as those groups that are thought to have similar genetic or inherent characteristics. However, others argue that the physical traits by which people are grouped into racial categories are not intrinsic but merely subjective. *Ethnic groups* are those groups that have common cultural traits and that believe they are a distinct group.

As we have seen, *prejudice* refers to biased beliefs about individuals based on their membership in a particular racial or ethnic group. Prejudice necessarily entails stereotyping. It can be thought of as a weapon used by a dominant group to maintain its dominance. Some argue that prejudice is learned through socialization. Others emphasize that prejudice has evident economic benefits.

We are a long way from achieving the society Durkheim imagined, built on organic solidarity and valuing different kinds of people for the different values, interests, and skills they bring to our society. Today Canada needs immigrants more than ever—to compensate for declining fertility and provide tomorrow's workers and taxpayers, and to continue to link us to other peoples and societies around the world. This means that ethnic and racial inequality and the politicization of migration will likely remain major, volatile issues. At the same time, the demographic and global patterns make it all the more important that these issues of inequality be resolved.

Questions for Critical Thought

1. Do you think that different ethnic groups can live together very harmoniously, without conflict? Use the terms *cultural mosaic, melting pot*, and *multiculturalism* in your answer.
2. Use Georg Simmel's definition of the *stranger* and briefly outline how this applies to the experience of minority ethnic groups. Discuss with reference to 'otherness'.
3. Elaborate on the notion that perception of conflict and competition is in essence a social construction.
4. There is a debate as to whether race should be considered biological or socially constructed. Discuss the arguments each side would offer and how the different theories justify and explain inequality and discrimination.
5. The chapter briefly discusses the role that Israel plays with regard to the diasporic Jews. Elaborate on how the Jews have maintained strong ties both to their birthplace and to their 'homeland' throughout history. In your answer, discuss the identity issues likely experienced by diasporic individuals and their children.

Recommended Readings

Kay J. Anderson, *Vancouver's Chinatown: Racial Discourse in Canada, 1875–1980* (Montreal and Kingston: McGill-Queens University Press, 1991).

This historical analysis is designed to examine how place is related to identity. The author uses government documents and other written evidence (such as letters to the editor) to document the changing role of Vancouver's Chinatown, from a ghetto to a slum to an advertised tourist attraction.

Raymond Breton, Wsevolod W. Isajiw, Warren E. Kalbach, and Jeffrey G. Reitz, *Ethnic Identity and Equality: Varieties of Experience in a Canadian City* (Toronto: University of Toronto Press, 1990).

Using eight ethnic groups in Toronto, this book looks at how ethnicity works as a sustaining factor Canada's socio-economic system. The book covers identity retention, residential segregation, concentrations in labour markets, and the ethnic group as a political resource.

Donald R. Kinder and Lynn M. Sanders, *Divided by Color: Racial Politics and Democratic Ideals* (Chicago: University of Chicago Press, 1996).

This book considers the historical context of and various arguments for and against affirmative action programs. Using analysis of opinion polls, the authors see indications that a sizeable majority of whites feel that enough has been done to redress past discrimination against minorities.

William F. Lewis, *Soul Rebels: The Rastafari* (Prospect Heights, IL: Waveland Press, 1993).

An overview of Rastafarian culture is offered with specific attention to peasant roots, group heterogeneity, and the possible classification of Rastafarians as an ethnic group based on cultural identity. The Rastafarian world view sees capitalist society as an extension of Babylon. There is also mistrust of money and technology, and a belief in natural living and in the use of marijuana as sacrament.

Anthony H. Richmond, 'Socio-demographic Aspects of Globalization: Canadian Perspectives on Migration', *Canadian Studies in Population*, 29, no. 1 (2002): 123–49.

Immigration and emigration trends in Canada are studied in global context. The author constructs a typology of migrants who move for work reasons. Recent concerns over security and border control are debated in terms of human rights.

Julia Roberts, ' "A Mixed Assemblage of Persons": Race and Tavern Space in Upper Canada', *Canadian Historical Review*, 83, no. 1 (2002): 1–28.

Whites, blacks, and Native people mixed together in public taverns in early Canadian history, but race boundaries were maintained through interactions in taverns in Upper Canada. This paper examines the ways that these boundaries were created.

Ella Shohat and Robert Stam, *Unthinking Eurocentrism: Multiculturalism and the Media* (London and New York: Routledge, 1995).

It is suggested here that Eurocentrism perpetuates stereotypes of marginalized people in both Western and non-Western mass media. These are reinforced in the media by casting, procedures, linguistic decisions, and audience expectations.

Jace Weaver, *That People Might Live: Native American Literatures and Native American Community* (New York: Oxford University Press, 1997).

This book deals with ethnic identity generally and looks at how identity is distinguished not only by blood, but also by both tribal and pan-Aboriginal identity.

Recommended Web Sites

World Conference on Racism
<www.un.org/WCAR/>
   The World Conference on Racism Web site provides a brief backdrop to the events leading up to the 2001 conference in Durban, South Africa. A great deal of information is also available relating to the conference itself and to its media coverage.

Canadian Race Relations Federation
<www.crr.ca/EN/default.htm>
   This Web site deals with issues around racism in Canada. A number of publications, research reports, and fact sheets are available online. In conjunction with this, the CRRF provides recent news information and information on current events and programs.

Citizenship and Immigration Canada
<www.cic.gc.ca>
   This site offers practical information, such as how to get a new passport. Also, it provides information of public policy in this government department. There are useful links, too. An example is <www.parl.gc.ca>, which offers transcripts of parliamentary debates.

References

Allotey, Pascale. 1998. 'Travelling with "Excess Baggage": Health Problems of Refugee Women in Western Australia'. *Women and Health*, 28, no. 1: 63–81.

Allport, Gordon W. [1958] 2000. 'The Nature of Prejudice'. In *Stereotypes and Prejudice: Essential Readings*, edited by Charles Stangor, 20–48. Philadelphia: Psychology Press.

Anderson, Kay J. 1991. *Vancouver's Chinatown: Racial Discourse in Canada, 1875–1980*. Montreal: McGill-Queen's University Press.

Arfken, Cynthia L., and Cheryl A. Houston. 1996. 'Obesity in Inner-City African Americans'. *Ethnicity and Health*, 1: 317–26.

Barsh, Lawrence. 1997. 'Aboriginal Peoples and Quebec: Competing for Legitimacy as Emergent Peoples'. *American Indian Culture and Research Journal*, 21, no. 1: 1–29.

Beauvais, Fred. 2000. 'Indian Adolescence: Opportunity and Challenge'. In *Adolescent Diversity of Ethnic, Economic and Cultural Contexts*, edited by Raymond Montemayor, Gerald R. Adams, and Thomas P. Gullotta, 110–40. Thousand Oaks, CA: Sage.

Brave Heart, M.Y. 1999. 'Gender Differences in the Historical Trauma Response Among the Lakota'. *Journal of Health and Social Policy*, 10, no. 4: 1–21.

Breton, Raymond. 1964. 'Institutional Completeness of Ethnic Communities and Personal Relations to Immigrants'. *American Journal of Sociology*, 70: 193–205.

———. 1978. 'Stratification and Conflict Between Ethnolinguistic Communities with Different Social Structures'. *Canadian Review of Sociology and Anthropology*, 15: 138–57.

Breton, Raymond, Jeffrey G. Reitz, and Victor Valentine. 1980. *Cultural Boundaries and the Cohesion of Canada*. Montreal: Institute for Research on Public Policy.

Broadhurst, Roderic. 1996. 'Aboriginal Imprisonment in Australia'. *Overcrowded Times*, 7, no. 3: 5–8.

Bogardus, E.S. 1928. *Immigration and Race Attitudes*. Boston: D.C. Heath.

Callan, Alyson, and Roland Littlewood. 1998. 'Patient Satisfaction: Ethnic Origin or Explanatory Model?' *International Journal of Social Psychiatry*, 44, no. 1: 1–11.

Canadian Council on Social Development (CCSD). 2000. 'Unequal Access: A Report Card on Racism'. *Perception*, 24, no. 3. Available at <www.ccsd.ca/perception/243/racism.htm>, accessed 21 January 2003.

Citizenship and Immigration Canada. 2000. *Facts and Figures 1999: Immigration Overview*. Available at <www.cic.gc.ca/english/pdf/pub/facts1999.pdf>, accessed 23 January 2003.

Clairmont, Donald. 1996. 'Alternative Justice Issues for Aboriginal Justice'. *Journal of Legal Pluralism and Unofficial Law*, 36: 125–57.

Coleman, Heather, Grant Charles, and Jennifer Collins. 2001. 'Inhalant Use by Canadian Aboriginal Youth'. *Journal of Child and Adolescent Substance Abuse*, 10, no. 3: 1–20.

Commander, M.J., S.P. Sashi Dharan, S.M. Odell, and P.G. Surtees. 1997. 'Access to Mental Health Care in an Inner-City Health District. II. Association with Demographic Factors'. *British Journal of Psychiatry*, 170: 317–20.

Cooper, Helen, Chris Smaje, and Sara Arber. 1999. 'Equity in Health Service Use by Children: Examining the Ethnic Paradox'. *Journal of Social Policy*, 28: 457–78.

Coser, Lewis A. 1965. *The Functions of Social Conflict*. London: Routledge & Kegan Paul.

D'Arcy, Carl. 1998. 'Social Distribution of Health Among Canadians'. In *Health and Canadian Society: Sociological Perspectives*, 3rd edn, edited by David Coburn, Carl D'Arcy, and George M. Torrance, 73–101. Toronto: University of Toronto Press.

Dubois, Laurent. 1996. 'A Spoonful of Blood: Haitians, Racism and AIDS'. *Science as Culture*, 6, no. 1: 7–43.

Duffy Hutcheon, Pat. 1998. 'Multiculturalism, Good Intentions and a Clouded Vision?' Paper presented at the annual meeting of the International Sociological Association.

Durkheim, Émile. [1895] 1964. *Division of Labor in Society*. Translated by George Simpson. New York: Free Press.

Farmer, Melissa M., and Kenneth F. Ferraro. 1999. 'Who Are the "Truly Disadvantaged" in Health? A 20-Year Examination of Race, Socioeconomic Status, and Health Outcomes'. Paper presented at the annual meeting of the American Sociological Association.

Farrales, Lynn L., and Gwen E. Chapman. 1999. 'Filipino Women Living in Canada: Constructing Meanings of Body, Food, and Health'. *Health Care for Women International*, 20: 179–94.

Fenton, Steve, Anthony O. Hughes, and Christine E. Hine. 1995. 'Self-assessed Health, Economic Status and Ethnic Origin'. *New Community*, 21, no. 1: 55–68.

Fontana, Barbara. 1997. *The State of Migration Research in South Africa*. Foundation for Global Dialog (FGD) Occasional Paper 8. Braamfontein, South Africa: Foundation for Global Dialog.

Franklin, Anderson J. 1998. 'Treating Anger in African American Men'. In *New Psychotherapy for Men*, edited by William S. Pollack and Richard F. Levant, 239–58. New York: Wiley.

Frideres, J.S., and Boni Robertson. 1994. 'Aboriginals and the Criminal Justice System: Australia and Canada'. *International Journal of Contemporary Sociology*, 31: 101–27.

Furniss, Elizabeth. 1999. 'Indians, Odysseys and Vast, Empty Lands: The Myth of the Frontier in the Canadian Justice System'. *Anthropologica*, 41: 195–208.

Gaertner, Samuel L., and Dovidio, John F. 2000. 'The Aversive Form of Racism'. In *Stereotypes and Prejudice: Essential Readings*, edited by Charles Stangor, 289–304. Philadelphia: Psychology Press.

Gee, Ellen M., and Steven G. Prus. 2000. 'Income Inequality in Canada: A Racial Divide'. In *Perspectives on Ethnicity in Canada: A Reader*, edited by Madeline A. Kalbach and Warren E. Kalbach, 238–56. Toronto: Harcourt Canada.

Gil, Vincent E. 1998–9. 'Empowerment Rhetoric, Sexual Negotiation, and Latinas' AIDS Risk: Research Implications for Prevention Health Education'. *International Quarterly of Community Health Education*, 18: 9–27.

Gilmour, Glenn A. 1994. *Hate-Motivated Violence*. (WD1994-6e). Ottawa: Department of Justice. Available at <http://canada.justice.gc.ca/en/dept/pub/hmv>, accessed 19 June 2001.

Gray, Bradley, and Jeffrey J. Stoddard. 1997. 'Patient-Physician Pairing: Does Racial and Ethnic Congruity Influence Selection of a Regular Physician?' *Journal of Community Health*, 22: 247–59.

Harrell, Shelly P. 2000. 'A Multidimensional Conceptualization of Racism-Related Stress: Implications for the Well-Being of People of Color'. *American Journal of Orthopsychiatry*, 70, no. 1: 42–57.

Hayward, Mark D., and Melanie Heron. 1999. 'Racial Inequality in Active Life Among Adult Americans'. *Demography*, 36: 77–91.

Henry, Frances. 1999. 'Two Studies of Racial Discrimination in Employment'. In *Social Inequality in Canada: Patterns, Problems, Policies*, 3rd edn, edited by James Curtis, Edward Grabb, and Neil Guppy, 226–35. Scarborough, ON: Prentice-Hall.

Henry, Frances, and Effie Ginzberg. 1985. *Who Gets the Work: A Test of Racial Discrimination in Employment*. Toronto: Urban Alliance on Race Relations in Employment and Social Planning Council of Metropolitan Toronto.

Hou, Feng, and T.R. Balakrisnan. 1996. 'The Integration of Visible Minorities in Contemporary Society'. *Canadian Journal of Sociology*, 21: 307–16.

Howard, Rhoda. 1998. 'Being Canadian: Citizenship in Canada'. *Citizenship Studies*, 2: 133–52.

Hunt, Wayne A. 1996. 'The First Peoples and the Quebec Question'. *Telos*, 108: 139–48.

Ignatieff, Michael. 1994. *Blood and Belonging: Journeys into the New Nationalism*. New York: Farrar, Straus & Giroux.

Johnson, Genevieve Marie, and Reinhild Boehm. 1995. 'Aboriginal Canadian University Students: A Comparison of Students Who Withdraw and Students Who Continue'. *Australian Journal of Adult and Community Education*, 35, no. 2: 141–56.

Johnson, Melissa A., Alyse R. Gotthofer, and Kimberly A. Lauffer. 1999. 'The Sexual and Reproductive Health Content of African American and Latino Magazines'. *Howard Journal of Communications*, 10, no. 3: 169–87.

Kim, Hyun Sook. 1997. 'The Construction of Asian Immigrants as a Social Problem'. *Sociological Imagination*, 34, nos 2–3: 129–47.

Klos, Nancy. 1997. 'Aboriginal Peoples and Homelessness: Interviews with Service Providers'. *Canadian Journal of Urban Research*, 6: 40–52.

Krieger, Nancy, Diane Rowley, Allen A. Herman, Byllye Avery, Monol T. Phillips. 1993. 'Racism, Sexism, and Social Class: Implications for Studies of Health, Disease, and Well-Being'. *American Journal of Preventive Medicine*, 9, no. 6 (suppl.): 82–122.

Kymlicka, Will. 1995. *Multicultural Citizenship: A Liberal Theory of Minority Rights*. Oxford: Clarendon Press.

Landrine, Hope, and Elizabeth A. Klonoff. 1996. 'The Schedule of Racist Events: A Measure of Racial Discrimination and a Study of Its Negative Physical and Mental Health Consequences'. *Journal of Black Psychology*, 22: 144–68.

Laroche, Mireille. 2000. 'Health Status and Health Services Utilization of Canada's Immigrant and Non-immigrant Populations'. *Canadian Public Policy*, 26: 51–73.

LaVeist, Thomas A., Chamberlain Diala, and Nicole C. Jarrett. 2000. 'Social Status and Perceived Discrimination: Who Experiences Discrimination in the Health Care System, How, and Why?' In *Minority Health in America: Findings and Policy Implications from the Commonwealth Fund Minority Health Survey*, edited by Carol J. Hogue, Martha A. Hargraves, and Karen Scott Collins, 194–208. Baltimore, MD: Johns Hopkins University Press.

Leck, Joanne D. Sylvie St. Onge, and Isabelle Lalancette. 1995. 'Wage Gap Changes Among Organizations Subject to the Employment Equity Act'. *Canadian Public Policy*, 21: 387–400.

Lee, David J., Kyriakos S. Markides, and Laura A. Ray. 1997. 'Epidemiology of Self-reported Past Heavy Drinking in Hispanic Adults'. *Ethnicity and Health*, 2, 1–2: 77–88.

Malin, Merridy. 2000. *A 'Whole of Life' View of Aboriginal Education for Health: Emerging Models*. Keynote address at the Australian Medical Association, Northern Territory, Conference 2000, 'Learning Lessons: Approaching Indigenous Health Through Education'. Available at <http://192.94.208.240/Crc/General/CRCPubs/Malin_AMA_2000.PDF>, accessed 20 June 2001.

Maxim, Paul S., Jerry P. White, Dan Beavon, and Paul C. Whitehead. 2001. 'Dispersion and Polarization of Income Among Aboriginal and Non-Aboriginal Canadians'. *Canadian Review of Sociology and Anthropology*, 38: 465–76.

Melancon, Hugues. 1997. 'A Pluralist Analysis of Indigenous Legal Conceptions Before the Criminal Law Courts of Canada'. *Canadian Journal of Law and Society*, 12: 159–86.

Moreau, Sylvie, Cecile Rousseau, and Abdelwahed Mekki Berrada. 1999. 'Immigration Policies and the Mental Health of Refugees: The Profile and Impact of Family Separations'. *Nouvelles Pratiques Sociales*, 11, no. 1: 177–96.

Nakamura, Raymond M. 1999. *Health in America: A Multicultural Perspective*. Boston: Allyn and Bacon.

Ontario. Commission on Systemic Racism in the Ontario Justice System. 1995. *Report of the Commission on Systemic Racism in the Ontario Justice System*. Toronto: The Commission.

Oppenheimer, Valerie K., and Matthijs Kalmijn. 1995. 'Life-Cycle Jobs'. *Research in Social Stratification and Mobility*, 14: 1–38.

Peikoff, Tannis Mara. 2001. *Anglican Missionaries and Governing the Self: An Encounter with Aboriginal Peoples in Western Canada, 1820–1865*. Unpublished doctoral dissertation, University of Manitoba.

Phipps, Etienne, Martin H. Cohen, Rorng Sorn, and Leonard E. Braitman. 1999. 'A Pilot Study of Cancer Knowledge and Screening Behaviors of Vietnamese and Cambodian Women'. *Health Care for Women International*, 20: 195–207.

Porter, John A. 1965. *The Vertical Mosaic: An Analysis of Social Class and Power in Canada.* Toronto: University of Toronto Press.

Rajaram, Shireen S., and Anahita Rashidi. 1999. 'Asian-Islamic Women and Breast Cancer Screening: A Socio-cultural Analysis'. *Women and Health*, 28, no. 3: 45–58.

Reed, Micheline, and Julian Roberts. 1999. 'Adult Correctional Services in Canada, 1997–98'. In Canadian Centre for Justice Statistics, *The Juristat Reader: A Statistical Overview of the Canadian Justice System*, 39–51. Toronto: Thompson Educational.

Reitz, Jeffrey G. 1998. *Warmth of the Welcome: The Social Causes of Economic Success for Immigrants in Different Nations and Cities.* Boulder, CO: Westview.

Reitz, Jeffrey G., and Raymond Breton. 1999. 'Prejudice and Discrimination Toward Minorities in Canada and the United States'. In *Social Inequality in Canada: Patterns, Problems and Policy*, 3rd edn, edited by James Curtis, Edward Grabb, and Neil Guppy, 357–70. Scarborough, ON: Prentice-Hall.

Roberts, Julian V., and Anthony N. Doob. 1997. 'Race, Ethnicity, and Criminal Justice in Canada'. In *Ethnicity, Crime and Immigration: Comparative and Cross-national Perspectives*, edited by Michael Tonry, 469–522. Chicago: University of Chicago Press.

Rodlandt, Theo J.A. 1996. 'Ethnic Stratification: The Emergence of a New Social and Economic Issue?' *Netherlands' Journal of Social Sciences*, 32, no. 1: 39–50.

Rogers, Angie, Jane E. Adamson, and Mark McCarthy. 1997. 'Variations in Health Behaviours Among Inner-City 12-Year-Olds from Four Ethnic Groups'. *Ethnicity and Health*, 2: 309–16.

Rollock, David, and Edmund W. Gordon. 2000. 'Racism and Mental Health into the 21st Century: Perspectives and Parameters'. *American Journal of Orthopsychiatry*, 70, no. 1: 5–13.

Russell, Gerald L., Diane C. Fujino, Stanley Sue, Mang-King Cheung, and Lonnie R. Snowden. 1996. 'The Effects of Therapist-Client Ethnic Match in the Assessment of Mental Health Functioning'. *Journal of Cross-Cultural Psychology*, 27: 599–615.

Russell, Peter. 1996. 'Aboriginal Nationalism: Prospects for Decolonization'. *Pacifica Review*, 8, no. 2: 57–67.

Ruttkay-Milkián, Eszter. 2001. 'Revival and Survival in Iugra'. *Nationalities Papers*, 29: 153–70.

Saldov, Morris. 1991. 'The Ethnic Elderly: Communication Barriers to Health Care'. *Canadian Social Work Review*, 8: 269–77.

Samson, Colin. 1999. 'The Dispossession of the Innu and the Colonial Magic of Canadian Liberalism'. *Citizenship Studies*, 3, no. 1: 5–25.

Segura Escobar, Nora. 2000. 'Colombia: A New Century, an Old War, and More Internal Displacement'. *International Journal of Politics, Culture, and Society*, 14: 107–27.

Silove, Derrick, Ingrid Sinnerbrink, Annette Field, Vijaya Manicavasagar, and Zachary Steel. 1997. 'Anxiety, Depression and PTSD in Asylum-Seekers: Associations with Pre-migration and Post-migration Stressors'. *British Journal of Psychiatry*, 170: 351–7.

Simmel, Georg. [1905] 1964. *The Sociology of Georg Simmel.* Translated and edited by Kurt Wolff. New York: Free Press.

Snowden, Lonnie R., Teh-wei Hu, and Jeannette M. Jerrell. 1995. 'Emergency Care Avoidance: Ethnic Matching and Participation in Minority-Serving Programs'. *Community Mental Health Journal*, 31: 463–73.

Spaulding, Richard. 1997. 'Peoples as National Minorities: A Review of Will Kymlicka's Arguments for Aboriginal Rights from a Self-determination Perspective'. *University of Toronto Law Journal*, 47: 35–113.

Spencer, N. 1996. 'Race and Ethnicity as Determinants of Child Health: A Personal View'. *Child: Care, Health and Development*, 22: 327–45.

St. Jean, Yannick. 1996. 'American Attitudes Towards Haitians: AIDS as Stigma'. *Comparative Social Research*, 2, suppl.: 153–64.

Statistics Canada. 2001. 'Canadian Statistics: The People: Population'. Available at <www.statcan.ca/english/Pgdb/People/popula.htm>, accessed 18 June 2001.

Stolcke, Verena. 1999. 'New Rhetorics of Exclusion in Europe'. *International Social Science Journal*, 51: 25–35.

'Study Reveals Disturbing Trends in Care of Minorities'. 2000. *Healthcare Benchmarks*, 8, no. 4: 40–1.

Symons, Gladys L. 1999. 'Racialization of the Street Gang Issue in Montreal: A Police Perspective'. *Canadian Ethnic Studies*, 31: 124–38.

Thomas, W.I., and Florien Znaniecki. [1919] 1971. *The Polish Peasant in America.* New York: Octagon Books.

Trovato, Frank. 2001. 'Aboriginal Mortality in Canada, the United States and New Zealand'. *Journal of Biosocial Science*, 33: 67–86.

Waldram, James P., Ann D. Herring, and T. Kue Young. 1996. *Aboriginal Health in Canada: Historical, Cultural, and Epidemiological Perspectives*. Toronto: University of Toronto.

Warburton, Rennie. 1997. 'Status, Class and the Politics of Canadian Aboriginal Peoples'. *Studies in Political Economy*, 54: 119–41.

Weinrath, Michael. 1999. 'Violent Victimization and Fear of Crime Among Canadian Aboriginals'. *Journal of Offender Rehabilitation*, 30: 107–20.

Whaley, Arthur L. 1998. 'Racism in the Provision of Mental Health Service: A Social-Cognitive Analysis'. *American Journal of Orthopsychiatry*, 68: 47–57.

Williams, David R. 1999. 'Race, Socioeconomic Status and Health: The Added Effects of Racism and Discrimination'. In *Socioeconomic Status and Health in Industrial Nations: Psychological and Biological Pathways*, edited by N.E. Adler, M. Marmot, B.S. McEwen, and J. Stewart, 173–88. New York: New York Academy of Sciences.

Williams, David R., Yan Yu, James S. Jackson, and Norman B. Anderson. 1997. 'Racial Differences in Physical and Mental Health: Socio-economic Status, Stress, and Discrimination'. *Journal of Health Psychology*, 2: 335–51.

Yeo, Gwen. 1991. 'Ethnogeriatric Education: Need and Content'. *Journal of Cross-Cultural Gerontology*, 6: 229–41.

Glossary

Antilocution The sharing of prejudiced behaviours among like-minded friends; considered the most benign level of prejudiced attitudes.

Aversive racism Aversive racists often sympathize with the victims of past injustice and support public policies that, in principle, promote racial equality. They try to reduce the harm of racism, and they identify more generally with a liberal political agenda, regarding themselves as non-prejudiced and non-discriminatory.

Chain migration The successful migration of one family member creates a chain of opportunities for the whole kin network. Migration is not random or disorganized, but is increasingly about networks, rational choices, economic opportunities, sponsorship, and kinship relations. Immigrants today are more likely to keep ties to their ethnic culture and homeland.

Charter groups The dominating powers in a country. Historically, the English and French Canadians determined the entrance status of immigrants.

Clique A small exclusive group of friends or associates; also, a friendship circle within which members are identical to each other sociometrically and are mutually connected. Cliques are social structures that create and control an exclusive information flow.

Culture The way of life of a society, which includes codes of manners, dress, language, and norms of behaviour. Humans both are acted on by culture and act back, and so generate new cultural forms and meanings. Thus, this framework of values and practices adapt to the changing historical and regional circumstances.

Diaspora The situation of any group of people dispersed, whether forcibly or voluntarily, throughout the world. Almost any migrant community with some degree of international linkage is referred to as *diasporic*.

Discrimination A more intense attitudinal level of discrimination with active attempts to subordinate the minority from employment, education, housing, and even political rights. Members of a socially defined group are treated differently because of their reference to features of race, ethnicity, gender, or religion.

Entrance status Because of processes of assimilation laid down by dominant groups, less preferred immigrants enter Canada's labour force in lower-level occupational roles. The low-status groups are then compelled to accept their inferior position and subjection.

Exclusion The selective ethnic and racial inclusion by a majority group delineates and defends group boundaries.

In-group and out-group The insiders in contrast to the outsiders in a relationship or set of interactions.

Institutional completeness Coined by Raymond Breton, this is a measure of the degree to which an immigrant ethnic group gives its own members the services they need through their own institutions. It usually gives off an impression of cohesiveness and solidarity among members of the group.

Out-group See **in-group**.

Prejudice Aversive or hostile attitude toward a person who belongs to a group; opinions and attitudes often unjustified by fact.

Racial socialization The process of social interaction whereby a person is exposed to and over time internalizes his or her racial or ethnic identity, including its set of beliefs, values, cultural history, language, and social and economic implications; the constant awareness of race in daily social interaction.

Social distance People feel varying comfort levels when interacting with members of other cultures and in different circumstances. Such feelings of aloofness and inapproachability are felt between members of different social strata. People are far more willing to have close relations with others who are culturally and racially similar. Distance comes with prejudices and discriminatory practices.

Transnationalism Marked by the globalization of capitalism and by a revolution in communication and transportation technologies; marked by decolonization and an expansion of human rights, and by the growth of social networks that facilitate transnational migration patterns.

Vertical mosaic This term, coined by John Porter, describes a hierarchy in which English and French Canadians exist at the top and other ethnic minorities are positioned below. This economic ladder categorizes the Canadian experience of opportunity stratification.

Chapter 5

Sexism and Gender Inequality

Chapter Objectives

After reading this chapter the student should understand:
- the definitions of *sexism* and *gender inequality*
- differences between *sex* and *gender*
- factors that reinforce gender inequality
- the significance of the 'glass ceiling'
- the different theoretical approaches to gender inequality
- social consequences of this type of inequity
- what is meant by the 'feminization of poverty'
- social-psychological and health consequences of gender inequality
- possible solutions to gender inequality

Introduction

This chapter is about gender and sex, men and women, and gender inequality, stereotyping, discrimination, and socialization—all of which can be found in homes, schools, and work settings throughout this country. Formally, Canadians appear to support rules that make it unlawful for employers to limit or segregate their employees by sex. Informally, however, many Canadians still discriminate against women or in favour of men. Sociologists study these processes.

Sociologists also study how the biology of sex translates into the sociology of **gender**. As parents, we raise children who are genetically female as 'girls'. We raise children who are genetically male in a different way as 'boys'. Many aspects of our social institutions reinforce this differential socialization. Gender stereotyping and gendered socialization occur at most levels of social life in Canada.

Far worse than job discrimination happens to women, however. Sexual assault against women is far too common. Rape offenders, who are usually male, often harbour misogynistic and sadistic attitudes toward their female victims. Of course, there are rapes of men too, but these are much less frequent than rapes of females.

Poverty is also a more common experience for women than for men. Researchers have shown that the high rates of female poverty are a result of women's vulnerable status in society, of their subordinate position compared with men, and of their exposure to risk in cases of abandonment, divorce, and widowhood. This chapter will explore these problems and others that affect in varying degrees over half the Canadian population.

Defining *Sexism* and *Gender Inequality*

We can define **sexism** as including discrimination and insulting attitudes and beliefs that stereotype people because of their gender. Sexism and gender stereotyping can be problems for both men and women. However, since males have traditionally dominated Canadian society, sexism has harmed women more than men. **Gender inequality** is any difference between men and women in gaining access to valued rewards. It can grow out of structural arrangements, interpersonal discrimination, or cultural beliefs, as we will see in this chapter.

Sex and Gender

All known societies have distinguished between male and female roles in some ways. However, the precise distinctions made between men and women, and the resulting divisions of labour, have varied considerably through time and across cultures. The gender distinctions are always socially constructed. They operate within social institutions to determine the roles that men and women can enter and the kinds of experiences they will have within these roles. So what begin as biological difference assume a vast importance through the social construction of gender roles. The use of the term *gender* by sociologists to apply to the social constructions suggests that biology is largely irrelevant to understanding the social distinctions people make between males and females.

From a purely biological standpoint, the Y chromosome must be present for the embryonic sex glands to develop in a male direction. Furthermore, hormones must be present in both sexes for either males or females to reach sexual maturity. However, hormones and chromosomes are only part of the story. From a social standpoint, gender is the social enactment of a biological difference. Males are treated as men because they play masculine roles, and females are treated as women because they play feminine roles. In the case of socially neutral roles (such as friend, guest, traveller, or stranger), men and women play them in gendered ways. Generally, our sex organs and genes are not in view, so biology is not immediately relevant to our social interactions.

Research has not revealed any simple dichotomy between the sexes or any direct link between genetics and the behaviour of each sex. Current thinking is that 'male' and 'female' are not discrete biological categories. It would be more accurate to view them as opposite poles along a continuum of sexual variation. The value of such subtle thinking is evident when we consider unusual cases. For example, consider the condition known as *adrenogenital syndrome*, in which an XX (46-chromosome) individual is exposed in the womb to abnormally high levels of androgens, a family of hormones that ordinarily predominates in the development of masculine features (Crooks and Baur, 1999). The result is an intersexed appearance, with normal internal genitalia (ovaries, uterus, inner vagina) and an external phallus that is intermediate in size between a clitoris and a penis. Male or female? For practical purposes, the answer is socially determined, through socialization and social interaction.

We have a hard time classifying the sex of people with mixed male and female features. Predicting their gender is even harder. Gender, unlike sex, is a purely social construct. It involves shared understandings of how women and men, girls and boys, *should* look and act. Gender is a label that includes a large variety of traits, beliefs, values, and mannerisms and that defines how we should practise social interactions. Like sex, gender is popularly (and wrongly) understood as comprising two mutually exclusive categories—'masculine' and 'feminine'—that neatly parallel the corresponding biological division between 'male' and 'female'.

Exceptions to Patterns of Male Dominance

There is much evidence, from across today's societies, of males having greater control, power, and status in many social situations. However, some anthropological studies underscore the point that gender roles are not always arranged in this way. Some pre-industrial societies treated men and women equally. Many hunting-and-gathering societies were egalitarian. Some were cross-gendered, in the sense that women played 'male' roles.

Consider the examples of cross-gendered females in Native North American tribes and selected African cultures. According to Evelyn Blackwood and Saskia Wieringa (1999), a pattern of consistent gender socialization of males to superior roles was not present in some Native American tribes. Cross-gendered women acquired a 'male' role by various accepted cultural channels, and took up adult tasks when mature.

In these cultures, girls were encouraged to take on the different role if they expressed any interest in it as they grew up: 'Adults, acknowledging the interests of such girls, taught them the same skills the boys learned' (Blackwood and Wieringa, 1999: 143). This possibility arose from social organization based on egalitarian cooperation among autonomous individuals. Though gender roles entailed the performance of specific tasks, there was considerable overlap between the sexes. Kinship was based on mutually advantageous ties between men and women. Cross-gendered women could have sexual relations with other women and marry them. This cross-gendered role disappeared with Western cultural influence.

In short, the female cross-gendered role in certain North American tribes constituted an opportunity for women to assume the male role permanently and to marry women. Its existence challenges Western assumptions about gender roles. Further, in certain African cultures, women seem to have had the highest-status roles: 'In this part of the world more than any other in pre-colonial times, women were conspicuous in "high places". They were queen-mothers, queen sisters, princesses, chiefs and holders of other offices in towns and villages, occasionally warriors, and in one well-known case, that of the Lovedu, the supreme monarch' (Sudarkasa, 1986: 152).

As we think about the male-dominated gendered pattern in Canadian society and other modern societies like Canada, these studies should serve to remind us that there is nothing inevitable or determined about male dominance as defined through gender roles and gender socialization. Indeed, as we will discuss below, there are various other examples of hunting-and-gathering societies, or even African societies that were horticultural or agricultural, that show little of this. So why does the male dominance pattern occur so often in Canadian society and in other modern societies? Part of the purpose of the present chapter is to provide alternative interpretations of this.

Factors That Reinforce Gender Inequality

At Home

Reproduction and child rearing continue to be mainly female activities in Canadian society, as they have been in most past cultures. Women's genes and hormones make childbearing possible. However, childbearing is no longer inevitable. Effective birth control, by reducing the risk of unwanted pregnancy, has made the outcome of sexual intercourse more predictable and controllable than at any other time in history. As a result, men and women can lead more similar lives today than ever before. Today, women spend less time bearing and raising children than they did in the past. Other parts of their lives—especially education, work, career, and marital companionship—are more important today than they once were. Even sexual practices and sexual ideas, like the traditional double standard, have changed as a result of this contraceptive revolution.

However, the family household remains a workplace for women more than for men (see Table 5.1). Before industrial capitalism, it was men's workplace too, but the separation of home and paid work largely brought this to an end (Tilly and Scott, 1987). Though each family has a characteristic and enduring division of labour, what is remarkable is how similar this division is across families and even across nations. Domestic labour, in short, is gendered labour (for a good Canadian overview of this, see Nakhaie, 1995). We still expect adult women to carry out more of the work than men, daughters to do more of the work than sons. This pattern also persists in caregiving. The primary caregiver is usually the wife, mother, or daughter. Women do more of the domestic work even if they engage in paid employment outside the home and are parenting infants, and even when they are taking care of sick or disabled family members.

A study comparing detailed data from Canada, the United States, Sweden, Norway, and Australia finds that the factors shaping men's and

TABLE 5.1
Canadian Population 15 Years and over, by Hours Spent on Unpaid Housework, 1996

	Males	Females
No hours	1,714,470	897,600
Less than 5 hours	3,319,100	1,819,665
5 to 14 hours	3,604,565	3,263,070
15 to 29 hours	1,572,235	2,776,115
30 to 59 hours	617,415	1,965,495
60 or more hours	194,660	884,520

SOURCE: Statistics Canada, 'Population 15 Years and Over by Hours Spent on Unpaid Housework, 1996 Census, Census Metropolitan Areas' (1996), available at <www.statcan.ca/english/Pgdb/famil56d.htm>, accessed 23 March 2003.

women's participation in housework vary little across countries, despite variations in ideology and sex-role attitudes:

> Households that have the most egalitarian divisions of labour are those in which both husband and wife are employed outside the home, both hold liberal sex role attitudes, and . . . wives contribute a significant proportion of the household income relative to their husbands. The data also show support for a number of other individual-level factors. In particular, older women do a greater proportion of indoor tasks than younger women, and having children in the household increases women's share of housework. (Baxter, 1997: 19–20)

Of course, families in each country do vary somewhat in this regard. In some studies, for example, remarried couples report a less complete or weaker version of gendered inequality than first-time married couples (Ishii-Kuntz and Coltrane, 1992). Couples who become parents in their twenties are somewhat more traditional in their gendering of domestic work than couples who make this transition in their thirties (Coltrane

and Ishii-Kuntz, 1990). Women who cohabit do much less household work than women who are legally married (Shelton and John, 1993). And dual-career couples often renegotiate their domestic division of labour as outside work duties change (Gregson and Lowe, 1994).

The Arrival of Children

Women's lives become much more complicated with the appearance of children. Helena Willen and Henry Montgomery (1996) refer to this fact as the 'Catch 22' of marriage: wishing and planning for a child increases marital happiness, but achieving this wish reduces that happiness. The birth of a child and the resulting intense mother-child relationship tend to strain marital relations (Erel and Burman, 1995). New parents are less happy with each other and experience more frequent, sometimes violent, conflicts with each other after the baby arrives (Crohan, 1996). For some, the conflict may begin even before the baby arrives.

With the arrival of children, wives have much less time for their husbands or for them-

Research investigating household division of labour in Canada indicates that married women do more domestic labour than cohabitating, non-married women, and that dual-earner couples often renegotiate their domestic division of labour as their outside work duties change. (Bill and Peggy Wittman)

selves, which may cause resentment. The birth of a child reduces by up to 80 per cent the proportion of activities wives do alone, or that parents do as a couple or with non-family members, until the child is school-aged (Monk et al., 1996; for Canadian evidence on this topic, see Cowan & Cowan, 1995).

This radical shift from spousal (adult-centred) activities to parenting (child-centred) activities creates an emotional distance that the partners find hard to bridge. Romance and privacy decline. Sleepless nights increase. Mothers, the main providers of child care, change their time use much more than fathers. Particularly after the birth of a first child, marital quality and quantity of time together declines immediately. Mothers report feeling more angry and depressed than before (Monk et al., 1996; for Canadian evidence on this topic, see Cowan and Cowan, 1995).

The transition to parenthood tends to increase gender inequality between partners (Fox, 2001). The social relationship between husband and wife changes. Wives, as mothers, devote more time to their infants and less time to their husbands. Husbands often resent this change, and wives may adopt a new, subservient way of dealing with husbands to reduce the resentment and conflict. This often produces resentment on the wife's side. As Bonnie Fox summarizes the evidence,

> how a woman defines mothering is partly a product of negotiation with her partner. Because intensive mothering requires considerable support, it is contingent upon the consent and active cooperation of the partner, which makes for all sorts of subtle inequalities in the relationship. . . . [A] strong relationship between the father and his child . . . is partly contingent upon the woman's active creation of it. And in encouraging the relationship, women cater to their partners' needs more than they otherwise might. (2001: 11–12)

Even the closest, happiest couples experience distress after having a baby, and few professional services are available to smooth this transition (Cowan and Cowan, 1995). After the initial euphoria and depression of parenthood wears off, reality sets in. The spouses are often too busy to spend even limited 'quality time' with each other. For example, sexual activity falls off dramatically and never returns to its original level (see, for example, Kermeen, 1995).

Typically, marital satisfaction, which decreases with the arrival of children, reaches an all-time low when the children are teenagers. The presence of children in the household, though pleasing in many respects, also increases the domestic workload for parents and increases conflict. Once the children leave home, creating what some sociologists have called an 'empty nest', many marriages improve to near-newlywed levels of satisfaction (Lupri and Frideres, 1981).

Parental (and other work) responsibilities decline, partly explaining this return of marital satisfaction in later life (Orbach, House, and Mero, 1996). Many couples rediscover each other because they have more leisure time in which to become reacquainted. Thus, older couples show much less distress, less desire for change in their marriage, and a more accurate understanding of the needs of their partners than do younger married couples (Rabin and Rahav, 1995).

Paid Work Versus Housework

In the last few decades, throughout the industrial world, women's labour-force participation and family lives have changed dramatically. For women, working outside the home has many benefits. It contributes to their satisfaction, increases the likelihood of equal treatment within the home, and provides security in case of marital dissolution (Chafetz and Hagan, 1996). However, women continue to do most of the housework and child care.

This results in overload, culturally induced stress, and spillover. By *overload*, we mean that women face an excessive amount of work. Often they are physically and emotionally unable to keep up with the demands. By *culturally induced stress*, we mean that the workload—and the failure to complete it all—carries guilt-inducing meanings in our culture. By *spillover*, we mean that the demands and stress from one domain spill over into other domains of a woman's life, affecting the functioning of the entire family.

The stress associated with the unequal division of domestic work is frequently intensified by the fact that women are equally as likely as or more likely than men to hold stressful jobs. Many of the jobs of women combine heavy continuing demands with a lack of decision-making authority (for example, sales, service, and clerical positions). This combination causes increased risk of stress and health problems, including cardiovascular disorders (Karasek and Theorell, 1990). Of course, men often have these and other forms of stress at work, too. However, their domestic workload is generally lighter. Because women spend more combined time on paid work and domestic work than men, they experience overload attached to a greater variety of activities, especially during early parenthood (Michelson, 1985, 1988). Also, women often have to work more hours than men because of their lower overall earning power (that is, their hourly differences in earnings). Further, they are much more likely to face the demands of being a single parent.

What many women face today is a third-millennium work pattern with a 1950s division of labour at home. Arlie Hochschild (1998) has suggested that domestic labour is even less manageable and egalitarian than paid work. This may be why many women do not take advantage of corporate arrangements such as job sharing. If they spend less time at work, it simply means that they'll be doing more domestic labour.

Caregiver Burden

Serious acute and long-term illnesses and disabilities (which we will group together as 'serious illnesses') can also put great strains on a family's ability to function and the well-being of its members—especially that of the main caregiver. Caregivers are usually female (see Figure 5.1). The caregiver in an elderly couple is usually the wife. If a spouse is not available, an adult daughter usually takes over. Men may provide occasional assistance but are much less likely to assist with, for example, daily chores (Stoller, 1990). Sons in our society tend to become caregivers to older parents only in the absence of an available female sibling (Horowitz, 1985).

Caregiving is an emotional, mental, and physical burden. As more care is given, the caregiver's well-being decreases. This is a growing problem because of the aging of the Canadian population, which means that more adults will be called on to

FIGURE 5.1
Who Feels the Burden of Caregiving to Seniors?

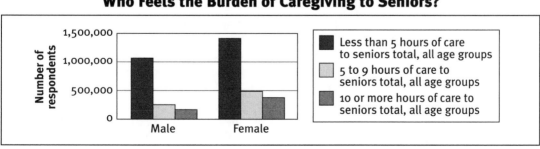

SOURCE: Kelly Cranswick, *Canada's Caregivers* (Ottawa: Statistics Canada, 1997), available at <www.hc-sc.gc.ca/seniors-aines/pubs/unsorted/survey.htm>, accessed 23 March 2003.

provide care for their aging parents and spouses. As well, medicine and health technologies have become more successful in prolonging the lives of chronically ill or disabled people. Family members today can expect to spend a larger fraction of their lives caring for other family members than was the case in the past.

Overall, unpaid caregivers to the sick and disabled—whatever the relationship or cause of disability—have a distinctive profile. Most are women, aged 30 to 59, and married. Most are the children, parent, or partner of the care recipient. The vast majority of the recipients they care for have multiple problems, frequently age-related. Except for caregivers whose relatives are in residential care, few receive any formal assistance, although many receive informal support from family and friends. Nearly half the caregivers report they have experienced major health problems of their own in the past year. Two-thirds say they feel exhausted at the end of each day. Half feel they have more to do than they can handle (Schofield and Herrman, 1993).

So women are far more likely than men to provide care. As a result, they suffer caregiving strain, work interference, income loss, and role strain (Fredriksen, 1996). When caregiving responsibilities are added to the regular demands of domestic work, parenting, and paid work, the dangers of caregiver burnout and family breakdown increase dramatically. Some women shift to part-time work, at least temporarily, when their caregiving burdens become onerous (Walsh, 1999). Others make different short-term arrangements or take a leave of absence (Franklin, Ames, and King, 1994). The result is a forced fluidity in women's lives as paid workers, despite their skills, training, and aspirations (Pohl, Collins, and Given, 1998). This fluidity can also have serious long-term consequences for social security benefits after retirement (Kingston and O'Grady-LeShane, 1993). Further, some women—especially single mothers—are forced to stay on welfare so that they can meet their parental obligations (Heymann and Earle, 1998).

Difficulties in balancing the demands of home and employment create considerable stress that, taken to extremes, contributes to life-threatening health conditions (see, for example, Ginn and Sandell, 1997; Scharlach and Fredriksen, 1994). Working women experience large increases in stress when they are forced to alter their work schedules to meet the home care needs of an impaired, elderly family member (Orodenker, 1990).

The socialization of women to view themselves as particularly responsible for caregiving makes guilt and shame potent additional sources of stress if caregiving becomes difficult to accomplish well. Even when faced with high care demands, women who are primary care providers use secondary providers merely to help in care tasks they are already carrying out (Stommel et al., 1995).

Individual psychosocial interventions, including respite programs, have been moderately effective in dealing with caregiver distress (Knight, Lutzky, and Macofsky-Urban, 1993). Increasingly, the social, medical, and helping professions are learning when and how to intervene most effectively to support families that are dealing with chronic illness (Woods, Yates, and Primomo, 1989). Some families adapt to this stressor so well that functioning returns to normal. However, the stressor may still be present. Support from family, friends, and community agencies eases the impact of caregiving for some people. A supportive work environment also reduces physical and emotional strains (Lechner, 1993).

Support for the caregiver can come from two sources: other caregivers who provide assistance (who help reduce the workload) and others outside the caregiving situation (who provide emotional support). Social networks often play a potent role in providing social support to families that are struggling to support chronically ill or disabled family members. A family's ability to support its members is, in large part, influenced by its ability to obtain external support to mitigate illness-related family stress. This is where networks of kin and friends can play an important part (Ell, 1996).

When caring for parents, as we have said, daughters take on more of the duties. Subsequently, they experience more distress due to interference with work and strained relationships with the parents being cared for (Mui, 1995). So far, there is little information on the extent of this type of caregiving in the general population or on types of work interference (Carswick, 1997; Tennstedt and Gonyea, 1994). Even so, regular caregiving adversely affects both personal and professional life—especially when crises arise, which is almost inevitable (Gottlieb, Kelloway, and Fraboni, 1994).

Caregiver stress, burnout, and psychosomatic symptoms may occur because of unresolved conflicts with or ambivalent feelings toward the ill or aged parent. Spending large amounts of time providing attentive and personal care to an elderly parent with whom he or she has a strained relationship is bound to take an extra toll on the caregiver's mental health. Family caregivers who put their relatives in nursing homes experience immediate relief from feelings of overload and tension. However, for many, a continuing concern and sense of guilt leads to long-term stress (Zarit and Whitlatch, 1993).

The problems that come with caring for a chronically ill parent, spouse, or other relative promise to become increasingly prevalent as lifespans lengthen (Blazer, 1982). These problems also come at a time when a decline in fertility rates means that people have fewer siblings to share duties with and fewer social supports to help them, given the drastic cuts in the numbers of hospital beds and nurses.

Gender Stereotypes in the Media

Portrayals of girls and women in the mass media, especially in television, keep gender stereotypes alive and, in this way, help keep women from achieving equality with men at home or at work

(see, for example, Merlo and Smith, 1994a, 1994b). In the mass media, we see gendered images all around us—gendered images of women and men, boys and girls. Even animals are presented as gendered (think about Disney cartoons, for example). These gendered images are parallelled in media advertisements for consumer items and in the items people end up buying—toys, clothes, books, and magazines. The media present items as proper for use by one or the other biological sex. Our culture makes assumptions about what male people and female people will typically want to do. The belief produces a self-fulfilling prophecy: often our children turn out to be how we expect them to be.

Look at Saturday morning children's television: cartoon shows interspersed with commercials. Advertisers aim the commercials directly at girls or boys, typically matched to the type of show—Barbie dolls (or the equivalent) for girls, GI Joe figures (or the equivalent) for boys. These programs entertain children, but they also teach them which toys are for them, how we expect them as girls or boys to behave, and what we expect them, as gendered beings, to want in our society.

The messages from TV are clear. Idealized boys will fight physically and push aside others whom they do not respect, making decisions about themselves and for others weaker than them. Girls will fight verbally (if at all), play with dolls, and wait to be chosen or told what to do. Storybooks and movies carry similar messages. Years later, young women follow the men whom they feel have chosen them, trying to appear not too aggressive, not too successful, in case they are perceived as a threat and rejected (Brinson, 1992; Furnham and Bitar, 1993; Salamon and Robinson, 1987).

Some have hailed the growing display of open sexuality in the mass media as liberating and empowering, for women as well as for men. Others, however, believe that some forms of sexually explicit display—for example, pornography—are not empowering. Pornography objectifies women by depicting women in dehumanizing ways. In doing so, it helps to maintain female submission and male domination. Like prostitution, pornography supports patriarchal culture and its gender hierarchy (Leuchtag, 1995). Straight pornography and gay pornography can also objectify and dehumanize males. Degrading pornography denigrates all its subjects, whether female or male.

Others have celebrated the way current popular culture embraces the word 'girl' as a term of female empowerment, especially as it is applied to high-profile female athletes. Supposedly, the new 'girl culture' of these female athletes offers young women role models that are better than prior images of girls as vulnerable, doll-like, and helpless. The newer image promotes confidence, health, and authority, and that is all to the good (Geissler, 2001).

The popular media in general, though, is more likely to describe women in terms of the number of children they have, men in terms of occupations or political affiliations. A woman who emphasizes politics in her life or a man whose priority is his children's care is pointed out as a curiosity not as a role model. These are only a few of the gender stereotypes that bombard us from the media (Livingstone, 1994; Media-Watch, 1991; Shaw and Martin, 1992).

Of course, members of some branches of the media see their role differently. They aspire to be forerunners and agents of change. Thus, they will

---

BOX 5.1
Radical Cheerleaders

Some groups take stereotyped media images of women and turn them on their head—for example, Radical Cheerleaders. That's right: they go to protests and do cheerleaders' routines . . . only a little differently than in high school. If you are lucky they will be at the next protest you attend. Or search on the Web for your local branch.

We're sexy, we're cute
We're sexy, we're cute, we're radical to boot!
We're angry, we're tough, and we have had enough!
. . . . .
Public service is privatized, do you want your health care super-sized?
. . . . .
We're sexy, we're cute, we're radical to boot!
We're angry, we're tough, and we have had enough!
Take back the power, fight corporate greed . . .

Riot Don't Diet
RIOT DON'T DIET
GET UP GET OUT AND TRY IT
RIOT DON'T DIET
GET UP GET OUT AND TRY IT
hey girl (clap clap clap)
get yer face out of that magazine
you are more than a beauty machine
you've got anger soul and more
take to the street and let it roar
RIOT DON'T DIET
GET UP GET OUT AND TRY IT
RIOT DON'T DIET
GET UP GET OUT AND TRY IT . . .

The Sarcastic One
totally, for sure, I just got a manicure
the sun, I swear, it's ruining my golden hair
36 to 44 does anybody know the score
rah rah fight fight
gee I hope I look all right

SOURCE: *Radical Cheers!* Available at <http://www.geocities.com/radicalcheerleaders/cheers.htm#cheerleading>, accessed 21 January 2003.

purposely show the female engineer or the male nurse or elementary teacher not as curiosities but as experts in their fields, deliberately chosen as role models. Some programs and magazines also typically show an awareness of diversity in race and ethnicity. Sadly, the rest of the media often stereotype these programs and magazines as 'educational' or 'feminist'. The public often receives them in the same terms; they are generally watched, read, or listened to by fewer people than other aspects of the media. Some socially conscious agencies are also now trying to use commercial media (for example, television advertisements) to promote change. We will occasionally see, for example, male sports stars talking about problems of violence against women in an attempt to promote models of masculinity that are concerned, caring, and nurturing though strong. However, the idea of a rapid direct imitative influence of media images on viewers, and so on society, may be too simplistic. The media may reflect and reinforce culture more than they are able to easily *change* culture and society.

Recent research by Melissa Milkie (2002) shows that editors of girls' magazines share in the critique of the depiction of girls in the media, recognizing they should change images but cannot. In these accounts, the editors reveal struggles at the organizational and the institutional levels over altering narrow images of femininity. At the same time, editors also undermine the girls' critique by suggesting that the (good) reader is *supposed* to understand the images. Here, editors claim that they can change images but *should* not. Ultimately, both sets of responses prevent the girls' critique from redefining femininity, and undermine the power of girls' resistance to media images.

Theories of Gender Inequality

In the past, sociology had a disappointing track record of attempts to adequately explain gender inequality. Part of the reason for this is that sociologists, like other academics, were mostly men

before the latter part of the twentieth century. They largely accepted, without questioning, the gendered division of labour as an aspect of social organization. With the increase in the number of female sociologists and with the rise of feminist scholarship, there has been an improved understanding of gender roles. The three broad theoretical perspectives of sociology and the feminist perspective have been applied to this understanding.

The Structural-Functionalist Perspective

The earliest sociologists viewed gender differences, including inequalities, as givens; these differences were therefore to be explained by their supposed social functions.

Structural-functionalists approach the issue of gender inequality as a problem stemming from a once effective household arrangement that has failed to develop with the times. This approach stresses that in pre-industrial societies, work and family life were closely intertwined. The entire economy was little more than a set of household economies. In this context, the classic division of labour developed between the sexes to ensure that the family would survive. Women, as the natural childbearers, were responsible for raising and nurturing children, but they were also responsible for gardening, gathering, and preparing farm produce. Men, being physically stronger, were responsible for the heavier or more dangerous work.

This delineation of tasks helped to ensure that all the necessary ingredients for survival would be present. The division of labour was practical and efficient and, over time, became accepted as the natural arrangement of the household. Eventually, however, with industrialization and the growth of work outside the household in offices and factories, the family sphere became increasingly separate from the work sphere. Women's roles in the family became increasingly confined to household nurturance, while men became the near-exclusive participants in the paid workforce. Though rural women might have continued to do the kinds of work they had always done, men socially devalued this work in comparison with wage work or salaried work.

Eventually, the traditional division of labour that had separated men's work from women's was no longer an effective means of balancing production and reproduction. It was no longer necessary, given a declining fertility rate; no longer secure, given an increasing divorce rate; and no longer affordable, given a new economy that demanded multiple sources of family income for a comfortable lifestyle. In short, that is why, according to the functionalist perspective, modern family structures are growing less rigid and traditional, the workplace is slowly becoming more gender-equal, and gender roles are creeping tentatively toward greater androgyny. Society is evolving or adapting—as it often does—to the new needs and demands of its members.

Conflict Theory

Conflict theorists have argued that gender inequality is essentially the result of a struggle for economic and social power. In pre-industrial hunting-and-gathering societies, men and women had more equal status despite an informal division of labour. Although women were the primary caregivers, their contribution to the food supply limited to the gathering of agricultural produce and the preparation of meals, they were hardly subordinate to their male, hunting counterparts. Neither was there a class system or ownership of private property. In short, there was little differentiation of functions in these societies, and what differentiation there was did not lead to wide social inequalities.

Even today, some hunter-gatherer cultures continue to live a near-egalitarian lifestyle, although such examples have become exceedingly rare. One is the !Kung society of the Kalahari Desert, a semi-nomadic hunting-and-gathering people. When asked, !Kung will state that there is

men's work and women's work, and they conceive of most individual jobs as sex-typed, at least in principle. In practice, however, adults of both sexes are willing to do the work of the opposite sex. No social disadvantages attach to being men or women (Lee, 1993; Howell, 2000).

Industrial societies, however, separate the family from the paid workforce. This is the result of a long developmental process, as Friedrich Engels explains in his classic work *The Origin of the Family, Private Property, and the State* ([1884] 1985). With settled agriculture and an agricultural surplus comes the rise of private property, and with private property, the rise of states and ruling classes. Religion becomes part of a ruling structure that legitimates class and gender inequality. With the rise of industrial production, the tendencies to private ownership, exploitation, and the ideological legitimation of inequality strengthen under the aegis of the state and the 'rule of law'.

Since the inheritance of property flows through kinship based mainly on blood, blood ties are critically important where there is significant private property to be inherited. However, only the maternity of children is known with certainty. To control property, men must oversee and control women's reproduction. This change marks the beginning of patriarchal control within families and societies. Out of this comes the general deprivation of women's rights, controls on their public behaviour, even seclusion.

Early conflict theorists, led by Engels, Marx, and the Marxists who followed, argued that capitalism was the source of this inequality. Later thinkers, led by Weber and the Weberians, have argued that inequality can arise from a variety of differences in power and authority, and not merely from private property under capitalism.

Symbolic Interactionism

Most of the variations that exist between men and women are cultural and learned. Symbolic interactionists stress that gender 'teaching', through stereotyping and socialization as well as other means, occurs at all levels of social life. Our values and norms, media, and religion, even our language use, also maintain controlling stereotypes.

Symbolic interactionists focus on the fact that individuals are 'meaning-seekers' who are trying to develop a stable sense of self. This process is gradual and continues throughout life, as people negotiate meanings in interaction with others, in the context of social institutions and cultural expectations. A sense of gendered self comes out of this process of gradual socialization and interpersonal experience.

It is in this context, for example, that women learn to do 'women's work' and to view themselves as suited for these tasks. (Along similar lines, women come to expect payment at the levels that they have received in the past.) 'Women's' jobs typically pay less, have lower prestige, and require longer hours of work than jobs in which most workers are men. Historically, men have tended to demand and receive more authority than women.

Consider the work relationship between nurses and doctors. By tradition, the nurse has been the 'handmaid' of the doctor. The doctor is viewed as the professional who possesses the most training, expert knowledge, authority, and prestige. The nurse's role is to carry out the doc-

tor's wishes with an attitude of obedience, competence, selflessness, loyalty, and total dedication to caring for patients. In short, the nurse serves as an 'instrument' or 'tool' of the doctor—not as the doctor's co-worker. Janet Kerr and Janetta MacPhail have studied how 'sex stereotyped views of nursing emphasize subservience, lack of assertiveness and domination of nurses who are primarily female, by physicians, who are primarily male' (1999: 21). Consider, also, how the term 'male nurse' is commonly (although irrelevantly) used to describe a man in the profession, a tacit intimation that the role of 'nurse' is by default a female occupation. (See also Figure 5.2.)

The Feminist Perspective

A fourth theoretical perspective that is becoming more and more influential in sociology is the feminist perspective. Like other sociological approaches, the feminist approach is composed of a wide variety of different points of view and diverse, sometimes conflicting theories. Nevertheless, there are a number of common themes and concerns that can be identified in the work of feminists.

Note first that feminism is not something new. It is an approach that goes back at least two centuries, to the English philosopher Mary

FIGURE 5.2
Nurses by Sex, 1991 and 1996

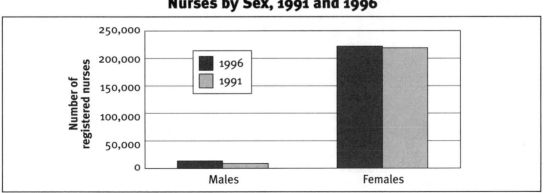

SOURCE: Statistics Canada, *1996 Census Nation Tables* (Ottawa: Statistics Canada, 2002), available at <www.statcan.ca/english/census96/nation.htm> accessed 1 March 2003.

Wollstonecraft ([1792] 1992). Since the mid-nineteenth century, there have been numerous bursts of visible feminist activity followed by periods of near invisibility. The first wave of feminism occurred between the middle of the nineteenth century and the early twentieth century. It culminated in women's gaining the right to vote in many Western countries. Then two strands of feminism emerged: one concerned with gaining equal rights with men in the public sphere, the other with gaining recognition of women's difference from men and improving their position in the private sphere of

Although women are also perpetrators of violence, they are disproportionately men's victims. Perhaps most disturbing is that it is not strangers but those closest to women who hurt them the most often. (Dick Hemingway)

the family. This second wave, or re-emergence, of feminism occurred in the 1960s. It is this wave that created the modern women's movement and that has influenced sociology through a feminist critique of the male-dominated discipline.

Up to the late 1960s, feminism was concerned with understanding the oppression believed to be commonly experienced by all women. More recent feminist scholarship has emphasized the diversity of women's experience as members of different countries, classes, and racial and ethnic groups. As a result, we have seen the growth of varied 'feminisms' that focus on one or another type of female experience. However, one widely accepted distinction is that between radical feminism and materialist (socialist or Marxist) feminism.

Radical feminism is characterized by a belief that patriarchy is the main and universal cause of women's oppression, owing to the superior power of men over women. This view has promoted the notion that women must organize separately from men to protect their own interests and foster a distinct women's culture. *Materialist feminism* traces its roots to Marxism and, like Marxism, views gender relations in a historical, economic context. It sees social class relations as determining the conditions women experience within capitalism. This approach calls for women to organize alongside men of the same social class to solve the problems women are suffering. What the two main types of feminism have in common is a belief that the subordination of women is not a result of biological determinism, but rather a result of socio-economic and ideological factors. Though they differ in thinking about the ways this might be achieved, both types are committed to eliminating the social inequality of women and men.

The application of feminism in sociology calls attention to the *androcentric* (male-dominated) history of sociological thinking. To remedy this, feminist sociologists emphasize the experiences of women 'because there can be no sociological generalizations about human beings as long as a large number of such beings are systematically excluded or ignored' (Sydie, 1986: 360). Feminist research often includes elements of symbolic interactionism and conflict approaches. However, it is typically informed by a unique set of assumptions about reality, namely,

- all personal life has a political dimension;
- the public and private spheres of life are both gendered (that is, the positions of men and women are unequal in both);
- women's social experience routinely differs from men's;
- patriarchy, or male control, structures the way most societies work; and
- because of routinely different experiences and differences in power, women's and men's perceptions of reality differ.

So, for example, feminists would point out how men and women typically have different views about divorce because they typically have very different experiences after divorce. For men, divorce means a brief reduction in the standard of living—if any reduction at all—and a huge reduction in parenting responsibilities. For women, it usually means a dramatic, long-term loss in income and standard of living. Poverty is common among single mothers and their children. It also means an increase in parental responsibilities, since mothers usually retain custody of the children. For all these reasons, divorce has a very different meaning for women than it does for men. For similar reasons sex, love, and marriage all have different meanings for men and women,

as we will see in later chapters. Each of these are topics studied by feminist sociologists.

This approach also leads one to consider how women are sometimes degraded or victimized. Indeed, along with children, women are often even in danger of their lives. More men kill women and children than are killed by women and children, for example (Gartner and Archer, 1984). Thus, women's acceptance of the female role is far more costly—even dangerous—than is men's acceptance of the male role.

Rosalind Sydie points out that feminist sociology is political because it shows how sociologists have previously justified intellectually the continuing existence of gender inequality (1986). So, for example, male sociologists were quick to defend gender inequalities in the family by creating functional theories that made gender inequality seem not only inevitable, but also desirable. Feminists emphasize that our notions of what it means to be male or female and our dealings with one another as male or female are a result of the social arrangements prevalent in our society. No one is ever 'naturally' male or female because gender is neither biological nor 'natural'.

Feminism is also a form of political activism that attempts to change the circumstances within which men and women lead their lives. Feminism, then, has an emancipatory goal. If gender relations always reflect the larger pattern of social relations in a society, then changing gender relations requires changing those social relations as well. In this respect, feminism is one of the social movements that—alongside the anti-war, youth, civil rights, anti-racism, and green movements—have in the last three decades reshaped modern politics. Like these other social movements in both spirit and organization, feminism has looked for grassroots support, affirmed subjectivity and spontaneity in politics, and sought to dramatize its struggle rather than submerge its efforts in the traditional party system using traditional electoral methods. Like these other movements, feminism has appealed to the social identity—the personal life experience—of its supporters. More than that, by arguing that 'the personal is political', feminism opened up new domains of social life—sexuality, housework, child rearing, and so on—to political debate and legislation. It also forced us all to examine the very roots of our being as gendered subjects—that is, how we get to be and think of ourselves as men versus women or mothers versus fathers.

Social Consequences of Gender Inequality

As we would expect from the foregoing discussion, issues of gender are implicated in pretty much all aspects of Canadian social life. In this section, we will provide selected examples from the areas of education and employment, domestic work, parenting, crime and violence, poverty, self-esteem, and political struggles.

Education and Employment

A frequently cited problem associated with gender inequality is the gap between men's and women's occupational attainments. Part of the problem, in other parts of the world, is educational. For example, literacy rates around the world are lower for women (72 per cent) than for men (84 per cent). In the least developed countries, the discrepancy is even higher, at 39 per cent and 59 per cent, respectively (UNDP, 1998). Families, governments, and economies simply do not give young women high priority in education and jobs.

In Canada, female enrolments in the university-level social sciences and humanities have been comparatively high for many years, and have even reached parity or near-parity with male enrolment in some traditionally male-dominated programs such as medicine. (See Figure 5.3.) However, in recent years, women's numbers have made only marginal progress in engineering, mathematics, and the physical sciences, and remain low in those areas (Normand, 1995).

A survey released by the Canadian Council of Professional Engineers found that although '24 per cent of all professional engineers born after 1970 are women' and 'women accounted for nearly 20 per cent of the students enrolled in

FIGURE 5.3
University Enrolment in Canada, by Sex, 1994/5–1998/9

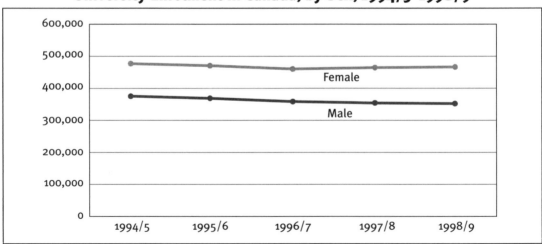

SOURCE: Statistics Canada, 'University Enrolment, Full-time and Part-time, by Sex', available at <www.statcan.ca/english/Pgdb/educ03a.htm>, accessed 23 March 2003.

Canadian undergraduate engineering programs during the 1998–99 academic year', low female entry rates into the engineering profession before the early 1980s mean that women account for fewer than 6 per cent of Canada's registered professional engineers (1999). Among those enrolled in undergraduate mathematics and physical science degrees in 1999, only 30 per cent were women. The gap between the sexes is even more dramatic in masters-level and doctoral-level programs, except in the social sciences.

These patterns are partly a consequence of the media processes we discussed earlier in this chapter. They also result from more general gender socialization that begins as early as elementary school, when we teach girls and boys through example and direct suggestion to aspire to different, gender-specific careers and fields of study.

Among young men and women with the same educational background in the same line of work, income differences virtually disappear. In 2000, Canadian university-educated women aged 25 to 29 who worked in the 10 most common occupations chosen by men of the same age group and qualifications earned about 89 cents for every dollar their male counterparts made. In four out of these 10 occupations, women made at least 90 per cent of what men earned. But overall, the most common occupations held by young women are lower paying than those men most commonly work in. The 10 most common occupations held by university-educated women aged 25 to 29 paid $37,185 on average. The 10 occupations most common to men of the same age group and level of education paid women an average of $41,509.

Thus, a large part of the gendered income difference is due to the segregation of work. Gender segregation affects people's earnings even after controlling for human capital variables (such as education level), organizational attributes (such as industry or size of organization), and job characteristics (such as job level), suggesting that the gender gap in pay is at least partly a function of the gendering of workplaces (Knudsen and Roman, 2000). However, women also receive a lower return on their investment in a university education because of tending to family responsibilities. In 1998, 62 per cent of men but only 49 per cent of women between the ages of 25 and 64 with a university degree were employed in high-level positions (Clark, 2001: 8). This largely reflects women's loss of income and opportunities because of maternity leave, employment in part-time work, or relocation to another town or province to accompany a male partner.

Job prestige may be tied to whether a job is considered men's or women's work. Office clerks in the early nineteenth century, for instance, were mainly male, and as a result, clerkships were highly admired. When typewriters and other technological innovations made office work more routine, men vacated the field and women moved in. The clerical job lost status and pay, and remains a low-status, low-paying position to this day.

In some workplaces, women have an equal opportunity. In many others, they still hit a 'glass ceiling' when they strive for advancement. This term, **glass ceiling**, points to the fact that women face nearly hidden obstacles when it comes to advancing into the highest-status jobs. Women are less often hired into these jobs, because in part of an 'old boys' club' mentality, a snobbish preference for men, and a belief (in some cases) that women are inferior.

In the past, many factors hindered better forms of employment for and promotion of women. Many people felt that women should not compete for men's management positions. Ideas about the different skills and abilities of women and men led to the idea that there were jobs women *could* not do, and those they *should* not do. Some men were embarrassed to have their wives working for pay since (they thought) it reflected badly on their ability to support a family and, in this way, reflected badly on their masculinity. Even as recently as 20 years ago, it was common for women to be explicitly paid less than men—the 'breadwinners'—for doing the same work. In reality, many women also had to support families, but social assumptions over-looked this. Women, many thought, could not give the same attention to difficult or complex tasks because of their responsibilities to spouses and children.

We have now removed some of these barriers. As the twentieth century progressed, women showed that they too could excel in mathematics, science, politics, and other 'male' fields of endeavour. Further, the economy needed the skills of talented women, as well as of men. In many parts of the Western world, discrimination against women is now illegal and employers commonly advertise jobs as 'open to women and men'. In today's schools, both girls and boys study mathematics, sciences, and arts. Barriers to the entry of women into law schools and medical schools are long gone. However, if we look at the distribution of occupations, we still find fewer women than men in high-paying positions, and, on average, full-time working women still earn about 70 cents for every dollar earned by counterpart men, calculated based on hourly wages.

To determine whether there is still a 'glass ceiling', we should look not at today's highest earners, but at people who are currently working their ways up the corporate and professional ladders. Generally, the evidence suggests that women with higher education do as

TABLE 5.2
Average Earnings in the Five Occupations Most Commonly Held by Those Aged 25 to 29 With a University Degree Working Full-year, Full-time,[a] by Sex, Canada, 2000

	Number		Average Earnings		Women's Earnings as a Percentage of Men's Earnings
	Men	Women	Men	Women	
Five occupations most commonly held by young men					
Computer and information systems	17,710	6,450	$54,052	$45,915	84.9
Financial auditors and accountants	4,155	5,280	$42,913	$39,990	93.2
Sales marketing and advertising managers	3,125	3,320	$56,440	$46,047	81.6
Retail trade managers	2,645	2,380	$38,122	$31,596	82.9
Secondary school teachers	2,425	4,120	$36,201	$35,546	98.2
Five occupations most commonly held by young women					
Elementary school and kindergarten teachers	1,625	9,255	$36,243	$35,535	98.0
Computer and information systems	17,710	6,450	$54,052	$45,915	84.9
Financial auditors and accountants	4,155	5,280	$42,913	$39,990	93.2
Registered nurses	360	4,820	$44,688	$41,088	91.9
Secondary school teachers	2,425	4,120	$36,201	$35,546	98.2

[a]Earners who worked 49 to 52 weeks during the year for 30 or more hours per week.

well as men with the same educational attainment and career goals—that is, until they marry and have children. At that point, their pay starts to dip in comparison with men's. At more senior levels, women may put off career plans to bear and raise children. If they do so, they will take longer to achieve more senior executive status. The existence of this 'Mommy track' shows that the women themselves make choices about their lives, choices that obviously affect their career plans.

Many women still seek entry into the traditionally female jobs of stenographer and secretary, sales clerk, bookkeeper and accounting clerk, cashier, nurse, elementary school teacher, general office clerk, and janitor and cleaning staff. However, if women do take these jobs, it is more often because they choose to do so. For a variety of reasons, many women still enter jobs that are low-paid or that do not lead to promotions and career paths. Sometimes the content of the job attracts them. Sometimes they think the job will fit in with their family responsibilities. For any given woman, raising a family may take priority at one point in her life, and she may emphasize her career later. (See also Table 5.2.)

Two facts are clear. First, women who gain the highest levels of education come closest to job and income equality with men. Higher education is an important way toward gender equality in Canada today. Though it does not solve all the problems, it solves many. Others must be solved through sharing family responsibilities. Second, women who marry and bear children move away from job and income equality with men, whatever their level of education. Family responsibilities continue to fall most heavily on wives and mothers, not husbands and fathers. For good reason, more and more women delay marriage, childbearing, or both to pursue higher education and high-paying careers. As a result, more women are running into age-related problems of infertility and often come to rely on new, costly reproductive technologies (Scritchfield, 1995).

Domestic Work

We have already discussed gender inequality in unpaid work at home. Here are a few additional facts on the matter: Statistics Canada estimates that women do a daily average of 4.3 hours of 'household work and related activities', including cooking, housekeeping, maintenance and repair, shopping, and child rearing, compared with 2.8 hours for men (1999: 5). Women usually do the chores that must be done daily, such as cooking and child care, while men are more likely to do the chores that require only occasional attention, such as mowing the lawn, automobile maintenance, and small household improvements (Statistics Canada, 1999). Not by accident, women's tasks usually require nurturance and sensitivity, while men's tasks often require power tools.

Gender equality indexes are statistics used to measure differences between men and women in a variety of domains, including income, work, and education. They are ratios by which a score of 1.00 means that women and men are exactly balanced; a ratio below 1.00 shows that women have less of something than men, and a ratio above 1.00 means that women have more. The Year 2000 edition of a report by Status of Women Canada, using such indexes, shows that women have scores over 1.00 in only two domains: amount of unpaid work (1.56) and amount of time spent on child care (1.72 for full-time working women living with a partner, 1.27 for single mothers). Women do more than their share of unpaid domestic duties. Women are equal with men only on measures of total workload and amount of employment training participation (Clark, 2001). Activities such as unpaid community work and family health care are still considered women's work, in our society as in others.

Let us consider child care a little further. With women in the paid workforce, who looks after their children? Some families rely on daycare provided by professional caregivers. More, however, rely on babysitters who come to the parents' houses, on small-scale child care operations, or on family members' voluntary care. Most babysitters are female, and comparatively few are male. Most non-household family members who 'help' with child care are female; only some are male. When researchers ask parents how they divide the responsibility of the household, they find women taking much more responsibility for the events or tasks of child care (Doucet, 2000; Tremblay, 2001). Thus, although men do take children to doctor's appointments, most often women will have made the appointments.

Crime and Violence

Although men are sometimes the victims of rape and sexual assault, these vicious crimes are primarily directed toward woman. Rape is devastating for the victim not only because of the physical and psychological violations involved, but also because the victim must come to terms with the unsettling fact that she was attacked solely for who she is, for her gender. Rape offenders, who are usually male, typically harbour women-hating, sadistic attitudes toward their victims *because they are women.*

According to the Ontario Women's Directorate, 83 per cent of all sexual assault victims in Canada during 1998 are women, while 98 per cent of the accused perpetrators are men. Young women are at particular risk: 24 per cent of single women aged 18 to 24 report having been victims of date rape, while another 12 per cent of married women in that same age group report at least one incident of violence by a marital partner in a one-year period, compared with an average of 3 per cent for all married or cohabiting women (2000). Statistics for the United States are equally grim. Despite a drop in the overall crime rate in 1999, there was a 20 per cent increase in rapes and a 33 per cent increase in sexual assaults. Nearly 7 in 10 rape and assault victims knew the offender as an acquaintance, friend, relative, or intimate partner (Rennison, 2000: 30, 1; see also Table 5.3).

In 1997/8, 15,257 women and 13,455 dependent children were admitted to shelters in Ontario (Ontario Women's Directorate, 2000), often to escape the reaches of a violent spouse or partner. Four out of every five Canadian victims of spousal homicide in 1998 were female, and women under 25 were at greatest risk. Today, steady lobbying from feminist groups and a growing public awareness of and sensitivity toward the dilemma of abused women has made spousal assault a higher priority and a better-understood crime than in the past.

Historically, women who faced violence in their homes could not rely on police protection. Because the larger community saw domestic violence as a private matter, police were trained to respond accordingly. In doing so, they reflected the expectation of the community and the criminal justice system that officers should be involved in only the most extreme cases. Police were taught to either defuse the situation quickly and leave or attempt to mediate the 'dispute'. This reinforced a view of the victim and assailant as equal parties with equal power over each

TABLE 5.3
Total Violations Against Female Victims, by Relationship of Accused to Victim, Canada, 1999

	Spouse/Ex-Spouse	Friend	Acquaintance	Stranger	Total
Total sexual assaults	4.8%	8.9%	32.2%	23.3%	8,116
Total non-sexual assaults	39.0%	11.2%	17.2%	11.8%	45,090
Total assaults	33.8%	10.8%	19.5%	13.6%	53,206

SOURCE: Statistics Canada, *Canadian Crime Statistics 1999* (Cat. no. 85-205-XIE) (Ottawa: Statistics Canada, 2000).

other's behaviour. Victims were left feeling confused and at fault. Having turned to the police for help, they were left blaming themselves for bothering to call.

Only recently have we come to understand that domestic violence is usually uneven. Whether or not men initiate physical violence, they use more physical force in domestic conflicts than women do. Further, men and women often have different goals in using force. Women are more likely to leave an unsatisfactory relationship, while men are more likely to use force to prevent their partner from leaving. Women will use violence mainly to protect themselves. Husbands will also use violence to compel partners to give them sex. Only recently have law enforcement agencies and the public come to accept spousal rape as a criminal offence. In the past, many considered such behaviour, like spousal abuse, to be a private matter between husband and wife.

Another problem that women sometimes must deal with is sexual harassment in the workplace. This comes in two forms: First, **quid pro quo sexual harassment** is the blatant demand by employers for sexual favours in exchange for promotion opportunities, salary increases, and preferential treatment. The second type of harassment is subtler; it involves fostering a hostile and unpleasant work environment through sexist remarks, jokes, and insults.

Feminization of Poverty

Women are overrepresented among the poor people of the world. Researchers have labelled this development the **feminization of poverty**. High rates of female poverty are usually the result of (1) women's occupational disadvantage in society, (2) women's subordinate position compared with men overall, and (3) women's difficulties in case of abandonment, divorce, or widowhood.

These gender differences increase with age. Old women are poorer, older, sicker, have less adequate housing and access to private transport,

and are more likely to experience widowhood, disability, and institutionalization than are old men (Gibson, 1996). The National Anti-Poverty Organization (NAPO) calculates the figures for Canada to be as follows: 40.9 per cent of non-elderly unattached women live in poverty, while 35.1 per cent of non-elderly unattached men are poor (1999). Not only are the women who head poor families affected by their impoverished state, but their children feel the consequences of poverty as well. Almost one in five of Canada's children, or 1,397,000 people under 18, live in poverty (NAPO, 1999). The effects on children can be both direct, such as nutritional insufficiencies or a shortage of adequate clothing, or indirect, as when they are forced to assume tasks for which their parents have no time.

Social-Psychological Consequences of Gendering

Gender discrimination also carries social-psychological costs. For women, decreased self-esteem, increased depression, and other psychological problems often result from derogation by men, awareness of their subordinate status in society, or a failure to achieve the stereotypical ideal female body. As we have already noted, one area in which this limitation occurs is in the choice of careers. Women are often reluctant to enter professions that involve dangerous, physically demanding work, such as firefighting or the military. By contrast, men are informally, and sometimes directly, cautioned against entering professions that seem to undermine their masculinity, such as early childhood education or nursing.

To protect their self-esteem, women often attribute negative criticisms made to them concerning their work, their abilities, and so on to prejudice by male evaluators, whether the men actually believe gender stereotypes or not (Crocker et al., 2000). This defensive strategy, although understandable, may lead some people to see prejudice where none exists. This becomes a problem when it leads a person to imagine that every member of the opposite sex is the 'enemy'.

Marriage counsellors and couples' therapists have long noted that power differentials can drive a wedge between partners. Trying to balance work, spousal/partner relations, and family life is difficult at the best of times. An unequal sharing of duties can create stress, frustration, and anger for the partner who is doing more of the work—and usually, that partner is a woman. Consistently, research finds that men are more satisfied with current household task arrangements than women. This finding cannot possibly be surprising considering that on average men do much less work around the home.

This type of imbalance poses no problem if the couple agrees that the man contributes more than his share in another aspect of the relationship, such as to the household finances, say, or to parenting duties. Often, however, men feel it unnecessary to make an equal contribution to the domestic workload, reasoning that their earnings are contribution enough to the household. Wives today are less willing to accept that premise. Modern views on love and intimate relationships are based on emotional compatibility. That, coupled with the increasing acceptance of divorce and ease of ending a marriage, means that partners who fail to nurture the relationship, or once too often take advantage of their significant others' willingness to compromise, may find themselves formerly married.

Women's and Men's Political Organizations

People have waged the 'battle of the sexes' for centuries, a struggle that has until recently been a lopsided victory for men. Only with the rise of

---

BOX 5.2
Record Number of Women in Swedish Parliament

Sweden's 349-seat parliament, the Riksdag, retained its title as the most gender equal in the world after elections in which 45 per cent of seats went to women, the Swedish election authority said.

Women won 158 of the seats up for grabs in the election, the highest proportion ever represented in Sweden. In the 1998 election, 149 women, or 43 per cent of MPs, were elected.

Sweden leads the world when it comes to female representation, according to figures from the Interparliamentary Union (IPU), with the Nordic countries claiming the top five spots.

Denmark is in second place with 38 per cent, followed by Finland with 36.5, Norway with 36.4, and Iceland with 34.9 per cent.

The number of women in world parliaments is on average 14.7 percent, according to IPU.

Canada's Parliament
The House of Commons in Canada is above the average, with 20.9 per cent of seats occupied by women as of 26 May 2002. However, in the Canadian Senate, which is appointed rather than elected, 35 per cent of the seats are occupied by women.

Question: Is it implicit in the logic of people who advocate for equal representation in Parliament that men and women are so different from each other that even their political views will necessarily be different? Are there areas of policy or morality on which men and women probably differ in their attitudes, for example, daycare accessibility, abortion, or Native land claims?

SOURCE: APF, 'Record Number of Women in Swedish Parliament', 1 October 2002, available at <http://pub75.ezboard.com/fwomensnewsclippingsfrm6.showMessage?topicID=8.topic>, accessed 21 January 2003.

the feminist movement and, consequently, more progressive views have women made headway in achieving equal standing with men. As with all political ideologies, feminism comes in a variety of forms and comprises a spectrum of factions, each with a different and gradually more radical opinion on how the struggle for women's rights should continue. Some observers have interpreted the most extremely radical positions as not so much pro-women as anti-men. Like sexist anti-women sentiments, anti-men sentiments create a feeling of 'them' versus 'us' that is no more constructive when applied to gender than it is when applied to racial differences.

Some men have viewed the rise of the women's movement less as a threat to their privileged position in society than as an attack on their cherished gender identity. They fear that feminists are motivated to strip men of their political and social power, to remove them from family life, and to represent them as potential rapists, abusers, and sexual predators. Men's claims of male-bashing victimization at the hands of 'castrating' and 'militant' women hold very little truth. For the most part, such allegations are exaggerated and based on sexist and misogynistic views.

The extreme position taken by some members of the feminist and men's movements aside, these political organizations have advanced our awareness and understanding of gender relations. Perhaps the greatest accomplishment of these movements has been to increase public acceptance of the fluidity of gender: the notion that men can be 'feminine' and women can be 'masculine'. Because of the work of these movements, the ideas of biological sex and sociological gender are not as rigidly paired and dichotomized as they used to be. Also, awareness of existing levels of gender inequality has been advanced by such groups. One hopes that the two movements will persist in their instructional activities, with the consequence that this will move society closer to flexible and tolerant understandings of gender roles and greater gender equality.

Health Consequences of Gender Inequality

Women's Health

As women's status in society improves, so does their health. In one study (Kawachi et al., 1999), women's status was assessed by four composite indices measuring political participation, economic autonomy, employment and earnings, and reproductive rights. Main outcome (health) measures were total female and male mortality rates, female cause-specific death rates, and mean days of activity limitation. Data were collected from the 50 US states. The researchers found that women experience higher mortality and morbidity in states where they have lower levels of political participation and economic autonomy. Living in such states has harmful consequences for the health of men as well, however, perhaps because states that limit women are characterized by a more general inequality and lack of social development.

Historically, men have controlled women's bodies—as fathers, husbands, and, more recently, employers. They have also controlled women's bodies as physicians, by defining how women's symptoms and experiences might be interpreted medically. A prime example is found in the work of Sigmund Freud. The field of psychoanalysis, which Freud established, had a great impact on all branches of psychotherapy, as well as on literature and popular culture more generally. Gendered thinking is central to psychoanalysis, which rests on several key assumptions that include the following: (1) all little boys want to murder their father and have sexual relations with their mother; (2) females naturally envy men's penises; and (3) women's illnesses, physical illnesses included, can often be explained by female hysteria—a derangement of female emotions.

It is easy to find, in such assumptions, the basis of 'scientific' legitimacy for the sexual objectification of women, for women's secondary social status and low self-esteem, and for the tendency to doubt and dismiss women's health complaints as unfounded. Throughout the mid- to late twentieth century, one could find in women's magazines the trivialization of potentially important and serious mental symptoms and the subordination of women's health problems to those of others around them, especially male partners. Depression was viewed as a women's mental health disability, and a form of 'gendered incompetence' (Beal and Gardner, 2000).

Even today, 'women's' illnesses and health conditions are often considered more trivial, ridiculous, or shameful than men's. Though sufferers of premenstrual syndrome (PMS) experience distressing—even disabling—psychological and somatic symptoms over a long period (Corney and Stanton, 1991), many men view PMS as a source of humour or irritation. Women experiencing urinary incontinence link their incontinence problems to personal history (childbearing, menopause, and aging) and also personal failings (such as lack of exercise or being overweight) and see the condition as a symbol of their lack of moral worth (Peake, Manderson, and Potts, 1999).

Menopause often offers women another opportunity for shame and embarrassment. Women going through menopause view their physical symptoms—unpredictable or unexpectedly heavy bleeding, intense hot flashes, sudden emotional outbursts—as potentially embarrassing or disruptive. They report struggling to conceal and maintain control of the changes, to keep up appearances (Kittell, Mansfield, and Voda, 1998). In Japan, the menopausal woman is sometimes blamed for her condition and condemned as selfish and lacking in willpower. Canadian research has shown that some doctors view the menopausal woman as depressed, lacking a meaningful occupation, and suffering from a multiplicity of losses (Kaufert and Lock, 1998).

Body image is a big concern for North American women, with the result that women are much more likely than men to starve their bodies into submission through anorexia or bulimia. Though historically African American women have not been as much afflicted by eating disorders because of a greater acceptance in their culture of fuller female figures, the tendency of mainstream culture to measure women's worth by their approximation to the slender, boyish supermodel figure has lately led even black women and girls to judge themselves physically inadequate (Williamson, 1998).

Adolescent fertility is another big problem for women in North America. Factors predicting non-marital teenage pregnancy include two proximate determinants of pregnancy—contraceptive use and frequency of intercourse—as well as a history of school problems, drug use, fighting, living with parents, length of relationship with boyfriends, and best friends experiencing pregnancies (Gillmore et al., 1997). In short, women without long-term goals and stable, cordial relationships are more likely to produce children in adolescence. The results are regrettable, for the children as well as for the mother: a termination of the mother's education, a limitation of the child's economic future.

Not every industrial society has had the same problem with teenage pregnancy as the United States because of a greater willingness elsewhere to acknowledge the sexual activity of teenagers and provide the information and contraceptive resources to prevent their childbearing (Furstenberg, 1998). The blame does not all lie at the feet of the poor or minority communities that produce these teenage pregnancies in large numbers. For example, contrary to popular notions that the African American community condones teenage pregnancy, single parenting, and reliance on welfare, the girls' mothers and grandmothers express feelings of anger, frustration, and disappointment over the situation (Kaplan, 1997).

Women overall, and single mothers in particular, are more likely to be impoverished than any other demographic group (Albelda and Tilly, 1997; see Figure 5.4). A variety of health consequences trouble women who are economically

FIGURE 5.4
Income of Lone-Parent Families, by Gender and
Visible Minority Status, 1996 (Number of Families)

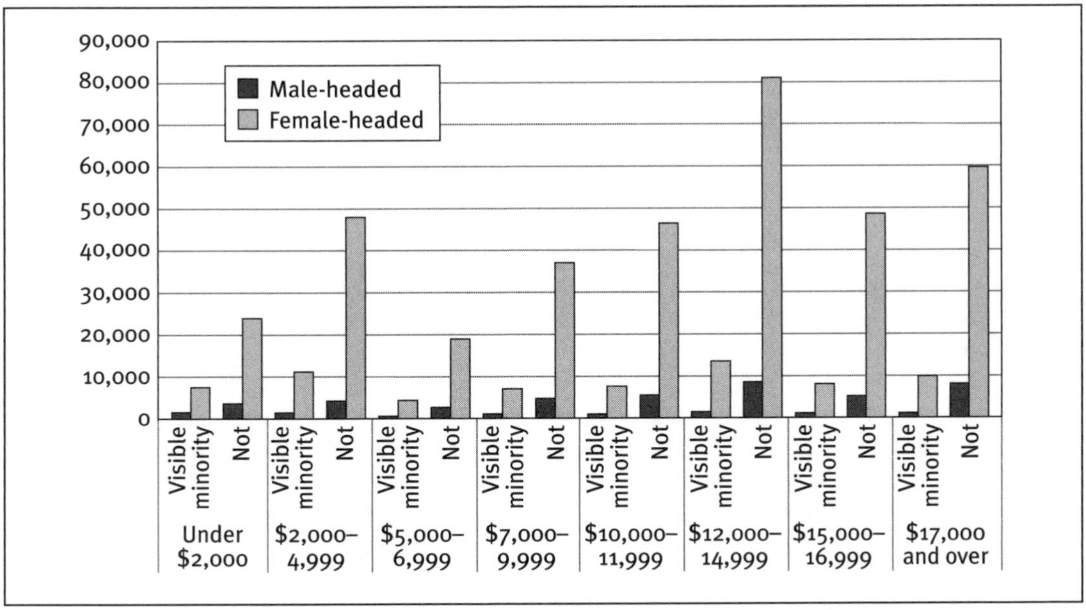

SOURCE: Statistics Canada, Census of Canada, 1996: Dimensions Series, (Cat. no. 94F0009XDB96094).

deprived, including increased vulnerability to infectious and other disease, arthritis, stomach ulcers, migraines, clinical depression, stress, vulnerability to mental illness, self-destructive coping behaviours, and increased risk of heart disease (Morris, 2002).

Because of poverty, iron-deficiency anemia (a blood disorder) affects twice as many women as it does men. Poverty causes health problems not only because of poor diet and unsanitary living conditions, but also because financial barriers obstruct access to health care services. For example, Rubye Beck, Caroline Jijon, and Joellen Edwards (1996) found that among rural populations, women perceive financial barriers to adequate health care more than do men, and report poorer health.

Patriarchy is, by its nature, pro-natal; it views women's primary role as bearing and raising children. Many societies press women to bear as many children as they can, stigmatizing them if they are childless (Inhorn, 1998). Yet often, high rates of pregnancy can bring high rates of illness and death to a society. Each year around the world, half a million women die needlessly from pregnancy-related complications, exacerbated by poverty and remoteness (WHO, 2000). Many women, especially in developing countries, die during pregnancy and childbirth. The figure is highest in the least developed nations (1,000 deaths/100,000 live births, compared with 21/100,000 in developed countries). The UN reported in 1997 that 585,000 women die each year from pregnancy-related causes; these deaths are preventable, and are symptomatic of women's vulnerability and the violation of their human rights—a matter of social justice (UNFPA, 1997).

The same pro-natal patriarchal sentiments that support high rates of pregnancy oppose abortion. The legalities of abortion affect women's lives in every society. Consider the example of Chile, where all abortion procedures are prohibited: illegal abortions are the leading cause of maternal death there. Poverty is an important factor in who is prosecuted for abortion in Chile, however. Poor, uneducated women have to rely on abortionists who are illiterate, without medical training, assisted by friends or relatives. Wealthier women who can afford less risky procedures and private care can avoid public hospitals that betray patient confidentiality (Casas-Becerra, 1997). Abortion providers in Latin America are subject to lack of medical support, the need for secrecy, and threats of violence, extortion, and prosecution (Rodriguez and Strickler, 1999). Policies that criminalize abortion elevate fetal rights over maternal rights, are sexist, and serve to victimize poor pregnant women around the world (Gustavsson and MacEachron, 1997).

In South Asia, abortions are common among women of all socio-economic statuses. However, the quality of the procedure sought varies according to economic circumstances: most poor women use non-medical services or perform self-induced abortions, whereas non-poor women are more likely to seek trained medical personnel (Singh, Wulf, and Jones, 1997).

In the least developed, most patriarchal societies, such as India and China, females still suffer grave risks of infanticide (the killing of infants) that are only recently diminishing. New technology that makes possible prenatal sex determination is likely to allow for the selective abortion of female fetuses. Legislation curbing prenatal sex determination and policy measures addressing societal female devaluation have had little effect, suggesting that female demographic disadvantage in India will continue (Sudha and Rajan, 1999).

Health care needs also arise from the spousal violence that occurs in some households. While women are slightly more likely to initiate a violent episode—usually by means of slapping,

kicking, or throwing an object—men are more likely to respond with more devastating force—beating, choking, or threatening to use a knife or gun. As a result, nearly half of women (49 per cent) who report being abused by a previous spouse in the past five years in Canada sustained physical injury, compared with 21 per cent of men. Fully 19 per cent of these women and only 5 per cent of these men received injuries severe enough to require medical attention. In retrospect, 48 per cent of female victims and 13 per cent of male victims feared for their lives during the ordeal (Statistics Canada, 2001: 40).

Not only gender roles, but also changing sex roles influence the rate of mental illness. Some believe that multiple roles—marriage, parenthood, paid work—provide a burden for women that creates mental problems. Research finds this is not the case. For women, multiple roles are associated with *improved* mental health status. There is some evidence, though, that men are having a problem with this. As women increasingly enter the labour force, the mental health status of men declines (Hankin, 1990). Employment has beneficial effects on health for unmarried women and little or no health effect on married women. Little evidence has been found that the combination of employment and motherhood results in harmful health effects (Waldron, Weiss, and Hughes, 1998).

Men's Health

To this point, this chapter has been mainly about women as a minority group and the problems they suffer because they are women. However, there are also important ways in which men become disadvantaged in health, by virtue of how society is organized. Let's turn to these processes.

Consider, for example, that men are more likely than women to drive, and to drive recklessly. Both factors mean that men have more accidents, and more severe accidents, than women. Men also are more likely to drink too much and to drink and drive, with the expected consequences of more drunk-driving accidents. Further, they are more likely to be victimized in a violent crime. Men also are more likely to work in dangerous work settings, and more likely to be victims of occupational accidents.

In our society, as in many others, male anti-social behaviours are often associated with striving for a masculine self-image. Our culture expects masculine men to behave in dangerous and anti-social ways. So, for example, young men who become unemployed often take to smoking and drinking heavily. Unemployment plays an important part in establishing lifelong patterns of hazardous behaviour in young men, but it is often because they are men that unemployment affects them so (Montgomery et al., 1998). Social practices that undermine men's health are often signifiers of masculinity, and instruments that men use to negotiate social power and status (Courtenay, 2000).

As a result, men suffer more severe chronic conditions, have higher death rates for all leading causes of death, and die, on average, nearly seven years younger than women (Keyfitz, 1988).

Though men and women have similar overall rates of mental disorder, women more often develop symptoms of depression and anxiety, while men more often develop symptoms of alcoholism, drug abuse, and anti-social personality (Hankin, 1990).

Solutions

Feminist and Men's Movements

The **suffrage movement**, or the 'first wave' of feminism, made important gains for women's rights in Canada through the late nineteenth and early twentieth centuries. Focusing primarily on three sets of issues—political rights, legal rights, and social reform—and represented nationally by the Woman's Christian Temperance Union, the Young Women's Christian Association, the National Council of Women of Canada, and the Federated Women's Institutes,

these early feminists fought for a conservative agenda that placed the 'woman's role on a more secure material footing' rather than attempt to shatter the traditional gender myths that deemed the man to be the provider and the woman to be the nurturer (Brooks, 1996: 337).

True to these goals, the tactics Canadian feminists employed were cautious and moderate: 'Unlike their sisters in Great Britain and the United States, Canadian suffragists did not resort to such confrontational methods as chaining themselves to the fences surrounding Parliament, physically resisting the police, or hunger strikes' (Brooks, 1996). These moderate tactics were successful, and brought women the vote. It was only in the last 30 years of the twentieth century that the 'second wave' of feminism began its attacks on the cultural and social bases of inequality. Without questioning gender roles, as the women's movement has done over several decades, it is unlikely that women would have made strides toward social and economic equality.

Also, without this impetus from the women's movement, the men's movement would never have begun. It was only after female activism began to explode traditional gender myths about women that men, in the later years stages of the last century, began to re-evaluate their own notions of masculinity. Only after women began to voice their dissatisfaction with the gender constraints placed on them did men begin to examine their own gender and the costs of living a myth. Many men came to feel frustration over the need to conform to masculine stereotypes.

Some men see that their role as primary breadwinner forces them into a too competitive and unrewarding career. Archaic notions of idealized masculinity prevent them from expressing 'softer' impulses toward their spouse and children. Men, like women, suffer social psychological consequences from gender stereotyping. Our culture judges men according to particular economic and physical ideals, so there are self-esteem issues whenever men earn less money than we expect them to, fail to act as appropri-

ately 'masculine' (read 'aggressive and dominant'), or choose to work in a traditionally feminine profession. Vague and latent homophobia
hampers them from forming genuine emotional
bonds with male colleagues and friends. Groups
in the men's movement have helped some men to
reject stereotypic ideas of masculinity and to
question an ideology that implicitly viewed men
to emotionally vacant and replaceable cogs in the
wheel of labour.

Thus, the women's and men's movements
have changed people's consciousness of themselves, their relationships (marital and otherwise), and their cultural biases. Such changes are
the necessary starting point for any major change
of society.

Policy and Institutional Changes

Many institutional policies are designed to
remove barriers that prevent women (and other
marginalized groups) from participating to a full
extent in public life. As the opening vignette
illustrated, discrimination in the workplace
based on sex or gender is no longer tolerated in
modern society, either by the judicial system or
by much public opinion.

However, policies are not yet in place that
would give women the same occupational freedom that men enjoy. For example, we know that
many women's employment and childbearing
has been affected by problems with child care.
Analysis suggests that policies to increase the
supply of child care or to lower its cost could
increase female labour supply substantially, with
an even greater rise among women most at risk
of poverty and reliance on public assistance, but
it probably would not raise fertility significantly
(Mason and Kuhlthau, 1989).

Likewise, more effective workplace sexual
harassment policies would likely improve
women's work lives by preventing male chauvin-
ism from impeding a woman's career ambitions.
Finally, employment discrimination remains a
problem. Canada's Employment Equity Act protects all workers against discriminatory hiring
procedures, whatever their gender, race, ethnicity, disability status, or sexual orientation, by
ensuring that employee composition reflects the
diversity of society. In specific relation to gender,
this means that the workforces of large companies and federal employees must have a roughly
equal number of men and women in all levels of
employment, at least in theory. In practice, the
division is not nearly as exact, although the gap
is closing.

Some critics argue that such 'quota systems'
lead to decreased productivity, since the employer, constrained by employment equity laws,
may occasionally be forced to pass over the most
qualified candidate because his or her gender is
already overrepresented in the present workforce. Other opponents point out that, like anti-
hate legislation, policies that force employers to
act in a gender-neutral fashion will not extinguish discrimination and, in fact, may serve to
intensify it or drive it underground. These criticisms have some merit: since gender inequality
remains a problem in society, the criticisms probably predict what will happen sometimes.
Discrimination on the basis of gender is unfair, it
is socially harmful, and it has indirect and direct
health consequences.

The solution process will continue to be difficult and wrought with opposition, as society
overcomes its inertia and undergoes the painful
process of unlearning centuries' worth of outdated gender socialization. The system has been
skewed in favour of men for generations. In
attempting to correct this problem, skewing
some policies temporarily in favour of the marginalized group may be necessary until the playing field has been levelled. In some communities
and some societies that are particularly patriarchal, as, for example, much of the Arab world, a
resistance to transformations such as reduced
fertility, new family forms, more education for
women, and gender equality at work and in politics may create a social crisis that may be mani-
fested in political violence (Fargues, 1977).

Cross-national research makes clear that women's concerns must be made into well-understood social problems before policy proposals are formulated and passed. Women have driven all issues such as equal pay, affirmative action, educational equality, child care, abortion, domestic violence, and sexual harassment policies forward. They have been addressed most directly and effectively in countries such as Norway, Sweden, and Finland where women play a key role in political legislation, largely through a history of effective mobilization in unions, social movements, and political parties (Bacchi, 1999; Tyyska, 1994).

Individual Strategies

Any thoroughgoing solutions to sexism and gender inequality will require changes to social structure and culture that go well beyond the scope of what any individual or a few individuals can accomplish. However, individual actions can always have some modest positive consequence. For example, we can each do our part to assure that sexism and discrimination are not practised around us—at work, at school, in the wider public community, or at home.

At least, we can make sure that we are not part of the problem. We can join and support voluntary associations and other interest organizations that are dedicated to, and working toward, the promotion of gender equality. Further, we can try to ensure that everything feasible is being done in our workplace to pursue gender inequality. And when faced with situations of sexism and gender inequality, whether directed at others or at ourselves, we can become whistle-blowers—we can point this out for what it is and make a referral to the proper investigating group.

Research on top scientists has shown that even at the highest levels of intellectual accomplishment, women still subordinate their careers to their marriages, husbands, and children—for example, choosing the location of a job or post-doctoral position to fit a partner's needs. Men at the same level of achievement do not do the same. There is a lesson in this for young women who have the ability and desire to accomplish a great deal in their lives.

Concluding Remarks

Because of discrimination in the workplace, women still do not earn as much income, on average, as men. This means that they often lack the means to live independently from men. Women who are not part of the paid workforce and who act solely as homemakers are often denied both wages and respect.

Gender discrimination and gender inequality are not due to the intrinsic or biological inferiority of one or the other sex. Instead, they are the result of political, economic, and ideological structures. Women have increasingly entered the workforce in both developed and less developed countries. Despite this, women are still subject to discrimination within the workforce. This discrimination often takes the form of sexual harassment and the 'glass ceiling'. Women who work for pay are also likely to face the *double shift*—heavy workloads both at the workplace and at home. Within the home, gender inequality extends across domestic work, child care, and caregiver duties with parents and spouses.

Socialization plays an important role in the subordination of women. Socialization causes people to internalize values that, in turn, lead them to enforce and act out gender roles. This socialization occurs not only in the family, but also through the media, language, schools, and religion. Images of, perceptions of, and beliefs about gender are acquired both in childhood and through adult socialization. From a sociological standpoint, male-female differences are not only constructed, they are defended and reconstituted generation after generation. These are topics that symbolic interactionism and feminist theory, in particular, can help us understand.

A functionalist theory of the origin of gender discrimination is based on the need of early human groups to engage in hand-to-hand combat. Men had the physical advantage but needed to be motivated to run the risks of becoming warriors. Women, offered as inducement for men to do battle, were assigned the drudgework of society. A second functionalist explanation is that because women were physically encumbered through childbearing and nursing, men became dominant, taking control of weapons, warfare, and trade.

Conflict theorists emphasize that the legal, political, and other social rights that North American women now enjoy resulted from a power struggle with men. The confrontations and violence between the sexes that marked the late nineteenth and early twentieth centuries in the West have given way to legal pressuring and economic and educational competition. The feminist movement has many branches and philosophies, but it is generally aimed at the explanation and elimination of gender inequality. To date, it has played a key role in helping remove some of this inequality at all levels of society. In Canada, women tend not to occupy positions of real power in political or legal spheres. For this reason, women's issues are often ignored or receive less political attention than they deserve. In other societies, where women are more powerful politically, gender issues are sometimes dealt with more firmly and thoroughly.

Questions for Critical Thought

1. Go to a toy store, or recall from memory the characteristics of the different aisles of toys. What do they look like? What toys seem to be for girls, and what toys seem to be geared toward boys? Do you think society has made any progress recently in coming toward more equal gender representation? Discuss in terms of gender socialization and identity formation.

2. There is a widely held belief that people creatively and actively shape their behaviour, making choices and acting by volition. What role, if any, does agency play in the process of socialization? Do people actively choose their paths, or are we just susceptible to the powerful macro forces of social norms?

3. Do you believe that a 'glass ceiling' still exists? Has there been any recent advancement that has helped to alleviate this? Bring in insights regarding the 'Mommy track' from current events and look on the Statistics Canada Web site at <www.statscan.ca> for recent figures and statistics.

4. This text illustrates that social-psychological costs are another common consequence of gender discrimination and stereotyping. The media, and specifically advertising, are constantly under scrutiny for imposing their own set of ideals that are often accused of being androcentric. Discuss the social-psychological costs of a media with beautiful models, unattainable wardrobes, and airbrushed faces with respect to the negative effects they have on a woman's self-esteem.

5. Describe the impact that the shift from agricultural to industrial societies had on the gendered division of labour.

Recommended Readings

Vanaja Dhruvarajan, ed., *Women and Well-Being / Les Femmes et le mieux-être* (Montreal and Kingston: McGill-Queen's University Press, 1990).

Dhruvarajan's book, a collection of 20 articles from the 1987 conference of the Canadian Research Institute for the Advancement of Women (CRIAW), seeks to identify conditions that promote or inhibit women's experiences of well-being. The collection may be faulted for giving little attention to the issue of reproduction, but it should be praised for its articles on rural women, an area to which feminist studies have devoted relatively little attention.

Donna Eder with Catherine Colleen Evans and Stephen Parker, *School Talk: Gender and Adolescent Culture* (New Brunswick, NJ: Rutgers University Press, 1995).

This highly recommended book is a page-turner. Eder and her colleagues provide a comprehensive qualitative study of modern adolescents.

Arlie Russell Hochschild, *The Managed Heart: Commercialization of Human Feeling* (Berkeley: University of California Press, 1983).

This text is a study of Marx's concept of alienation applied to the 'pink-collar' labour force, with a focus on flight attendants. An analysis of various implications of 'emotional labour' is the topic of much of the book.

Arlie Hochschild with Anne Machung, *The Second Shift: Working Parents and the Revolution at Home* (New York: Viking, 1989).

Using data from interviews, the authors explore the tensions in two-income families.

Christine Overall, ed., *The Future of Human Reproduction* (Toronto: Women's Press, 1989).

Overall's book, a collection by women activists and scholars, offers a multidisciplinary assessment of the consequences of technological developments in human reproduction for Canada and other industrial societies. In particular, the implications of the medicalization of pregnancy and the proliferation of reproductive technologies are analyzed.

Chris Shilling, *The Body and Social Theory*, 2nd edn (Newbury Park, CA: Sage, 2003).

This book, part of the Theory, Culture and Society series, offers a critical analysis of the sociological literature on the body, treating such issues as sexuality and bodily image, developments in genetic engineering, the role of the body in consumer culture, and social theories of the body.

Recommended Web Sites

Status of Women Canada
www.swc-cfc.gc.ca

Status of Women Canada is a federal government agency that promotes gender equality and the increased participation of women in political, social, cultural, and economic life in Canada. The Web site provides information on publications, programs, news, and related Web sites.

Canadian Research Institute for the Advancement of Women
www.criaw-icref.ca

The Canadian Research Institute for the Advancement of Women is a national not-for-profit
organization committed to advancing women's equality through research. Founded in 1976, the CRIAW is a bilingual, membership-based organization that intends to bridge the gaps between the community and academe, and between research and action. The CRIAW provides research grants, resource links, facts, and publications for researchers and interested individuals.

Ontario Women's Directorate
www.gov.on.ca/mczcr/owd/

The Ontario Women's Directorate is an agency committed to the full participation of all women in provincial affairs. Information on publications, resources, statistics, facts, and grants are provided.

References

Albelda, Randy, and Chris Tilly. 1997. *Glass Ceilings and Bottomless Pits: Women's Work, Women's Poverty*. Boston: South End Press.

Bacchi, Carol Lee. 1999. *Women, Policy and Politics: The Construction of Policy Problems*. London: Sage.

Baxter, Janeen. 1997. 'Gender Equality and Participation in Housework: A Cross-National Perspective'. *Journal of Comparative Family Studies*, 28: 220–48.

Beal, Bruce A., and Carol Brooks Gardner. 2000. 'Gendered Advice and Mental Health Practices'. *Perspectives on Social Problems*, 12: 203–16.

Beck, Rubye W., Caroline R. Jijon, and Joellen B. Edwards. 1996. 'The Relationships Among Gender, Perceived Financial Barriers to Care, and Health Status in a Rural Population'. *Journal of Rural Health*, 12, no. 3: 188–96.

Blackwood, Evelyn, and Saskia E. Wieringa, eds. 1999. *Female Desires: Same-Sex Relations and Transgender Practices Across Cultures*. New York: Columbia University Press.

Blazer, Dan. G. 1982. 'The Epidemiology of Late-Life Depression'. *Journal of the American Geriatrics Society*, 9: 587–92.

Brinson, Susan L. 1992. 'TV Fights: Women and Men in Interpersonal Arguments on Prime-Time Television Dramas'. *Argumentation and Advocacy*, 29, no. 2: 89–104.

Brooks, Stephen. 1996. *Canadian Democracy: An Introduction*, 2nd edn. Toronto: Oxford University Press.

Canadian Council of Professional Engineers. 1999. *Women in Engineering*. Available at <www.ccpe.ca/e/prog_women.cfm>, accessed 20 February 2003.

Carswick, Kelly. 1997. 'Canadian Caregivers'. *Canadian Social Trends*, 2.

Casas-Becerra, Lidia. 1997. 'Women Prosecuted and Imprisoned for Abortion in Chile'. *Reproductive Health Matters*, 9: 29–36.

Chafetz, Janet Saltzman, and Jaqueline Hagan. 1996. 'The Gender Division of Labor and Family Change in Industrial Societies: A Theoretical Accounting'. *Journal of Comparative Family Studies*, 27: 187–219.

Clark, Warren. 2001. *Economic Gender Equality Indicators 2000*. Status of Women Canada. Available at <www.swc-cfc.gc.ca/pubs/egei2000/egei2000_e.html>, accessed 15 March 2003.

Coltrane, Scott, and Masako Ishii-Kuntz. 1990. 'Men's Housework and Child Care: A Life Course Perspective'. Paper presented at the annual meeting of the American Sociological Association.

Cook, Rebecca J. 1999. 'The Human Rights Dimensions of Maternal Mortality'. Paper presented at the annual conference of the International Union for the Scientific Study of Population.

Corney, Roslyn, and Ruth Stanton. 1991. 'A Survey of 658 Women Who Report Symptoms of Premenstrual Syndrome'. *Journal of Psychosomatic Research*, 35: 471–82.

Courtenay, Will H. 2000. 'Constructions of Masculinity and Their Influence on Men's Well-Being: A Theory of Gender and Health'. *Social Science and Medicine*, 50: 1385–401.

Cowan, Carolyn Pape, and Philip A. Cowan. 1995. 'Interventions to Ease the Transition to Parenthood: Why They Are Needed and What They Can Do'. *Family Relations*, 44: 412–23.

Crocker, Jennifer, Kristin Voelkl, Maria Testa, and Brenda Major. 2000. 'Social Stigma: The Affective Consequences of Attributional Ambiguity'. In *Stereotypes and Prejudice: Essential Readings*, edited by Charles Stangor, 353–68. Philadelphia, PA: Psychology Press.

Crohan, Susan E. 1996. 'Marital Quality and Conflict Across the Transition to Parenthood in African American and White Couples'. *Journal of Marriage and the Family*, 58: 922–44.

Crooks, Roberts, and Karla Baur. 1999. *Our Sexuality*, 7th edn. Toronto: Nelson Canada.

Doucet, Andrea. 2000. '"There's a Huge Gulf Between Me as a Male Carer and Women": Gender, Domestic Responsibility, and the Community as an Institutional Arena'. *Community, Work & Family*, 3, no. 2: 163–84.

Ell, Kathleen. 1996. 'Social Networks, Social Support and Coping with Serious Illness: The Family Connection'. *Social Science Medicine*, 42: 173–83.

Engels, Friedrich. [1884] 1985. *The Origin of the Family, Private Property, and the State*. Harmondsworth, UK: Penguin.

Erel, Osnat, and Bonnie Burman. 1995. 'Interrelatedness of Marital Relations and Parent-Child Relations: A Meta-analytic Review'. *Psychological Bulletin*, 118: 108–32.

Fargues, Philippe. 1977. 'State Policies and the Birth Rate in Egypt: From Socialism to Liberalism'. *Population* and Development Review, 23, no. 1: 115–38.

Fox, Bonnie. 2001. 'The Formative Years: How Parenthood Creates Gender'. Canadian Review of Sociology and Anthropology, 38: 373–90.

Franklin, Susan T., Barbara Ames, and Sharon King. 1994. 'Acquiring the Family Eldercare Role: Influence on Female Employment Adaptation'. Research on Aging, 16, no. 1: 27–42.

Fredriksen, Karen I. 1996. 'Gender Differences in Employment and the Informal Care of Adults'. Journal of Women and Aging, 8, no. 2: 35–53.

Furnham, Adrian, and Nadine Bitar. 1993. 'The Stereotyped Portrayal of Men and Women in British Television Advertisements'. Sex Roles, 29: 297–310.

Furstenberg, Frank F. 1998. 'When Will Teenage Childbearing Become a Problem? The Implications of Western Experience for Developing Countries'. Studies in Family Planning, 29: 246–53.

Gartner, Rosemary, and Dane Archer. 1984. Violence and Crime in Cross-national Perspective. New Haven, CT: Yale University Press.

Geissler, Dorie. 2001. 'Generation "G"'. Journal of Sport and Social Issues, 25: 324–31.

Gibson, Diane. 1996. 'Broken Down by Age and Gender: "The Problem of Old Women" Redefined'. Gender and Society, 10: 433–48.

Gillmore, Mary R., Steven M. Lewis, Mary J. Lohr, Michael S. Spencer, and Rachelle D. White. 1997. 'Repeat Pregnancies Among Adolescent Mothers'. Journal of Marriage and the Family, 59: 536–50.

Ginn, Jay, and Jane Sandell. 1997. 'Balancing Home and Employment: Stress Reported by Social Services Staff'. Work, Employment and Society, 11: 413–34.

Gottlieb, Benjamin H., E. Kevin Kelloway, and Maryann Fraboni. 1994. 'Aspects of Eldercare that Place Employees at Risk'. Gerontologist, 34: 815–21.

Gregson, Nicky, and Michelle Lowe. 1994. 'Waged Domestic Labor and the Renegotiation of the Domestic Division of Labor Within Dual-Career Households'. Sociology, 28: 55–79.

Gustavsson, Nora S., and Ann E. MacEachron. 1997. 'Criminalizing Women's Behavior'. Journal of Drug Issues, 27: 673–87.

Hankin, Janet R. 1990. 'Gender and Mental Illness'. Research in Community and Mental Health, 6: 183–201.

Heymann, Jody, and Alison Earle. 1998. 'The Work-Family Balance: What Hurdles Are Parents Leaving Welfare Likely to Confront?' Journal of Policy Analysis and Management, 17: 313–21.

Hochschild, Arlie R. 1998. The Time Bind: When Work Becomes Home and Home Becomes Work. New York: Henry Holt.

Horowitz, Amy. 1985. 'Sons and Daughters as Caregivers to Older Parents: Differences in Role Performance and Consequences'. Gerontologist, 25: 612–17.

Howell, Nancy. 2000. Demography of the Dobe !Kung. 2nd edn. Hawthorne, NY: Aldine de Gruyter.

Inhorn, Marcia C. 1998. 'Infertility and the Quest for Conception in Egypt'. In Reproductive Health and Infectious Disease in the Middle East, edited by Robin Barlow and Joseph W. Brown, 114–29. Brookfield, VT: Ashgate.

Ishii-Kuntz, Masako, and Scott Coltrane. 1992. 'Remarriage, Stepparenting, and Household Labor'. Journal of Family Issues, 13: 215–33.

Kaplan, Elaine Bell. 1997. Not Our Kind of Girl: Unraveling the Myths of Black Teenage Motherhood. Berkeley: University of California Press.

Karasek, Robert A., and Tores Theorell. 1990. Healthy Work: Stress, Productivity, and the Reconstruction of Working Life. New York: Basic Books.

Kaufert, Patricia A., and Margaret Lock. 1998. '"What Are Women For?" Cultural Construction of Menopausal Women in Japan and Canada'. In Health and Canadian Society: Sociological Perspective, 3rd edn, edited by David Coburn, Carl D'Arcy, and George M. Torrance, 187–200. Toronto: University of Toronto Press.

Kawachi, Ichiro, Bruce P. Kennedy, Vanita Gupta, and Deborah Prothrow Stith. 1999. 'Women's Status and the Health of Women and Men: A View from the States'. Social Science and Medicine, 48: 21–32.

Kermeen, Patricia. 1995. 'Improving Postpartum Marital Relationships'. Psychological Reports, 76: 831–4.

Kerr, Janet, and Janetta MacPhail, eds. 1999. Canadian Nursing: Issues and Perspectives. 3rd edn. Toronto: Mosby.

Keyfitz, Nathan. 1988. 'On the Wholesomeness of Marriage'. In Readings in Sociology: An Introduction, edited by Lorne Tepperman and James Curtis, 449–62. Toronto: McGraw-Hill Ryerson.

Kingson E.R., and R. O'Grady-LeShane. 1993. 'The Effects of Caregiving on Women's Social Security Benefits'. Gerontologist, 33: 230–9.

Kittell, Linda A., Phyllis Kernoff Mansfield, and Ann M. Voda. 1998. 'Keeping Up Appearances: The Basic Social Process of the Menopausal Transition'. Qualitative Health Research, 8: 618–33.

Knight, Bob G., Steven M. Lutzky, and Felice Macofsky-Urban. 1993. 'A Meta-analytic Review of Interventions for Caregiver Distress: Recommendations for Future Research'. *Gerontologist*, 33: 240–8.

Knudsen, Hannah K., and Paul M. Roman. 2000. 'Gender Segregation in Work Groups in the United States: An Analysis of Earnings'. Paper presented at the annual conference of the Southern Sociological Society.

Lechner, Viola M. 1993. 'Support Systems and Stress Reduction Among Workers Caring for Dependent Parents'. *Social Work*, 38: 461–9.

Lee, Richard B. 1993. *The Dobe Ju/'hoansi*. 2nd edn. Fort Worth, TX: Harcourt Brace.

Leuchtag, Alice. 1995. 'The Culture of Pornography'. *Humanist*, 55, no. 3: 4–6.

Livingstone, Sonia. 1994. 'Watching Talk: Gender and Engagement in the Viewing of Audience Discussion Programmes'. *Media, Culture and Society*, 16: 429–47.

Lupri, Eugen, and James Frideres. 1981. 'The Quality of Marriage and the Passage of Time: Marital Satisfaction over the Family Life Cycle'. *Canadian Journal of Sociology / Cahiers canadiens de sociologie*, 6, no. 3: 283–305.

Mason, Karen Oppenheim, and Karen Kuhlthau. 1989. 'Determinants of Child Care Ideals Among Mothers of Preschool-Aged Children'. *Journal of Marriage and the Family*, 51: 593–603.

Media-Watch. 1991. 'Two Years of Sexism in Canadian Newspapers: A Study of 15 Newspapers'. *Resources for Feminist Research*, 20, no. 1/2: 21–2.

Merlo, Joan M. Reidy, and Kathleen Maurer Smith. 1994a. 'The Feminine Voice of Authority in Television Commercials: A Ten-Year Comparison'. Paper presented at the annual conference of the American Sociological Association.

———. 1994b. 'The Portrayal of Gender Role in Television Advertising: A Decade of Stereotyping'. Paper presented at the annual conference of the Society for the Study of Social Problems.

Michelson, William. 1985. *From Sun to Sun: Daily Obligations and Community Structure in the Lives of Employed Women and their Families*. Totowa, NJ: Rowman & Allanheld.

———. 1988. 'Divergent Convergence: The Daily Routines of Employed Spouses as a Public Affairs Agenda'. In *Life Spaces: Gender, Household, Employment*, edited by Caroline Andrew and Beth Moore Milroy, 81–101. Vancouver: University of British Columbia Press.

Milkie, Melissa. 2002. 'Contested Images of Femininity: An Analysis of Cultural Gate Keeper Struggles with the Real Girl Critique'. Paper presented at a conference on Gender and Society.

Monk, Timothy H., Marilyn J. Essex, Nancy A. Snider, Marjorie H. Klein, et al. 1996. 'The Impact of the Birth of a Baby on the Time Structure and Social Mixture of a Couple's Daily Life and Its Consequences for Well-Being'. *Journal of Applied Social Psychology*, 26: 1237–58.

Montgomery, Scott M., Derek G. Cook, Mel J. Bartley, and Michael E.J. Wadsworth. 1998. 'Unemployment, Cigarette Smoking, Alcohol Consumption and Body Weight in Young British Men'. *European Journal of Public Health*, 8, no. 1: 21–7.

Morris, Marika. 2002. *Women and Poverty*. Canadian Research Institute for the Advancement of Women (CRIAW). Available at <www.criaw-icref.ca/Poverty_fact_sheet.htm#50>, accessed 23 March 2003.

Mui, Ada C. 1995. 'Caring for Frail Elderly Parents: A Comparison of Adult Sons and Daughters'. *Gerontologist*, 35: 86–93.

Nakhaie, M.R. 1995. 'Housework in Canada: The National Picture'. *Journal of Comparative Family Studies*, 26: 409–26.

National Anti-Poverty Organization (NAPO). 1999. *Poverty in Canada: Some Facts and Figures*. Available at <www.napo-onap.ca/nf-figur2.htm>, accessed 27 June 2001.

Normand, Josée. 1995. 'Education of Women in Canada.' *Canadian Social Trends*, 39: 17–21.

Ontario Women's Directorate. 2000. *Students and Teachers: Facts and Statistics for Students*. Available at <www.gov.on.ca/mczcr/owd/english/students/facts.htm>, accessed 21 January 2003.

Orbach, Terri L., James S. House, and Pamela S. Mero. 1996. 'Marital Quality over the Life Course'. *Social Psychology Quarterly*, 59: 162–71.

Orodenker, Sylvia. 1990. 'Family Caregiving in a Changing Society: The Effects of Employment on Caregiver Stress'. *Family Community Health*, 12, no. 4: 58–70.

Peake, Susan, Lenore Manderson, and Helen Potts. 1999. '"Part and Parcel of Being a Woman": Female Urinary Incontinence and Constructions of Control'. *Medical Anthropology Quarterly*, 13 (n.s.): 267–85.

Pohl, Joanne, Clare E. Collins, and Charles W. Given. 1998. 'Longitudinal Employment Decisions of Daughters and Daughters-in-Law After Assuming Parent Care'. *Journal of Women and Aging*, 10, no. 1: 59–74.

Rabin, Claire, and Giora Rahav. 1995. 'Differences and Similarities Between Younger and Older Marriages Across Cultures: A Comparison of American and Israeli Retired Nondistressed Marriages'. *American Journal of Family Therapy*, 23: 237–49.

Rennison, Callie M. 2000. *Criminal Victimization 1999: Changes 1998–99 with Trends 1993–99*. Washington, DC: Bureau of Justice Statistics, US Department of Justice.

Rodriguez, Karen, and Jennifer Strickler. 1999. 'Clandestine Abortion in Latin America: Provider Perspectives'. *Women and Health*, 28, no. 3, 59–75.

Salamon, E.D., and B.W. Robinson, eds. 1987. *Gender Roles: Doing What Comes Naturally?* Toronto: Methuen.

Scharlach, Andrew E., and Karen I. Fredriksen. 1994. 'Elder Care Versus Adult Care: Does Care Recipient Age Make a Difference?' *Research on Aging*, 16: 43–68.

Schofield, Hilary, and Helen Herrman. 1993. 'Characteristics of Carers in Victoria'. *Family Matters*, 34: 21–6.

Scritchfield, Shirley A. 1995. 'The Social Construction of Infertility: From Private Matter to Social Concern'. In *Images of Issues: Typifying Contemporary Social Problems*, edited by Joel Best, 131–46. Hawthorne, NY: Aldine de Gruyter.

Shaw, Donald L., and Shannon E. Martin. 1992. 'The Function of Mass Media Agenda Setting'. *Journalism Quarterly*, 69: 902–20.

Shelton, Beth Anne, and Daphne John. 1993. 'Does Marital Status Make a Difference? Housework Among Married and Cohabiting Men and Women'. *Journal of Family Issues*, 14: 401–20.

———. 1996. 'The Division of Household Labor'. *Annual Review of Sociology*, 22: 299–322.

Singh, Susheela, Deirdre Wulf, and Heidi Jones. 1997. 'Health Professionals' Perceptions About Induced Abortion in South Central and Southeast Asia'. *International Family Planning Perspectives*, 23, no. 2: 59–67, 72.

Statistics Canada. 1998. *Canada Yearbook 2000*. Ottawa: Minister of Industry.

———. 1999. *Overview of the Time Use of Canadians in 1998*. (Cat. no. 12F0080XIE). Ottawa: Minister of Industry.

———. 2001. *Family Violence in Canada: A Statistical Profile 2001*. (Cat. no. 85-224-XIE). Ottawa: Minister of Industry.

Stoller, Eleanor Palo. 1990. 'Males as Helpers: The Role of Sons, Relatives, and Friends'. *Gerontologist*, 30: 228–36.

Stommel, Manfred, Barbara A. Given, Charles W. Given, and Clare Collins. 1995. 'The Impact of the Frequency of Care Activities on the Division of Labor Between Primary Caregivers and Other Care Providers'. *Research on Aging*, 17: 412–33.

Sudarkasa, Niara. 1986. '"The Status of Women" in Indigenous Africa Societies'. *Feminist Studies*, 12: 91–103.

Sudha, S., and S. Irudaya Rajan. 1999. 'Female Demographic Disadvantage in India, 1981–1991: Sex-Selective Abortions and Female Infanticide'. *Development and Change*, 30: 585–618.

Sydie, Rosalind A. 1986. *Natural Women, Cultured Men: A Feminist Perspective on Sociological Theory*. Toronto: Methuen.

Tennstedt, Sharon L., and Judith G. Gonyea. 1994. 'An Agenda for Work and Eldercare Research: Methodological Challenges and Future Directions'. *Research on Aging*, 16: 85–108.

Tilly, Louise A., and Joan W. Scott. 1987. *Women, Work, and Family*. New York: Routledge.

Tremblay, Diane-Gabrielle. 2001. 'Polarization of Working Time and Gender Differences: Reconciling Family and Work by Reducing Working Time of Men and Women'. In *Restructuring Work and the Life Course*, edited by Victor W. Marshall, Walter R. Heinz, Helga Kruger, and Anil Verma, 123–41. Toronto: University of Toronto Press.

Tyyska, Vappu Kaarina. 1994. *The Women's Movement and the Welfare State: Child Care Policy in Canada and Finland, 1960–1990*. Unpublished doctoral dissertation, University of Toronto.

United Nations Development Programme (UNDP). 1998. *Human Development Report 1998: Gender-Related Development Index*. Available at <www.undp.org/hdr2000/english/presskit/gdi.pdf>, accessed 20 February 2003.

United Nations Population Fund (UNFPA). 1997. *State of World Population 1997*. Available at <www.unfpa.org/swp/1997/swpmain.hm>, accessed 5 May 2003.

Waldron, Ingrid, Christopher C. Weiss, and Mary Elizabeth Hughes. 1998. 'Interacting Effects of Multiple Roles on Women's Health'. *Journal of Health and Social Behavior*, 39: 216–36.

Walsh, Janet. 1999. 'Myths and Counter-myths: An Analysis of Part-time Female Employees and Their Orientations to Work and Working Hours'. *Work, Employment and Society*, 13: 179–203.

Willen, Helena, and Henry Montgomery. 1996. 'The Impact of Wishing for Children and Having Children on Attainment and Importance of Life Values'. *Journal of Comparative Family Studies*, 27: 499–518.

Williamson, Lisa. 1998. 'Eating Disorders and the Cultural Forces Behind the Drive for Thinness: Are African American Women Really Protected?' *Social Work in Health Care*, 28, no. 1: 61–73.

Wollstonecraft, Mary. [1792] 1992. *A Vindication of the Rights of Woman*. London: Penguin.

Woods, Nancy Fugate, Bernice C. Yates, and Janet Primomo. 1989. 'Supporting Families During Chronic Stress'. *Image: Journal of Nursing Scholarship*, 2, no. 1: 46–50.

World Health Organization (WHO). 2000. *Gender, Health and Poverty*. (Fact Sheet 251). Available at <www.who.int/inf-fs/en/fact251.html>, accessed 22 January 2003.

Zarit, Steven H., and Carol J. Whitlatch. 1993. 'The Effects of Placement in Nursing Homes on Family Caregivers: Short- and Long-Term Consequences'. *Irish Journal of Psychology*, 14, no. 1: 25–37.

Glossary

Feminization of poverty Women are clearly overrepresented among the impoverished people of the world. In the West, economic liberalization and the dominance of the market have meant that those with least earning power—single mothers with children—have suffered most.

Gender A social division referring to the social and social-psychological attributes by which human are categorized as 'male' or 'female'. Biology is deemed somewhat irrelevant to understanding social distinctions between males and females. Gender encompasses the shared understandings of how women and men, girls and boys should look and act. It is a label that subsumes a large assortment of traits, beliefs, values, and mannerisms, and that defines how we should practise social interactions.

Gender inequality The difference between men and women when gaining access to valued rewards tends to stem from structural arrangements, interpersonal discrimination, and cultural beliefs.

Glass ceiling Women can have considerable success, but only up to the point of reaching top-level positions. For women at high levels of achievement, further advancement becomes especially difficult.

Quid pro quo sexual harassment The blatant demand by employers for sexual favours in exchange for promotion opportunities, salary increases, and preferential treatment.

Sexism Discrimination and derogatory attitudes and beliefs that promote stereotyping of people because of their gender. Sexism and gender stereotyping are two problems for both men and women that are most often experienced in institutions and social relationships.

Suffrage movement Considered within the 'first wave' of feminism, in the late nineteenth and early twentieth centuries. The movement focused primarily on three sets of issues: political rights, legal rights, and social reform.

Chapter 6

Work and Unemployment

Chapter Objectives

After reading this chapter the student should understand:
- how work and employment may be considered as social problems
- some basic facts about work and unemployment
- the role of multinationals in the global economy
- the relationship between bureaucratization and unemployment
- alternative major sociological theories about work and unemployment
- the role technology plays in unemployment and work
- health consequences of work and unemployment, and possible solutions

Introduction

This chapter is about employment and unemployment, workers and workplaces, productivity, labour, industry, profits, manufacturing, and health. In particular, it is about work in Canada under **capitalism**. Modern technology is an important part of this modern Canadian workplace. Increasingly, Canadian companies need fewer, better-educated, and more highly skilled workers to operate the machinery of production. The result is less job security.

In some ways, work under capitalism has not changed in a century. Despite automation, modern workplaces still have human relations problems. We have already discussed the problem of gender inequality in the workplace. In this chapter, we will discuss aspects of class exploitation and class conflict in the workplace. Modern society has not eliminated the class structure, though it has blurred class distinctions. The division between social classes, first emphasized by Karl Marx, who distinguished between owners and the working class, or the *bourgeoisie* and the *proletariat*, continues to exist in our post-industrial, service- and information-based society.

Nor has modern work eliminated unemployment. People who are forced out of work by

mass layoffs are, usually, workers on the lowest rungs of the occupational ladder. Ironically, these workers who are the most in need of a stable income are the first to lose their jobs whenever a recession occurs. However, in a few important ways, work *has* changed in the past half-century. For example, work has become more flexible, family-friendly, and woman-friendly. It is easier for people to work at home, for example. Another worker-friendly program, flextime, allows employees to decide when they begin and end the workday. Researchers are still debating whether these are genuine improvements in working life or mere window dressing.

Work and Employment as Social Problems

Most of us view work as a central part of our lives. It gives us a sense of identity, produces income, and contributes to the community's prosperity. Work rewards people with both intrinsic satisfaction—the feeling of a 'job well done'—and extrinsic rewards: money, prestige, respect, and social recognition.

Despite all the benefits that work offers to individuals and society, it is also a highly flawed activity. Problems of workplace health and safety are important. Injuries suffered by the workforce become social problems when they occur often or as a result of wilful negligence by owners and management. As we will see, some jobs are naturally more harmful to health than others. While health-and-safety risks are an inescapable hazard for some occupations (for example, police officer or firefighter), they are also avoidable but common among workers in low-wage jobs.

Work-related risks are often the result of corporate cost-cutting in the name of profits. Violation of worker rights is another cause for concern. Capitalism benefits the wealthy at the expense of the poor. To boost personal profits, owners and managers often take advantage of their employees' dependence by offering them low wages, few benefits, and little job flexibility. In some workplaces, racism, sexism, and homophobia are still major problems, particularly when prejudice excludes some types of people from jobs or prevents them from receiving raises, benefits, or promotions.

Though employment is better than unemployment, all jobs are not created equal. Jobs vary in salary, benefits, degree of challenge, novelty of the work, level of independence granted to the worker, and amount of social recognition conferred on the position. As well, some types of people are more likely to get the better jobs and are less likely to suffer unemployment. Thus, work and its discontents—including unemployment—are socially structured and unevenly distributed.

Some Basic Aspects of Work

Work becomes a social problem when it makes workers unhappy, harms their health, or supports other social problems, such as racism, sexism, and economic inequality. This section will focus on some basic aspects of work. We will discuss unemployment as a social problem further in later sections.

Capitalism and Socialism

Two economic approaches control the world's economy: capitalism and socialism. **Capitalism** refers to the economic system in which private individuals or corporate groups own the means of production and distribution and invest private capital to produce goods and services to be sold for profit in a competitive market. **Socialism** is an alternative economic and political ideology that flourished in the nineteenth and twentieth centuries. It favours public ownership of the means of production and distribution and the investment of public capital in producing goods and services. Currently, most modern economies are a mixture of capitalism and socialism, with some tending more in the capitalist direction (for example, Japan and the United States) and others tending more in the socialist direction (for example, Sweden and Canada—Sweden more than Canada).

Under capitalism, private individuals own and operate the means of production for profit. In contrast, socialism is based more on public ownership than on private ownership. It stresses the needs of the whole society over the desires of individuals. At least in theory, it proposes that goods and services be spread equally among members of society as dictated by their needs. Socialists argue that since many human needs can be satisfied only through cooperation with others, it is in everyone's interest to work together to serve the collective interest, thus bringing about economic prosperity.

Arguments can be made for both sides. Capitalist societies have tended, on average, to achieve a higher standard of living than socialist nations. However, economic inequality is also more pronounced in those societies that regulate capitalism least. In the twentieth century, countries such as Canada, Germany, France, and Sweden adopted strategies that included elements of both capitalism and socialism. The United States continues to resist regulation and socialism most vigorously. As a result, the standard of living is lower in Canada than in the United States, as indicated by (among other things) the value of the Canadian dollar compared with the American dollar. On the other hand, inequality in Canada is narrower; here, we are not as likely to find the same dire extremes of poverty and degradation as one finds in the United States (for example, in urban ghettos).

Industrialism and Post-industrialism

Since the late eighteenth century, industrialism has transformed the way we work. In pre-industrial societies, people worked collectively in mainly agricultural settings. Because of the small, localized scale of rural communities and the interconnectedness of people's experiences, work was largely inseparable from family and personal life. People led similar lives and held similar moral, religious, and political beliefs.

The Industrial Revolution, which began in the late eighteenth century, ushered in a new approach to production. No longer did farmers and artisans produce only enough to match their consumption. Instead, the new factory system created a surplus, which the capitalist factory owners then sold for profit. Machines began to replace human hands and tools, while steam (and later, electrical) power began to take over from human effort as the source of energy. As the manufacturing process became more complex, jobs were divided and became more specialized. Assembly lines were invented. Cities began to grow as people came together in factory towns to seek work in return for wages. Earlier, family life and work life had been carried out in the same place. Now the two realms of activity became distinct and exclusive, the one still located at home, the other in a factory or office. This began a new marked separation of men and women, men's work and women's work, adult work and children's formal education.

Transnationals and the Global Economy

In the late twentieth century, industrialism became post-industrialism. *Post-industrialism* refers to the shift from a manufacturing-intensive economy to an economy based on services and information. Because of recent advances in computer-based and telecommunications technology, production is now often exclusively an automated process in which information is both the main input and the main output.

With post-industrialism, geography, distance, and national borders have lost much of their importance. Information can flow across great distances quickly, cheaply, safely, and easily. Other factors have also speeded the flow of information, products, and people, including multinational trade agreements, such as the North American Free Trade Agreement (NAFTA) and the more recently proposed Free Trade Area of the Americas (FTAA), and international economic organizations, such as the World Trade Organization (WTO), the World Bank, and the International Monetary Fund (IMF). However, these are not mere 'techniques' for improving the flow of resources: they are also profoundly political arrangements.

Trade agreements are aimed at removing tariffs for import and export. International organizations pressure less developed countries to open their borders to global trade. As this happens, corporate transnationals find it easier to gain access to raw materials in foreign countries, to employ cheap labour overseas, and to steer clear of government regulation concerning workers' rights and environmental pollution. Many believe this process benefits rich nations at the expense of poorer ones, and large multinational organizations at the expense of smaller organizations and nation-states. As a result, free trade and other aspects of economic globalization have been the focus of organized protest at meetings in Canada (Montreal), the United States (Seattle), and elsewhere.

In the end, global capitalism has supported the growth of huge transnational corporations with revenues much larger than the revenues of the majority of nation-states. They are the new political and economic force in the post-industrial world. In some instances, they produce jobs and new wealth. In other instances, they destroy jobs—leading to unemployment—and put more wealth in the pockets of the already wealthy.

The Bureaucratization of Work

Along with factories and cities, bureaucracies are a defining feature of modern work life. **Bureaucracies** are large, complex organizations employing highly specialized workers who work within the context of what Max Weber (1947) called a *legal-rational* authority structure. This form of authority is distinguished by thorough written rules governing how people are to perform their jobs.

Under capitalism, a system devoted to the pursuit of utmost profits, the rich quickly found that some forms of social and economic organization yield higher rates of profit on investment. Bureaucratic organization is well suited to the pursuit of profits: it is usually prudent, cautious, and shrewd. Bureaucracies as a whole are rarely impulsive or petty, as despots and dictators might be. Moreover, a bureaucratic organization can grow as large as necessary yet remain highly controlled from the top. Growth is much more limited in organizations that rely on personal attachment and duty, such as family businesses.

Another aspect of modern bureaucracy is the legal idea of *limited liability*, which allows a corporation to manage investment and profits impersonally, in a way that protects both the owners and the workers. Under this legal principle, organizational officers are protected (in most cases) from lawsuits arising out of the legal operation of their company. The same impersonality also makes bureaucracy different from patronage and other personalized systems (such as the Mafia, described in chapter 3). In principle,

bureaucracies distinguish between the rights and obligations attaching to a position and the characteristics of the person who (temporarily) holds a position of authority.

Industrialization favoured the rise of bureaucracies. Bureaucracies are good at controlling large workforces—even highly educated and differentiated workforces. As organizations grow, their differentiation usually increases. Problems of coordination and control—formalization, decentralization, and supervision—are bound to arise. Often, reorganization is needed, especially if the number of personnel is large and growing rapidly. As industrial enterprises grow with the mechanization of work, control structures (that is, for management and administration) have to grow too.

Ideally, every member of a bureaucratic organization is enmeshed in a network of **reporting relationships**. In graphic form, the ideal bureaucracy is a Christmas-tree-shaped structure that repeatedly branches out as you go down the hierarchy. Ideally, at the bottom of the hierarchy many people have to (1) carry out orders from above, (2) report work-related information up the tree to their superiors, and (3) uphold linkages between the organization and its client or customer base. At the top of the hierarchy, a few people get to (1) issue orders to their subordinates, (2) process information received from below, and (3) uphold linkages between the organization and other organizations—political, economic, and social. Also, those at the top of the structure ideally share information between the heads of planning, manufacturing, shipping, public relations, and other sectors of the organization.

In theory, all information in a bureaucratic organization is stored and expressed in writing. Ideally, all written information is recorded and reported up the ladder. Ideally, workers never leak work-related information outside the organization, to superiors other than their own, to workmates in other branches of the structure, or even to workmates with the same superior. Accordingly, and ideally, a shop supervisor would hear about a problem related to shipping, sales, or customer satisfaction only after this information had made its way up the structure from the bottom to the top and then back down to the factory floor. Ideally, most employees of a large bureaucracy are strangers to one another, and they are encouraged to remain strangers.

However, reality is different. The gap between fact and fiction is often a source of problems. In practice, there is a 'politics from below' that includes all the actions that defy, oppose, or sidestep the rules and roles of the organization. Below the surface of the ideal, or formal, structure—which prescribes how a bureaucracy *ought* to work—there is an actual, or informal, structure, which is how it *really* works. The basis of this informal organization is informal communication based on trust. Trust, in turn, relies on friendship, acquaintanceship, and gossip about third parties to strengthen existing ties. People form stronger attachments to other workers than they do to 'the organization' as an abstract entity. Thus, personalistic patterns of patronage, friendship, and informal decision making develop even within bureaucracies (see, for example, Crozier, 1969; Perrow, 1984).

Bureaucracies and Misconduct

As bureaucratic organizations have grown in power, they have opened opportunities for new forms of misconduct by people who are hidden by the corporate structure. So-called collective decisions—taken by the top executives—are liable to be foolish, harmful, or even criminal. Corporate and government entities are unique in that their deviant behaviour may be caused by systemic patterns in their organizations rather than by individual malfeasance. However, once deviant behaviour has occurred, the perpetrators are well positioned to evade responsibility. Managers may often refuse responsibility by hiding behind organizational structures or by adopting the view that they were merely following orders.

The misconduct of big business and big government sometimes occurs because of limited information, the establishment of norms and rewards that encourage deviant outcomes, or the actions of organizational elites. Such deviance is initiated by managerial elites and then institutionalized into organizational culture. It often continues unchecked until it is challenged. Almost no one in the organization has enough information to assess the decisions taken or the reasons they are taken. People are actively discouraged or even prevented from gaining this information. **Whistle-blowers**—employees who bring forward valid information about wrongdoing or illegal conduct by their organization—are often punished for doing so. Even organizations that publicly say that they want employees to 'participate' and that they hold high ethical standards move to discredit whistle-blowers and to fire them as soon as they report information about waste, fraud, or abuses of power in the organization.

Corporations stage-manage their public image and take pains to hide what they do not want people to know (consider, for example, the recent case of the Enron Corporation scandal and investigation, in 2001–2). They use public relations tactics to improve their image. Ironically, it is the front-line workers of the organization—the people who actually deliver goods and services to customers—who have the most contact with the outside world and know the most about it. This fact creates an asymmetry in the organization. Those with the most knowledge about the environment have the least authority to influence corporate relations with that knowledge, and vice versa.

Sociologists since Weber have pointed out that bureaucracy has a vast potential for enslavement, exploitation, and cruelty. It also has a vast potential for promoting human progress through economic development and scientific discovery, high-quality mass education, and the delivery of humane social services to the needy. However, bureaucracies are founded on principles of efficiency and procedural rigidity that are potentially in conflict with humane values and public service. Like automobiles, which can take you to good places or bad, depending on the wishes of the driver, bureaucracies are only as good as the people in charge.

Theories of Work and Unemployment

As in other areas of sociological research, sociologists in research on work and unemployment employ alternative theoretical approaches. The three broad theoretical perspectives of structural functionalism, conflict theory, and symbolic interaction all provide interpretations for work and unemployment.

The Structural-Functionalist Perspective

This perspective stresses that, along with the family, work is the most basic of social institutions. Everyone needs love, work, and hope, functionalists like to think. Work must be seen as especially important because it lets people obtain the necessities of life—food, water, shelter, and clothing—for themselves and their families.

Not only does paid work give workers an opportunity to satisfy their physical needs, it also allows them to satisfy their emotional needs. These include the desires to be a productive and valued member of society, to gain recognition and praise, and to interact and cooperate with others. Thus, work has social functions. It provides a basis for social interaction, social solidarity and cohesion, and the sharing of lifestyles and meanings. The workplace, ideally, permits people to exercise all of their social and creative impulses while earning a living.

As work has changed with industrialization, societies have had to change too. Émile Durkheim ([1893] 1964) was among the first to note that in the pre-industrial era, societies were primarily small, rural settlements with little division of labour based principally on age and sex. People did not really have 'jobs'. They worked at various tasks, sharing the same experiences and lifestyles. As a result, they developed similar values, norms, and identity—what Durkheim called the *common conscience*. This all changed with industrialization and modernity. In modern societies, we hold highly specialized jobs and lead varied lives. As sociologists, we have not yet learned how different kinds of people, with different jobs and different experiences, can live together happily and harmoniously. The problem we face is learning how to use our 'human capital' and highly specialized labour power in peaceful, non-coercive ways and adapting continuously to change in the workplace.

For functionalists, then, work is a human necessity; the problem we face is knowing how to organize ourselves efficiently, flexibly, and peacefully in the face of complex and rapidly changing demands.

Conflict Theory

Conflict theorists, by contrast, focus on how the economic system promotes social inequality. The problem is not efficiency per se, because people with different amounts of wealth and power will have different ideas about the value of efficiency and the ways we might pursue it. As a result, there will inevitably be conflict over how to organize work best for everyone involved.

Karl Marx (for example, [1887] 1936) claimed that capitalism is the root cause of all conflict within and between societies. To his mind, the members of society could be divided into two factions. The ruling class, or *bourgeoisie*, comprises the wealthy owners of the means of production, and the working class, or *proletariat*, comprises the labourers who work for the bourgeoisie. One group wants to hire labour for the lowest possible price; the other wants to sell its labour for the highest possible price. Given their opposed interests, the two classes are locked in a conflict that plays itself out largely in the workplace, which economist Richard Edwards (1979) called a 'contested terrain'. In this contested terrain, there can never be peace and cooperation, or a universally accepted definition of efficiency, because the interests of workers and capitalists are opposed.

Whereas the structural-functionalist perspective views employment as benefiting all members of society equally, conflict theory—to which Marx contributed—argues that some benefit more than others from the work relationship. Specifically, the ruling class controls and manipulates the economy—and other related institutions such as the media, education, the legal system, and governmental politics—for their own benefit, while exploiting the working class in the process.

From this point of view, the workplace is not a place for sociability and creativity. It is a place for repression and mistreatment, a place in which some groups of workers are even more vulnerable than others. In this system, low-end workers—the most vulnerable workers, those most in need of a stable income—are often the first to lose their jobs when the economy goes into a slump.

Conflict theorists believe that many corporate initiatives—for example, telework—give the false impression of concerned and well-meaning management, when in fact they are based on more selfish motives. These policies outwardly appear to place the employee's family and personal needs ahead of company interests. However, they serve to profit the corporate leaders who apply them by increasing worker productivity and lowering costs. Take, as another instance, the example of on-site daycare facilities for working parents. A conflict theorist might argue that the employer provides this service because it ensures that the employee will not have to take an extended paternity leave to raise his or her newborn child, saving the employer the cost of hiring and training a temporary replacement.

Another worker-friendly program, flextime, allows employees to determine when they begin and end the workday, as long as they log the necessary hours per week. While this may allow, say, working mothers to leave at 3 p.m. to pick up their children after school, it also means they have to either arrive at work at 7 a.m. or make up the lost time by working on weekends. In either case, these 'family-oriented' policies are, at best, a mixed blessing.

According to conflict theory, the power elite also uses unemployment to boost profits. In the conflict perspective, unemployed people are necessary to the operation of the capitalist system because they depress wages. They provide a 'reserve army' of labour that can be drawn into service when unionized wages are too high, for example. Workers who protest too hard in times of high unemployment will find themselves replaced by people from the great pool of the unemployed. In this way, powerful industrialists use the unemployed as a way of quashing employee unrest. Workers are less likely to demand higher wages if they fear they will be replaced by cheaper labour.

Symbolic Interactionism

Symbolic interactionists, by contrast, are inclined to focus on the meanings of work and unemployment for the individual. Work, particularly in a modern, individualistic culture, provides a major part of our identity. Because a person's line of work is so central to his or her identity, others often use it as a source of information. 'So what do you do for a living?' is possibly the second most popular question asked whenever two strangers strike up a conversation (the first being, 'Come here often?').

The reasoning is simple: we like to believe that people choose their occupations freely, based on their interests and dispositions. Therefore, knowing what someone does for a living (for example, nun or rock musician) should provide clues to that person's character—his or her personality and interests. Many people also treat occupational titles as status symbols and use them as a way of making judgments about someone's 'station in life'. Stereotypes about various careers are plentiful. Yet in the end, people base their assessments of jobs largely on the amount of prestige and income those jobs receive.

Symbolic interactionists are also interested in how face-to-face contact between people in the workplace can alter people's views of their boss and fellow workers. An entire seminar-based industry has emerged, for example, that gives corporate managers the interpersonal skills they need to interact with their employees in a way that maximizes worker productivity, job satisfaction, and company loyalty. Likewise, go-getting workers learn to interact with their employers and co-workers in ways that ease their ascent up the corporate hierarchy.

Regarding unemployment, some symbolic interactionists would argue that chronic unemployment is a learned trait. This 'culture of poverty' viewpoint argues that constant job insecurity, unemployment, and underemployment result in a culture in which the disadvantaged develop distinctive patterns of behaviour and belief. This includes *learned helplessness*, a pessimistic concession of one's impoverished state that reduces

people's ability to break free of their hopeless situation. Of course, as we suggested in chapter 1, helplessness may be a response to confronting a persistently bad job market. The opportunity structure can be so poor that it grinds down one's will.

Social Consequences of Work and Unemployment

As we have already seen in earlier chapters, work and unemployment are connected to a great many other social problems. We will touch on a few of these in this section.

Gender Discrimination

In spite of a steady advancement in gender equality over the past several decades, discrimination against women remains an important problem. Gender stereotyping and inequality continue to occur in the workplace. Because the issue of sexism was discussed in detail in chapter 5, this section will only briefly remind us of some aspects of this problem.

BOX 6.1
Gender Equity in the Universities

A group of Canadian academics is attacking a federal agency for paying universities what it calls 'girl money' to hire female professors instead of men. Since 1998, the Natural Sciences and Engineering Research Council has spent close to a million dollars a year encouraging Canadian universities to hire women into entry-level science professorships, by paying most of their salaries for the first five years of employment. Women supported under the University Faculty Awards program also receive a large research grant. Tim Nau, a council spokesman, says the program is designed to boost the representation of female professors in science and engineering, fields in which men traditionally dominate.

However, Doreen Kimura, president of Canada's Society for Academic Freedom and Scholarship, says the program flagrantly discriminates against men. 'These things are not available to men and there are no equivalent scholarships that men can apply for', Dr Kimura, a professor at Simon Fraser University in British Columbia, says. 'This is more than affirmative action, this totally excludes men.'

Mr Nau says any women hired under the program have already been granted research funds after a separate peer review process. Mr Nau says only 6% of all engineering and applied science professors in Canada are women. He says if there were more women role models in these

continued

fields, there would be more female students. 'If you don't have any women professors and you're a woman student looking for a career in these areas, it probably is a bit of a turnoff', he says. 'But I can't prove it.'

Dr Kimura calls it nonsense. 'The fact is that women just show less interest in these programs', she says. 'They apply to these fields in much smaller numbers than to other ones.' Studies consistently show that Canadian universities hire a greater proportion of women into faculty positions than the percentage of women who apply for the work. Andrew Irvine, a University of B.C. professor, found that in the mid '70s women made up 27% of applicants for faculty jobs at universities across the country but received 42% of all appointments. A study of hiring practices at the University of Western Ontario between 1984 and 1999 said 10% of all female applicants were hired into faculty positions compared to 5.4% of all male applicants.

SOURCE: Richard Foot, 'Academics Attack Funding Program as Discriminatory: Schools Get "Girl Money"', *National Post*, national edition, 8 January 2000, A6.

The 'glass ceiling' that results in earning differences between women and men, along with other gender-related workplace concerns, such as harassment, are discussed at length in chapter 5. The problem of gender inequality in the workplace is important because the income derived from work affects a person's access to the necessities of life, education of children, and leisure. Women are overrepresented in the lower end of the primary work sector and in the secondary sector of the dual-market system (see Table 6.1). This stratification leads to further problems. The low wages and job instability of the secondary work sector often mean that even full-time workers must live in poverty. Because of stereotypes of women as largely nurturing and emotional and of men as more dominant and rational, female workers have customarily been excluded from occupations requiring broad education and skill development. For these reasons, even today, women are still underrepresented in leadership positions.

For women, employment does not always mean an escape from poverty. The jobs that are obtainable are part of the problem. 'Women's work'—clerical jobs, sales, light manufacturing, and the catch-all category 'service work', which includes nurses' aides, elementary-school teachers, waitresses, and welfare caseworkers—tends to pay poorly. In general, women's work not only pays less than men's, but is also less inflation-proof. The occupational segregation of women in our society makes for a vital difference between women's poverty and men's. For men, poverty is often a result of unemployment and is curable by getting a job. But for women, concentrated in the low-wage stratum of the workforce, a job may not eliminate poverty, only reduce it.

Another important issue women face at work is that, particularly on a global scale, women's labour is not recognized as work that is deserving of compensation. For example, even when cash exchanges are involved, the involvement of women is not included or is discounted in national statistics. Yet, in rural areas, women not only prepare but also grow most of the family food, and it is mainly girls and women who collect water, fuel for cooking, and fodder for domestic animals. Women's unpaid household labour may account for as much as one-third of the world's economic production. When unpaid agricultural work and housework are considered along with wage labour in developing countries, women's work hours are estimated to exceed men's by 30 per cent (United Nations Population Fund, 2000: 38).

TABLE 6.1
Reasons for Part-time Employment by Gender, 2002

	Women				Men			
	Total	15–24	25–44	45+	Total	15–24	25–44	45+
Own illness (%)	2.8	0.4	2.6	5.5	3.3	0.6	5.3	7.0
Caring for children (%)	14.7	1.9	33.6	4.0	0.9	unr.[a]	2.8	0.6
Other personal/family responsibilities (%)	5.9	0.8	8.1	8.3	1.4	0.4	2.6	2.1
Going to school (%)	24.9	72.3	5.9	0.8	41.9	75.1	14.3	unr.
Personal preference (%)	25.0	4.8	17.5	54.4	20.9	4.8	15.3	56.5
Other voluntary (%)	1.2	0.4	1.6	1.5	1.5	0.3	2.9	2.8
Other[b] (%)	25.6	19.4	30.7	25.7	30.2	18.4	56.8	30.4
Total employed part-time	1,983,770 (27.7%)	612,900 (52.9%)	761,400 (21.2%)	609,400 (25.4%)	900,000 (10.9%)	461,800 (38.2%)	199,500 (4.9%)	238,700 (8.0%)

[a] 'Unr.' indicates that the data for these categories are considered too unreliable to publish; as a result, percentages may not add up to 100.
[b] Includes business conditions and inability to find full-time work.

SOURCE: Statistics Canada, 'Reasons for Part-time Work' (2003), catalogue no. 89F0133XIE; available at <www.statcan.ca/english/Pgdb/labor63c.htm>.

Racial and Ethnic Discrimination

Another widespread and institutionalized form of discrimination in the workplace is ethnic and racial prejudice, as we saw in chapter 4. Workers who belong to ethnic and racial minorities or who are recent immigrants are particularly disadvantaged in the search for jobs, in the incomes they receive once hired, and in opportunities to advance based on merit. In part, these problems are due to stereotypes and social distance. Employers are unwilling or unable to imagine that certain types of people can do good work. Equally important, these problems are due to social networks, as we will see later in this chapter. People with more **social capital** are better able to hear about good jobs, and employers are more likely to hear about them.

Poverty and Wealth Inequalities

Work also influences the widening income gap between the haves and the have-nots. Even as corporations post record profits, 'downsizing' continues to leave many lower- and middle-class labourers underemployed and unemployed. The clear division between haves and have-nots, first noted by Marx when he distinguished between the bourgeoisie and the proletariat, continues to exist in our post-industrial, service- and information-based society. The capitalist imperative to take full advantage of profits and reduce production costs creates a mentality in which company executives are eager to ignore or override the needs and rights of workers if doing so promises greater corporate wealth.

Work-Family Concerns

As gender roles, demographics, and family structures have changed, the dual-income household has emerged as the norm in Canada and elsewhere. These changes have had effects on both the workplace and the family. A once-patriarchal and male-dominated workforce has come under pressure to provide for women's career aspirations and desires for financial independence. These changes progressed steadily throughout the twentieth century, but as we saw in chapter 5, women still have a lot of ground to make up if real equality is to be achieved.

Parents must now learn the difficult task of balancing work, family, and personal needs on a daily basis, often with neither the financial means to pay for child care nor the traditional assistance of extended family support networks. (See Figure 6.1.) One major problem of the new century is figure out how families can organize themselves most effectively to deal with the multiple problems of work, companionship, child rearing, and increasingly, elder care. We will have more to say about this in the next chapter, on families.

Technology and the Changing Workplace

Other consequences of the workplace flow from its adoption of new technology. Whereas manufacturing jobs dominated the Industrial Revolution of the late eighteenth century and the nineteenth century, service- and information-oriented jobs dominate the economy today. The explosion of telecommunications and computer technology in the last quarter of the twentieth century has resulted in the growth of jobs requiring highly skilled workers with advanced education and professional training.

The pace of development in our current epoch is unrivalled by any other period in history. For workers, this means that skills are becoming outdated faster than ever. Our abilities require constant upgrading to remain competitive in a continually changing job market. However, not everyone can achieve this. This spirited self-improvement is largely limited to those with the financial and educational means to do so and those who work in a sector of the economy that requires and promotes such changes. For workers mired in low-wage, dead-end positions—manufacturing or retail, for example—the market may not force them to rapidly adapt to technical change, but neither does

Over the last decade, one increasingly popular solution to the work-family crunch has been teleworking. However, anyone who has tried it will tell you that it presents its own challenges. Balancing work and home life in the same environment is often more difficult than separating the two spheres. (Dick Hemingway)

it offer many opportunities for greater self-improvement and wealth.

Workers in the manufacturing industry are also increasingly being threatened with job cuts because of the automation of production. Computer-controlled machinery benefits corporate managers for several reasons. First, it eliminates human error in jobs that are boring and repetitive. Consider computer-assisted production with lasers: because of the precision and specificity that can be achieved with modern laser and fibre-optic technology, computer-based production cuts down on human error and variability in the final product. Second, computerization replaces human workers with machines, resulting in significant financial savings. Third, computerization and mechanization more generally reduces human conflict between workers and bosses by reducing the number of humans

FIGURE 6.1
Shift Work

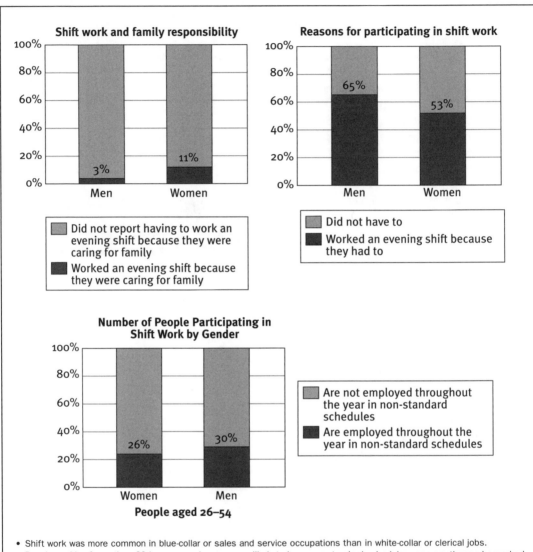

- Shift work was more common in blue-collar or sales and service occupations than in white-collar or clerical jobs.
- People working fewer than 30 hours a week were more likely to have non-standard schedules, as were those who worked on weekends.
- The likelihood of working shift decreased with advancing age, possibly because older workers with seniority have more choice in their hours than do younger, less experienced workers.
- Single or previously married workers were more likely than those who were married to have non-standard schedules.

SOURCE: Statistics Canada, 'Shift Workers and Health', *Health Reports* (25 July 2002), based on data from the Canadian Community Health Survey (2000/01), the National Population Health Survey (1994/95, 1996/97, and 1998/99), and the Survey of Work Arrangements (1991 and 1995).

involved. Computing devices do not demand an income, never go on strike, never tire or get bored of their work, and can work around the clock. Rather than employing dozens of workers to run a production floor, managers and owners can now hire only a few well-trained employees to program, supervise, and maintain the otherwise robotic manufacturing process.

The microelectronics revolution is transforming many aspects of our society. With proper use, computers can become instruments of human betterment. With wrong use, they can become instruments of domination. In the twentieth century and the beginning of the twenty-first, we have seen that this is true of much technology.

Worker Dissatisfaction and Alienation

In the literature on utopias—places that do not really exist anywhere except our imagination—work is invigorating, satisfying, and socially useful. It fulfills the individual's need for meaningful labour and society's need to get work done. In reality, however, many jobs are *not* stimulating and challenging. They are repetitive and boring, and often not even socially useful.

At least as far back as Marx, thinkers have noted that industrialization and the division of labour have separated the worker from the work process, from the object he or she produces, and from his or her fellow workers. This experience of **alienation** involves feelings of powerlessness, meaninglessness, normlessness, estrangement, and social isolation in the workplace. Highly specialized work roles mean that each individual worker is given few responsibilities, performing narrowly defined tasks lacking in variety and challenge, so that the worker is performing below his or her full intellectual, physical, and emotional potential, as demanded by the employer. Sociologists have tended to disagree about the origins of these problems: Marx attributed them to capitalism, Durkheim to specialization, and Weber to rationalization.

Whatever the source, these problems are made worse in tall, hierarchical bureaucracies, in which workers at the bottom have no control of, or say in, the work process. In many cases, employees become just another cog in the wheel, mindlessly churning out the products required by their employers in the form of a factory line, a clerical office, a filing department, or a retail shop. As a result, worker loyalty and production often decline, since employees are no longer dedicated to doing a particularly good job. Many studies have shown that low levels of perceived work satisfaction result from these work circumstances.

In one survey, only half of the respondents reported being happy with their present job (Stafford, 2000). In particular, most employees were unhappy about income, bonus packages, and training programs. They also reported less satisfaction with supervisors or their physical work environment than in earlier years. On the other hand, most reported greater feelings of job security and affection for co-workers. Though these attitudes vary somewhat over time and place, they indicate the kinds of feelings that are typical among North Americans today.

To be sure, not everyone requires complete control and stability in their jobs for their work to be enjoyable and fulfilling. Still, several factors have been consistently shown to be involved in surveys of job satisfaction. They include safe working conditions, job security, challenge and stimulating work content, pleasant and like-minded colleagues, respect and consideration from superiors, and opportunities for creativity, initiative, and advancement. Moreover, it is important that the worker's expectations of the job match with the actual work experience. When the two diverge, resentment, job dissatisfaction, and alienation arise. Perhaps most important, people crave some measure of autonomy and control over their work. We will have more to say about this in the section on health later in this chapter.

Social Consequences of Unemployment

As unpleasant as work is—for many people, it is a soul-destroying and unrewarding experience—the alternative, unemployment, is even worse. Unemployment is a major social problem. Since everyone needs money to buy what they need and want and since most people can get money only by working, unemployment deprives most people of the bases for material survival. Unemployment also takes an economic toll on society at large. With people out of the work-force, the economy cannot reach its utmost potential for production. Another reason unem-ployment affects the overall economy is the cost of maintaining a social support network to assist those who are currently between jobs.

From a social-psychological perspective, unemployed people are often marked with the stigma of being lazy people who are unwilling to work. People who think this way think that unemployment insurance and welfare under-mine the work ethic that has allowed so many others to succeed in life. Public attitudes to inequality are mixed and confused, and so are public attitudes to unemployment. People who see themselves (and others) as victims of forces beyond their control are able to believe that unemployment resulting from ill health, discrim-ination, recession, or corporate downsizing deserves assistance. People who see themselves as masters of their own fate hold those who are unemployed responsible and do not think these people deserve public assistance.

The amount of assistance made available to unemployed people varies with the duration and perceived causes of unemployment. Those who are physically disabled receive the most help, since people tend to consider them the blameless 'deserving poor'. They sometimes consider chronically unemployed people the 'undeserving poor'. To some extent, their thinking operates on

---

BOX 6.2
Rights of the Unemployed

The cartoon on your editorial page for Oct. 17 is a graphic example of 'poor-bashing'.

The cartoon stereotypes a poor person as a long-haired male with a beard and a paunch and of course smoking a cigarette—a lazy per-son, unwilling to work and of course spending our tax dollars on cigarettes.

How dare a poor person have addictions like the rest of us!

It has been my experience over many years in my personal contacts as well as in my vari-ous vocations as social worker, priest and high school principal, that most people want to work and they find a sense of meaningfulness and value in having work.

Article 25 (1) of the International Declaration of Human Rights sets out the obli-gations of a government towards its citizens. It states in part, 'Everyone has the right to food, clothing, housing, medical care and necessary social services, and the right to security in the event of unemployment or other lack of liveli-hood'. Canada's signature is on that declara-tion. Canada has a responsibility to change the policies and structures that cause poverty and gross inequality.

It needs to address the lack of meaningful work for far too many people in our society. It needs to ask why many countries in Europe have child poverty rates of less than five per cent, while child poverty in Canada is 20 per cent.

Thank you for your attention to this very important concern.

SOURCE: Bud Godderis, Letter to the editor, *Trail Daily Times*, 25 October 2001, 4. Reprinted by permission of Mr Godderis.

the assumption that, after a while, unemployed people should have taken retraining or moved to another city and found a new job. People who have failed to do this have failed to act in their own interests. As a result, they receive less generous and secure assistance. Social assistance payments to chronically unemployed people fail to meet actual living expenses, especially for people who live in large cities like Toronto and Vancouver where rents are high.

Many believe that if social assistance payments were to exceed the minimum-wage level, unemployed people would be reluctant to get off welfare and take a job, though hundreds of thousands *cannot* find a job. There is the supposition that only motivation is at issue: anyone who tries to can find a job. This supposition ignores the evidence of discrimination against racial minorities and the disappearance of work for the less educated. Certain groups, such as female lone parents of small children, cannot afford to pay the daycare costs that would allow them to take a job. Others, such as the physically disabled, cannot find a job that fits their abilities.

Researchers base their measures of unemployment on the percentage of the workforce currently without jobs, actively seeking employ-ment, and available to work. This definition excludes **discouraged workers**, those who have turned their back on the traditional work system and abandoned any effort to be gainfully employed. These discouraged workers consist disproportionately of women and racial minorities. Other people do not take part in the labour force because they are in school, retired, or injured, sick, or otherwise unable to work. (See Table 6.2.)

Because of these exclusions, most official unemployment rates understate the actual percentage of people who are not working. This in turn underestimates the size of the unemployment problem. Official employment rates also do not distinguish between full-time and part-time work, nor do they recognize odd jobs, temporary work, and other forms of underemployment as unique work experiences. A person who reports working as little as one hour per week is formally considered 'gainfully employed', for example. This too minimizes the visible problem of unemployment. So, in the end, our estimates of unemployment tend to provide too rosy a picture of the world.

Researchers distinguish between discriminatory and structural unemployment. **Discrimi-**

TABLE 6.2
Canadian Labour-Force Activity, 1981–1996[a]

	1981	1986	1991	1996
Total population 15+ years	18,609,285	19,634,100	21,304,740	22,628,925
Total labour force	12,054,155	13,049,860	14,474,945	14,812,700
Employed	11,167,915	11,702,215	13,005,500	13,318,740
Unemployed	886,235	1,347,640	1,469,440	1,493,960
Not in the labour force	6,555,130	6,584,240	6,829,795	7,816,225
Participation rate	64.8%	66.5%	67.9%	65.5%
Employment–population ratio	60.0	59.6	61.0	58.9
Unemployment rate	7.4%	10.3%	10.2%	10.1%

[a] Figures are as published by Statistics Canada.

SOURCE: Statistics Canada, 'Population 15 Years and Over by Sex, Age Groups and Labour Force Activity, for Canada, Provinces and Territories, 1981–1996 Censuses (20% Sample Data)', available at <www.statcan.ca/english/census96/mar17/labour/table6/t6p00a.htm>, accessed 23 January 2003.

natory unemployment, as the name implies, is unemployment resulting from discrimination against particular groups, such as ethnic minorities and women. **Structural unemployment**, on the other hand, results from social and economic factors that affect workers equally across all groups. These factors include corporate downsizing, capital flight (caused by corporate mergers and the move of operations to another geographic region— so-called runaway plants), and automation (the replacement of human labour with machinery).

Predictors of Unemployment

Some explanations of unemployment focus on the individuals who lose their jobs; others focus on the social and financial environment in which jobs are lost. In the latter category, research has been done on the causes and consequences of down-sizing. For example, researchers found that downsizing eliminated about 60 per cent of the workforce and one-quarter of the job titles in the British Columbia sawmill industry, largely in response to an economic recession in the early 1980s. The youngest workers lost their jobs. The result was a reduced workforce and a more hierarchical structure of control (Ostry et al., 2000).

Other researchers focus on the personal characteristics of people who lose their job or are at particular risk of losing their job in the event of an economic recession. Often they focus on human capital characteristics, such as educational attainment or particular job-related skills. Some focus on the mental or physical health of the workers themselves. We will discuss later in this chapter the health consequences of job insecurity and unemployment.

Some have argued that health problems often predate and cause unemployment; they are not merely consequences of unemployment. So, for example, aggression in childhood predicts school maladjustment at age 14, which is directly and indirectly (through problem drinking, insufficient schooling, and a lack of occupational alternatives at age 27) related to long-term unemployment (Kokko and Pulkkinen, 2000). Unhealthy lifestyle behaviours, such as smoking and heavy use of alcohol, are correlated with unemployment (Liira and Leino, 1999). Family characteristics play a part, too. For example, single marital status predicts unemployment after a layoff among construction and forest workers (Liira and Leino, 1999). Parental divorce, low parental emotional involvement, and, for males only, parental unemployment predict the unemployment of youth (de Goede et al., 2000).

Age itself predicts unemployment. Older workers (over age 40) who have been laid off find it harder than younger workers to get a job, especially in work, like construction, that demands physical strength (Leino et al., 1999). Poor physical health may result in unemployment, even among youth (Hammarstrom and Janlert, 1997). A study of job mobility over a five-year period in the Netherlands found that health problems were significantly associated with a higher risk of mobility out of employment in 1991 and a lower likelihood of mobility into employment in 1995. The least healthy people remained economically inactive over the period (Van de Mheen et al., 1999). Mental as well as physical health is linked to transitions to early retirement or other unemployment (Wray, 2000). Above-average mental health plays a protective role in keeping workers in the workforce rather than laid off, on sick leave, or unemployed.

To some degree, the effects of illness on working life depend on the duration of a disability. Over half of the workers who become limited in activities of daily living as adults have unemployment spells lasting less than two years. Few disabled people who remain outside the workforce for four years re-enter the workforce (Burchardt, 2000). More than half the non-working disabled report that economic, social, and job-based barriers contribute to their inability to work, and one-fourth of working disabled people report having experienced discrimination in the last five years because of their disability (Druss et al., 2000).

However, health problems do not always lead to long-term unemployment. Specific health conditions, such as asthma or visual impairment, may be associated with work limitation, yet they are reportedly not among the principal determinants of continuous unemployment (McCarty, Burgess, and Keeffe, 1999; Yelin et al., 1999). The risk of unemployment for chronically ill people is largely dependent on active labour market policies—specific efforts made by government to stimulate employment, job training, and worker mobility—and employment protections, as illustrated by lower rates of unemployment and inactivity in Sweden than in Britain (Burstrom et al., 2000).

Re-employment

As we will see later in this chapter, unemployment brings a variety of social and health consequences. It is good to know, then, that a majority of unemployed people eventually find jobs. What's more, re-employment typically brings good results, such as reductions in psychological distress (Creed, 1999). Mental health improves (Pernice and Long, 1996). Re-employed persons' sense of time structure—the degree to which they perceive their use of time as structured and useful—returns (Wanberg, Griffiths, and Gavin, 1997). Even temporary job creation brings positive health effects (Swart and Machler, 2000). And even long-term unemployed people improve their mental health after entering a job (Claussen, 1999b). Leaving unemployment resolves economic difficulties and the uncertainty faced during unemployment. Entering permanent employment means an even larger increase in mental well-being than entering temporary employment or self-employment (Strandh, 2000).

Such recovery is not universal. People who, during the intervening period of unemployment, suffered a marital breakup or financial hardship and had never suffered comparable psychological distress before may continue to suffer persistent distress even after finding a job (Halvorsen, 1998).

Job Insecurity

Uncertainty and insecurity cause people problems. Chronic job insecurity produces adverse physiological changes in people's bodies because of increased stress and worry (Ferrie, Shipley, et al., 2001). Insecure jobs can be as detrimental to health as actual unemployment. This fact leads us to conclude that employment and unemployment are points on a continuum (Hallsten, Grossi, and Westerlund, 1999).

Involuntary unemployment caused by workplace closure or downsizing can have enormous physical, mental, and financial effects on people's lives (Ferrie, 1997; Ferrie, Martikainen, et al., 2001). A study of Swedish police inspectors threatened with unemployment, for example, traced chemical changes in their bodies over a three-year period, reflecting worry about employment and symptoms of burnout during the reorganization of a police district. Reports of lowered work satisfaction, perceived decline in the ethical and moral standards of the organization, and favourable changes in the employment status and work environment all registered appreciably in blood samples taken before and after the reorganization (Grossi et al., 1999).

Because of this negative effect of uncertainty, people can suffer from economic recessions even if they are not immediately affected. The trade cycle affects the health mainly of people who are not long-term unemployed since they are the ones with jobs to lose. Distress and dissatisfaction increase during economic recessions because of increased job demands and ever less adequate pay (Tausig and Fenwick, 1999). During a recession, young job holders report more physical and psychological symptoms than they do during a boom. The effects of a recession on young people's—especially young women's—health are mediated by pessimism about the future, high work demands, and financial problems (Novo, Hammarstrom, and Janlert, 2001). Among men, recessions increase the prevalence of binge drinking, even among those who remain employed

(Dee, 2001). Similarly, people who live in communities where the unemployment rate is high are at a greater risk of ill health even if they are employed full-time (Bellaby and Bellaby, 1999).

A high level of job insecurity lowers self-rated health and increases distress and the use of medications. Job insecurity reduces people's sense of control over their environment and their opportunities for positive self-evaluation. These experiences have harmful health consequences that cut across genders, educational levels, income levels, marital status, and other social categories (McDonough, 2000). Another study finds that job insecurity—fear of unemployment—has a more unfavourable effect on the health of highly educated employees than on the health of the less educated (Domenighetti, D'Avanzo, and Bisig, 2000).

Along similar lines, people in organizations where layoffs have occurred because of downsizing and who have any kind of personal contact with laid-off people are more likely to experience job insecurity, and more symptoms of poor health, depression, and eating changes, than are people who have no such contact. People who are laid off and rehired suffer more work-related injuries and illnesses and more missed work days than people who were employed throughout the same period (Grunberg, Moore, and Greenberg, 2001).

The Social Process of Getting a Job

One tricky part of the work experience is finding a job. You would be wrong to think that the best way of finding a job is by approaching strangers with a résumé in hand. Yet this is what our culture seems to tell us to do: take your résumé and go talk to a stranger with an advertised job opening.

Members of our culture like to believe that people who are talented and work hard will inevitably get the best jobs, and that the best jobs will inevitably find the best employees. In theory, a job market operates invisibly to link job seekers and job providers. People who get bad jobs, by this reasoning, probably deserve bad jobs. We assume they lack the training, or even the skills of self-presentation that are important when interviewing for a job. Likewise, jobs that fail to find good candidates probably also deserve to fail. They must not have presented candidates with a positive corporate image, for example.

However, these beliefs are very often not true. Often, employers do not know how hard-working, meritorious, or qualified you are. As well, you may have a problem finding out about the best job and then reporting your credentials to the right employer. In other words, there may be an information problem and a matching problem in the so-called job market (see Figure 6.2). Both the job applicant and the employer need to

Work affects people's health in a variety of ways. In the long term, work that gives a person too little autonomy and control can produce stress that has dire consequences. In the short term, work can cause illness and death by exposing workers to workplace hazards. Further to this, safety in the workplace is a major concern.
(Bill and Peggy Wittman)

FIGURE 6.2
Vacant Jobs: The 'Matching' Problem

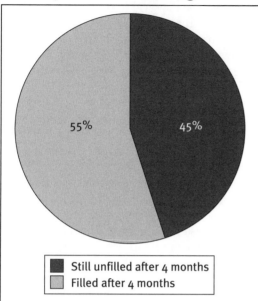

55%   45%

■ Still unfilled after 4 months
□ Filled after 4 months

The report from which this data, showing the proportion of all industries in Canada that had vacation positions unfilled for four months or more, is derived suggests that there are two kinds of industries with job vacancies of more than four months: (1) workplaces with high skill requirements and low turnover, and (2) the opposite, most commonly service and retail jobs, characterized by low pay and no unionization.

SOURCE: Diane Galarneau, Howard Krebs, René Morissette, and Xuelin Zhang, *The Quest for Workers: A New Portrait of Job Vacancies in Canada* (The Evolving Workplace 2, Cat. no. 71-584-Xie) (Ottawa: Statistics Canada and Human Resources Development Canada, 2001), 16; see also page 35 in the same source.

find out about each other, and they also need to evaluate each other. Hiring a new employee is like adopting an innovation—for example, a new hybrid corn seed. You need to become aware of the new possibility, then you need to evaluate it and become confident of the adoption decision before you take an important action: planting the seed, in one case, or hiring the applicant, in the other.

However, other factors also influence who gets jobs, especially good jobs. Reasons for failure to get a (good) job may include relying unduly on impersonal means of job searching—for example, answering advertisements, sending out unbidden résumés—or excessive reliance on highly personal means of job searching—for example, seeking a job through close relatives or close friends. Other strategies often work better. Sociologist Mark Granovetter (1974) discovered that most managers he studied had found their job through an acquaintance—what he called a **weak tie** to distinguish it from a close friend or relative, which would be a **strong tie**. In fact, Granovetter's managers had found the best jobs through weak ties.

The reason is simple: we have more acquaintances than close friends, and our acquaintances often do not know each other. As a result, our acquaintances are likely to have different information about job opportunities. The information reaching our best friends is little different from the information we already have. Some of our closest friends know each other. They may even be kin, friends, neighbours, or acquaintances of each other. Therefore, they may know the same things. So, taken altogether, we find relatively little new information by polling our closest friends and a lot of new information by polling our acquaintances.

Acquaintances turn up the best jobs, and best job-to-person matches, because they give both applicants and employers the best combination of *awareness*, or information quantity, and *evaluation*, or information quality. Strong ties provide reliability and obligation. The advantage of weak ties lies not in their individual effectiveness, but in their numbers. Like fruit flies, weak ties have an impact because they multiply prodigiously. Overall, then, the best job information flows through a combination of weak and strong ties.

Weak ties were important for finding good jobs in the booming economy of the late 1960s when Granovetter studied managers in Boston. Weak ties may be more important in finding and filling jobs—even good jobs—that are plentiful when the economy is growing. In boom times, filling a vacant position causes people more concern than finding a vacant position to fill. Under conditions of scarcity (recession or unemployment), people collect and use information in their own interest and that of their closest friends and family. Under conditions of plenty, they give information away, even to acquaintances. Thus, the strength of weak ties probably depends on the ratio of vacant jobs to job candidates.

People vary in the size and quality of their social network. People with more education, income, and social status have larger networks of acquaintances made up of more varied people. This gives them what sociologists call **social capital** (Portes, 1998; Putnam, 2000). Therefore, they and their children have an advantage in finding good jobs. The best a person can do to compete against superior networks is to develop **cultural capital**, especially educational credentials. Whatever their social and cultural capital, job seekers should create and preserve networks of acquaintanceships, and they should 'network' their acquaintances when they are looking for a job.

Minorities are often at a disadvantage in finding jobs because of the importance of networks (for example, see Lin, 2000). In a profession where there are few black people, for example, good information about jobs in that profession will be hard for a black person to get because good information typically comes only from people already in that profession. If firms hire through personal contact, and if blacks talk mainly to blacks and whites talk mainly to whites (which is often the case), then no black people will be recruited because there is nobody in the firm who is black. Employers will not get good information about groups lacking in contacts or social capital because the employers personally know no people in that group.

The implication is that some kind of quota system or policy is needed to ensure that a certain number of people from the group in question will begin to practise this profession or occupy jobs of that kind. Such a policy not only benefits people who directly occupy the job, but also has a multiplier effect. Once you have mem-

bers of that group in the profession, they will start to bring in other members of that same group because they will have information about people from that group. Employers, in turn, will come to trust the information they receive about the credentials of these people and will not feel the same hesitation they feel when they are unable to get good information.

Exploitation of Workers

What happens in the workplace has even more impact on a person's health than success or failure in finding a job and keeping it. The health consequences of employment and unemployment are directly contingent on the quality of work. The highest levels of health risk are found among dissatisfied workers, the lowest levels among satisfied workers (Graetz, 1993). Two conditions influence a person's experience of stress and depression on the job. One is *job strain*: a combination of high demand and low control at work. The other is *job injustice*: high effort with low reward (Tsutsumi et al., 2001). Both relate to the problem that Marx called *alienation*.

As Marx said over a century ago, power in society comes out of power in the workplace: control of the means of production. Those people who control the means of production—the capitalists, or bourgeoisie—control the creation and destruction of jobs, hiring and firing, promotion and demotion. They also control wages and working conditions to a large degree, that degree depending on whether the workers are unionized. Workers in some (typically, nonunionized) occupations are paid below minimum wage, offered no overtime or benefits, and made to work upward of 50 or 60 hours per week in unsafe and crowded factories.

Conditions are even worse in developing countries, where unemployment rates are higher and unions are weak or non-existent. According to a report by the International Labour Organization's International Programme on the Elimination of Child Labour (Ashagrie, 1998), an estimated

250 million children between the ages of 5 and 14 are currently working full-time in developing countries. Most of these children do not even earn a wage, and those who do are paid only a fraction of the country's official minimum wage. Often governments are unwilling to legislate better working conditions because they do not want to scare off foreign capitalists who are willing to relocate their factories to these low-wage countries.

In recent years, protestors in Canada and other developed countries have called on consumers to recognize the extent of worker exploitation abroad and also to understand that this exploitation—though outside their immediate view—has consequences for their own lives. As long as workers are exploited in developing countries, Canadian consumers will be able to buy logo-branded clothing, smart household furnishings, and up-to-date electronic items for low prices. As consumers, we all like this. As workers, however, we should know that the consequence is continued exploitation abroad and the migration of high-paying jobs from Canada to low-wage countries. It remains to be seen whether Canadians, as consumers and as voters, will take the appropriate actions.

Health Consequences of Work and Unemployment

Work affects people's health in a variety of ways. In the long term, work that gives a worker too little autonomy and control can produce stress that has dire consequences. In the short term, work can cause illness and death by exposing workers to workplace hazards. Further, unemployment

---

BOX 6.3
Tell Your Subordinates 'Great Job!' or Else . . .

Being someone's employee is often thought of as being synonymous with having less power than the employer. In bureaucracies, but also in smaller organizations, the wielders of power in one relationship are the powerless in another exchange. Indeed, employment is defined legally by a reference to control or power. When power is questionable or not present, then legally a relationship is not employment; rather, it is a partnership or a contractor-client arrangement.

Employment relationships in market economies are sometimes theorized to be contracts that are freely made. Marx argued against this view, claiming that employees were not free agents because if they did not work, they would starve. This is relevant to health and safety because, particularly during the period when Marx was writing, working conditions in the UK specifically were horrible and workers had trouble finding the leverage or power they required to force employers to improve conditions in factories and mines.

Power relations in the workplace affect health. There are two empirically verified theoretical paradigms that are best conceptualized as stressors on workers. One is the demand/control model, which is characterized by having little influence or control over the day-to-day organization of one's work combined with high demand in the form of imposed deadlines. The outcomes of working under these stressors include higher rates of infectious disease, cardiovascular disease, mental health problems, alcohol and drug dependence and certain types of injuries.

The second stressor is a paradigm called the effort reward imbalance model, in which a worker perceives little or low compensation or acknowledgment, whether in the form of status, a raise or career advancement, and high effort in the form of either high mental or physical energy.

continued

This type of stressor leads to a variety of adverse health outcomes, prominent among which are cardiovascular disease and mental health problems such as anxiety and depression. It is interesting that on the face of it, a worker's unequal status to his or her employer impacts their health and yet, perhaps, simple courtesies like acknowledging a job well done would help to counteract these effects.

Questions: Do you think that these stressors are 'real' or the result of lazy whiners? What kind of public policy initiative could address these stressors?

SOURCE: Abridged from *Fairness in Families, Schools and Workplaces: Implications for Healthy Relationships in these Environments* (Cat. no. H46-2/01-251E) (Ottawa: Minister of Public Works and Government Services Canada, 2001), 20–4.

can have strong health consequences, as we will see. Let us begin with consequences of work.

Work and Health

In 1998, 798 Canadian workers were killed as a result of an occupational injury and another 793,666 injured while on the job. Of these, almost half (375,360, or 47 per cent) were classified as *time-loss injuries*, which comprise those that involved compensation for lost wages as a result either of time spent off work recovering from the injury or of a permanent disability. Direct reimbursements and workers' compensation board payments concerning work-related injuries total over $4.5 billion, a figure that doubles when indirect costs are figured in as well. The total number of work days lost as a result of occupational injuries is over six times the number lost as a result of worker strikes or lockouts (HRDC, 2000: 11–12).

Health-and-safety hazards in the workplace are, therefore, an obvious social problem. Moreover, some industries are more dangerous than others. The manufacturing sector, in particular, is a hazardous place to work, accounting for nearly 30 per cent of the total occupational injuries reported in Canada in 1998. Incidence rates were highest among the logging and forestry, construction, and manufacturing industries, and lowest within the finance and insurance sector. In general, the occupations with the highest risk of occupational injury or fatality are those that involve semi-skilled manual labour, such as equipment operator and installer, manufacturer, and machine assembler. The occupations with the lowest risk of work-related injury or death are senior management executive and the business and finance professions (HRDC, 2000).

These official statistics often underrate the severity of the health risks in dangerous workplaces since they measure only directly observable medical conditions. Many other job-related injuries and fatalities can result not from a specific incident but from years of exposure to poor air quality and toxic or carcinogenic (cancer-causing) substances. These hazards may be understood and accepted parts of the job. They may also be the result of company negligence. Firefighters, for example, are at a higher risk of developing cancer than the average person, a direct result of their constant exposure to toxic smoke and burning materials. However, most of the people who choose to enter this profession have been made aware of the dangers in advance. Firefighting units try to minimize the hazards by wearing protective gear and breathing with oxygen tanks.

Many workers in other occupations do not have the luxury of preventive technologies, or even the awareness of harm. For example, James Coleman points out that although people had been aware of the dangers of asbestos exposure since 1918, the industry did not make any attempts to protect workers until as late as the

1960s. As a result, of the half-million labourers exposed, at least 100,000 will die from lung cancer, 35,000 from mesothelioma, and 35,000 from asbestosis (Coleman, 1994: 74). Even today, workers continue to be exposed to dangerous levels of asbestos, sometimes with the full knowledge of corporate management.

Owens Corning, a major US insulation-making company, filed for bankruptcy in 2000 after paying out more than $6 billion in lawsuit settlements over asbestos-based pipe insulation it had stopped producing in 1972. The insulation was used in power plants and shipyards, and has recently been found to be a cause of cancer. Since that discovery, Owens Corning has received over 250,000 lawsuits ('Owens Corning', 2000).

Biological hazards in the workplace include viruses, bacteria, fungi, and parasitic organisms. Dangerous chemicals include liquids such as gasoline and mercury, paint and pesticide vapours, and toxic gases such as ammonia. Environmental hazards include radiation, ultraviolet, and microwaves, extreme temperatures and humidity, and insufficient interior lighting.

Another health-related aspect of employment that is increasingly being studied is work-related stress. This can lead to burnout as well as other significant physical and mental health consequences. Any time that the requirements and demands of the job exceed the abilities, resources, or needs of the worker, job stress occurs. Several studies cited by the National Institute for Occupational Safety and Health found that between 26 and 40 per cent of workers surveyed report their work as being stressful; 75 per cent of employees believe that there is more on-the-job stress than a generation ago (1999: 4–5, 9). Work-related problems are more strongly associated with health complaints than are financial problems, family problems, or any other life stressors.

Work conditions that may lead to stress include a heavy workload and infrequent rest breaks, ambiguous or excessive job responsibilities, and routine, repetitive, unchallenging, and inherently meaningless tasks. A lack of decision-making opportunity, poor communication with superiors, and insufficient support from co-workers can also cause stress.

Statistics on hours spent at work cannot capture either the full amount of time spent working or the stress associated with work. It is possible to be 'at work' without actually working. It is possible to be at home, 'away from work', yet preoccupied with work issues. It is possible to work 10 hours a day in a leisurely fashion yet do less work and feel less stressed than someone who works 7 intense hours a day. Increasingly, for example, professional and managerial workers are expected to take their work home with them and to be on call as needed. The continuous availability of these workers to one another—through telephone, voice mail, fax, and e-mail—means that we need subtle and comparable measures of work, and of stress, if we are to make meaningful international comparisons.

The health consequences of prolonged workplace strain are obvious and serious. After reviewing 14 studies, Paul Landsbergis and colleagues (1993) reported that a clear connection exists between job stress and heart disease. High demand—that is, the requirement that someone be 'on call' and responsive all the time—can be offset by high control over the work environment. However, when the tasks are demanding but the employee lacks control over the situation, stress may encroach upon both productivity and health. Prime examples of people in these occupations are waitresses, nurses, schoolteachers, and social workers—note that they are overwhelmingly 'women's occupations'. Most of the people in these occupations who report stress and burnout reveal that their desire to assist others and solve problems is 'frequently thwarted by the need to deal with an excessive number of clients, limited resources, and administrative policies that make it difficult to be effective' (Krahn and Lowe, 1993: 362).

Unemployment and Health

Research shows that unemployment causes a wide range of social and personal pathologies. Inadequate employment can be as depressing as unemployment (Dooley, Prouse, and Rowbottom-Ham, 2000). However, unemployment deprives people of money, meaning, and sociability in a way that no job can do. We will briefly review a few of the health consequences of unemployment.

Mortality

Unemployed people are at a higher risk of death from causes that are associated with unhealthy lifestyles. Specifically, unemployment produces anxiety and depression, which leads to increased smoking, alcohol consumption, and drug use, which may, over the long term, produce cirrhosis, bronchitis, emphysema, and various forms of cancer (Pasarin, Borrell, and Plasencia, 1999). A review of the literature on mortality and morbidity rates shows a causal relationship between unemployment and mortality from cardiovascular disease and suicide (Jin, Shah, and Svoboda, 1997).

Unemployment does not usually cause death in the short term, except by means of linkages to suicide, homicide, and driving accidents (Martikainen and Valkonen, 1998). The longer the period of unemployment, the more physical and psychological health problems emerge. So, for example, unemployment in 1973 among both women and men showed an association with higher than expected mortality by 1996 among people under age 70 (Nylen, Voss, and Floderus, 2001), for both men and women, even after controlling for social, behavioural, work-related and health-related factors (for example, smoking, alcohol, and lifestyle behaviours). Unemployment also raised the risks of death among young people studied over a shorter period, for example, Australian youth studied over a five-year period. Researchers found that young men suffer an increased risk of death as a consequence of being neither employed nor a student (Morrell et al., 1999).

Suicide

Unemployment is not the only disturbing life event that interacts with existing psychological problems (for example, hopelessness, psychological distress, or drug abuse) to raise the risk of suicide, but it is an important one (Foster et al., 1999). Others include death of a close relative, illness of a relative, personal illness, and marital conflict or separation (Chrostek et al., 2001).

Most research concludes that unemployment increases the risk of suicide (Brown et al., 2000; for contrary views, see Goldney et al., 1995; Hagquist et al., 2000). After nine years of follow up, unemployed women were over three times more likely to kill themselves than were their employed counterparts (Kposowa, 2001). Unemployment increases the risk of a wide variety of suicide attempts, including deliberate self-poisoning (Carter et al., 1999), often carried out on repeated occasions. Unemployment may be the single best predictor of deliberate self-poisoning, even when all related variables are controlled for (Kelleher, Kelleher, and Corcoran, 1996).

After controlling for other confounding associations, unemployment remains significantly associated with suicidal ideas, substance abuse, and criminal behaviours (Fergusson, Horwood, and Woodward, 2001). Suicide rates for unemployed people are clearly and consistently higher than those for employed people (Preti and Miotto, 1999). The connection between unemployment and suicide can be observed on both the individual level and through ecological (community) analysis. The latter shows that areas experiencing the lowest increase in unemployment rates experience the lowest increase in rates of suicide (Crawford and Prince, 1999).

Suicide rates have always been higher for men than for women, though women make more suicide attempts. Men are more likely to succeed because of the more lethal means they use, because of their higher levels of alcohol and drug use, and because they are less likely to seek medical or psychiatric help when they are feeling suicidal (Russell and Judd, 1999). Few people who kill themselves contact mental health services beforehand (Rose, Hatcher, and Koelmeyer, 1999). Young unemployed men are particularly likely to kill themselves; often they succeed after earlier attempts had failed (Hawton, Houston, and Shepperd, 1999). The associations between unemployment and suicide, in both men and women, are stronger for young people. The same factors influencing suicide influence men and women, to the same degree (Gunnell et al., 1999).

Substance Abuse

Unemployment increases the risk of consumption of alcohol, tobacco, and other drugs, particularly in young men (Fillmore et al., 1998; MacDonald and Pudney, 2000; Montgomery et al., 1998). As we have said, the mortality rate is significantly higher among unemployed young men and women, especially by means of suicide and accidents, which are often associated with alcohol and drug use. Alcohol abuse, associated with unemployment, is correlated with a heightened risk of death in connection with suicide, violence, and driving accidents (see, for example, Stefansson, 1991).

Increased alcohol consumption is one mechanism connecting unemployment and suicide (Hintikka, Saarinen, and Viinamaki, 1999). Unemployment increases the risk of alcohol abuse, and re-employment reduces the prevalence of alcohol abuse (Claussen, 1999a, 1999b). In turn, alcohol abuse increases the risk of violence, especially family violence (Rodriguez, Lasch, and Mead, 1997). If we control for alcohol use, unemployment has no effect on family violence. Alcohol abuse also increases the likelihood of fatal car crashes at night; the crashes decline only to the extent that unemployment reduces the numbers of kilometres people drive (Gonzalez and Rodriguez, 2000).

Drug and alcohol dependence is associated with both lower employment rates and fewer hours of work. In particular, co-morbidities—

multiple drug dependencies—play a critical role in the relationship between substance use and employment (Bray et al., 2000).

Depression and Anxiety

More than anything else, unemployment affects health by increasing anxiety and depression (Comino et al., 2000; Montgomery et al., 1999; Viinamaki et al., 1993, 1996; Ytterdahl, 1999). Job loss typically arouses defensive feelings, lowers self-esteem, and creates uncertainty about the future. It puts stress on people's coping abilities and often causes them to become passive and to withdraw from social life, further harming their mental health (Underlid, 1996). Unemployed people report more stress, boredom, uncertainty, and dissatisfaction with themselves and their lives than do other people (Gien, 2000). Typically, unemployment causes people's resources to diminish, having a negative impact on their perceptions of themselves, their aging process, and the possibility of leading a productive life (Schmitt, 2001).

It is easy to understand why unemployed people become depressed. Work is not only instrumental for the fulfillment of material needs, for most adults it is a human need in itself. Most people have a psychosocial need for work (Nordenmark and Strandh, 1999).

However, some people feel unemployment more keenly than others. People who are highly committed to work for non-financial reasons have the highest risks of poor mental health after losing their job (Nordenmark, 1999a). People with strong feelings of commitment to being employed feel particularly distressed if they are unemployed for extended periods (Hannan, O'Riain, and Whelan, 1997). Additionally, people who lost a stimulating job and have only a weak attachment to non-employment activities, such as housework and leisure activities, are particularly likely to miss their job. Conversely, people who find a stimulating job have a stronger level of non-financial commitment to their work and greater mental well-being than people who are continuously unemployed or who acquire a job with a mainly economic value (Nordenmark, 1999b). (Likewise, employees who are highly invested in their jobs are most adversely affected by job insecurity; see Probst, 2000).

Unemployed people in low-unemployment areas are also more likely to be depressed, particularly if they have a college-level education (Turner, 1995). Further, people who believe the world is 'just' experience job loss more negatively, with more depressive symptoms, than people who do not hold that belief (Benson and Ritter, 1990).

Researchers disagree about whether unemployment has the same effects on women and men. Some state that men experience job loss as more existentially threatening than do women, with a resulting higher frequency of depression among unemployed men than among unemployed women (Lahelma, 1992; Ytterdahl and Fugelli, 2000). Women can usually invest themselves in the private sphere of housework, if necessary, though unemployment for women also involves a loss of personal identity (Desmarais, 1991). Others observe that women can suffer great distress from unemployment, even after giving birth, when women are very much involved in their maternal role (Saurel et al., 2000). In responding to unemployment, women and men are more similar than they are different (Nordenmark, 1999b). They may show their distress in slightly different ways, however. Job loss results in anxiety disorders in women, while unemployed men often fall victim to substance abuse and depression as well as anxiety. When a spouse loses a job, women suffer both the economic consequences and increased marital conflict (Avison, 1996).

Unemployment produces distress, fatalistic attitudes, feelings of a lack of control over the labour market, and feelings of personal inefficacy. Poor mental health, in turn, reduces the likelihood of finding a job. Depression caused by unemployment may lead to continued

unemployment. Conversely, finding a job is predicted by a positive attitude and an active way of dealing with unemployment (Schaufeli, 1997).

Other Health Problems

Unemployment and its social and health consequences carry secondary consequences one might not imagine:

- Unemployment predicts higher smoking rates. Higher smoking rates increase the risk of sudden infant death syndrome (SIDS)—any otherwise unexplained death of an infant during sleep (Mehanni et al., 2000).
- Unemployment increases the risk of domestic violence; factors involved include alcohol abuse, drug use, intermittent employment, and recent unemployment (Kyriacou et al., 1999).
- Unemployment among husbands increases stress and illness in wives and the incidence of very low birth weights in babies born to pregnant wives (Catalano, Hansen, and Hartig, 1999).
- Unemployment, by increasing anti-social behaviour, increases the incidence of foster-home placements for children in families that lose jobs or income (Catalano, Lind, and Rosenblatt, 1999).
- Unemployment of all household members is associated with the risk of a very preterm birth within the first 22 to 32 weeks of pregnancy (Ancel et al., 1999).
- Unemployment reduces the likelihood that a woman will have a periodic cervical (pap) smear, increasing the likelihood that doctors will fail to detect cervical cancer early (Rohlfs et al., 1999).
- Unemployment increases the risk of obesity because of increased fat consumption, reduced exercise, and increased alcohol consumption (Karvonen and Rimpela, 1997; Sarlio-Lähteenkorva and Lahelma, 1999).
- Unemployment increases the likelihood of a gunshot-wound-induced spinal cord injury (McKinley, Johns, and Musgrove, 1999).

As we have seen, unemployment sets in motion a long line of mental and physical health problems, which in turn make it harder for a person to find and keep a job. Long-term unemployed men experience more ill health than employed men in terms of depressive and somatic complaints and of self-reported chronic diseases (Leefland, Hesselink, and Spriut, 1992). With each successive job loss, or recurrence of unemployment, the return to full-time employment becomes more difficult and the health consequences also compound. Unemployment risks for unhealthy workers are strongly correlated with attributes of social inequality. The accumulation of risks strongly disadvantages workers who are already social and politically vulnerable (Arrow, 1996).

Entering unemployment is a drastic form of downward social mobility, which substantially impacts a person's future mobility chances. Ill health is often a consequence of unemployment. The longer the unemployment period, the more physical and psychological health problems are likely to arise (Buffat, 2000). The more health problems a person has, the harder it is to find a good job. In short, ill health increases the risk of both becoming and remaining unemployed (Korpi, 2001).

Solutions

Unemployment leads to both poverty and ill health. This tells us that a society that does not invest money in jobs for the poor will have to invest money in more jails and more health care. Losing a job diminishes a person's well-being— her or his confidence, self-esteem, and health. In the end, we all pay for this social problem. The chronically unemployed often put a heavy burden on health, social support, and welfare assistance programs. So ordinary taxpayers end up paying for the employment decisions (and high salaries) of the corporate elite.

There are no quick and easy solutions to the various problems associated with unemployment and work, but there are some practical options.

Unemployment Interventions

Interventions for the problem of unemployment might take the form of reducing the numbers of individuals who experience unemployment, reducing the stresses of unemployment, strengthening individuals' life skills and psychosocial resources, and providing counselling and clinical interventions (Avison, 2001). Job-creation programs can reduce some unemployment. Here, it is important that jobs created be mainly in the primary work sector. Such 'good' positions are less likely to result in a return to unemployment further down the road. Jobs that are temporary and fail to build new skills and contacts are a waste of effort.

As well, since education is the best weapon against unemployment, governments should ensure that schooling is made available to as many people as possible. Schooling opportunities are particularly needed by those whose economic situations might otherwise prevent them from attaining higher education, including poor people, rural people, disabled people, and Aboriginal people. This initiative should include adult education programs, which can be another effective tool for increasing the probability of re-employment and career advancement.

Labour unions, which have historically been effective tools in pressuring employers to provide better wages and working conditions for employees, have experienced a decline in recent years. Initiatives that support unions and political parties that promote working-class interests, such as the New Democratic Party in Canada and equivalent parties abroad (for example, the Labour Party in Britain), are key to ensuring that wages and working conditions remain on the legislative agenda. However, given the global mobility of capital and the power of transnational corporations, the interests of local workers have taken a back seat to concerns about job loss and job attraction. The result has been less worker-friendly legislation.

No one has taken responsibility for the health problems of unemployed people. Existing and newly created institutions will need to take responsibility for counselling, referral, and treatment of people who suffer from unemployment-related health problems (Schiffer, 1999). Many factors are involved in a return-to-work outcome, and physicians need to know how to identify and track the factors that facilitate or impede return to work; this implies a change in way physicians are trained (Guirguis, 1999). People need to be taught job-search skills, helped to prevent declines in mental health, and helped to cope with involuntary unemployment (Turner, Kessler, and House, 1991).

While they are without a job, people need money to live on. However, the kind of support they receive also makes a difference. Unemployed people who receive means-tested benefits (such as welfare) are more likely to be depressed than people who receive unemployment benefits (Rodriguez, 2001; Rodriguez, Lasch, and Mead 1997; Rodriguez et al., 2001). When socio-economic characteristics and previous health and employment status are controlled for, means-tested benefits do not seem sufficient to reduce the effect of unemployment on health.

Unemployment appears to hurt people's health, particularly when it humiliates them and makes them insecure. Welfare benefits are best when they provide income security without humiliating the recipient. (See also Table 6.3 for other international comparisons.) Means-testing humiliates benefit recipients and, therefore does nothing to reduce the harm of unemployment. By contrast, benefits that replace lost income, as in Sweden, provide income security without humiliating the recipient (Strandh, 2001). Such a policy is not only fair and equitable, it is also economically efficient, since it keeps the working-age population healthy even when they are unemployed. As a result, organizations committed to redistributive policies, such as social democratic parties, are generally more successful in improving the health of populations (Navarro and Shi, 2001).

Workplace Health and Safety

To reduce the number of annual occupational injuries and fatalities, governments will have to oblige employers to protect the health-and-safety concerns of their workers more effectively. It will likely cost more to do business this way, which is why the government will have to take the initiative and impose penalties for non-compliance. Already, there is strong evidence of support for such changes. In recent years, closer public and media scrutiny, combined with constant pestering by anti-corporate and human rights groups, have forced some companies to improve their workplace conditions, particularly in the overseas factories of transnational organizations. More of the same pressure, and change to the workplace, is needed.

Increasingly, workers and lobby groups want more than a minimally hazard-free workspace. They want a higher standard of quality of life at work. In response, many of today's more progressive employers, aware of the link between employee well-being and corporate profitability, are offering workers on-site health education and medical care facilities. Some have begun to outfit their workplaces with gyms, swimming pools, and volleyball, tennis, and basketball courts, as well as to provide their workers with lunchtime aerobics workouts and healthy food options in the cafeteria. These attempts to improve employee health and fitness, regardless of how sincere or self-serving such actions may be, can help ensure that work itself does not become a health risk.

Job Satisfaction

If we accept the view that a happy worker is a productive worker, then it is in the employer's best interest to ensure that job satisfaction levels remain high. This means designing jobs, careers, and workplaces that provide meaning and stimulation, and opportunities that allow workers to apply the full scope of their abilities. The most satisfying work allows workers to participate in consequential decision-making processes. It also allows room for workers' needs and commitments outside of the workplace.

Communication among workers should also be encouraged, as should harmonious employee-employer relations (National Institute for Occupational Safety and Health, 1999). Regardless of the particular strategy or incentive chosen by the employer, any attempt to improve job satisfaction will necessarily involve an awareness of what people wish to take from working. Extrinsic concerns are important too, so income, recognition, promotions, and benefit packages all need to be distributed in a way that mirrors both personal performance and company prosperity.

TABLE 6.3

Participation and Unemployment Rates in Canada and Other First World Nations, 1999 (Percentages)

	Canada	United States[a]	Japan	Australia	New Zealand
Participation rate[b]					
Both sexes	75.9	77.2	72.4	72.9	75.2
Men	82.0	84.0	85.3	82.1	83.2
15–24	65.3	68.0	47.7	70.8	66.9
25–54	91.1	91.7	97.1	90.0	91.1
55–64	60.7	67.9	85.2	61.7	71.6
65 and over	9.8	16.9	35.5	9.2	10.8
Women	69.8	70.7	59.5	63.6	67.4
15–24	61.7	62.9	46.7	65.9	59.6
25–54	78.2	76.8	66.4	69.2	73.5
55–64	39.4	51.5	49.8	31.7	48.4
65 and over	3.4	8.9	14.9	2.9	4.2
Unemployment rate					
Both sexes	7.6	4.2	4.7	7.0	6.8
Men	7.8	4.1	4.8	7.2	7.0
15–24	15.3	10.3	10.3	14.7	14.6
25–54	6.5	3.0	3.7	5.5	5.5
55–64	6.3	2.7	6.7	6.3	5.5
65 and over	3.0	3.0	2.9	0.9	2.0
Women	7.2	4.3	4.5	6.7	6.5
15–24	12.6	9.5	8.2	12.0	12.8
25–54	6.3	3.4	4.4	5.3	5.3
55–64	5.3	2.6	3.3	4.7	4.2
65 and over	–	3.2	0.5	0.8	1.0

[a] Estimates are for people aged 16 and older.
[b] The participation rate for all ages is defined as the total (or civilian) labour force for all ages divided by the total population for ages 15–64.

SOURCE: Organisation for Economic Co-operation and Development (OECD), *Labour Force Statistics 1978–1999* (Paris: OECD, 2000).

BOX 6.4
Is Your Company Cool?

Q: We just lost a promising employee who told us the main reason she was leaving was because our company is not 'cool', but she did not clarify what she meant. I am not an out-of-touch manager, but I don't know what it means to be a cool company. What do you think?

C.S. A: The notion of cool companies has become a hot topic. Some people say that if you have to ask if your company is cool, then it's not. Cool companies try to understand and respect their employees as individuals and provide them with real opportunities to be heard. They also foster employee learning, development and growth. They consider the balance between work and life, and implement policies with this in mind, such as flex time, on-site child care and telecommuting.

Cool companies act honestly and with integrity, and there is a genuine respect for employee diversity. These companies have a real appreciation of the value that diversity of backgrounds, experiences and cultures can bring to the organization. Such companies embrace the newest technological advances and they tend to have a more casual atmosphere, not only in terms of attire but in terms of the physical and organizational structure. In fact, their corporate structure is not a pyramid, but tends to be rather flat. Research is already showing that turnover in cool companies is relatively low, and that's pretty cool too.

SOURCE: Ken Lloyd, 'Is Your Company Cool? Here's How to Tell', *Vancouver Sun*, final edition, 27 November 1999, C10.

Equally or more important, however, are the intrinsic benefits of work, which vary from job to job and from worker to worker. Job satisfaction is an intricate, and possibly inseparable, mix of **intrinsic** and **extrinsic rewards**. Some people, for instance, crave a high degree of independence and lack of structure (freelance writers or entrepreneurs, say), while others find themselves most comfortable and happiest in a job that is rigidly rule-bound and delineated (chartered accountants). Some demand constant appreciation and attention in their careers (musicians or actors), while others prefer to work quietly and without fanfare behind the scenes (social workers or organizers for non-profit associations). Some choose a job that allows them to help people spiritually (priests and rabbis), while others choose careers that allow them to help people physically (physicians and therapists). Some enjoy working in intellectually and academically rigorous professions (professors or scientists), while others opt for careers that require less extensive academic achievement (construction workers, truck drivers, or some political positions).

To maximize job satisfaction, executives, administrators, and workers must recognize that a paycheque is important but not enough. To keep workers happy, employers must be able to match employee interests with job characteristics while providing benefits and perks that make work intrinsically satisfying. Further, workers must be able to move between jobs, to match their interests and needs to positions.

Individual Solutions

The unemployment rate and the mix of available jobs in your community are very much outside of your control as an individual, as we emphasized above and in the chapter on poverty and economic inequality. However, there are things you can do to find work and improve your economic circumstances. One strategy is suggested in an earlier section of this chapter on the social process of getting a job.

We have seen that there is a danger that an unemployed person will become fatalistic, passive, and depressed. This must be avoided at all costs. Jobs must be sought, and for this to happen, the unemployed person must fight the negative psychological effects of unemployment. Some training programs based on cognitive behavioural therapy have been effective in preparing people for this (Proudfoot et al., 1999). Problem-focused coping and cognitive restructuring programs reduce emotional distress (Grossi, 1999). Interrupted career group therapy encourages people to discuss their feelings of envy, shame, inferiority, rage, and humiliation associated with their unemployment. Some participants in this group benefit from the technique and are able to resume their career-building efforts; the remainder cannot (Ronningstam and Anick, 2001).

Though networking is important in finding a job, as we saw earlier, networking intensity—increasing personal actions such as contacting friends, acquaintances and referrals to get information, leads, or advice on getting a job—does not increase a person's chance of achieving re-employment rapidly, compared with other methods (Wanberg, Kanfer, and Banas, 2000). Job-search intensity—engaging a high degree of commitment, persistence, and focus—predicts re-employment status, though not necessarily re-employment quality (Wanberg, Kanfer, and Rotundo, 1999).

When faced with difficulty in getting a job, we should, whenever possible, draw upon our 'weak' social ties as well as our 'strong' ties to seek information and contacts concerning available jobs. This advice, as we have seen, is based on the principle that each person has a different social network of acquaintances and that these social networks can be used as resources in our searches for jobs. The evidence from studies of job searches shows that weak ties, which are more numerous and more far-reaching in their social contacts, will generally pay off better than strong ties of close friends and relatives in finding jobs. This is certainly true compared with simply answering job ads in the newspapers and job listings.

Most of the readers of this textbook will already be in the process of doing the single most important thing for ensuring that a better job and income will be obtained and for ensuring that the risks of unemployment, at least for a very long period, are minimized: getting a college or university degree. Education level is used as a screening, and exclusionary, mechanism at most places in the job world. People with higher education are the least likely to be unemployed at any particular time, or, if unemployed, to stay unemployed for very long.

What else can you do to combat the risk of unemployment? One other strategy worth considering is to become acquainted with information on current trends of expansion and contraction of the labour market and to consider steering one's studies and career preparation toward types of jobs that are of interest among those jobs that are increasing in numbers.

Thus, one might take note of the current trend toward expansions of jobs, and scarcity of trained people, in the areas of teaching, nursing, and other applied health services, in gerontology and other services for the elderly, and so on. If some of these areas of work are of interest, one can prepare for the work through courses, with the knowledge that there will likely be jobs out there to be had over the near future. Sources of information on labour market expansion and contraction include newspapers and magazines, Internet sources, government resources, and college and university courses on work in sociology and economics.

People also should acquaint themselves with information, where it is available, on work-related health risks such as those we have described above, and make their job choices, or change their jobs, based on this information. Some of these strategies may be easier said than done, though, in geographic areas with limited choice of jobs and for people who have not had, or will not have, an opportunity to undertake higher education. For such individuals, the strategy of making use of both weak and strong ties in job searches is an even more important strategy. And in the end, we need to use our individual energies as voters and consumers to pressure government and business. This can best be done through unions, movements, parties, and other associations.

Social supports are important in buffering the effect of unemployment and financial strain on health and emotional well-being. In particular, partner and family support are important immediately after the loss of a job (Shams, 1993). Social support and contact with close friends can have a moderating effect on nervous symptoms in women but not in men (Hammer, 1993). The presence of a confidante significantly reduces the odds that depression and anxiety will produce illness (Harrison et al., 1999).

Concluding Remarks

A small elite mostly controls the level of employment and unemployment in any society, ours included. For example, this elite controls private bureaucracies that employ large numbers of people. Employment and workplace problems can arise when these elites act exclusively in their own interest, and not also in the interest of their employees.

As we have seen, different sociological approaches focus attention on different aspects of the work and unemployment issue, or provide different interpretations. The functionalist perspective emphasizes the importance of human capital in a post-industrial society and argues that inequality (as well as poverty and unemployment) motivates talented people to develop their skills. The conflict perspective emphasizes that class conflict is a central feature of the modern economy, one that shapes relations between employers and employees. Even as corporations post record profits, downsizing continues to leave many lower- and middle-class workers underemployed and unemployed. Symbolic interactionists show that the experiences and meanings of work, unemployment, and social class vary considerably. As our experiences change, so do our beliefs and expectations.

We have seen that people's beliefs and expectations also shape their experiences of work. Individualist ideology teaches that people get what they deserve. This common ideology is used to justify inequality and ignores economic exploitation and the handicaps (that is, discrimination) that are placed on the poor. The 'culture of poverty' explanation suggests that the learned cultural habits of an economic minority are the cause of their poverty.

Other, more structuralist explanations focus on bureaucratic and economic mechanisms. Bureaucratic structures, as we have seen, organize and control large numbers of people. The problem with these structures is that they do not always work to the benefit of employees and that they cause alienation and unhealthy work conditions.

With the increase of automated technology and the flight of the manufacturing industry to Third World countries, there are increasing problems of unemployment for blue-collar workers. These blue-collar workers often lack the resources they need to increase their training and education. At the same time, these structural and technological changes create more employment demand for white-collar workers. The outcome of these changes is a widening gap between social classes, and no increase in the security or enjoyment of work.

Questions for Critical Thought

1. Take a quick survey to discover which kind of jobs give people the most stress. Which jobs have the highest wage and highest prestige? Using the data you collect, consider how peoples' perceptions of jobs support a neo-conservative approach to economics and public policy. For example, if financial managers are thought to have high stress, high wages, and high prestige, should they be let off easy for white-collar crime?
2. Evaluate the conflict perspective's view on unemployment. Does the interpretation ring true? How would you criticize or elaborate upon it?
3. This chapter argues in part that work means something quite different for men than it does for women. For example 'pink-collar' workplaces like the service industry are not as often unionized as 'blue-collar' workplaces are. Review the occupations of 10 or 20 people you know well. Is it fair to say that the work of the women has different meaning than that of the men?
4. What is *alienation*? Formulate an outline of an essay that describes possible connections between alienation and the Protestant work ethic and meritocracy as described in this chapter.
5. How are family life and gender inequality in the workplace connected? Discuss.

Recommended Readings

Morton Beiser and Feng Hou, 'Language Acquisition, Unemployment and Depressive Disorder Among Southeast Asian Refugees: A 10-Year Study', *Social Science and Medicine*, 53 (2001): 1321–34.

Although unemployment increases the risk of mental health difficulties, this study looks at the mediating effects of language facility among Southeast Asian refugees resettling in Canada. English-language proficiency did not mediate depression or employment rates, but after 10 years in Canada, English-language proficiency had become a factor, especially among refugee women.

Nicole W. Biggart, *Charismatic Capitalism: Direct Selling Organizations in America* (Chicago: University of Chicago Press, 1989).

Biggart looks at direct-selling organizations and examines the ideologies that compel them. The integration of the family and work spheres for workers is also explored.

Barry Glassner, *Career Crash: America's New Crisis—And Who Survives* (New York: Simon and Schuster, 1994).

This text uses ethnographic methods and interviews to examine how men and women have reinvented their relationship to work. Glassner shows how work is a major component of the structure of self-identity. He notes that career crashes among baby boomers are common, and so baby boomers are forced to re-evaluate their relationships to work and to other members of the community.

Selahadin A. Ibrahim, Fran E. Scott, Donald C. Cole, Harry S. Shannon, and John Eyles, 'Job Strain and Self-Reported Health Among Working Women and Men: An Analysis of the 1994/5 Canadian National Population Health Survey', *Women and Health*, 33, nos 1–2 (2001): 105–24.

Using the Canadian national population health survey of 1994/5, this article looks at the association between high-strain jobs and self-rated health.

High-strain jobs were classed in terms of decision latitude and psychological demands. Among both men and women, high-strain jobs predicted worse self-rated health.

J. Lait and J.E. Wallace, 'Stress at Work: A Study of Organizational-Professional Conflict and Unmet Expectations', *Industrial Relations*, 57 (2002): 463–90.

Anyone who has worked in service, and anyone who plans on doing so, should know that the pleasure of interpersonal contact can also be a stressful way to make money. Using data from a survey of human-service providers in Alberta, this study tests a model that posits that organizational conflict and bureaucratic conditions result in service provider's stress. Interestingly, decreasing service providers' control over their work does not increase their job stress.

Victor W. Marshall, Philippa J. Clarke, and Peri J. Ballantyne, 'Instability in the Retirement Transition: Effects on Health and Well-Being in a Canadian Study', *Research on Aging*, 23 (2001): 379–409.

This study looks at the little-researched, yet increasingly common, transition between post-retirement work and full retirement. The subjects are a group of early retirees from a Canadian telecommunications corporation, and ill health is found to be associated with instability.

Peggy McDonough, Vivienne Walters, and Lisa Strohschein, 'Chronic Stress and the Social Patterning of Women's Health in Canada', *Social Science and Medicine*, 54 (2002): 767–82.

Social roles and socio-economic position do affect women's health, but why? This research uses data from a 1994 Canadian national probability sample of women between the ages of 24 and 64. Employment, marriage, and living with children enhanced women's lives, as did income and education. This article is one of many in this volume of *Social Science and Medicine* on women's health, socio-economic status, and work.

Richard Ogmundson and Michael Doyle, 'The Rise and Decline of Canadian Labour / 1960 to 2000: Elites, Power, Ethnicity and Gender', *Canadian Journal of Sociology*, 27 (2002): 413–54.

Unions are thought to have declined in importance of late, although the elite labour leaders are still powerful. Among the changes in labour have been an influx of women and a decrease of people of British origin. Interestingly, however, there has not been and increase in visible minority groups within labour.

Jeremy Rifkin, *The End of Work: The Decline of the Global Labor Force and the Dawn of the Post-market Era* (New York: Tarcher/Putnam, 1995).

This volume studies the relationship between transformations of family life and gender roles on the one hand and employment on the other hand. The roles of technologies and changing labour markets are also studied. Rifkin goes on to argue that political and social stability can be threatened by increasing structural unemployment.

Paul Ryan, 'The School-to-Work Transition: A Cross-national Perspective'. *Journal of Economic Literature*, 39, no. 1 (2001): 34–92.

Looking at results alone in seven advanced economies and focusing on young people without postsecondary education, Ryan examines the flows of unemployment and their duration, and the effects of social disadvantage on unemployment.

Michel Tremblay and Denis Chênevert, 'Managerial Career Success in Canadian Organizations: Is Gender a Determinant?' *International Journal of Human Resource Management*, 13 (2002): 920–41.

The future of Canadian women at work is of critical importance. Using research on 3,060 Canadian managers, the importance of human capital, family context, socio-economic origin, work investment and reward expectations, and structural factors were analyzed. Successful female managers are found to be successful for different reasons than successful male managers.

Recommended Web Sites

Human Resources Development Canada
www.hrdc-drhc.gc.ca

Human Resources Development Canada (HRDC) provides information for both employers and employees, and for the unemployed. Labour publications and information pertaining to children, youth, and senior citizens are also available.

The HRDC Web site also offers information about job opportunities for Canadians, with additional specific categories for Aboriginal people, the disabled, and seniors. There are also reports about employment trends in Canada.

International Labour Organization
www.ilo.org

As the Web site of the US branch of this international organization indicates, the ILO is 'a specialized agency of the United Nations', it 'brings governments, workers and employers together to promote decent work', and it 'transfers know-how to 138 countries through technical cooperation'. In recent years, it has focused its attention particularly on the effects of globalization.

Canadian Labour Congress
www.clc-ctc.ca

The Canadian Labour Congress (CLC) promotes decent wages and working conditions and improved health-and-safety laws. It also lobbies for fair taxes, strong social programs, job training, and job-creation programs. Considerable information is provided on the Web site on topics ranging from social and economic labour policies to anti-racism and human rights links.

Canadian Centre for Occupational Health and Safety
www.ccohs.ca

The Canadian Centre for Occupational Health and Safety promotes safe and healthy working environments by providing information and advice. Their Web site covers products and services provided by the CCOHS, education and training programs, resource links, and general information about workplace safety.

References

Ancel, P.Y., M.J. Saurel Cubizolles, G.C. Di Renzo, E. Papiernik, and G. Breart. 1999. 'Social Differences of Very Preterm Birth in Europe: Interaction with Obstetric History'. *American Journal of Epidemiology*, 149: 908–15.

Arrow, J.O. 1996. 'Estimating the Influence of Health as a Risk Factor on Unemployment: A Survival Analysis of Employment Durations for Workers Surveyed in the German Socio-economic Panel (1984–1990)'. *Social Science and Medicine*, 42: 1651–9.

Ashagrie, Kebebew. 1998. *Statistics on Working Children and Hazardous Child Labour in Brief*. International Labour Organization (ILO), International Programme on the Elimination of Child Labour. Available at <www.ilo.org/public/english/standards/ipec/simpoc/stats/child/stats.htm>, accessed 23 January 2003.

Avison, William R. 1996. 'What Determines Health? Summary of *The Health Consequences of Unemployment*.' National Forum on Health. Available at <http://wwwnfh.hc-sc.gc.ca/publicat/execsumm/avison.htm>, accessed 23 January 2003.

Avison, William R. 2001. 'Unemployment and Its Consequences for Mental Health'. In *Restructuring Work and the Life Course*, edited by Victor Marshal, Walter R. Heinz, Helga Kruger, and Anil Verma, 177–200. Toronto: University of Toronto Press.

Bellaby, Paul, and Felix Bellaby. 1999. 'Unemployment and Ill Health: Local Labour Markets and Ill Health in Britain, 1984–1991'. *Work, Employment and Society*, 13: 461–82.

Benson, D.E., and Christian Ritter. 1990. 'Belief in a Just World, Job Loss, and Depression'. *Sociological Focus*, 23: 49–63.

Bray, J.W., G.A. Zarkin, M.L. Dennis, and M.T. French. 2000. 'Symptoms of Dependence, Multiple Substance Use, and Labor Market Outcomes'. *American Journal of Drug and Alcohol Abuse*, 26: 77–95.

Brown, G.K., A.T. Beck, R.A. Steer, and J.R. Grisham. 2000. 'Risk Factors for Suicide in Psychiatric Outpatients: A 20-Year Prospective Study'. *Journal of Consulting and Clinical Psychology*, 68: 371–7.

Buffat, J. 2000. 'Unemployment and Health'. *Revue Medicale de la Suisse Romande*, 120: 379–83.

Burchardt, Tania. 2000. 'The Dynamics of Being Disabled'. *Journal of Social Policy*, 29: 645–68.

Burstrom, B., M. Whitehead, C. Lindholm, and F. Diderichsen. 2000. 'Inequality in the Social Consequences of Illness: How Well Do People with Long-term Illness Fare in the British and Swedish Labor Markets?' *International Journal of Health Services*, 30: 435–51.

Carter, G.L., I.M. Whyte, K. Ball, N.T. Carter, A.H. Dawson, V.J. Carr, and J. Fryer. 1999. 'Repetition of Deliberate Self-poisoning in an Australian Hospital-Treated Population'. *Medical Journal of Australia*, 170: 307–11.

Catalano, Ralph, Hans Tore Hansen, and Terry Hartig. 1999. 'The Ecological Effect of Unemployment on the Incidence of Very Low Birthweight in Norway and Sweden'. *Journal of Health and Social Behavior*, 40: 422–8.

Catalano, Ralph, Samuel L. Lind, and Abram B. Rosenblatt. 1999. 'Unemployment and Foster Home Placements: Estimating the Net Effect of Provocation and Inhibition'. *American Journal of Public Health*, 89: 851–5.

Chrostek, Maj J., A. Polewka, S. Kroch, Boba M. Mikolaszek, W. Rachel, and W. Datka. 2001. 'Significance of Subjective Evaluation of Life Events as Risk Factors for Predicting Future Suicide Attempts'. *Przeglad Lekarski*, 58: 340–3.

Claussen, Bjørgulf. 1999a. 'Alcohol Disorders and Re-employment in a 5-Year Follow-up of Long-term Unemployed'. *Addiction*, 94: 133–8.

———. 1999b. 'Health and Re-employment in a Five-Year Follow-up of Long-term Unemployed'. *Scandinavian Journal of Public Health*, 27, no. 2: 94–100.

Coleman, James. 1994. *The Criminal Elite: The Sociology of White-Collar Crime*, 3rd edn. New York: St. Martins Press.

Comino, E.J., E. Harris, D. Silove, V. Manicavasagar, and M.F. Harris. 2000. 'Prevalence, Detection and Management of Anxiety and Depressive Symptoms in Unemployed Patients Attending General Practitioners'. *Australian and New Zealand Journal of Psychiatry*, 34: 107–13.

Crawford, M.J., and M. Prince. 1999. 'Increasing Rates of Suicide in Young Men in England During the 1980s: The Importance of Social Context'. *Social Science and Medicine*, 49: 1419–23.

Creed, Peter A.. 1999. 'Predisposing Factors and Consequences of Occupational Status for Long-term Unemployed Youth: A Longitudinal Examination'. *Journal of Adolescence*, 22: 81–93.

Crozier, Michel. 1969. *The Bureaucratic Phenomenon*. Translated by Michel Crozier. Chicago: University of Chicago Press.

Dee, Thomas S. 2001. 'Alcohol Abuse and Economic Conditions: Evidence from Repeated Cross-sections of Individual-Level Data'. *Health Economics*, 10: 257–70.

de Goede, M., E. Spruijt, C. Maas, and V. Duindam. 2000. 'Family Problems and Youth Unemployment'. *Adolescence*, 35: 587–601.

Desmarais, Danielle. 1991. 'Linking Unemployment, Health and Employment in Women's Accounts of Unemployment: Understanding As a Prerequisite to Social Intervention'. Paper presented at the annual meeting of the Sociological Practice Association/ISA Working Group in Clinical Sociology.

Domenighetti, Gianfranco, Barbara D'Avanzo, and Brigitte Bisig. 2000. 'Health Effects of Job Insecurity Among Employees in the Swiss General Population'. *International Journal of Health Services*, 30: 477–90.

Dooley, David, Joann Prouse, and Kathleen A. Rowbottom-Ham. 2000. 'Underemployment and Depression: Longitudinal Relationships'. *Journal of Health and Social Behavior*, 41: 421–36.

Druss, B.G., S.C. Marcus, R.A. Rosenheck, M. Olfson, T. Talielian, and H.A. Pincus. 2000. 'Understanding Disability in Mental and General Medical Conditions'. *American Journal of Psychiatry*, 157: 1485–91.

Durkheim, Émile. [1893] 1964. *The Division of Labor in Society*. Translated by George Simpson. New York: Free Press.

Edwards, Richard. 1979. *Contested Terrain: The Transformation of the Workplace in the Twentieth Century*. New York: Basic Books.

Fergusson, D.M., L.J. Horwood, and L.J. Woodward. 2001. 'Unemployment and Psychosocial Adjustment in Young Adults: Causation or Selection?' *Social Science and Medicine*, 53: 305–20.

Ferrie, Jane E. 1997. 'Labour Market Status, Insecurity and Health'. *Journal of Health Psychology*, 2: 373–97.

Ferrie, Jane E., P. Martikainen, M.J. Shipley, M.G. Marmot, S.A. Stansfeld, and G.D. Smith. 2001. 'Employment Status and Health After Privatization in White Collar Civil Servants: Prospective Cohort Study'. *BMJ*, 322: 647–51.

Ferrie, Jane E., M.J. Shipley, M.G. Marmot, P. Martikainen, S.A. Stansfeld, and G.D. Smith. 2001. 'Job Insecurity in White-Collar Workers: Toward an Explanation of Associations with Health'. *Journal of Occupational Health Psychology*, 6: 26–42.

Fillmore, Kaye Middleton, Jacqueline M. Golding, Karen L. Graves, Steven Kniep, E. Victor Leino, Anders Romelsjo, Carlisle Shoemaker, Catherine R. Ager, Peter Allebeck, and Heidi P. Ferrer. 1998. 'Alcohol Consumption and Mortality, I. Characteristics of Drinking Groups'. *Addiction*, 93: 183–203.

Foster, T., K. Gillespie, R. McClelland, and C. Patterson. 1999. 'Risk Factors for Suicide Independent of DSM-III-R Axis I Disorder: Case-Control for Psychological Autopsy Study in Northern Ireland'. *British Journal of Psychiatry*, 175: 175–9.

Gien, L.T. 2000. 'Land and Sea Connection: The East Coast Fishery Closure, Unemployment, and Health'. *Canadian Journal of Public Health*, 91, no. 2: 121–4.

Goldney, Robert D., Anthony H. Winefield, Marika Tiggerman, and Helen R. Winefield. 1995. 'Suicidal Ideation and Unemployment: A Prospective Longitudinal Study'. *Archives of Suicide Research*, 1: 175–84.

Gonzalez, Luque J.C., and Artalejo F. Rodriguez. 2000. 'The Relationship of Different Socioeconomic Variables and Alcohol Consumption with Nighttime Fatal Traffic Crashes in Spain: 1978–1993'. *European Journal of Epidemiology*, 16: 955–61.

Graetz, Brian. 1993. 'Health Consequences of Employment and Unemployment: Longitudinal Evidence for Young Men and Women'. *Social Science and Medicine*, 36: 715–24.

Granovetter, Mark S. 1974. *Getting a Job: A Study of Contacts and Careers*. Cambridge, MA: Harvard University Press.

Grossi, G. 1999. 'Coping and Emotional Distress in a Sample of Swedish Unemployed'. *Scandinavian Journal of Psychology*, 40: 157–65.

Grossi, G., T. Theorell, M. Jurisoo, and S. Setterlind. 1999. 'Psychophysiological Correlates of Organizational Change and Threat of Unemployment Among Police Inspectors'. *Integrative Physiological and Behavioral Science*, 34, no. 1: 30–42.

Grunberg, L., S.Y. Moore, and E. Greenberg. 2001. 'Differences in Physiological and Physical Health Among Layoff Survivors: The Effect of Layoff Contact'. *Journal of Occupational Health Psychology*, 6: 15–25.

Guirguis, S.S. 1999. 'Unemployment and Health: Physician's Role'. *International Archives of Occupational and Environmental Health*, 72, suppl: S10–13.

Gunnell, D., A. Lopatazidis, D. Dorling, H. Wehner, H. Southall, and S. Frankel. 1999. 'Suicide and Unemployment in Young People. Analysis of Trends in England and Wales, 1921–1995'. *British Journal of Psychiatry*, 175: 263–70.

Hagquist, C., S.R. Silburn, S.R. Zubrick, G. Lindberg, and G. Ringback Weitoft. 2000. 'Suicide and Mental Health Problems Among Swedish Youth in the Wake of the 1990s Recession'. *International Journal of Social Welfare*, 9: 211–19.

Hallsten, L., G. Grossi, and H. Westerlund. 1999. 'Unemployment, Labour Market Policy and Health in Sweden During Years of Crisis in the 1990s'. *International Archives of Occupational and Environmental Health*, 72, suppl: S28–30.

Halvorsen, Knut. 1998. 'Impact of Re-employment on Psychological Distress Among Long-Term Unemployed'. *Acta Sociologica*, 41: 227–42.

Hammarstrom, Anne, and Urban Janlert. 1997. 'Nervous and Depressive Symptoms in a Longitudinal Study of Youth Unemployment: Selection or Exposure?' *Journal of Adolescence*, 20: 293–305.

Hammer, Torild. 1993. 'Unemployment and Mental Health Among Young People: A Longitudinal Study'. *Journal of Adolescence*, 16: 407–20.

Hannan, Damian F., Sean O'Riain, and Christopher T. Whelan. 1997. 'Youth Unemployment and Psychological Distress in the Republic of Ireland'. *Journal of Adolescence*, 20: 307–20.

Harrison, J., S. Barrow, L. Gask, and F. Creed. 1999. 'Social Determinants of GHQ Score by Postal Survey'. *Journal of Public Health Medicine*, 21: 283–8.

Hawton, K., K. Houston, and R. Shepperd. 1999. 'Suicide in Young People: Study of 174 Cases, Aged Under 25 Years, Based on Coroners' and Medical Records'. *British Journal of Psychiatry*, 175: 271–6.

Hintikka, J., P.I. Saarinen, and H. Viinamaki. 1999. 'Suicide Mortality in Finland During an Economic Cycle, 1985–1995'. *Scandinavian Journal of Public Health*, 27, no. 2: 85–8.

Human Resources Development Canada (HRDC). 2000. *Work Safely for a Healthy Future: Statistical Analysis: Occupational Injuries and Fatalities Canada.* Available at <http://info.load-otea.hrdc-drhc.gc.ca/~oshweb/naoshstats/naoshw2000.pdf>, accessed 23 January 2003.

Jin, Robert L., Chandrakant Shah, and Tomislav J. Svoboda. 1997. 'The Impact of Unemployment on Health: A Review of the Evidence'. *Journal of Public Health Policy*, 18: 275–301.

Karvonen, Sakari, and Arja H. Rimpela. 1997. 'Urban Small Area Variation in Adolescents' Health Behaviour'. *Social Science and Medicine*, 45: 1089–98.

Kelleher, Michael J., Michael J.A. Kelleher, and Paul Corcoran. 1996. 'Deliberate Self-Poisoning, Unemployment, and Public Health'. *Suicide and Life-Threatening Behavior*, 26: 365–73.

Kokko, K., and L. Pulkkinen. 2000. 'Aggression in Childhood and Long-Term Unemployment in Adulthood: A Cycle of Maladaptation and Some Protective Factors'. *Developmental Psychology*, 36: 463–72.

Korpi, Thomas. 2001. 'Accumulating Disadvantage: Longitudinal Analyses of Unemployment and Physical Health in Representative Samples of the Swedish Population'. *European Sociological Review*, 17: 255–73.

Kposowa, A.J. 2001. 'Unemployment and Suicide: A Cohort Analysis of Social Factors Predicting Suicide in the US National Longitudinal Mortality Study'. *Psychological Medicine*, 31: 127–38.

Krahn, Harvey J., and Graham S. Lowe. 1993. *Work, Industry, and Canadian Society*, 2nd edn. Scarborough, ON: Nelson Thompson Canada.

Kyriacou, D.N., D. Anglin, E. Taliaferro, S. Stone, T. Tubb, J.A. Linden, R. Muelleman, E. Barton, and J.F. Kraus. 1999. 'Risk Factors for Injury to Women from Domestic Violence Against Women'. *New England Journal of Medicine*, 341: 1892–8.

Lahelma, Eero. 1992. 'Unemployment and Mental Well-Being: Elaboration of the Relationship'. *International Journal of Health Services*, 22: 261–74.

Landsbergis, Paul A., Susan J. Schurman, Barbara A. Israel, Peter L. Schnall, Margrit K. Hugentobler, Janet Cahill, and Dean Baker. 1993. 'Job Stress and Heart Disease: Evidence and Strategies for Prevention'. *New Solutions*, 3, no. 3: 42–58.

Leefland, R.L.I., D.J. Klein Hesselink, and I.P. Spruit. 1992. 'Health Effects of Unemployment. I. Long-Term Unemployed Men in a Rural and an Urban Setting'. *Social Science and Medicine*, 34: 341–50.

Leino Arjas P., P. Mutanen, A. Malmivaara, and E. Matikainen. 1999. 'Predictors and Consequences of Unemployment Among Construction Workers: Prospective Cohort Study'. *BMJ*, 319: 600–5.

Liira, J., and Arjas P. Leino. 1999. 'Predictors and Consequences of Unemployment in Construction and Forest Work During a 5-Year Follow-up'. *Scandinavian Journal of Work, Environment and Health*, 25, no. 1: 42–9.

Lin, Nan. 2000. 'Inequality in Social Capital'. *Contemporary Sociology*, 29: 785–95.

McCarty, C.A., M. Burgess, and J.E. Keeffe. 1999. 'Unemployment and Underemployment in Adults with Vision Impairment: The RVIB Employment Survey'. *Australian and New Zealand Journal of Ophthalmology*, 27, nos 3–4: 190–3.

MacDonald, Z., and S. Pudney. 2000. 'Illicit Drug Use, Unemployment, and Occupational Attainment'. *Journal of Health Economics*, 19: 1089–15.

McDonough, Peggy. 2000. 'Job Insecurity and Health'. *International Journal of Health Services*, 30: 453–76.

McKinley, W.O., J.S. Johns, and J.J. Musgrove. 1999. 'Clinical Presentations, Medical Complications, and Functional Outcomes of Individuals with Gunshot Wound-Induced Spinal Cord Injury'. *American Journal of Physical Medicine and Rehabilitation*, 78, no. 2: 102–7.

Martikainen, Pekka, and Tapani Valkonen. 1998. 'The Effects of Differential Unemployment Rate Increases of Occupation Groups on Changes in Mortality'. *American Journal of Public Health*, 88: 1859–61.

Marx, Karl. [1887] 1936. *Capital: A Critique of Political Economy.* Translated by Samuel Moore and Edward Aveling. New York: Modern Library.

Mehanni, M., A. Cullen, B. Kiberd, M. McDonnell, M. O'Regan, and T. Matthews. 2000. 'The Current Epidemiology of SIDS in Ireland'. *Irish Medical Journal*, 93, no. 9: 264–8.

Montgomery, Scott M., Derek G. Cook, Mel J. Bartley, and Michael E.J. Wadsworth. 1998. 'Unemployment, Cigarette Smoking, Alcohol Consumption, and Body Weight in Young British Men'. *European Journal of Public Health*, 8, no. 1: 21–7.

———. 1999. 'Unemployment Pre-dates Symptoms of Depression and Anxiety Resulting in Medical Consultation in Young Men'. *International Journal of Epidemiology*, 28: 95–100.

Morrell, Stephen, Richard Taylor, Susan Quine, and Charles Kerr. 1999. 'A Case-Control Study of Employment Status and Mortality in a Cohort of Australian Youth'. *Social Science and Medicine*, 49: 383–92.

National Institute for Occupational Safety and Health. 1999. *Stress . . . at Work*. (Cat. no. 99-101). US Department of Health and Human Services, Centers for Disease Control and Prevention. Available at <www.cdc.gov/niosh/pdfs/stress.pdf>, accessed 23 January 2003.

Navarro, Vicente, and Leiyu Shi. 2001. 'The Political Context of Social Inequalities and Health', *Social Science and Medicine*, 52: 481–91.

Nordenmark, Mikael. 1999a. 'Employment Commitment and Psychological Well-Being Among Unemployed Men and Women'. *Acta Sociologica*, 42: 135–46.

———. 1999b. *Unemployment, Employment Commitment, and Well-Being: The Psychological Meaning of (Un)employment Among Women and Men*. Unpublished doctoral dissertation, Umeå University (Sweden).

Nordenmark, Mikael, and Mattias Strandh. 1999. 'Towards a Sociological Understanding of Mental Well-Being Among the Unemployed: The Role of Economic and Psychological Factors'. *Sociology*, 33: 577–97.

Novo, Mehmed, Anne Hammarstrom, and Urban Janlert. 2001. 'Do High Levels of Unemployment Influence the Health of Those Who Are Not Employed? A Gendered Comparison of Young Men and Women During Boom and Recession'. *Social Science and Medicine*, 53: 293–303.

Nylen, L., M. Voss, and B. Floderus. 2001. 'Mortality Among Women and Men Relative to Unemployment, Part-time Work, Overtime Work, and Extra Work: A Study Based on Data from the Swedish Twin Registry'. *Occupational and Environmental Medicine*, 58: 52–7.

Ostry, Aleck, Steve A. Marion, L. Green, Paul A. Demers, Kay Teshke, Ruth Hershler, Shona Kelly, and Clyde Hertzman. 2000. 'The Relationship Between Unemployment, Technological Change and Psychosocial Work Conditions in British Columbia Sawmills'. *Critical Public Health*, 10: 179–91.

'Owens Corning Files for Bankruptcy: Reorganization a Move to Force Settlement of Huge Asbestos Claims'. 2000. *Ottawa Citizen*, 6 October, H6.

Pasarin, M., C. Borrell, and A. Plasencia. 1999. 'Two Patterns of Social Inequalities in Mortality in Barcelona, Spain?' *Gaceta Sanitaria*, 13: 431–40.

Pernice, Regina, and Nigel Long. 1996. 'Long-term Unemployment, Employment Attitudes, and Mental Health'. *Australian Journal of Social Issues*, 31: 311–26.

Perrow, Charles. 1984. *Normal Accidents: Living with High-Risk Technologies*. New York: Basic Books.

Portes, Alejandro. 1998. 'Social Capital: Its Origins and Applications in Modern Sociology'. *Annual Review of Sociology*, 24: 1–24.

Preti, A., and P. Miotto. 1999. 'Suicide and Unemployment in Italy, 1982–1994'. *Journal of Epidemiology and Community Health*, 53: 694–701.

Probst, T.M. 2000. ' "Wedded to the Job": Moderating Effects of Job Involvement on the Consequences of Job Insecurity'. *Journal of Occupational Health Psychology*, 5: 63–73.

Proudfoot, J., J. Gray, J. Carson, D. Guest, and G. Dunn. 1999. 'Psychological Training Improves Mental Health and Job-Finding Among Unemployed People'. *International Archives of Occupational and Environmental Health*, 72, suppl: S40–4.

Putnam, Robert D. 2000. *Bowling Alone: The Collapse and Revival of American Community*. New York: Simon and Schuster.

Rodriguez, Eunice. 2001. 'Keeping the Unemployed Healthy: The Effect of Means-Tested and Entitlement Benefits in Britain, Germany, and the United States'. *American Journal of Public Health*, 91: 1403–11.

Rodriguez, Eunice, K.E. Lasch, P. Chandra, and J. Lee. 2001. 'Family Violence, Employment Status, Welfare Benefits, and Alcohol Drinking in the United States: What Is the Relation?' *Journal of Epidemiology and Community Health*, 55: 172–8.

Rodriguez, Eunice, Kathryn Lasch, and June P. Mead. 1997. 'The Potential Role of Unemployment Benefits in Shaping the Mental Health Impact of Unemployment'. *International Journal of Health Services*, 27: 601–23.

Rohlfs, Izabella, Carme Borrell, M. Isabel Pasarin, and Antoni Plasencia. 1999. 'The Role of Sociodemographic Factors in Preventive Practices: The Case of Cervical and Breast Cancer'. *European Journal of Public Health*, 9: 278–84.

Ronningstam, E., and D. Anick. 2001. 'The Interrupted Career Group: A Preliminary Report'. *Harvard Review of Psychiatry*, 9: 234–43.

Rose, J., S. Hatcher, and T. Koelmeyer. 1999. 'Suicide in Auckland 1989 to 1997'. *New Zealand Medical Journal*, 112: 324–6.

Russell, D., and F. Judd. 1999. 'Why Are Men Killing Themselves? A Look at the Evidence'. *Australian Family Physician*, 28: 791–5.

Sarlio-Lähteenkorva, S., and E. Lahelma. 1999. 'The Association of Body Mass Index with Social and Economic Disadvantage in Women and Men'. *International Journal of Epidemiology*, 28: 445–9.

Saurel Cubizolles, M.J., P. Romito, P.Y. Ancel, and N. Lelong. 2000. 'Unemployment and Psychological Distress One Year After Childbirth in France'. *Journal of Epidemiology and Community Health*, 54: 185–91.

Schaufeli, Wilmar B. 1997. 'Youth Unemployment and Mental Health: Some Dutch Findings'. *Journal of Adolescence*, 20: 281–92.

Schiffer, J. 1999. 'Concept on Health Promotion about the Unemployed in Switzerland'. *International Archives of Occupational and Environmental Health*, 72, suppl: S23–5.

Schmitt, E. 2001. 'Significance of Employment and Unemployment in Middle and Advanced Adult Age for Subjective Perception of Aging and Realization of Potentials and Barriers of a Responsible Life'. *Zeitschrift fur Gerontologie und Geriatrie*, 34: 218–31.

Shams, Manfusa. 1993. 'Social Support and Psychological Well-Being Among Unemployed British Asian Men'. *Social Behavior and Personality*, 21, no. 3: 175–86.

Stafford, Diane. 2000. 'Workplace Discontent on the Rise, Survey Finds'. *Ottawa Citizen*, 21 October, K2.

Stefansson, Claes Goran. 1991. 'Long-Term Unemployment and Mortality in Sweden, 1980–1986'. *Social Science and Medicine*, 32: 419–23.

Strandh, Mattias. 2000. 'Different Exit Routes from Unemployment and Their Impact on Mental Well-Being: The Role of the Economic Situation and the Predictability of the Life Course'. *Work, Employment, and Society*, 14: 459–79.

———. 2001. 'State Intervention and Mental Well-Being Among the Unemployed'. *Journal of Social Policy*, 30: 57–80.

Swart, E., and H. Machler. 2000. 'Does Health Status Improve After Resumption of ABM Employment?' *Gesunheitswesen*, 62: 335–41.

Tausig, M., and R. Fenwick. 1999. 'Recession and Well-Being'. *Journal of Health and Social Behavior*, 40, no. 1: 1–16.

Tsutsumi, A., K. Kayaba, T. Theorell, and J. Siegrist. 2001. 'Association Between Job Stress and Depression Among Japanese Employees Threatened by Job Loss in a Comparison Between Two Complementary Job-Stress Models'. *Scandinavian Journal of Work, Environment, and Health*, 27, no. 2: 146–53.

Turner, J. Blake. 1995. 'Economic Context and the Health Effects of Unemployment'. *Journal of Health and Social Behaviour*, 36: 213–29.

Turner, J. Blake, Ronald C. Kessler, and James S. House. 1991. 'Factors Facilitating Adjustment to Unemployment: Implications for Intervention'. *American Journal of Community Psychology*, 19: 521–42.

Underlid, Kjell. 1996. 'Activity During Unemployment and Mental Health'. *Scandinavian Journal of Psychology*, 37: 269–81.

United Nations Population Fund. 2000. *State of World Population 2000: Lives Together, Worlds Apart: Men and Women in a Time of Change*. Available at <www.unfpa.org/swp/2000/english/index.html>, accessed 23 January 2003.

Van de Mheen, H., K. Stronks, C.T.M. Schrijvers, and J.P. Mackenbach. 1999. 'The Influence of Adult Ill Health on Occupational Class Mobility and Mobility out of and into Employment in the Netherlands'. *Social Science and Medicine*, 49: 509–18.

Viinamaki, Heimo, Kaj Koskela, and Leo Niskanen. 1993. 'The Impact of Unemployment on Psychosomatic Symptoms and Mental Well-Being'. *International Journal of Social Psychiatry*, 39: 266–73.

———. 1996. 'Rapidly Declining Mental Well-Being During Unemployment'. *European Journal of Psychiatry*, 10: 215–21.

Wanberg, Connie R., Rich F. Griffiths, and Mark B. Gavin. 1997. 'Time Structure and Unemployment: A Longitudinal Investigation'. *Journal of Occupation and Organizational Psychology*, 70, no. 1: 75–95.

Wanberg, Connie R., R. Kanfer, and J.T. Banas. 2000. 'Predictors and Outcomes of Networking Intensity Among Unemployed Job Seekers'. *Journal of Applied Psychology*, 85: 491–503.

Wanberg, Connie R., R. Kanfer, and M. Rotundo. 1999. 'Unemployed Individuals: Motives, Job-Search Competencies, and Job-Search Constraints As Predictors of Job Seeking and Reemployment'. *Journal of Applied Psychology*, 84: 897–910.

Weber, Max. 1947. *The Theory of Social and Economic Organization*. Translated by A.M. Henderson and Talcott Parsons. New York: Free Press.

Wray, Linda A. 2000. 'Does Mental Health Affect Transitions out of the Labour Force in Older Workers?' Paper presented at the annual meeting of the American Sociological Association.

Yelin, E., J. Henke, P.P. Katz, M.D. Eisner, and P.D. Blanc. 1999. 'Work Dynamics of Adults with Asthma'. *American Journal of Industrial Medicine*, 35: 472–80.

Ytterdahl, T. 1999. 'Routine Health Check-ups of Unemployed in Norway'. *International Archives of Occupational and Environmental Health*, 72, suppl: S38–9.

Ytterdahl, T., and P. Fugelli. 2000. 'Health and Quality of Life Among Long-term Unemployed'. *Tidsskrift for Den Norske Laegeforening*, 120: 1308–11.

Glossary

Alienation Marx noted that industrialization and the division of labour have separated the worker from the work process, from the object he or she produces, and from his or her fellow workers. This experience involves feelings of powerlessness, meaninglessness, normlessness, estrangement, and social isolation in the workplace.

Bureaucracy A large, complex organization employing highly specialized workers who work within the context of what Max Weber called a *legal-rational* authority structure.

Capitalism The economic system in which private individuals or corporate groups own the means of production and distribution. Capitalists invest capital to produce goods and services, which they sell for profit in a competitive free market.

Cultural capital Developed through educational credentials and through knowledge of the dominant culture in terms of language, arts, and so forth.

Discouraged workers Those people who are not actively seeking employment. Specifically, they are thought to have turned their backs on the traditional work system and to have abandoned any desire to be gainfully employed. Most discouraged workers are qualified to work only within the secondary job market. They consist unduly of women and racial minorities. Also left out are individuals who do not take part in the labour force because they are in school, retired, or injured, sick, or otherwise unable to work.

Discriminatory unemployment Unemployment resulting from discrimination against particular groups, such as ethnic minorities and women.

Extrinsic rewards When work rewards the worker with money, prestige, respect, and social recognition.

Intrinsic rewards When work rewards the worker with the feeling of a 'job well done'.

Reporting relationships A network in a bureaucratic organization that enmeshes each individual worker into a Christmas-tree-shaped structure that repeatedly branches out as you go down the hierarchy. Thus, at the bottom of the hierarchy many people have to (1) carry out orders from above, (2) report work-related information up the tree to their superiors, and (3) uphold linkages between the organization and its client or customer base. At the top of the hierarchy, a few people get to (1) issue orders to their subordinates, (2) process information received from below, and (3) uphold linkages between the organization and other organizations—political, economic, and social.

Social capital Some people have more education, income, and social status; often these people have larger networks of acquaintances with more varied people among them. Sociologists call this 'having greater social capital'.

Socialism An alternative economic and political ideology that flourished in the nineteenth and twentieth centuries. It favours the public ownership of the means of production and distribution, and the investment of public capital in producing goods and services.

Strong ties Social linkages with close friends or relatives; they are distinguished from *weak ties* with acquaintances by sociologist Mark Granovetter.

Structural unemployment Results from social and economic factors that affect workers equally across all groups, such as corporate downsizing, capital flight (caused by corporate mergers and the move of operations to another geographic region—'runaway plants'), and the automation of work processes (that is, the replacement of human labour with mechanical equipment).

Weak ties See **Strong ties**.

Whistle-blowers Employees in a bureaucratic organization who bring forward valid information about wrongdoing or illegal conduct by their organization and who are often punished for doing so. Even organizations that publicly say that they want employees to 'participate' and that they hold high ethical standards move to discredit whistle-blowers and to fire them as soon as they report information about waste, fraud, or abuses of power in the organization.

Chapter 7

Family

Chapter Objectives

After reading this chapter the student should understand:
- the difference between the myth and the reality of the family
- what makes Canadian families unique
- the modern conception of the nuclear family
- the competing and conflicting theories on the family
- the social significance of the 'double shift'
- the presence of domestic violence in Canadian families and how it is recorded
- how everyone in the family experiences divorce differently
- potential health consequences of family problems
- possible solutions to family issues such as domestic abuse

Introduction

This chapter is about husbands and wives, parents and children, marriage and separation, family life and work life, divorce and violence. At bottom, family life is about three main social relationships: between spouses or partners, between parents and children, and between siblings (brothers and/or sisters). In the chapter, we will discuss many concerns that people feel about modern family life. As we will see, an important feature of family life is that family members interact with each other on a micro level, but the macro level of society plays a large part in framing the circumstances—economic, political, legal, religious, and otherwise—that shape these interactions.

Many people with family problems face a double difficulty: the problems themselves, and the shame and guilt they associate with feeling that no one else has similar problems. We begin this chapter by examining some of the disabling myths people hold about family life. We then put these myths against the backdrop of real Canadian families, noting the discrepancy. We briefly discuss the role of sex and sexuality in

family life, recognizing that families have always regulated sexuality. We then review competing sociological theories about families. After considering the social problems that families face, we judge the health consequences of family life. We finish with some thoughts about the ways that family problems might be remedied.

Family life is central to our whole society. It is the **family** that produces and socializes the next generation of citizens. Families have always been basic to society, providing the emotional sustenance and economic security that people need. People have always relied on families, especially in hard economic times. Because families are so important, problems in family living become important social problems for society as a whole.

Today, more than ever, we lack clear guidelines about the best ways to fulfill our family duties or to deal with the failings of other family members. There is no sure guide to good spousal, parental, or sibling behaviour. We are in a time of change. In this context, the work of sorting out modern family life is made a great deal more difficult by the survival of myths about an imaginary golden age of family life.

Myths of the Family

Throughout the period that makes up the supposed golden age of the family, television and Hollywood—ever the sentimentalists—promoted the image of an ideal family. In shows such as *Leave It to Beaver* (1957–63), *Ozzie and Harriet* (1952–66), *I Love Lucy* (1951–7), *Father Knows Best* (1954–62), and *The Donna Reed Show* (1958–66), television actors played out peaceful family scenes to the delight of audiences. Father was the breadwinner, Mother the bread maker. The phrase 'till death do you part' was taken literally. Stories made no mention of prior marriages, divorces, and separations, let alone children born to unmarried women. The children were clean-cut and well behaved, respectful of parents, and eager in school. They may have broken some rules, but when they did, parental discipline was fair and loving and the children learned their lessons.

BOX 7.1
Convocation Survival Tips

Along with the ideal family image of the 1950s, there are rituals and events that implicitly centre on this false gold standard of familial support. For example, what is the role of the bride's stepfather in a traditional wedding ceremony? The humorous piece here explores convocations.

By now, you've probably noticed the swarms of dapper young Queen's University graduates who have descended upon Kingston for Spring Convocation. Unfortunately for some graduates, not all of this celebratory merriment may be as merry as it seems. Consider the predicament of those students whose family situation does not resemble society's nuclear-family ideal—two happily married, heterosexual parents who provide more-than-adequate income for themselves, their two-point-five children, and a loyal golden retriever named Shep.

Unless it was of the incredibly rare, amicable variety, divorce creates a rather unique family dynamic when the folks (a.k.a. both halves of the 'Couple Formerly Known As Unhappily Married') re-unite to celebrate the success of the one thing they still have in common—their children. This awkwardness becomes exponentially compounded by the number of remarriages undertaken by each parent since the divorce, as well as by the number of step-parents present at the ceremony. A handy equation for remembering this is Remarriage 3 1 5 Tension 3 3, while Present Step-parent 3 1 5 Tension 3 7, although this varies slightly based on the attractiveness of the new husband/wife.

By the end of the weekend, the frazzled graduate may have to remind his/her parents that, although personal differences may necessitate that they sit in separate bleachers, they are still cheering for the same team. Of course, this is strictly a worst-case scenario. I'm sure there are divorced families who get along so very well that their only concern this weekend will be whether or not Dad will make rabbit ears behind Stepdad's head in the big group photo. My point is this: although Convocation is a time that was designed to celebrate a family's unified sense of pride in one member's accomplishments, the graduate's finest accomplishment of his/her university career, ironically enough, might very well be the survival of their own convocation.

If you work at one of the city's finer dining establishments and happen to spot a glum-looking graduate sitting in your section, do that student a favor and keep the wine a comin'. It's probably been a rough weekend.

SOURCE: Jessica Aldred, 'Convocation Survival Tips for Grads from Non-nuclear Families', *Kingston Whig-Standard*, final edition, 29 May 1998, 6.

This image of the family was never more than an ideal, even in the 1950s. It did not represent a majority of families at the time. Even back in those days, some brides were pregnant and some marriages ended in separation or divorce. Still, this ideal remained prominent and desirable to many contemporary North Americans. But it was always wishful thinking, and it proved the power of television to create fantasy worlds in people's minds.

In North American culture today, the ideal family is still based on a formal marriage between two people of different sexes who have come together freely to build a monogamous and enduring relationship with children present. Many members of the public still view alternatives to this as 'departures' from the 'norm', if not even as actually 'deviant'. Single-parenting, stepfamilies, common-law relationships, and same-sex couples may be growing in familiarity (and therefore acceptance), but they remain 'departures' from the cultural ideal. (See Table 7.1.)

In real life, most of us experience tensions between individualism and familism, and attempts to reinvent the family along democratic lines have been largely unsuccessful. The white, Western European nuclear family remains a powerful ideological device in our society. By giving us an image

TABLE 7.1
Families by Family Structure, Canada, 1995 and 2001[a]

	1995		2001	
	(000s)	%	(000s)	%
Total families	**8,363**	**100.0**	**8,790**	**100.0**
Couples with no children	**3,048**	**36.4**	**3,334**	**37.9**
Married	2,489	29.8	2,720	30.9
Common-law	559	6.7	614	7.0
Couples with children	**4,165**	**49.8**	**4,271**	**48.6**
Intact families	3,734	44.6	3,768	42.9
Married	3,506	41.9	3,438	39.1
Common-law	228	2.7	330	3.8
Stepfamilies	430	5.1	503	5.7
Married	217	2.6	251	2.9
Common-law	213	2.5	252	2.9
Blended families	161	1.9	200	2.3
Her children	216	2.6	253	2.9
His children	54	0.6	50	0.6
Total married couples (with children)	3,723	44.5	3,688	42.0
Total common-law couples (with children)	442	5.3	583	6.6
Lone-parent families	**1,151**	**13.8**	**1,185**	**13.5**
Male parent	168	2.0	209	2.4
Female parent	982	11.7	976	11.1

[a]The sum of values categories may not add to total due to rounding.
SOURCES: General Social Survey, 1995 and 2001.

SOURCE: Statistics Canada, *Family History* (Cat. no. 89-575) (Ottawa: Statistics Canada, 2002), 5; available at <www.statcan.ca/english/freepub/89-575-XIE/89-575-XIE2001001.pdf>, accessed 25 January 2003.

of what is 'proper', the fantasy family image serves to control and socialize race, class, gender, and sexual orientation (Chambers, 2000).

Basic Aspects of Canadian Families

In reality, families are more different and more varied than the media suggest. In place of an idealized nuclear family, we find a wide variety of families and more tolerant attitudes toward different family types. However, the number and variety of families is far from infinite. In many respects, Canadian families today are similar to families in other Western societies, such as the United Kingdom, France, and the United States. Urban industrial societies like Canada have certain typical family forms.

Like most urban industrial societies, Canadian society is organized around married couples. Society provides less protection for the property rights of partners in common-law relationships than for those of legally married partners, for example. Yet Canadian family policies differ from those of other countries, and they often vary from one province to another. The most progressive patterns are found in Quebec, where the rates of cohabitation, divorce, and births out of wedlock are highest. Quebec aside, family practices vary from east to west, with the western provinces being least traditional in their ways and the Atlantic provinces most traditional.

Like many terms sociologists use, **family** has a variety of definitions devised for different purposes. For purposes of the census, the Canadian government defines the *economic family* as 'a now married couple (with or without never-married sons and/or daughters of either or both spouses), a couple living common-law (again with or without never-married sons and/or daughters of either or both partners), or a lone parent of any marital status, with at least one never-married son or daughter living in the same dwelling' (Statistics Canada, 2001a). A broader sociological definition of the family, one that sociologists would be more likely to support, is as a group of individuals, related by blood, marriage, or adoption, who support one another financially, materially, and emotionally (see, for example, Murdock, 1949). This definition, though better, does not apply well to same-sex partnerships between people who are not related by blood, legal marriage, or legal adoption. To cover these relationships, we need to recast the concept of family to focus on the important processes that typify marriage, such as financial, material, and emotional support.

The most common forms of family structure in Canada today are nuclear families and extended families. A **nuclear family** comprises one or two parents and any dependent children who live together in one household separate from other relatives. This type of arrangement is typical of families in industrialized countries like Canada. Because adult children in industrial societies are economically independent, they tend to form their own households after starting a family, separate from parents, siblings, and extended kin.

By contrast, the **extended family** is a nuclear family that lives with other kinfolk under one roof. The kinfolk are most commonly drawn from grandparents, aunts, uncles, and dependent nephews and nieces. Extended-family households are often found in pre-industrial societies. There, the agricultural basis of survival often means that a larger household, with more workers to help grow and harvest the crops, is better able to support the entire family. In Canada, extended families are common among newly arrived ethnic groups, such as Asian Canadians, that come from an agricultural background. Often they place a strong value on upholding intergenerational ties with elders. However, overall, the popularity of extended families in North America declined rapidly in the twentieth century.

Though most Canadian families today are nuclear families, they vary widely. For one thing, the fraction of families with a traditional two-parent structure is declining. Today, Canadian nuclear families include married couples without

A nuclear family comprises one or two parents and any dependent children who live together in one household. The extended family is a nuclear family that lives with other kinfolk under one roof. (Dick Hemingway)

children, couples cohabiting (that is, living in a common-law relationship), single parents (never-married or divorced), same-sex families, and blended families. *Blended families* are remarriages in which one or both partners have a child from an earlier relationship.

Most Canadian families, 73 per cent in 2001, are still classifiable as a 'married-couple union', to use Statistics Canada's term. However, this group has declined since 1986, when 80 per cent of all families were based in legal marriage (Statistics Canada, 1997). Alongside the decreased rate of marriage, we see a corresponding increase in common-law unions. Statistics Canada defines a *common-law couple* as 'two persons of opposite sex who are not legally married to each other, but live together as husband and wife in the same dwelling' (Statistics Canada, 1997). Although

historically Canadians frowned on couples that lived together without marrying, today the stigma against non-marital cohabitation has diminished if not disappeared (Vanier Institute, 2000).

The common-law union is the fastest-growing family category today. There were 1.2 million cohabiting couples in Canada in 2001, a 20 per cent increase since 1995. Non-marital cohabitation is most prevalent in the province of Quebec, where one in four couples live common-law and where 43 per cent of all such relationships in Canada occur (Bélanger et al., 2001: 34–5).

Sex and Sexuality

Families typically begin through the forming of bonds between partners. In the beginning, this process is driven as much by sexuality as by the desire to satisfy social norms and achieve economic security. In a society like ours, in which most mating is based on romance, sexual norms are central to mating and family formation.

Sexuality continues, over the course of family life, to cement a partner relationship or, often, to create conflict. As such, it both enlivens and endangers family life. On the one hand, many couples come together to form a family because of sexual passions that emerge between them. These passions, which may last for several years in their original form, help the couple ride out the many storms that come up as they learn to live and work together. Their relationship is based on *romantic love*, a type of love that is found mainly in societies that allow both males and females to give and withhold love freely. As a result, the power of romantic love and sexual passion to bring couples together and keep them together is a result of sexual equality.

Societies that allow premarital sex for both men and women rate romantic love considerably higher than societies that have a double standard or that disapprove of female sexuality outside marriage (de Munck and Korotayev, 1999). Said another way, societies that regulate female sexuality more closely than male sexuality are societies in which romantic love and passionate sex are relatively unimportant in marriage. However, ironically, in 'romantic' societies marriages are less secure. Marriages based on choice and passion are always at risk of ending through the discovery of new choices, partners, and passions. This is the paradox of modern marriage.

Societies also vary in the degree to which women exercise control over the frequency, timing, and conditions of sex (for example, over the use of condoms). In Sweden, a highly egalitarian society, people in stable relationships typically plan the choice and use of contraceptive method with their partners. A failure to agree on the method often results in no intercourse (Lindell and Engberg, 1999). This suggests that Swedish women exercise far more control over marital sex than their North American counterparts. Some view the new female condom as a technology that is likely to empower women by protecting them better and giving them more control over the consequences of sex (Kaler, 2001).

Like marital sex, premarital sex is socially structured. Sexual initiation depends, first of all, on the availability of partners. The same factor that reduces the likelihood that a woman will become sexual active—a shortage of potential marriage partners—increases the likelihood that a sexually active woman will enter unwed motherhood (on this, see Lloyd, 2001, discussing Latinas in the United States). Marriage and sexual 'markets' are limited by ethnic and racial endogamy, in the sense that people initially look for partners within their own ethnic or racial group. Immigrants, in particular, often put pressure on their children to obey traditional sexual rules (for example, the double standard) and to avoid socializing (and sexualizing) with members of other ethnocultural communities. For a variety of reasons, these markets vary considerably in size and diversity. For example, within ethnic or racial groups, women are unlikely to find potential male partners who are older and better educated than they are. This often leads people to look for mates in other markets.

Ironically, the less contact groups have had with each other, the more likely they are to believe sexual myths and stereotypes about those groups. So, for example, Filipino Americans view their wives and daughters as models of sexual morality while viewing Anglo-Americans as morally inferior. 'We don't sleep around like white girls do', they say (Espiritu, 2001). Such myths may cause parents great anxiety, and they likely increase the appeal and excitement of *exogamy*—mating outside one's own group.

Same-Sex Couples

Same-sex relationships are like families in many of the most important ways, except that they are less concerned with childbearing or child rearing and, presumably, more concerned with sex, romance, and attraction. Same-sex relationships fall outside the usual pattern that links sexual behaviour to reproduction, so they are more likely to be based on sexual attraction and personal compatibility. Beyond this, same-sex relationships differ from opposite-sex relationships in a few other respects. For example, same-sex relationships appear to have a much more equalitarian attitude toward the distribution of household labour.

Many people, especially older, more religious, and less sexually experienced people, tend to be homophobic. Attitudes toward gay men are typically more negative than attitudes toward lesbians. As well, men are more typically homophobic than women, and less educated people more homophobic than those who are more educated (Schellenberg, Hirt, and Sears, 1999). Other things being equal, Canadians are much less homophobic in their attitudes than Americans or Mexicans (Tepperman and Curtis, 2003). However, in Canada as elsewhere, religious ideas continue to fuel discrimination against homosexuals and their right to form families (Howard-Hassmann, 2001).

Many gay and lesbian people are deeply embedded in familial structures as parents, children, siblings, aunts, uncles, grandchildren, and so on (O'Brien and Goldberg, 2000). Yet in most industrialized countries, gays and lesbians are unable to marry legally since marriage continues to be defined as a union between a man and a woman. There are signs that this is changing. Indeed, the legal treatment of lesbian and gay families in the United States and Canada has been changing since the late 1970s, as is evident in both countries in child custody, access, and adoption cases in which sexual orientation was a factor (Arnup, 1999). By challenging the definition of 'spouse' and applying to the courts to formalize their relationships with their children by way of adoption, lesbian parents have challenged the normative content of spousal relations and the law itself as a gendering strategy (Gavigan, 1999).

Same-sex couples have recently received more recognition and benefits, making these more similar to those granted heterosexual couples. In February 1998, the province of British Columbia became the first jurisdiction in North America to redefine the term 'spouse', in their Family Relations Act, to include same-sex couples. The amendment gave same-sex couples the privileges and obligations automatically granted to heterosexuals, including custody of children, access, and child support (O'Brien and Goldberg, 2000).

In 1999 and 2000, Quebec, Ontario, and the federal government of Canada adopted omnibus bills granting same-sex common-law spouses almost all the same rights as heterosexual couples under the tax system, social security programs, and family law (O'Brien and Goldberg, 2000; Rose, 2000). In 2000, the government of Canada passed the Modernization of Benefits and Obligations Act, giving same-sex couples the same rights as heterosexual couples under 68 federal laws (EGALE, 2001). Additionally, in 2001, Statistics Canada included questions about same-sex unions in the national census for the first time.

Quebec's Bill 84, which came into effect at the end of July 2002, gave same-sex couples the chance to seal their commitment in a marriage-like civil ceremony. Those who sign the registry will be entitled to spousal property rights, as well as life insurance, health, succession, and pension benefits. Already, same-sex marriages have been carried out in Quebec. Efforts to do the same in Ontario, in July 2002, were rebuffed when a court clerk refused to issue the required marriage licence.

Public opinion polls prove that Canadians are becoming more tolerant of same-sex unions. (See Table 7.2 on the prevalence of same-sex unions in Canada.) In a 2001 Leger Marketing poll, 65.4 per cent of those surveyed agreed that we should grant same-sex couples the right to legally marry and 75.7 per cent felt that we should give homosexuals the same rights as

TABLE 7.2
Canadian Same-Sex Couples by Province or Territory, 2001

	Total Couples	Same-Sex Couples[a]	Male Couples	Female Couples
Newfoundland and Labrador	131,330	0.14%	88 (0.07%)	93 (0.07%)
Prince Edward Island	32,120	0.17%	23 (0.07%)	33 (0.10%)
Nova Scotia	218,765	0.39%	388 (0.18%)	468 (0.21%)
New Brunswick	180,485	0.28%	250 (0.14%)	260 (0.14%)
Quebec	1,683,955	0.62%	6,348 (0.38%)	4,015 (0.24%)
Ontario	2,704,885	0.46%	7,005 (0.26%)	5,495 (0.20%)
Manitoba	253,690	0.34%	420 (0.17%)	445 (0.18%)
Saskatchewan	223,550	0.21%	210 (0.09%)	268 (0.12%)
Alberta	694,760	0.36%	1,258 (0.18%)	1,265 (0.18%)
British Columbia	917,610	0.63%	2,985 (0.33%)	2,808 (0.31%)
Yukon	6,265	0.57%	8 (0.13%)	28 (0.45%)
Northwest Territories	7,670	0.39%	10 (0.13%)	20 (0.26%)
Nunavut	4,720	0.34%	8 (0.17%)	8 (0.17%)
Total Canada	7,059,830	0.48%	19,001 (0.27%)	15,206 (0.22%)

[a] All percentages are of total couples; percentages may not add up because of rounding.

SOURCE: Statistics Canada, Canada: 2001 Census Information on Same-Sex Couples, Same-Sex Couples by Province or Territory (Statistics Canada, 2001), available at <www.gaydemographics.org/canada/gen.htm>.

heterosexuals. However, these tolerant attitudes do not extend to issues related to children. For example, only 53.1 per cent of those surveyed agreed that we should permit homosexuals to adopt children (Leger Marketing, 2001). This disapproval of adoption by gays and lesbians likely reflects an unsupported belief that homosexual parenting will harm children's sexual development (O'Brien and Goldberg, 2000). However, research finds no evidence that children raised by gays and lesbians tend more toward homosexuality or differ significantly in gender identity or gender behaviours from children raised by heterosexual parents (O'Brien and Goldberg, 2000).

Childhood: Theory and Fact

We know from French historian Philippe Ariès (1958) that childhood is a social invention. Its spread coincided with the development of schooling, city life, and industrialization. When most children lived with their parents on farms or in small villages, they helped out with the family work from an early age onward. Differentiation of roles and status by age was minimal. People learned to do adult tasks from birth onward and took on adult responsibilities as soon as they were able. The further differentiation of people by age resulted, in the nineteenth century, in the invention of adolescence. Possibly, we will have further age differentiation of young people in the twenty-first century, as people continue to extend their education and delay their entry into full adult earning status.

This creation of age groups through age differentiation meant an increased distinction, separation, isolation, and segregation of different-aged people from one another. As well, with the invention of childhood came a mythologizing of children's innocence, ignorance, and purity. Adults liked to believe that children could be

BOX 7.2
Children and Domestic Violence

Children don't have to have scars to be victims of conjugal violence. Simply being exposed as a witness—watching it, hearing it or seeing the aftermath—can have devastating, long-term consequences for children, according to a growing body of literature and research. For instance, males who witness their father being violent are more likely than other men to be violent in intimate relationships. And females with a violent father are more likely to gravitate to abusive men: they may get skewed messages of what is OK and believe that domination means caring.

In one study, more than half of young offenders charged with crimes against people were found to have been exposed to domestic violence as children. There is research to suggest that being exposed to violence puts children at more risk than actually being subjected to violence—the theory being that it is somehow more insidious, observed Peter Jaffe, a world expert in the field and the keynote presenter at a community panel discussion to be held Wednesday. There are programs to help these children, the experts say, but first, awareness that they are silent victims needs to be raised—in the community at large and among the people who encounter them, including police, teachers, lawyers and social-service professionals.

SOURCE: Susan Schwartz, 'Domestic Violence Can Have Hidden Effects', *The Gazette* (Montreal), 21 October 2002, D4. Reprinted by permission The Gazette.

moulded like clay. People who were 'bad' adults had been born 'good' but must have been abused or neglected in childhood. Thus, a strong responsibility rested and rests on the shoulders of adults to raise their children in a loving, protective way.

This enshrinement of childhood likely led to a reduction of childbearing. We tend to idolize what is rare and to cut down on activities that are costly. With their idolization, children became more costly and less common. As a result, fertility began to decline in the West in France in the late eighteenth century, with similar declines in the United States, Britain, and Western Europe in the mid- to late nineteenth century. English Canada's main fertility decline dates from the late nineteenth century, with French Canada's a little later. (See Figure 7.1 for more recent data.) Many explanations have been offered for the fertility decline, including the increases in gender equality and control over conception and the growing availability of contraceptive knowledge and

technology. However, the single most likely factor is the declining economic value and increasing cost of children in urban industrial societies. With stronger child-labour laws, children become less valuable for producing an income. And with extended periods of education and economic dependency, children become more expensive to raise.

The reduction in childbearing has been important for women. With fewer children to bear and raise, women have had more opportunity to achieve equality with men, both within families and within the labour force. Since the end of the baby boom, ever more women have delayed or avoided marriage altogether, preferring to establish stable careers and economic independence before becoming parents. Increasingly, the choice of a suitable partner is being based on emotional compatibility and companionship rather than on financial or social necessity or on the willingness to produce many children.

FIGURE 7.1

Live Births, by Age Group of Mother, 1987–97

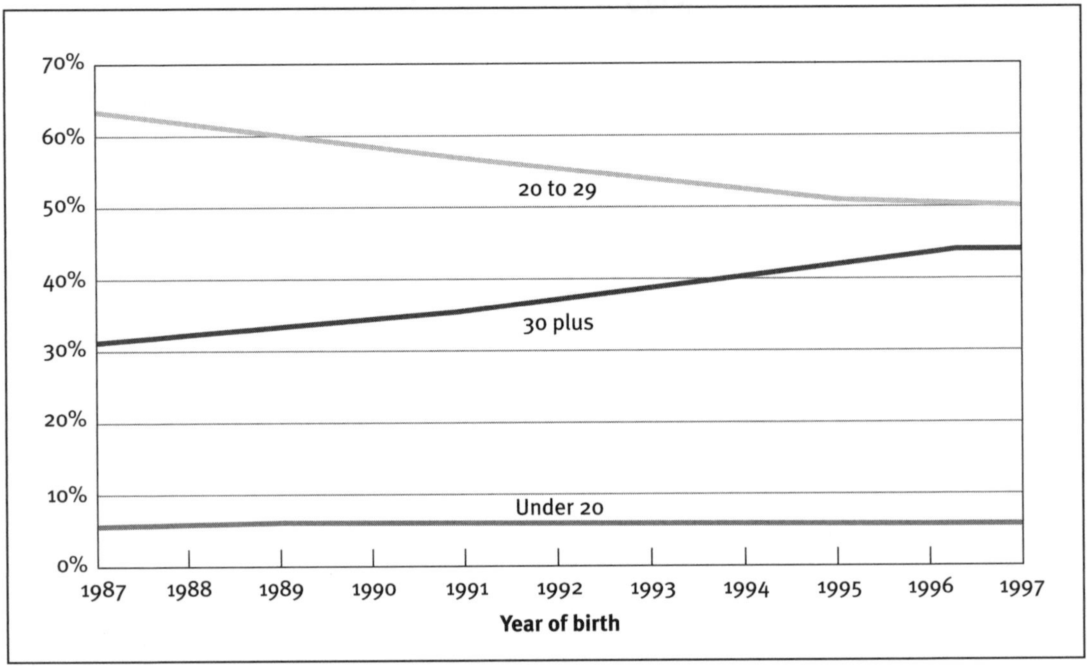

SOURCE: Statistics Canada, *The Daily*, 16 June 1999; available at <www.statcan.ca/Daily/English/990616/d990616b.htm>, accessed 25 January 2003.

Theories of the Family

As in other areas of sociology, the analysis of family life varies according to the perspective of the analyst. Different approaches to the study of families provide different explanations of why families evolve as they do and why family problems arise.

The Structural-Functionalist Perspective

Functionalists view the family as a central institution in society. They see the family as a microcosm of society, with individual family members coming together in a unified and productive whole (Lehmann, 1994). In Talcott Parsons and Robert Bales's functionalist analysis (1955), the family's division of labour is the key to a family's success. In a traditional family, the husband of the household performs an *instrumental* role as

the breadwinner, decision maker, and source of authority and leadership, while the wife fulfills an *expressive* role as homemaker, nurturer, and emotional centre of the family.

Though these roles of the husband and wife have changed since 1950, functionalists still view the family institution as accomplishing several important functions. One is the regulation of sexual behaviour and reproduction. Reproduction is crucial to the survival of all species, and mating is a highly organized behaviour throughout the animal kingdom. For people as for other animals, the structure regulating most sexual intercourse has traditionally been the family. Regulated sex increases the likelihood that children will have two parents to care for them, that mothers will have husbands to help pay the bills, and that fathers will have some assurance that a newborn is their own biological offspring.

Another function of the family is to provide for the physical (food, shelter, and so on) and psychological (nurturance, learning, and so on) needs of its members. A third function of the family is to socialize children. The ways in which parents teach children the values and norms of their particular culture vary from one society to another. Finally, the family confers membership in a social unit, which in turn confers social status and identity in relation to class, race, ethnicity, and religious affiliation. In this way, family membership provides both a sense of location within a family history or genealogy and a sense of location within the community.

Functionalism today surfaces in arguments about the naturalness or inevitability of certain family forms. For example, psychiatrists Ronald Immerman and Wade Mackey (1999) argue that almost all marriage systems across the world support monogamous pair bonding. This suggests there may be something wrong with a pattern of multiple partners within a social group. In communities where people have multiple partners, sexually transmitted diseases increase. So do a variety of societal dysfunctions, such as out-of-wedlock births, infant morbidity, violent crime, and lower educational attainment. These outcomes reduce the ability of the community to compete with other societies that have maintained pair bonding. This, in turn, reduces the survival capacity of the community.

Others make structural arguments to show that cohabitation is inferior to traditional (legal) marriage. Therefore, Linda Waite (1999–2000) argues that cohabiting relationships are less often permanent, fail to provide many benefits of marriage to both participants, are less likely to involve extended families, and provide less support for the cohabiting partners during a crisis. Additionally, domestic violence rates are higher in cohabiting relationships, cohabiting partners are less sexually exclusive, partners are less likely to share domestic work and income, psychological well-being is less, and separation rates are higher. By implication, society should encourage legal marriage and do what it can to discourage cohabitation.

Conflict and Feminist Theories

Unlike functionalists, conflict theorists do not assume that families operate as units, perform functions, or accomplish tasks for the good of society. Conflict theorists take a historical approach and focus on political and economic changes.

They note that with industrialization, families moved from being self-sustaining economic units to consumption units. In doing so, they became dependent on outside sources of income to meet their survival needs. This meant that working-class men had to sell their labour power to the bourgeoisie in exchange for an income. In this process, women gained exclusive control over the home, becoming responsible for child rearing, food preparation, and the provision of emotional support. However, as conflict theorists emphasize, women did this work without financial remuneration, despite the importance of the tasks. This amounted to exploitation of women that benefited their husbands' employers. Thus, sexual inequality increased under industrial capitalism.

In short, gender inequality arises out of economic exploitation, not the need of 'society' or even of a given family for task differentiation based on gender. There are historical reasons for this development, and for the association of this development with the rise of industrial capitalism. Feminist theorists argue that, just as factory workers depend on capitalists for a living wage, wives depend on their husbands. This dependence easily turned into subordination. Women have historically endured not only economic reliance on men in the household, but also political and social inferiority; they did not receive the right to vote in Canada until 1918. Though these patriarchal tendencies are very old, the capitalist economy affirmed them by providing men a different access to the labour market than women.

For feminist sociologists, an important element is the *ideology of gender*, an aspect of socialization that serves to explain how males and females are different, justifying treatment of the sexes as two distinct and separate kinds of persons. Men, for example are assumed to be more aggressive and competitive than women, yet at the same time also more rational and objective. It is men who invent, explore, and explain. Women are considered to be more passive and supportive than men, yet at the same time more emotional and dependant. It is women who consume, nurture, and create.

Like other cultural behaviours, people learn their gender-based habits of behaviour through **gender socialization**. The socialization process links gender to personal identity in the form of *gender identity* and to distinctive activities in the form of gender roles. The major agents of social-ization—family, peer groups, schools, and the mass media—all serve to reinforce cultural definitions of masculinity and femininity. Gender socialization begins as soon as an infant's sex is identified and continues through preschool and primary school. Young children learn gender identities when they experiment with hair and clothing styles, role-play-ing games, and body decoration, and also by observing others at nursery school or daycare. Their imitative efforts all reflect enormous pres-sures to conform to assigned gender identities.

Parents routinely assign more household tasks to daughters than to sons. The tasks people assign to their sons are more often 'handyman' tasks, not cleaning, child care, or meal preparation. Not sur-prisingly, children form traditional gender-based attitudes toward housework before the end of high school. In this way, they perpetuate age-old

---

BOX 7.3
A Critique of Women's Studies and Feminism

What do you think? The author seems to argue (1) that women's studies programs should not be publicly funded and (2) that the content of women's studies programs does not represent Canadians' attitudes, which the author shows by citing statistics on the importance of the family to many Canadians. Are you convinced on either point, and are her statistics sufficient to prove her points?

Would you hire a woman with a degree in Women's Studies? What would they bring to the table? This is a puzzlement to me because we do turn out such young women, from a score of such departments in Canada, and have been doing so for 30 years. So what are they learn-ing anyway?

Luckily, last week, the Independent Women's Forum in Washington, DC, published Lying in a Room of One's Own, How Women's Studies Miseducate Students. The report, by

Christine Stolba, analyzes the standard, com-monly used texts of this quasi-discipline, and, what is even more valuable, fact-checks those texts. If someone from Women's Studies turns up at your personnel department, this is what they have been learning:

'Hidden away in many of those suburban homes of the 1950s, were drinking problems, bickering spouses and bored wives.' 'Women who take traditional gender norms at face value and become full-time mothers and homemak-ers are rewarded by being the most economi-cally and psychologically vulnerable of all women.' 'The modern form of the family leads women to be economically and emotionally dependent on men and, as a result, the tradi-tional family is a source of social conflict and a haven only for men.'

Had enough? Luckily, the Patriarchy released its own study this Monday in the guise of the Strategic Counsel, which used actual

continued

statistical analysis. It is called Canadian Attitudes on the Family. The unconscious enslavement thing must be working quite well.

Canadians, men and women, 80% of them, consider maintaining a stable marriage as their top priority, and 76% consider being good parents as the second. Work? Way down on the list. Eighty-eight per cent say that having children was the best thing that ever happened to them. Seventy-six per cent say that they'd rather one parent be able to stay at home with their children. An equal number say that both parents work because they have to, not because they want to.

Eighty-two per cent say that taxes should be reduced so that one parent can stay home.

Most desired family size? Growing. Edging towards four. Yes, four. Double the number that Gallup found in 1994. The younger the respondent, the more likely he or she was to disagree with divorce as a solution to family problems. Seventy-eight per cent believe that 'the importance of family life is undervalued in Canadian society today' and 83% agree that encouraging strong families should be a top priority of governments in Canada'.

Well. Two entirely different pictures have emerged. Now I know many people who cherish their families, but almost no one who subscribes to the intellectual blather we pay universities to teach young women.

SOURCE: Elizabeth Nickson, 'The Charter Challenge Ladies Are Dangerous', *National Post*, national edition, 21 June 2002, A18.

stereotypes without being aware of doing so. Men, older people, and poor people are particularly likely to hold and teach traditional, gendered attitudes. As a result, fathers raising teenage daughters demand more help from their children than fathers who are raising teenage sons.

Media images of gender roles still influence children, who end up holding stereotyped ideas of male and female behaviour. So, for example, when asked to write stories on any topic, students aged 9 to 16 show strong evidence of media-influenced sex-role stereotyping. They depict men in a variety of occupations and using violent means to resolve conflict. Women are portrayed in more traditional female roles, are less active, and use less violence.

The maintenance of a sharp cultural dichotomy between men and women is facilitated if we conceive of separate locations for the two groups—women's 'place' is in the home, for example, while men have a place in public affairs. Men and women have separate activities and schedules. They wear different kinds of clothing (that is, uniforms), with women's clothing often discouraging vigorous physical activity.

Historically, men and women were also treated in different ways, as in the idealized 'gallantry' whereby men's caring attentiveness has emphasized the weakness and dependence of women. These symbolic distinctions have weakened over time, with more gender equality in practice.

Patriarchy

By **patriarchy**, we mean male dominance that is justified in a society's system of values. This dominance is tied to the ideology of gender and can be found in every society.

Most known societies are patriarchal to some extent, a fact that has never been satisfactorily explained. Perhaps the universality of patriarchy is due to the universality of social differentiation by sex, which is due in turn to the physical vulnerability and dependence of women under conditions of frequent pregnancy and childbirth. If so, it follows that with the worldwide reduction in childbearing, we can expect to see a worldwide reduction in patriarchy, and, in fact, this change is evident. An increase in women's educational and job opportunities makes it possible for lower fertility to translate into less male domination.

Like class inequality, the degree and form of inequality between the sexes already varies a great deal from one society to another. So too does the excuse or justification for gender inequality. In many societies, the excuse is sacred (based on religious texts and teachings). Major religions of the world—Catholicism, Judaism, and Islam among them—give different and less powerful roles to women than to men.

The struggle over cultural and religious patriarchy is critical to the future of families. Consider the clash of ideologies evident in the recent celebration of World Youth Day in Toronto, where 200,000 Catholic youth from around the world gathered to celebrate their faith. The Church and the faith they celebrated are in conflict with many of the dominant beliefs of Canadian society, such as women's right to choose contraception, divorce, and have a legal abortion; the increasing necessity for women of all cultures to work outside the home; and an increasing acceptance of gay relationships and marriage.

Thus, there are degrees of patriarchy. In mainstream Canadian culture, common ways of expressing gender inequality are everywhere, though they are intangible. In a marriage, for example, one spouse may control the way money is spent. In a dating couple, one person may decide how to spend an evening or whether there will be sexual intercourse. In conversation, one person will cut off or break in on the speech of another.

Conflict and feminist theories are useful in understanding the causes for gendered inequality and conflict. However, they have difficulty accounting for the near universality of gender differentiation and male domination across societies and cultures. Moreover, like functionalist theories, conflict theories tend to ignore the processes by which meanings and inequalities are constructed interpersonally.

Symbolic Interactionism

As we have seen throughout the book, interactionists focus on the micro level of sociological phenomena. With respect to families, symbolic interactionists study the ways members of a family talk and interact with one another and how they resolve conflicts within the boundaries of their roles in the family. An important part of this process is the creation and revision of family myths.

Like people in any social relationship, couples enter a marriage as initially separate individuals with distinct identities. However, as time passes, a married couple builds a shared definition of their family—its goals, identity, and values. They may even change their views about themselves as individuals to make them more consistent with the family subculture (Berger and Kellner, 1964). For example, a couple may develop stories about how they met and fell in love that are congruent with their current beliefs about their relationship. As children are born and the family grows larger, they may again revise their stories and identities to incorporate new roles and goals.

Symbolic interactionists also study how people view the institution of marriage overall and how they come to imbue it with values. Although modern Western culture stresses that romantic love is the basis of a solid marriage, this has not always been the case. For much of the history of marriage, passionate love—although undeniably experienced both within and without the bounds of wedlock—was not a necessary factor in deciding who wedded whom. Instead, people often based marriage on complementarity and companionship. They intended marriage to weld two people into a single economic unit of production, consumption, and reproduction. Only in the modern era has romantic love become paramount as the assumed basis for choosing a mate (as opposed to, say, money or convenience).

Other symbolic interactionists have studied the way in which wives and husbands differently interpret the objective reality of their marriage. Research has shown that although spouses share many experiences, they often interpret these events in different ways (Safilios-Rothschild,

1969). As a result, many researchers find that men report much higher levels of happiness and satisfaction with their marriage than do women (Bernard, 1982). Presumably, this has something to do with the inequalities of power and status we discussed earlier. It may also reflect the different expectations that men and women bring to marriage and parenthood.

Social Consequences of Family Life

Elements in family life such as abuse, employment and unemployment, and divorce all have serious social and health consequences that can affect the individual, his or her family, and society as a whole. Every family has problems to deal with, and in this section we will mention only a few of the more common ones and their social consequences.

Employment

Canada's higher cost of living than one or two generations ago prevents most families from surviving comfortably on a single income. As a result, both parents usually have to work to make enough money to cover the necessities, pay for the occasional luxury, and still save enough for their children's postsecondary education and their own retirement. The demands of employers for workers' time are often in direct conflict with the needs of the family.

Findings from a major study of time stress among working parents suggest the size of the problem. When asked 'Do you ever consider yourself a workaholic?' one-third of surveyed fathers and one-fifth of mothers answered yes. One out of three said his or her partner was a workaholic. Many admitted they experienced a problem of 'time famine' (Hochschild, 1997: 199–200).

Research finds that mothers whose work has stressed them are more likely to ignore their children. By contrast, fathers whose work has stressed them are more likely to generate conflict with their children—to pick a fight with them. Both child neglect and conflict increase the likelihood of problem behaviour among adolescents. Parent-adolescent conflict is highest when work stresses both parents.

On the other hand, data from the US Child Outcomes Study (Zaslow et al., 1999) point to more positive child outcomes across a variety of measures of development for children of employed mothers in families with some history of welfare receipt. Employment yields an income that reduces family poverty, thus improving child health and educational outcomes. It also increases the mother's independence and equality, which improves her mental well-being. Employment, as well as income and control, benefits mother's mental health (Davies and McAlpine, 1998).

Family life is hard to reconcile with a career, especially if you are a mother. As a result, many highly educated women today delay marriage, preferring to go to school, work, and establish financial independence before bearing children. Others avoid marriage altogether, opting instead to have a career and pursue only those romantic relationships that do not hinder their professional lives. The higher we look in the occupational hierarchy, in professional or managerial jobs, the more likely we are to find women who never married, who married and divorced, who married early but did not have children, or who married late and had few if any children.

Whatever their education and career goals, women who marry and bear children usually face a **double shift**: modern women's dual roles as both breadwinner and homemaker. Most wives have yet to break free from the stereotype that they are inherently suited—and therefore obliged—to play the role of nurturer in the family.

One home characteristic and three work characteristics put particular pressure on the interface between work and home life: (1) a spouse who often works overtime, (2) a bad work schedule, (3) a heavy workload, and (4) a troubled relationship with the boss. These work-home interference factors produce emotional exhaustion, psychosomatic health complaints, and sleep deprivation (Geurts, Rutte, and Peeters, 1999). So, in the end, motherhood and employment are not opposite categories, but activities woven together throughout life. More research needs to be done on social and policy implications of making work and motherhood compatible.

Children and Adolescents

For many people, children still define family life. They are the reason for settling down with one partner. Though more couples have only one or two children rather than three or four, there are few couples who choose to have no children. So even though childbearing has declined more or less continuously for the last century, there has not been—and is not today—a desire to eliminate children from the family agenda.

Moreover, children have improved their social situation in modern societies. Though many children are still neglected and abused, as a group children today have rights against neglect and abuse that they lacked a century ago. The brutal workhouse—and child labour, more generally—that Charles Dickens wrote about and that still lingers on some parts of the world is not to be found in Canada. Increasingly, we have moved to extend childhood as a time of care, protection, and education.

Children today are no longer considered the property of their parents. Parents are expected to obey the rules of Canadian society, regardless of their own background and parenting preferences. Children have individual rights in law, and the state has set out to protect them. The tolerance for spanking and harsh discipline, for example, is diminishing steadily. This has not, however, eradicated child abuse. Parenting values are still being fought over in court cases, and parents, surrogate parents, or teachers still have the right to use force against a child if the force is reasonable under the circumstances and so long as they do not use an instrument or leave marks.

So the dangers of abuse and neglect remain real enough, as evidenced by the large numbers of children who run away from home to live on the streets on reaching adolescence.

Though the legal rights afforded to children are increasing, their social rights and social opportunities are not improving. The numbers of children who live in poverty are increasing as more Canadian families at the bottom of the economic ladder encounter hardship (see Figure 7.2). This means that more children experience the use of food banks, used clothing, and life in a shelter. In Toronto, for example, the family occupancy rate in shelters was 29 per cent higher in 2002 than it was in 2000 (Toronto, CYAC, 2002).

Beyond that, Canada is still without a federal child care program. Quebec is the only province that provides a universally accessible and affordable child care system. Some provinces, like Ontario, have even reduced social assistance and used the federal money ($1.7 billion) mandated for a National Children's Agenda for purposes other than child care. They have emphasized 'encouraging' single mothers to accept minimum-wage jobs that leave them below the poverty line while depriving their children of parenting. Increasingly, grandparents are called on to take on the parenting role because of the biological parents' work pattern, inability to cope, or substance abuse, or because of allegations of child mistreatment.

Adolescents suffer from abuse, neglect, and poverty, too, but have somewhat different concerns over and above these. Concerns about heterosexual relationships peak around the age of 11, concerns about peer acceptance around 15, and concerns about relationship to and independence from parents at 15 for girls and 17 for boys. This is probably an oversimplified account (Kloep, 1999). However, it does capture some of the major stages in youth development and notes that family life continues to be important in the lives of young people through much of their second decade.

FIGURE 7.2
Poverty Rates for Children, 1980–1999

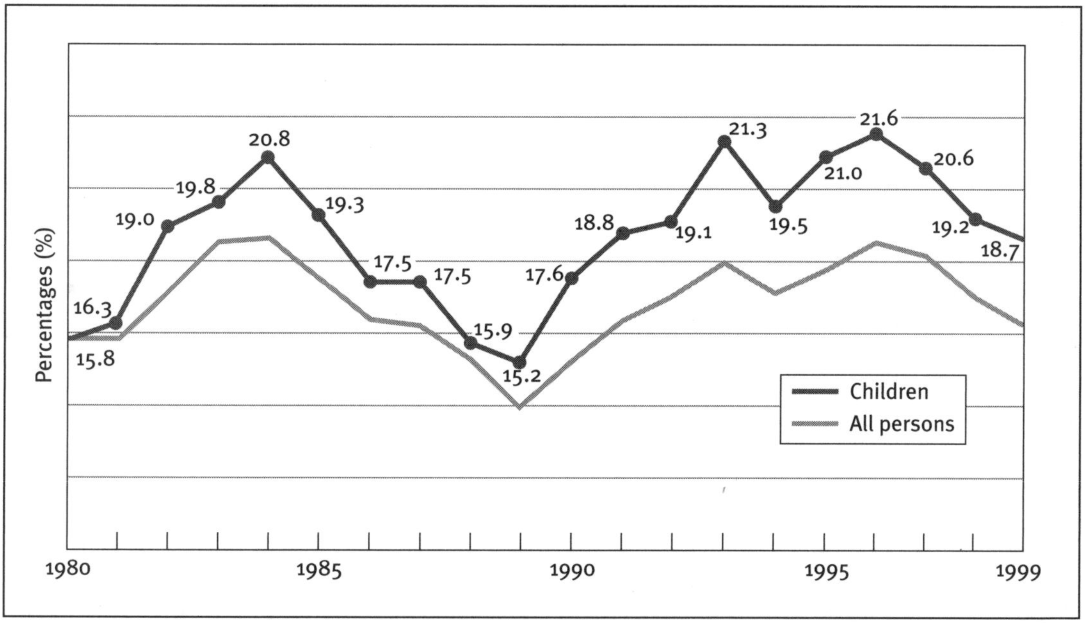

SOURCE: National Council of Welfare (2002), data available at <www.ncwcnbes.net/htmdocument/reportpovertypro99/>.

Adolescence is a period of many changes, with outcomes for physical health, social and emotional well-being, and school attendance and performance. Risks of suicide, drug use, drinking and driving, violence in school, homicide, pregnancy, single parenthood, sexually transmitted diseases, crime, and running away all emerge at this time (Males, 1992). Tobacco use, unhealthy dietary behaviours, physical inactivity, carrying a weapon, and other risk-taking activities that begin in adolescence can have consequences immediately or decades later. Roughly three-quarters of all deaths among persons aged 10 to 24 result from only four causes: motor vehicle crashes, other unintentional injuries, homicide, and suicide (Kann et al., 2000).

Like younger children, adolescents benefit from a continued attachment to their parents. Adolescents who are closely connected to their parents enjoy the greatest emotional well-being

(Svetaz, Ireland, and Blum, 2000). Under these conditions, parental monitoring, communication, and attitude all influence adolescent behaviour significantly, and predict adolescent behaviour much better than family-structure variables (such as the number of parents in the household). Parental thinking shapes adolescents' educational aspirations, plans, and activities—even, their tendency to engage in risky sexual behaviour (Miller, Forehand, and Kotchick, 1999).

Teen pregnancy poses problems for the adolescent and her family, among others. The pregnancy, unless aborted, may mean the young woman will drop out of school, have to work early, abandon her parental family, get married, go on welfare, and generally have children without experiencing her own youth. This is all to be avoided if possible. Yet adolescents' access to contraception and abortion services continues to spark debate in some parts of the world, including the United States. Innovative programs are needed to address issues such as poverty and access to health care in the management and prevention of adolescent pregnancies (Carter et al., 1994).

Much of the current concern about teen pregnancy is due to teenage pregnancies' representing other worrisome changes in society—changes to do with sexual permissiveness, family responsibility, parental authority, and economic dependency, and more. Perceptions and stereotypes about the 'kinds of people' who become teenage mothers also raise anxieties. In solving the teen pregnancy problem, we need to separate the real problems and their solutions—for example, sex education and available contraception—from the more confused undercurrent of concern (Luker, 1996).

Divorce

At the beginning of the twentieth century, divorce was rare in Canada. In 1900, a mere 11 divorces were registered (Snell, 1983, cited in Eichler, 1997: 10). People widely disapproved of divorce, as expressed both in religion and popular opinion and in the law that restricted it. Until 1968, adultery was the only ground for divorce. The introduction of the Divorce Act in 1968 brought about a massive change in family behaviours. This law allowed judges to grant divorces on the grounds of 'marriage breakdown' after a couple had been separated for at least three years. Between 1968 and 1970, the number of divorces nearly doubled (Oderkirk, 1994). An amendment to the Divorce Act in 1986 reduced the minimum period of separation to one year.

In 1968, before the reforms, a marriage that ultimately ended in divorce lasted an average of 15 years. The liberalization of divorce laws speeded up the process. At the beginning of the twenty-first century, the figure was 12.7 years. Based on 1996 divorce rates, we expect 37 per cent of current Canadian marriages to end in divorce. Canadian divorce rates are higher than one finds in other Western nations: 2.6 divorces

per 1,000 people, compared, for example, with 2.2 in Sweden and 2.0 in Germany, based on 1996 data (Ambert, 2002). Canada's divorce rate also surpasses those of Australia and the Netherlands (Statistics Canada, 1994). However, the American divorce rate still outdoes that of Canada. In 1996, there were 4.3 divorces per 1,000 people in the United States—nearly twice Canada's rate.

Divorces affect men and women differently because of gender inequalities in the wider society. Economically, divorce affects women much more negatively than men. A formal separation lowers women's standards of living by 73 per cent on average, but raises men's by 42 per cent (Mahoney, 1995: 18). Fully 40 per cent of ex-wives lose half their family income following the separation, compared to less than 17 per cent of ex-husbands (Arendell, 1995: 38). The fact that custody of children is usually granted to mothers compounds the economic burden on women: not only is income reduced compared to before the divorce, but that smaller income must go toward caring for dependants as well.

Taking on the role of primary caregiver also consumes a lot of time. Lone working mothers often report severe time stress and a feeling of being overwhelmed by responsibilities. The combination of work, child rearing, and household maintenance leaves little time to develop a social life. The alternative, giving up custody to the father, is usually unacceptable to the mother because she loves and wishes to be close to her children. As a lesser consideration, she would face the disapproving eye of a patriarchal society if she gave up custody.

Following a separation or divorce, husbands are usually better off financially than are wives, because they were the dominant income earners during the marriage and they continue to be bigger earners after the divorce. Although their ex-wives' incomes are no longer available to them, the decrease in expenses partially offsets this loss. As well, men tend to experience more freedom following a divorce, since children of a marriage usually end up living with the mother. Thus, men have more opportunities to work, travel, return to school, and go on dates.

The negative impact of divorce on children has also been well documented. Much of the effect of divorce on children can be predicted by conditions that existed well before the separation occurred, and 'at least as much attention needs to be paid to the processes that occur in troubled, intact families as to the trauma that children suffer after their parents separate' (Cherlin, Chase-Lansdale, and McRae, 1991: 1388). Family and personal distress, whether caused by conflict, by poverty, or by unemployment, leads to less effective parenting—a complex notion that involves insufficient surveillance, lack of control over the child's behaviour, lack of warmth and support, inconsistency, and displays of aggression or hostility by parents or older siblings.

Depression is common among children of divorce, as are declines in academic performance, higher rates of emotional problems, and increased probability of anxious or anti-social behaviour (Roizblatt et al., 1997). These problems can continue into adulthood. Paul Amato and Bruce Keith (1991), for instance, report that adult children of divorced parents register poorer psychological well-being (in the form of depression and low self-reported life satisfaction); lower educational attainment, income, and occupational prestige; an increased risk of undergoing a divorce themselves; and poorer physical health.

The debate over divorce and children's well-being has been particularly fierce. Extreme positions—on the one side, that divorce does enormous harm, and on the other side, that it does no harm whatsoever—have not given a clear picture of the consequences of growing up in a single-parent family or stepfamily (Cherlin, 1999). In general, the results are mixed.

Lone Parenthood

Single-parent families, along with young parents, are at the highest risks of poverty and other disadvantage. Having said that, many women—and possibly men—are consciously deciding to parent alone and may be doing an excellent job.

Of Canadian marriages that dissolved in 1995, child custody was a concern in approximately 70 per cent of cases. In more than two out of three of these cases, judges granted mothers sole custody of their children (Vanier Institute, 2000). These women, in their transition from marriage to post-divorce, mainly joined the ranks of the Canadian lone parent. Of the 1.1 million single parents enumerated in 1996, 58 per cent were separated or divorced, 22 per cent were single or never-married, and 20 per cent were widowed. The vast majority, 83 per cent, were women (Vanier Institute, 2000: 70; see Figure 7.3). This gender difference is significant because female-headed lone-parent families are more likely to suffer from lower incomes—indeed, poverty—than are male-headed lone-parent families. In 1998, lone-parent families headed by women made up the largest fraction of all low-income families. Female-headed families were more than twice as likely as male-headed families to be living in poverty (42.0 per cent versus 17.5 per cent) (Glossop and Mirabelli, 2002).

The number of Canadian lone-parent families has increased dramatically since the 1970s—almost 250 per cent between 1971 and 1996, compared with an overall increase of only 55 per cent in the total number of Canadian families (Vanier Institute, 2000: 70). These rates mark a return to proportions seen in the early decades of the twentieth century. In 1931, for example, 13.6 per cent of Canadian families were headed by one parent, compared with a very similar 15 per cent in 1996 (Vanier Institute, 2000: 70). However, the reasons for lone parenthood have changed. Whereas in the first half of the twentieth century most single-parent households were a result of the death of a spouse, in the second half of the century they were mainly the result of separation, divorce, or non-marriage (Oderkirk and Lochhead, 1992).

FIGURE 7.3
Lone-Parent Families by Sex of Parent, Canada, 1986, 1991, and 2001 (Number of Families)

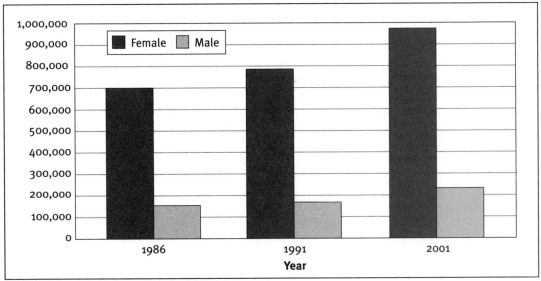

SOURCE: Data derived from Statistics Canada, *Census Families Time Series, 1931–2001*, available at <www.statcan.ca/english/census12/01/products/analytic/companion/fan/family.cfm>, accessed 9 May 2003.

Caring for the Elderly

Canada's population is aging. This results from a combination of lowered fertility and general increases in life expectancy for both men and women. In 2000, 12.5 per cent of the Canadian population was 65 years of age or older (Bélanger et al., 2001: 9). With continued declines in fertility, this proportion will continue rising. This trend can be seen in all Western societies, especially those in Europe.

With the greying of the population, concerns have increased about the costs of caring for an aging population (McDaniel, 1994). In the last few decades, governments have made an effort to move elder care outside institutional settings, making it increasingly the responsibility of informal caregivers, most frequently female family members (McDaniel, 1996). Health care services that were previously offered in institutional settings are now being performed in community health centres, day clinics, and people's own homes. This has created a difficult situation for elderly people, especially in rural Canada. Alongside limited formal health care supports in these areas, depopulation, aging communities, smaller family sizes, limited community resources, and volunteer burnout have resulted in fewer informal community supports (Blakley, 1999).

This development, in turn, has led to widespread unease that the middle-aged children of elderly parents will be 'squeezed' or 'sandwiched' by the multiple roles and obligations associated with dependent children, elderly parents, and work obligations (Martin-Matthews, 2000). Women show greater engagement with caregiving and more willingness to travel to provide assistance, even to the point of relocating residentially themselves to improve caregiving (Hallman and

The structural-functional perspective views the family as a key social institution, a microcosm of society. In this view, the division of labour is essential to a family's success. (Jean-Paul Lemieux, *Les beaux jours*. Photo: Patrick Altman)

Joseph, 1999). Living nearby and being without siblings may force men into being more involved in the care of aged parents (Campbell and Martin-Matthews, 2000a, 2000b).

Elder care can drastically affect the availability of personal time for other family relationships, as well as for work and leisure. Research has shown that so far, this problem is not typical for the vast majority of middle-aged Canadians. Few provide frequent help to their elderly parents (Rosenthal et al., 1996). In fact, until parents reach the age of 75, the flow of support favours the children: they receive more help from parents than they give to them (Spitze and Logan, 1992). Using data from Canada, the United States, the United Kingdom, West Germany, and Japan, Harald Kunemund and Martin Rein (1999) found that the giving of services by older people to their adult children

increases the probability that they will receive help from them. In this way, generous welfare systems that give resources to elderly people help to increase rather than to undermine family solidarity.

The return of grown children to their parental home, usually for financial reasons, is a particularly vivid example of the generational transfer of wealth from older to younger adults. Canadian young adults are much more likely to return to the parental home if their mother tongue is English. Other factors influencing a return to home include the father's education, the number of siblings, gender, age at home-leaving, and the initial reason for home-leaving (Mitchell, Wister, and Gee, 2000). Parental satisfaction with the arrangement is greater when children reciprocate exchanges of support, are more autonomous, and are closer to the completion of adult roles (Mitchell, 1998). Normatively, adulthood involves completing one's education, finding a job that pays an income, mating with a partner, establishing a separate household, and (sometimes) producing children. Completion of adult roles would ideally involve these accomplishment.

The majority of Canadian seniors continue to live on their own well into advanced age, and most of the care they receive comes not from their children, but from other members of the same generation, usually a spouse (Martin-Matthews, 2000). Friends and neighbours may, however, provide essential help when seniors live alone (Martel and Legare, 2000).

Poverty

Poverty affects family lives through a concentration and accumulation of disadvantages, from childhood on. It starts by creating stress and danger in the child's environment. This directly harms a child's health and school readiness. Poverty also harms the child indirectly by stressing his or her parents and by its association with worse parenting, which also harms the child. The increased concentration of poverty in urban neighbourhoods has been associated with a variety of other disadvantages, such as teenage pregnancy, unemployment, and crime (Wilson and Hernnstein, 1987).

Children in poverty are more likely to report or to be reported to have higher than average rates of depression, anxiety, and anti-social behaviour. The negative effects of poverty are somewhat less for African Americans, Native Americans, and Hispanics because of protective factors such as perceived social support, deep spirituality, extended families, and maternal coping strategies (Samaan, 2000).

Sometimes poverty can combine with other types of disadvantage, such as racism and sexism, that result in exclusion and discrimination. Exclusion and segregation of the disadvantaged can intensify the problems associated with individual poverty and discrimination (Jargowsky, 1998). Often, poverty is associated with a number of other conditions that also work against the well-being of the family and its members—conditions such as immigrant status, parental absence, the number of siblings in the home, parental literacy and educational attainment, parental labour-force participation, and overcrowded housing conditions (Hernandez, 1998). Though immigrants may work hard and earn well, they may still have high poverty rates as a group (Flores, 1999).

The number of poor children has grown in the last decade. Reasons for this include teenage pregnancy, parents' low educational achievement, and domestic violence (Shirk, Bennett, and Aber, 1999). Lack of good-quality, affordable child care continues to be a central problem facing poor parents—especially single parents—who want to seek work. Poverty increases the number of child care constraints (availability, quality, affordability, reliability, convenience) for poor minority women in particular (Press, 2000).

Health Consequences of Family Life

Generally, research shows that marriage adds to people's health and happiness, especially that of men and especially when contrasted with divorce and separation. In fact, marriage is probably the single best way humans have devised to prevent alcoholism, drug abuse, risky driving, suicide, and other lifestyles associated with early death. In these respects, marriage is not necessarily better than cohabitation. What matters is the stability and quality of the relationship, not its legal status. However, some common aspects of family life are not very healthy at all.

Domestic Violence

Domestic and intimate-partner abuse, child and adolescent physical and sexual abuse, and elder abuse constitute family violence. Such violence is responsible for a significant portion of intentional injury and, as such, is a major health problem (Kaplan, 2000).

Elder Abuse

Elder abuse, which we will discuss in the next chapter, includes physical injury, neglect, financial abuse, abandonment, and psychological traumatization. Spouses and children are frequent abusers, although most abusers of the elderly are institutional caregivers. Elder abuse in families has apparently increased in recent years, for a variety of reasons. These reasons include the increasing proportion of older adults in the total population, the related increase in chronic disabling diseases, and the increasing involvement of families in caregiving with elders (Schiamberg and Gans, 2000). The elderly population will continue to grow, and with it the risks of elder abuse.

Child Abuse

Child abuse can take the form of physical or mental harm, sexual abuse, neglect, or maltreatment. Of these, neglect is the most common form of reported child abuse. Children also run the risk of sexual abuse, more likely by a stepfather or a mother's boyfriend than by their biological father. Stepfathers are apparently not hindered by the same culturally imposed incest taboos as biological fathers (Blankenhorn, 1995).

Abused children tend to display anti-social behaviour, aggression, low self-esteem, depression, and poor school performance. In adulthood, self-destructive behaviours often continue to manifest themselves, including depression, low self-esteem, anxiety, and an increased risk of alcohol or drug abuse and suicide. Children who witnessed or were victims of physical abuse have an increased risk of becoming abusers themselves when they enter adulthood (Gelles and Conte, 1991).

Even after controlling for other socio-demographic variables, poverty, substance abuse, and (young) maternal age are strong predictors of substantiated reports of all types of child maltreatment. Young mothers and poor mothers are at particular risk of abusing their children. This suggests that we need a comprehensive approach to the problem of child abuse, one that lessens the economic stress on young mothers while improving their parenting skills (Lee and George, 1999).

Partner Abuse

In a 1999 national survey, Statistics Canada found that 8 per cent of women (approximately 690,000 individuals) and 7 per cent of men (549,000 individuals) reported experiencing at least one incident of violence at the hands of a current or previous partner sometime in the past five years (2000: 5).

Both married and unmarried couples inflict violence on each other. One study found severe violence to be five times more likely among cohabiting couples than among married couples (Yllo and Straus, 1981). Further, Douglas Brownridge and Shiva Halli (2001) showed that Canadian women who cohabit, those who cohabited with someone other than their husband before getting married, and those who did not cohabit before

marriage are three distinct groups. Women in these marital-status groups differ in the prevalence of their victimization by violent partners. Research confirms that cohabitors are still more likely than spouses to engage in violent relationships (Jackson, 1996). Other variables likely to distinguish partners who batter their wives are presence of alcohol abuse, low education, frequent arguments with the spouse, and frequent drug use. Abusing husbands typically also have a (childhood) background of family violence and marital arguments (Coleman, Weinman, and Bartholomew, 1980).

Many women have trouble leaving an abusive relationship, or even seeking help when they are in the abusive relationship. As women, they typically earn less than their husbands, so leaving is often not financially viable for them. Should they divorce, they are often left with the care of the children and a lack of financial child support from the children's father. Thus, the codependency of abused people is as often a financial problem as it is a psychological or emotional one.

Often, psychologically and physically abusive men fear the loss of their partner, whom they consider their sexual and emotional property. Men are more likely to batter—or kill—to protect what they think of as their sexual property, whereas women are likely to batter or kill only to protect themselves. Men are likely to kill themselves after killing their 'property'. Women kill their partners because the partner has battered them systematically and they fear being battered even more. Compared with non-battered women, battered women use more violence, receive lower levels of social support, and experience higher levels of self-blame. Battered women, therefore, are more likely to use violence against their spouse when they feel are receiving little social support, and even if they feel they are to blame for the conflict (Barnett, Martinez, and Keyson, 1996).

Same-sex relationships are also subject to partner abuse. Lesbians and transsexual people are not always comfortable in women's shelters, as they may experience homophobia from heterosexual women. Shelter clients, for their part, having escaped from abusive relationships with a man, may not feel safe being with a transsexual person. As well, lesbians have little safety from their partners in a women's shelter that is open to women. Gay men have no shelters they can use other than homeless shelters, which offer little security from abusive partners and no long-term housing.

Divorce and Remarriage

Other health problems, particularly those that are psychological in nature, are experienced by divorced adults and children of divorce. As we have said, divorce increases the risk of poverty for many women, resulting in health risks linked to poor nutrition, unsanitary living conditions, and lack of access to health care services. Far more common are emotional problems resulting from divorce. Usually, these are short-term difficulties arising from the stressful changeover in moving to a new living arrangement. Rates of psychiatric care, suicide rates, accident rates, and postmarital stress are all higher among divorced men than women, although women are more likely than men to report emotional problems such as depression (Ambert, 1982; Gove, 1970).

Some observers have added that research on emotional problems among divorced men and women should be treated with some caution because divorced individuals who appear to experience emotional problems after the divorce may have already had emotional problems before the divorce. These problems may have led to divorce, rather than the other way around (Rushing, 1979).

Divorce is an emotionally draining and highly stressful experience. This is not surprising because divorce results in the loss of a partner, possible decrease in contact with children, lower financial standing, single parenthood, and so on. Children of divorced parents have, for instance, many more substance-using friends and fewer coping and social skills than children whose

parents are married (Neher and Short, 1998). Some research suggests that parental divorce increases the risk of poor mental health in adulthood (Cherlin, Chase-Lansdale, and McRae, 1998). Children face other difficulties as well. One study, for example, found that children who grow up without a male presence are at a higher risk of dropping out of school, experimenting with drugs and alcohol, being unemployed as teenagers and adults, and suffering mental problems (Shapiro and Schrof, 1995).

One controversial issue concerns the circumstances under which it is in the child's best interest for parents to separate rather than stay together. An investigation by Jaap Dronkers examined whether serious conflicts between non-divorced parents have a stronger negative effect on the well-being of their children (in terms of use of drugs, illness, violence and crime, mental health, etc.) than living in a single-mother family caused by divorce (1996).

Three of Dronkers's findings are relevant to the current discussion. First, the well-being of children living in single-mother families was higher than that of children living in two-parent homes with a high level of parental conflict. Second, the well-being of children living in single-mother families with a low level of parental conflict and with a high degree of contact with the non-residential father was still lower than that of students living in two-parent families with an equally low level of parent conflict. Finally, the degree of parental conflict after divorce was more important for the well-being of the children than was contact with the departed father. These results suggest that, as measured by well-being outcomes, divorce may or may not be the best option for children depending on the level of parental conflict in the marriage. Conflict is bad for children—worse than divorce, it seems (Dronkers, 1996).

Researchers have also linked health consequences to single parenthood for both mothers and their children. Teenage women and unmarried women are less likely to seek prenatal care and more likely than older women and married women to smoke, drink alcohol, and take drugs. Often, negative health effects are caused by the poverty that many teenage mothers find themselves living in. As well, the need for two incomes among married households has created a shortage of time, which may lead indirectly to further health problems for families. Sylvia Hewlett links the time crunch experienced by today's working parents with a lack of child supervision and, as a result, higher rates of developmental impairment; young people today are more likely to 'underperform at school, commit suicide, need psychiatric help, suffer a severe eating disorder, bear a child out of wedlock, take drugs, be a victim of a violent crime' (1991: 81).

Work as a Family Health Problem

As we have noted, paid work is a key source of stress. Questionnaire data on nearly 80,000 employees from 250 work sites in the United States reveal that the greatest sources of stress in people's lives are job, finances, and family (Jacobson et al., 1996). Once they become parents, men and women approach the workplace in different ways. Fathers are more likely to work extended hours when possible. Mothers work shorter hours and require more flexibility in their working arrangements. Mothers working full-time are more likely to ask for and receive parental leave from their employers than are mothers working part-time or fathers.

When work increases the stress on a husband, it increases the likelihood of a hostile marital relationship and interactions. In that way, stress reduces the quality of both marital and family functioning (Larson, Wilson, and Beley, 1994). As work increasingly interferes with family life, both emotional and practical supports within the family deteriorate.

With rising stress and complexity, many families fear further government cuts to the health care system—even, the privatization of medical services. Some fear that if private

companies take over essential services and create a two-tiered health care system, middle- and working-class families will not be able to afford the treatment available to more affluent households. Others merely fear increased complexity in their lives.

Solutions

Work-Family Solutions

Many families suffer from the conflict between work life and family life. Currently, efforts are being made to solve this problem, with variable success. Arlie Hochschild (1997) finds, however, that even within family-friendly companies that offer their workers various programs designed to increase the time available to spend with family, few employees took advantage of the programs.

Even though many workers state a desire to cut back on their 'workaholism' and spend more time with spouses and children, 'programs that allowed parents to work undistracted by family concerns were endlessly in demand, while policies offering shorter hours that allowed workers more free or family time languished. . . . Only flextime, which rearranged but did not cut back on hours of work, had any significant impact on the workplace' (Hochschild, 1997: 25–6).

Three explanations have been offered to account for these worker preferences. One is that workers cannot afford to cut back on work hours, despite their wishes to the contrary. This is most evidently true among lower-tier workers whose combined household incomes bar either partner from scaling back in order to meet family needs. However, this theory does not explain why top-level executives, whose salaries are large enough to permit the adoption of a shorter work-week, also choose against such policies as job sharing and part-time work.

A second explanation is that workers choose not to use family-friendly programs because they are afraid of being laid off. Although company policies often encourage employees to spend more time with their families, workers doubt the sincerity of such offers, particularly since the policies are devised by top-level executives concerned with public relations and company image and are carried out by practical-minded middle managers and supervisors concerned with meeting quotas, budgets, and deadlines. This argument implies that family-friendly programs are often mere ornaments designed to soothe external critics but not to solve workers' problems.

A third explanation is that despite what workers say about wanting to spend more time with their families, they find that the time spent at work is often more pleasant and rewarding than time spent at home. In her three-year study of a top US company, Hochschild (1997) found that the duties of home life—caring for the children, sharing household duties, trying to maintain a sense of intimacy and love with one's spouse, and so on—were often highly stressful. As a result, one's family becomes in many ways like work—in fact, a second shift.

For these reasons, work-based solutions to the family-work issue are helpful steps in the right direction, but they must be fine-tuned, made more widely available, and accepted more widely by workers and management. At the same time, families need to seek new answers through the reorganization of domestic work.

Caregiving is a fundamentally *social* activity, and increasingly, it is a family activity. Social support networks are critically important for caregivers and care recipients alike. Clear and continuing communication between informal and formal caregivers, on the one hand, and health care and social service providers, on the other, is a necessity. Family and community organization is central to good caregiving.

Rosalie Kane and colleagues (1999) followed the experiences of family caregivers of older people hospitalized for stroke or hip fracture in three US cities. The researchers studied the families for one year after the hospitalization, tracking the demands that providing care placed on the families and how families responded to those demands. They found that the primary caregiver—often aged 65 or older—regularly spent 20 hours or more every week caring for their relative. What surprised the researchers was the tremendous variety in *how* the families reorganized to meet these new demands.

Perhaps the most striking information to come from this study was that the difficulties that caregivers reported facing were related less to specific task performances than they were to dealing with feelings, managing time, and adjusting to changing relationships and life plans. This tells us that understanding how caregiving affects a family and its organization might significantly contribute to efforts to help families deal with the many problems associated with long-term care. Once we understand how some families effectively reorganize to provide care, it will become possible to assist other families trying to do the same.

Researchers must seek information that may lead to solutions to problems of family organization and restructuring around home care obligations. As well, researchers must determine how much and what kinds of public support—services and funding—families need in order to provide their members with desirable levels of health care, and they must communicate this information to relevant policy makers.

Individual Solutions

Families can be helpful in overcoming life's adversities. To make the home more supportive and less stressful, husbands and male common-law partners can increase their presence in the domestic area. They can accept that just earning an income is no longer a sufficient contribution to their family's well-being. (See Figure 7.4.) A complete and equal contribution will also have to include providing assistance in raising the children, performing household chores, and supporting their wives' personal ambitions.

Also, as Reginald Bibby and Donald Posterski say, we need a 'new father movement':

FIGURE 7.4
Average Minutes per Day Spent by Parents on Child Care

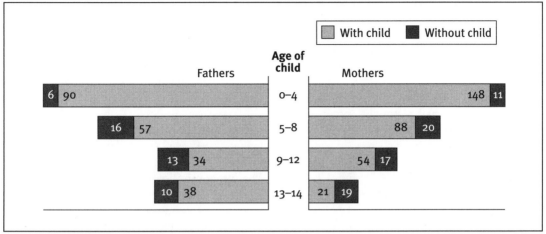

SOURCE: Cynthia Silver, 'Being There: The Time Dual-Earner Couples Spend with Their Children', *Canadian Social Trends*, 26 (2000), 28; available at <www.statcan.ca/english/indepth/11-008/feature/star2000057000s2a04.pdf>, accessed 25 January 2003.

Concerned fathers can begin rocking a few boats in the workplace. Employers need to hear more often an employee say that he can't work the weekend or stay late because he has a date with his daughter. A father needs to be able to say good night to colleagues without apology when his son is waiting to go to the hockey game. (1992: 210)

When divorce is necessary, we must be careful not to exaggerate the extent or permanence of harm done. The stresses include economic hardship, parental adjustment, interpersonal conflict, and parental loss. Developing resources and protections can reduce the negative effect of these stresses. Higher levels of coping resources support a greater optimism about the future, fewer financial problems, more confidence in parenting ability, and a more satisfactory relationship with the former spouse (O'Leary, Franzoni, and Brack, 1996).

Factors that reduce the adverse effect of divorce on children include a strong and clear sense that both parents still love them, an understanding that they are not to blame for the divorce, and regular visits with the non-custodial parent. Children of divorce may need some help coming to terms with irrational beliefs about divorce and with feelings of sadness, guilt, and anxiety (Skitka and Frazier, 1995). Involved and caring parents can help a child adjust to divorce. Parental distance, on the other hand, is likely to produce maladjustment. Parental conflict, as we have said so often, has a bad effect in both intact and divorced families.

Though divorce may sometimes cause problems, it also often solves problems. It may even bring benefits. People whose parents divorced during their adolescent years display a much higher level of moral development than those whose parents did not divorce (Kogos and Snarey, 1995). Underlying the development of moral judgment is an increased perspective-taking, necessary for children of divorce who witness differences in opinions between their parents.

Violence is a major factor causing women to leave marriages. Often, violence continues throughout the separation and divorce process, affecting negotiations for assets and custody (Kurz, 1995). Protective measures need to be put in place by government to ensure that this isn't the case. Individuals who are experiencing violence need to come forward and seek help. They may have to leave the home and relationship to do so.

Programs that attempt to address abuse directly—such as civil restraining orders, treatment programs for batterers, and policies requiring mandatory arrest and no dropped charges—are generally not effective in solving the problem of domestic violence (Davis and Smith, 1995). By contrast, treatments aimed at reducing alcohol and drug abuse may make a long-term difference to the likelihood of future violence (Brannen and Rubin, 1996; O'Farrell and Murphy, 1995).

In the end, however, there will be no major decline in violence within families until societies reduce the stresses on family members. If we want to reduce family stresses, we must create a society that is family-friendly, with increased social support and practical assistance to working parents with small children, to caregivers, and others. Research shows us that the health and social service professions are, sadly, far behind the times. For those that work in areas in which they are likely to come into contact with people who are stressed or violent or who are the victims of stress and violence, better training is the key to progress.

Societies must also dismantle the cultural justifications for domestic violence and deprive those who are violent of opportunities to hide or repeat their behaviour. Ending domestic violence must be a societal project in which we all participate. The time for acting surprised by violence is over. Violence has become all too common, and all too costly to society, its families, and their family members.

Concluding Remarks

The modern family is the product of a post-industrial economy, in which economic production is not part of the household. The typical conception of what constitutes a family is an ideological notion. This ideology often differs from real patterns of family life that occur in post-industrial society.

There can be little doubt that people have turned their backs on the traditional, idealized family of 50 years ago. Today, people are getting married later in life and having fewer children. The proportion of childless couples has also increased. Closely related to this trend has been an increase in the number of couples who cohabit. The divorce rate has increased dramatically in the last few decades. Yet people continue to come together in long-term relationships and, for the most part, struggle to make them survive.

Despite the fact that more women have been entering the workforce, women still tend to do more housework than men in dual-paycheque households. This so-called double shift has harmful health consequences, and places stress on the relationships between spouses and between parents and children.

As we have seen, families often have to deal with serious problems. The negative consequences of divorce, both emotional and financial, tend to be greatest for women and children. One-seventh of all Canadian families are single-parent households. A woman heads about 90 per cent of these single-parent families. These single-parent families are more prone to financial and emotional strain. However, most families, single-parent or not, are experiencing financial and emotional strain these days. Family violence is more common than many people recognize. Although women and men are just as likely to participate in violence, women are the ones hurt most often.

Questions for Critical Thought

1. It is an unfortunate fact that teenage mothers constitute the majority of single parents. Not only are they young and alone in struggling to support their child, they also lack the earning power of men and are at much greater risk of impoverishment than single fathers. The Internet provides a wealth of information on teenage pregnancy, offering social support resources and statistics, but more important, the Internet offers personal testimonies. Isolate one such case and chronicle what it must be like for that specific teenager to be a single mother. What type of issues does she deal with on a daily basis? Who is there for support? What is the role of the father in raising the child? Imagine a day in the life of a teenage parent.

2. A myth of suburbia has permeated society's collective consciousness since the 1950s. A nostalgic desire for block parties, green grass, Cadillacs, and TV dinners shaped the ideology of the perfect nuclear family for decades. However, a lot has changed with respect to the portrayal of the family since the *Leave It to Beaver* era. Examine a TV show like *The Simpsons* and ask yourself if this is an accurate portrayal of the family in the twenty-first century. If it is, how so? And if not, where is it erroneous? Be detailed in your analysis using specific characters, examining their role within the family. How are familial relationships portrayed?

3. Families around the world were not created equal. There are many cultures that do not fit Westernized notions of who is considered 'family'. Look in anthropological studies and research family structure in different cultures. Who lives in the household? Are the structures matrilineal or patrilineal? Contrast with our own dominant notion of family.

4. Undoubtedly women today are pursuing further education and desiring occupational careers and economic independence. However, women still want to raise families and desire a major role in child rearing. To some, the daycare that would be necessary for both parents to be at work all day is not an option. Thus, there is a conflict for women: part of them wants to raise a family, yet another part wants to pursue a full-time career where, all too often, starting a family may be seen as a disadvantage to the company. How do we reconcile this conflict? Should the government further develop maternity-leave programs? Or is this just an inevitable conflict of feminism? How has the role of 'supermom' changed with more women in the labour force?

5. Most often, abusive situations are not reported by the victims. Why do you feel they choose to not report such traumatic events? Discuss how statistics might not be as representative as they claim to be. Research a trauma hotline; if possible, contact the hotline and ask what kind of calls they get and how they help victims of domestic, sexual, drug, or alcohol abuse.

Recommended Readings

Lourdes Benería and Shelley Feldman, eds, *Unequal Burden: Economic Crisis, Persistent Poverty, and Women's Work* (Boulder, CO: Westview Press, 1992).

This edited volume draws connections between some of the social problems we have addresses within the family as it relates to the international economy. Most interesting among the articles is one regarding the Mexican debt crisis, in which Benería relates the debt crisis to familial adaptations through increased women's work and a change in the actual social problems that develop within family.

Ruth Schwartz Cowan, *More Work for Mother: The Ironies of Household Technology from the Open Hearth to the Microwave* (New York: Basic Books, 1983).

Cowan's work addresses the notion that as technology increases we lighten the burden of labour on women in particular. Although this simplistic notion cannot be utterly refuted, Cowan identifies the way that technological change, instead of lightening women's work in the home, served to alter the conditions in which it was performed, creating a 'women's sphere' and ultimately serving the profits of the commodity producers.

Bette J. Dickerson, ed., *African American Single Mothers: Understanding Their Lives and Families* (Thousand Oaks, CA: Sage, 1995).

This volume focuses on female history, identity, and empowerment in relation to the lives and families of women of colour as described in their own voices. The collection offers a historical review of research on female-headed African American families.

Rebecca Dobash and Russell Dobash, *Violence Against Wives: A Case Against the Patriarchy* (New York: Free Press, 1979).

Particularly interesting among the authors' work here is an article on becoming a wife that explains the gradual isolation of battered women and the initial connection between possessiveness and love in a dating relationship. This helps explain the difficulty we have in aiding battered women and the confusion outsiders feel, continually asking, 'Why doesn't she just leave?'

Jennifer Glass, 'Envisioning the Integration of Family and Work: Toward a Kinder, Gentler Workplace', *Contemporary Sociology*, 29, no. 1 (2000): 129–45.

The family, as we have identified, is a unit of economic cooperation, and its ability to amass and distribute resources is addressed in this article. Glass suggests some radical and some simple policy changes that would address these issues.

Meg Luxton, *More Than a Labour of Love: Three Generations of Women's Work in the Home* (Toronto: Women's Press, 1980).

Luxton's work shows some of the changes in Canadian rural society in the last 100 years, using interviews made in Flin Flon, Manitoba. She includes insightful chapters regarding women's feelings toward the sexual exchange in their marriage as well as a chapter on housework. The technological changes associated with these two areas of women's family life cause fewer attitudinal changes than one might expect.

Marion Lynn, ed., *Voices: Essays on Canadian Families* (Toronto: Nelson Canada, 1996).

This volume offers contemporary Canadian families an analytical mirror in which to view themselves. The articles emphasize the meaning of trends in the Canadian family and the attitudes that accompany these changes.

Joy Parr, ed., *Childhood and Family in Canadian History* (Toronto: McClelland and Stewart, 1982).

This older edited volume shows the deep roots of some of the trends we have discussed in this chapter. The point is made explicitly with evidence that the ideal 1950s family modal was a rooted in its time, not in moral authority.

Arlene S. Skolnick and Jerome H. Skolnick, eds, *Family in Transition*, 10th edn. (New York: Longman, 1999).

This edited volume includes a fascinating view on the ideal egalitarian marriage in Pepper Schwartz's article. Schwartz uses a snowball sample and discovers the major stumbling blocks in achieving what she deems to constitute an egalitarian marriage.

Kath Weston, *Families We Choose: Lesbians, Gays, Kinship* (New York: Columbia University Press, 1991).

Looking at the contemporary experiences of gays and lesbians in the United States, Weston develops a new and looser concept of the family, which she sees exemplified in the gays and lesbians she interviews.

Recommended Web Sites

National Clearinghouse on Family Violence
www.hc-sc.gc.ca/hppb/familyviolence

The National Clearinghouse on Family Violence (NCFV) is a resource centre for those seeking information about violence within the family. It provides a number of publications that deal with violence against children, women, and older adults. The NCFV Web site also allows visitors to search its online library for both books and video aids on family violence.

Family Service Canada
www.familyservicecanada.org

Founded in 1982, Family Service Canada is a not-for-profit national voluntary organization representing the concerns of families and family service agencies across Canada. It provides a wide range of services and programs to individuals and families, designed to assist and strengthen people in their relationships, both in critical times and in day-to-day living.

Childcare Resource and Research Unit
www.childcarecanada.org

The Childcare Resource and Research Unit seeks to further the idea of publicly funded, not-for-profit early childhood daycare. They provide information on past, current, and future research projects on child care, and also provide links to global governmental policies that have been enacted regarding child care. The CRRU Web site also provides a resource section containing past CRRU publications, print and Web resources, and links relating to the topic of child care.

References

Amato, Paul R., and Bruce Keith. 1991. 'Parental Divorce and Adult Well-Being: A Meta-analysis'. *Journal of Marriage and the Family*, 53: 43–58.

Ambert, Anne-Marie. 1982. 'Differences in Children's Behavior Towards Custodial Mothers and Custodial Fathers'. *Journal of Marriage and the Family*, 44: 73–86.

———. 2002. *Divorce: Facts, Causes, and Consequences*. Rev. edn. Ottawa: Vanier Institute of the Family. Available at <www.vifamily.ca/cft/divorce/divorcer. htm>, accessed 24 March 2003.

Arendell, Terry. 1995. *Fathers and Divorce*. Thousand Oaks, CA: Sage.

Ariès, Philippe. 1958. *Centuries of Childhood: A Social History of Family Life*. Translated by Robert Baldick. New York: Vintage Books.

Arnup, Katherine. 1999. 'Out in This World: The Social and Legal Context of Gay and Lesbian Families'. *Journal of Gay and Lesbian Social Services*, 10, no. 1: 1–25.

Barnett, Ola W., Tomas E. Martinez, and Mae Keyson. 1996. 'The Relationship Between Violence, Social Support, and Self-Blame in Battered Women'. *Journal of Interpersonal Violence*, 11: 221–33.

Bélanger, Alain, Yves Carrière, and Stéphane Gilbert. 2001. *Report on the Demographic Situation in Canada 2000*. (Cat. no. 91-209-XPE). Ottawa: Statistics Canada.

Berger, Peter, and Hansfried Kellner. 1964. 'Marriage and the Construction of Reality'. *Diogenes*, 46: 1–32.

Bernard, Jessie. 1982. *The Future of Marriage*. New Haven, CT: Yale University Press.

Bibby, Reginald W., and Donald C. Posterski. 1992. *Teen Trends: A Nation in Motion*. Toronto: Stoddart.

Blakley, Bonnie M. 1999. 'The Impact of Health Care Reforms on Elderly Caregivers in Rural Canada'. Paper presented at the conference of the Society for the Study of Social Problems.

Blankenhorn, David. 1995. *Fatherless America: Confronting Our Most Urgent Social Problem*. New York: Basic Books.

Brannen, Stephen J., and Allen Rubin. 1996. 'Comparing the Effectiveness of Gender-Specific and Couples Groups in a Court-Mandated Spouse Abuse Treatment Program'. *Research on Social Work Practice*, 6: 405–24.

Brownridge, Douglas A., and Shiva S. Halli. 2001. 'Marital Status as Differentiating Factor in Canadian Women's Coping with Partner Violence'. *Journal of Comparative Family Studies*, 32: 117–25.

Campbell, Lori D., and Anne Martin-Matthews. 2000a. 'Caring Sons: Exploring Men's Involvement in Filial Care'. *Canadian Journal on Aging*, 19: 57–79.

———. 2000b. 'Primary and Proximate: The Importance of Coresidence and Being Primary

Provider of Care for Men's Filial Care Involvement'. *Journal of Family Issues*, 21: 1006–30.

Carter, Debra M., Marianne E. Felice, Jeannie Rosoff, Laurie Schwab Zabin, Peter L. Beilenson, and Andrew L. Dannenberg. 1994. 'When Children Have Children: The Teen Pregnancy Predicament'. *American Journal of Preventive Medicine*, 10, no. 2: 108–13.

Chambers, Deborah. 2000. 'Representations of Familism in the British Popular Media'. *European Journal of Cultural Studies*, 3: 195–214.

Cherlin, Andrew J. 1999. 'Going to Extremes: Children's Well-Being, and Social Science'. *Demography*, 36: 421–8.

Cherlin, Andrew J., P. Lindsay Chase-Lansdale, and Christine McRae. 1998. 'Effects of Parental Divorce on Mental Health Throughout the Life Course'. *American Sociological Review*, 63: 239–49.

Cherlin, Andrew J., Frank F. Furstenberg, Jr, P. Lindsay Chase-Lansdale, Kathleen E. Kiernan, Philip K. Robins, Donna Ruane Morrison, and Julien O. Teitler. 1991. 'Longitudinal Studies of Effects of Divorce on Children in Great Britain and the United States'. *Science*, 252 (7 June): 1386–9.

Coleman, H.H., M.L. Weinman, and P.H. Bartholomew. 1980. 'Factors Affecting Conjugal Violence'. *Journal of Psychology*, 105: 197–202.

Davies, Lorraine, and Donna D. McAlpine. 1998. 'The Significance of Family, Work, and Power Relations for Mothers' Mental Health'. *Canadian Journal of Sociology*, 23: 369–87.

Davis, Robert C., and Barbara Smith. 1995. 'Domestic Violence Reforms: Empty Promises or Fulfilled Expectations?' *Crime and Delinquency*, 41: 541–52.

de Munck, Victor C., and Andrey Korotayev. 1999. 'Sexual Equality and Romantic Love: A Reanalysis of Rosenblatt's Study on the Function of Romantic Love'. *Cross-Cultural Research*, 33: 265–77.

Dronkers, Jaap. 1996. 'The Effects of Parental Conflicts and Divorce on the Average Well-Being of Pupils in Secondary Education'. Paper presented at the annual meeting of the American Sociological Association.

EGALE. 2001. '2001 Census to Recognize Same-Sex Couples'. Press release. Available at <www.islandnet.com/~egale/pressrel/010510-e.htm>, accessed 24 March 2003.

Eichler, Margrit. 1997. *Family Shifts: Families, Policies, and Gender Equality*. Toronto: Oxford University Press.

Espiritu, Yen Le. 2001 ' "We Don't Sleep Around Like White Girls Do": Family, Culture, and Gender in Filipina American Lives'. *Signs*, 26: 415–40.

Flores, Ronald J. Ortiz. 1999. 'The Recently Arrived Foreign-Born in New York State, 1990'. In *New York State in the 21st Century*, edited by Thomas A. Hirschi and Tim B. Heaton, 203–27. Westport, CT: Praeger.

Gavigan, Shelley A.M. 1999. 'Legal Forms, Family Forms, Gendered Norms: What Is a Spouse?' *Canadian Journal of Law and Society / Revue canadienne droit et société*, 14: 127–57.

Gelles, Richard, and Jon R. Conte. 1991. 'Domestic Violence and Sexual Abuse of Children: A Review of Research in the Eighties'. In *Contemporary Families: Looking Forward, Looking Back*, edited by Alan Booth, 327–40. Minneapolis, MO: National Council on Family Relations.

Geurts, Sabine, Christel Rutte, and Maria Peeters. 1999. 'Antecedents and Consequences of Work-Home Interference Among Medical Residents'. *Social Science and Medicine*, 48: 1135–48.

Glossop, Robert, and Alan Mirabelli. 2002. *The Current State of Canadian Family Finances, 2002 Report*. Ottawa: Vanier Institute of the Family. Available at <www.vifamily.ca/PR/releases/state02pr.htm>, accessed 15 March 2003.

Gove, W.R. 1970. 'Sex, Marital Status, and Psychiatric Treatment: A Research Note'. *Social Forces*, 58: 89–93.

Hallman, Bonnie C., and Alun E. Joseph. 1999. 'Getting There: Mapping the Gendered Geography of Caregiving to Elderly Relatives'. *Canadian Journal on Aging*, 18,4: 397–414.

Hernandez, Donald J. 1998. 'The Changing Lives of Immigrant and Nonimmigrant Families in the USA from 1910 to 1990'. Paper presented at the annual meeting of the International Sociological Association.

Hewlett, Sylvia. 1991. *When the Bough Breaks: The Cost of Neglecting Our Children*. New York: Basic Books.

Hochschild, Arlie Russell. 1997. *The Time Bind: When Work Becomes Home and Home Becomes Work*. New York: Henry Holt.

Howard-Hassmann, Rhoda E. 2001. 'Gay Rights and the Right to a Family: Conflicts Between Liberal and Illiberal Belief Systems'. *Human Rights Quarterly*, 23: 73–95.

Immerman, Ronald S., and Wade C. Mackey. 1999. 'The Societal Dilemma of Multiple Sexual Partners: The Costs of the Loss of Pair-Bonding'. *Marriage and Family Review*, 29, no. 1: 3–19.

Jackson, Nicky Ali. 1996. 'Observational Experiences of Intrapersonal Conflict and Teenage Victimization: A Comparative Study Among Spouses and Cohabitors'. *Journal of Family Violence*, 11: 191–203.

Jacobson, Neil S., John M. Guttman, Eric Gortner, Sara Berns, and JoAnn Wu Shortt. 1996. 'Psychological Factors in the Longitudinal Course of Battering: When Do the Couples Split Up? When Does the Abuse Decrease?' *Violence and Victims*, 11: 371–92.

Jargowsky, Paul A. 1998. 'Urban Poverty, Race, and the Inner City: The Bitter Fruit of Thirty Years of Neglect'. In *Locked in the Poorhouse: Cities, Race, and Poverty in the United States*, edited by Fred R. Harris and Lynn A. Curtis, 79–94. Lanham, MD: Rowman and Littlefield.

Kaler, Amy. 2001. '"It's Some Kind of Women's Empowerment": The Ambiguity of the Female Condom as a Marker of Female Empowerment'. *Social Science and Medicine*, 52: 783–96.

Kane, Rosalie A., James Reinardy, Joan D. Penrod, and Shirley Huck. 1999. 'After the Hospitalizatioin Is Over: A Different Perspective on Family Care of Older People'. *Journal of Gerontological Social Work*, 31: 119–41.

Kann, L., S.A. Kinchen, B.I. Williams, J.G. Ross, R. Lowry, J.A. Grunbaum, and L.J. Kolbe. 2000. 'Youth Risk Behavior Surveillance—United States, 1999, State and Local YRBSS Coordinators'. *Journal of School Health*, 70, no. 7: 271–85.

Kaplan, S.J. 2000. 'Family Violence'. *New Directions for Mental Health Services*, 86: 49–62.

Kloep, M. 1999. 'Love Is All You Need? Focusing on Adolescents' Life Concerns from an Ecological Point of View'. *Journal of Adolescence*, 22: 49–63.

Kogos, Jennifer L., and John Snarey. 1995. 'Parental Divorce and the Moral Development of Adolescents'. *Journal of Divorce and Remarriage*, 23: 177–86.

Kunemund, Harald, and Martin Rein. 1999. 'There Is More to Receiving Than Needing: Theoretical Arguments and Empirical Explorations of Crowding In and Crowding Out'. *Ageing and Society*, 19, no. 1: 93–121.

Kurz, Demie. 1995. *For Richer or for Poorer: Mothers Confront Divorce*. New York: Routledge.

Larson, Jeffrey H., Stephan M. Wilson, and Rochelle Beley. 1994. 'The Impact of Job Insecurity on Marital and Family Relations'. *Family Relations*, 43: 138–43.

Lee, Bong Joo, and Robert M. George. 1999. 'Poverty, Early Childbearing, and Child Maltreatment: A Multinomial Analysis'. *Children and Youth Services Review*, 21: 755–80.

Leger Marketing. 2001. 'Canadian Perceptions of Homosexuality'. Available at <http://www.legermarketing.com/english/set.html>, accessed 20 March 2003.

Lehmann, Jennifer M. 1994. *Durkheim and Women*. Lincoln: University of Nebraska Press.

Lindell, Marianne, and Ingegerd Bergbom Engberg. 1999. 'Swedish Women's Partner Relationship and Contraceptive Methods'. *European Journal of Women's Studies*, 6, no. 1: 97–106.

Lloyd, Kim Marie. 2001. *Contextual Influences on Sexual Initiation and Family Formation Throughout the Life Course of Young Latino/Latina Americans*, Unpublished doctoral dissertation, State University of New York–Albany.

Luker, Kristin. 1996. *Dubious Conceptions: The Politics of Teenage Pregnancy*. Cambridge, MA: Harvard University Press, 1996.

McDaniel, Susan A. 1994. 'Health Care Policy in an Aging Canada: Forward to the Past?' Paper presented at the annual meeting of the International Sociological Association.

———. 1996. 'The Family Lives of the Middle-Aged and Elderly in Canada'. In *Families: Changing Trends in Canada*, 3rd edn, edited by Maureen Baker, 195–211. Toronto: McGraw-Hill.

Mahoney, Rhona. 1995. *Kidding Ourselves: Breadwinning, Babies, and Bargaining Power*. New York: Basic Books.

Males, Mike. 1992. 'The Code Blue Report: Call to Action, or Unwarranted "Dirism"?' *Adolescence*, 27: 273–82.

Martel, Lauren, and Jacques Legare. 2000. 'L'orientation et le Contenu des Relations Reciproques des Personnes Agees'. *Canadian Journal on Aging*, 19: 80–105.

Martin-Matthews, Anne. 2000. 'Gerontology in Canada: A Decade of Change'. *Contemporary Gerontology*, 7, no. 2: 53–6.

Miller, Kim S., Rex Forehand, and Beth A. Kotchick. 1999. 'Adolescent Sexual Behavior in Two Ethnic Minority Samples: The Role of Family Variables'. *Journal of Marriage and the Family*, 61, no. 1: 85–98.

Mitchell, Barbara A.. 1998. 'Too Close for Comfort? Parental Assessments of "Boomerang Kid" Living Arrangements'. *Canadian Journal of Sociology / Cahiers canadiens de sociologie*, 23: 21–46.

Mitchell, Barbara A., Andrew V. Wister, and Ellen M. Gee. 2000. 'Culture and Co-residence: An Exploration of Variation in Home-Returning Among Canadian Young Adults'. *Revue canadienne de sociologie et d'anthropologie / Canadian Review of Sociology and Anthropology*, 37: 197–222.

Murdock, George P. 1949. *Social Structure*. New York: Macmillan.

Neher, Linda S., and Jerome L. Short. 1998. 'Risk and Protective Factors for Children's Substance Use and Antisocial Behavior Following Parental Divorce'. *American Journal of Orthopsychiatry*, 68: 154–61.

O'Brien, Carol-Anne, and Aviva Goldberg. 2000. 'Lesbians and Gay Men Inside and Outside Families'. In *Canadian Families: Diversity, Conflict, and Change*, 2nd edn, edited by Nancy Mandell and Ann Duffy, 115–45. Toronto: Harcourt Canada.

Oderkirk, Jillian. 1994. 'Marriage in Canada: Changing Beliefs and Behaviours, 1600–1990'. *Canadian Social Trends*, 33: 3–7.

Oderkirk, Jillian, and Clarence Lochhead. 1992. 'Lone Parenthood: Gender Differences'. *Canadian Social Trends*, 27: 16–19.

O'Farrell, Timothy J., and Christopher M. Murphy. 1995. 'Marital Violence Before and After Alcoholism Treatment'. *Journal of Consulting and Clinical Psychology*, 63: 256–62.

O'Leary, Micky, Janet Franzoni, and Gregory Brack. 1996. 'Divorcing Parents: Factors Related to Coping and Adjustment'. *Journal of Divorce and Remarriage*, 25, nos 3–4: 85–103.

Parsons, Talcott, and Robert F. Bales. 1955. *Family Socialization and Interaction Process*. New York: Free Press.

Press, Julie E. 2000. 'Child Care as Poverty Policy: The Effect of Child Care on Work and Family Poverty'. In *Prismatic Metropolis: Inequality in Los Angeles*, edited by Lawrence D. Bobo, Melvin L. Oliver, James H. Johnson, and Abel Valenzuela, Jr, 338–82. New York: Russell Sage Foundation.

Roizblatt, Arturo, Sheril Rivera, Tzandra Fuchs, Paulina Toso, Enrique Ossandon, and Miguel Guelfand. 1997. 'Children of Divorce: Academic Outcome'. *Journal of Divorce and Remarriage*, 26, nos 3–4: 51–6.

Rose, Ruth. 2000. 'Les Droits des lesbiennes au Quebec et au Canada'. *Recherches Feministes*, 13: 145–8.

Rosenthal, Carolyn J., Anne Martin-Matthews, and Sarah H. Matthews. 1996. 'Caught in the Middle? Occupancy in Multiple Roles and Help to Parents in a National Probability Sample of Canadian Adults'. *Journals of Gerontology: Series B, Psychological Sciences and Social Sciences*, 51B, no. 6: S274–83.

Rushing, W.A. 1979. 'Marital Status and Mental Disorder: Evidence in Favor of a Behavioral Model'. *Social Forces*, 58: 540–56.

Safilios-Rothschild, Constantina. 1969. 'Family Sociology or Wives' Family Sociology? A Cross-Cultural Examination of Decision-Making'. *Journal of Marriage and the Family*, 31: 290–301.

Samaan, Rodney A. 2000. 'The Influences of Race, Ethnicity, and Poverty on the Mental Health of Children'. *Journal of Health Care for the Poor and Underserved*, 11, no. 1: 100–10.

Schellenberg, E. Glenn, Jessie Hirt, and Alan Sears. 1999. 'Attitudes Toward Homosexuals Among Students at a Canadian University'. *Sex Roles*, 40: 139–52.

Schiamberg, L.B., and D. Gans. 2000. 'Elder Abuse by Adult Children: An Applied Ecological Framework for Understanding Contextual Risk Factors for the Intergenerational Character of Quality of Life'. *International Journal of Aging and Human Development*, 50: 329–59.

Shapiro, Joseph P., and Joanna M. Schrof. 1995. 'Honor Thy Children'. *U.S. News and World Report*, 27 February, 39, 49.

Shirk, Martha, Neil G. Bennett, and J. Lawrence Aber. 1999. *Lives on the Line: American Families and the Struggle to Make Ends Meet*. Boulder, CO: Westview.

Skitka, Linda, and Michele Frazier. 1995. 'Ameliorating the Effects of Parental Divorce: Do Small Group Interventions Work?' *Journal of Divorce and Remarriage*, 24: 159–79.

Snell, James G. 1983. ' "The White Life for Two": The Defence of Marriage and Sexual Morality in Canada, 1890–1914'. *Histoire Sociale / Social History*, 16, no. 31: 111–28.

Spitze, Glenna, and John R. Logan. 1992. 'Helping as a Component of Parent-Adult Child Relations'. *Research on Aging*, 14: 291–312.

Statistics Canada. 1994. *Families, 1991*. Census Technical Reports. (Cat. no. 92-327E). Ottawa: Statistics Canada.

———. 1997. 'Formation of First Common-Law Unions'. *The Daily*, 9 December.

———. 2000. *Family Violence in Canada: A Statistical Profile 2000*. (Cat. no. 85-224-XIE). Ottawa: Statistics Canada.

———. 2001a. 'Changes to Family Concepts for the 2001 Census'. Available at <www12.statcan.ca/english/census01/Meta/fmlycncpts.cfm>, accessed 24 March 2003.

———. 2001b. *Divorces*. Available at <www.statcan.ca/english/Pgdb/People/Families/famil02.htm>, accessed 12 July 2001.

Svetaz, M.V., M. Ireland, and R. Blum. 2000. 'Adolescents with Learning Disabilities: Risk and Protective Factors Associated with Emotional Well-Being: Findings from the National Longitudinal Study of Adolescent Health'. *Journal of Adolescent Health*, 27: 340–8.

Tepperman, Lorne, and James Curtis. 2003. *Orientations Toward Outgroups*. Unpublished paper.

Toronto. Children and Youth Action Committee (CYAC). 2002. *Toronto Action Plan for Children: 2002*. Toronto: Children and Youth Action Committee. Available at <www.torontochildren.com/all/action_plan2002.pdf>, accessed 16 February 2003.

Vanier Institute of the Family. 2000. *Profiling Canada's Families II*. Ottawa: Vanier Institute of the Family.

Waite, Linda J. 1999–2000. 'The Negative Effects of Cohabitation'. *The Responsive Community*, 10, no. 1: 31–8.

Wilson, James Q., and Richard J. Herrnstein. 1987. *Crime and Human Nature*. New York: Simon and Schuster.

Yllo, K., and M.A. Straus. 1981. 'Interpersonal Violence Among Married and Cohabiting Couples'. *Family Relations*, 30: 339–47.

Zaslow, Martha, Sharon McGroder, George Cave, and Carrie Mariner. 1999. 'Maternal Employment and Measures of Children's Health and Development Among Families with Some History of Welfare Receipt'. *Research in the Sociology of Work*, 7: 233–59.

Glossary

Double shift Modern women's dual roles as both breadwinner and homemaker.

Extended family Where more than two generations of relatives live together in a household. The arrangement often includes grandparents, aunts, uncles, and dependent nephews and nieces.

Family A group of people related by kinship or similar close ties in which the adults assume responsibility for the care and upbringing of their natural or adopted children. Members of a family support one another financially, materially, and emotionally.

Gender socialization The process by which people learn their gender-based behaviour. The socialization process links gender to personal identity in the form of gender identity and to distinctive activities in the form of gender roles. The major agents of socialization all serve to reinforce cultural definitions of masculinity and femininity.

Nuclear family A family unit comprising one or two parents and any dependent children who live together in one household separate from relatives.

Patriarchy Male dominance that is justified in a society's system of values. This dominance is tied to the ideology of gender and can be found in every society.

Chapter 8

Aging and Ageism

Chapter Objectives

After reading this chapter the student should understand:

- how aging is a social process and how one's individual perception of aging changes throughout one's lifetime
- some basic facts about aging, and where elderly people are more concentrated in Canada
- the major tenets of the prominent competing theories on aging and ageism
- how the experience of aging differs along gender, ethnicity, and class lines
- the face of retirement in Canada
- what is meant by a *generation clash*
- the social significance and function of inheritance
- how filial responsibility is causing a burden on the baby-boom generation
- major health consequences of aging, especially with regards to elder abuse
- the different lobby groups and social support programs initiated by the government

Introduction

This chapter is about seniors and younger people, ageism and aging, retirement, youth, and decline. As we shall see, the average age of Canadians is rising each decade. Yet despite our growing awareness of older people and age variation, many Canadians openly practise **ageism**—direct or indirect discrimination against people on the basis of their age. This includes denying qualified and willing candidates employment because of stereotypic attitudes toward older or younger people—indeed, toward any people who appear to violate the age norms and expectations that are common in our society.

We begin this chapter with a discussion of the life course and related ideas about the progression through life that is associated with aging. We introduce some ideas about age and aging, as both individual and societal processes, and further consider the notion of ageism. We see that age stratification exists in our society, in much the same sense that income stratification

or racial stratification exists. Following a brief discussion of different theoretical approaches to the sociology of aging, we examine some of the main social and health consequences of aging and ageism. We conclude with a consideration of possible solutions to the problems of aging and ageism.

The Idea of a 'Life Course'

Sociologist Glen Elder (1999), currently considered the most eminent researcher studying this topic, states that the life course approach rests on five main elements or assumptions, and each is very important to our understanding of age and aging.

First, directing us away from age-specific studies—for example, studies exclusively of elderly people, of infants, or of teenagers—is the observation that 'human development and aging are life-long processes' (Elder, 1999: 7). They start at birth and never stop. We cannot understand the ideas, actions, and beliefs of people at any given age without some understanding of how they got to that age—that is, their developmental pathway. This means that longitudinal studies are the best ways of understanding all people, and especially old people.

Second, Elder notes that 'the developmental antecedents and consequences of life transitions, events, and behaviour patterns vary according to their timing in a person's life' (1999: 9). Said simply, it makes a difference at what age you make a key life transition—whether you divorce at 25 or at 55, for example, or graduate from college at 20 or at 40. Earlier and later life transitions affect the ways people view themselves, for example, since their self-image is often based on a comparison with others.

Third, 'lives are lived interdependently and socio-historical influences are expressed through this network of shared relationships' (Elder, 1999: 10). Since our lives are embedded in social relationships with others, we may find ourselves entering new statuses or speeding through the life course *because of* the actions of others. The teenage pregnancy of her daughter may make a woman a grandmother 'before her time', just as the early death of her husband may make a woman a widow 'before her time'. Our degree of preparation for new roles and statuses is important for how we experience and perform those roles and statuses.

Fourth, 'the life course of individuals is embedded in and shaped by the historical times and places they experience over their lifetime' (Elder, 1999: 13). Coming of college age means something different in wartime (for example, in the 1940s) than it does in peacetime (as in the 1980s), in a period of prosperity (the 1950s) than one of economic depression (the 1930s), in a period of gender equality (the 1990s) than one of male dominance (the 1890s). The historical period affects the opportunities available to us and the actions we are likely to take, and these in turn will affect other opportunities and actions throughout our lives.

Fifth, 'individuals construct their own life course through the choices and actions they take

within the opportunities of history and social circumstances' (Elder, 1999: 15). Said simply, though social forces influence our opportunities and actions, we continue to have a measure of choice in our own lives. This means several things. First, it means that within any social category or historical period, we will find variations in the human life course, because people are free to choose different paths and they do so. Second, cultural values and psychological dispositions—along with social norms concerning the life course—also influence people's choices. This produces predictable variations in the life course across regions and across ethnic, religious, and other subcultures, as well as between people with different personality types.

The life course model is a useful way of viewing age and aging. It helps us to understand why all 20-year-olds are not the same, nor are all 50- or 80-year-olds. On the other hand, it also helps us understand why people have a fairly predictable sequence of life experiences as they move from 20 to 50 to 80, and why they feel uncomfortable when they depart from that sequence.

However, age and aging are not merely about passage through the life course. John Mirowsky and Catherine Ross (1999) identify five aspects of age: maturity, decline, generation, survival, and life cycle. First, with age comes experience and maturity. For most people, this shows itself in lower crime rates, safer habits, a more orderly lifestyle, greater satisfaction, and a more positive self-image. Second, decline is also evident with age. Often with aging we see an accumulation of failures, faults, injuries, and errors. Over time, these changes may gradually promote physical and mental decline.

Third, different age groups represent different generations, or *cohorts*, and in this way reflect historical events and trends. For example, twentieth-century trends included increased education, income, female employment, and life expectancy but decreased family size and rural residence (Bianchi and Spain, 1986). These trends are evident in successive cohorts of people. Older people are, for example, on average less educated and more likely than younger people to have grown up in large families or rural areas.

Age groups within a society also represent survivorship. By definition, aging means surviving from birth until today. However, the chance of survival itself varies over time. As historical cohorts, different age groups have to survive different dangers at different ages. For example, the polio epidemic of the 1950s posed different risks if you were an infant, a teenager, or a mature adult at the time. The older you were, the less risk you faced. Each period also brings new challenges to survival. In recent decades, HIV/AIDS has posed a new risk to young people. Increasingly, depression and depression-related risks (such as suicide and alcoholism) pose a growing risk. Severely depressed people die at two to four times the rate of others who are similar in terms of age, sex, socio-economic status, pre-existing chronic health problems, and apparent fitness (Bruce and Leaf, 1989).

Finally, *life cycle* refers to the age-related passage through a common sequence of roles. As people grow older, they typically advance from school to job to retirement, from single to married to widowed, and so on. Changes in marital, employment, and economic status accompany the process of aging. No wonder some have compared life to a journey, others to a river. Still others think of it as a life 'cycle', as though life repeats itself or returns to its origins, like a wheel. And others speak of a life 'course', meaning a route, path, or track, as though a predictable but not exactly repeated sequence of events awaits us between birth and death.

The way sociologists think about it, the *life course* is a patterned sequence of individual experiences over time, subject to varied social, historical, and cultural influences (Gubrium and Holstein, 1995). There is, in each society—indeed, in each social group—an *expected* life course, which fits

(more or less) with the *experienced* life course (Handel, 1997). However, these life courses, ideal and actual, are not identical. The gap between the life courses we expect and those we experience may cause much distress. Actual living may sometimes mean 'breaking the rules' or failing to live up to age-related expectations.

Despite this gap, we all expect life to follow known patterns, and these patterns are age-related. As people get older, their lives change. At each stage, certain concerns become paramount and others become trivial. Certain important life events are typically concentrated in certain periods of a person's life. Social institutions also play a part, as gatekeepers. They segment and regulate life-course transitions, pushing people in and out of school, in and out of marriage, in and out of jobs, and so on (Heinz, 1996). They also establish, teach, and reward the social expectations connected with a life course.

People experience important transitions or passages in their lives: from full-time students to full-time workers, from economically dependent children to economically independent adults, from single people to people with partners (de Vaus, 1995). Leaving home, for example, is accompanied by a host of individual, gender-related, and familial (for example, interpersonal) factors, and it is often a momentous turning point in a person's life (Sherrod, 1996). Each transition typically carries new rights and responsibilities. Because these life stages imply different activities, people's activity patterns change over the course of their lives. The presence or absence of children, a partner, or a job all affect time allocation and activity selection, for example (Singleton and Harvey, 1995).

In short, changing ages often means changing roles, locations, skills, and identities. With each new age of life, people are led to congregate with others of the same age, to carry out age-related activities and share age-related lifestyles. As a result, people tend to change their friends and associates as they age and pass through life.

Early in life, we are most concerned about relations with our parents. Our childhood home is the culture and society we know best, and we measure everything else—our wishes, our hopes, our self-esteem—against what we have learned there. As we age, this process changes radically. We become acquainted with a much larger world at school; the peers we encounter there are much more varied than are our parents and siblings. For the first time, we feel moral uncertainty. The question we face is not 'Should I obey the rules?' but 'What *are* the rules?' In adolescence, our needs for peer acceptance are increasing at the same time as we are searching for an identity and purpose of our very own. We often feel torn between the conflicting goals of finding our own true selves and gaining social acceptance as one of the crowd.

Much of growing up is the learning of age-related rules of behaviour. Drawing on their own experiences, elders often give young people advice about how to travel the life course. Often, parents tell their children not to marry before they can support themselves, which means finishing their education and getting started in a career. Speaking of the United States, Dennis Hogan (1981) calls this the 'normative pattern'. In large part, it has also applied in Canada and other Western societies.

Many factors conspire against this normative pattern. Economic recessions, for example, disrupt traditional patterns; they make it harder for young people to find work and achieve economic security. Under these conditions, getting married seems no more foolish than does not getting married. This aside, Hogan senses a continuing movement away from the normative pattern: a trend toward marriage before the completion of education and career-building, for example. Reasons for this change include the gradual lengthening of formal education, the growing availability of student loans and married-student housing, the increase in full-time and part-time work for students and their spouses, the rise of part-time education, and, of course, the increased protection from unwanted pregnancy that modern birth control provides.

Basic Aspects of the Sociology of Age

With aging, an individual's physical and mental abilities gradually decline in a process known as **senescence**. However, exactly at what age and in what form the decline takes place varies widely from one person to another. Today, older people can look forward to a longer and healthier old age than in the past. Yet our culture has not fully kept up with these changes in the social definition of who is elderly and what elderly people are like.

Age Socialization

Because so many factors are involved, aging as a social process is hard to understand and hard for people to enact. The mass media oversimplify the process, with regrettable results. Both through its programming and through advertisements, the mass media in Canada contribute to *age socialization*, which teaches us about age roles. Typically, the media present young people as attractive, spirited, up to date, humorous, sexy, and rash; they present middle-aged and elderly people as the opposite. A few elderly television characters, such as Dick Van Dyke's Dr Mark Sloan, a crime-fighting doctor on the drama series *Diagnosis Murder*, are depicted as active and healthy individuals. (In real life, Dick Van Dyke is over 75 years old.) However, such cases remain the exception rather than the rule. Elderly roles in commercials are rare, with old people appearing almost exclusively in advertisements for life insurance, age-related health care items (such as adult diapers), and other products targeted specifically at the elderly market.

Because the popular media mislead us about aging, as they do about everything else—marriage, crime, politics, economics, and so on—most of us enter old age saddled with ignorance and wrong ideas. We all have to figure out how to live as elderly people in a world that is made more complicated and cruel by media images. In large part, our age socialization is a matter of teaching ourselves and learning from our peers.

Perceptions of Aging

In Western culture, people never seem to enjoy the stage of life they currently occupy. Adolescents, for example, rather than enjoying their lack of social and economic responsibility, dream of breaking free of parental authority and starting lives of their own.

As people move from one stage in life to another, they switch roles, from student to employee or employer, single to married, child-free to parent, married to divorced or widowed, worker to retiree. In every society, there are suitable ages by which we expect the changes to have

---

BOX 8.1
Happiness Over the Life Course

As they age, people pass through a life cycle— a sequence of typical, important stages. At each stage, certain concerns become paramount and others trivial.

Certain important life events are typically concentrated in certain periods of a person's life. Early in life, we are most concerned about relations with our parents. Our childhood home is the culture and society we know best, and we measure everything else—including our wishes, hopes, and self-esteem—against what we have learned there.

As we age, all this changes radically. We become acquainted with a much larger world at school; the peers whom we encounter there are much more varied than our parents and siblings. For the first time, we feel moral uncertainty. In adolescence, our needs for peer acceptance are increasing at the same time as we are searching for an identity and purpose of our very own. We often feel torn between the conflicting goals of finding our own true selves and gaining social acceptance as 'one of the crowd'.

Our cultural norms invite this rejection of family life and re-integration into it as part of normal development and the passage from childhood to adulthood. Teenagers typically rate acceptance, success and comfort more highly than adults do. To adults, material success and comfort are indicators of family well-being and security. To teenagers, they are

means of freeing themselves from family constraints and proof that they have achieved full membership in adult society.

People's values and goals continue to change as they get older. People under 30 are focused on establishing themselves in careers. Marital and family concerns become increasingly important in the thirties and forties, while leisure and health considerations become more important for people facing retirement.

The same factors that contribute to life satisfaction in old age contribute to good health and longevity. Research shows the growing importance of social and family support to the life satisfaction of the elderly. What is important is affiliation and the sense of being integrated into a community. Among the elderly, loneliness and boredom are particularly likely to be associated with low life satisfaction.

Changes in satisfaction associated with aging are even more profound for women than for men: in fact, young women start out life more satisfied than men and end up in old age much less satisfied than men. The physiological effects of aging interact with marital status, income, health, and social support to produce these changes in life satisfaction over the life course. Typically, however, healthy older people who are integrated into family and friendship groups, and continue to lead active lives, are very satisfied with life indeed.

occurred. For example, we expect marriage by 30 and retirement at or before 65 in most parts of Canada. These changes are meaningful to us. We carefully track and celebrate age in our society. We recognize birthdays, anniversaries, graduations, retirements, and other important time-based landmarks in our lives. We treat turning 18, 21, 30, 40, 50, and 65 as occasions worthy of gifts and cake.

Other cultures revere their elderly members as vessels of wisdom and authority. By contrast, Western culture worships youth, or at least the appearance of youth. Members of our culture fear the aging process, perhaps because of a fear of physical decline or death. They view a receding hairline or crow's feet around the eyes as glaring reminders of decline and the imminent end. The result is a tendency to stereotype and exclude old people.

In a culture like ours that dreads aging and that stereotypes elderly people, ageism affects many people who become old. Myths about the old abound. One common myth about aging is that most seniors are frail and ailing, and that the majority require full-time care in nursing homes or other institutional settings. In truth, only 1.4 per cent of men and 1.7 per cent of women aged 65 to 74 live in a special care institution, while the vast majority live with family members or alone (Novak, 1997; Statistics Canada, 1998). Another popular but wrong belief is that most elderly people are senile or heading in that direction. In fact, most of them retain their cognitive and perceptual functions for many years. Alzheimer's disease, the most common form of neurological dementia, affects only 3 per cent of people aged 65 to 74. The prevalence rate rises to nearly 50 per cent only after people pass 80 years of age (Alzheimer's Disease Education and Referral Center, 1995).

Stereotypes of elderly people as isolated, depressed, weak and physically inactive, mentally confused, and living in the past all perpetuate a negative image of aging and of being old. Because of our tendency to socialize with people whose age is similar to our own, most young people know few elderly people. As a result, they often believe that elderly people all have the same abilities, interests, needs, characteristics, or lifestyles. However, old people are no more homogeneous than young or middle-aged people.

In growing up, we all learn negative attitudes toward aging and older people, derived in part from the mass media and from jokes and cartoons. Many of these stereotypical images are myths. Nonetheless, if accepted as fact they can influence expectations about and reactions to aging and aged people, even among elderly people themselves. By shaping the popular perceptions of older people, the media create a self-fulfilling prophecy in which elderly individuals begin to think and behave as expected, thus reinforcing the stereotype. For example, they may come to believe that shows of sexual interest are inappropriate.

Negative stereotypes can also devalue the status of elderly people. One result is a decrease in the frequency and quality of social interaction between young and old. Another is the allocation of fewer social services to elderly people. These outcomes are unfortunate and unwarranted. People in their sixties who would have been considered old a generation ago are considered middle-aged today; they are active, healthy, and socially involved. This proves that, to a large degree, age and ageing are relative.

Age Stratification

Every known society distinguishes people according to their age. Probably because chronological age is associated with physical and mental ability and with social experience, most social roles carry assumptions about age, however hidden these may be. In high-fertility societies, where young people are very numerous, old people are relatively rare, highly valued, and socially dominant. As fertility falls, the population grows older and old people become more numerous. Then a conflict often develops with traditional expectations about age and aging. Older people become more numerous but less powerful and less respected—sometimes even resented. Younger people come to dominate the social and cultural agenda.

Age stratification theory focuses on the role of social structures in the process of individual aging and the stratification, or vertical segregation, of people by age. It also analyzes the movement of age cohorts over the life cycle. Thus, people born in the same period usually experience the same role transitions around the same time, since they are subject to the same age-related rules and institutional arrangements.

Aging and ageism pose a variety of problems for society. First, ageism, like discrimination based on race or gender, is repellent to a society like ours that is pledged, in principle, to judging people by what they do rather than who they are. We say we believe in rewards based on achievement not ascription. Thus, ageism is a sign that we do not, as a society, live up to our own proclaimed values of justice and equality. Second, ageism poses practical problems for the victims

of this discrimination. Like all discrimination, ageism has both material and psychological effects. Materially, it limits people's opportunities to get the jobs and incomes they may need to survive. Psychologically, ageism makes people feel rejected, excluded, and demeaned. They feel they are less than they want and need to be as human beings.

In 1901, only 5 per cent of the population was aged 65 or older. In the past century, this fraction has more than doubled to 12.3 per cent. Though the Canadian population is aging rapidly, it is far from the oldest population. Many Northern and Central European populations have been aging for generations, with much higher proportions of elderly people than one finds in North America. Canada is expected to have about 14.0 per cent of the population aged 65 and older by 2011 and 21.7 per cent in 2031 (Statistics Canada, 1994: 25).

We might best describe Canada's **age pyramid** today as a diamond shape, with a small base among the youngest groups, spreading out gradually as age groups increase in size until the 45- and 55-year-old

FIGURE 8.1
Age Pyramid of Population of Canada, 1 July 2001 (Thousands)

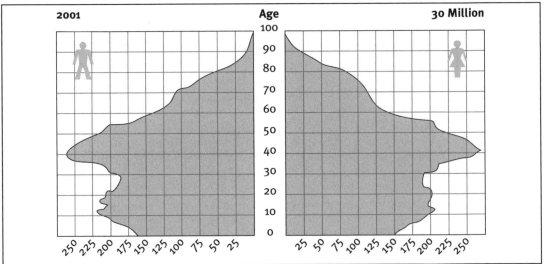

SOURCE: Statistics Canada, 'Age Pyramid of Population of Canada July 1, 1901–2001'; available at <www.statcan.ca/english/edu/power/ch1/examples/examples.htm>, accessed 9 May 2003.

levels, before tapering off into a high, thin peak around the eighties and nineties (Statistics Canada, 2000; see Figure 8.1). A diamond shape reflects a population undergoing change—a triangle that is gradually becoming a rectangle as the birth rate slows. The wide middle of the diamond represents the large number of births during the baby-boom period. The pointed ends represent the small number of surviving older people (at the one end) and the small number of births in recent decades.

Regionally, Saskatchewan has the highest proportion of seniors aged 65 and over (14.5 per cent) of any other Canadian province or territory. The Yukon, Northwest Territories, and Nunavut have the lowest proportions, at 5.4, 4.1, and 2.6 per cent respectively (Statistics Canada, 2001). Several factors contribute to the greying of a region such as Saskatchewan. One is that young people migrate out of the area for economic, social, or personal reasons. Another factor is an influx of seniors into an area because of more favourable climates, suitable housing, and presence of resources, as is the case in Victoria, Vancouver, and the Okanagan Valley in British Columbia. However, the most important factor is the birth rate. Under good health conditions, a low birth rate means an old population, depicted by a rectangular age distribution. Some Canadian

regions, in particular the northern territories, have higher birth rates (and lower life expectancies) than the national average, resulting in younger populations and pyramidal age distributions.

Stereotyping aside, aging poses problems for a society of a very real kind. Generally, populations with a high proportion of very old or very young people—that is, low-fertility populations like our own, or high-fertility populations like Iraq's—consume a high proportion of their national economy in the form of supports for dependent populations: health, education, welfare, housing, and so on. Populations with a high proportion in the workforce, aged 25–65, are able to invest more of their economy in development, savings, or war, without significantly reducing their spending on human capital.

Sociological Theories of Aging

The Structural-Functionalist Perspective

As we have seen throughout this book, structural-functionalists think that society is like a well-oiled machine, made up of mutually supporting parts that together function as an efficient, productive whole. This perspective also views society as being only as strong as its weakest members.

There are those who would challenge the disengagement theory, arguing that many elderly people are far more active than many younger people. (Bill and Peggy Wittman)

One structural-functional theory of aging, first promoted by Elaine Cummings and William Henry (1961), is **disengagement theory**. This theory holds that elderly people are among the weakest members of the population and that society has, therefore, devised a means of displacing them from its central positions of power and influence. As people age, their bodies undergo a natural process of physical and mental deterioration, Cummings and Henry note. Muscles weaken, bones become fragile, perceptual abilities worsen, and cognitive faculties decline. Elderly people are also more prone to illness and disability. At work, elderly individuals are often less efficient than their younger, stronger, and more energetic counterparts. For the good of society and for themselves, the disengagement theory argues, elderly people must finally give up their positions and withdraw to the edges of society, where they can prepare for their inevitable death.

Retirement from work serves several functions for society as a whole: (1) it vacates a position to allow someone from the next generation to move up the social hierarchy; (2) it allows the retiring member a moment of recognition—for example, a retirement party—for his or her contribution; and (3) it ensures that society replaces outdated skills and ideas with more useful ones. Structural-functionalists stress that this process of change is both natural and crucial to society's effectiveness. Without such turnover, the economy would be less efficient and less equipped to compete globally.

However, many disagree with the assumptions of functionalism, particularly with the assumption that the exclusion of older people from economically rewarding and socially important roles is good for society. Nor is age-related discrimination against the young necessarily useful to society.

Conflict Theory

Conflict theorists believe that ageism does not serve society as a whole but is merely a form of inequality exercised by the younger majority to further its own interests.

Many scholars have criticized disengagement theory as too simplistic. It depicts humans as robots who contribute to the economic institution for many years before voluntarily consigning themselves to the dust heap in later life, waiting listlessly for death to overtake them in retirement communities. This view is wrong. Contrary to what disengagement theory predicts, many elderly individuals remain active and fight against retirement and obsolescence. Elderly people rarely withdraw from society of their own will. Instead, employers and retirement rules push them out of the workforce. Without these pushes, many elderly people would remain active for as long as possible, because people value being active. Even after retirement, many stay active as long as opportunities in the family and the wider community will allow. To the extent that elderly people disengage, it is other people's idea, not their own. This is the perspective taken by most conflict theorists.

Conflict theorists note that social programs designed to aid young people and elderly people are undergoing intense political and social debate. Clashes over funding for public schools, health care, social security, and health insurance all represent conflicts between the needs of young people and elderly people on the one hand and middle-aged people on the other. Age groups hold different interests, and each group competes against the others to maximize its yield of society's resources. A problem with this arrangement is that the young and the old are less able to prevail since they lack the organization and the power to influence public policy that the middle aged have. As a result, the interests and needs of elderly people and children are often ignored or set aside by decision makers.

Many assumptions about aging lead directly to the dependence of elderly people on the rest of society. These are false perceptions that isolate age as the cause of dependence. In fact, financial assistance is needed for only a portion, not all, of the elderly population with physical and mental problems. Mandatory retirement, in particular, forces some elderly people without health problems to become financial vulnerable. Many elderly people would rejoin the workforce if permitted and if the perception of elderly people were not so negative. (See Figure 8.2.)

Conflict theorists view this as a vicious cycle: if the government did not enforce mandatory retirement, social assistance programs would not have to be so costly. The cost that younger members of society incur for these problems causes frustration with and anger against elderly people, who are viewed as expensive and economically inefficient (Matcha, 1997).

Finally, conflict theorists point out how social class, gender, and race divide the elderly population in much the same way as they divide every other age group. Elderly people are not free of other social inequalities. Therefore, some among them are subject to double jeopardy. Elderly women or racial minorities suffer discrimination both because of their age and because of their gender or race.

Symbolic Interactionism

Symbolic interactionists focus their attention on how we symbolize elderly people and enact the process of aging in society. They study how socially constructed definitions of age and aging affect a person's experience of growing old. The symbolic interactionists stress that age is a state of mind that is shaped by the labels society applies. For example, they might note that remaining happy and satisfied in the later stages of life depends largely on the perspective on aging accepted by the individual. Interactionists stress that satisfaction with aging means rejecting the definition of old age as incapacitating.

Activity theory (Havighurst and Albrecht, 1953) argues that, contrary to disengagement theory (which holds that people give up roles as they age), people in fact take on *new* roles as they age. Such continued activity maintains a sense of continuity, helps people preserve their self-concept and thereby maintain a high level of life satisfaction. People who keep up a high level of

FIGURE 8.2
You Are What You Do: Canadian Labour Force by Age, 1996

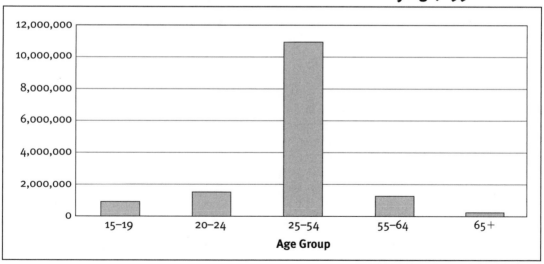

SOURCE: Statistics Canada, 1996 Census Nation tables.

activity age more 'successfully' than people who do not. This can be considered a symbolic inter-actionist theory because it relates role play to self-identity and psychological well-being.

Other symbolic interactionists have exam-ined how society, and its media in particular, portrays elderly people. These portrayals both reflect society's stereotypes about older people and help reinforce those images. Elderly actors find little work in mainstream film and prime-time television. Recently, for example, there was a great furor caused by the firing of network commentators and news anchors whom net-work bosses felt were too old. Younger people were hired for these roles in the hope of attract-ing a younger audience to view news programs.

Women are chiefly targeted for elimination from the media on the grounds of age. As male lead actors continue to make Hollywood movies, same-aged women actors lose their marketability. They are no longer allowed to serve as compelling love interests since the largest group of ticket-buying moviegoers is young men in their teens and twenties. The result is a much-remarked-on tendency for male leads such as Robert Redford, Clint Eastwood, and Harrison Ford to be acting alongside, and make fictional love to, women 10, 20, or 30 years their junior. More will be said about this in the next section, on feminist theories.

Feminist Theories

The experience of aging is different for men and women, largely because for women, aging is associated with a culturally defined loss of youth and glamour—a less critical concern for men. Women and men 'age' differently owing to differ-ent constitutions. Women and men also bring different resources to old age. And they are sub-ject to different expectations as young, middle-aged, and elderly humans (Ginn and Arber, 1995). Women in our culture dread getting older in a way that most men do not.

Today, women and men lead somewhat more similar lives, in the sense that both may pursue careers. However, their careers are likely to be in different sectors of the workforce. While in the workforce, most women earn less pay than men and are less likely to qualify for a private pension during the years in which they are work-ing. Because of this, and because their spouses or partners usually die before them, women are at particular risk of finding themselves living alone on a meagre income in their senior years. As well, a reduced income and depleted savings may mean that elderly women are forced to sell their family homes and move to rental or institu-tional homes. In addition to their heavier weight of disadvantage in connection with aging, older

---

BOX 8.2
Facts About Elderly Women

- People aged 65 years and older are the fastest-growing segment of Canadian society.
- About 58 per cent of the people over 65 in Canada —1.9 million of them—are women.
- There are about 138 women for every 100 men over the age of 65 in Canada.
- Eighty-eight per cent of women aged 65 and over have a health problem.

- Living on average six years longer than men, women's later years are characterized by dis-ability and illness.
- Women continue their caregiving roles in their senior years. For example, wives care for two thirds of the disabled or bedfast men not in institutions.

SOURCE: Women's Health Bureau, 'The Health of Senior Women', available at <www.hc-sc.gc.ca/english/women/facts_issues/facts_seniors.htm>, accessed 3 May 2003.

women have more domestic duties and social responsibilities than older men. They have a different role in the family division of labour. For example, they typically play a vital role in kin-keeping, through social networks and caregiving, that older men do not play.

These social responsibilities over the entire life course carry important consequences in old age. The family caregiving roles women take on at younger ages often remove women from the labour force, so women accumulate fewer pension benefits than men do (Moody, 2000). This limits their lifetime earnings and may result in economic insecurity after retirement.

The feminization of poverty in old age has many causes, including sex discrimination, patterns of economic dependency, and widowhood (Smolensky, Danziger, and Gottschalk, 1988). Aging means an increased risk of divorce, widowhood, and isolation for both sexes. However, the life course is generally very different for men and women with regard to marriage and divorce. For men, divorce may mean a brief reduction in the standard of living and a huge reduction in parenting responsibilities. For women, it usually means a dramatic, long-term loss in income and standard of living. Poverty is common among single mothers and their children, as it is among widows. Divorce also means an increase in parental responsibilities, since mothers usually retain custody of the children.

Finally, caring (or caregiving) is a gendered activity, unduly expected of women, with resulting hardships in terms of physical and mental health and material well-being. Informal caregiving for elderly people can have negative consequences on the caregivers' physical and emotional health (Montoro Rodriguez, 1999; however, for a finding of no effect, see Taylor, Ford, and Dunbar, 1995). Professionals have offered women carers less support in the way of public services than they have offered their male counterparts, perhaps believing that women are naturally equipped to deal with the stresses of caring (Bywaters and Harris, 1998).

Social Consequences of Aging

Poverty, Wealth, and Social Class

The higher a person's socio-economic status (SES), the longer he or she is likely to live. This is because affluent people have better access to health care services, take better advantage of available health care, live in more comfortable and more sanitary housing, suffer less stress, and are more sheltered from dangerous work than others. Higher SES is also related to fewer residential moves, more leisure time, and greater self-reported life satisfaction. All of this is true among elderly people as well. It is better to be a rich old person than a poor one.

While many of Canada's elderly are poor, Canada does not have as great a problem in this regard as many nations. In Canada, the elderly population is less destitute than in some other countries, with a low-income rate of only 4.8 per cent, compared to 6.0 per cent in Sweden and 22.4 per cent in the United States (Ross, Scott, and Smith, 2001, chapter 9). Still, economic strain remains a problem for many of Canada's elderly.

People are living longer in Canada, and they are staying healthy, energetic, and at work for longer periods of life. This has meant that age is becoming a worse predictor of employment status (Hogan, 1981). Still, elderly people often face discrimination in the workplace, and mandatory retirement policies force all but the self-employed to retire at age 65. Employers and co-workers worry about older people's physical health and cognitive ability and about their ability to handle a full workload. Others believe that because the education and training of elderly people are not as recent, they tend to lack the marketable skills required in a technologically advanced workplace, compared with younger workers. Still others openly practise ageism, denying qualified and willing candidates employment because of stereotypic attitudes toward members of older generations.

Most important, perhaps, employers sometimes target elderly members of the workforce when first looking to cut expenses during downturns in the economy. Other things being equal, older employees cost more in wages and salaries than younger employees. Even if they were equally productive, the younger employees would represent a more efficient choice for employers.

Powerlessness is an aspect of inequality, discussed in chapter 1, that increases stress and the likelihood of illness and early death. Longitudinal research finds that powerlessness is associated with more limitation of activity and more psychosocial symptoms among older adults. Increasing powerlessness predicts worsening health and heightened risks of mortality among both older men and older women (Seeman and Lewis, 1995).

Sense of control, which is related to powerlessness, is an inverted U-shaped function of age: people start life with little sense of control, gain more sense of control as they mature, then experience a diminished sense of control with widowhood and retirement. Scott Schieman (2000) finds that higher education slows the erosion of sense of control during the later years, hence reducing the likely health consequences. Locus of control (a person's sense of whether he or she is in control or is controlled by others) is a reliable predictor of health, particularly for men (Pilisuk et al., 1993).

People's experience of old age reflects a variety of accumulated experiences up to that point. A history of employment instability, for example—that is, frequent unemployment and re-employment—leads to the accumulation of large work experience deficits among inner-city minority people (Tienda and Stier, 1996). This has consequences for later well-being: pensions will be smaller, health will be worse.

Unfavourable life courses are characterized by low education, moves from manual work to early retirement, and poor housing conditions at the beginning and end of the life course.

Reduced mortality at each stage is correlated with marriage, good housing, and non-manual employment, while favourable life courses are characterized by marriage, better education, better initial SES, and upward socio-economic mobility during the life course (Wunsch et al., 1996).

Canadian research finds that the relationship between SES and health is the same for men and women and strongest among the elderly population. Both income and education contribute to better health among elderly people (Veenstra, 2000). Financial assets, especially liquid assets (that is, money rather than property), are associated with lower mortality throughout adulthood and old age, at least until age 85; and financial assets become more important relative to education and income at older ages for some measures of health (Robert and House, 1996).

Canada's retirement income system currently consists of three tiers:

1. government benefit programs, such as Old Age Security (OAS), which as of January 2003 was set at a maximum of $443.36 per month (except pensioners with an annual income above $57,879, who must repay part or the entire amount), and the Guaranteed Income Supplement (GIS)
2. the government-sponsored Canadian Pension Plan (CPP) and Quebec Pension Plan (QPP), which are based on a worker's income between the ages of 18 and 65 (the maximum CPP and QPP amounts in 2003 were $801.25 if taken at age 65)
3. personal savings, investment portfolios, and Registered Retirement Savings Plans (RRSPs)

The government introduced the GIS in 1966 to supplement the incomes of seniors whose main source of income was the OAS. The amount of the monthly benefit varies according to marital status, pensioner's income, and spouse's income. In 2003, $538.80 was available to a pensioner who was single or whose spouse or partner was a non-pensioner, while $350.94 was provided to those whose partner was on a pension. In addition, the government offers Spouse's Allowances (SPAs) to those between the ages of 60 and 64 whose spouses have passed away ($887.98 per month) or are recipients of an OAS pension ($804.31 per month).

A Clash of Generations

Another social problem related to aging is the clash of generations associated with a shift in our thinking about youth and aging. In earlier centuries, advanced age brought respect, authority, and attention from others. It also brought envy and impatience. In Ireland, for example, sons waited for their father to die so they could inherit land, marry, and begin a family. Sometimes they had to wait until well into their thirties, forties, or beyond. As a result, marriages were late and birth rates were low. Because women were much younger than their husbands, they were more likely to become widows. Most important, the old enjoyed a high degree of control over their children, and over young people overall (see Lasch, 1977).

As Western populations industrialized, children could more readily strike out on their own as earners. They no longer had to rely on their fathers. With increased mobility, young people married, set up their own households, and made themselves less available (or willing) to provide assistance. This process, which unfolded throughout the West during the nineteenth and twentieth centuries, also began in the East in the second half of the twentieth century (see Gottlieb, 1993).

Compared with other societies, kinship is unimportant in Canadian society. Consider our kinship terms. North America's kinship terms are few and uninformative. For example, we make no gender or generational distinctions among the terms we apply to our cousins. Cousins are called 'cousins' whether they are related to us through father or mother, through a parent's brother or sister, by blood or by marriage, or are distant from us by one generation, two generations, or more. By such vague indifference to detail, we suggest that cousins are unimportant. We still make gender and generational distinctions between our siblings (brother, sister) and by gender between their children (nephew, niece). However, we do not distinguish terminologically between, for example, our brother's sons and our sister's sons.

Problems of Inheritance

Generational differences in families have always involved control of resources and property that are passed on after death as inheritance. *Inheritance* is the flow of property after death along kinship lines and from the older to the younger generation. In nearly all societies, it is assumed, unless other instructions are provided, that close kin (spouses, parents, and children) will have first call on the property of a deceased person.

Inheritance practices influence marriage patterns, the quality of relationships between parents and children, and the quality of relationships between siblings. However, inheritance practices vary over time and from one society to another. Societies like our own make it easy for people to leave their wealth to whichever kin they prefer, or even to non-kin. They even make it easy for women and men to receive equal treatment under succession rules.

Wealth tends to flow downward from older to younger generations. However, cultures vary in whether the dominant inheritance pattern is one of **primogeniture**, that is, the eldest son gets everything, or the property is split among the surviving children. Historically, primogeniture has been a conservative strategy for ensuring the survival of the family by keeping the family's property intact. Children who are unlikely to inherit are more likely than others to leave the family home. In nineteenth-century Japan, where primogeniture prevailed, the children who stayed at home were children without siblings, eldest sons, and eldest daughters with only sisters. Larger proportions of sons than of daughters remained in the home village. Those who left were younger sons with elder brothers, and younger daughters. They left for various destinations through marriage, adoption, service, and work migration.

In traditional societies in which men and women are treated unequally, women may be barred from inheriting family property, yet they are expected to provide continuous care for their aging parents or in-laws. Even today in Canada, we expect daughters to provide more care to parents than we do sons, who (as men) are more advantaged socially and economically.

Filial responsibility is the moral responsibility of a grown child to look after his or her aging parent. Notions of filial responsibility, or filial piety, are particularly marked in China and other societies influenced by the teachings of Confucius (for example, Korea and Japan). Recent social changes associated with urbanization and industrialization have weakened these traditional norms. With the nuclearization of the family, newlyweds in Asia, too, have been setting up their own households, with the result that daughters-in-law and mothers-in-law no longer have the same home. This has deprived mothers-in-law of a traditional source of caregiving (Kim, 1996).

Fertility decline has also affected Asian patterns of caregiving. With the increased longevity of old people added to declining fertility, Chinese kinship networks will continue to change from the broad, short (one- or two-generation) structures of a century ago to narrow, long (three- or four-generation) structures over the course of the twenty-first century. Each of these many generations will contain few members. This means, first, that there will be fewer children and grandchildren in future to care for elderly people. It also weakens traditional family values, such as filial responsibility. In Japan, as in China and Korea, rapid population aging puts a strain on the social security system, and the governments of these countries are trying to shift the costs of elder care back onto families.

Health Consequences of Aging

Health consequences of aging and ageism fall into several categories: physical consequences of aging, psychological consequences of aging and ageism, and elder abuse.

BOX 8.3
Asian Family Structure in Canada

The provincial distribution of households reveals strong associations between three-generation households and the immigrant population. Overall, nearly half of all three-generation households in Canada were headed by immigrants. This average, however, masks some widely varying scenarios; in both British Columbia and Ontario, immigrants headed every six out of ten three-generation households, while the proportion was closer to four out of ten in Alberta and just three out of ten in Quebec. . . .

Among immigrants who arrived between 1986 and 1996, Asians made up the majority (75%) of three-generation household heads.

This gain of Asian immigrants may explain, at least in part, the recent rise of three-generation households in Canada. People born in Asia are more culturally accustomed to live in a large, extended family system. And because most Asian immigrants are recent arrivals, they are more likely to uphold the traditions of their country [of origin] than immigrants who have been in Canada longer.

SOURCE: Janet Che-Alford and Brian Hamm, 'Under One Roof: Three Generations Living Together', *Canadian Social Trends*, 53 (Summer 1999): 6–9.

Physical Illness

Quality of life often declines in old age. One reason for this is that physical and mental abilities decline in the process of senescence, although exactly at what age and in what form the decline takes place is variable from one individual to the next. Scientists are continuing to study the genetic and physiological processes involved in aging-related ailments.

However, health problems often arise alongside changes in the life course, and often because of these changes. Widowhood and divorce are associated with health problems, particularly in men. Some research says that poorer health status is related to both retirement plans and actual retirement for women but not for men (Midanik et al., 1990). Loss of independence can also be a significant cause of emotional and physical problems (Lazzarini, 1990).

People who are in good health in old age were often in good health during their youth. In short, good health tends to be maintained, after we take into account factors such as SES and health behaviours that may distort the connection

(Swallen, 1997). (See also Table 8.1.) This being so, it is important for people, and for society as a whole, to develop strategies for 'aging well'. These would include strategies for maintaining health and independence, for improving quality of life, for developing coping strategies when needed, and for preventing or postponing disabilities during the later years (Perry, 1995).

Factors that increase the likelihood of a healthy old age include a strong constitution, an ability to cope with stressful events, and a variety of social supports. Successful aging means more than the avoidance of disease and disability. It means the maintenance of high physical and cognitive functioning, and sustained engagement in social activities (Rowe and Kahn, 1997). Successful aging also means prolonging security, involvement, satisfaction, autonomy, integration, and creativity over the life course (Earle, 1999). Healthy older people remain active and engaged with others. Societies differ in the help they give old people to lead such lives.

Perceived health, in turn, is a good indicator of actual current health, but it is influenced by past health, current health, functional limitations,

TABLE 8.1

Expected Number of Deaths Before Age 70 in Four Cohorts of 100,000 Individuals Now Aged 15, Based on 1990 Canadian Mortality and Smoking Prevalence Data

Cause of Death	Males			Females		
	Current Smokers	Never-Smokers	Attributable to Smoking	Current Smokers	Never-Smokers	Attributable to Smoking
Coronary heart disease	9,372	4,391	4,981	4,276	1,666	2,610
Cerebrovascular disease	1,776	727	1,049	1,474	492	982
Cancer	14,577	5,116	9,461	10,833	6,263	4,570
Chronic obstructive pulmonary disease	1,031	93	938	825	77	748

SOURCE: Larry F. Ellison, Howard I. Morrison, Margaret de Groh, and Paul J. Villeneuve, 'Short Report: Health Consequences of Smoking Among Canadian Smokers: An Update'. *Chronic Diseases in Canada*, 20 no. 3 (2000): 36–9.

depression, and attitudes toward aging (Erickson, 1997). Age, race, educational attainment, and economic status all affect the ways that people rate their own health (Peek, 2000; Peters and Rogers, 1997). People with a poor psychosocial adjustment and poor perceived health pose particular problems to the health care system. They cost considerably more than people who are moderately or well adjusted. On the other hand, older poorly adjusted people are no more costly than younger poorly adjusted people (Watt, Roberts, and Browne, 1997).

Social and cultural factors mediate these relationships. A study by Becca Levy and Ellen Langer (1994) comparing mainland Chinese and American elderly people, for example, found that the Asian group held more positive attitudes toward aging than their American counterparts. They also scored much higher on memory tasks, so much so that there was virtually no difference in performance between young and old Chinese participants. Chinese elderly people also display a culture-specific strategy of not complaining about their health, even if miserable, thus perpetuating the stereotype of the Chinese elderly as having few life or health problems (Lam, 1994). Finally, though Chinese seniors prefer Western health care and Western-trained doctors, about half also use traditional Chinese care, owing to their religious beliefs and a preference for Chinese medicine (Chappell and Lai, 1998).

Happiness and Mental Well-Being

Health status is highly correlated with happiness, life satisfaction, and general well-being. In turn, health status and well-being are both correlated with social integration and economic security. The same factors that contribute to life satisfaction contribute to good health and longevity (Lowry, 1984; Palmore, 1985). These include the following:

- nutritious diet
- avoidance of obesity
- exercise and recreation (see also Russell, 1990)

- avoidance of tobacco
- moderate use of alcohol
- work satisfaction
- high SES or good income (see also D'Amato, 1987; Doyle and Forehand, 1984)
- marriage (see also D'Amato, 1987; Yahya, 1988)
- satisfying sexual activity

Social and family support continue to contribute to the life satisfaction of the elderly population (D'Amato, 1987; Levitt et al., 1985). Indeed, social integration is critical, whether in work or in leisure. What is important is not so much active involvement as affiliation (Duff and Hong, 1982; Lowry, 1984; Salamon, 1985) and the sense of being integrated into a community (Steinkamp and Kelly, 1985; see also Steinkamp, 1987). Among the elderly population, loneliness and boredom are particularly likely to be associated with low life satisfaction (Brown and Orlando, 1988; Doyle and Forehand, 1984). With fewer family and job concerns for them to think about, social and health concerns take on much greater importance.

Many people entering their sixties and seventies are faced with retirement, the change to a work-free lifestyle, economic uncertainty, the loss of their spouse or partner, increased frequency of health concerns, a possible move to institutional or private care, and a growing awareness of the proximity of death. The quick succession of these events within a short period often makes the change to elderly status a difficult one. The happiness of elderly people is determined in part by living arrangements. Living with a spouse is most preferred, followed by living alone and living with one's children. Other factors affecting happiness include health status, marital status, and religious commitment, of which we will say more shortly (Kehn, 1995).

Marital status is enormously important to mental and physical health. Divorce at a later stage of life is harmful since it worsens the financial situation and raises the risk of mortality. Divorced elderly people are more likely to suffer from poor health than married, widowed, or single elderly people (Dooghe, 1996). Longitudinal research on widowhood shows that mental health, morale, and social functioning all decline with the death of a spouse. Even physical health declines for a period. Men are particularly affected by the loss of a partner (Bennett, 1998).

People who engage in higher levels of religious activity tend to have better health outcomes, including better mental health (Levin and Chatters, 1998). The effects of religion on subjective health seem to be greatest for people who suffer from physical health problems. This suggests that religion comforts people (Musick, 1996). Religious involvement even reduces disability, depression, and the risk of dying in the month before an important religious holiday (Idler and Kasl, 1992). Religious involvement gives elderly people a renewed sense of meaning and social integration, and it facilitates adjustment to the later stages of life (Broyles and Drenovsky, 1992). It may encourage people to help others, which contributes to a higher subjective health rating (Krause et al., 1990). Perhaps for these reasons, church attendance has a statistically significant positive effect on subjective health, even when other possible explanatory variables are controlled for (Morris, 1997).

Elder Abuse

Living longer brings unprecedented opportunities but also presents personal and social challenges related to quality of life, including the controversial relationship between elderly people and caregivers (Daichman et al., 1998). Elder abuse occurs in a variety of settings. Typically, the older person is mistreated in the victim's private place of residence by someone with whom he or she is intimately connected, such as a spouse, sibling, child, friend, or trusted caregiver. As well, elder abuse occurs at the hands of staff and professional caregivers in facilities for elderly people.

As the National Centre on Elder Abuse (2001) has shown, several categories of abuse occur across each of these settings. These include physical abuse, sexual abuse, emotional or psychological abuse, neglect, abandonment, and financial or material exploitation. This last category includes improper use of an elderly person's personal savings, property, or assets without authorization or beyond the terms set out in a caregiver–patient contract; such offences may include stealing money or material possessions, forging signatures, and improper use of guardianship or power of attorney rights. The National Centre on Elder Abuse (2001) also emphasizes that self-neglect can be a problem among the elderly population. Self-neglect shows itself in an older person's refusal or failure to give himself or herself adequate food, water, clothing, shelter, personal hygiene, medication (when suggested), and safety precautions.

One study estimates that five times as many incidents go unreported as are reported, with self-neglect the most frequent type of abuse, women the most frequent victims, and relatives reporting abuse most often but also perpetrating abuse and neglect (Cyphers, 1999). Data on elder abuse have shown that the typical perpetrator of domestic elder abuse is the adult child or spouse of the victim, although older family members and non-relatives may also be perpetrators. Often, the abuser depends on the victim for shelter, financial assistance, or emotional support. Also commonly associated with abuse of elders are histories of alcohol addiction on the part of the abuser or of prior abuse by the victim.

Safety

Many elderly people surveyed fear being victimized, often to the extent that they become prisoners in their own homes. However, except for purse snatching, pickpocketing, and home burglary, fewer crimes are committed against elderly persons than against any other age group (see Table 8.2). Strangers do not victimize elderly people as often as the prevailing belief would have it. One reason for this lower rate of victim-

TABLE 8.2
Selected Total Violations Against the Person, Canada, 1999

	Total Victims	Total Victims 60+	Percentage of Victims 60+
Homicide	277	39	14.1
Criminal negligence	51	11	21.6
Attempt/conspire murder	486	13	2.7
Total sexual assaults	9,449	85	0.9
Total non-sexual assaults	98,195	2,456	2.5
Total assaults	107,644	2,583	2.4
Total violations against the person[a]	163,664	5,074	3.1

[a] Multiple violations against individual victims mean that these totals will not reflect the column figures.

SOURCE: Statistics Canada, *Canadian Crime Statistics 1999* (Ottawa: Statistics Canada, 2000), cat. no. 85-205-XIE.

ization is that elderly people go out less often at night. Many incidents occur at home and involve family members who have their own problems or who can no longer cope with the stress of providing care to an older relative.

Solutions for Problems of Aging

Many conditions contribute to well-being in old age, including economic prosperity (or at least security), marriage and parenthood, good health and physical functioning, a sense of autonomy and personal control, a sense of connectedness to the community, and a more general sense of purpose or meaning. In this last respect, one finds repeatedly that people who are older, more religious, married, and healthy are the people most satisfied with their lives. When asked how happy they are, older people typically say they are happier than younger people, although the differences are not great (Wood, 1990).

Informal and Formal Social Supports

Solving the problems of aging will involve strengthening the individuals and institutions that provide social integration: caregivers, families, support networks, and community organizations.

As children enter middle life and parents enter their later years, interactions between them may increase, especially if an elderly parent becomes partially or totally dependent on a child for support. This shift from independent parent to dependent parent represents a shift in power and responsibility from parent to offspring. Depending on the quality of the relationship between parent and child throughout life, this onset of dependence may provide an occasion to repay the parent for past debts or to seek revenge for real or imagined injustices. With increased life expectancy, shrinking kinship networks, and diminished public support, the need for informal support for aging parents and grandparents has increased. Elderly siblings' help is given when an elderly person has functional impairments and when support from other family members is unavailable (Cicerelli, Coward, and Dwyer, 1992).

At the same time, the need for aging parents to support middle-aged children who have become unemployed or divorced is also on the rise. Several factors influence the frequency and quality of these relationships, including the older generation's need for independence or support, the intergenerational interaction patterns established early in the life of the family, social class, the gender of the offspring, and the location and type of living arrangements (Connidis, 1989).

Said another way, the unfolding of relations between children and their aging parents will reflect a variety of factors that include the larger culture (for example, notions of filial responsibility), the ethnic culture, family traditions, long-standing relations between parents and particular children, the availability of children (especially daughters), and the financial ability of children to care for their dependent parents.

All four types of social support—informational, tangible, emotional, and integrating—mitigate the impact of stress on elderly individuals (Krause and Markides, 1990). There is by now a huge literature on social support networks as they affect elderly, chronically ill, and other dependent people. Men rely emotionally on spouses, while women diversify their emotional supports when possible (McDaniel and McKinnon, 1993). Social contacts with friends are related to well-being; consequently, fewer contacts lead to lower well-being (Lennartsson, 1999).

Some of the support provided is instrumental, some of it emotional. Instrumental support and subjective social support protect elderly people against decline. Subjective social support buffers the detrimental effect of depression on risk of physical decline (Hays et al., 1997). Both types of support are needed; neither can compensate for the lack of the other (Ikkink and van Tilburg, 1998). More resourceful and diversified networks, including friends and neighbours, are consistently associated with better scores on measures of basic and instrumental activities of daily living and self-rated health than are narrow family-focused networks (Litwin, 1998).

Increasingly, researchers have become aware that we need supports both to maintain the health of elderly people and to support the health of caregivers. Patients have to play their part, doctors theirs. The supporting cast of friends and relatives also has an important part to play in this culturally scripted drama. Diaries reveal the importance of social support in the lives of elderly people, particular those dealing with a chronic condition.

Chronic illness can often be stigmatizing and can cause social isolation for the sufferer (Warner et al., 1998). The elderly sick person's attitudes toward illness and medical care are important. Cancer patients, for example, have much regard for their physicians and expect a lot from them. They want doctors to provide professional support, information, help in learning personal coping strategies, regular updates from other professionals, and education about the nature of the disease they are caring for.

Interpersonal trust depends on the degree to which patients see their doctors as competent, responsible, and caring. Continuities of care and encounter time that allows opportunities for response, patient instruction, and patient participation in decision making encourage trust. For example, a larger social network is more important for sick people who are less trusting than average. Because they are distrustful, they use the resources available in their networks less efficiently. For people who are more trustful, and therefore better able to mobilize support from their networks, network size is less important.

Social supports help caregivers and patients, whether it is a doctor, a group, a network, or a technology that delivers the support. Social support pushes sick people away from harmful behaviours in the direction of healthy behaviours. Thus, social support is a form of social control and a means of influencing behaviour and delivering benefits. One way it does this is by influencing sick people to comply with the treatment advice they receive from their doctors.

Technology and Support Groups

Since elderly people and their caregivers cannot get all the support they need from doctors, support groups, or social networks, technology may have to play a greater role.

In recent years, researchers have studied the possible uses of the telephone and the Internet as means of delivering social support. In one study of caregivers to patients with Alzheimer's disease,

There is a great deal of literature on social support networks as they affect the elderly, the chronically ill, and other dependent people. Social contacts with friends are related to well-being; consequently, fewer contacts lead to less well-being. (Bill and Peggy Wittman)

researchers tried two types of intervention. One intervention used the telephone to create discussion groups. Four or five caregivers held regularly scheduled, supportive conversations with one another over the telephone. The other intervention delivered taped informational lectures over the telephone. After three months, caregivers in both programs showed less psychological distress, more satisfaction with the support they were receiving, and more sense that they were receiving social support. After six months, however, these gains had levelled off or declined. Caregiver burden and social conflict increased again. Of the two programs, participants learned more by listening to the informational lectures. However, they contacted family and friends more while waiting to enter a peer conversational network (Goodman, 1990).

Health professionals have also set up telephone support groups for AIDS caregivers. Use of the telephone offers people a sense of privacy not afforded in face-to-face groups. It also offers support to people who are isolated because of the stigma associated with HIV/AIDS and the lack of adequate support networks in their communities. In one telephone-based program, semi-structured groups of caregivers used conference calls to share information about resources and coping strategies. After eight such calls, participants report having valued the group experience highly (Meier, Galinsky, and Rounds, 1995). However, the other results were mixed. Measures of social isolation and self-efficacy improved, but measures of social support and coping did not. Said another way, the caregivers felt more effective than before, but they still did not know what to do or who would help them do it (Rounds, Galinsky, and Despard, 1995).

Like telephone-mediated groups, computer-mediated groups have the potential to help people who are unable or unwilling to take part in traditional face-to-face support groups. They do away with the barriers of time and distance, can be of any size, and provide for an increased variety and diversity of supports. Membership is anonymous, participants have an opportunity to express themselves in writing, and the process offers potential training experiences for group leaders. As a result, health professionals have adapted computer technology to a variety of self-help and mutual-aid groups. These have included computer-based 12-step groups for problems with alcohol, narcotics, eating, gambling, compulsive sexuality, relationships, smoking, and more.

Where addiction is the problem, online communication provides more access to support, a growth in or spreading around of dependency, and more attention to the needs of people with unusual concerns. Barriers related to social status cues are lowered. Reluctant group members are

---

BOX 8.4
Innovation in Social Support

The transition from caring for small children in her home to minding frail seniors was a natural for Joy Ward, who found the needs of both groups to be quite similar. The 47-year-old Scarborough resident is participating in a pioneering alternative home care program. She and 16 other trained care providers open their homes to seniors for respite care on a daily basis or overnight.

Lena Jankulovski, co-ordinator for the three-year-old program, run by Scarborough Support Services for the Elderly, says many of the seniors come from different backgrounds. 'Scarborough has a large ethnic community of Chinese, Asian and Caribbeans and so we endeavour to match caregivers and clients with similar cultural backgrounds', she says. Ward, who has taken special training with the elderly and is studying gerontology part-time at a community college, was chosen to give one-on-one care for special needs clients.

At the moment, Ward is caring for 61-year-old Vindy, who suffers from brain damage after an accident and needs almost constant supervision. 'In Vindy's case, her husband and daughter both work and nobody can stay home and care for her', says Ward. Jankulovski says many families from different cultures aren't comfortable with placing elderly parents in institutions.

'That's why this program suits those clients because their elderly parents are receiving customized services to meet the unique needs of ethnic seniors in a home environment that is sensitive to their language and cultural needs', she says.

The care providers are given a course in caring for the elderly at George Brown College. They also undergo a police safety check. 'All the care providers' homes must be equipped with special grab bars in the washroom, and have a spare bedroom so the senior can rest or stay overnight', says Jankulovski. Every home is checked for adequate lighting, railings on stairs and safe floors to minimize falls. Ward, like the other caregivers, often takes her charges on outings to shop or visit a child care centre, which, she says, the seniors love.

She also hosts a day for other clients and their care providers at her home so there is a break in the seniors' routines and a chance to socialize. 'We make crafts, do exercises, listen to music and share food from different cultures', Ward says. 'It also gives the care providers an opportunity to network'.

SOURCE: Judy Creighton, 'Caring Begins at Home: Clients Matched with Providers of Similar Cultural Background', *The Toronto Star*, 18 March 1999, F6. Reprinted by permission of The Canadian Press.

more likely to participate, relational communications improve, and people with interpersonal difficulties find themselves opening up more readily.

Possible disadvantages of going online include destructive interactions and lack of clear and accountable leadership. The same elements that promote ease of online communication, especially anonymity and invisibility, can also promote recklessness and cruelty. This may mean social isolation, ostracism, or stigmatization for some. Beyond that, non-computer-using populations will have no access to this interaction. In any event, we currently lack research about its benefits and about user satisfaction.

Personal Efforts to Adapt

Some elderly people have a harder time than others making use of services and supports. Because of low levels of education, language problems, and lack of job skills, many elderly members of ethnic groups, especially those who came to Canada during the 1940s, are now retired without a pension. However, they may underuse social and health care services because of lack of knowledge about the availability of services and programs or because they cannot be served in their own language. Likewise, they may be unwilling to enter long-term care institutions because of differences in language, customs, beliefs about medical practices and death, food preferences, or the need for privacy.

Elderly people need to learn how to age effectively. For this purpose, they often require training, a complex process that seeks to integrate each new individual and group into society, and into specific institutions or positions within society, by transmitting current cultural behaviours, beliefs, and values. We can anticipate role changes, such as marriage and retirement, and individuals can begin planning to help themselves adjust to these changes. Other changes, however, such as widowhood or becoming a father at the age of 55, may occur unexpectedly.

Still others, though expected, can be stressful and can lead to an identity crisis or loneliness and to a decreased quality of life. Examples include the *empty nest syndrome*, which occurs when children leave home for university or marriage.

Anticipatory socialization can ease later-life role changes. Important aids in making these age-related changes include the social support of friends and family, the development of personal coping skills, and the presence of age peers who serve as role models (George, 1980). Aging always involves change—in friendships, health, economic status, role relationships, and more. Changes in daily routines can generate stress because of the constant need of coping with a new life situation.

Widowhood is one of the most problematic of all changes because it can occur so suddenly and endure for so many years. In 1991, 13 per cent of Canadian men and 47 per cent of Canadian women over 65 years of age were widowed. The reasons for the large discrepancy include the greater life expectancy of women, the fact that husbands are typically two to three years older than their wives, and men's greater propensity to remarry after the death of their spouse. Thus, not only do more women experience this tragic life event, they also live longer in the role of widow. Even a woman who becomes a widow at the age of 80 can expect an average of almost nine more years of life as a single person.

A large body of research literature has established that the death of a spouse is one of the most stressful role changes in the life cycle and *the* most stressful in the later years (Martin-Matthews, 1991). Most of the literature has focused on the experience of widows. However, the few studies of widowers suggest that while they are not often faced with economic burdens, widowers have more difficulty in adapting to their new role, as evidenced by higher suicide rates, higher rates of remarriage, and higher rates of mortality following bereavement.

People have little opportunity to prepare for the change from married person to widow or widower unless their spouse has been ill for a long time. Adjustment to widowhood normally begins with a stage of mourning, which may last up to two years. Unlike in earlier times, there is no formal mourning period, and mourning clothes to signify the new status are seldom worn in this society. Instead, the widowed person must develop a social support network.

The adjustment is easier if the survivor has a friendship group containing age peers who have already been widowed. They have in effect created community-based 'widow-to-widow' programs to provide emotional and social support. After the immediate and acute period of grief and mourning, the widowed person must begin to rebuild a new identity and lifestyle—being alone, having no spouse to share thoughts and feelings with, cooking for one person, losing friends who were more closely tied to the deceased spouse, managing financial affairs alone, and, for a widow who loses the pension rights of the deceased spouse, living on a reduced income.

While adjustment is initially difficult, most eventually make a successful changeover. However, though they may adjust to the loss of their spouse, they may not cope as well with the consequences of being widowed—loss of income, of companionship, of friends, and, for men especially, of a homemaker. Many widows become closer to their children or move into a social circle comprising other widows.

One of the most difficult adaptations for older widows is the beginning of new intimate or sexual relationships, especially if female friends, children, or siblings disapprove. Still, as social values and norms have changed in recent years, cohabitation or remarriage has become a more socially acceptable option for the elderly widowed person. At the same time, with the onset of the women's movement, fewer older women are likely to remarry merely to play nurse, cook, and homemaker. Given the greater sharing of domestic tasks because of dual careers, widowers may be less likely to remarry mainly to find domestic assistance. Future generations of older widows will probably also have more personal economic and social resources so they will not have to remarry for sheer economic survival.

The pattern of interaction among parents, children, and grandchildren varies at different stages in the life cycle. It can also vary in frequency, quality, and type, depending on the ages, interests, and needs of the generations. For instance, conflict over values and behaviour may characterize the relationship between adolescent children and parents. As the children reach adulthood and establish their own nuclear families, conflict may change in intensity and frequency since the demands of child rearing and careers leave the young adults little time for interaction with their parents.

Government Legislation

There is considerable disagreement about the extent of the state's obligation to support retired individuals. This issue is particularly significant because of the impoverished status of many older adults, particularly elderly widows, and because of fears that public old age security funds and private pension plans may become bankrupt in the future (Brown, 1991).

Income after retirement depends on the individual's pattern of lifetime employment (regular or sporadic), place of employment (whether it offers a private pension), and level of income while in the labour force, and on his or her pattern of savings, investments, and expenditures over the life course.

From a demographic perspective, there is no evidence to suggest that fertility rates will increase or that life expectancy will decrease significantly. The median age of the population will therefore continue to rise, to as high as 41 years in 2006 and 48 years in 2031. This means that 20 to 25 per cent of the population will be over 65 years old by the time you reach 50 years of age (assuming that you are now in your early twenties). Contrary to prevailing concerns, however, this large group of elderly persons will not, for the most part, be impoverished, institutionalized, or sedentary. There is no valid evidence right now for such media-based fear-generating scenarios as a bankrupt public pension system, the abolition of universal medicare, generational conflict over scarce resources, the warehousing of elderly people in institutions, or poverty among young people because of the cost of support programs for the aged population. Recognition is growing that we can shape the physical environment to increase the independence and mobility of elderly people (Satariano, 1997).

Older age groups will be healthier, more physically and mentally active, more independent, and more satisfied with their life situation than the current elderly population. This optimistic scenario is based on the belief that personal, private, and government interventions will create a more viable system in which to age. This elderly-friendly environment would include creative social policies and programs; enhanced private-sector products and services; changing attitudes toward health, nutrition, physical activity, and stress; political involvement and empowerment; new attitudes toward retirement and leisure; and innovative long-range economic planning during the early and middle years of adulthood. It remains for us to bring about these changes.

Canadians will also have to focus on creative fiscal management of private and public pension funds. This will mean dealing with the issue of mandatory retirement, examining options for both early and late retirement as labour surpluses and shortages occur overall or in specific regions or occupational groups. Finally, they will have to address such ethical issues as the right to die, the creation of living wills, guardianship for the dependent elderly, empowerment of the elderly population, and equity across genders, races, ethnic groups, and religions in the development of policies and the delivery of services.

The role of elderly people may change drastically if they are once again needed by the economy. With an increasingly aged population, a relative lack of suitable workers creates a vicious cycle of smaller revenues to support larger pension expenses. One possible solution is to promote a privately funded and managed pension system to reinforce the possible shortfall of the public system, as Mexico began to do in 1997. Replacing the Mexican public pension system with a system of mandatory private pension plans for all working Mexicans has alleviated the problem of maintaining a government-sponsored benefit plan. Such procedures can boost the country's insurance sector while providing more secure pensions for employees (Souter, 1997).

Lobbying Efforts by Elderly People

As a heterogeneous group, elderly people have experienced widely different life situations and have not voted with a common voice. However, through such voluntary organizations as the United Seniors Citizens of Ontario, One Voice, CARP, the National Academy of Older Canadians, and the Fédération de l'age d'or du Québec, Canada's older adults have been making their concerns known to politicians, business, and younger voters.

Currently, the largest lobby group for the elderly population in Canada is CARP. This set of initials once stood for the Canadian Association of Retired Persons, but because of the changing characteristics of its membership, the group's name was changed to Canada's Association for the Fifty-Plus. Formed in 1984 by a husband-and-wife team, Murray and Lillian Morgenthau, CARP was initially composed of 10 friends who met around kitchen tables to share their experiences of being elderly. CARP is a non-profit organization and refuses funding from government bodies; it has a mandate dedicated to the promotion of the rights and quality of life of mature Canadians. The organization publishes an award-winning magazine, *CARPNews 50Plus*; gives its members discounts for homes, cars, medical expenses, retirement planning, and health insurance; and acts as a voice of Canada's elderly.

CARP fights for an improved quality of life for seniors and helps make policy makers and the

BOX 8.5
What's There to Lobby For? Long-term Effects of Divorce

Hundreds of thousands of women in their 60s, caught in the surge of divorces that started a generation ago, are finding that they have to stay in the work force because they lack enough money to retire. Wages in effect are becoming their pensions. Women alone in old age have always been at greater risk of falling into poverty than married women. But until recently, women alone generally were widows, who at least had the pensions and savings their husbands had left them, and a tradition of living with children. Widows greatly outnumbered older divorced women until the late 1990s, but now for the first time the divorced outnumber widows.

Divorced women are increasingly the group among the elderly that is most at risk. Susan Smith Parkhurst, who lives in Denver, is one. Like so many women of her generation, Parkhurst, 63, stopped working when she began having children in the 1960s. Her husband earned enough as an investment adviser and she busied herself with motherhood and volunteer work. Then after 20 years of marriage she found herself divorced at 48. Her divorce settlement prodded her to work by removing her name from her husband's health insurance and giving her very little income. Nor did she get a stake in any future pension.

The women's movement had opened opportunities in the workplace, however, and Parkhurst soon landed at an investment firm. She rose in the ranks, received raises and now, nearly 16 years later, she is closing in on retirement age. But she cannot afford to give up a salary: she has not worked long enough to earn the pension of someone who worked a lifetime.

To avoid this pitfall, Hounsell advises married women to keep retirement and divorce always in mind. 'And I tell young women: "Don't stay home and take care of the children unless you make sure there is a personal pension set up for you, an IRA [RRSP]. You don't redo the kitchen or the baby's room until you are sure there is enough saved in that IRA."'

SOURCE: Louis Uchitell, 'Lacking Pensions, Older Divorced Women Remain at Work', *New York Times*, 26 June 2001. Copyright © by the New York Times Co. Reprinted with permission.

public aware of elderly people's unique perspective on social, economic, financial, and political issues. Among its many actions, CARP has organized several national forums on scams and frauds against seniors, on home care, and on the environment; addressed health care issues such as long-term care, hospital closures and mergers, the national health strategies, and the funding, availability, cost, and taxation of drugs; persuaded the government in Ottawa to change the legislation regarding Registered Retirement Income Funds (RRIFs) to remove the 90-year age limit and allow increased withdrawals; identified and combated

incidences of ageism and elder abuse; helped to design strategies to provide safe, affordable living accommodations and transportation for seniors; and released many reports, publications, seminars, and videos on various topics concerning and of interest to the elderly population (CARP, 2001). Such lobby groups play an invaluable role in pursuing the interests of elderly people.

Like racism and sexism, ageism is now considered an inappropriate form of discrimination. Government policies have, therefore, been enacted in an attempt to ensure that age does not act as a barrier to equal opportunity. Regulators have applied these to the work environment, where older people have traditionally been over-looked in job hiring and promotions. However, the burden of proving age discrimination at work is difficult. It is well documented that age is associated with increased risk of serious health complications. Therefore, the line between failing to meet valid qualifications for the position and being dismissed or overlooked because of discriminatory attitudes is often difficult to discern.

Concluding Remarks

Medicine, disease control, and biotechnology have led to large increases in life expectancy in the past century or so, and the process is probably not yet complete. As scientists improve their knowledge of how the human body ages and deteriorates, they will likely be able to design treatments and drugs that can compensate for or delay these processes. Not only will people live longer, they will also experience a better quality of life in the later stages of life. Though we are unlikely to discover a magical fountain of youth any time soon, medical technology may at least be able to reduce the significant discrepancy in physical and mental functioning between young adults, middle-aged people, and the elderly population.

The mass media, in both programming and advertisements, are the main vehicle of socialization about the meaning of age in Canada. In part, the media are giving viewers what they want. What appears on television, in movies, and in print is a reflection of what society values and derides. However, the media are also an active force that shapes how we view the world. Largely, the media promote images of elderly people that are outdated, disrespectful, and ridiculous.

These images support ageism, which in turn often leads to economic disadvantage of elderly people since they are discriminated against in the workforce. This discrimination includes mandatory retirement and the placement of elderly individuals in low-paying positions. Elderly people may not receive the economic support they require because

ageism in the political realm discourages those with political power from spending resources on programs designed to help the elderly population. Ageism may also lead to emotional and physical abuse. Stereotypes associated with ageism may be the reason that we sometimes institutionalize elderly individuals unnecessarily. It also may be why institutions set up to support elderly people can be underfunded. Once institutionalized, elderly individuals are often neglected socially since institutions may place them in isolating situations. Elderly people may also experience physical malnutrition and unnecessary drug use.

From the functionalist perspective, aging is a social problem because the institutions of modern society are failing to meet the needs of the dependent aged. Conflict theorists view the problems of the elderly population as stemming from older people's lack of power to shape social institutions to meet their needs. Symbolic interactionists believe elderly people are stigmatized because they do not conform to the images, ideals, and norms of a youth-oriented culture. Feminist theorists note that among the elderly population, the most economically disadvantaged are women, minorities, and those who live alone.

The jobs of successful aging and age reform cannot be left to governments and voluntary associations, but these agencies, along with informal and formal social networks, are important for successful aging. Also, elderly people need to learn to play a role in their own well-being. Various studies have confirmed that social contact with friends and relatives enhances physical and mental well-being among elderly people. Social relationships can markedly improve quality of life by reducing stress and increasing positive health practices. For example, they can foster awareness of health care alternatives and of the importance of compliance with treatment. People who lack social and community ties are likely to die earlier than those with more extensive social activities. More media attention to health promotion among elderly people will go a long way to solving age-related problems.

We have seen that aging is inevitable and that every society takes note of this process in its own culturally meaningful way. Increasingly, however, every society has to deal with the public responsibility for increased longevity and reduced family care.

Questions for Critical Thought

1. There is definitely a widespread discomfort and fear associated with growing old. As mentioned in the text, while some cultures revere their elderly members, Western culture seems to worship the appearance of youth. Discuss the role of the media and mention specific products that appeal to this fear in aging. For instance, even in *Seventeen* magazine, targeted at preteen adolescents, there are advertisements for firming creams. Why, in your opinion, does Western culture so highly prioritize looking young and feeling fit? Is this obsession dangerous? Or is it just a reflection of insecurities of the influential baby-boom cohort as they are aging?

2. Quite often elderly individuals feel that they are absent from and misrepresented in popular-culture media and feel that their selective presence in commercials for such products as denture cleaners unfairly represents who they are. Further, Grandpa Simpson in the very popular TV series *The Simpsons* also does not help: he is depicted as senile, belligerent, and often terrified. What do you feel is the impact of this portrayal on people's opinions on elderly people, and how do you feel this affects elderly people themselves as they watch these commercials and shows? Discuss this using personal examples and references.

3. The text outlines physical, sexual, and emotional or psychological abuse, neglect, abandonment, and financial exploitation as forms of abuse particular to the elderly. Using the Internet as a tool, find examples, whether in news stories or on Web sites that deal specifically with elder abuse. Is there one type of abuse that seems most prevalent? Are there patterns that occur (for example, who is being abused and who is abusing)? What do you feel are possible solutions or remedies to the examples you found? In other words, could the abuse have been avoided?

4. The text suggests that elderly people and their caregivers cannot get all the support they need from doctors, support groups, or social networks. It is at this point that technology begins to play a greater role. In recent years, the Internet has come to play an increasing role as a means for delivering social support. Go on the Internet and find support Web sites for elderly persons seeking companionship, answers, and assistance. What are the main features of these sites, and what services do they provide? Also in your discussion outline possible drawbacks to Internet support groups.

5. There is incessant controversy over the government's role in providing for the aging cohort of the population. What, in your opinion, is the purpose of government interventions such as social policies, economic planning programs, and enhancing products and services? What do you feel their role is, if any, in changing popular opinion and attitudes surrounding elderly issues?

6. Do you agree with a mandatory retirement program? Why or why not?

Recommended Readings

Pamela T. Amos and Steven Harell, eds, *Other Ways of Growing Old: Anthropological Perspectives* (Stanford, CA: Stanford University Press, 1979).

Among the interesting cross-cultural perspectives on aging in this volume is an eye-opening vignette by Megan Biesele and Nancy Howell entitled 'The Old People Give You Life', describing the !Kung of the Kalahari.

Patrice Bourdelais, *Le Nouvel age de la vieillesse: histoire du vieillissement de la population [The New Age of Old Age: History of the Aging of the Population]* (Paris: Odile Jacob, 1993).

The author presents an essential history of demographic aging, exploring various popular, political, and scientific approaches to demographic aging in France and elsewhere. He discusses the use of age as a category and develops the notion of equivalent age, arguing that the onset of old age changes because of improved health and other factors.

Barry D. McPherson, *Aging as a Social Process: An Introduction to Individual and Population Aging*, 3rd edn (Toronto: Harcourt Brace Canada, 1998).

A comprehensive discussion of theories of aging and trends for individual and population aging in Canada. This volume also features material consequences of individual and population aging, including health consequences.

Kyriakos S. Markides and Charles H. Mindel, *Aging and Ethnicity* (Newbury Park, CA: Sage, 1987).

This text deals with some of the ethnographic components of aging. It looks at the cultural distinctions concerning aging and the aged population, at demographic concerns, and at policy issues.

David R. Phillips, ed., *Ageing in East and South-East Asia* (London: Edward Arnold, 1992).

Elderly people are the fastest-growing population segment in Southeast Asia. Phillips's book deals systematically and comprehensively with aging in the region. The author is in touch with the issue that family care for the aged population may have to change with changing demographic and economic circumstances.

Eloise Rathbone-McCuan and Betty Havens, eds, *North American Elders: United States and Canadian Perspectives* (New York: Greenwood Press, 1988).

This text is designed to offer a cross-national analysis and includes the following topics: income security in old age, long-term care in Canada, the rural elderly, the chronically mentally ill, aging veterans, Native elders, and cross-national intergenerational families.

James H. Schulz, Allan Borowski, and William Crown, *Economics of Population Aging: The 'Graying' of Australia, Japan, and the United States* (Westport, CT: Auburn House, 1991).

This interdisciplinary work includes demographic data on aging in Japan, Australia, and the United States. The authors' argument relating economic factors to decreases in fertility rates and increases in the aging population is discussed as particularly relevant.

Jay Sokolovsky, ed., *The Cultural Context of Aging: Worldwide Perspectives* (New York: Bergin & Garvey, 1990).

This text addresses the functioning of older adults in diverse societies, discussing aged ethnic families and informal supports; families of black women and church roles; Native American grandparents; Irish, Jewish, and Italian widowers; Bowery men; a Latino Alzheimer's support group; and nursing-home liminality.

John van Willigen, *'Gettin' Some Age on Me': Social Organization of Older People in a Rural American Community* (Lexington: University of Kentucky Press, 1989).

The rural elderly in Kentucky are the focus of van Willigen's ethnography, which provides a framework by which to examine their social networks, focusing on kin networks. The text suggest that support networks and informal economies generally emerge as reactions to low socio-economic status and increased dependence on the market economy.

C.R. Victor, *Health and Health Care in Later Life* (Milton Keynes, UK: Open University Press, 1991).

This book focuses on the current health status of older people and on their patterns of use of health and social services. It is suggested that future research consider issues of work and leisure, black and ethnic-minority elder issues, homosexuality, and social deviance.

Recommended Web Sites

National Center on Elder Abuse
www.elderabusecenter.org

The NCEA Web site aims at assisting users to locate data, publications, assistance, and information. It provides a number of links to subject areas relating to publications, elder-abuse laws, statistics, conferences, research, and a number of other topics related to the issue of elder abuse.

The Care Guide
www.thecareguide.com

The Care Guide is a resource centre providing information and knowledge to empower both consumers and providers of seniors' housing and health care. It provides considerable information to seniors who are looking into housing, as well as medical information that is relevant to seniors.

Canadian Association on Gerontology
www.cagacg.ca

The Canadian Association on Gerontology (CAG) is a national multidisciplinary scientific and educational association established to provide leadership in matters related to the aging population. CAG seeks to improve the lives of older Canadians through the creation and dissemination of knowledge of gerontological policy, practice, research, and education.

References

Alzheimer's Disease Education and Referral Center. 1995. *Alzheimer's Disease Fact Sheet*. Available at <www.alzheimers.org/pubs/adfact.html>, accessed 27 January 2003.

Bennett, Kate Mary. 1998. 'Longitudinal Changes in Mental and Physical Health Among Elderly, Recently Widowed Men'. *Mortality*, 3: 265–73.

Bianchi, Suzanne M., and Daphne Spain. 1986. *American Women in Transition*. New York: Russell Sage Foundation.

Brown, Robert. 1991. *Economic Security in an Aging Population*. Toronto: Butterworths.

Brown, W., and D. Orlando. 1988. 'Enhancing Life Satisfaction for Older Adults'. *Journal of Applied Sociology*, 5: 73–87.

Broyles, Philip A., and Cynthia K. Drenovsky. 1992. 'Religious Attendance and the Subjective Health of the Elderly'. *Review of Religious Research*, 34: 152–60.

Bruce, M.L., and P.K. Leaf. 1989. 'Psychiatric Disorders and 15-Month Mortality in a Community Sample of Older Adults'. *American Journal of Public Health*, 79: 727–30.

Bywaters, Paul, and Alison Harris. 1998. 'Supporting Carers: Is Practice Still Sexist?' *Health and Social Care in the Community*, 6: 458–63.

CARP. 2001. *What Is CARP?* Available at <www.fiftyplus.net/CARP/about/main.cfm>, accessed 8 July 2001.

Chappell, Neena, and David Lai. 1998. 'Health Care Service Use by Chinese Seniors in British Columbia, Canada'. *Journal of Cross-Cultural Gerontology*, 13, no. 1: 21–37.

Cicirelli, Victor G., Raymond T. Coward, and Jeffrey W. Dwyer. 1992. 'Siblings as Caregivers for Impaired Parents'. *Research on Aging*, 14: 331–50.

Connidis, Ingrid. 1989. *Family Ties and Aging*. Toronto: Butterworths.

Cummings, Elaine, and William Henry. 1961. *Growing Old: The Process of Disengagement*. New York: Basic Books.

Cyphers, Gary C. 1999. 'Elder Abuse and Neglect'. *Policy and Practice*, 57, no. 3: 25–30.

Daichman, Lia Susana, Rosalie A. Wolf, Gerald Bennet, Bridget Penhale, and Elizabeth Podnieks. 1998. 'Action on Elder Abuse: An Overview'. *Australasian Journal on Ageing*, 17, no. 1, suppl.: 17–18.

D'Amato, T.J. 1987. 'Factors Causing Variation in the Life Satisfaction of the Elderly'. *National Journal of Sociology*, 1, no. 1: 54–72.

de Vaus, David. 1995. 'Adult–Parent Relationships: Do Life Cycle Transitions Make a Difference?' *Family Matters*, 41: 22–9.

Dooghe, Gilbert. 1996. 'Effects of Divorce at an Advanced Age'. *Tijdschrift Voor Sociale Wetenschappen*, 41: 406–28.

Doyle, D., and Forehand, M.J. 1984. 'Life Satisfaction and Old Age: A Reexamination'. *Research on Aging*, 6: 432–48.

Duff, R.W., and Hong, L.K. 1982. 'Quality and Quantity of Social Interactions in the Life

Satisfaction of Older Americans'. *Sociology and Social Research*, 66: 418–34.

Earle, Leon D. 1999. 'Celebrating the International Year of Older Persons: Younging Longer or Ageing Younger?' *Journal of Family Studies*, 5: 258–65.

Elder, Glen H., Jr. 1999. 'The Life Course and Aging: Some Reflections'. Distinguished Scholar lecture given at the annual meeting of the American Sociological Association. Available at <www.unc.edu/~elder/asa/asacharts.pdf>, accessed 25 March 2003.

Erickson, Mary Ann. 1997. 'The Life Course and Physical Health: Perceived Health, Health Events and Health Trajectories'. Paper presented at the annual meeting of the American Sociological Association.

George, Linda. 1980. Role *Transitions in Later Life*. Monterey, CA: Brooks/Cole.

Ginn, Jay, and Sara Arber. 1995. '"Only Connect": Gender Relations and Ageing'. In *Connecting Gender and Ageing: A Sociological Approach*, edited by Sara Arber and Jay Ginn, 1–14. Buckingham, UK: Open University Press.

Goodman, Catherine. 1990. 'Evaluation of a Model Self-Help Telephone Program: Impact on Natural Networks'. *Social Work*, 35: 556–62.

Gottlieb, Beatrice. 1993. *The Family in the Western World: From the Black Death to the Industrial Age*. New York: Oxford University Press.

Gubrium, Jaber F., and James A. Holstein. 1995. 'Life Course Malleability: Biographical Work and Deprivation'. *Sociological Inquiry*, 65: 207–23.

Handel, Gerald. 1997. 'Life History and Life Course: Resuming a Neglected Symbolic Interactionist Mandate'. Paper presented at the annual conference of the American Sociological Association.

Havighurst, Robert, and Ruth Albrecht. 1953. *Older People*. New York: Longman, Green.

Hays, Judith C., W.B. Saunders, E.P. Flint, B.H. Kaplan, and D.G. Blazer. 1997. 'Social Support and Depression as Risk Factors for Loss of Physical Function in Late Life'. *Aging and Mental Health*, 1: 209–20.

Heinz, Walter. 1996. 'Life Course and Social Change in Germany: The Interchange Between Institutions and Biographies'. Paper presented at the annual conference of the American Sociological Association.

Hogan, Dennis P. 1981. *Transitions and Social Change: The Early Lives of American Men*. New York: Academic Press.

Idler, Ellen L. and Stanislav V. Kasl. 1992. 'Religion, Disability, Depression, and Timing of Death'. *American Journal of Sociology*, 97: 1052–79.

Ikkink, Karn Klein, and Theo van Tilburg. 1998. 'Do Older Adults' Network Members Continue to Provide Instrumental Support in Unbalanced Relationships?' *Journal of Social and Personal Relationships*, 15, no. 1: 59–75.

Kehn, Diane J. 1995. 'Predictors of Elderly Happiness'. *Activities, Adaptation and Aging*, 19, no. 3: 11–30.

Kim, Myung-Hye. 1996. 'Changing Relationships Between Daughters-in-Law and Mothers-in-Law in Urban South Korea'. *Anthropological Quarterly*, 69, no. 4: 179–92.

Krause, Neal, Berit Ingersoll-Dayton, Jersey Liang, and Hideihiro Sugisawa. 1990. 'Religion, Social Support, and Health Among the Japanese Elderly'. *Journal of Health and Social Behavior*, 40: 405–21.

Krause, Neal, and Kyriakos Markides. 1990. 'Measuring Social Support Among Older Adults'. *International Journal of Aging and Human Development*, 30: 37–53.

Lam, Lawrence. 1994. 'Self-Assessment of Health Status of Aged Chinese-Canadians'. *Journal of Asian and African Studies*, 29, nos 1–2: 77–90.

Lasch, Christopher. 1977. *Haven in a Heartless World: The Family Besieged*. New York: Basic Books.

Lazzarini, Guido. 1990. 'Paths of the Elderly'. *Studi di Sociologia*, 28: 371–85.

Lennartsson, Carin. 1999. 'Social Ties and Health Among the Very Old in Sweden'. *Research on Aging*, 21: 657–81.

Levin, Jeffrey S., and Linda M. Chatters. 1998. 'Religion, Health, and Psychological Well-Being in Older Adults'. *Journal of Aging and Health*, 10: 504–31.

Levitt, M.J., T.C. Antonucci, M.C. Clark, J. Rotton, and G.E. Finley. 1985. 'Social Support and Well-Being: Preliminary Indicators Based on Two Samples of the Elderly'. *International Journal of Aging and Human Development*, 21: 61–77.

Levy, Becca, and Ellen Langer. 1994. 'Aging Free from Negative Stereotypes'. *Journal of Personality and Social Psychology*, 66: 989–97.

Litwin, Howard. 1998. 'Social Network Type and Health Status in a National Sample of Elderly Israelis'. *Social Science and Medicine*, 46: 599–609.

Lowry, J.H. 1984. 'Life Satisfaction Time Components Among the Elderly: Toward Understanding the Contribution of Predictor Variables'. *Research on Aging*, 6: 417–31.

McDaniel, Susan A., and Allison L. McKinnon. 1993. 'Gender Differences in Informal Support and Coping Among Elders: Findings from Canada's 1985 and 1990 General Social Surveys'. *Journal of Women and Aging*, 5, no. 2: 79–98.

Martin-Matthews, Anne. 1991. *Widowhood*. Toronto: Butterworths.

Matcha, Duane A. 1997. *The Sociology of Aging: A Social Problems Perspective*. Needham Heights, MA: Allyn and Bacon.

Meier, Andrea, Maeda J, Galinsky, and Kathleen A. Rounds. 1995. 'Telephone Support Groups for Caregivers of Persons with AIDS'. *Social Work with Groups*, 18, no. 1: 99–108.

Midanik, Lorraine T., Krikor Soghikian, Laura J. Ransom, and Michael R. Polen. 1990. 'Health Status, Retirement Plans, and Retirement: The Kaiser Permanente Study'. *Journal of Aging and Health*, 2: 462–74.

Mirowsky, John, and Catherine E. Ross. 1999. 'Economic Hardship Across the Life Course'. *American Sociological Review*, 64: 548–69.

Montoro Rodriguez, Julian. 1999. 'The Psychosocial Consequences of Informal Caregiving to Older People'. *Revista Internacional de Sociologia*, 23: 7–29.

Moody, Harry R. 2000. *Aging: Concepts and Controversies*, 3rd edn. Boston: Pine Forge Press.

Morris, David C. 1997. 'Health, Finances, Religious Involvement, and Life Satisfaction of Older Adults'. *Journal of Religious Gerontology*, 10, no. 2: 3–17.

Musick, Marc A. 1996. 'Religion and Subjective Health Among Black and White Elders'. *Journal of Health and Social Behavior*, 37: 221–37.

National Centre on Elder Abuse. 2001. *The Basics: What Is Elder Abuse?* Available at <www.elderabusecenter.org/basic/index.html>, accessed 27 January 2003.

Novak, Mark. 1997. *Aging and Society: A Canadian Perspective*. 3rd edn. Scarborough, ON: Nelson Thompson.

Palmore, E.B. 1985. 'How to Live Longer and Like It'. *Journal of Applied Gerontology*, 4, no. 2: 1–8.

Peek, Chuck W. 2000. 'Correlates of Dynamic Profiles of Self-Rated Health'. Paper presented at the annual conference of the Southern Sociological Society.

Perry, Daniel. 1995. 'Researching the Aging Well Process'. *American Behavioral Scientist*, 39: 152–71.

Peters, Kimberley, and Richard G. Rogers. 1997. 'The Effects of Perceived Health Status and Age on Elders' Longevity'. *International Journal of Sociology and Social Policy*, 17, nos 9–10: 117–42.

Pilisuk, Marc, Mary Beth Montgomery, Susan Hillier Parks, and Curt Acredolo. 1993. 'Locus of Control, Life Stress, and Social Networks: Gender Differences in the Health Status of the Elderly'. *Sex Roles*, 28, nos 3–4: 147–66.

Robert, Stephanie, and James S. House. 1996. 'SES Differentials in Health by Age and Alternative Indicators of SES'. *Journal of Aging and Health*, 8: 359–88.

Rounds, Kathleen A., Maeda J. Galinsky, and Mathieu R. Despard. 1995. 'Evaluation of Telephone Support Groups for Persons with HIV Disease'. *Research on Social Work Practice*, 5: 442–59.

Ross, David P., Katherine J. Scott, and Peter J. Smith. 2001. *Canadian Fact Book on Poverty—2000*. Ottawa: Canadian Council on Social Development.

Rowe, John W., and Robert L. Kahn. 1997. 'Successful Aging'. *Gerontologist*, 37: 433–40.

Russell, R.V. 1990. 'Recreation and Quality of Life in Old Age: A Causal Analysis'. *Journal of Applied Gerontology*, 9, no. 1: 77–90.

Salamon, M.J. 1985. 'Sociocultural Role Theories in the Elderly: A Replication and Extension'. *Activities, Adaptation and Aging*, 7, no. 2: 111–22.

Satariano, William A. 1997. 'Editorial: The Disabilities of Aging—Looking to the Physical Environment'. *American Journal of Public Health*, 87: 331–2.

Schieman, Scott. 2000. 'Age, Education, and the Sense of Control: A Test of the "Cumulative Advantage" Hypothesis'. Paper presented at the annual conference of the American Sociological Association.

Seeman, Melvin, and Susan Lewis. 1995. 'Powerlessness, Health and Mortality: A Longitudinal Study of Older Men and Mature Women'. *Social Science and Medicine*, 41: 517–25.

Sherrod, Lonnie R. 1996. 'Leaving Home: The Role of Individual and Familial Factors'. *New Directions for Child Development*, 71: 111–19.

Singleton, Jerome F., and Andrew Harvey. 1995. 'Stage of Lifecycle and Time Spent in Activities'. *Journal of Occupation Science (Australia)*, 2, no. 1: 3–12.

Smolensky, E.S., S. Danziger, and P. Gottschalk. 1988. 'The Declining Significance of Age in the United States: Trends in the Well-Being of Children and the Elderly Since 1939'. In *The Vulnerable*, edited by J.L. Palmer, T. Smeedling, and B. Torrey, 29–54. Washington, DC: Urban Institute Press.

Souter, Gavin. 1997. 'Costs, Restrictions Criticized in Mexico's Pension Reform'. *Business Insurance*, 31, no. 33 (18 August): 33.

Statistics Canada. 1994. *Population Projections for Canada, Provinces and Territories, 1993–2016.* (Cat. no. 91-520.) Ottawa: Statistics Canada.

———. 1998. *Canada Yearbook.* (Cat. no. 11-402-XPE.) Ottawa: Statistics Canada.

———. 2000. 'Age Pyramid of the Population of Canada, July 1, 1974 to 2004'. Available at <www.statcan.ca/english/kits/animat/pyca.htm>, accessed 3 July 2001.

———. 2001. 'Population by Age Group'. Available at <www.statcan.ca/english/Pgdb/People/Population/demo31a.htm>, accessed 3 July 2001.

Steinkamp, M.W. 1987. 'Social Integration, Leisure Activity, and Life Satisfaction in Older Adults: Activity Theory Revisited'. *International Journal of Aging and Human Development*, 25: 293–307.

Steinkamp, M. W., and Kelly, J.R. 1985. 'Relationships Among Motivational Orientation, Level of Leisure Activity and Life Satisfaction in Older Men and Women'. *Journal of Psychology*, 119: 509–20.

Swallen, Karen C. 1997. 'Do Health Selection Effects Last? A Comparison of Morbidity Rates for Elderly Adult Immigrants and US-Born Elderly Persons'. *Journal of Cross-cultural Gerontology*, 12: 317–39.

Taylor, Rex, Graeme Ford, and Martin Dunbar. 1995. 'The Effects of Caring on Health: A Community-Based Longitudinal Study'. *Social Science and Medicine*, 40: 1407–15.

Tienda, Marta, and Haya Stier. 1996. 'Generating Labor Market Inequality: Employment Opportunities and the Accumulation of Disadvantage'. *Social Problems*, 43: 147–65.

Veenstra, Gerry. 2000. 'Social Capital, SES and Health: An Individual-Level Analysis'. *Social Science and Medicine*, 50: 619–29.

Warner, Camille D., Marie R. Haug, Carol M. Musil, and Diana L. Morris. 1998. 'Illness Narratives and Health Diaries of Older Adults'. Paper presented at the annual conference of the American Sociological Association.

Watt, Susan, Jacqueline Roberts, and Gina Browne. 1997. 'Age, Adjustment, and Costs: A Study of Chronic Illnesses'. *Social Science and Medicine*, 44: 1483–90.

Wood, F.W., ed. 1990. *An American Profile: Opinions and Behavior, 1972–1989.* Detroit: Gale Research.

Wunsch, Guillaume, Josianne Duchene, Evelyne Thitges, and Mohammed Salhi. 1996. 'Socio-Economic Differences in Mortality: A Life Course Approach'. *European Journal of Population*, 12: 167–85.

Yahya, H.A.Q. 1988. 'Factors Influencing the Satisfaction of Muslim Organization Members in a University Town in the United States (Lansing, Michigan)'. *Journal Institute of Muslim Minority Affairs*, 9: 280–95.

Glossary

Age pyramids Graphs used to illustrate the composition by age and sex of a given population.

Ageism Direct or indirect forms of discrimination against the young, the elderly, or other groups on the basis of their age.

Disengagement theory Holds that the elderly are among the weakest members of the population and that society has therefore devised a means of steadily displacing them from its core to its periphery.

Filial responsibility The moral responsibility of a grown child to look after his or her aging parent.

Primogeniture A system of inheritance in which the eldest son gets everything.

Senescence The process in which physical and mental abilities gradually decline with aging.

Chapter 9

Urban Problems and Homelessness

Chapter Objectives

After reading this chapter the student should understand:
- the problem of homelessness in cities
- different theoretical contributions that have historically founded urban sociology
- the social significance of neighbours and neighbourhoods
- the historical and social significance of suburbanization
- the different sociological perspectives explaining the urban way of life
- what is meant by *gentrification*
- the controversy surrounding deinstitutionalization
- the meaning of traffic as an urban problem
- environmental issues of metropolitan areas
- possible solutions to urban problems

Introduction

This chapter is about cities and neighbourhoods, housing and homelessness, urban life, wealth, and poverty. It examines the problems people encounter living in cities. Cities, as Max Weber (1968, 1981) pointed out, are among humanity's great social inventions. Most important, cities make possible a range of experiences that are unavailable in smaller rural areas or small towns. The sheer size and heterogeneity of city populations allow for specialization and diversity in the goods and services on offer.

Yet, for all that, city life has been surrounded by controversy since the beginning. Some have hailed cities as affording liberty, especially the freedom to think and act as one wishes. Others have viewed cities as lacking in neighbourliness and community spirit. They have depicted city-dwellers as lonely atoms, deprived of purpose and control.

Much of twentieth-century American sociology was addressed to examining these competing views of cities. At first, research on cities was skewed by the dominance of research on the city of Chicago, owing to the overwhelming presence

of the Department of Sociology at the University of Chicago. During the heyday of Chicago-style sociology, roughly 1900–40, Chicago was a living laboratory for the study of city populations, especially the poor, the marginal, and the stigmatized.

In the last half of the twentieth century, the main goals of urban sociologists were to understand **suburbanization**, urban renewal, and the development of enormous cities in the Third World. All of these topics came under the scrutiny of sociologists then, and we touch on all of these topics in this chapter. With the collapse of social spending and the social safety net under neo-liberal governments in the last decades of the twentieth century, more concern arose about the city's most vulnerable populations: the poor, racial minorities, the chronically ill, the unemployed or unemployable, and the homeless. Increasingly, cities became the venue, once again as during the heyday of the University of Chicago, for studying inner-city populations and their social and health problems.

Few of the issues we discuss in this chapter are unique to cities. Most, like crime and poverty, are found in rural areas as well. However, these problems are particularly pronounced in cities. The prevalence of crime and poverty, for example, is much greater in cities than in the countryside. Likewise, marked economic and ethnic segregation is more marked in cities (see, for example, Higley, 1995).

Some urban problems are more common in some regions than others. Rural-to-urban migration is a bigger problem in the developing world than in North America and Europe, for example. The assimilation of foreign immigrants is a bigger problem in North America than it is in most developing nations. Other urban problems are similar worldwide. These problems do not only affect developing or developed societies, they affect all societies. Every city in the world has to find solutions to many of the problems we discuss in this chapter. More than half of the world's population now lives in cities and towns rather than in rural areas.

The number one urban problem in the world today is unemployment, according to a report by the United Nations Development Programme. This report tabulated the results of a survey of mayors who rated problems in their respective cities on a scale running from 'mild' to 'severe'. The second most serious problem, according to this same report, is insufficient solid waste disposal, and the third most important problem—one that may be related to unemployment—is poverty. Other high-ranking problems in the world's cities, in descending order, are inadequate housing stock, insufficient solid waste collection, inadequate water and sanitation facilities, inadequate public transportation, traffic congestion, poor health services, insufficient participation in civil society, inadequate education services, air pollution, and urban violence, crime, and personal safety (International Survey of Mayors, 2002).

Contrasting Images of Cities

Given the many problems of cities, it is amazing how many people every year flock to them to live, work, and play. There is something appealing about city life. It may be the grandeur of urban architecture, the way city streets weave through a mix of intriguing landmarks and national monuments, residential areas, and commercial venues. Even the sheer congregation of lives is exciting, with its dense mass of strangers who live side by side, each expecting civility but not necessarily friendship from their neighbours. Yet for all the glamour and excitement that major cities offer, urban life has its problems.

Some people manage to avoid these problems. Experiences of city life vary widely from one person to the next depending on each person's position in the social structure: racial, class, gender, and age characteristics. A social problem affecting many people in the city may have no serious consequence for many others. This said, most city-dwellers are at least aware of some common city problems—crime, poverty, pollution, and traffic congestion, for example.

The leading theories about cities and city life—by Ferdinand Tönnies, Louis Wirth, and Georg Simmel, and others—were first developed a long time ago. We cite their theories not because sociologists have failed to develop theories since that time, nor because we imagine that cities have gone unchanged for 50, 100, or 200 years. On the contrary, cities have changed dramatically and continue to change today. There are some aspects of modern city life—for example, the modern suburb and its relation to 'downtown'—that never entered into the thinking of Tönnies, Wirth, and Simmel for the simple reason that suburbs did not exist in a modern sense or, in Wirth's case, to any significant degree before 1950.

However, these earliest theorists addressed some of the basic questions about cities, and we have no reason to think that the answers have changed significantly. For example, Tönnies ([1887] 1957) asked, what social bonds tie together people in small, stable communities, compared with large, fluid communities? For Tönnies, the movement from rural to city life meant a loss of **Gemeinschaft**—that is, community, intimacy, and emotional meaning.

Gemeinschaft refers to the typical characteristics of rural and small-town life. These characteristics include a stable, homogenous group of residents with a strong attachment to one particular place. Residents of the community interact around similar qualities and lead similar lives. In terms of social structure, the *Gemeinschaft* is marked by dense or highly connected networks, centralized and controlling elites, segregated or status groups, and multiple social ties. Even today, in rural areas, relatives and neighbours are closely linked, and others constantly observe their behaviour. Someone deviating from the prevailing social norms would feel social pressures to conform.

According to Tönnies, the ties among people in a city take the form of a **Gesellschaft**. The residents have different personal histories and impersonal brief relationships. They interact around similar interests, not similar characteristics or histories. There are few shared moral values and few moral custodians to enforce a common moral code. In terms of social structure, city networks are less connected, less centralized, less cliquish, and less redundant. In short, there is less cohesion and less control in the *Gesellschaft*.

Following Tönnies's lead, early American sociology considered cities anonymous and stressful. In his article 'Urbanism as a Way of Life' (1938), Louis Wirth explained why cities have less social integration or cohesion than smaller communities and why, as a result, cities develop their way of life, like the one Tönnies described. The experience of cities, Wirth said, arises out of their immense population size, variety, and fluidity.

A large population *size* ensures that most people will not know one another. Because they are strangers, they do not feel tied to one another in ways that control deviance and support cooperation in a smaller community. As a result, city people are less willing to help one another, especially when helping carries a personal cost. A high degree of *variety*—the presence of people with widely varying values, norms, and interests—is a second problem people have to solve in the city. Confusion, if not outright conflict, is bound to arise between strangers who see the world differently and who compete with one another for jobs, housing, and political influence. Finally, a high degree of *fluidity* makes it hard for people to anticipate one another's actions. City people will have many interactions and communications with strangers. The potential for uncertainty in their interactions leads people to develop strategies for avoiding strangers or keeping them emotionally at a distance. It also encourages them to develop institutions, such as police forces, to control or pacify strangers in public places.

Cities also concentrate poverty and unemployment in a small area. In particular, the population density of young men in cities is high, and young men are statistically the most likely to perpetrate common crimes. Cities bring young men together in a critical mass, making it possible for gangs to organize for criminal purposes. In short, crime results because cities marginalize—that is, concentrate, ghettoize, and segregate—both unwanted land uses and unwanted people. As well, cities are innovation centres in everything, even crime. New crimes, such as computer fraud and credit-card counterfeiting, are always being invented. In big cities, organized criminal 'mobs' perfect older crimes, such as drug trafficking, prostitution, and illegal gambling.

The Ideas of Georg Simmel

It was the German sociologist Georg Simmel from whom Wirth took many of his ideas. Simmel (1950) was the first to sense how life in a large city affects people psychologically and emotionally. City life is too stimulating, Simmel wrote. Strangers surround us on all sides. We experience countless strange noises, smells, sights, dangers, and opportunities. Walking a city street, we must pay constant attention to our environment. In the end, sensation overload takes its toll on our nervous systems.

Research supports at least some of these suppositions. The tempo of life *is* faster in a large city—more costly, arousing, and engaging than in a small town. People walk faster, talk faster, and even eat faster, mostly because more people must crowd into the same spaces every hour. City people also make more noise: the larger the city, the more car horns there are for irritated people to honk and the more people honk their horns. In these various ways—through isolation,

---

BOX 9.1
Mouth-to-Mouth Revelations

It turns out there's more to urban legends than you might think. They play on our deepest fears and warn us against risky behaviours by pointing out what supposedly happened to others who did what we might be tempted to try. Think of them as mini morality plays.

A teenage couple parks on a dark country road to listen to the radio and fool around. Suddenly, the music is interrupted by an announcer who says there is an escaped convict in the area who has served time for rape and murder. He is described as having a hook instead of a right hand. The girl, frightened, insists on being driven home immediately. The boy, frustrated, floors the accelerator and takes off. When they arrive at the girl's home, the boy goes around to open the car door for her only to discover a bloody hook hanging from the door handle.

This grisly gem has been making the rounds for decades. It even appeared in a 1960 Dear Abby column. The moral here of course is that teens shouldn't have sex. But more than that, it is because the girl cuts the necking short that the couple is saved—it's up to the girl to apply the brakes.

University of Toronto sociologist Walter Podilchak, a specialist in popular culture, says such legends serve to reinforce existing social structure which blames women for sexual seduction. 'The hierarchies in society are re-legitimated in the re-telling of the story', he says. But he says that when it comes to urban legends, regional variations abound. The AIDS Mary story is a case in point. The standard yarn is about a young man who meets a woman in a bar and brings her home. The couple enjoy an incredible night of lovemaking but when the man wakes in the morning, the woman is gone. He goes to the bathroom but is stopped dead in his tracks when he sees written in lipstick across the mirror 'Welcome to the world of AIDS'.

The Newfoundland variation on this story has two young women who save up for years for a once-in-a-lifetime trip to Florida. The one falls in love with a local man and after a whirlwind courtship he proposes marriage. Convinced this is the man for her and secure in the knowledge they will be married, the woman agrees to spend her last night in Florida with him. The next day, he gives her a small box and tells her not to open it until she gets home. The woman can't contain her excitement and she opens the box on the plane. Inside, she finds a tiny wooden coffin inscribed with, you guessed it, 'Welcome to the world of AIDS'.

Koven says it is a story that speaks volumes about Newfoundlanders. 'This was a good girl. She didn't do anything wrong. When she did decide to give up her virginity, they were going to be married. AIDS entered Newfoundland from without. It's not our fault. It exonerates Newfoundlanders', says Koven.

SOURCE: Sharon Oosthoek, 'Mouth-To-Mouth Revelations: Urban Legends Play on Our Deepest Fears and Can Be Considered Mini Morality Plays', *The Hamilton Spectator*, 5 January 1999, C4. Reproduced courtesy of the Hamilton Spectator.

higher risks of crime, and stresses on mental health—the city enslaves people who may have expected to gain freedom through city life.

At least, this is one view of cities. On the other side, many people think that city life is worth the psychic costs because city life is freer than life elsewhere. For example, Karl Marx was a fan of cities; that is why he referred in passing to the 'idiocy of rural life' (Marx and Engels, [1848] 1968: 36). Marx himself spent much of his adult life in London, perched day after day on the same chair in the great round Reading Room of the British Museum, sifting through books for evidence of patterns in world history. His was a uniquely urban activity, especially in the quasi-aristocratic setting of Great Russell Street in London's Bloomsbury. Until recently, such scholarly activity was impossible on the farm, or even in the suburbs. (The coming of the Internet and electronic access to worldwide libraries has changed this.) In the past, scholarship meant gathering vast knowledge and culture in one place; since at least Alexandria in ancient times, the city has been that place.

The vast storehouse of knowledge concentrated in cities liberates people, first by giving them intellectual freedom. But cities are not only great accumulations of knowledge, they are also accumulations of people, capital, and corporate institutions. Just about every activity is possible in a city, so just about every activity occurs there. Social control is weaker than in rural areas. People are freer to indulge their whims in cities.

Urbanity, today, remains the 'solution' to suburban alienation, urban sprawl, segregation, economic redevelopment, and boredom. For theorist Henri Lefebvre, the urban is not only a mode of cognition and a distinct process in capitalism, it is also a way of being-in-the-world. The urban is an *oeuvre* (creation) produced, made in the everyday by the inhabitants. The everyday is both the residual of organized and planned life and the product of the social whole (Boudreau, 1998). High rates of population growth show that urban areas are a desirable place to live, despite the urban problems associated with these dynamic areas. However, what of the fear that people in cities would lack a sense of community? Is this fear warranted?

The Importance of Neighbours and Neighbourhoods

Tönnies was wrong to suppose that cities lack communities or community sentiments, or that city-dwellers would not care about such sentiments. Residential segregation by race and social class is a common feature of life in North American cities (Emerson, Yancey, and Chai, 2001) and has an enormous impact on people's social relations and social identities. This voluntary assortment of people into urban communities based on culture, language, and ethnicity, and on resulting distinct identities, is a major source of Canada's continuing multiculturalism.

Social Similarity

People who are similar achieve closer neighbouring relationships, especially within ethnic or racial minority communities (Hallman, 1984). The desire to live among socially similar people may be due to a belief that this will produce comfort and security. Similarity also gives people less need to exercise control over their neighbours, an issue that would worry people whose lack of wealth and power gives them little ability to control others.

The neighbouring relationship is part of a hierarchy of relationships that range from close to distant. We discussed this hierarchy in chapter 4 on race and ethnic relations, in relation to E.S. Bogardus's measurement of *social distance* (1959). Not as close as marriage but closer than mere acquaintance, neighbouring—like every close or semi-close relationship—is based on a desire for similarity. Where similarity is lacking, people tend to exclude, reject, or drive others away. Thus, residential segregation, like clique formation, fences some people in while fencing others out. By becoming a neighbour, you tacitly agree to be like the people nearby.

Different groups of people may crave different kinds of similarity. For example, immigrants may select themselves into communities where they share the same language, religion, ethnicity, or race with their neighbours, regardless of social class. Native-born people of the same ethnic group may select themselves into communities where they share the same social class with their neighbours, regardless of religion, ethnicity, or race. Members of visible minorities or minorities who have historically experienced discrimination and prejudice may look for neighbours who share the same religion, ethnicity, or race, regardless of when they or their ancestors immigrated. Because of this self-selection, people vary widely across city neighbourhoods but vary little within neighbourhoods. Therefore, seen from a distance, cities look extremely varied. However, people only experience city variety when they travel outside their own neighbourhoods. Otherwise, their experience is little different from life in a small town a century ago.

Despite the homogenizing tendencies of mass education and the mass media, neighbours and neighbourhoods are still important today. They are important enough to evoke hostile NIMBY ('not in my backyard') reactions under certain circumstances—for example, reactions to the placement in their neighbourhood of public housing, halfway houses, or treatment facilities for recovering drug addicts (Oakley, 1999). To a large degree, it is precisely because cities are *not* agglomerations of undifferentiated strangers, and because people feel so strongly about keeping strangers and people unlike themselves at a distance, that cities have trouble solving typical problems such as homelessness and fear of victimization.

Satisfaction with Neighbourhood and Community

Neighbourhood satisfaction grows out of a mix of elements: the **objective characteristics** of a neighbourhood (for example, its appearance, upkeep, and access to resources and services), the **social and demographic characteristics** of the respondents (for example, their age, income, and length of residence), and residents' social ties and subjective definitions of the neighbourhood—how residents see it and feel about it (Fried, 1984; LaGory, Ward, and Sherman, 1985).

Over a lifetime, people leave a community if they do not like it. People who remain in a community come to like it even more with the passage of time. People generally accept their surroundings more readily as they age. Finally, the older generation has generally lower, and less fluid, expectations than the younger generation (Van Es and Schneider, 1983).

Satisfaction with neighbours, home, and the aesthetic quality of the community are all very important to people (Widgery, 1982). Residents in high-status neighbourhoods tend to be more satisfied with their neighbourhoods than other people (Rigby and Vreugdenhil, 1987). Of all neighbourhood characteristics, the things that people feel most satisfied about—their neighbours and other homes and buildings in the neighbourhood—are the ones most highly correlated with neighbourhood satisfaction (Gruber and Shelton, 1987). In short, neighbourhood satisfaction reflects the quality and quantity of social interaction within the neighbourhood (Connerly and Marans, 1985).

Problems Caused by Urban Growth

Contrary to what some believe, cities existed thousands of years ago. Babylon, Jerusalem, Byzantium, Alexandria, Athens, and Rome were all large and important cities before Christ was born. Paris, London, Venice, and Florence were all large and important before massive economic developments in the late eighteenth century kick-started rapid **urbanization**, the process by which a large portion of the human population came to shift from rural to urban homes (see Sjoberg, 1965; Weber, 1968).

However, modern cities are new in human history, only a few centuries old. Technological innovations that allowed better sewage disposal and water supply, mass transportation, and electrical lighting—all central to modern city life—contributed to the faster rate of urban growth throughout the nineteenth and early twentieth centuries. For example, a distinctive feature of the modern city is the high-rise office building. Such buildings only began to spread with the invention of elevators, telephones, and new building techniques in the nineteenth century. High-rise buildings (or skyscrapers), in turn, not only changed city skylines, they also drove urban population sizes through the roof, so to speak. This, in turn, led to new problems, including crowding, traffic congestion (for example, rush-hour traffic), and smog.

The growth of commerce, industry, and national governments also created new kinds of cities, and new city problems. In particular, the location of factories in cities, huge influxes of immigrants to work in the factories, and capitalist exploitation of workers led to inner-city poverty, homelessness, traffic congestion, rising crime rates, and other problems. These problems all intensified as cities grew.

Then the period following World War II changed the landscape of North American urban life in a different way. As North America entered an economic boom, spending and birth rates were high, unemployment was low, and families prospered. The purchase of homes outside the urban core exploded in the 1940s and 1950s, causing land developers to expand residential housing into outlying regions. In this way, the modern suburb was born.

Suburbanization

Like cities themselves, suburbs existed long before the mid-century economic boom made them popular. Railways, for example, made suburban living possible in the nineteenth century. However, twentieth-century suburbs differed markedly from the suburbs built in earlier times. For one thing, the new housing developments were almost entirely residential in function, with little land set aside for commercial or industrial use. More important, however, was that buyers of houses in the suburban housing projects owned automobiles. This allowed residents to commute long distances between where they lived and where they worked. (See Table 9.1.) More than any other single factor, the spread of the family car allowed suburbanization to take place. In this way, Henry Ford, who invented the assembly-line production of cheap automobiles, also invented the suburb and transformed modern city life.

Suburbanization is the process by which housing spreads almost unhindered into once-rural regions surrounding the city core. This process greatly expanded the geographic size of cities. For instance, Chicago's population has increased only 4 per cent in the past

TABLE 9.1
Time Spent in Minutes Commuting in 1986 and 1998

	1986	1998
By bus or subway, Canada	85	100
By car		
Canada	56	58
Montreal	63	60
Toronto	67	70
Vancouver	58	70
Mid-sized CMAs[a]	61	57
Small CMAs[b]	48	49
Rural areas	50	56

[a] Ottawa-Hull, Edmonton, Quebec City, Hamilton, Kitchener, London, Winnipeg, and Calgary.
[b] St. Catharines–Niagara, Halifax, Victoria, Saint John, Thunder Bay, Trois Rivières, Sudbury, Chicoutimi, Sherbrooke, Regina, Saskatoon, Oshawa, and Windsor.

SOURCE: Warren Clark, 'Traffic Report Weekday Commuting Patterns', *Canadian Social Trends* no. 56 (Spring 2000): 20. Data from Statistics Canada, General Social Survey 1998.

20 years, yet its spatial geography has increased by 46 per cent between 1980 and 2000. Those who first moved to the suburbs were mainly wealthy middle- to upper-class whites. This movement increased the racial and ethnic segregation of minorities in urban centres. Further, as more affluent residents migrated to the outskirts of the city, their property taxes went with them, leaving the city's centre with less revenue for schools, roads, and other services.

Suburbanites who work in the city used the city's services, such as roads and sanitation, but do not pay for them. As a result, while the suburbs flourished amid a surplus of property tax income, downtown areas stagnated and dried up. Business and industry owners, seeing the cheaper land values and lower property tax rates in the suburbs, began to move, taking much-needed jobs away from urban cores.

In the first half of the twentieth century, most architects who were asked to describe the utopian city life envisioned soaring skyscrapers and multi-level networks of roads and pedestrian promenades. However, in the second half of the twentieth century, cities grew outward rather than upward. Today, the traditional functions of cities—as employment, recreational, and cultural centres—have been decentralized and taken up by individual urban villages, pods that are ever farther away from the central metropolitan area (Garreau, 1991). The best-paying new jobs in Canada are often located in suburban Mississauga (outside Toronto), Kanata (outside Ottawa), and Richmond (outside Vancouver).

Yet, while the best-paying jobs are to be found in formerly remote fringe towns, the people most in need of a stable income and decent place to live—the urban poor—continue to suffer, unaided and unable to take advantage of these opportunities. Financial institutions have also abandoned troubled urban areas. Some banks and insurance companies, for example, have redlined cities and metropolitan areas. Redlining refers literally to the drawing of red lines on the map and making loans and providing insurance on one side of the line—and not on the other, in what are deemed undesirable areas.

Sprawl

As an urban form, sprawl has been loudly attacked by some social scientists as an inefficient and ineffective urban form that contributes to (if not directly causes) a variety of social ills. At the same time, it has been accepted by other social scientists as a positive force in today's urban form (Schmidt, 1999). Urban sprawl is most often characterized as haphazard or unplanned growth, or in terms of undesirable land-use patterns. It includes such patterns as scattered development, 'leapfrog' development, strip or ribbon development, and continuous low-density development (Redburn, 2002). In Canadian cities, large low-density, low-rise bedroom suburbs dotted by strip malls, shopping centres, and industrial parks epitomize suburban sprawl.

The vast highway programs of the 1950s and 1960s fostered massive migration to the suburbs and corresponding deterioration of urban centres, though more so in the United States than in Canada. Policy research since the 1960s has been dedicated to investigating the relationship between transportation policy and land use and to devising policies that might improve the worst effects of suburban sprawl and the corresponding urban blight. Scarcity of federal funds, shortage of highway capacity, and the limited ability of the environment to absorb additional pollution were all determinants of transportation and land use decisions since the 1970s (Hyman and Kingsley, 1996).

We cannot underestimate, in this story, the effects of the automobile, the world's leading mass-produced durable good, on the global economy and social organization of space. The very same three nations (the United States, Germany, and Japan) that dominate the world economy also have a disproportionate share of auto production and consumption. The prevalence of auto-centred transport systems (ACTS) largely determines a nation's pattern of transportation and urban sprawl (Freund and Martin, 2000).

Today, developing nations of the South are adopting Western standards of 'automobility' but face unique problems such as unequal access, inadequate roads and infrastructure, and the cost of importing oil. These nations represent a major new market as well as an environmental threat. China, for example, faces a shortage of arable land that will be further compromised by ACTS. Similar problems beset South Africa, Mexico, India, and other countries (Freund and Martin, 2000).

The tendency for technology, capital, and industry to drive urban development has not been limited to the Third World. In North America, since early in the twentieth century, governments have been under continuing pressure from the auto, oil, and rubber monopolies to promote the use of the automobile over public rail transportation. This pushed metropolitization outward, to the detriment of the working class, who often did not own automobiles. In the 1980s, suburban development began to change, emphasizing office parks and subcities with higher-density metropolitan subcentres. This change has benefited the working class. However, the locations of future subcities and public transportation links in North America need to be planned, as they have been in Europe. The lack of such planning in North America has resulted in a chaotic spatial spread of workers because of suburban sprawl (Zeitlin, 1990).

California is a particularly vivid and well-known example of the sprawl problem. Until recently, the history of California has been characterized by meteoric growth in all aspects: population, economic output, housing construction, and the global impact of its cultural values. Yet this growth has come at a price: sprawl and traffic congestion, distressed older neighbourhoods, air pollution, inadequate urban services, and a decline in quality of life.

These consequences were predicted if trends continued unabated, undirected by some plan for managing growth. Calls for growth management

at the state and regional levels can be traced to at least the late 1950s, but they were systematically defeated. The explanation for this defeat involves issues related to conflicts between regional level governance structures and local control, questions of accountability and democracy, and the complex of meanings embodied in the terms *growth* and *region* (Pincetl, 1994).

However, not everyone is critical of the outcome or sees this outcome as a failure to achieve some other kind of order. Some view the evolution of economics, politics, and culture in Los Angeles—historically depicted as outside the mainstream of US urban culture—as having successfully established a new style of urban life. Some believe that the media have exaggerated the images of urban sprawl, inconsequential architecture, freeways, sun, surf, and smog in Los Angeles. In their view, Los Angeles actually bears a strong resemblance to many emerging world cities and US urban centres.

Contrary to the legacy of industrial metropolis advocated by the Chicago school, the emerging 'Los Angeles school' of urban studies has presented a more contemporary depiction of modern urban centres, characterized by dispersed patterns of low-density growth, multicultural and ethnic enclaves, and an array of urban centres in a single region (Hise, Dear, and Schockman, 1996).

Alternative Theories of Urban Areas

As with other social problems we discuss in this book, different sociological approaches discuss the problems of cities in different ways, leading to different proposed solutions.

The Structural-Functionalist Perspective

Some structural-functionalists would view social problems in the city as resulting naturally from growth and specialization.

With the growth of wealth in cities, there is more to steal than in the countryside, hence, more theft and robbery. With the growth of density, there is more intense competition for scarce resources—jobs, housing, recreational opportunities, and so on—hence, more need for criminal 'innovation'. With the development of neighbourhoods where people are anonymous—indeed, virtually invisible—there is more likelihood of every kind of private vice, for example, drug use and the satisfaction of unusual sexual tastes. Homelessness, a peculiarly urban problem, is the result of the attempts of many vulnerable people—runaways from abusive families, mentally ill people without anyone to care for them, and people below the poverty line who cannot afford shelter—to survive and, despite adversity, their finding it easier to survive in cities than in small towns or rural areas.

Thus, as Robert Merton (1957) pointed out in his theory of adaptations to anomie, discussed in chapter 3 on crime and violence, people pursue the American dream in many ways. Cities make more of these ways of pursuit possible and likely. Since the Middle Ages, people have known this and have steadily chosen city life over village life.

Other structural-functionalists focus on those tendencies of the city—its size, variety, and fluidity in particular—that promote social disorganization, weak social controls, and consequent deviance and distress. From this perspective, social problems such as crime, addiction, and mental illness are foreseeable consequences of urbanization.

These theorists argue that three main processes have markedly changed the normal functioning of social institutions in cities. First, the massive influx of workers into urban centres during the Industrial Revolution weakened personal ties with family and religion. The Industrial Revolution brought millions into cities, where they broke off into specialized groups that occupied a particular position within the increasingly stratified division of labour. Second, huge waves of immigrants flooding into cities throughout the nineteenth and twentieth centuries overwhelmed acculturation mechanisms, making it difficult for many people quickly to assimilate into society.

These first two processes led to cities being comprised of many strangers coexisting in a highly dense environment, with little real relationship between them. In contrast, pre-industrial societies were mainly small, rural settlements in which members shared the same experiences and developed similar values, norms, and identity. Émile Durkheim ([1893] 1964) called this *common conscience*. Moreover, the lives of these people were often interconnected in a tight, homogeneous social order (which Durkheim called **mechanical solidarity**). The new social order was based on interdependent, though not necessarily intimate, relationships. Under this **organic solidarity** (also Durkheim's term), no member of society was entirely self-sufficient; all people were dependent on others for survival and prosperity.

The third process, suburbanization, involved the flight of the affluent out of the urban centre to the surrounding area. Functionalists believe that this also contributed to social disorganization, in much the same way that the mass migration of workers into the city a century earlier weakened personal relationships. Suburbanization at least created conflict between the traditional urban dwellers and the new suburbanites that intensified already existing urban problems.

Conflict Theory

Unlike functionalists, conflict theorists always ask whose interests are served by the actions of the dominant groups in society and by their ideology. These theorists attribute urban problems such as homelessness and poverty not to the effects of size, variety, and fluidity, but to the workings of capitalism. By their reckoning, cities suffer problems—even 'die'—because it is in no powerful group's interest to prevent this from happening.

Unlike functionalists, conflict theorists do not believe that modest economic incentives to business will revive a dying city; they believe that there is more to urban problems than a lack of economic growth. Unequal power, competing class interests, capital investment decisions, and government subsidy programs mediate the growth of cities. The distribution of urban wealth, not merely its creation, determines whether the majority of city-dwellers will live or die.

Because of their emphasis on class relations as the source of most urban social problems, conflict theorists call for decisive changes in public policy by government, to direct tax dollars and corporate profits toward rebuilding cities. Such a change will, in turn, likely require collective political action by the underclasses to gain the attention of government. Some observers have pointed to examples where this has begun to happen, linking the economic and social marginalization of inner-city inhabitants with patterns of civil unrest. The Los Angeles riots of 1992 are a prime example of explosive tension and hostility that had been brewing among economically deprived urban ethnic groups and that targeted a supposedly racist white majority.

Symbolic Interactionism

Symbolic interactionists study the ways people experience city life on an everyday basis. One of the earliest writers on urban social relations to take this approach was the German sociologist Georg Simmel (1950). As noted earlier, he argued that cities were so inherently stimulating and quick-paced that to prevent sensory overloading, inhabitants needed to reduce their sensitivity to events and people around them.

However, symbolic interactionists tend to doubt that everyone in the same structural setting has the same experience. Some symbolic interactionists have focused on how the meaning of city life varies from one group to another. Herbert Gans (1982) noted that people experience urban life in different ways, depending on their neighbourhood and their personal characteristics, such as age and cultural background. For example, *cosmopolites*, a category to which students, artists,

writers, and professionals belong, view the city as a place where they can meet others with similar cultural values and interests; *ethnic villagers* reside in ethnic enclaves because of the experiences and perspectives they share with other members of their own group; and the *trapped* and *deprived* live in the city because they believe that they have no other option.

Gans's work is one example of symbolic interactionists' study of the formation of subcultures in the city. A **subculture** is a group of people who shares some cultural traits of the larger society but that, as a group, also has its own distinctive values, beliefs, norms, style of dress, and behaviour. Subculture membership allows individuals who are otherwise isolated within an impersonal city to form connections with those around them. An ethnic community is an example of a subculture, as are skinheads and youth gangs. The corporate elites, who have determined the future of urban areas, are also by this view a subculture.

Social and Health Consequences of Urban Areas

Poverty

Among the most visible urban problems are poverty and homelessness. Today, North American poverty is mainly an urban problem, although rural poverty also exists.

In 1995 in Canada, roughly 5.5 million people, or one in five Canadians, qualified as poor. While the total population in census metropolitan areas (CMAs) increased by 6.9 per cent between 1990 and 1995, the poor population in CMAs rose by 33.8 per cent, nearly five times as quickly. In 1995, 63.2 per cent of Canada's total population and 69.3 per cent of all poor people lived in a CMA. In contrast, in 1959, only 27 per cent of the poor in the United States lived in major cities, while the rest were confined to rural areas. Now that figure has risen to nearly 50 per cent (Wilson, 1996: 11–12).

Of all Canadian cities, Montreal has the highest ratio of high-poverty census tracts. *High-poverty census tracts* are those geographic areas with an economic family poverty rate equal to or greater than 32.6 per cent, twice the national rate. While most CMAs have at least some high-poverty neighbourhoods, three-fifths of the nation's total are in Montreal and Toronto (Lee, 2000).

One of the most serious problems associated with urban poverty is the lack of affordable housing for low-income families and individuals. Currently, affordable housing is scarce in many major Canadian and US cities, including Toronto (see Table 9.2 and Figure 9.1), Vancouver, and New York. There are several reasons for this scarcity. First, the ownership of rental housing is being concentrated in the hand of a few property owners. In New York and Houston in the 1980s, for example, 5 per cent of all landlords controlled more than 50 per cent of the rental units

TABLE 9.2
Vacancy Rate (Percentages), Private Rental Housing, All Units and Two-Bedroom Units, Toronto (formerly Metropolitan Toronto), 1989–98[a]

	All Units	Two-Bedroom Units
1989	0.4	0.3
1990	0.8	0.7
1991	1.6	1.6
1992	2.0	1.7
1993	1.9	1.6
1994	1.2	0.9
1995	0.8	1.2
1996	1.1	1.3
1997	0.8	0.8
1998	0.9	0.7

[a] All data are from the month of October.

SOURCE: Data drawn from Ontario Non-Profit Housing Association and Co-operative Housing Federation of Canada, *Where's Home? A Picture of Housing Needs in Ontario*; available at <www.housingagain.web.net/whome/#complete>, accessed 24 March 2003.

available; in Boston, 20 people owned 40 per cent (Gilderbloom, 1991: 131). As owners form an oligopoly over rental housing, they can cooperate to raise rents without fear of competition.

Another reason for the housing shortage is that developers stand to make larger profits by investing in and constructing housing solely for the middle and upper classes. As a result, upscale homes are in relative abundance for people who can afford them, while low-income housing remains scarce.

Other forms of real estate investment include condominium conversion and gentrification. *Condominium conversion* is the transformation of rental units into apartments for sale. Again, this practice creates a supply of housing for those who can afford a downpayment and a mortgage out of the financial reach of the urban poor. **Gentrification** involves the purchase of cheap, rundown properties in economically disadvantaged neighbourhoods and their renovation into middle- and upper-class housing. As property values in the area rise in response to the inflow of capital and public interest, the poor who once lived there are forced to move elsewhere.

As 'undesirables' are evicted and impoverished neighbourhoods made over to reflect upper- and middle-class tastes, the poor concentrate in inner-city neighbourhoods that are economically stagnant and physically decayed. In these areas, rates of crime, violence, and drug use are typically higher than elsewhere in the city. Some who are unable to afford even the most modest of places to live grow increasingly reliant on urban shelters for a place to sleep at night.

Given the common stereotype of the poor as shiftless and unattached, it is shocking to find that the most rapidly increasing category of shelter users in Toronto is two-parent families with children. The number of children staying in shelters rose from 2,700 in 1988 to 6,000 in 1998 (City of Toronto, 2001). As desperate and humbling as any reliance on shelters may be for poor people, the alternative—homelessness—is even less appealing.

FIGURE 9.1
Rent Increases, Toronto, 1989–98

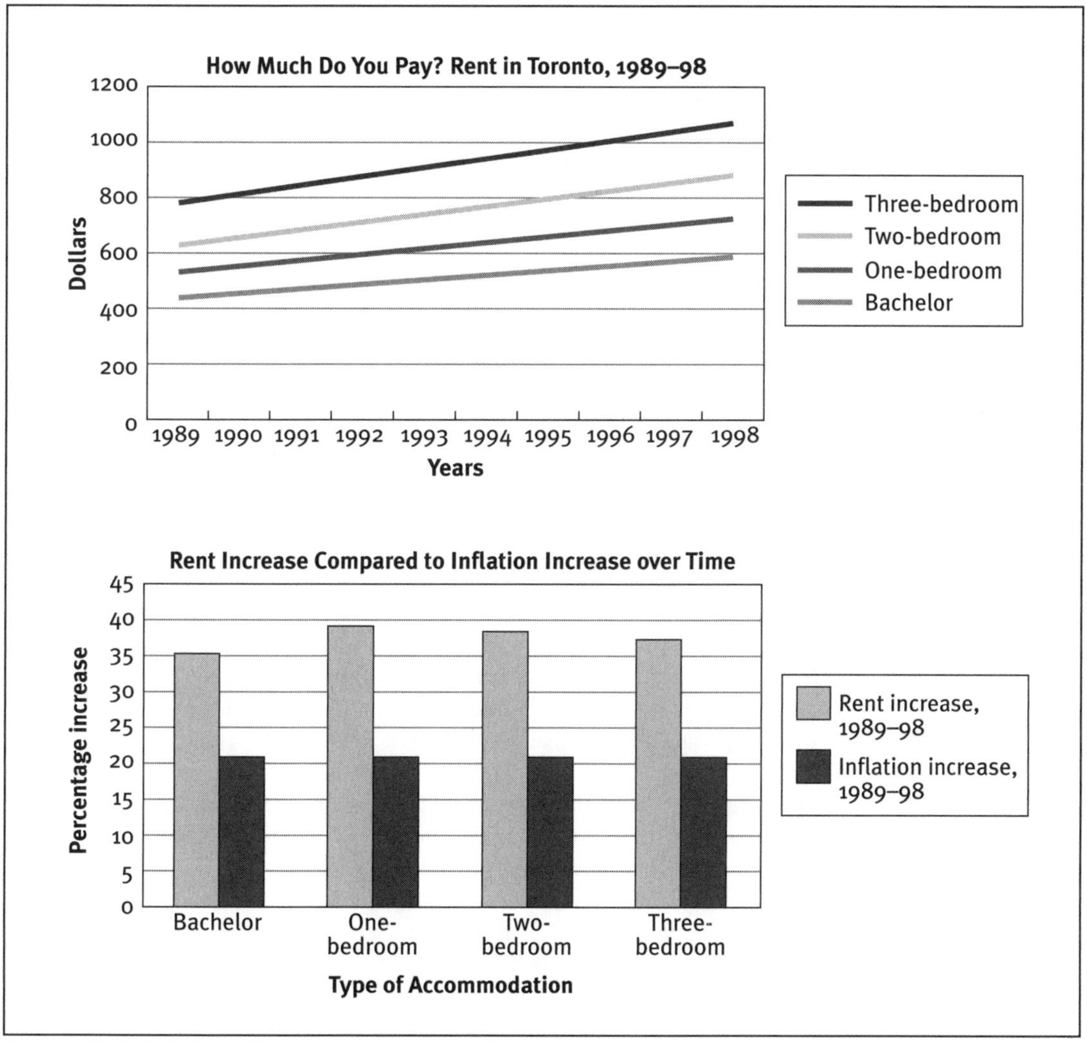

How Much Do You Pay? Rent in Toronto, 1989–98

(Line graph. Y-axis: Dollars, from 0 to 1200. X-axis: Years, 1989 to 1998.)

Legend:
- Three-bedroom
- Two-bedroom
- One-bedroom
- Bachelor

Rent Increase Compared to Inflation Increase over Time

(Bar graph. Y-axis: Percentage increase, from 0 to 45. X-axis: Type of Accommodation — Bachelor, One-bedroom, Two-bedroom, Three-bedroom.)

Legend:
- Rent increase, 1989–98
- Inflation increase, 1989–98

SOURCE: Linda LaPointe, 'Change in Average Rents for Private Rental Compared to Inflation Toronto (Formally Metropolitan Toronto). 1989–1998'; available at <www.housingagain.web.net/whome/88toronto.pdf>, accessed 28 February 2003. Data from CMHC and Statistics Canada; analysis by LaPointe Consulting.

Health Perspectives

Health problems, to be found in all population densities, are most concentrated in urban areas. This is in part the result of a large number of people's gathering in a small area. (See also Table 9.3.) Rates of illness and disease are bound to go up because of population size. It is often acknowledged that city life is much more stressful, and this too poses health problems. The rush of traffic, the pace of change, the cost of living, jostling with strangers, the fear of victimization, economic competition, noise—all of these characteristics are common to the city, and all are

TABLE 9.3
Food-Bank Clients' Self-Evaluations of Health

With public health care on the public's mind at present, it is timely to look at the health of certain population groups beyond merely medicare and hospitalization issues. For low-income people in general, nutrition is inadequate and health in general is poorer. This year's survey shows, too, that health has declined as incomes have declined.

Food recipients were asked how they compared their health to others of the same age.

	1993	2002
Rated health excellent	17.2%	11.8%
Rated health very good	16.2%	17.2%
Rated health good	30.2%	28.6%
Rated health fair	19.0%	24.4%
Rated health poor	12.5%	16.4%

Furthermore, the health of food recipients is not only declining but is also considerably lower than that of the general population. 41.8% of food recipients rated their health as fair or poor. If one asks middle-income earners the same question, only 10% or 12% say their health is fair or poor.

SOURCE: Daily Bread Food Bank, *Poorer People, Poorer Health: The Health of Food Bank Recipients, Spring Food Drive* (Toronto: Daily Bread Food Bank, 2002).

stress-inducing. Though the occasional experience of acute stress is a healthy and manageable stimulus, chronic exposure to high stress levels can lead to serious health problems, including heart disease and an ailing immune system.

However, this is probably not why mentally ill people are disproportionately common in cities, or among the urban homeless. Instead, cities gather all kinds of people into a small space and then leave them to struggle for survival.

Homelessness

Runaways

The homeless are a varied mix of single men and women, young people, families, Aboriginal people, and some individuals with serious health problems (such as HIV/AIDS). Many are able bodied, free from substance or alcohol abuse, and willing to work—indeed, some even have jobs but lack sufficient income to afford to pay the high rent of the most bare of city apartments. And in large cities, many of the homeless are young people who have run away from home because they would rather live on the street than under the same roof as an abusive parent.

Research shows that runaways overlap, in experience and background, with a variety of other social types. To their parents, they are 'missing children'. Malcolm Payne (1995) identifies five different kinds of young people who go missing: runaways, pushaways, throwaways, fallaways, and take-aways. Gerald Adams, Thomas Gullotta, and Mary Anne Clancy (1985) identify three categories of homeless adolescents: runaways, throwaways, and societal rejects. As the names suggest, young people have a variety of reasons for leaving home.

The population of runaway and homeless youth has changed in recent decades, with youth running away from abuse, neglect, and disintegrated families rather than seeking economic opportunities or excitement. Most street youth are from families suffering serious emotional, mental, or substance abuse problems. These youth are not necessarily on the street because of socio-economic pressures (Price, 1989), though

---

BOX 9.2
Tallying the Homeless

In its first stab at counting the number of people who sleep in homeless hostels and abused women's shelters, Statistics Canada appears to have missed some heads. Counting people in shelters as a distinct category in the census for the first time, the agency has pegged the population living in hostels with nowhere else to turn at 14,145 on the day the census was taken in May last year. Nearly 1,500 were children under 15.

The demographers at Statscan are swift to caution that the number is not a measure of Canada's homeless population, but merely a snapshot of the hordes sleeping in shelters across Canada on a particular spring night. It ignores the thousands more who slumber on park benches or squat in abandoned buildings.

'It's a fairly good estimate of the population in shelters on census day', said Pierre Turcotte, a family demographer at Statscan. 'Its certainly not an estimate of the homeless population.' But with its count for some cities fallen far short of those municipalities' own statistics, the Statscan numbers would seem to understate the growing social blight of people crowded into the country's homeless shelters.

In Calgary, where the city has counted its homeless population in shelters and on the streets every other year for the past decade, Statscan has pinned the number in hostels at 1,135; the city's own outreach workers counted 1,620 people in shelters last May.

But counting the people who drift in and out of shelters is tricky business. Not only are homeless people hard to track, but as their numbers increased over the past decade, cities like Toronto flung open the odors of low-budget motels and church basements to shelter those turned away from mainstream hostels. So plenty of people in makeshift shelter system were lumped into other categories under the Statscan criteria. Excluded from the count of people in shelters, for example, where those living in at the YMCA or in discount motels who, in Toronto, comprise 750 of those in the shelter system.

SOURCE: Margaret Philp, 'Tallying the Homeless in Canada', *The Globe and Mail*, 6 November 2002, A9. Reprinted with permission *The Globe and Mail*.

---

family financial difficulties increase the likelihood of physical abuse.

Les Whitbeck, Danny Hoyt, and Kevin Ackley (1997) conclude that families of runaways tend, on average, to give their children less support, supervision, and acceptance than other families. Even parents at times concede they may have been guilty of minor abusive acts, though they are less willing than their children to report more severe forms of abuse.

In short, most runaways are children escaping dysfunctional families. Abuse aside, the children tend to come from 'chaotic/aggressive families' and to reveal a mixed pattern of youth aggression and parental skill deficiency (Teare, Authier, and Peterson, 1994). Running away is most often, but not always, a response to neglect, abandonment, and physical or sexual violence (Côté, 1992). Abused runaways are even more likely than those who were not abused to describe their parents in ways that suggest serious anti-social personality and drug problems (Stiffman, 1989a). Evidence also suggests that the parents of runaways themselves had a history of running away from home when they were children (Plass and Hotaling, 1995).

Common to runaways studied in Toronto are problem families; high rates of delinquency, depression, tension, and low self-image; and a history of physical abuse (Janus, Burgess, and McCormack, 1987). Sexually abused male runaways show extreme withdrawal from all types of interpersonal relationships. Other runaways associate with deviant or criminal peers, engaging in deviant survivor strategies such as prostitution (Whitbeck and Simons, 1990).

Runaways run a heightened risk of suicide attempts: 30 per cent of runaways report having attempted suicide in the past. Suicide attempters in runaway shelters have many more behavioural and mental health problems, and report having more family members and friends with problems

Homelessness, a particularly harrowing urban social problem, is the result of many vulnerable people trying to survive and, despite adversity, finding it easier to survive in cities than in small towns or rural areas. (Dick Hemingway)

than do other runaways (Stiffman, 1989b). Suicide attempts by runaway youth are most commonly caused by trouble at home, arguments, disappointments, humiliations, trouble at school, assault, and sexual abuse (Rotherham-Borus, 1993).

Accordingly, the main reason that runaways remain on the street, refusing to return home or to try foster care, is their stated belief that family conflict is inevitable. Runaways develop their own surrogate families on the street, largely among other street people, rather than risk further rejection or further abuse (Holdaway and Ray, 1992). Some runaways who become residents of child-welfare institutions opt not to run away. What determines whether they stay or run is the perceived level of emotional warmth or coldness in the institution (Angenent, Beke, and Shane, 1991).

Many chronic runaways grow up to be homeless adults. Homeless adults who display higher than average rates of criminal behaviour, substance abuse, and other forms of deviant behaviour tend to come from more abusive and deprived childhoods (Simons and Whitbeck, 1991). A history of foster care, group-home placement, and running away is particularly common among homeless adults (Susser et al., 1991).

Deinstitutionalized People

In large cities, many of the homeless are mentally ill people who have been released from institutional care—**deinstitutionalized**—and left to fend for themselves with little money or social support. People who suffer from mental illness also suffer from the negative stigma associated with mental illness. When asked to consider mental illness and the mentally ill, people tend to think of ideas of danger, uncleanness, instability, and people who are unable to conform to basic social standards (Baron, 1981). For example, researchers find that the adjectives most closely ascribed to ex-mental patients include *excitable*, *strange*, *tense*, *strong*, *uncertain*, *unsure*, *unpredictable*, *convincing*, *active*, and *mysterious* (Fracchia et al., 1976).

Many believe that former mental patients are still a potential threat to the community (Fracchia et al., 1976). The public associates mental disorders with violent behaviour (Monohan, 1992), and continues to stigmatize mental illness (Borinstein, 1992). Considering the negative stereotypes the notion of mental illness evokes, it is not surprising that many people have opposed the deinstitutionalization of the mentally ill.

In Canada as in the United States, deinstitutionalization began in the 1960s. Within the first twenty years, the number of beds in mental institutions was reduced by more than 60 per cent (Aubry, Tefft, and Currie, 1995: 39–40). This was supposed to coincide with the development of community supports, since the primary goal of deinstitutionalization was to integrate the mentally ill with other members of the community. Administrators were to develop support systems and aid in their 'normalization' (Aubry, Tefft, and Currie, 1995). Deinstitutionalization, then, ideally involves not only the individuals who are mentally ill, but also the members of an ex-patient's neighbourhood.

Some community members have feared that the new neighbours would endanger them, or lower property values. These fears prove largely unwarranted. After a few years of living near a community mental health home, most neighbours report no negative effect of the home on property values and no one reports problems in selling their home (Arens, 1993: 241). Likewise, community mental health facilities do not affect house marketability (Dear and Taylor, 1982). Despite this, 15 to 24 per cent of survey respondents, depending on the question asked, remain worried about the potential dangers associated with the mentally ill (Borinstein, 1992: 190).

Some people are not as fearful of or as opposed to mental health facilities as other people; nor do they all want to keep their distance from the mentally ill. In the end, however, issues of stigmatization, stereotyping, NIMBYism, and deinstitutionalization are all the results of large social processes at work—of government policies to marginalize the poor and vulnerable economically, politically, and legally. Deinstitutionalization was, largely, a cost-saving tactic by governments. Money that could have facilitated patients' integration into society did not materialize after they were released from hospital (Sigurdson, 2000). The integration of these people back into society was not planned, nor was any scientific research conducted on how to go about reintroducing them into society. Much cost-shifting between the federal government and state governments also surrounded the advent of deinstitutionalization, so that the issue was no longer patient care but who would pay for the care of the mentally ill.

Many mentally ill people end up in jail, since the number of police—unlike other public employees—was never reduced and money continues to be available to build jails, if not hospitals and halfway houses. Chris Sigurdson (2000) reports that because of this emphasis on law and order, the Los Angeles County Jail holds the largest population of mentally ill people in America. Paradoxically, given the costs of keeping a person in jail—an estimated $20,000 (US) per year in 1997—it might have been cheaper to provide more hospitals and halfway houses after all. Therefore, in the end, improper planning of the reintegration process and short-sighted thinking by politicians eager to show taxpayers a tax reduction produced higher costs for the government.

Traffic

Another major problem that is mainly urban is traffic congestion. Each year, thousands of people suffer death or injury in traffic-related accidents. In Third World countries, the numbers are even more dramatic than in North America. In Nigeria, for example, traffic accidents are the leading cause of death among Nigerian adults aged 30 to 40. Road traffic accidents are also the major cause of death in Ireland. In North America, pedestrian injuries are a leading cause of childhood mortality.

Generally, traffic accidents are caused by our increased dependence on autos and the hegemony of the automobile over social space. Under conditions of dense auto traffic, as in cities, accidents are bound to occur. Further, as long as there is poverty, there will be poor people driving vehicles in poor repair. The spreading use of larger, heavier vehicles—vans, SUVs, and light trucks—also seems likely to increase the risks of injury and death for people who are struck by vehicles.

Congestion is another problem caused by traffic. Canadians are travelling farther to get to their usual workplace locations in 2001 than in 1996—a median distance of 7.2 kilometres in 2001. These commuting distances vary from region to region, however. For example, nearly one-third of the workers in the Oshawa census metropolitan area, east of Toronto, travel more than 25 kilometres to reach their workplace. The cost of traffic congestion, in lost time, wasted fuel, and higher insurance rates, is considerable and mounting fast. Related to the growth of congestion is the increase in air pollution, noise, and lack of green space in and around cities. Environmental harm also includes the damage to roads. Highways currently carry more and heavier trucks than they were originally designed to carry. The dramatic increase in heavy traffic results in faster road deterioration.

At present, a great many car users choose the car over alternative modes of transport because it is more convenient, it saves time, and they think the alternatives are bothersome. They see road traffic as less serious for the environment than people's use of other transport modes. They are also less positive toward measures that benefit public transportation, walking, and cycling.

Given their many problems, it is amazing how many people flock to cities to live, work, and play. For all of the excitement and glamour that major cities offer, urban life faces tremendous problems. (Dick Hemingway)

In most North American cities, cars are given greater priority than pedestrians. Consider the amount of urban space that cities devote to the automobile. On average, a pedestrian takes up 0.5 square metres of room when standing and 0.9 square metres when in stride. A car, on the other hand, requires 28 square metres when parked and 280 square metres of forward clearance when travelling at 60 kilometres per hour (Kay, 1997: 67). The importance attached to the automobile is also reflected in the amount of parking space dedicated to it. In Paris and Amsterdam, two cities renowned for their metropolitan charm and pedestrian-friendly design, there is only one parking space for every three people living in the central area. Houston, with its sprawling web of highways slicing through the urban core, allots 30 parking spaces per resident (Lowe, 1995: 131). In the suburbs, where space is widely available, the room apportioned to the automobile is even greater. For instance, the parking lots of major suburban shopping centres are typically much larger than the malls themselves (Duany, Plater-Zyberk, and Speck, 2000: 13).

Traffic interferes with people's enjoyment of their neighbourhood. For example, it complicates residents' street crossing, visiting, and outdoor activity, and it reduces people's desire to settle in an area. In short, traffic has a negative effect on neighbourhood cohesion and community integration. The growth of street traffic increases fearfulness among people who are less socially integrated by increasing the number of strangers on the street. Traffic modifications can reduce the rate of growth in crime and reduce the fear of crime even more.

The effects of traffic are particularly obvious in areas that are heavily travelled by tourists. Tourism-related traffic congestion, noise, and pollution are evident even in the rural communities of Ohio, where people come to see the old-fashioned Amish people. There, an increase in automobile traffic at a rate of 13 per cent per year since 1993 has led to an almost five-fold increase in the cost of farmland and to a growing economic dependency on tourism. Changes in ecology and environment because of tourism—which include deforestation in and around cities, traffic congestion, scarce housing, inadequate supplies of safe drinking water and health services, and problems of garbage and waste disposal—are likely to repel tourists in the long run (Kreps, Donnermeyer, and Kreps, 1996; Sharma, 1998).

Since traffic causes problems that are many and varied, so are the proposed solutions. Where drunk driving is the problem, behaviour change, rather than technology, holds the greatest promise of reducing auto crashes. People use a variety of ways to regulate their own drunk driving. The most common self-regulatory techniques are limiting drinking, arranging rides, using taxis, and delaying or avoiding driving. People who use the drink-limitation technique are less likely to drive drunk than those who use other self-regulatory techniques. However, informal deterrence through peer intervention has been developed as an alternative in lowering DUI (driving under the influence) rates.

Increasingly, people intervene to prevent others from driving while intoxicated. An estimated one-third to one-half of all the people faced with a potential drunk-driving situation intervene. Techniques used include threatening to drive, taking the keys, and actually driving the person home. Decisions to intervene are motivated primarily by concern for the immediate physical well-being of the drinking driver, and secondarily by concern for the physical well-being of others and by friendship with the drinking driver. Willingness to accept help is influenced by the quality of relationship between the drunken person and the intervener and by some characteristics of the situation (for example, whether it is public or private) in which the offer is made. Educational programs to reduce alcohol and marijuana use and improve driving behaviours report good immediate success but no long-lasting effects. A study by Knut-Inge Klepp, Steven Kelder, and Cheryl Perry (1995), for example, describes good intermediate success but no results after four years.

Another problem with the dependence on automobile transportation in cities is that cars give off high levels of carbon monoxide in their exhaust fumes. Carbon monoxide has been a major contributor to global warming. As well, the greenhouse gases produced by cars and other machines are involved in the creation of smog, that thick, dirty cloud of air that can be seen hanging over many car-heavy cities. These problems are made all the worse because more urban drivers are driving alone, for longer periods, and for greater distances than ever before, particularly during weekday commutes to and from work. In the United States, overall ridership on mass transit systems is declining. In 1940, public transportation accounted for 30 per cent of all the miles covered by passengers of any mode of vehicular travel in the United States. By 1970, the number had dwindled to 6 per cent. By 1983, it was only 3 per cent (Shannon, Kleniewski, and Cross, 1991: 159–61). The same did not happen in Canada. (See Figure 9.2.)

The development of environment-friendly and city-friendly transportation systems depends on institutionalized public behaviour—on making people more willing to leave their cars at home and use public transit. Canadians make good use of public transit—when it is cheap, clean, and available. According to a report commissioned for a review of the Canada Transportation Act, nearly 1.5 billion Canadians rode in public transit vehicles in 1999. Most of the rides were in large cities, especially Toronto, Montreal, and Vancouver. In 2001, Toronto ridership increased for the fifth consecutive year as passenger trips totalled 420 million. The highest single-day ridership in 2001 was reached on Friday, 30 November, when passenger trips peaked at 1.5 million. The TTC, the only public transit system in Canada that carries more than 400 million annual riders, has surpassed that 400-million mark two years running. This level of use means about 370 million fewer auto trips a year.

In many Third World cities, such as Cairo, traffic is even more chaotic than in European and US cities. Participant observation comparing Seattle in Washington and Hyderabad in India shows that traffic moves in the most orderly fashion where, as in Seattle, public space is controlled and the number of transactions between drivers is reduced. Road plans (for example, the use of stoplights, speed bumps, one-way streets, and roundabouts) and law enforcers mediate the social order in traffic, reducing accidents, congestion, delay, and pollution.

The use of bicycles by police forces in Vancouver and Toronto offers an example of a powerful and respected group's modelling the benefits of participating in environmentally friendly transportation. Bicycling has become a superior form of transportation in cities, allowing the police to travel quickly through traffic-congested streets (Gardner, 1998). Additionally, bicycles are cheap to fix, easy to use, and health-inducing. (But see Figure 9.3 on helmet use.) They are also appealing to many members of the public, especially younger people. The cost of operating a bicycle is much less than that of a car. Running a car costs an estimated 7.5 cents per kilometre, as opposed to just over half a penny per kilometre for a bicycle. In addition, bicycle riding reduces the number of casualties caused by traffic every year.

In Europe, support for bicycling is even stronger; there, bicycles are now used for 20 to 30 per cent of all trips made within city boundaries (Gardner, 1998: 16). In the Netherlands, for example, the length of bicycle paths doubled between 1978 and 1992. The country saw deaths from car accidents drop by 30 per cent, injuries by 25 per cent, as more people began riding bicycles. There is also evidence to suggest that the use of bicycles in business considerably lowers expenses, and bicycles are just as efficient and quick. For example, in San Salvador, a Pepsi distributor switched from trailer delivery to bicycle delivery and was still able to deliver 900 cases of Pepsi per month, and at much lower cost. This

FIGURE 9.2
Means of Commuting in Canada, by Province and by Mode of Transportation[a]

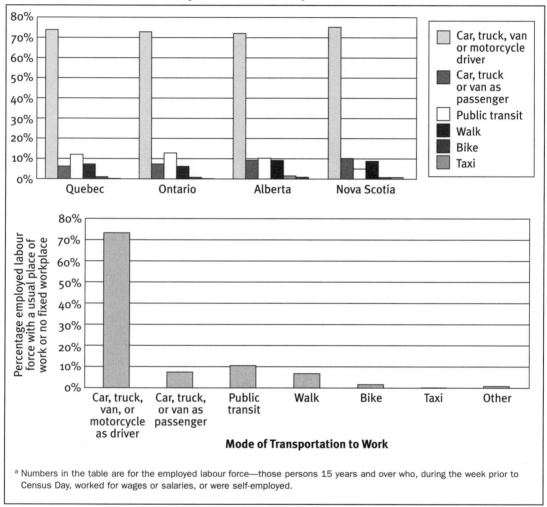

[a] Numbers in the table are for the employed labour force—those persons 15 years and over who, during the week prior to Census Day, worked for wages or salaries, or were self-employed.

SOURCE: Statistics Canada, 'Employed Labour Force by Mode of Transportation to Work, 1996 Census', 1996 Census Nation tables; available at <www.statcan.ca/english/Pgdb/labor42a.htm>, accessed 25 March 2003.

mode of delivery was particular suited for deliveries that were located close to one another (Gardner, 1998: 19).

It takes government incentive to make city roads and the urban environment bicycle-safe and bicycle-friendly, providing people with the opportunity to choose an alternative to automobiles. However, bicycles are used less often when people in authority do not support bicycle use, as in the city of Jakarta, Indonesia, where they are thought of as a backward technology to be eradicated. There, 20,000 bicycle rickshaws were destroyed and 30,000 more were confiscated under government order in the 1980s. Authorities

FIGURE 9.3
Use of Bike Helmets in Canada

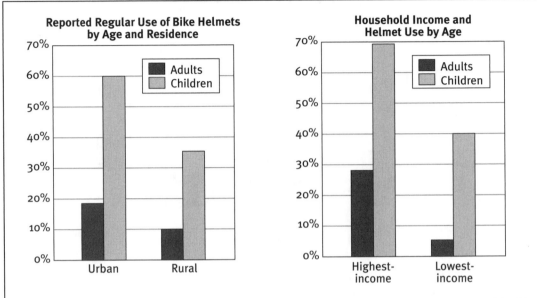

One reason suggested to explain the relationship between high income and regular helmet use may be knowledge of the risks. The same study found that only 42 per cent of parents in the lowest-income households were aware that injuries are the leading cause of death among children, whereas 82 per cent of parents in the highest-income households claimed to be aware of this information.

SOURCE: Wayne J. Millar and I.B. Pless, 'Factors Associated with Bicycle Helmet Use', *Health Reports*, 9, no. 2 (1997): 33, 36. Data from 1994/95 National Population Health Survey.

were, apparently, more interested in the profits that the car industry, car licensing, and the road construction industry would yield, and pro-bicycle policies were dropped to the bottom of the agenda (Gardner, 1998).

Two new developments tend to affect driving accidents in different ways. On the one hand, the use of cell phones increases the risk of a collision by 4 to 16 times. Analysis of 699 drivers in Toronto who were involved in motor-vehicle collisions that resulted in substantial property damage but no personal injury found that 24 per cent had used a cellular telephone during the 10-minute period before the collision (Redelmeier and Tibshirani, 1997: 455).

On the other hand, telework and homework (that is, work performed in the home rather than at another worksite) reduce the number of acci-

dents by reducing the amount of commuter travel and introducing flexibility into the timing of traffic flow. However, telecommunications will never entirely take the place of physical transportation and face-to-face contact. So we cannot rely on a simple substitution of new communication methods for old to reduce transportation and eradicate traffic congestion and pollution. The answer will have to come from another source.

Urban Environmental Problems

Another urban environmental concern, along with traffic, is the massive amount of sewage, litter, and solid waste produced by the millions of people crowded into a small area. Not surprisingly then, some areas of the city are heavily polluted. For example, of the 162 Chicago sites considered highly polluted, 98 (60 per cent) are in the predominantly African American South Side neighbourhood. All 10 of the city's communities with the highest levels of lead poisoning (caused by toxic levels of lead in the paint used in residential buildings) were made up of at least 70 per cent minorities (Cohen, 1992).

This problem has been labelled **environmental racism** by some researchers. It is the result of several factors: fewer public services—sanitation workers, garbage disposal units, road maintenance crews, and so on—being devoted by local governments to the undesirable areas; a perception among corporate polluters that the local residents lack the political clout to prevent the dumping of industrial trash in their communities; and a shared sense of general demoralization by the economically deprived residents that precludes any concerted effort to preserve and improve the neighbourhood.

Among other effects, increased dependence on the car for urban mobility has allowed urban planners in the half-century since World War II to spatially segregate land uses. Before this automobile culture took hold, communities were designed to ensure that all the services required for daily life were within walking distance or a short bus or bicycle ride away (Rybczynski, 1995). Today, however, current zoning regulations in most North American cities distinguish between residential, industrial, commercial, and recreational spaces.

This type of urban design has its benefits. For instance, building a homogenous project is cheaper for the developer than mixing functions. However, it also forces people to get the use of a vehicle before they can have access to the necessities of daily life. For most individuals not living along the border between a residential and commercial zone, even an errand as mundane as purchasing a carton of milk or a bar of soap will likely involve a car ride to the nearest supermarket.

The maze of high-speed, multi-lane roads that separates different land uses is often too hazardous for children to pass through alone,

resulting in their dependence on parents to accompany them everywhere: to and from school, sports practices, leisure pursuits, visits to their friends' homes, and more. In a study comparing 10-year-olds in a traditional, light-traffic, small Vermont neighbourhood with their counterparts in a new Orange County, California, suburban development, the Vermont children enjoyed three times as much mobility as their Californian peers (cited in Calthorpe, 1993: 9).

Given the choice, most people would choose to live in a walkable neighbourhood rather than a heavily driven district. Study after study has shown that what urban people want is less traffic and more neighbourhood activity. Visual Preference Surveys, created by urban planner Anton Nelessen, use photo comparisons to learn what homebuyers want from home developers. The responses from more than 50 such polls are clear: people consistently prefer light-traffic, highly populated districts where the density of residents and services is high (cited in Kay, 1997: 298).

Even sidewalks are important to people. More than just a strip of concrete to carry pedestrians, the space between a building and the curb can function simultaneously as a 'playground' for some users and an impromptu meeting place for others. Café patios transform the sidewalk into a social hub, and occasional street performers convert it into a temporary outdoor stage. Unlike a motorist in a car—itself a private space—no single user can claim ownership or control of a public domain.

Crime and Fear of Crime

Much has been much written on the fear of crime and on anxiety over potential victimization because they are such widespread phenomena. The concern is so serious that some believe the fear of crime has become a problem as grave as crime itself (Clemente and Kleiman, 1977).

A commonly reported finding is that various forms of media affect fear of crime. For example, television viewing is correlated with fear of crime (Sparks and Ogles, 1990). People who watch a lot of television become more fearful. Coupled with social isolation, televised information about crime intensifies fears of victimization (Taschler-Pollacek and Lukesch, 1990). Newspaper coverage also has a positive correlation with fear of crime (Williams and Dickinson, 1993). In particular, the many crime stories in which the crimes are local, random, and sensational increase people's fear. Researchers believe that people who express the most fear over crime are not necessarily people who are particularly vulnerable, but are often isolated people. Isolated people have less independent information about the conditions outside their home, so they are more reliant on 'objective' news reports and more suggestible.

People typically learn of crime events through the mass media. The media exploit their feeling of insecurity when they highlight random and impersonal violent attacks (Lagrange, 1993). This increased fear of crime, in turn, can have a negative effect on the development of community programs designed to help people with criminal records. Mary Holland Baker and colleagues (1983) suggest that fear of crime elicits avoidance behaviour and can inhibit normal social interaction and alter everyday routines.

Solutions to Urban Problems

High unemployment, crumbling infrastructure, little access to business capital, and loss of hope all represent notable challenges to inner cities. These problems have arisen because of the political, economic, and social abandonment of troubled and stigmatized city centres, so the solutions may have to include reversing these trends.

Economic and Political Solutions

Empowerment zones (EZs), enterprise communities (ECs), and other economic incentives may help in attracting business and industry back to the central cities. A program initiated in the United States, the formation of urban empowerment zones, has coordinated efforts by the federal government and private corporations to revitalize ailing neighbourhoods in major cities. These empowerment zones receive tax breaks, development grants for housing projects, and job-creation programs. HUD, the federal body responsible for making these policies, has outlined four key principles guiding the initiatives: (1) a strategic vision for change, (2) community-based partnerships, (3) economic opportunity, and (4) sustainable community development. Corporations are asked to provide a physical presence in the community, setting up their operations nearby to stimulate employment and flow of capital. In Detroit, for instance, the automotive industry, with big players like General Motors and DaimlerChrysler, has pledged billions of dollars toward the city's empowerment zone. Such programs would likely meet with success in Canada as well.

Increasingly, large cities are trying to make a global impact and participate fully in the global economy. However, there are significant costs in moving to that level of competition. Consider the globalization of Chicago, Illinois. Although Chicago's history and location facilitate the process, globalization might cost hundreds of thousands of manufacturing jobs, lead to increased social and economic disparity between ethnic groups, and increase problems in governing the city. Despite Chicago's role in national trade, international finance, and the quality of its universities, medical centres, and research facilities, the city may lack the cosmopolitan culture of Los Angeles and New York City (see the HUD Web site, <www.hud.gov>).

Strategies for success appear to include (1) establishing new governmental institutions to effectively manage public resources, reduce social and racial inequalities, and constrain urban sprawl; (2) creating an environment that accelerates and nurtures economic activity; and (3) building mechanisms of social responsibility for industry and finance (Moberg, 1997).

Geographer Richard Florida (2002) has also emphasized the need for a city to attract creative, or 'bohemian', elements, including artists and designers of various types, if it is going to achieve excellent standing. People who work with ideas and symbols are as central to the creation of a global city as are the people who command capital. They are as essential to the production of city wealth in an information age as skilled crafts workers—electricians, pipe fitters, toolmakers— were to the production of city wealth in an earlier industrial era.

Urban Planning

Another urban problem has been the decentralization of cities and the uncontrolled rate of suburban sprawl. The spread of characterless bedroom communities in the suburbs and of segregated poverty in the downtown core could be

---

BOX 9.3
Inclusionary Zoning

The only province with anything remotely approaching inclusionary zoning is BC, which recently passed legislation saying community plans must include 25 per cent affordable housing. But it hasn't defined 'affordable', and municipalities have barely begun to grapple with the new legislation. The city of Vancouver, under then-mayor Gordon Campbell—now leader of BC's Liberal party—pushed for something like inclusionary zoning with a requirement that developers of mega-projects set aside 20 per cent of their land for social housing. But the developers only had to promise to reserve the land for social-housing groups. They still got paid for the land and didn't have to build anything themselves.

Why hasn't inclusionary zoning caught on in Canada? Richard Drdla, a Toronto housing researcher who has studied inclusionary zoning in the US and Canada, says that he believes it's because Canadians never had to come up with ways to get the private sector involved the way the Americans did. 'Our non-profit housing programs removed the responsibility for cities or states to do anything', he says.

Linda Lapointe, a Toronto planning consultant who helped many municipalities write their housing policies when Ontario was pushing the 25-per-cent solution, sees two other factors behind the American moves to inclusionary zoning: segregation and the law. 'It all goes back to discrimination', she says. Residential segregation is an unavoidable issue in the US. Poor white people tend to get integrated into middle-class communities. But poor blacks are much more likely to be isolated in ghettos with high concentrations of poverty. Many American regions effectively kept Hispanics and blacks, who were also poor, shut out by using 'exclusionary zoning', which prohibited smaller and, therefore, less expensive kinds of housing, like apartments and townhouses.

But the US does have the Fair Housing Act that allows people to challenge any policy that has the effect of discriminating against particular groups. Housing-advocacy groups use it all the time to challenge municipalities that seem to be trying to pull up the drawbridge to keep the poor out. Canada doesn't have the poor-equals-black situation the US does and it doesn't have a law, which has left municipalities relatively free of any social pressure to be more integrated.

SOURCE: Vancouver based journalist Frances Bula investigated affordable housing policies and possible solutions in Canada as a recipient of the J. E. Atkinson Fellowship in Public Policy in 1998. 'No Place Like Home' was published in *The Toronto Star*, 23–30 October 1999. Reprinted by permission of the Atkinson Charitable Foundation.

halted if land developers were forced to build mixed-use neighbourhoods. The principle of mixed-use construction is that communities should be built so that all necessities—occupational, commercial, and recreational—are within easy reach of one's home, either on foot or by public transit.

Urban theorist Jane Jacobs has described this blending of 'primary uses' as one of the four conditions needed to generate diversity in a city's streets; the other conditions are short city blocks, a mingling of buildings that vary in age and condition, and a sufficient density of people in the area to sustain the neighbourhood's businesses and institutions ([1961] 1993). It is this type of development that characterizes many desirable (and expensive) urban communities: Toronto's Annex, New York City's Greenwich Village, and London's Notting Hill, for example. The principle could be extended to areas with middle-class and low-income housing.

However, mixed-use developments are often prohibited by strict building regulations that separate the various aspects of daily life. Until the middle of the twentieth century, this segregation applied only to incompatible land uses (for example, residential and industrial); today, it applies to every use (Rybczynski 1995). These ordinances were originally developed to promote the health, safety, morals, and general welfare of the city's inhabitants. It was assumed that people wanted private homes and distance between themselves and the less attractive aspects of city life. So it is ironic that a recent study conducted in Los Angeles found that residents in both middle- to upper-income and low-income communities wanted more diversity and services, such as markets, drug stores, and libraries, than present zoning codes allow (Lowe, 1995). These same respondents ranked sociability and friendliness as their first and second most wanted characteristics in an ideal community.

Mixed-use communities also allow less reliance on cars for transport, which has environmental benefits. For instance, the city of Vancouver was advised in its 1990 *Clouds of Change* report to improve air quality by curtailing the use of motor vehicles and encouraging greater density through multi-unit residential developments. Among the specific recommendations were proposals to 'decentralize commercial and community services to reduce travel distance, creating self-contained communities with a better balance between employment and population' and to 'encourage the development of high-quality walking and bicycling facilities, including alternatives to private automobile use' (Vancouver, Task Force on Atmospheric Change, 1990: 11–12).

Urban developers and government officials need to pay closer attention to these types of report. In a study examining why some of New York City's parks and plazas consistently attracted larger crowds than others, sociologist William Whyte (1996) found that people congregate wherever there are places to sit down. Aware of the obviousness of his conclusion, he nevertheless emphasized that many urban spaces have neglected to provide seats.

Besides providing a variety of places to sit—ledges, steps, moveable chairs, grassy areas—what distinguishes the most popular places from the others is the way in which seating satisfies their users. Other details include the height and depth of ledges, how chairs can be moved around to create different sitting arrangements, the circulation of people within and through the space; and the unimpeded relationship between the plaza and the street (Whyte, 1996). Whyte's observations highlight the importance of convenience in public spaces.

The Congress for the New Urbanism (CNU), an international coalition of New Urbanists founded in 1994 by architects, urban designers, engineers, journalists, and public citizens, is calling for an end to suburban sprawl and a return to traditional planning and neighbourhood-based design. They believe in

the restoration of existing urban centers and towns within coherent metropolitan regions, the reconfiguration of sprawling suburbs into communities of real neighborhoods and diverse districts. . . . Neighborhoods should be diverse in use and population; communities should be designed for the pedestrian and transit and the car; cities and towns should be shaped by physically defined and universally accessible public spaces and community institutions. (<www.cnu.org>)

An increase in government funding to public transportation systems, encouragement of programs that support recycling and composting, and new policies that reduce the number of garbage bags disposed of per home are partial solutions to the environment problem. Regulatory monitoring accompanied by higher levels of water treatment to raise quality would deal with inadequate water sanitation.

Health Promotion

The 'healthy city', a common concept in developed societies, has only recently been adopted in developing countries. From 1995 to 1999, the World Health Organization (WHO) supported healthy city projects (HCPs) in Cox's Bazaar, Bangladesh; Dar es Salaam, Tanzania; Fayoum, Egypt; Managua, Nicaragua; and Quetta, Pakistan.

Throughout the developing world, urbanization has brought significant health problems. Infectious diseases that are common in rural areas combine with urban problems such as pollution and stress. The urban poor are particularly victimized, and health services simply cannot cope. An HCP attempts to integrate preventive health care into all the other planning and development decisions. It attacks the causes of ill health, most of which are beyond the reach of curative medicine.

Trudy Harpham, Salma Burton, and Ilona Blue (2001) recently evaluated four of these projects, the first major evaluation of HCPs in developing countries. Using a variety of methods, the researchers found that in these cities, municipal

health plan development—one of the main components of the healthy city strategy—was limited. Evaluations of HCPs in Europe came up with similar findings (Harpham, Burton, and Blue, 2001).

The evaluation found that stakeholder involvement varied in relation to (1) the level of knowledge of the project, (2) the location of the project office, (3) the project management structure, and (4) the type of activities involved. There was evidence to suggest that the understanding of environment–health links was increased across stakeholders.

The evidence suggested that stakeholders increased their understanding of environment–health links by participating in these projects. However, political commitment to the healthy city projects was limited, perhaps because most of the municipalities had not requested the projects. Consequently, the projects had little influence on written or expressed municipal policies. Some of the projects mobilized considerable resources, and most achieved effective intersectoral collaboration.

Concluding Remarks

A middle-class flight to the suburbs began in the 1950s. This migration occurred because people wanted cheap housing; additionally, it signified an attempt to escape urban problems and gain distance from ethnic minorities. As residential segregation has occurred, inner cities have lost jobs, business, and their tax base. Business and financial instructions have tended to divest from cities and invest in suburban communities. Manufacturing business has moved to the suburbs or Third World countries, leaving unskilled inner-city residents at a disadvantage.

Lack of efficient public transportation in many cities has put low-income people at a disadvantage since they cannot afford the automobiles necessary to reach jobs in the suburbs and urban fringe. Where public transportation does flourish, it encourages suburban development.

The poor and ethnic minorities often live in the deteriorating inner city, while the middle class live in the newer suburbs. Those living in the inner city have more health problems, including higher rates of tuberculosis, infant mortality, asthma, and sexually transmitted diseases. Inner cities also have high rates of crime, violence, and drug use. Often these sorts of problems are the result of gangs and organized crime.

Along with deinstitutionalization, gentrification and urban renewal programs have added to the homeless population by decreasing the housing stock that is available to low-income people. Despite government efforts to provide affordable housing, homelessness has increased in cities. There is simply not enough affordable housing available to low-income people.

Additionally, cities continue to suffer from problems that have plagued cities throughout the world. Traffic continues to impose problems of safety and environmental degradation. Many cities continue to grapple with serious problems of air and water pollution. Cities continue to offer the freedom and variety that they always did; however, until they also provide safety, good housing, and economic security, this freedom and variety will continue to be out of the reach of society's most vulnerable citizens.

Questions for Critical Thought

1. There is no doubt that suburbanization is a major force permeating the modern urban landscape. What effect has this had on your own life? Do you live in a suburb? If so, how often to you go into the city centre, and for what reasons? What do you feel about the myth of suburbia? Do you feel that living near the city centre offers a different lifestyle than suburban living? Discuss using specific examples and figures.

2. The text uses the 1992 Los Angeles riots as an example of the explosive tension and hostility that can arise among economically deprived urban ethnic groups against a perceived racist white majority. Can you think of any similar situations? How are they similar and how are they different? Use your knowledge of conflict theory to help gain insight into the possible motives and reasons for such clashes.

3. It seems as though in a big city there is something for everyone. Pick a certain subculture, such the gay and lesbian subculture, and discuss its presence in your city. Are certain services, facilities, restaurants or bars, and shops concentrated in a certain area? Do they share similar characteristics? Where are they found? Discuss how living in a big city makes for greater opportunity for subcultures to emerge and flourish.

4. Considering the negative stereotypes evoked by the notion of mental illness, it is not surprising that the deinstitutionalization of the mentally ill has been met with opposition. Is society acting out of ignorance and being fearful of the unknown, or is this 'threat' based on fact? Search the Internet and various newspaper articles and look for specific cases in which deinstitutionalization has been either welcomed or met with apprehension.

5. In December 2001, a drunken Ralph Klein, the premier of Alberta, approached a homeless shelter and told inhabitants to stop being lazy and get jobs. After much press coverage and controversy, the problem of homelessness was again brought into public focus. Where do you feel the problem is rooted, and what measures, if any, should the government take to help rectify this issue? Are homeless people in control of their own fate, or are they victims of a capitalist society?

Recommended Readings

Elijah Anderson, *Streetwise: Race, Class and Change in an Urban Community* (Chicago: University of Chicago Press, 1990).

The cornerstone of this book is Anderson's use of personal observations of Philadelphia's inner city. Anderson intertwines the themes of his title to support his argument that unrest in inner cities is a result of hopelessness derived from unavailable opportunities for upward mobility.

Henry C. Binford, *The First Suburbs: Residential Communities on the Boston Periphery, 1815–1860* (Chicago: University of Chicago Press, 1985).

This text looks at two US towns, Cambridge and Somerville, Massachusetts, through a process of suburbanization that is different from the suburbanization of the 1950s. Suburbanites were active in forging transportation links, and Binford also examines residential patterns.

Bernard J. Frieden and Lynne B. Sagalyn, *Downtown, Inc.: How America Rebuilds Cities* (Cambridge, MA: MIT Press, 1989).

The two authors look at American cities and emphasize the positive effects that malls have had on urban life.

Herbert J. Gans, *People, Plans, and Policies: Essays on Poverty, Racism, and Other National Urban Problems* (New York: Columbia University Press and the Russell Sage Foundation, 1991).

This text investigates the underlying issues that cause urban poverty. Gans criticizes the physical determinism argued by some social scientists; instead, he suggests that addressing poverty with jobs and eliminating racial intolerance will go further in ending urban poverty.

Dennis Hardy, *From Garden Cities to New Towns: Campaigning for Town and Country Planning, 1899–1946* (London: Spon, 1991).

This text traces the history of the 'garden city' model and identifies the proponents of the model in the United Kingdom. Hardy claims that without a re-evaluation of the adequacy of the model from an environmental standpoint, the original utopian vision will never be realized.

Tanis Hinchcliffe, *North Oxford* (New Haven, CT: Yale University Press, 1992).

Hinchcliffe looks at Oxford, England, between the 1860s and the 1970s to examine the growth of suburbs and the relations between the colleges of Oxford and the city's predominately middle-class townspeople.

Charlotte Ikels, Jennie Keith, Jeanette Dickerson-Putman, Patricia Draper, Christine Fry, Anthony Glascock, and Henry Harpending, 'Perceptions of the Adult Life Course: A Cross-Cultural Analysis', *Aging and Society*, 12 (1992): 49–84.

This interesting article examines the different perceptions of the life course in places with varying degrees of urbanization.

Stefanie Knauder, *Globalization, Urban Progress, Urban Problems, Rural Disadvantages: Evidence from Mozambique* (Burlington, VT: Ashgate, 2000).

Knauder looks at the rural-urban divide in Mozambique. She is thorough and takes into account social status and the legacies of colonialism.

Brian Ladd, *Urban Planning and Civic Order in Germany, 1860–1914* (Cambridge, MA: Harvard University Press, 1990).

Ladd traces the history of urban planning through the twentieth century and identifies problems with the German 'healthy city' model.

Peter McGahan, *Urban Sociology in Canada* (Toronto: Harcourt Brace Canada, 1995).

A comprehensive review of urban issues in Canada, including ethnic concentration and segregation, geographic mobility, and social inequality.

Susan D. Tolliver, 'Movers and Shakers: Black Families and Corporate Relocation', *Marriage and Family Review*, 19, nos 1–2 (1993): 113–30.

This article describes the interrelations between race and relocation. Tolliver identifies the specific challenges facing black families when relocating to a new city.

Recommended Web Sites

Canadian Urban Institute
www.canurb.com

The Canadian Urban Institute (CUI) is a non-profit organization dedicated to enhancing the quality of life in urban areas in Canada and internationally. The CUI is actively engaged in applied research and training for public- and private-sector clients. It stimulates debate and fashions solutions through policy research, publications, seminars, and conferences, and also provides information on a regular basis regarding current research, current events, and publications.

Canadian Council on Social Development
www.ccsd.ca

The Canadian Council on Social Development (CCSD) is one of Canada's most authoritative voices promoting better social and economic security for all Canadians. A national, self-supporting, non-profit organization, the CCSD's main product is information and its main activity is research, focusing on concerns such as income security, employment, poverty, child welfare, pensions, and government social policies.

Urban Institute
www.urban.org

The Urban Institute is a non-profit, non-partisan policy research and educational organization established to examine the social, economic, and governance problems facing the United States. It provides information and analysis to public and private decision makers to help them address these challenges, and strives to raise citizen understanding of these issues and of trade-offs in policy making.

References

Adams, Gerald R., Thomas Gullotta, and Mary Anne Clancy. 1985. 'Homeless Adolescents: A Descriptive Study of Similarities and Differences Between Runaways and Throwaways'. *Adolescence*, 20: 715–24.

Angenent, Huub L., Balthasar M. Beke, and Paul G. Shane. 1991. 'Structural Problems in Institutional Care for Youth'. *Journal of Health and Social Policy*, 2, no. 4: 83–98.

Arens, D.A. 1993. 'What Do the Neighbors Think Now? Community Residences on Long Island, New York'. *Community Mental Health Journal*, 29: 235–45.

Aubry, T.D., B. Tefft, and R.F. Currie. 1995. 'Public Attitudes and Intentions Regarding Tenants of Community Mental Health Residences Who Are Neighbours'. *Community Mental Health Journal*, 31, no. 1: 39–52.

Baker, Mary Holland, Barbara C. Nienstedt, Ronald S. Everett, and Richard McCleary. 1983. 'The Impact of a Crime Wave: Perceptions, Fear, and Confidence in the Police'. *Law and Society Review*, 17: 319–35.

Baron, R.C. 1981. 'Changing Public Attitudes About the Mentally Ill in the Community'. *Hospital and Community Psychiatry*, 32: 173–8.

Bogardus, E.S. 1959. *Social Distance*. Los Angeles: Antioch.

Borinstein, A.B. 1992. 'Public Attitudes Toward Persons with Mental Illness'. *Health Affairs*, 11: 186–96.

Boudreau, Julie-Anne. 1998. 'Inhabitants of a Megacity: The Urbanity of Citizens for Local Democracy'. Paper presented at the annual meeting of the International Sociological Association.

Calthorpe, Peter. 1993. *The Next American Metropolis: Ecology, Community, and the American Dream*. New York: Princeton Architectural Press.

Castells, Manuel. 1977. *The Urban Questions*. London: Edward Arnold.

City of Toronto. 2001. *The Toronto Report Card on Homelessness 2000*. Available at <www.city.toronto. on.ca/homelessness/>, accessed 17 January 2003.

Clemente, Frank, and Michael B. Kleiman. 1977. 'Fear of Crime in the United States: A Multivariate Analysis'. *Social Forces*, 56: 519–31.

Cohen, Linc. 1992. 'Waste Dumps Toxic Traps for Minorities'. *Chicago Reporter*, 21, no. 4: 6–9, 11. Available at <www.chicagoreporter.com/1992/04-92/0492WasteDumpsToxicTrapsforMinorities.htm>, accessed 27 February 2003.

Connerly, C.E., and Marans, R.W. 1985. 'Comparing Two Global Measures of Perceived Neighborhood Quality'. *Social Indicators Research*, 17, no. 1: 29–47.

Côté, Marguerite-Michelle. 1992, 'A Painful Situation Still Crying Out for a Solution: Montreal's Street Youth'. *Revue internationale d'action communautaire*, 27: 145–52.

Dear, M.J., and S.M. Taylor. 1982. *Not on Our Street: Community Attitudes to Mental Health Care*. London: Pion.

Duany, Andres, Elizabeth Plater-Zyberk, and Jeff Speck. 2000. *Suburban Nation: The Rise of Sprawl and the Decline of the American Dream*. New York: North Point Press.

Durkheim, Émile. [1893] 1964. *The Division of Labor in Society*. Translated by George Simpson. Glencoe, IL: Free Press.

El-Badry, Samia, and Peter K. Nance. 1992. 'Driving into the 21st Century: Smart-Car Research'. *American Demographics*, 14: 46–53.

Emerson, Michael O., George Yancey, and Karen J. Chai. 2001. 'Does Race Matter in Residential Segregation? Exploring the Preferences of White Americans'. *American Sociological Review*, 66: 922–35.

Florida, Richard L. 2002. *The Rise of the Creative Class: And How It's Transforming Work, Leisure, Community and Everyday Life*. New York: Basic Books.

Forstall, Richard L. 1993. 'Going to Town'. *American Demographics*, 15: 42–7.

Fracchia, J., D. Canale, E. Cambria, E. Ruest, and C. Sheppard. 1976. 'Public Views of Ex-Mental Patients: A Note on Perceived Dangerousness and Unpredictability'. *Psychological Reports*, 38: 495–8.

Freund, Peter, and George Martin. 2000. 'Driving South: The Globalization of Auto Consumption and Its Social Organization of Space'. *Capitalism, Nature, Socialism*, 11, no. 4: 51–71.

Fried, M. 1984. 'The Structure and Significance of Community Satisfaction'. *Population and Environment*, 7, no. 2: 61–86.

Gans, Herbert. 1982. *The Urban Villagers: Group and Class in the Life of Italian-Americans*. 2nd edn. New York: Free Press.

Gardner, Gary. 1998. 'When Cities Take Bicycles Seriously'. *World Watch*, 11, no. 5: 16–22.

Garreau, Joel. 1991. *Edge City: Life on the New Frontier*. New York: Doubleday.

Gilderbloom, John I. 1991. 'Housing in America: It's Time for a New Strategy'. *USA Today Magazine*, November, 30–2.

Gruber, K.J., and G.J. Shelton. 1987. 'Assessment of Neighborhood Satisfaction by Residents of Three

Housing Types'. *Social Indicators Research*, 19: 303–15.

Hallman, Howard W. 1984. *Neighborhoods: Their Place in Urban Life*. Beverly Hills, CA: Sage.

Harpham, Trudy, Salma Burton, and Ilona Blue. 2001. 'Healthy City Projects in Developing Countries: The First Evaluation'. *Health Promotion International*, 16, no. 2: 111–25.

Higley, Stephen Richard. 1995. *Privilege, Power and Place: The Geography of the American Upper Class*. Lanham, MD: Rowman and Littlefield.

Hise, Greg, Michael J. Dear, and H. Eric Schockman. 1996. 'Rethinking Los Angeles'. In *Rethinking Los Angeles*, edited by Michael J. Dear, Eric H. Schockman, and Greg Hise, 1–14. Thousand Oaks, CA: Sage.

Holdaway, Doris M., and JoAnn Ray. 1992. 'Attitudes of Street Kids Toward Foster Care'. *Child and Adolescent Social Work Journal*, 9: 307–17.

Hyman, William A., and G. Thomas Kingsley. 1996. 'Transportation and Land Use'. In *Reality and Research: Social Science and U.S. Urban Policy*, edited by George Galster, 113–30. Washington, DC: Urban Institute Press.

International Survey of Mayors. 2002. Available at <http://magnet.undp.org/docs/urban/maysur.htm>, accessed 28 February 2003.

Jacobs, Jane. [1961] 1993. *The Death and Life of Great American Cities*. New York: Random House.

Janus, Mark David, Anne W. Burgess, and Arlene McCormack. 1987. 'Histories of Sexual Abuse in Adolescent Male Runaways'. *Adolescence*, 22: 405–17.

Kay, Jane H. 1997. *Asphalt Nation: How the Automobile Took Over America and How We Can Take It Back*. New York: Random House.

Klepp, Knut-Inge, Steven H. Kelder, and Cheryl L. Perry. 1995. 'Alcohol and Marijuana Use Among Adolescents: Long-Term Outcomes of the Class of 1989 Study'. *Annals of Behavioral Medicine*, 17: 19–24.

Kreps, George M., Joseph Donnermeyer, and Marty W. Kreps. 1996. 'A Study of the Impact of Tourism on a Rural Community with Specific Attention to the Amish Subculture of That Community'. Paper presented at the annual meeting of the American Sociological Association.

LaGory, M., R. Ward, and S. Sherman. 1985. 'The Ecology of Aging: Neighborhood Satisfaction in an

Older Population'. *Sociological Quarterly*, 26: 405–18.

Lagrange, Hugues. 1993. 'Media and Insecurity'. *Revue internationale d'action communautaire / International Review of Community Development*, 30: 181–95.

Lee, Kevin K. 2000. *Urban Poverty in Canada: A Statistical Profile*. Ottawa: Canadian Council on Social Development. Available at <www.ccsd.ca/pubs/2000/up>, accessed 30 January 2003.

Lowe, Marcia. 1995. 'Reclaiming Cities for People'. In *Beyond the Car: Essays on the Auto Culture*, edited by Sue Zielinski and Gordon Laird, 129–36. Toronto: Steel Rail Publishing.

Marx, Karl, and Friedrich Engels. [1848] 1968. *Manifesto of the Communist Party*. Peking: Foreign Languages Press.

Merton, Robert K. 1957. 'Social Structure and Anomie'. In *Social Theory and Social Structure*, rev. edn, 131–60. New York: Free Press.

Moberg, David. 1997. 'Chicago: To Be or Not to Be a Global City'. *World Policy Journal*, 14: 71–86.

Monohan, J. 1992. 'A Terror to Their Neighbours: Beliefs About Mental Disorder and Violence in Historical and Cultural Perspective'. *Bulletin of the American Academy of Psychiatry and the Law*, 20: 191–5.

Oakley, Deirdre A. 1999. 'Keeping Homeless Individuals Homeless: City Politics and the Zoning of Permanent Housing for Street Alcoholics'. Paper presented at the annual meeting of the American Sociological Association.

Payne, Malcolm. 1995. 'Understanding "Going Missing": Issues for Social Work and Social Services'. *British Journal of Social Work*, 25: 333–48.

Pincetl, Stephanie. 1994. 'The Regional Management of Growth in California: A History of Failure'. *International Journal of Urban and Regional Research*, 18: 256–74.

Plass, Peggy S., and Gerald T. Hotaling. 1995. 'The Intergenerational Transmission of Running Away: Childhood Experiences of the Parents of Runaways'. *Journal of Youth and Adolescence*, 24: 335–48.

Price, Virginia Ann. 1989. 'Characteristics and Needs of Boston Street Youth: One Agency's Response'. *Children and Youth Services Review*, 11: 75–90.

Redburn, David E. 2002. 'Urban Sprawl in the Upstate of South Carolina: Do City and County Residents; Attitudes Diverge?' Paper presented at the annual meeting of the Southern Sociological Society.

Redelmeier, Donald A., and Robert J. Tibshirani. 1997. 'Association Between Cellular-Telephone Calls and Motor Vehicle Collisions'. *New England Journal of Medicine*, 336: 453–8.

Rigby, K., and A. Vreugdenhil. 1987. 'The Relationship Between Generalized Community Satisfaction and Residential Social Status, *Journal of Social Psychology*'. 127: 381–90.

Rotherham-Borus, Mary J. 1993. 'Suicidal Behavior and Risk Factors Among Runaway Youths'. *American Journal of Psychiatry*, 150: 103–7.

Rybczynski, Witold. 1995. *City Life: Urban Expectations in a New World*. Toronto: HarperCollins.

Schmidt, Robert R. 1999. *An Analysis of the Causes and Consequences of Urban Sprawl on the Las Vegas Valley*. Unpublished doctoral dissertation, University of Nevada at Las Vegas.

Shannon, Thomas R., Nancy Kleniewski, and William M. Cross. 1991. *Urban Problems in Sociological Perspective*, 2nd edn. Prospect Heights, IL: Waveland Press.

Sharma, Satish K. 1998. 'Environment and Change in an Urban Society: The Case of an Himalayan City'. Paper presented at the annual meeting of the International Sociological Association.

Sigurdson, Chris. 2000. 'The Mad, the Bad and the Abandoned: The Mentally Ill in Prisons and Jails'. *Corrections Today*, 62, no. 7: 70–8.

Simmel, Georg. 1950. *The Sociology of Georg Simmel*. Translated by Kurt Wolff. Glencoe, IL: Free Press.

Simons, Ronald, and Les Whitbeck. 1991. 'Running Away During Adolescence as a Precursor to Adult Homelessness'. *Social Science Review*, 65: 224–47.

Sjoberg, Gideon. 1965. *The Preindustrial City, Past and Present*. New York: Free Press.

Sparks, Glenn G., and Robert M. Ogles. 1990. 'The Difference Between Fear of Victimization and the Probability of Being Victimized: Implications for Cultivation'. *Journal of Broadcasting and Electronic Media*, 34: 351–8.

Stiffman, Arlene Rubin. 1989a. 'Physical and Sexual Abuse in Runaway Youths'. *Child Abuse and Neglect*, 13: 417–26.

———. 1989b. 'Suicide Attempts in Runaway Youths'. *Suicide and Life-Threatening Behavior*, 19: 147–59.

Susser, Ezra S., Shang P. Lin, Sarah A. Conover, and Elmer L. Struening. 1991. 'Childhood Antecedents of Homelessness in Psychiatric Patients'. *American Journal of Psychiatry*, 148: 1026–30.

Taschler-Pollacek, Heidrun, and Helmut Lukesch. 1990. 'Fear of Victimization as a Consequence of Television Viewing? A Study of Older Women'. *Publizistik*, 35: 443–53.

Teare, John F., Karen Authier, and Roger Peterson. 1994. 'Differential Patterns of Post-shelter Placement as a Function of Problem Type and Severity'. *Journal of Child and Family Studies*, 3: 7–22.

Tönnies, Ferdinand. [1887] 1957. *Community and Society (Gemeinschaft und Gesellschaft)*. New York: Harper and Row.

Vancouver. Task Force on Atmospheric Change. 1990. *Clouds of Change: Final Report of the City of Vancouver Task Force on Atmospheric Change*. Vol. 1. Vancouver: City of Vancouver.

Van Es, J.C., and J.B. Schneider. 1983. 'Age Relates Positively to Community Satisfaction: Some Explanations and Implications'. *Journal of the Community Development Society*, 14, no. 1: 31–8.

Weber, Max. 1968. *The City*. Translated by Don Martindale and Gertrud Neuwirth. New York: Free Press.

———. 1981. *General Economic History*. New Brunswick, NJ: Transaction Books.

Whitbeck, Les B., Danny R. Hoyt, and Kevin A. Ackley. 1997. 'Families of Homeless and Runaway Adolescents: A Comparison of Parent/Caretaker and Adolescent Perspectives on Parenting, Family Violence, and Adolescent Conduct'. *Child Abuse and Neglect*, 21: 517–28.

Whitbeck, Les B. and Ronald L. Simons. 1990. 'Life on the Streets: The Victimization of Runaway and Homeless Adolescents'. *Youth and Society*, 22; 108–25.

Whyte, William H. 1996. 'The Design of Spaces from City: Rediscovering the Center'. In *The City Reader*, edited by Richard T. Legates and Frederic Stout, 483–90. New York: Routledge.

Widgery, R.N. 1982. 'Satisfaction with the Quality of Urban Life: A Predictive Model'. *American Journal of Community Psychology*, 10: 37–48.

Williams, Paul, and Julie Dickinson. 1993. 'Fear of Crime: Read All About It? The Relationship Between Newspaper Crime Reporting and Fear of Crime'. *British Journal of Criminology*, 33, no. 1: 33–56.

Wilson, William J. 1996. *When Work Disappears: The World of the New Urban Poor*. New York: Knopf.

Wirth, Louis. 1938. 'Urbanism as a Way of Life'. In *On Cities and Social Life*, 60–83. Chicago: University of Chicago Press.

Zeitlin, Morris. 1990. 'Land Use, Transportation, and Working-Class Politics in the Modern Metropolis'. *Nature, Society, and Thought*, 3: 325–40.

Glossary

Deinstitutionalized The label given to mentally ill individuals who have been released from the institutional care of mental hospitals, prisons, convents, or military camps.

Environmental racism Occurs when certain social groups and areas within a city are discriminated against. This concept is a result of several factors, including fewer public services being devoted by local governments to undesirable areas and a perception on the part of polluters that local residents are so politically weak that residents are unable to prevent exposure from pollutants.

Gemeinschaft Social situations in which those involved treat one another as ends rather than as means; primary relationships based on sentiment, found most often in rural life.

Gentrification The restoration and upgrading of deteriorated urban property by middle-class or affluent people, often resulting in displacement of lower-income people.

Gesellschaft Social situations in which those involved treat one another as means rather than as ends; secondary relations based primarily on calculation and individual interest, found most often in city life.

Mechanical solidarity Coined by Émile Durkheim, this term describes the social and psychological bonds prevailing between people and groups in a homogenous society in which there is a minimal division of labour and little individualism.

Objective characteristics Characteristics of a neighbourhood that have a strong effect on quality of life, such as its appearance, its upkeep, and access to resources and services. In other words, these are the specifics of a local environment that have a general physical appearance.

Organic solidarity The practical bond prevailing between people and groups in a heterogeneous society in which people are functionally dependent upon one another and in which the division of labour is highly developed.

Social and demographic characteristics Characteristics that describe a locality, such as age, income, and length of residence. For example, people become more satisfied with their community (as with other domains of life) as they age.

Subculture A group of people who share some cultural traits of the larger society but that also has its own distinctive values, beliefs, norms, style of dress, and behaviour. Subcultures allow individuals who are otherwise isolated within an impersonal city to form connections with those around them with similar values.

Suburbanization The process by which housing spreads almost unhindered into once-rural regions surrounding the city core. This greatly expands the geographic size of cities, and there is a noticed shift of the affluent out of the urban centre to these surrounding areas.

Urbanization The growth in the proportion of the population living in urbanized areas. There is also an increasing appearance in rural and small-town areas of behaviour patterns and cultural values associated with big-city life.

Chapter 10

Environment and Technology

Chapter Objectives

After reading this chapter the student should understand:
- the basic facts of environmental problems in Canada today
- the impact technology historically had on the environment
- what is meant by the *demographic transition*
- how population growth is depleting resources
- the significant role immigration plays in sustaining the Canadian population
- the contributions of such theories as 'technological dualism' and 'the tragedy of the commons'
- what is meant by *post-materialism*
- how the different theoretical paradigms help to add more insight into these issues
- the social and health consequences of our continued depletive actions
- possible solutions to environmental problems

Introduction

This chapter is about the relationships among environment, technology, population, society, and economy. It deals with such problems as pollution, environmental damage, natural disasters, consumerism, and resource depletion.

Let's begin by acknowledging that the problems discussed so briefly in this chapter are complex and we cannot hope to do justice to them in so short a space. Readers interested in learning more about these problems should certainly pursue them in the appropriate sources.

Further, population growth, far from being a problem, can be a benefit. Without population growth in human history, there would not have been agricultural growth. The denser a population is, the more intensive cultivation becomes (Boserup, 1965). In turn, agricultural surplus and population density make possible social differentiation, institutional growth, and, eventually, industrialization.

Finally, let us acknowledge, with Julian Simon (1996) and others, that human beings are 'the ultimate resource'. Humans have proven immensely creative in the face of adversity. Therefore, we may need not fewer people but, instead, better-equipped and better-educated people; not less use of non-renewable resources, but more effort and creativity in finding substitutes (as humanity has done throughout its history); and not a suspicion of technology, but rather a commitment to developing and using technology purposefully, for the good of humanity. The problems we discuss in this chapter are not environment, technology, and population per se—they are the human failure to handle these raw materials more creatively and effectively. Humanity, then, is the problem we are discussing, and a better-organized humanity is the solution.

Having said that, we haven't yet figured out how to achieve that needed organization. Without it, most scientists today acknowledge that humanity faces important population problems; these problems include 'overpopulation' and population aging (which we discussed in chapter 8). Humanity also faces momentous

environmental problems, such as global warming, air and water pollution, the depletion of certain key resources, and the gradual extinction of
living species. Finally, we face dangers to our survival and way of life as a result of technological
developments such as atomic fission, genetic
engineering, and the ability of computerized
information systems to monitor and manipulate
every part of our lives.

Each of these concerns—population, environment, technology—poses enormous challenges to
our scientific ingenuity, economic well-being, and
political organization. Each also poses new ethical
concerns. Each touches on the creation, modification, and extinction of life. Most important for the
purpose of this chapter, all three are related. Each
influences the other, and each affects all of us.
Increasingly, a change in the population, environment, or technology in any part of the world affects
everyone.

We begin this chapter by reviewing some
facts about the Canadian environment. Then,
since technology both affects the environment
and responds to problems in the environment,
we discuss the processes of technological innovation, adoption, and **diffusion**. These processes
affect humanity's ability to use technology creatively, to solve its problems, and, sometimes, to
unwittingly create new problems.

We go on to discuss human populations—
the people who live in this global environment
and use this modern technology. We emphasize
the global character of all three sets of problems—environmental, technological, and demographic. We end by considering the social and
health consequences of these problems and considering some possible solutions. What we hope
to accomplish in this chapter is to outline a way
of thinking about these interrelated problems,
rather than present a set of facts, questions, and
answers.

To clarify the connections among environment, technology, and population that we discuss

in this chapter, it is useful to imagine a time
100,000 years ago. At that time, everyone lived in
small bands. The human population of the world
existed solely as nomadic hunters and gatherers,
living off whatever the surroundings offered and
moving to more fertile regions when food became
scarce. As far as we can tell, people led lives that
were short but healthy. These nomads probably
had enough to eat. To judge from hunter-gatherer
peoples living today, they were also sociable,
cooperative, and contented. At some point, however, humans developed tools and skills that
enabled them to farm the land, and all this began
to change (see, for example, Lee, 1979).

Humans first began to artificially transform
their natural environment with the invention of
agricultural tools and practices. Farming, by providing a steady supply of food, allowed people to
settle down. With settlement came a rapid rise in
childbearing, longevity, and population size.
These changes, in turn, led to increases in social
differentiation, inequality, and conflict. People
began to separate themselves from the natural
world and to make efforts to dominate it.
Technology, which helped them do that, also
brought new social and health problems. A growing population, which succeeded for a while in
conquering the environment, also carried
unforeseen side effects. It increased human
reliance on technology and began to transform
the natural environment (see, for example, Farb,
1978).

Severe damage to the environment, through
technology and population growth, began two
centuries ago, with industrialization in the West.
Since then, governments have often ignored environmentally harmful practices, perhaps because
the industries responsible for much of the pollution in our skies, land, and water also power the
economy. In less developed countries, environmental damage has occurred mainly because governments are trying to attain the affluence that
older industrial countries enjoy.

Facts About the Canadian Environment

Air Pollution

In large cities around the world—whether Los Angeles, Paris, Budapest, or Beijing—smog has become a major problem. There and elsewhere, the air is thick and the sky yellowish-grey in the vicinity of a major thoroughfare. The stench of gasoline fumes is literally nauseating. In Taipei, Tokyo, and other large Asian cities, one commonly sees people walking on the street—or, ironically, driving motor scooters—with faces covered by masks to strain out the air pollutants. This daily experience of air pollution has become a universal, urban sensation, part of human sensory experience around the world.

What's more, the air we breathe, particularly in large urban centres, is getting dirtier. Emissions from cars mixed with other chemicals released by industrial processes and other forms of fuel combustion have created high levels of pollution by carbon monoxide, sulphur dioxide, and lead in the atmosphere. Transportation vehicles are major contributors to air pollution—particularly trucks, minivans, and SUVs, all of which consume much more gas and release more pollutants than smaller passenger cars.

In principle, nature can repair itself. Through the process of **photosynthesis**, trees and other vegetation remove the carbon dioxide that humans and other organisms produce in the air, replacing them with breathable oxygen. However, the available amount of greenery—trees and other vegetation—limits these natural processes and their ability to process air. Trees and bushes can remove only so much pollution in any given period, and when the level of pollutants exceeds what they can remove, pollutants accumulate in the atmosphere, making the air potentially dangerous to inhale.

Ozone Depletion

The *ozone layer* is a thin veil in the stratosphere that shields the planet against the sun's harmful ultraviolet (UV) radiation. Without this protective layer, UV rays would seriously damage most of the life on the earth's surface. Unfortunately, certain industrial chemicals—including chlorine chemicals, halons, and the chlorofluorocarbons (CFCs) used in most

Population, environment, and technology pose enormous challenges to our scientific ingenuity, economic well-being, and political organization. Each also poses new ethical concerns. Each touches on the creation, modification, and extinction of life. (Bill and Peggy Wittman)

refrigerators, aerosol cans, and solvents—have weakened the ozone layer, allowing UV rays to penetrate it. This is the *ozone depletion problem*. The damage has been most severe in the Antarctic region, where a hole in the ozone layer has grown to a record size of 28.3 million square kilometres as of September 2000 (slightly larger than Canada, the United States, and Mexico combined) and is beginning to stretch over more densely populated areas of South America.

Global Warming

Climate change, as caused by global warming, is arguably the single biggest environmental threat humans collectively face today because people can do little to reverse the process. All we can do is slow down the change. Certain greenhouse gases, such as CFCs, carbon dioxide, and methane, tend to accumulate in the atmosphere, trapping the heat reflected off the earth's surface. This causes global temperatures to rise. The process is known as the *greenhouse effect*. (See Figure 10.1).

In 1998, the World Meteorological Organization declared the year the warmest on record, surpassing the mark set only 3 years before. The next year, 1999, was slightly cooler, ranking as the 5th warmest since measurements began in 1860. The 10 warmest years have all occurred within the last 2 decades, with 8 of these occurring since 1990. The 1990s were estimated to be the warmest decade in the past millennium. These patterns of climate change have been attributed to the greenhouse effect (WMO, 2000).

Even a small increase in global temperatures can lead to elevated sea levels and to devastating changes in precipitation rates. Such climate changes, in turn, harm the natural vegetation and wildlife of the local ecosystem, alter the crop yields of agricultural regions, and allow deserts to take over fertile regions. As a striking example of the effects of global warming, Greenpeace recently reported that entire islets in Kiribati in the Pacific Ocean have disappeared as a result of rising sea levels (Greenpeace, 2001).

FIGURE 10.1
The Greenhouse Effect

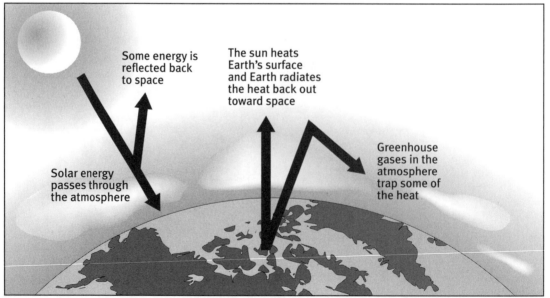

Regrettably, almost one-third of the 84 countries that have agreed to the Kyoto Protocol, which aims to cut greenhouse gas emissions, have yet to officially ratify it (as of February 2003). Canada did not sign until December 2002, and even then it did so in the face of a vocal lobby. The United States, for its part, has called the Kyoto Accord irresponsible because the reduction in the use of fossil fuels (which lead to greenhouse gas emissions) required by the accord would hinder the American oil industry and economic growth more generally.

Water Pollution and Scarcity

Water pollution is another environmental problem, and it is largely caused by technological and industrial practices. Fertilizers, waste from industrial plants, oil spills, and acid rain have all contaminated much of the world's drinking water. For example, the Great Lakes, a major source of fresh water in North America, have experienced much pollution. Pollutants from the surrounding regions, comprising heavily farmed and densely populated communities, have found their way to the lakes, contaminating the water, promoting excessive growth of algae, and poisoning the aquatic life. Today, most of the beaches along the shores of the Great Lakes are too polluted for authorities to allow swimming. Similar situations have been reported for various areas along the North American ocean coastlines.

Global water use also increased greatly in the latter half of the twentieth century, especially for agricultural purposes, further straining the supply of clean, drinkable water. Canada has been among the worst offenders. Among the 29 members of the Organisation for Economic Co-operation and Development (OECD), the most developed industrial nations, 'only Americans use more water than Canadians':

Canada uses 1,600 cubic metres of water per person per year. This is more than twice as much water as the average person from France, three times as much as the average German, almost four times as much as the average Swede and more than eight times as much as the average Dane. Canada's per capita water consumption is 65% above the OECD average. (Boyd, 2001)

At the same time, more and more countries are experiencing *water stress*, a condition in which supplies are so low that each person has available an average of only 1,000 to 2,000 cubic metres of water per year. Other countries are at the level of *water scarcity*, defined as when the availability of water per person is less than 1,000 cubic metres of water per year. Canada's per capita per year water availability, in contrast, is 120,000 cubic metres (IFPRI, 1997).

Deforestation

As noted above, trees remove carbon dioxide from the air and convert it to oxygen. However, as forests have been continuously harvested, mostly by commercial logging operations, the rate of carbon dioxide removal from the atmosphere has notably decreased. Up to 30 per cent of the atmospheric accumulation of carbon dioxide, which is directly responsible for global warming, is due to deforestation, according to an estimate by the World Resources Institute (1998: 1).

Forests are also vital to the health of a region because they help to protect the thin layer of fertile topsoil from wind erosion. Widespread clear-cutting of wooded areas for harvesting or to make room for expanding farmlands often results instead in the expansion of deserts. The rich topsoil may be depleted too quickly or may be carried away by wind. Deforestation of the world's rainforests also results in the displacement of indigenous people and of many animal species from these natural habitats. In extreme cases, peoples and species risk extinction because of deforestation.

It may be useful to reflect on the fact that once upon a time, the barren Sahara Desert in

Africa was woodland. All of the parched and sandy beach land around the Mediterranean Sea was covered with trees. Today, there are few trees there and the land cannot be farmed, only used for grazing, fishing, or tourism communities. Having said that, we should recognize that devastation done to the environment is not necessarily irreversible and permanent. The land around Lake Ontario and the Pacific Ocean may not necessarily become like the Sahara.

Waste Disposal and Pollution

The mass production process also creates useless by-products that require disposal. People generate a great deal of leftover paper, clothing, food, metals, plastics, and other synthetics. These materials are used and then thrown away. For example, across Canada in 1996, governments and businesses disposed of 20.6 million tonnes of trash.

There are two main methods of disposal: landfills and incinerators. As well, many products produced by today's industries, and ending up in these sites, consist of plastics and other synthetic materials. Unlike organic materials, which decompose naturally in a short period if appropriately disposed of, plastics can survive intact indefinitely when left in a landfill site. Another option is to burn the plastics, along with other forms of waste, using incinerators. However, this process converts many synthetics into hazardous chemicals, which are then released into the air as pollutants.

Compared to citizens of the developed world, citizens of developing countries have low levels of resource use and high levels of recycling. This is generally more out of necessity than out of environmental consciousness. City authorities in the Third World, however, appear set on replicating the solid waste management systems of developed countries while giving little consideration to those who make their livings from picking waste (Paccione, 2001). It is entirely possible that when these cities make economic headway, they will be less environmentally friendly than the average North American city is today.

Non-renewable Resources

All industrial societies consume massive amounts of energy because some type of energy powers each of their forms of technology. The most frequently harnessed energy sources are petroleum, coal, and natural gas, which are resources that we cannot renew once we have exhausted the planet's supplies. The US Energy Information Administration estimates that the world's energy consumption will increase from 382 quadrillion (1,015) Btu (British thermal units) in 1999 to 607 quintillion Btu in 2020 (2001).

Already we are beginning to suffer the economic consequences of the world's declining fossil fuel reserves, with gas prices in Canada and elsewhere increasing significantly since the early 1980s. The exchange of Western money for Eastern oil results in a huge transfer of funds from the West to Arab and other developing countries.

Used as a substitute, coal (when burned) contributes appreciably to the carbon dioxide and sulphur dioxide production that has added to global warming and acid rain. But since people became aware of the potential energy crisis, some attention has been given to renewable energy sources, such as hydroelectric, solar, wind, and geothermal energy. Of these alternative options, the cleanest, least expensive, and therefore most widely used is hydroelectric power. Even so, hydroelectricity is not without its drawbacks, mainly in the form of environmental damage caused to the local wildlife, waterways, and ecosystems by the massive dams that we must construct to harness the water's energy.

Industrialization and Technological Innovation

As we noted earlier, the problems of industrialization and technological innovation are new in human history. They arose only a century or two ago, and we are still learning how to deal with them. That is because they are part of the rise of industrial society.

Industrial Society

The term **industrial society** refers to a society in which industrial or mass production prevails. Whatever the political system or economic ideology, industrialization promotes certain characteristic features:

- Subsistence farming disappears.
- The number of farmers declines.
- People produce food for exchange, not for their own consumption.
- Workers begin to produce goods in large factories.
- Large machines increasingly help production.
- Jobs and workers become highly specialized.
- The number of industrial wage labourers increases.
- More people come to live in large cities.
- More people learn how to read and write.
- Scientific research changes industrial production.
- People become more concerned with efficiency.

The adoption of new, complex technology goes hand in hand with a secular culture focused on efficiency, consumerism, and a high standard of living. Citizens expect a highly developed state that provides health, education, and welfare benefits. An urban middle class dominates the class structure (numerically, if not politically).

The growing similarity of industrial societies around the world has produced what sociologists call a **convergence** of social and cultural forms. Industrial societies differ mainly in whether they merge selected 'modern' ideas with their existing culture, as Japan has done, or rearrange their cultures around these ideas, like Singapore.

Innovation Through Diffusion

Historically, people believed that change was beyond human understanding, a result of fate or God's will. Others believed that social change is the result of great minds toiling in hidden laboratories, or of great leaders pushing humanity to new heights of accomplishment in business, politics, or war. Today, many believe that many changes are 'blind' results of great forces operating without purpose or expectation. For example, some of the changes—environmental, technological, or demographic—that occurred during industrialization are due to the invention of new social arrangements, in response to demands for technological innovation (for example, the development of research capabilities) and for a more highly skilled workforce (for example, the development of universal public education). Even the growth in gender equality can be traced, ultimately, to unexpected changes in society that are rooted in industrialization and 'modernity'.

However, in this chapter we emphasize the importance of the 'common person' in bringing about momentous social changes. Mere people are the actors in all of the large accomplishments and disasters of humanity. Social changes occur because people like us change. However, we need to consider why people adopt technologies whose social, cultural, and ethical implications they do not understand. We also need to reflect on why people change their thinking about 'the good life' and at some stages in history believe, for example, that large families are a blessing and at other stages come to think that they are a burden.

In some instances, people independently 'invent' new behaviours, for example, sexual practices whose aim is the prevention of pregnancy despite an absence of modern contraceptive knowledge or technology. In some places, they may share this information secretly and informally, giving each other social support for the adoption of what religious authorities may deem improper behaviour. In some communities, particular individuals may possess special expertise and be looked to for advice and encouragement.

More generally, major social changes depend on the spread of new ideas and practices from one person to another and from one community to another. The study of this information flow is called the study of **diffusion**. Diffusion includes the spread of cultural information from one society to another, the spread of investment information, the transmission of rumours in a community, the passing along of job information and the inside dope on job candidates, and advice about birth control or safe sex. Diffusion is important in several processes that are central to modernization, including the spread of scientific information and new technology, and of information about ways to control fertility.

Industrialism increases the global and national flow of technologies, ideas, and practices, both between and within nations, and between social groups. This flow is facilitated by the rise of global media, global capitalism, multinational corporations, and international travel.

The flow and adoption of new ideas and practices typically has several stages. First, the ideas and practices have to arrive, and some people are better placed than others to monitor and receive new ideas. Generally, people with larger and looser social networks receive more new ideas. And generally, people with higher social status and more geographic mobility have larger, looser networks (Klonglan et al., 1971).

Second, people have to consider these new ideas and practices. People with particularly high or low social standing are the most likely to innovate. Neither group has anything to lose by trying: the high-status group has a secure enough status to try new things, while the low-status group has no status to lose. Additionally, people are more likely to try new practices if they know others whose judgment they respect and who can offer them information, opinion, or support on this matter. These are what we might call *community opinion leaders*. If the opinion leaders are supportive, people will be more likely to try something new.

Third, 'adopters' of these new practices will typically try to evaluate the results of their innovation in a cautious, modest way. The more consequential the innovation, the longer and more slowly they will evaluate it. People are not fools;

they will not change patterns of a lifetime, risking everything, just to try something that will not work for them. So before they adopt the change on a large scale, they are likely to adopt it on a small scale and watch for good results.

This adoption of new ideas and technologies has a particular, well-documented mathematical pattern. A defining feature of diffusion is the *S-curve*, which plots the cumulative percentage of adopters in a population as a function of time. Gradually, people substitute the new technology for the old technology. Gradually, the new technology takes an ever-larger share of the market. For example, mainframe computers replace filing clerks, then stand-alone desktop computers replace mainframe computers, then computer networks replace stand-alone computers, and so on. In each instance, an initial slow diffusion is followed by rapid diffusion.

If you plot this process on graph paper, with 'time' along the x-axis and 'percentage of farmers who have adopted the seed' (or 'organizations that have adopted mainframe computers') along the y-axis, you will have drawn an **S**-shaped curve with a long, rapidly rising middle section. This characteristic shape tells us that diffusion processes always feature a slow start by the courageous and well connected; a rapid, ever faster mania of copying; and a slow finish, with late adoptions by the fearful and the uninformed. Most important, this pattern applies to a wide range of phenomena.

The Case of Fertility Control

It is important to emphasize the general applicability of this process. A great many important human transformations of the last millennium have been processes of diffusion. Consider the *demographic transition*, by which the human race gave up its historic pattern of high mortality and high fertility for a new pattern of low mortality and low fertility. The last part of the transition, fertility reduction, moved like a wildfire in the twentieth century, thanks to diffusion.

Historical demographic evidence shows that the 1870s were a watershed in world history. It was in that decade that Western European, Northern European, and North American countries' childbearing rates began their steep, never-to-be-reversed downward trend—in effect, the middle section of the S-curve for fertility decline. This change marked the beginning of the end of high fertility for the human race, a pattern that has since spread to Southern and Eastern Europe, Latin America, Asia, and Africa. This pattern continues today. In 2001, the continent of Africa still had a fertility rate of 5.2 childbirths per woman, much higher than the world's average rate of 2.8. The percentage of married women in Africa aged 15 to 49 and using any form of contraception was a mere 26 per cent in 2001 compared to the 60 per cent average of the world (Population Reference Bureau, 2001: 2). However, there is every sign in Africa of a continuing growth in fertility control and a decline in childbearing.

The transition has happened in at different rates in different regions of the world, and in some regions it is still going on today, two centuries or so after it began. However, in the scheme of human history, this has been a brief and sudden process with a clearly definable outline.

None of the social and economic variables associated with industrialization fully predicted this downturn. Large increases in urbanization and literacy and large reductions in mortality all played a part, and together they predicted some fertility reduction. However, none of these variables was as strong an influence as theorists had expected. In industrializing countries, fertility declined more rapidly than would have been expected, and the decline did not always occur in the most highly industrialized locations. Fertility reduction diffused from Northern and Western Europe to Eastern and Southern Europe, and then to the Middle East and Asia.

The entire process has taken humanity 150 to 200 years, though the process sped up after World War II because of the 'broadcasting' of new birth control technology through the developing world. In the less developed world, the role of industrialization was less influential in reducing fertility in the twentieth century than it had been in Europe and North America a century earlier. There, fertility reduction was just as likely to occur without industrialization and urbanization as with it—if, that is, birth control information, technology, and the motivation to limit childbearing were present.

The missing link was diffusion. There are clear signs that diffusion played a key part in the European demographic transition. For example, researchers have found that geographic proximity to low-fertility areas predicted low fertility in areas that were not themselves urban or industrial (van de Walle and Knodel, 1980).

This evidence suggests that social relations influence people's decisions to limit their childbearing. Fertility reduction diffuses because, as with other important decisions, people consult others they know and respect before taking such an important action. They need advice about how to limit their fertility and encouragement to limit it from people they trust. For people traditionally committed to producing large families, the decision to produce small families is an important one. People take it only after consulting with kin, friends, and respected elders who have some experience in these matters.

Diffusion and Location

A telling feature of diffusion is that it is locational. Usually, diffusion is taking place when we see geographic concentrations of a given behaviour—for example, concentrations of low fertility in a particular region—and a gradient in that behaviour at increasing distances from that region. The suspicion is strengthened if the behaviour appears to spread out from the source in stages over time. In a diffusion process, the extent of geographic spread is a joint function of time and distance. Information that diffuses penetrates first locations that are nearest to the source. As time passes, the information reaches the closest locations first and influences them most. Locations equidistant to the source are usually influenced equally and at the same time. How much time has elapsed since the process began determines how much the information has influenced a distant location.

However, not all instances of diffusion have this characteristic locational pattern. Non-locational diffusion occurs when, for example, the instrument of diffusion is what is called a *culture carrier*. Any one of many mobile people and things can be culture carriers, including migrants, books, photographs, and memories. Media of communication are also culture carriers. Books, magazines, movies, television shows, and videos all carry cultural ideas from one end of the earth to another. Research into distant and electronic communication (for example, e-mail or webcasting) will gradually reveal just how closely people can simulate face-to-face, trusting, or intimate relationships technologically. This will reveal how much diffusion processes can be freed from location.

Historically, then, the spread of new ideas and practices—the basis of most important changes in the environment, technology, and population—has occurred through locational diffusion. This has meant the movement of people from one place to another. The more people travelled, the more widely ideas and practices were diffused and the more rapidly changes occurred in the environment, technology, and population. With the development of mass media—books, newspapers, journals, and, more recently, radios, movies, and television—travel took a back seat to mass communication as a means of spreading new ideas.

Problems of Population Growth

In understanding humanity's assault on the environment, one other element besides industrialization is important: the worldwide growth of population, especially in the last 200 years.

Population and Power

Like the flow of ideas, the flow of people is critical. People are also the basis for agricultural and industrial growth in society: larger populations create larger economies—if they are well organized. Likewise, large populations are the basis for large armies, though military power depends on more than population size alone. Large populations are also attractive to industrialized commercial societies as potential consumers of their products.

Thus, the aggregation of people through birth and migration is a politically and economically important factor in human history. However, because population size affects social organization, the movements of large numbers of people can be socially disruptive. In the past century, migration has become an explosive concern throughout the world, as the casualties of famine, war, and other disasters have spilled across borders and forced other nations to take note of their plight. Even within nations, demographic, economic, and environmental changes have the effect of leading people to move from one region to another and thereby changing the social order.

Demographer Kingsley Davis (1988) points to three critical moments in the history of world migration during the last five centuries: Europe's discovery of the New World; the Industrial Revolution; and the demographic transition, which saw major declines in mortality after 1770 and major declines in fertility after 1870. Each had a dramatic impact on the demand for and supply of labour.

The discovery of the New World launched international exploration, colonization, and slave trading. The peopling of the Americas with Europeans marked a major shift in the balance of location of the human race and a shift in the international balance of power. The Industrial Revolution launched the creation of new cities and suburban communities, as well as the large-scale movement of people off the land and out of agriculture. It also encouraged migration from less developed to more developed countries.

Finally, the demographic transition connected high economic productivity—and high standards of living—with low fertility. This made aging, prosperous industrial societies particularly attractive to potential immigrants and young, fertile potential immigrants particularly attractive to industrial societies.

Emigration from poorer countries benefits local community development and provides labour power for the developed world. However, migration has negative effects as well. For example, it may bring depopulation and underdevelopment to the rural (sending) region. It may also segregate people—for instance, older people from younger people (Rogers, Watkins, and Woodward, 1990). On an international scale, migration may produce hostile, intolerant and fearful reactions from the nations receiving large numbers of new immigrants.

It is hard to gauge the seriousness of the world's immigration problem since, for many parts of the world, demographers have only a rough idea of how many people have migrated. Indeed, it is difficult to obtain anything like accurate counts of migrants from any part of the world where there is war, famine, desperate poverty, or political oppression.

Canada's Population History

Few countries have been shaped by migration as rapidly and dramatically as Canada. It has grown substantially in some periods and to a limited extent in others. The decades before World War I and after World War II were times of rapid growth; growth was slower during the late nineteenth century, during the 1930s, and after 1965. The reasons for these shifts lie in changing patterns of international migration as well as in natural increase.

When Europeans 'discovered' North America in the early 1600s, between 200,000 and 1,000,000 people already lived in what is now Canada. Their ancestors had arrived in the Americas from Asia not less than 10,000 years earlier, and possibly as much as 50,000 years earlier (Farb, 1978). Thus, *all* Canadians are descended from immigrants.

By 1763, French, English, and other European immigrants and their descendants had increased the local population by 100,000. Greater numbers of immigrants, from a wider range of countries, arrived during the nineteenth and twentieth centuries. The population grew about 4 per cent annually during the century before Confederation, and 2 per cent annually during much of the century that followed. The growth of Canada to over 31,000,000 people has taken two centuries. It is the result of high rates of both childbearing and immigration—two factors that have created an extremely high ratio of newcomers to tradition-carriers, adults who were born into and grew up with Canadian culture. (For further discussion of the concept of *tradition-carriers* among Canadians, see Bell and Tepperman, 1979; see also Li, 2003.)

But emigration from Canada was often so common that it largely offset the effects of immigration. Since 1851, about 12 million immigrants have entered Canada and 7.5 million emigrants have left. (See Table 10.1.) Thus, the net gain through migration was about 4.5 million people. In the same period, there was a net gain through natural increase of some 20.5 million people—more than four times the gain through migration. Therefore, especially in French Canada, fertility has influenced Canada's population history much more significantly than immigration (Beaujot and McQuillan, 1982: 55; Foot, 1982: 3–7).

Nonetheless, immigration has distinctively coloured Canada's history, culture, and social organization. Much more than any European, Asian, or African society, Canada is a nation of immigrants and descendants of immigrants. Consequently, we cannot understand Canadian society without examining the contribution of migration to Canada's population history.

TABLE 10.1
Canadian Demographics: Population and Growth Components, 1851–1996 (Thousands)[a]

	Census Population at the End of Period	Total Population Growth[b]	Births	Deaths	Immigration	Emigration
1851–61	3,230	793	1,281	670	352	170
1861–71	3,689	459	1,370	760	260	410
1871–81	4,325	636	1,480	790	350	404
1881–91	4,833	508	1,524	870	680	826
1891–1901	5,371	538	1,548	880	250	380
1901–11	7,207	1,836	1,925	900	1,550	740
1911–21	8,788	1,581	2,340	1,070	1,400	1,089
1921–31	10,377	1,589	2,415	1,055	1,200	970
1931–41	11,507	1,130	2,294	1,072	149	241
1941–51[c]	13,648	2,141	3,186	1,214	548	379
1951–6	16,081	2,433	2,106	633	783	185
1956–61	18,238	2,157	2,362	687	760	278
1961–6	20,015	1,777	2,249	731	539	280
1966–71[d]	21,568	1,553	1,856	766	890	427
1971–6	23,450	1,882	1,755	824	1,053	358
1976–81	24,820	1,371	1,820	843	771	278
1981–6	26,101	1,280	1,872	885	677	278
1986–91	28,031	1,930	1,933	946	1,199	213
1991–6	29,672	1,641	1,936	1,024	1,137	229

[a] Numbers may not add up evenly because of rounding.
[b] Total population growth is the difference in census population counts at the end and beginning of each period.
[c] Beginning in 1951, Newfoundland is included.
[d] Beginning in 1971:
   • The population estimates are based on census counts adjusted for net undercount, and the reference date is July 1 instead of census day (the 1 July 1971 population adjusted for net census undercount is 21,962,100).
   • Immigration figures include landed immigrants, returning Canadians, and the net change in the number of non-permanent residents.
   • Population growth calculated using the components will produce a different figure than is reported in table. Beginning in 1971, an independent estimate of emigration is produced. Prior to 1971, the emigration figures are 'residual' estimates and include the errors in the other three growth components—births, deaths, and immigration—as well as errors in the census counts.

SOURCE: Statistics Canada, Demography Division data, available at <www.statcan.ca/english/Pgdb/demo03.htm>, accessed 20 February 2003.

The Wide Fluctuations of Immigration

The effects of migration to and from Canada have fluctuated widely with time and place, while the effects of natural increase have not. Mirroring Western Europe's demographic transition, Canada's birth and death rates have dropped slowly and predictably since about 1851. True, the economic depression of the 1930s pushed fertility below the expected level and the post-war baby boom pushed births above it. In general, however, the downward trend has been slow and steady.

By contrast, migration into and out of Canada has varied a great deal from decade to decade. Canadian economic development has gone on rapidly, almost crazily, from one resource-driven economic boom-and-bust cycle to another. With each resource discovery has come the opening of a new portion of the country. Willing workers extract the resource, whether fish, furs, timber, wheat, gold, or oil. The resource industry creates new communities and new jobs in manufacturing, services, communications, and transportation. In fact, often more jobs are created than can be filled by native-born Canadians with the right skills. Canada then opens its doors to immigrants, liberalizing legislation, increasing quotas, even searching out immigrants in preferred countries (Hawkins, 1972; Kalbach, 1970).

How long this need for workers will last depends on foreign demand for the resource. Today, there's a stiff international demand for Canadian hydroelectric power and water. However, the future demand for Canadian timber, precious metals, and wheat on the world markets is uncertain. Sales of these natural resources are always affected by international tariffs and competition. Political as well as economic issues are involved. Additionally, popular tastes change. No one wears beaver hats anymore, and fewer people want sealskin coats. The codfish are almost gone from ocean waters, and fewer people want to eat codfish anyway. Canada—the country built on beaver, cod, and timber, and later on wheat, gold, oil, and uranium—has had to repeatedly rethink its economic foundations.

When the demand for a natural resource dies down, as it always does, the need for immigrant labour collapses. Immigration laws tighten up again and fewer immigrants are admitted. The 'quality' and quantity of immigrants are controlled more systematically through, for instance, the tightening of medical inspection (Sears, 1990). As opportunities within Canada evaporate, more people leave the country, chiefly for the United States.

This sequence of migration is most noticeable when we focus on a single region, such as Alberta.

Consider, for example, the rapid population growth of Edmonton and Calgary in the 1970s, followed by a slowdown in the 1980s. More dramatic still, as Rex Lucas (1972) has pointed out, are the effects of migration on resource-based, single-industry company towns. A psychology of population instability results from (and, in turn, causes) a movement of migrants. Its effect is out of all proportion to the number of migrants in the population (Porter, 1965).

Or consider the massive shift of migrants away from an increasingly separatist Quebec during the 1980s. Migration has been a particular problem for French Canada from two standpoints. Throughout the early part of the twentieth century, many French Canadians migrated to the United States (Lavoie, 1972). This trend led some to believe that emigration could end the French presence in Canada. Francophone Canada has also suffered an opposite problem: an influx of immigrants who cannot speak French and who are unwilling to learn it. The evidence of French language loss outside Quebec has led to concern among francophone demographers (Henripin, 1974) and policy makers. However, this anxiety may be unwarranted. Within Quebec, the French language is apparently alive and well (Caldwell and Fournier, 1987; Lachapelle, 1980; Statistics Canada, 2002).

In 1990, the federal government opted to raise the ceiling on the number of immigrants to Canada. The decision was informed by a prediction based on current demographic trends that, unless more immigrants are allowed in, Canada's population by the year 2025 would be smaller than it was then.

'Demographic Problems' Worldwide

Often when people react against changes in population size, composition, or distribution, they are reacting against the growth in numbers of people who are unlike themselves. This is presently a serious and escalating problem throughout the world, as shown by violent ethnic, religious, and racial conflicts.

In Israel, the 'demographic problem' focuses on concern that the non-Jewish portion of the population is growing more rapidly than the Jewish portion (Vining, 1989). In South Africa, the policy of apartheid was foreshadowed by differential treatment of white and non-white women in the event of births outside marriage—so-called illegitimate births—during the first decades of the twentieth century (Burman and Naude, 1991). As in the other cases cited, these population events were problems for the dominant society because they represented a growth in the size (and potential power) of a subordinate community. In the end, then, change in the composition of a population affects the real and perceived balance of power in a society.

The Malthusian Debate

Modern scientific theories about population growth and its effect on societies begin with Thomas Malthus ([1798] 1959). A population growing exponentially (that is, in a series 1, 2, 4, 8, 16) at a constant rate adds more people every year than the year before. Consider a population of 1,000 women and 1,000 men. Each woman marries and has 4 children. If all survive, in the next generation there are roughly 2,000 women and 2,000 men. If all of those women have 4 children each, then in the next generation there are roughly 4,000 women and 4,000 men, and in the generation after that, 8,000 women and 8,000 men. With a constant pattern of 4 births per woman, the population doubles every generation (roughly 30 years). In only 300 years, the original population of 2,000 has grown to a million people! (As you can verify, this is due to 10 doublings.) This is the power of exponential growth.

On the other hand, Malthus said that increases in the food supply are only additive, or arithmetic (that is, in a series 1, 2, 3, 4, 5). Limits on available land, soil quality, and technology all constrain the growth in food supplies. Malthus believed that there is a real risk of populations outgrowing the food supply. The chance of running out of food thus poses a real threat to humanity. For that reason, checks (or limits) are needed to keep population growth in line with growth in the food supply. Welfare schemes to help the poor by redistributing wealth are futile, said Malthus. If we feed the hungry, they will procreate until they run out of food and are hungry again.

The only sure solutions are positive checks and preventive checks. **Positive checks** prevent overpopulation by increasing the death rate. They include war, famine, pestilence, and disease. **Preventive checks** prevent overpopulation by limiting the number or survival of live births. They include abortion, infanticide, sexual abstinence, delayed marriage, and contraceptive use. Among these preventive options, the pious Reverend Malthus approved of only delayed marriage and sexual abstinence.

Today, people who argue that there is still a 'population problem', that the world is becoming 'overpopulated', or that the world is a population 'time bomb' make some of the same arguments Malthus did two centuries ago. World population is still growing. Even allowing for slower growth, experts predict that in 30 years the current world population of just under six billion people will be three billion larger. (See Figure 10.2.)

One consequence of population growth, hinted at above, is a growing shortage of non-renewable resources that include land, fresh water, petroleum fuel, and minerals needed for manufacturing. Another major consequence of rapid growth is a population in which a large proportion is school-aged or younger. Since people need an education, rapidly growing societies must spend a large portion of their budget on schools and schooling. Along with old people and the infirm, children require much public spending on health and welfare. Finally, overpopulation strains the ability of governments to prevent and deal with economic and natural disasters. Today, famines and epidemics continue to rage throughout the world, especially in the countries where the population is growing most rapidly.

FIGURE 10.2
End-of-the-World Population

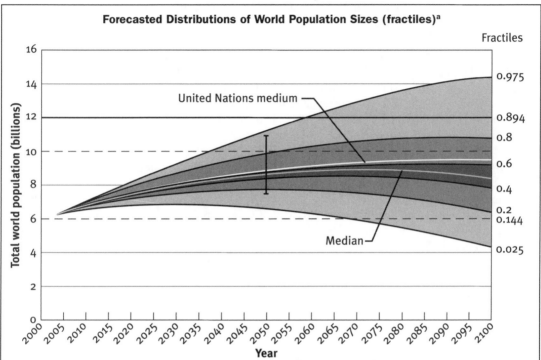

Forecasted Distributions of World Population Sizes (fractiles)[a]

There has been enormous concern about the consequences of human population growth for the environment and for social and economic development. But this growth is likely to come to an end in the foreseeable future. Improving on earlier methods of probabilistic forecasting, here we show that there is around an 85 per cent chance that the world's population will stop growing before the end of the century. There is a 60 per cent probability that the world's population will not exceed 10 billion people before 2100, and around a 15 per cent probability that the world's population at the end of the century will be lower than it is today. For different regions, the date and size of the peak population will vary considerably.

[a] Forecasted distributions of world population sizes (fractiles). For comparison, the United Nations medium scenario (white line), and 95 per cent interval as given by the NRC on the basis of an ex post error analysis (vertical line in 2050) are also given.

SOURCE: Wolfgang Lutz, Warren Sanderson, and Sergei Scherbov, 'The End of World Population Growth', *Nature*, 412 (2001): 543–5. Copyright 2001 Macmillan Magazines Limited.

However, we cannot rely on the occurrence of changes—for example, more equality, better government, or new technology—that will make Earth able to support many more people. Second, few of us are willing to give up many 'goods'—material prosperity, long life, political liberty, a low-risk future—merely to have more people on Earth. Obviously, humanity must take measures, for environmental and other reasons, to lower world fertility.

The Future of World Population

Italian demographer Massimo Livi-Bacci notes, 'developing countries will account for approximately 95 per cent of world population increase in the period 1990–2025. . . . [As a result] between 1950 and 2025 the developed country share of world population will decline from 33.1 per cent to 15.9; Europe's share will decline still faster, from 15.6 per cent to 6.1' (1992: 202).

European countries whose populations were in the world's 'Top 20' in 1950—Germany, the United Kingdom, Italy, France, Spain, and Poland—will be off the list entirely in 2025. Newcomers to the list will include Ethiopia, Zaire, and Tanzania. As Livi-Bacci points out, 'though relations between countries are conditioned primarily by political, cultural, and economic factors, large changes in their relative population sizes are bound to have an effect' (1992: 202).

It is not clear that the planet's carrying capacity will be strained, however. Writing in 1949, the eminent demographer Alfred Sauvy described potential overpopulation as a 'false problem' and argued against attempts at global population control (Sauvy and Demeny, 1990). He suggested examining countries on a case-by-case basis to see whether they lack the raw materials and natural resources that can support a larger population. Otherwise, we run the risk of underpopulating a country (such as Canada) that could support a much larger population.

Demographers continue to debate the merits of different theories of population growth. For this reason, it is difficult, if not impossible, to foresee the future of the world's population. All that can be said with certainty is that population processes cannot and will not continue indefinitely in the way they did during the twentieth century. Modern Malthusians would add that otherwise, we would also start running out of breathable air, drinkable water, fuel, and natural resources to feed industrial machinery. In short, modern industrial civilization would collapse without a reduction in world population growth.

Demographic transition theorists likewise foresee an ultimate reduction in population growth, but they suggest a very different way of getting there. In their scenario, worldwide modernization and the spread of cheap, safe contraception will cause fertility to continue dropping, as it has done for the last century or so. Some societies might follow China's example and promote below-replacement fertility (for example, one child per family). World population size might reach a plateau around the middle of this century, at 10 to 20 billion people, and then slowly start to decrease. By 2200, the world's

---

BOX 10.1
Pass the Condoms

Quick, pass the condoms, someone just gave birth to the earth's six billionth human! The alarmists would have us believe that a population spread is a bad thing; that the Earth will soon be stripped of food, leaving swollen-bellied children to starve. Depending on who you talk to, the numbers will nod: The world hosted its first billion in 1804. At least 123 years passed before man and womankind doubled to two billion, but it took only 33 years (1960) for us to reach three billion, and 14 years to reach four (1974).

Then growth started to ease up: another 13 years passed before we saw five billion and

an additional 12 years flew by before we topped six billion this week. But the expansion we've experienced is because humans' lifespans have doubled—not because we're copulating like rabbits. Harvard University researcher Nicholas Eberstadt recently concluded that Canada is one of 61 countries where women aren't producing enough to replace the population—global fertility levels today are believed to be at least 40 per cent lower than they were in the early 1950s.

If this continues, we could start falling back. Indeed, Mark Leonard, director of the

continued

U.S.-based Foreign Policy Center goes further: He predicts a world population shortage that will see affluent countries jockeying for immigrants to fill a chronic labour shortage.

It all boils down to women's lib, they say; women around the world are climbing the status ladder, and that means choices, and that translates into fewer pregnancies. It may also translate into a world that's shrinking, rather than multiplying. Okay, wiseguy (you might reply), but what about the increasing demands we put on the environment?

Glad you asked. Research indicates that developed countries aren't paying a whole lot more for the Earth's riches—cereals, timber, oil, minerals, etc.—than the going rate a century ago. Yes, we've near exhausted some 'natural resources', but we've created others in their stead.

Frankly, there's no need to panic about the growing number of mouths to feed, what we should be freaking out about is the sloppy, inefficient, over-regulated way governments manage the resources we have.

Global communities need to learn how to nurture, harvest and replenish the vast treasures on Earth. Then there'll be plenty to go around.

SOURCE: 'Family Planning Is a Good Thing, Resources Planning Is One Better', *The Province* (Vancouver), 14 October 1999, A46. Reprinted by permission of Pacific Newspaper Group Inc.

population could even be back to what it is today, some 5 or 6 billion people.

Demographers have proven notoriously wrong whenever they have tried to predict the future with any exactitude. For one thing, fertility responds very sensitively to changes in people's values and economic opportunities, in government policies, and in contraceptive technology. Mortality and migration also respond sensitively to changes in the social and political climate, particularly modern statecraft and warfare. Like everyone else, demographers are poorly equipped to predict changes in values, economic opportunities, new technologies, government policies, and warfare.

In the end, 'population problems' such as high fertility and high rates of immigration are social problems in a society that has not worked out ways of putting its population to good use, in good health. Population problems are environmental problems in a society that does not know how to protect its environment in the face of increased population pressure. In this sense, environmental problems arise not because of new technology or too many people, but because of poor social organization.

Environmental Problems as Global Problems

Unlike most other social problems, environmental issues are global in their consequences. They affect us all in a way that many social problems, such as alcohol and drug abuse or race and ethnic relations, may not. The latter can vary greatly across societies and groups in their consequences. Still, there are important connections between the social problems of the natural environment and the economic strength of a society or group. Some groups and societies pay a heavier cost for, and receive less benefit from, technological change and environmental decay than others.

Most forms of technology, from computers to medical treatments to manufacturing processes, are first invented and used by wealthy, industrialized nations before spreading to less developed societies. Researchers have estimated, for example, that up to 50 per cent of the world's population have yet to make their first phone call, let alone log on to the Internet (Norman Wagner, cited in Sharpe, 2000). Technological change widens the gap between developed and developing nations.

Paradoxically, many of the raw materials that advanced nations use come from less developed regions, creating a dilemma for the poorer countries. These countries continue to increase their economic output in an attempt to close the gap between themselves and their more advanced counterparts, but that economic output (as exported raw materials) is largely responsible for maintaining that gap.

In a time when Western countries are becoming electronically integrated in cyberspace through the Internet and other forms of wireless telecommunications, less developed nations struggle to maintain food and water supplies, shelter, and basic infrastructure. Unequal technological growth affects the environmental impact of developed and less developed countries in different ways. In wealthy societies, the environmental problems result from both consumption and pollution. Large amounts of energy are used and massive pollution and environmental damage occur, all because of a technologically advanced lifestyle.

Canadians are no less guilty than others of sacrificing the environment through heavy consumption. The Canadian Environmental Law Association estimates that no less than a trillion litres of raw and partially treated sewage are released into our waterways every year (1999). Governments often ignore or accept environmentally harmful practices, of which this is only one example, possibly because the industries responsible for pollution in our skies, land, and water are thought to be necessary to power the economy.

Environmental damage in less developed countries occurs primarily because governments are trying to approach more closely the level of economic affluence that their wealthier counterparts enjoy. They treat economic development as the highest priority, at the expense of the environment. For example, since the 1940s, overgrazing by cattle has destroyed nearly 800 million hectares of pasture and rangeland—one-third of all depleted lands. Much of this has occurred in sub-Saharan Africa. The constant beating of animal hooves on the ground compacts the exposed, sun-scorched earth, preventing water from penetrating it and allowing wind and water to sweep the soil away. Elsewhere, the growing scarcity of arable land has led farmers to attempt to grow crops in semi-arid regions, leading to the expansion of neighbouring deserts that eventually overtake the area (Postel, 1994).

Technology widens the gap separating the rich from the poor not only between nations, but within nations too. In Canada and other developed countries, most people enjoy the convenience offered by computers, fax machines, and automobiles. However, in every society there are many people who cannot afford these innovations. These technological have-nots, often living in rural areas or poor urban areas, are at risk of becoming further marginalized and left behind even as the bulk of society advances at a vigorous pace.

Sociological Theories

As always, sociology provides multiple perspectives on the environmental problems we discuss in this chapter, and on the interactions between technology and population in creating these environmental problems.

The Structural-Functionalist Perspective

Functionalists are not surprised that modern people's values and activities have contributed to the pollution of our natural surroundings and the overharvesting of resources. Several types of cultural ideologies particularly help support ecologically harmful practices, and functionalists study these. Researchers have called one example the **cornucopia view of nature**. According to this belief, people view nature as a storehouse of resources that exist only for use by humans—especially for currently living humans. Another environmentally unfriendly belief is an unrealistic faith in the ability of technology to miraculously solve all the problems in the world, including those that technology itself has caused. The *growth ethic*, which is especially popular in North America and has been embraced by many advertisers, promotes the view that things can always progress further and therefore encourages the discarding of just about everything in favour of the production and consumption of new items.

Closely related to this ethic is the ideology of *materialism*, the notion that the consumption of material wealth is a direct indicator of life success and that more is always better. Finally, the Western notion of *individualism*, which advocates personal goals and desires over collective interests, is the driving force behind the tragedy of the commons, to be discussed later in this chapter.

Conflict Theory

Sociologists following the conflict theory focus on how the social structure benefits some individuals at the expense of others. Like functionalists, conflict theorists are concerned with the consequences and implications of how society is arranged. However, a conflict theorist studying environmental and technological problems will emphasize that when environmental problems arise, they generally tend to negatively affect the poor more often and more severely than the rich. These theorists view the capitalist mode of production as a means for wealthy industry leaders to maximize corporate and personal profits at the expense of others.

The work of conflict theorists shows that when disasters occur, the poor tend to lose their lives while the rich tend to lose only their financial investments. Over 90 per cent of disaster-related deaths, for instance, occur within the poor populations of developing countries, while developed nations experience 75 per cent of disaster-related economic damage. Of the 25 per cent of the world's population currently living in a natural-disaster-prone region, most live in less developed countries (Smith, 2001: 26–7).

Famines and droughts provide some examples of the differential effects of natural disasters on rich and poor areas. In developed regions, agricultural droughts, such as those that sometimes take place in areas of Canada's prairies and the United States, result in reduced crops but almost no deaths. In underdeveloped regions, in contrast, famine droughts, such as those that occur frequently in parts of sub-Saharan Africa, are devastating in both their economic and their human costs.

Sociological research shows that disasters that occur in less developed nations result more often from 'the spread of capitalism and the marginalization of the poor than from the effects of geophysical events' and offer possible solutions that involve 'the redistribution of wealth and power in society to provide access to resources rather than . . . the application of science and technology to control nature' (Smith, 2001: 50–1).

The situation is similar in highly industrialized nations. Again, the rich alone possess the economic means to shelter themselves from health consequences of locally occurring disasters, such as floods and hurricanes, a luxury that the poor must learn to cope without. Less economically well-off families disproportionately own mobile homes, for instance, which are more vulnerable to hurricane, tornado, or flood damage than are more rooted and stable homes. The risk to mobile-home owners is increased by their tendency to put homes in cheaper, more disaster-prone areas, such as flood plains and tornado regions. The wealthy are also more often able to physically extricate themselves from an area once disaster occurs, permanently or temporarily moving to stable geophysical regions where they can (literally and figuratively) weather the storm.

Symbolic Interactionism

The symbolic interactionist perspective investigates how the meanings and labels learned through social interaction affect environmental problems, with a particular focus on how they alter the perception of these problems at the individual level.

Here, the social constructionist framework is particularly relevant. Sociologists approaching environmental problems from this perspective ask why and how certain environmental problems enter public consciousness: what kinds of 'claims' make the greatest impact, and under what circumstances. For instance, sociologists Clay Schoenfeld, Robert Meier, and Robert Griffin (1979) have looked at how environmental issues have become a 'problem' in the public's eye. How and why does the greenhouse effect become a widespread public concern one year, and AIDS or women's rights or child labour in India become a concern another year?

The symbolic interactionist perspective also offers insights into how environmental polluters manipulate symbols to protect themselves from criticism. Many companies and businesses, facing increasing levels of public scrutiny in recent years over their impact on the environment, have attempted to boost their image and profits by using a public relations strategy known as *greenwashing*. This technique involves redesigning and repackaging their products as 'environmentally friendly' or 'green', soothing consumers' concerns about possibly contributing to the environmental problem by purchasing ecologically harmful items.

Social Consequences

The Tragedy of the Commons

The tragedy of the commons is sometimes used to explain why people knowingly pollute and damage the environment with seemingly no regard for their actions. The **tragedy of the commons** refers to what happened when medieval English lords opened their uncultivated pastures to allow commoners to freely graze their herds. These open fields became known as the *commons*. Soon the number of cattle in these areas grew to the point at which the pastures could no longer sustain themselves. As competition for resources increased between commoners, each was faced with a difficult decision: to add more cows to his own herd, which would lead to greater personal yields but would also create an additional burden on all those occupying the pasture, or to limit his personal gains in the

---

BOX 10.2
Kyoto and the Tragedy of the Commons

In December 1997 thousands of delegates from 160 countries came together to hammer out a plan to stop global warming. Their goal was to cut back the greenhouse gases that human beings were pumping into the atmosphere—dramatically. It was a historic moment—the culmination of almost half a century of studying the impact of manmade emission on the environment. And Kyoto's mandate was to find a solution to global warming once and for all—and come up with a plan that would have obligations and consequences for everyone. Many people there believed that they were saving the world. . . .

In the five years since Kyoto only one thing has changed. One of former Texas oilman George W. Bush's first acts as US President was to pull the US out of the agreement. With the US out and Mexico exempt from the agreement the Prime Minister had became the only North American leader whose country still had to meet its Kyoto target.

Every day, Alberta produces about 3 million barrels of oil. It is home to 75% of the oil and gas industry in Canada. And Jean Chrétien's ongoing commitment to Kyoto has—as predicted—caused hostility and serious political problems there. . . .

continued

It's a widely accepted theory that the trapped carbon dioxide warms the earth and destabilizes the climate. But there are some who say that these weather disasters are perfectly natural. Alberta's Environment Minister, Lorne Taylor, says, 'I think that's a bunch of what I would call hokey science. The South Saskatchewan River was dry in 1862. Are you going to tell me that that was caused by global warming?' . . .

Alberta's Minister of the Environment, Lorne Taylor, claims that the costs of Kyoto could be catastrophic. 'Let's deal with it. 450 thousand jobs, $1.10 a liter of gas . . . now in terms of actual dollars, we're saying the cost to the Alberta economy could be as high as 8 billion dollars a year.'

But Ottawa's Environment Minister David Anderson claims that 'Mr. Taylor comes up with these figures, never supported with any analysis' and assures Albertans that—despite what their government says—Kyoto will not unfairly affect them.

It's led to an all out PR battle with commercial ad campaigns running across the country. But the latest polls indicate that Alberta seems to be winning—at least inside the province.

SOURCE: 'The Canadian Debate on Kyoto', *The Fifth Estate* (2002), available at <http://cbc.ca/fifth/kyoto/index.html>.

interest of others. This conflict between the interests of the individual and the interests of the group as a whole is what occurs for problems of depletion of non-renewable resources or accumulating levels of pollution.

Technological Dualism

Technology is inherently neither good nor bad. Technological innovations have both positive and negative effects. Like all other human advances, it is how we apply these developments that determines whether they will make positive or negative contributions to society.

We can readily illustrate this using the example of the automobile. This invention has made possible travel across vast distances, the freedom to dictate one's pace and destination, and the convenience of a speedy mobile private space. Today, the automobile allows people to travel in one hour a distance that would otherwise take all day to complete by foot. On the other hand, cars and trucks have helped lead to dangerous levels of carbon monoxide and smog in the atmosphere, contributed to global warming, and allowed for the expansion of suburban sprawl and chronic traffic jams. Today, thanks to traffic congestion, it is sometimes faster to travel through urban centres by foot than by car.

The rapid growth of technology also has immediate and practical consequences for work life in the industrialized world. As technology continues to transform the workplace, more efficient and less costly machines replace tasks once done by human labour. Automation and mass production often create unemployment for some individuals and leave others—almost exclusively those in the working and middle classes, as opposed to the members of the more affluent upper class—to work in monotonous and deskilled jobs that lack autonomy and challenge. Some think that the owners of the means of production are the only ones who benefit from technological change in the workplace. The conventional point of view is that technological innovation is bad for workers because machines take their jobs. However, opinion on this issue is divided.

Research in the United Kingdom, for example, studied the diffusion of microelectronics throughout the manufacturing industry and asked surveyed workers about the impact of the new technology on jobs. They found that fewer than half of the establishments reported a change in jobs. Overall, the average net decrease was only about two jobs per factory per year, mainly unskilled jobs. Among new-technology adopters, the losses were larger in factories using the new technology the most and in those with the more advanced applications. Over the same period, however, technology non-users lost about three times as many jobs as users. The number of jobs increased, not decreased, in the plants that used robots. (See Daniel, 1987; Newton and Lockie, 1987; Northcott, Fogarty, and Trevor, 1985; Northcott and Walling, 1988.)

Technology has both positive and negative effects on social interaction and social relationships. On the positive side, telephones, fax machines, e-mail, and Internet chat rooms allow people separated by great physical distance to remain in real-time contact with one another, either over a wire or in cyberspace. On the negative side, however, these and other technological inventions have also reduced the need for face-to-face contact. Often, we have replaced activities that once involved a human interface with a mechanical interface. For instance, the answering machine can replace the secretary, automatic teller machines (ATMs) can replace bank tellers, and online shopping Web sites can replace salespeople.

Finally, some scholars have said that the increased use of in-home computers and increased TV consumption have led to a decrease in levels of interaction with others in the community (Putnam, 2000). Barry Wellman and Keith Hampton dispute this claim, however. Their year-long ethnographic study of a fully 'wired' community outside Toronto found that, in fact, in-home computers increased neighbourhood interaction and general 'neighbouring' activities (Wellman and Hampton, 1999). James Curtis, Douglas Baer, and Edward Grabb (Baer, Curtis, and Grabb, 2001; Curtis, Baer, and Grabb, 2001) have presented comparative data from some 33 countries, Canada and the United States included, that show that activity in voluntary associations tends to be highest in nations with high levels of personal computing and television use. They also find no trend toward declines in association activity for the 1980s to 1990s, whether for the nations with high levels of use of the two communication technologies or for those with low use levels.

Health Consequences

Environmental problems have harmful health consequences. This is particularly striking in the poorer regions of the developing world. The World Health Organization (WHO) estimates, for instance, that 'poor environmental quality is directly responsible for 25% of all preventable ill-health in the world today, with diarrheal diseases and respiratory infections heading the list' (1999).

These health consequences are socially structured, too: a majority of all preventable ill health resulting from environmental conditions affects children; further, children and adults living in rural and peri-urban areas are more affected than those in urban areas (WHO, 1997; see also Aronwitz and Cutler, 1998; Helfgott, 1988). Even in developed nations, various forms of pollutants, chemicals, and other environmental hazards constantly bombard people. A major Canadian example occurred during the summer of 2000, when an outbreak of *E. coli* bacteria in the water supply of Walkerton, Ontario, killed nine people and infected thousands more. Although a board of inquiry looking into the deaths eventually blamed insufficient government regulations and human error, this event dramatically showed that water supplies in even the most technologically advanced regions are not safe from environmental contamination.

The list of health consequences is too long to present here, but consider just a few examples. The number of asthma cases treated in hospital emergency departments increases after a period of severe air pollution. Noise pollution, most apparent in dense urban environments and a result of our industrialized lifestyle, has been shown to contribute to hearing loss. The thinning of the ozone layer has meant an increase in the amount of harmful UV rays that are penetrating the atmosphere. This has resulted in a parallel increase in the number of skin cancer cases, particular in melanomas, which have increased 15-fold in prevalence in the past 60 years. This upsurge in UV-caused cancer accounts for 8 out of every 10 skin-cancer deaths. The use and haphazard dumping of ecologically harmful chemicals into the local environment has allowed persistent organic pollutants (POPs), such as pesticides, to accumulate in the food chain and, eventually, in human food supplies. On a global scale, climate changes resulting from global warming have led to a rise in the occurrence of droughts and famines, particularly in Africa and in regions along the equator, and to increases in the number of natural disasters such as floods.

Not everyone is affected to the same degree. For example, age differentiates who is exposed to environmental health risks. Children in both developed and developing nations are particularly vulnerable to chemical, physical, and biological pollutants in the environment since their immune systems are only partly developed. Indoor air pollution caused by fossil-fuel combustion for the purposes of cooking and heating is responsible for respiratory infections that account for 20 per cent of mortality in children under five years of age. Diarrheal diseases claim another 2 million children a year, mainly because of unclean drinking water and lack of hygiene. Ailing and elderly members of society are also at a higher risk because of their declining health status.

Technology, too, can have adverse health implications. Types of technology that pose severe health risks to the general population include nuclear power plants, automobiles, X-rays, food preservatives, breast implants, and pesticides. As we suggested above, industrialized societies are also increasingly experiencing technological emergencies and disasters, including accidents involving hazardous materials or nuclear power and mass transportation (for example, airplanes, buses, and trains).

Technology is not all bad. Biotechnology, the marriage of molecular biology research and applied engineering, has, among other accomplishments, produced slower-ripening tomatoes and pest-resistant corn and potato crops. However, critics are wary that a failure to consider the long-term health and environmental effects of this new technology may lead to the creation of new allergies and other, more serious forms of technology-induced disease. Already, for example, studies have shown that populations of monarch butterfly larvae have been harmed after eating genetically modified corn (WHO, 1999). Whether or not the artificial manipulation of other species will, in the future, introduce novel health problems for humans as well remains to be seen.

It is most important of all to realize that, in a highly technological society like ours, technological problems—even disasters—are predictable and almost inevitable. In that sense, such problems are what sociologist Charles Perrow (1999) has called 'normal accidents'. Perrow examines a variety of different kinds of technological disaster, including the nuclear accidents at Three Mile Island in Pennsylvania and Chernobyl in the Ukraine, and, more generally, nuclear power as a high-risk system for producing energy. He also examines a variety of records on aircraft accidents, marine accidents, and accidents at dams, mines, petrochemical plants, and elsewhere.

For Perrow, the key variables in all these cases of catastrophe are system complexity, on the one hand, and subsystem coupling, on the other. Conventional engineering tries to ensure safety by building in extra warnings and safeguards. However, this approach fails because it increases system complexity. Adding to complexity not only makes system failure more likely, it creates new kinds of accidents. Said simply, more complex systems have more chances of failing and more ways to fail. Additionally, the more tightly connected (or coupled) a system's parts, the more inevitable that one part's failure will trigger another failure. Thus, simplicity and loose coupling are preferable from a safety standpoint, but complexity and tight coupling are increasingly the norm. Technological catastrophes are often blamed on human error, but invariably such error is only the social side of a built-in technological risk.

Solutions

Population Control

Industrialization, urbanization, education, mass literacy, and the emancipation of women were all key parts of the voluntary reduction in child-bearing in recent history.

Invariably, birth rates have fallen wherever women have received more education, delayed marriage, and generally enjoyed more social, economic, and political equality with men. Several developing societies—among them Costa Rica, Sri Lanka, and Kerala State in India—have enjoyed notable success in lowering the birth rate. There, low mortality and fertility rates are the result of a long process that began with fairer income distribution, better nutrition, more education (especially for women), more autonomy for women, higher rates of political awareness and participation for all, and universal access to health services. In particular, income or land redistribution and political involvement gave people more sense of involvement in their own lives—hence, more to gain from changing their fertility decisions. This is particularly true of women, who with more education and autonomy are no longer as reliant on children for social status and income security.

In Canada today, by any standard, there are not too many people for the land to support. Nor is the population growing too quickly through high rates of fertility. Yet some people view high rates of immigration as a population problem, and as a social problem. Immigration has recently become an explosive political issue. Many people inside the country want the chance to bring their relatives over to Canada. Many outside the country want a chance to get in. However, a weak economy leads many native-born Canadians to resist the push for more immigrants. Some even want the immigration rate cut back.

Should immigration be more limited? As usual, there are conflicting views on this question. People who argue that immigration should be more limited make three main points that

---

BOX 10.3
India Takes Aim at AIDS

In 1952, just four years after winning independence from Britain, the Indian government created the Indian Family Planning Program. Although its goal of reducing the birth rate remained constant, the manner in which the goal was achieved became less voluntary, and during a state of emergency in the 1970s, 8 million Indians were forcefully sterilized.

India's health and family welfare ministry has launched a countrywide campaign to contain a burgeoning population and provide protection against contracting AIDS by demystifying the condom and encouraging its usage.

It plans to set up condom vending machines at airports and public washrooms, persuade hotels to stack them along with soap and shampoo in bathrooms and convince restaurateurs to distribute them free after meals along with the traditional betel nut and aniseed normally served as a digestive.

Three-million to five-million people in India are affected with HIV, the virus that leads to AIDS, the world's highest according to a recent United Nations report. But the main stress on using condoms is to stem a burgeoning population in India, set to overtake China as the world's most populous nation by 2010.

continued

India adds 20-million people each year to its population as only 40 per cent of 145-million couples in the reproductive age group practice contraception.

India launched its family planning program in 1952, but the 19-month internal emergency imposed by prime minister Indira Gandhi in the mid-1970s severely jeopardized it and succeeding governments were forced to abandon any aggressive population control measures and even renamed the Ministry of Family Planning as the Family Welfare Ministry. Ever since, no party has dared to involve itself in family planning work, considering it political suicide.

Members of parliament said that until the state of emergency, doctors were equated with gods and goddesses in most Indian villages but when a program of forcible sterilizations began, often of teenagers and octogenarians merely to bolster statistics, it turned doctors into feared and hated 'body snatchers' synonymous with infertility.

SOURCE: Rahul Bedi, 'India Takes Aim at AIDS, Population', *The Hamilton Spectator*, 5 February 1998, B7. Reproduced courtesy of The Hamilton Spectator.

focus on economic, cultural, and social issues respectively. (In Australia, many now also make the case against immigration on ecological grounds, arguing that it speeds population growth, which in turn spurs environmental degradation.) First, they claim that immigration poses an economic problem in a slow-growing economy. Second, they say that immigrants pose a problem of assimilation and cultural unity, an issue we discussed in chapter 4. Third, they raise the concern that high rates of immigration produce problems of social cohesion and conflict. (For a general discussion of these issues, see Banton 1992; Dei 1996; Reitz 1994, 1998.)

People who want to limit or reduce immigration on economic grounds argue that immigrants use too many public services. Health care is particularly important for older immigrants, educational services for younger immigrants, and welfare for unemployed immigrants. On the one hand, critics complain that too many immigrants fail to get (or keep) jobs, so they increase the unemployment rate. On the other hand, they complain that too many immigrants take jobs away from native-born Canadians in a tight job market. Increasingly, immigrants come from countries and cultures that are different from the dominant white North American culture. As with rapid population

change because of high rates of fertility, rapid change stemming from high rates of immigration strains a society's capacity to adapt.

High rates of immigration press society to rapidly acculturate the new immigrants or, alternately, to rapidly adopt multiculturalist policies that many reject. Often, immigrants develop a self-protective strategy that the sociologist Raymond Breton has called *institutional completeness*. It is this that gives the impression of clannishness. Institutional completeness is a measure of the degree to which an immigrant ethnic group gives its own members the services they need through its own institutions. The success of these services evokes the envy of poor native-born people.

Note, in closing, that because population is not the cause of environmental damage or misused technology, population control cannot solve these problems. However, social organization is harder to improve and social problems harder to solve when a population is large and growing rapidly. This is because so much effort and money is being diverted to dealing with population issues—for example, the care and education of the young, and the creation and maintenance of housing, roads, and other infrastructure—that money is not available for new initiatives.

Environmental Policies

Environmental problems, because of their broad, snowballing nature, are difficult and expensive to solve. Still, all levels of society must plan remedies because of the seriousness of the problems and their costs for humanity and the planet. At the highest levels, national and international policies need to be formulated to ensure that we follow a common plan cooperatively. Under this approach, governments should try to establish policies that will make it profitable for industries to clean up the environment and exercise ecologically friendly practices. We must also demand greater preparedness of emergency response organizations, including local government, fire, and police departments and special response teams.

Post-materialist Values

A new theory, proposed by Ronald Inglehart, a political scientist at the University of Michigan, notes that there is wide public support for solving the problems of technology and environment we discuss here. He puts this new environmental activism down to a culture shift that originates in a generation accustomed to prosperity. Inglehart (1990; see also Tepperman, 2001) argues that people who grow up in prosperous and secure conditions develop high personal and social goals. These include the goals of belonging, self-esteem, and self-actualization. Throughout the Western world, the post-war (that is, post–World War II) generation grew up with these goals.

Over time this post-war generation replaced earlier generations as voters and in elite positions of influence. In the West, the result is a new political culture. The new generation's goals have increasingly come to define the political agenda of Western democracies. The new political culture links a variety of political, social, and economic views. As a result, it represents a new outlook on life. It is *post-materialist* in the sense that it places little importance on personal wealth, economic development, and economic determinants of social life. In this respect the new outlook is also post-Marxist. The new post-materialist culture contains political attitudes and potentials for action. It encourages more political involvement, and more protest, than the materialist culture did. However, much of this activity occurs outside the framework of elections and traditional political parties.

Inglehart's research examines anti-establishment, grassroots politics and skepticism about

---

BOX 10.4
Canada's First National Park

Canada's national parks system was established in 1885 when 26 square kilometres around hot mineral springs near Banff Station, Alberta, were set aside for public use. Parks Canada has its origin as the oldest, continuous national park service in the world, created in 1911. The National Parks Act was enacted in 1930. This act also provided a legislative framework for the setting aside of federal lands for historical purposes.

The first national historic site was Fort Anne in Annapolis Royal, Nova Scotia, recognized in 1917. The Historic Sites and Monuments Act of 1953 provided statutory authority for the designation of national historic sites, regardless of ownership, as well as a legislative basis for acquiring and for contributing directly to the care and preservation of these sites.

Source: Canada, *What Is Sustainable Development?* (n.d.), available at <www.sdinfo.gc.ca/what_is_sd/history_e.cfm?id=100>, accessed 30 January 2003.

material progress. One major component of this post-materialist shift is the growing support for environmentalism and for movements that seek solutions to these problems. Linked as they are to preferences for specific political issues and parties, these 'new' needs produce 'new' political behaviours, including shifts in goals and partisanship. Post-materialists, who also report higher levels of material satisfaction, are said to be more politically active than materialists (Inglehart, 1977).

If Inglehart's theory is valid, the problems we have discussed in this chapter are already on the way to being solved. The new environmentalist movements and political parties will gain ever more support, form governments, and ban environmentally unsound practices. Human life will become healthier and happier. However, evidence does not entirely support the theory's predictions (on this, see Tepperman, 2001). Some say that Inglehart's approach is surprisingly simple or naive—a one-dimensional view of political culture that pits materialism against post-materialism. Some say that we cannot assume that a shift in cultural values toward environmentalism will translate into political action.

We may not be able to rely on a new political culture of post-materialism to bring about environmental or technological change, to improve our health and well-being. People will have to mobilize to consider, discuss, protest, and enact new policies. And a number of factors, including global capitalism, stand in the way.

Individual Strategies

Actions by average citizens, in groups, are clearly called for, of course, because of the dire consequences for future generations of the problems of technology and the environment. As with several other social problems discussed in this book, individuals can have significant consequences for these problems only through sustained organized

Governments should try to establish policies that will make it profitable for industries to clean up the environment and exercise ecologically friendly practices. All levels of society must plan remedies because of the seriousness of environmental problems and their costs for humanity and the planet. (Dick Hemingway)

activity by many people leading to changes in social policies and collective values. There are actions that each individual can take with respect, for example, to personal fertility planning, environmental practices, and restrained and enlightened use of technology. But given the magnitude of the problems, only widespread adoption of these practices in the general population will have significant impact.

To live an environmentally friendly, technologically uncluttered life means to make major sacrifices in convenience and cost. The simplest 'green' activities include recycling household items such as newspapers and aluminum pop cans instead of throwing them in the trash, and turning off lights and water taps when they are not being used. Other options, more inconvenient and costly but also more eco-friendly, include choosing to bicycle, carpool, or use public transit instead of driving from one place to another, and purchasing organic foods (which are not treated with pesticides) and energy-efficient fluorescent light bulbs, the use of which has to date saved the equivalent of about 100 coal-burning power plants.

Concluding Remarks

Environmental destruction is a problem that occurs on the global level. This destruction will increase as a function of increased population, urban concentration, and technologies connected to industrial production. Disposing of solid and toxic waste is a major problem as it requires the availability of new landfills and can cause disruption of the ecosystem. The depletion of non-renewable natural resources is also a serious problem. Developed countries are most to blame here as they are far more wasteful than developing countries. Since industry is profit-oriented, it is not likely to take responsibility for pollution; more governmental regulation will be needed.

We have seen that environmental problems have harmful health consequences. Those affected the most are the poor living in rural areas. Environmental harm accounts for 3 million premature deaths from exposure to air pollution alone, of which 90 per cent occur in developing countries. Climate changes resulting from global warming have led to a rise in the occurrence of droughts and famines, particularly in Africa and in regions along the equator, and to increases in the number of natural disasters such as floods.

Beliefs in progress in the nineteenth and twentieth centuries assumed that changes to the structure and culture of 'Third World' countries—making them more like 'First World' countries—would enrich the countries and their people, after a Western Industrial Age pattern. But in some cases, change of this kind has even resulted in impoverishment and environmental destruction. This has happened most often when too little attention was paid to cultural or social conditions that limit or pervert the use of Western technology and productive practices.

Likewise, we have often been told in North America that the world has a population problem but that the problem resides in other countries, not the countries of the North (or the industrialized West). Some think a 'population explosion' is taxing the resources of the earth and must be controlled. In line with this thinking, 'aid' programs offered by countries of the North are often tied to requirements for 'underdeveloped' countries to promote birth-control programs—with, however, limited success, as we have seen.

Demographers who have studied the composition of the population in Europe and North America during the eighteenth and nineteenth centuries warn that popular thinking on this issue may be upside down. Children who survived infancy were the support of their parents in later life and contributed to the family income as economic producers from their childhood on. In the towns of England and France, it was common for working-class townswomen to be engaged in paid jobs while their children were too small to contribute economically but to leave their jobs to become household managers when the children entered the paid workforce.

History (and demographic transition theory) shows that, in Europe, lower rates of childbearing followed after and were associated with more security and a higher likelihood of children's survival. Materialists (that is, Marxists and other conflict theorists) have concluded from this that once people have enough to eat, so that they are reasonably sure their children will not die, they are motivated to produce fewer children. It is the practicalities of life—having food and security—that come first and that influence people's ideas and opinions about how many children to have.

Despite differences of opinion about process, both demographic transition theory and modernization theory agree on one thing: the importance of technology and industrialization. In both theories, it is the improving lifestyle that drives fertility reduction, and technology that drives an improving lifestyle. But is affluence really all a result of technological change?

Remember that the eighteenth and nineteenth centuries were times of European colonial expansion. People were going out from Europe to other parts of the world, and claiming these for, say, Germany or Britain or France. Many of the people who left Europe were poor, and many did not leave of their own volition. Social changes in Europe had created millions of landless people whose ancestors were peasants but whose land had been claimed by large-scale landowners. Part of the prosperity of nineteenth-century Europe should be traced to its habit of exporting poverty along with its manufactured products. It was this export of poverty, as much as technological change, that led to the growth of wealth in industrial Europe.

Another part can be traced to the reckless use of technology and concern with short-term gain, in the Old World and the New, and to wilful ignorance about environmental consequences. Even today, many are still willing to sacrifice the environment for short-term gains in comfort or wealth. This will not change without large-scale change in attitudes and legislation to protect the environment.

Questions for Critical Thought

1. Along with deforestation comes the displacement of indigenous peoples and many animal species from these natural habitats. Also, peoples and species may be at risk of extinction because of such activities. Chart out the advantages and disadvantages of deforestation. Do you feel it is an ethical practice? Should the government set limits? Research specific examples to back up your claims.

2. People, as well as objects, can be culture carriers, for example, foreign students who come to Canada and then return to their country of origin, bringing back with them a variety of Canadian artifacts, customs, and values. Recall vacations you have gone on or situations in which you were such a carrier. Think of the various souvenirs you have bought over the years and try to imagine what values of that place they represent. Also, was there ever a time where you brought your own values and customs and imprinted them onto others of another culture?

3. China is famous for its one-child policy, with governmental policy formally reducing the birth rate of one of the most populous countries in the world. Generally, this is seen as very successful and productive. However, some believe it may produce more problems than it solves (for example, a proliferation of rules and the creation of an all-powerful state). What are some other drawbacks to such a policy, or do you believe the advantages outweigh the possible disadvantages? Do you feel other countries should adopt such a law?

4. There has recently been a great increase in the controversy over human cloning and genetic engineering. Go on the Internet and research some of the latest developments surrounding the debate. Prepare a brief written document outlining what you feel to be the major concerns and be sure to include ethical concerns about the 'new genetics'.

5. Everything around us, from bank machines to movie-ticket sales, is becoming automated. People's jobs are being replaced by machines, and human interaction seems to be a nostalgic idea of the past. Read sociologist Georg Simmel's essay 'Metropolis and Mental Life' ([1917] 1950), paying special regard to his ideas about people's becoming calculating and rational actors. Link his theory to the time-saving technologies automation provides. Also, what would Simmel offer on this apparent shift away from personalized and intimate relationships?

Recommended Readings

John W. Bennett, *Human Ecology as Human Behavior: Essays in Environmental and Development Anthropology* (New Brunswick, NJ: Transaction Publishers, 1993).

This book suggests solutions to the problem of relations between humans and our environment. Taking a grand macro perspective, Bennett claims that the most useful analysis is not to look at human actions individually as the source of environmental degradation; instead, he advocates an analysis of the historical, cultural, and economic contexts in which humans create these problems.

Stephen Dale, *McLuhan's Children: The Greenpeace Message and the Media* (Toronto: Between the Lines, 1996).

This book is a good and entertaining resource for those interested in the symbolic integrationist perspective, which is concerned with the construction of an environmental problem. Dale also addresses the political implications of constructing a claim of environmental damage.

Mary Douglas and Aaron Wildavsky, *Risk and Culture: An Essay on the Selection of Technological and Environmental Dangers* (Berkeley: University of California Press, 1982).

This text examines the connections between the structure of human societies and the environment in which we live.

Samuel P. Hays and Barbara D. Hays, *Beauty, Health, and Permanence: Environmental Politics in the United States, 1955–1985* (New York: Cambridge University Press, 1987).

Since World War II, the American public has become more involved in environmental issues. Hays and Hays argue that this is because the increased standard of living makes the concept of environmental 'balance' more reasonable.

Wayne Lutton and John Tanton, *The Immigration Invasion* (Petoskey, MI: Social Contract Press, 1994).

This text addresses global population growth and immigration in Europe. Europeans find that as their own level of technology and wealth increases, the birth rate decreases and the state requires more workers. But immigration is often seen as a threat to national identities, and latent racism is expressed by connecting immigrants with crime rates.

Recommended Web Sites

World Wildlife Fund
www.worldwildlife.org
The World Wildlife Fund (WWF) is dedicated to protecting the world's wildlife and wildlands. The WWF directs its conservation efforts toward three global goals: protecting endangered spaces, saving endangered species, and addressing global threats. Through the use of its educational services, the WWF provides insightful information on the issues of wildlife and wildlands.

Environment Canada
www.ec.gc.ca/envhome.html
Environment Canada's mandate is to preserve and enhance the quality of the natural environment, including water, air, and soil quality; to conserve Canada's renewable resources; to conserve and protect Canada's water resources; to carry out meteorology; to enforce the rules made by the Canada–US International Joint Commission relating to boundary waters; and to coordinate environmental policies and programs for the federal government.

Canadian Technology Network
http://ctn.nrc.ca/
The Canadian Technology Network links federal and provincial government labs and agencies, universities, community colleges, industry associations, technology centres, and economic development agencies. Together, these organizations provide innovative Canadian companies with quick and personal access to expertise, advice, and information about how to meet technology and related business challenges.

References

Aronowitz, Stanley, and Jonathan Cutler, eds. 1998. *Post-Work: The Wages of Cybernation*. New York: Routledge.

Baer, Douglas, James Curtis, and Edward Grabb. 2001. 'Has Voluntary Association Activity Declined? Cross National Analyses for Fifteen Countries'. *Canadian Review of Sociology and Anthropology*, 38: 249–74.

Banton, Michael. 1992. 'The Nature and Causes of Racism and Racial Discrimination'. *International Sociology*, 7: 69–84.

Beaujot, Roderic. 1991. *Population Change in Canada: The Challenges of Policy Adaptation*. Toronto: McClelland & Stewart.

Bell, David, and Lorne Tepperman. 1979. *The Roots of Disunity: A Look at Canadian Political Culture*. Toronto: McClelland & Stewart.

Boserup, Ester. 1965. *The Conditions of Agricultural Growth: The Economics of Agrarian Change Under Population Pressure*. Chicago: Aldine.

Boyd, David. 2001. *Canada vs. the OECD: An Environment Comparison*. Victoria, BC: Eco-Research Chair, University of Victoria. Available at <www.environmentalindicators.com/htdocs/PDF/CanadavsOECD.pdf>, accessed 25 March 2003.

Burman, Sandra, and Margaret Naude. 1991. 'Bearing a Bastard: The Social Consequences of Illegitimacy in Cape Town, 1896–1939'. *Journal of Southern African Studies*, 17: 373–413.

Caldwell, Gary, and Daniel Fournier. 1987. 'The Quebec Question: A Matter of Population'. *Canadian Journal of Sociology*, 12: 16–41.

Canadian Environmental Law Association. 1999. 'Water Watch Summit a Huge Success' (media release). Available at <www.web.net/~cela/mr990919.htm>, accessed 19 September 1999.

Curtis, James E., Douglas E. Baer, and Edward G. Grabb. 2001. 'Nations of Joiners: Explaining Voluntary Association Membership in Democratic Societies'. *American Sociological Review*, 66: 783–805.

Daniel, W.W. 1987. *Workplace Industrial Relations and Technical Change*. London: PSI/Frances Pinter.

Davis, Kingsley. 1988. 'Social Science Approaches to International Migration'. *Population and Development Review*, 14, suppl.: 245–61.

Dei, George J. Sefa. 1996. *Anti-Racism Education: Theory and Practice*. Halifax, NS: Fernwood.

Farb, Peter. 1978. *Man's Rise to Civilization: The Cultural Ascent of the Indians of North America*. 2nd edn. New York: Bantam.

Foot, David K. 1982. *Canada's Population Outlook: Demographic Futures and Economic Challenges*. Toronto: Lorimer.

Greenpeace. 2001. 'Pacific in Peril'. Available at <www.greenpeace.org>, accessed 14 May 2001.

Hawkins, Freda. 1972. *Canada and Immigration: Public Policy and Public Concern*. Montreal: McGill-Queen's University Press.

Helfgott, Roy B. 1988. *Computerized Manufacturing and Human Resources: Innovation Through Employee Involvement*. Lexington, MA: Lexington Books.

Henripin, Jacques. 1974. *Immigration and Language Imbalance: Green Paper on Immigration*. Ottawa: Manpower and Immigration, 1974.

Inglehart, Ronald. 1977. *The Silent Revolution: Changing Values and Political Styles Among Western Publics*. Princeton, NJ: Princeton University Press.

———. 1990. *Culture Shift in Advanced Industrial Society*. Princeton, NJ: Princeton University Press.

International Food Policy Research Institute (IFPRI). 1997. 'Report Finds World Water Supplies Dwindling While Demand Rises; World Food Production, Health, and Environment at Risk' (press release). Available at <www.ifpri.org/pressrel/030997.htm>, accessed 25 March 2003.

Kalbach, W.E. 1970. *The Impact of Immigration on Canada's Population*. Ottawa: Dominion Bureau of Statistics.

Klonglan, Gerald E., George M. Beal, Joe M. Bohlen, and E. Walter Coward, Jr. 1971. 'Conceptualizing and Measuring the Diffusion of Innovations'. *Sociologia Ruralis*, 11, no. 1: 36–48.

Lachapelle, Réjean. 1980. 'Evolution of Ethnic and Linguistic Composition'. In *Cultural Boundaries and the Cohesion of Canada*, edited by Raymond Breton, Jeffrey Reitz, and Victor Valentine, 15–43. Montreal: Institute for Research on Public Policy.

Lavoie, Yolande. 1972. *L'émigration des Canadiens aux États-Unis avant 1930*. (Collection Demographie canadienne 1). Montreal: Presses de l'Université de Montréal.

Lee, Richard B. 1979. *The !Kung San: Men, Women and Work in a Foraging Society*. Cambridge, UK: Cambridge University Press.

Li, Peter S. 2003. *Destination Canada: Immigration Debates and Issues*. Toronto: Oxford University Press Canada.

Livi-Bacci, Massimo. 1992. *A Concise History of World Population: An Introduction to Population Processes*. Translated by Carl Ipsen. Cambridge, MA: Blackwell.

Lucas, Rex. 1972. *Minetown, Milltown, Railtown: Life in Canadian Communities of Single Industry*. Toronto: University of Toronto Press.

Malthus, Thomas R. [1798] 1959. *Population: The First Essay*. Ann Arbor: University of Michigan Press.

Newton, Keith, and Norm Lockie. 1987. 'Employment Effects of Technological Change'. *New Technology, Work and Employment*, 2, no. 2.

Northcott, Jim, Michael Fogarty, and Malcolm Trevor. 1985. *Chips and Jobs: Acceptance of New Technology at Work*. London: PSI.

Northcott, Jim, and Annette Walling. 1988. *The Impact of Microelectronics*. London: PSI.

Paccione, Michael. 2001. *Urban Geography: A Global Perspective*. New York: Routledge.

Perrow, Charles. 1999. *Normal Accidents: Living with High Risk Technologies*, 2nd edn. Princeton, NJ: Princeton University Press.

Population Reference Bureau. 2001. *World Population Data Sheet, 2001*. Washington, DC: Population Reference Bureau.

Porter, John. 1965. *The Vertical Mosaic: An Analysis of Social Class and Power in Canada*. Toronto: University of Toronto Press.

Postel, S. 1994. 'Carrying Capacity: Earth's Bottom Line'. In *State of the World 1994*, edited by Lester R. Brown, 3–21. New York: Norton.

Putnam, Robert D. 2000. *Bowling Alone: The Collapse and Revival of American Community*. New York: Simon & Schuster.

Reitz, Jeffrey G. 1994. *The Illusion of Difference: Realities of Ethnicity in Canada and the United States*. Toronto: C.D. Howe Institute.

———. 1998. *Warmth of the Welcome: The Social Causes of Economic Success in Different Nations and Cities*. Boulder, CO: Westview.

Rogers, Andrei, John F. Watkins, and Jennifer A. Woodward. 1990. 'Interregional Elderly Migration and Population Redistribution in Four Industrialized Countries: A Comparative Analysis'. *Research on Aging*, 12: 251–93.

Sauvy, Alfred, and Paul Demeny. 1990. 'Alfred Sauvy on the World Population Problem: A View in 1949'. *Population and Development Review*, 16: 759–74.

Schoenfeld, A. Clay, Robert F. Meier, and Robert J. Griffin. 1979. 'Constructing a Social Problem: The Press and the Environment'. *Social Problems*, 27: 38–61.

Sears, Alan. 1990. 'Immigration Controls as Social Policy: The Case of Canadian Medical Inspection 1900–1920'. *Studies in Political Economy*, 33: 91–112.

Sharpe, Sydney. 2000. 'Digital Divide Assailed'. *Calgary Herald*, 24 September, A11.

Simmel, George. [1917] 1950. 'The Metropolis and Mental Life'. In *The Sociology of Georg Simmel*, translated by Kurt H. Wolff, 409–24. New York: Free Press.

Simon, Julian L. 1996. *The Ultimate Resource 2*. Princeton, NJ: Princeton University Press.

Smith, Keith. 2001. *Environmental Hazards: Assessing Risk and Reducing Disaster*. 3rd edn. New York: Routledge.

Statistics Canada. 2002. 'English-French Bilingualism'. Available at <www12.statcan.ca/english/census01/products/analytic/companion/lang/bilingual.cfm>, accessed 24 March 2003.

Tepperman, Lorne. 2001. 'The Postmaterialist Thesis: Has There Been a Shift in Political Cultures?' In *Political Sociology: Canadian Perspectives*, edited by Douglas Baer, 15–36. Toronto: Oxford University Press.

United States. Energy Information Administration. 2001. 'World Primary Energy Consumption (Btu) 1990–1999, Table E1'. Available at <www.eia.doe.gov/emeu/iea/tablee1.html>, accessed 30 January 2003.

van de Walle, Etienne, and John Knodel. 1980. 'Europe's Fertility Transition: New Evidence and Lessons for Today's Developing World'. *Population Bulletin*, 34: 6.

Vining, Daniel L. 1989. 'The "Demographic Problem" in Israel'. *Mankind Quarterly*, 30, nos 1–2: 65–9.

Wellman, Barry, and Keith Hampton. 1999. 'Netville On-line and Off-line: Observing and Surveying a Wired Suburb'. *American Behavioral Scientist*, 43: 475–92.

World Health Organization (WHO). 1997. *Health and Environment in Sustainable Development: Five Years After the Earth Summit*. Geneva: WHO.

———. 1999. *World Health Organization Report on Infectious Diseases*. Geneva: WHO. Available at <www.who.int/infectious-disease-report/index-rpt99.html>, accessed 23 February 2003.

World Meteorological Organization (WMO). 2000. 'WMO Statement on the Status of the Global Climate in 1999'. (WMO No. 913). Available at <www.wmo.ch/web/wcp/wcdmp/statement/html/913-1999.html>, accessed 14 May 2001.

World Resources Institute. 1998. *Climate, Biodiversity, and Forests: Issues and Opportunities Emerging from the Kyoto Protocol*. Baltimore, MN: World Resource.

Glossary

Convergence The growing similarity of industrial societies around the world. Industrialization brings with it certain needs or requirements that will be solved in similar ways from one industrial society to another.

Cornucopia view of nature According to this belief, people view nature as a storehouse of resources that exist only for use by humans, especially by those currently living.

Diffusion The social process through which cultural knowledge and practices spread from one social system to another. Some diffusionists seek to prove that all human culture originated in one place and spread out from there by diffusion. This process is usually facilitated by the rise of global media, global capitalism, multinational corporations, and international travel.

E. coli A bacteria (*Escherichia coli*) normally found in the human gastrointestinal tract and existing as numerous strains, some of which are responsible for diarrheal diseases. Other strains have been used experimentally in molecular biology.

Industrial society Refers to a social system whose mode of production focuses primarily on finished goods manufactured with the aid of machinery. These societies promote the rationalization of social life, formal education, and mass media.

Photosynthesis The process in green plants and certain other organisms by which carbohydrates are synthesized from carbon dioxide and water using light as an energy source. Most forms of photosynthesis release oxygen back into the atmosphere as a by-product.

Positive checks Part of Malthusian theory, these prevent overpopulation by increasing the death rate. They include war, famine, pestilence, and disease.

Preventive checks In Malthusian theory, these prevent overpopulation by limiting the number or survivals of live births. They include abortion, infanticide, sexual abstinence, delayed marriage, and contraceptive technologies.

Tragedy of the commons The belief that one is not personally responsible for one's own actions and will put the burden of responsibility on someone else. It is sometimes used to explain why people knowingly pollute and damage the environment with seemingly no regard for their actions.

Chapter 11

War and Terrorism

Chapter Objectives

After reading this chapter the student should understand:
- some basic facts concerning war
- the role religion may play in war and terrorism
- how gender socialization affects attitudes toward violence
- the defining features of a globalized society
- the contribution of world systems theory to an understanding of war and terrorism
- different definitions of war
- what each of the different theoretical perspectives adds to the academic study of the violence of war
- the extremities of war crimes and genocide
- the social and health consequences of war
- possible solutions to global war and terrorism

Introduction

As we write these lines, US-led troops are attacking Iraq on a mission to oust Saddam Hussein from power. Around the world, people are watching the war with intense interest. Thousands close to the battleground are sheltering from attack. Thousands are changing their travel plans to stay out of harm's way. Thousands around the world are protesting the war. Some—numbers unknown—are modifying their homes or workplaces to protect against terrorist reprisals. Investors are uncertain, so the world's stock markets are fluctuating more than usual. All of this makes it clear that war is very much part of our lives, and very much a social problem needing study.

Accordingly, this chapter is about war and terrorism, conflict and combat, soldiers and civilians. At no point in recorded history has there been a complete absence of conflict between groups of humans. It seems that when people are around, wars occur. There are no societies that are known to have avoided war entirely. Thus, warfare appears to be a human universal.

At the same time, we note that warfare has always varied over time and space, and the tendency to make war has varied from one society to another and from one century to another. Some groups are more warlike than others. Some periods are more warlike. This tells us that there are likely sociological variables to explain this variation. So even if we can never find ways of eliminating war altogether, we can hope to find ways of reducing war's prevalence or virulence.

No less important, the scale and nature of war has changed with the rapid pace of technological innovation. In the last century, it became possible to kill thousands with the push of a button, to kill at long distances without seeing the faces of victims, and to kill large number of civilians both intentionally and unintentionally. Before the Industrial Revolution, people fought most wars on a local scale, against neighbouring groups. From 1500 until the mid-twentieth century, most wars were fought in Europe, with a few in the Americas. Since then, many of the world's wars have been fought in developing nations outside Europe, even when European or North American states were involved. In short, the territorial scope of war has expanded. The duration of war has also expanded. The conflict between secularism and Shiite Islam, for instance, has lasted over 1,400 years (Lewis, 1990).

As we shall see in this chapter, much of the variation in warfare is connected with politics. We cannot understand warfare without understanding politics and statecraft since, as the early eighteenth-century Prussian military thinker Carl von Clausewitz opined, 'war is the continuation of politics by other means'. More precisely, he wrote, 'war is not merely a political act, but also a real political instrument, a continuation of political commerce, a carrying out the same by other means. . . . For the political view is the object. War is the means, and the means must always include the object in our conception' (1993).

Some political contingencies make war more likely. For example, a ruling party's need to deflect criticism by focusing national attention on external enemies, real or imagined, increases the likelihood of war. Said another way, the *function* of conflict with an outside group—as in a war—is to increase social cohesion and conformity within the conflicting groups. Warfare clarifies the social boundaries between insiders and outsiders, loyal citizens and traitors.

War has psychological and cultural as well as political and economic aspects, as we shall see. In times of war, politicians use a special language to legitimize combat and reduce the emotional impact of the massive numbers of death that will follow. Propaganda plays a large part in storytelling about war and in other efforts to increase public engagement. In their recruitment materials, the military always stresses honour, courage, and sacrifice for the greater good as defining characteristics of the 'ideal soldier'. War is, therefore, a response to internal conflict and a means of restoring consensus, however short-lived.

As we shall also see, **globalization** has affected warfare as much as it has affected everything else. With better transportation and communication, we are made continuously aware of events in other parts of the world. Moreover, factors affecting the outbreak of wars, such as ethnic conflicts, reverberate throughout the world, through the diasporic networks of immigrants that we discussed in chapter 4.

As always, these and other changes in warfare have been examined by a variety of sociological approaches, and different conclusions have been reached. What is certain is that war continues to have important social and health consequences. Though often good for the economy, war is generally bad for living things, and with the development of nuclear, chemical, and bacterial weapons, it is getting worse. Though social problems related to poverty and conflict may often be improved by warfare in the short run, in the long run everyone suffers.

As we shall see, the health consequences of war are varied and immense. Even surviving a war physically unharmed does not guarantee a soldier complete well-being. Many war veterans suffer the slow torture of psychological distress. However, though researchers have studied the effects of war on soldiers in the medical literature since the US Civil War, only within the past few decades have they studied civilian suffering in military conflicts. Research on civilians caught in war finds that exposure to terrorism leads to psychiatric difficulties in later life. The less visible injuries of war simply add to the numerous, more visible ones—to the lost lives and limbs, add lost wives and parents, lost opportunities, and lost futures.

To begin then, we note that wars and their associated glories and horrors are both widespread and recurrent over time.

War as Recurrent and Widespread

War—the pattern of large groups of people methodically trying to kill one another—is a common and persistent fact of human life. One has to wonder why people have repeatedly undertaken war in the face of massive human casualties, property damage, and public expense. In view of war's persistence, peace scarcely seems to have a real meaning except in short outbursts.

Consider the last century. In his book *The Age of Extremes* (1994), historian Eric Hobsbawm divided the twentieth century into three periods based on their levels of warfare and violence: the first period had two large-scale global conflicts; the second had relative peace (or at least the relative absence of warfare) for a little more than 20 years; and the last period saw the resurgence of many inter- and intra-national hostilities. In Hobsbawm's words, people of the century

> lived and thought in terms of world war, even when the guns were silent and the bombs were not exploding. . . . For those who had grown up before 1914 the contrast was so dramatic that many of them refused to see any continuity with the past. 'Peace' meant 'before 1914': after that came something that no longer deserved the name. (6)

For innocent civilians caught in the middle, the effects of war can be devastating. Unlike soldiers, who at the least can rationalize their participation as military personnel, civilians do not fight often (except when they require self-protection); they are coerced participants in the horrors of war.

For both people in uniform and for civilians, war is a recurrent nightmare. To understand its recurrence, we need to understand war's roots in politics, ideology, and religion. Only then will we start to understand why people let their children go off by the hundreds of thousands to be killed in battle.

Politics, the State, and Warfare

The Role of the State

Within any social unit—family, school, community, state, or otherwise—any conflict over resources is a political conflict. However, among social units, the State has a special part to play, for it always monitors and seeks to control the ways that other groups compete.

The State is that set of public organizations that makes and enforces decisions that are binding upon every member of a society (Weber, 1946). It includes the elected government, civil service, courts, police, and military. At one extreme of political life, we find the *authoritarian state*, which tries to fully dominate civil society and represses political dissent. It penetrates everyday life fully and, compared with the type of government we have in Canada, it is extremely repressive.

Fascist authoritarian states appear where a landed aristocracy remains in power during industrialization, keeping the middle class small, weak, and disorganized (Moore, 1967). With the aid of the military, the Church, and the bankers, the landed aristocrats control the State in their own interest. In most if not all authoritarian political states, the military is ready—along with the Church, the landed aristocracy, and the business class—to support the ruling party or dictator. Typically, military officers and institutions are culturally sympathetic to the goals of authoritarian regimes—order over liberty, tradition over modernity, for example. Military people also see opportunities for enrichment and career advancement in supporting war, and in supporting authoritarianism. Thus, warfare is a secondary consequence of the connection between the military and the State in authoritarian regimes.

Additionally, authoritarian regimes, in their need to suppress dissident elements like the peasantry and workers, often resort to warfare to engender patriotic cohesion and justify cracking down on political dissidents as 'traitors'. The dominant cultural imagery of authoritarian regimes—including various representations of past glory, racial purity, defence of the fatherland (as by the Nazis) or motherland (as by the Soviets), mythic figures, and national heroes—brings war to the forefront as a measure of the nation's courage, pride, and strength. Thus, war is viewed as an activity that carries a glorious past on to new glories. By contrast, non-authoritarian regimes use economic competition or sports competition to achieve a national sense of achievement.

In Canada, the military has never played an important role in the ruling elite, compared with many African and South American countries (for example, Brazil, Paraguay, or Nigeria). There and in other countries with less developed economic and bureaucratic elites, the military strongman or junta (cadre or ruling group) is a fixture of political life. More often than not, military dictators and juntas draw their strength from the assistance, cooperation, or tacit approval of bureaucratic and economic elites in other, more developed societies.

A society like Canada's, in which power is fragmented and shared among competing political, bureaucratic, and economic elites, is likely to have difficulty mobilizing the will and the resources to make war. Put another way, decentralized leadership is likely to be less warlike than centralized or, particularly, dictatorial leadership.

Another factor influencing politics and war is the role of ideology. An **ideology** is a system of beliefs that 'explain' how society is, or should be, organized. Ideologies are important for social change because they motivate and control people. Before people can change their political order, they must imagine a new order worth working for. People must have faith in that vision of the future and in the political leaders whom they expect to carry out that vision.

In recent years, organized religions and religious leaders have gained more power than they had in much of the twentieth century. This resurgence of religion testifies largely to the downfall of communism, an ideology and political system that had tried to destroy organized religion, which Karl Marx had viewed as 'the opiate of the masses' (see Tucker, 1978). In many parts of the world today, fundamentalist religions are gaining power. Christian fundamentalism is politically important in the United States, Jewish fundamentalism in Israel, and Islamic fundamentalism in Pakistan and other so-called Islamic states in Africa and Asia.

Fundamentalist religions seek to control the minds, hearts, and loyalties of their members, and fundamentalist religious leaders can have great political influence. This was certainly true of Billy Graham in the United States, Ayatollah Khomeini in Iran, and, more recently, the Taliban government and rebel terrorist Osama bin Laden in Afghanistan. Often, such fundamentalist movements and their leaders are created or propped up by capitalists outside the country to prevent the election to power of liberal, socialist, or Marxist critics of capitalism. For example, the US government supported both Saddam Hussein and Osama bin Laden as foes of Iran and the Soviet Union, respectively, before they became vilified foes of the United States.

On the other side, some religious activists work in less violent ways to change the political order. Catholic Nuns, for example, have campaigned for increased status for women and an end to spousal abuse; many leading religious figures have campaigned for peace; and in a few outstanding cases, a single individual, as spokesperson for a religious movement, has become associated with a civil cause. Looking to the recent past, anyone who has heard of South Africa's successful move to racial equality knows the name of Archbishop Desmond Tutu, and anyone who has heard of the US Civil Rights movement knows about the achievements of Dr Martin Luther King.

In many societies, the Church—like the military—was until recently a major social institution that not only controlled large amounts of land and wealth, but also trained a large portion of the younger generation and otherwise controlled ideology and popular thinking. In these societies, the Church was a major means of upward social mobility and, for those who reached the top, a means of political influence. In countries like Canada where the religion and politics are constitutionally separate, there is no church that enjoys this degree of political or ideological power.

Though there is no state church in the United States, in recent years fundamentalist Protestantism has exercised a disproportionate political influence at the highest political levels. This fact points both to the more important role of religion in American culture and to the superior organization of American religion through the formation of cults, sects, and churches, all of which are protected in the US Constitution far more than they are in Canada. In particular, American religious organizations have been successful in raising money for their political work, often through televangelism.

The Role of Social Movements

In every society, people mobilize to influence public policy. Then we speak of them forming **social movements**. **Relative deprivation theory** argues that movements arise when many people feel deprived in comparison with other people. They feel there is a gap between the social rewards they are getting and those they are entitled to get. Or they feel cheated when they compare their own lives with those of others. These people want to join a social movement whose goal is to change the distribution of social rewards. Compared with *absolute deprivation*—a serious, visible, and lengthy lack of social rewards—relative deprivation is largely subjective and even temporary. Yet relative deprivation is more likely than absolute deprivation to produce social movements.

Social movements gain the strongest support when there is a 'revolution of rising expectations' (Runciman, 1967). That is, people typically protest under improving conditions, not grinding, desperate poverty. Improving conditions make it easier for people to protest because they are not so fully preoccupied with the struggle to survive. Also, when people's lives improve, their expectations for change often grow faster than the rate at which change is taking place. A sense of deprivation causes feelings of frustration and discontent. Such feelings are necessary for social

---

BOX 11.1
When Social Movements Don't Have Access to Decision-Making Bodies

From April 20 to 22, Quebec City has the dubious honor of hosting the Summit of the Americas, which brings together all the so-called leaders of North, Central and South America (except Cuba). For a few days, Quebec will be turned into a militarized zone as these heads of state, and their big business pals, gather for a series of meetings, photo-ops and posh dinners.

The stated purpose of Summit meeting is to put the final touches on the Free Trade Area of the Americas agreement (FTAA) which aims to extend the North American Free Trade Agreement (NAFTA) to the entire hemisphere.

The FTAA is supposed to be adopted no later than 2005.

Like the WTO, IMF, WB, APEC and the rest of the insidious alphabet soup, the FTAA is another engine—in the form of a 'free' trade accord—which drives capitalist globalization.

In the spirit of Seattle, and the anti-IMF/WB demonstrations in Washington on A16/17, we've started to organize to make sure the Summit is effectively short-circuited. We want to go beyond symbolic protest or reformism to making sure the Summit of the Americas is shut down.

SOURCE: WTOaction.org, 'Stop the Summit of the Americas!' (25 September 2001). Available at <www.wtoaction.org/ftaa.phtml>, accessed 31 January 2003.

movements to emerge, and movements will not form without them. Still, they are not enough by themselves to start a movement. Many discontented people never join, let alone form, social movements. Leaders must satisfy another condition, resource mobilization, before a movement forms.

Resource mobilization theory addresses the methods leaders use to put forward their views. This theory looks not at *why* people want to promote or resist social change, but at *how* they launch social movements. It sees social movements in terms of the ability of discontented people to organize. Without discontent, there would be no social movements. Yet discontent is a constant of human life, always lurking in the background, waiting to express itself. Without the movement of resources, discontent can never express itself as a social force. It remains hidden or comes out in non-political, personal pathologies—as random violence, mental illness, heavy drinking, domestic violence, and so on.

Important elements in political organization include resources such as effective leadership, public support, money, legal aid, ties with influential officials and public personalities, and access to the mass media. Occasionally, organizing also means getting, and learning to use, weapons. Without access to such key resources, discontented people cannot change society or resist the powerful, and they rarely attempt it. Thus, the successes and failures of social movements show a change in access to key resources, and not necessarily a change in levels of contentment. Likewise, the absence of protest movements does not prove that people are contented.

World System Theory

Politics occur between states, as well as within them. One theory that examines the relations between states in a global system is **world system theory**. This theory explains the uneven pace of development in the world by looking at the unequal relations between different countries. Industrial *core states* take much of the raw materials and cheap labour they need from less developed *peripheral states*. Because they are economically and politically dominant, core states have the power to extract an economic surplus from the periphery. Investors from the core states effectively control the economies of peripheral states. As a result, profits made in the periphery drain out of the local economy and flow back to the core.

Core states are said to engage in **imperialism**—the exercise of political and economic control by one state over the territory of another, often by military means. However, domination today does not always require military conquest and colonization. In fact, economic domination is far safer, less costly, and usually more stable than military or political domination. This is precisely how first Britain and then the United States have controlled Canada. Some think that the end of old-style military imperialism may also mean the end of old-style world wars, which were largely driven by colonial interests.

Globalization Processes

Globalization is the trend of increasing interdependence between the economies and societies of the world. Some view it as just another name for US imperialism and others view it as the highest stage of what Émile Durkheim ([1893] 1960) called *organic solidarity*, or interdependence based on difference. The global economy as it exists today is a form of world social organization with six defining features. To understand the current state of global politics and war, we must take note of these characteristics:

- First, as noted, there is global economic interdependence. This means that most societies trade goods and services with one another: people are all buyers and sellers in a single world market.
- Second, a driving force for change is scientific and technological innovation. New methods

for producing goods and services are continuously developed.

- Third, the key actors in a global economy are 'constructed' or corporate entities, especially multinational corporations (like General Motors, IBM, Toyota, and Exxon). Individuals, small local firms, and even nationwide businesses lose in the competition for international markets.
- Fourth, cultures and polities are *polycentric*; that is, they are found in, and influenced by, activities in many nations. More cultures today are everywhere, with centres of activity throughout the world.
- Fifth, an evolving 'world culture' homogenizes human aspirations, narrowing the variety of desires and lifestyles. More people everywhere act like Americans. More Europeans think and act like the French, English, and Germans—

the dominant actors in the European Union. (See also Figure 11.1.)

- Sixth, and most relevant to this discussion, economic globalization forces nation-states to change. With less influence over the culture and economy, governments have less influence over the people they rule. With these changes come political stresses and upheavals, and the formation of new social movements and ideologies.

The key actors in a global economy are multinational corporations. Currently, multinational corporations control half the world's total economic production. Multinationals, consequently, have immense political importance. Some have budgets larger than most countries. They gather and spend huge amounts of money, create and eliminate many jobs. As a result,

FIGURE 11.1
World Trade of Cultural Goods (in Millions of Dollars), 1980–98

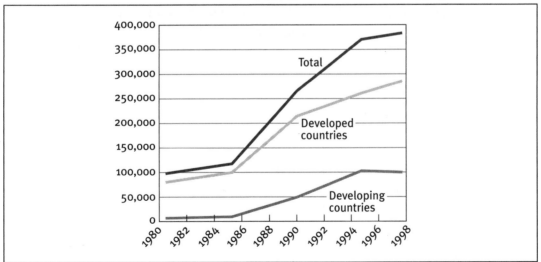

SOURCE: UNESCO, 'Study on International Flows of Cultural Goods Between 1980–98' (2000). UNESCO Framework for Cultural Statistics includes the following categories: printed matter and literature (books, newspapers and periodicals, other printed matters), music (phonographic equipment, records and tapes, music instruments), visual arts (paintings, drawings and pastels, engravings, prints and lithographs, sculpture and statuary), cinema and photography (photographic and cinematographic cameras and supplies), radio and television (television and radio receivers), games and sporting goods. Available at <www.unesco.org/culture/industries/trade/html_eng/question2.shtml#1980-98>, accessed 31 January 2003. Reproduced by permission of UNESCO.

multinationals are important members of every economic community—yet they are loyal to none. They move their operations wherever they can increase their profits, whatever the consequence for the countries in which they do business. (See Figure 11.2.)

Hybridization

Globalization does not, however, eliminate the role of traditional cultures, nor does it reduce the number of world cultures:

As the changing pattern of world trade profoundly shapes our national living standards and the vitality of our local communities, it is also dramatically transforming the social and cultural foundations of many so-called 'developing' nations. The rapidity of these changes, together with heightened fears over preserving their national sovereignty, envi-

ronmental standards, and traditional cultural values, is contributing to growing social and political movements in developing countries in order to resist the growing political and culture influence of multinational corporations. (Harper and Leicht, 2002)

As states and local cultures influence the uses made of foreign cultural products, the result is a 'hybrid', or crossbreed, of the two cultures, something entirely new. This process of hybridization is dialectical, a result of opposing currents. According to political scientist Benjamin Barber (1996), there is on the one hand a 'McWorld' influence—Western cultural domination and homogenization. This brings uniformity and secular cultural detachment from a nation's own history and identity. On the other hand, there is a 'jihad' influence—a reaction against Euro-Americanism. Named after the

FIGURE 11.2
Number of Export Processing Zones and Free Trade Zones by World Areas, 1996

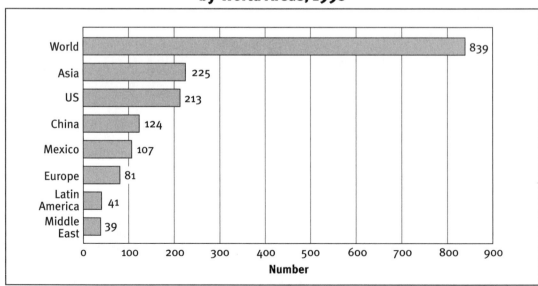

SOURCE: Based on UNCTAD (1998) *World Investment Report 1998: Trends and Determinants* (New York and Geneva: UN: 59). Available at <www.globalpolicy.org/globaliz/charts/exptzne1.htm>, accessed 31 January 2003.

Islamic word for a holy war against infidels, the jihad influence brings conflict, even war. Neither influence—McWorld or jihad—can prevail because each represents hundreds of millions of people and each reflects a genuine cultural commitment. The two impulses are locked in conflict in a great many less developed societies.

The Nature of War

Definitions

Most people consider **war** to be an armed conflict between two countries or between groups within a country. However, we should further expand the definition of *war* to include as well undeclared battles, guerrilla wars, covert operations, and even terrorism (Wright, 1964). Many countries even possess a *war system*, in which components of their social institutions, such as economies and governments, and their cultural practices promote warfare as a normal aspect of life (Cancian and Gibson, 1990).

War is an institution of collective violence. **Collective violence** is organized or group violence used to promote an agenda or resist an oppressive other. Unlike **interpersonal violence**, which is more episodic, unorganized, and impulsive, modern warfare relies on unemotional killing and high technology. Because of advances in military technology over the past century, people can now wage wars against enemies thousands of kilometres away, so that the killers and the killed may never even see one another face to face. As well, the weaponry used in modern combat is exponentially more deadly than even a century ago. Arrows, rifles, and swords require proximity to the target and usually claim only one life per shot or swing. In contrast, a single precision-guided missile released by a B-52 bomber many thousand feet above the war zone can kill hundreds of enemy soldiers. No wonder then that the twentieth century was the bloodiest hundred years in the history of human warfare.

There is continued disagreement about the causes of wars and terrorist incidents, and about the ways we might prevent them. People still argue about the causes and consequences of the two world wars of the twentieth century. To take a more current case in point, consider the current disagreement about a recent warlike event: the terrorist attacks on the World Trade Center and the Pentagon on 11 September 2001.

The Case of 11 September 2001

Intellectual opinion is strongly divided on the causes of and remedies for terrorism. This comes out clearly in sociological analyses of the attacks on the World Trade Center and Pentagon.

The events of 11 September 2001 changed the world as we know it. Intellectual opinion is strongly divided on the causes and remedies of terrorism and global inequality. (© 2001 Denton Tillman)

Aquiel Ahmad (2002), for example, notes that terrorism, as a means of gaining social, economic, and political advantage locally, has been around for a long time. The recent emergence of global society has merely given modern terrorism a wider dimension, both in terms of its goals and as a means for achieving these goals. With the rapid cross-national flow of information, ideas, people, and technologies at terrorists' disposal, tracking and forecasting the global roots and outreach of terrorism poses enormous challenges. Governments have responded tactically with the use of intelligence, prevention, and punishment. Intellectually, however, there seems to be a gap in our understanding. For example, policy analysts seem to lack theory to explain the background and causes of terrorism in contemporary society. As a result, the tactical responses fall short, and we lack what is needed for a longer-term response to the problem.

Seyla Benhabib (2002) agrees that we have no theory to deal with the new types of terrorism. The 11 September 2001 terrorist attacks defied conventional categories of war, international law, and nation-statism, he writes. Non-state actors, such as al-Qaeda, carry out Islamic jihadist terrorism with no apparent political goals other than destruction. These elements challenge the United States, its allies, and international bodies such as the United Nations to come up with new responses in the areas of international law, multilateralism, and foreign policy that do not shore up repressive regimes simply for the sake of oil.

A variety of factors support terrorism, in Benhabib's view. The failures of modernity and modernization, along with the worldwide discrediting of communism, have created an ideological vacuum in the Middle East that radical Islamism has rushed to fill. Globalization has helped erode the distinction between sacred and secular spheres in the Islamic world while spreading the 'decadent' values of the West by means of media images, travel, and migration. The West's challenge, then, is to respond with an awareness of the cultural and political complexities of the Middle East, and with a commitment to discussion.

Robin Blackburn (2002) is most concerned about US politics and its pretence. He notes that Congress granted President Bush virtually unlimited power to carry out the vaguely defined 'war on terror'. This has strengthened the administration's already evident leaning toward unilateralism and given the presidency imperial powers, despite the potential for multilateralism to quash al-Qaeda and its affiliated terrorist groups. Past US policy decisions to strengthen Saudi Arabia, Pakistan, and anti-communist Afghani 'freedom fighters' all backfired. All three have supported al-Qaeda and other Islamic jihadists. Once the United States even supported Islamic fundamentalism because of its perceived compatibility with capitalism and property rights as well as with US oil interests.

Blackburn urges Washington to engage diplomatically with Iran. Other potential allies are Pakistan and Uzbekistan. Most important, a multilateral approach through the United Nations must displace US crusading, not only to get rid of terrorism, but also to foster economic and democratic reform in the Middle East and promote global disarmament.

Echoing these sentiments, Carl Boggs (2002) notes that US history is full of military conquest, territorial enlargement, and forceful power-seeking. Today, he writes, the United States preaches international order, democracy, and human rights. Yet not so long ago it was conducting precision-strike military campaigns in Grenada, Nicaragua, Haiti, Serbia, Sudan, Somalia, Afghanistan, Panama, and Iraq; exporting weapons to 'unfriendly' nations; stockpiling and using weapons of mass destruction; and testing more nuclear weapons than any other country. The United States, animated by a neo-liberal ideology, also exercises control over international funding bodies and militarized drug wars. Terrorism and increased authoritarianism in other countries are merely unexpected consequences of such US militarism.

David Held (2002) notes that the 11 September 2001 terrorist attacks violated not only Western values, but also cosmopolitan (that is, basic and universal) human rights principles that go beyond borders and ethnic differences. However, responding to these attacks militarily is impractical against an enemy that does not act in the name of a state, according to Held. The United States needs to work with the UN and other alliances to shore up the role of international law in fighting terrorism, regardless of its source. It should also help to create tribunals to prosecute terrorist acts as war crimes. At the same time, Islamic countries need to recognize their duty to curb rather than promote anti-democratic, anti-modern ideologies. The entire international community must recommit to world order.

Patricia Ticinet Clough (2002), for her part, is troubled by the popular position that the United States should retaliate with force against those connected to the planning and execution of the terrorist attacks. She suggests that American citizens should have expected these attacks in light of the extent of economic injustice throughout the present-day world. Strategies that promote the intensification of national security are problematic and potentially dangerous. It would make more sense to question current global practices, especially American ones, she writes.

Thomas Badey (2002) notes that over the past decade, the topic of religion has played an increasingly prominent role in discussions of international terrorism. Fears concerning the rebirth of what some have called 'fundamentalist Islam' have produced visions of inevitable clashes of civilizations (Huntington, 1996).

Even before the terrorist attacks on the United States on 11 September 2001, the term *religious terrorism* had established itself in the vocabulary of many policy makers. However, in view of recent events, we now must answer essential questions concerning the ideologies of violence and the true role of religion in international terrorism.

Badey wonders, does 'religious terrorism' really exist? What is the function of religion in international terrorism? Is religion really the cause of terrorist violence, or is it simply a convenient way of polarizing populations? Badey states that religion is *not* the cause of international terrorism. Instead, it is an ideology that, like communism and nationalism, is used to mobilize populations toward political violence, given certain precipitating conditions.

Hester Eisenstein (2002), along similar lines, argues that emphasizing the supposed Islam-versus-modernity dichotomy hides the role of the United States as an enforcer of capitalism that has consistently crushed movements abroad aimed at establishing self-government and economic self-sufficiency. Islam as a political force goes beyond religious instruction to provide basic necessities to the poor who have been ignored in the neo-liberal model of development. Eisenstein contends that the US 'war on terrorism' merely continues the international war on social justice waged by the United States using the economic weapons of the international financial institutions.

John Michael (2002) also examines the misleading metaphor of 'the West and the rest (Islam)' that structures official statements about the 11 September 2001 attacks and the responses to them. Such language allows Americans to view opposition to the United States as a mistaken product of Islamic civilization and an opposition to modernity rather than a response to US policies of imperialist domination and military aggression. This formulation keeps American citizens from critically examining grievances against destructive political and military actions carried out by the United States. Identifying the 'enemy' as Islamic civilization has, not surprisingly, produced a backlash against Muslims in the United States. It seems ironic to speak out against this backlash, as some American politicians have done, while continuing to condemn the supposedly wrong values of Islamic culture.

Max Elbaum and Bob Wing (2002) view the misunderstanding of Islam within a broader context, in which the goal of the US government is not to bring the perpetrators to justice under international law, but to achieve a new level of international dominance under the guise of a 'global war on terrorism'. In this context, the racist element of the 'war on terrorism' is not a matter of accident.

Likewise, Victor Wallis (2002) argues that the US government is using the events of 11 September 2001 to support an agenda of global domination, and that it is linking the destruction of the World Trade Center to opposition to the World Trade Organization. Paradoxically, the terrorist network al-Qaeda—the perpetrator of a

---

BOX 11.2
The Definition of Terrorism in Canada

Bill C-36, the Anti-Terrorism Act, received royal assent on 18 December 2001 and defines terrorism as follows:

This enactment amends the *Criminal Code*, the *Official Secrets Act*, the *Canada Evidence Act*, the *Proceeds of Crime (Money Laundering) Act* and a number of other Acts, and enacts the *Charities Registration (Security Information) Act*, in order to combat terrorism. . . . Part 1 amends the Criminal Code to implement international conventions related to terrorism, to create offences related to terrorism, including the financing of terrorism and the participation, facilitation and carrying out of terrorist activities, and to provide a means by which property belonging to terrorist groups, or property linked to terrorist activities, can be seized, restrained and forfeited. It also provides for the deletion of hate propaganda from public web sites and creates an offence relating to damage to property associated with religious worship.

Part II.I Terrorism interpretation
'terrorist activity' means
(*b*) an act or omission, in or outside Canada,
(i) that is committed (A) in whole or in part for a political, religious or ideological purpose, objective or cause, and (B) in whole or in part with the intention of intimidating the public, or a segment of the public, with regard to its security, including its economic security, or compelling a person, a government or a domestic or

an international organization to do or to refrain from doing any act, whether the public or the person, government or organization is inside or outside Canada, and
(ii) that intentionally (A) causes death or serious bodily harm to a person by the use of violence, (B) endangers a person's life, (C) causes a serious risk to the health or safety of the public or any segment of the public, (D) causes substantial property damage, whether to public or private property, if causing such damage is likely to result in the conduct or harm referred to in any of clauses (A) to (C), or (E) causes serious interference with or serious disruption of an essential service, facility or system, whether public or private, other than as a result of advocacy, protest, dissent or stoppage of work that is not intended to result in the conduct or harm referred to in any of clauses (A) to (C), and includes a conspiracy, attempt or threat to commit any such act or omission, or being an accessory after the fact or counselling in relation to any such act or omission, but, for greater certainty, does not include an act or omission that is committed during an armed conflict and that, at the time and in the place of its commission, is in accordance with customary international law or conventional international law applicable to the conflict, or the activities undertaken by military forces of a state in the exercise of their official duties, to the extent that those activities are governed by other rules of international law.

devastating attack against the imperialist cen-tre—is also a product of imperialism.

S. Ravi Rajan (2002) also sees fault on both sides. Characterizing the perpetrators and plan-ners of the 11 September 2001 atrocities as geno-cidal criminals, Rajan feels it is an insult to compare them to revolutionary anti-colonial freedom fighters. However, Rajan also fears that the principles of democracy and freedom are in danger of destruction in the name of increased security. Other trends in world history related to this terrorist incident are just as frightening as the 11 September catastrophe, he writes, includ-ing the persistence of imperialism, the backing of evil leaders by Western governments, and the gradual dilution of democracy.

The Nature of Terrorism

In short, terrorism is best viewed as a 'poor man's war', a war that is evidently fought by new rules. Most generally, *terrorism* can be defined as

> the calculated use of unexpected, shocking, and unlawful violence against noncombat-ants (including, in addition to civilians, off-duty military and security personnel in peaceful situations) and other symbolic tar-gets perpetrated by a clandestine member(s) of a subnational group or a clandestine agent(s) for the psychological purpose pub-licizing a political or religious cause and/or intimidating or coercing a government(s) or civilian population into accepting demands on behalf of the cause. (Hudson and Den Boer, 2002: 1)

Yet the real definition of *terrorism* is difficult because it is an ideological and value-laden term as well as a description of events. An even broader, simpler definition, which shows the political undercurrent clearly, defines *terrorism* as any act by an individual or by a group that is intended to undermine the legitimate authority of a government or state.

The roots of terrorism can be found in the religious, ethnic nationalist, political, economic, and social differences that prevent people from living together in peace. There is currently no evidence to suggest a common reason for terror-ism, but the most generally accepted hypothesis is that participants feel that violence is the best course of action, all things considered. A rational cost-benefit analysis—not reckless impulse—leads them to this conclusion, often in view of various frustrating or limiting social, political, economic, and personal conditions. Valerie Hudson and Andrea Den Boer (2002) report that terrorists are primarily men with a higher than average education, from middle- to upper-class backgrounds, with specific skills and strong political motivation. Increasingly, terrorist organ-izations in the developing world recruit younger members. Often the only role models these young people have to identify with are terrorists and guerrillas.

Some think that terrorism is the behaviour of barbarians and madmen. Experts generally view terrorism as only a different form of sol-diering, with the usual motives: to protect home and country. As Jeffrey Simon writes, 'what lim-ited data we have on individual terrorists sug-gests that the outstanding common characteristic is normality' (2001: 338). As in the formation of social movements, the formation of terrorist groups relies on social networks to recruit mem-bers. Because terrorist activities are generally organized and carried out in secret, social net-works are important as a source of social control over the recruits, in order to ensure their trust-worthiness (see, for example, Erickson, 1981, on secret organizations).

State-sponsored terrorism is the state-sanc-tioned use of terrorist groups to facilitate to pur-sue foreign-policy objectives. In the eyes of the current US government there are currently seven countries on the 'terrorism list': Cuba, Iran, Iraq, Libya, North Korea, Sudan, and Syria (US Department of State, 2003). Of the seven coun-tries, five are Middle Eastern or other Islamic nations with mainly Muslim populations. Other governments might compile other lists. In the eyes of some, the United States itself might be viewed as a state that sponsors terrorism, with the aim of destabilizing foreign governments and undermining progressive political movements.

In certain areas, state sponsorship remains an important driving force behind terrorism. This is likely true in Israel, the West Bank, and the Gaza Strip today, where 'state-sponsored groups gain instant access to money, sophisticated weapons, training, false passports, safe passage, and protection both before and after their attacks' (Simon, 2001: 328). The CIA has often been implicated as a go-between, providing these kinds of resources to the citizens of various South American countries.

The irony of state-sponsored terrorism is that while it can be a powerful form of terrorism—given the resources and expertise that governments pass on—it can also be vulnerable to shifts in the international political arena. On various occasions, Third World rebel groups, like various governments, have found themselves suddenly deprived of support from the foreign sponsors that they had relied on. So, for example, Saddam Hussein was enlisted by the United States as an ally again Iran only to be dropped later. A variety of religious fundamentalists, including the Taliban and even Osama bin Laden, received support from the United States and its allies in an effort to undermine the Russians, only to be dropped and vilified later.

It is difficult to measure the progress of terrorism. Conventional wars are fought for territory; gains and losses are easily measured on a map. However, terrorism, and the war against it, covers many dimensions other than the geographic. These dimensions would have to include, for example, changes in the numbers of incidents and casualties.

Because terrorism sometimes involves the use of technology, even advanced weaponry, there is some reason to think the prevention of future attacks will mean involving the scientific community. Some have suggested tightening security measure to regulate the flow of scientific information, thus limiting the publication of scientific findings. Others have thought of enlisting the scientific community to improve tools to prevent, detect, protect, and treat victims of terrorist attacks. The improvement of airline security systems is one example; such improvements will increase the capacity to detect weapons of terror.

However, science and technology cannot solve what is ultimately a social and political problem. Improved technologies are not absolute guarantees against future terrorist attacks or criminal sabotage. Terrorist tactics will continue to improve as long as detection techniques improve and as long as new weapons of destruction are perfected. Additionally, the more complex we make each new technology, the more vulnerable it becomes to misuse, sabotage, and catastrophic failure. Finally, note that on 11 September 2001, the terrorists used low-tech weapons to take over the planes, which they then used as high-tech weapons. It takes little imagination to see how dedicated terrorists might easily and calamitously bring about mass death by infiltrating a city's water or subway system, the ventilation system in a skyscraper, or a country's food distribution system.

What this means is that we must concentrate on changing the motives of terrorists, because we cannot control their opportunities. Without understanding terrorist motives, no war against terrorism can succeed. Preventing future attacks will mean considering the historical, political, economic, and other factors that lead normal humans to see mass terror as legitimate and death by martyrdom as appealing.

Changing Contexts of Warfare

Not only has the nature of warfare changed over time, but so have the settings in which conflicts take place. At the turn of this twenty-first century, there were an estimated 40 active military conflicts in the world, many of them intra-national. Many wars are being 'played out on the terrain of subsistence economies; most conflict involves regimes at war with sectors of their own society—generally the poor and particular ethnic groups' (Summerfield, 2000: 232). As well, with the growing popularity of terrorist tactics that target civilian populations rather than military personnel, warfare has shifted from secluded outposts and isolated bases to crowded urban centres.

As a result, the numbers of civilian casualties has risen steadily since the middle of the twentieth century (Renner, 1993a; see also Figure 11.3). Researchers estimate that civilian deaths accounted for 75 per cent of all war-related fatalities in the 1980s and almost 90 per cent in the 1990s. The September 2001 attacks on the World Trade Center in New York City and the Pentagon in Washington, DC, are but two dramatic examples of how war has tended to

become urban. Atrocities against civilians overall, not just in terrorist attacks, have increased. They include illegal execution, torture, disappearances, and sexual violation.

One of the most common causes of war is a dispute over natural resources, such as land, oil, and water. As the only superpower remaining after the Cold War, the United States controls and consumes a disproportionate share of the world's resources and wealth. Such was the case for many nations that depended on Middle Eastern oil supplies when Iraq invaded Kuwait in 1990. Joyce Starr and Daniel Stoll, for example, are among those who state that soon 'water, not oil will be the dominant resource issue of the Middle East' (1989: 1).

Another common cause of war is defence against possible hostile attacks from others. When Germany invaded Poland at the onset of World War II, Britain and France declared war

FIGURE 11.3
Mortality in Armed Conflicts, 1950–94

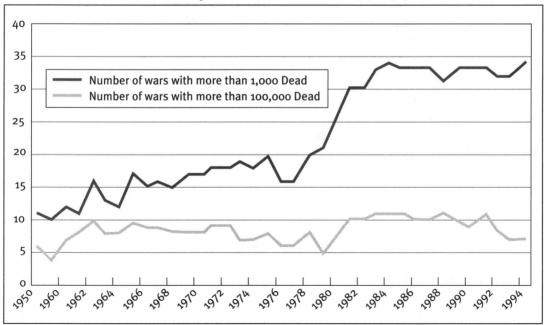

SOURCE: Benjamin Holt (Worldwatch Institute, 1999). Available at <www.globalpolicy.org/nations/numdead2.htm>, accessed 1 March 2003.

on Germany out of fear that their geographic proximity and opposing ideological stances would make them the next logical targets of attack. Japan bombed Pearl Harbor because it wished to avoid a later confrontation with the US naval fleet in the Pacific.

War Crimes

Despite the saying that 'all's fair in love and war', several nations have formally declared that at least some actions are unacceptable even in the madness of war. Having atrocities committed during war defined as *war crimes* may seem strange, given the fundamental ambition of combat—to kill your enemies—and the barbaric way warriors typically carry out much of the killing. However, the leadership of many nations seems to hold the view that the slaughtering of soldiers is an acceptable cost of war but that the intentional slaughtering of civilians is an indefensible horror.

A particularly horrific aspect of war is *genocide*, the systematic execution of a national, ethnic, racial, or political group. The most infamous case of genocide was the attempted extermination of Jews and Gypsies by Nazi Germany during World War II. In all, an estimated 6 million people were killed, many in concentration camps like Auschwitz, where an estimated 1 million died.

More recently, Slobodan Milosevic, the president of Yugoslavia during the 1998–9 conflicts in Kosovo in Yugoslavia's republic of Serbia, was extradited to the War Crimes Tribunal in The Hague and formally indicted for committing war crimes against ethnic Albanians. Among other things, the prosecutor accused him of ordering the dumping of at least 50 Kosovo Albanians into the Danube River in 1999, approving the deaths of hundreds of others, displacing up to 700,000 more, and carrying out other 'ethnic cleansing' policies while in power. Milosevic is the first head of state to ever face international war crimes charges.

Environmental Destruction

The wilful destruction of the environment as a strategy of war or as punishment for the defeated occurred at least as early as Roman times, and it has persisted to the present. Roman armies routinely destroyed crops and salted the earth to ruin the land's fertility. A millennium later, the Russians burned their own crops and homes not once but twice to prevent the invading armies of Napoleon and, later, Hitler, from making use of them.

When the Allied forces pushed the Iraqi forces out of Kuwait in 1990, the Iraqis set fire to 732 of the country's approximately 900 oil wells, producing one of the worst natural disasters in history. Black smoke from the fires blocked out the sun and produced record low temperatures along a 950-kilometre tract of land. Rescue operations recovered over 22 million barrels of oil, but more is thought to have leaked from the destroyed oil fields into the local environment, contaminating soil and water supplies. Saddam Hussein also ordered the release of an estimated 11 million barrels of oil into the Arabian Gulf, greatly damaging the local marine life.

Military operations also harm the environment during peacetime. According to Martin Calhoun, the US military is the largest producer of hazardous materials in that country, and 'decades of improper and unsafe handling, storage and disposal of hazardous materials while building and maintaining the world's most powerful fighting force have severely polluted America's air, water and soil' (1996: 60). Disposal is a major problem, and the drafters of disarmament treaties are often at a loss to suggest a safe place for disposal of missiles, mines, bombs, and nuclear warheads.

Population Control

As Thomas Malthus ([1798] 1959) pointed out over two centuries ago, war—along with disease and starvation—is a 'positive check' on population. Whether or not we choose to view war in this benevolent way, there can be no doubt that to a dramatic degree wars have reduced the population of humanity. In the thousand years between AD 1000 and 2000, wars killed approximately 175 million people. Of these, 111 million were killed in the twentieth century alone, owing to the increased scope and efficiency—the industrialization—of warfare in that century. An estimated 9 million were killed in World War I and another 61 million—over half of them civilians—were killed in World War II. The Soviet Union alone lost over 25 million people in World War II (on this, see Coupland and Meddings, 1999; Rummel, 1992, 1994, 1998).

UN and other projections estimate that had these 70 million people not been killed in World Wars I and II, the world's population today would have been 6.95 billion instead of 6.24 billion (on this, see two Web sites: Matthew White's *Historical Atlas of the Twentieth Century*, <http://users.erols.com/mwhite28/20century.htm>, and Rudolph Rummel's democide site, <www.hawaii.edu/powerkills>. Thus, the deaths of 70 million people in two world wars prevented the births of 710 million people who, but for these wars, would have been alive today. Though we implied in the previous chapter that the world may not need—indeed, may not be able to feed—another 710 million people, there are other ways to think about this kind of population control. Among the 710 million people who were never born, there might have been another Einstein, Mozart, Shakespeare, or Picasso; another Mother Teresa; or even your own uncle or cousin. Under some circumstances, you yourself might not have been born.

Theories of War and Terrorism

Given warfare's universal quality, we can readily understand why something so complex and consequential would have theoretical explanations at different levels of analysis—at the social level, but also the psychological and even the biologi-

cal levels. We shall now examine these different explanations and levels of explanation.

Biological Perspectives

Proponents of a biological theory of the origins of war and terrorism state that humans (and other species) are naturally prone to violent behaviour.

The argument in favour of an evolutionary basis for aggression finds support in Richard Wrangham and Dale Peterson's research on primates, the species most similar to humans, summarized in their book *Demonic Males: Apes and the Origins of Human Violence* (1996). They conclude that both human and non-human animals, and male members in particular in each species, have an inborn capacity for planned violence. Researchers have known male chimpanzees, for instance, to declare war on neighbouring groups of chimpanzees to secure resources and dominance, reasons similar to those that sometimes send humans into warfare.

Further research suggests hormonal and neurological bases for violent behaviour. Testosterone, a hormone found in greater proportion in males but also present to varying degrees in females, is higher among groups—both male and female—with aggressive, confrontational personalities, such as prison populations, police officers, and corporate lawyers. Similarly, researchers cited in the same publication (Wrangham and Peterson, 1996) have linked low levels of the neurochemical serotonin to increased aggression in both primate and human subjects. However, causality has yet to be established.

Psychological Perspectives

Competition between groups is a natural phenomenon that can develop over time into hostile forms if the resources fought over are scarce or if superiority and victory are central to the groups' identities. Jordan Peterson (1998) states, for example, that the horrible acts committed during

World War II were due to adherence to group ideology (then, Nazi ideology and a belief in the 'final solution'). Such behaviour is helped by a denial of contradictory information and of personal moral reservations and by an inability to think independently outside prescribed boundaries (Peterson, 1998).

Other social psychologists examine how otherwise 'normal' and mild-mannered citizens can change during wartime into soldiers capable of killing and injuring others seemingly without hesitation or remorse. Philip Zimbardo (1971) states that taking on a role, such as 'soldier', causes a person to internalize that role's identity. Similarly, ordinary citizens called upon to defend their country can readily identify themselves as 'soldiers' temporarily. They take on a role that justifies the brutal slaughter of their enemies. The degree of role socialization to violence is, of course, even greater among career soldiers whose entire adult lives have been spent in the military.

In a classic study of this process, Zimbardo (1971) simulated a prison in the Stanford University psychology department, assigning student volunteers at random to play the role of guards and prisoners. To the guards, he gave uniforms, billy clubs, and whistles; to the prisoners, prison outfits and jail cells. After only one day, all participants had become engrossed in their roles. 'Guards' cruelly disparaged and degraded 'prisoners'; prisoners suffered anguish and rebelled against their captors. Intense social conflict emerged, forcing Zimbardo to end the experiment after only six days, a week earlier than planned.

In another classic experiment, Stanley Milgram (1974) enlisted Yale University students supposedly to participate in a study on learning and memory, but he was actually studying the role of authority in maintaining obedience among subordinates. The reason for the research was Milgram's desire to learn how the atrocities of World War II, in particular the Holocaust, could have been committed by German soldiers who claimed they were only 'following orders'.

In Milgram's study, a stern experimenter in a lab coat explained that the experiment was investigating the effects of punishment on learning. The experimental subject's job was to teach a second participant a list of word pairs and to punish errors by delivering increasingly intense shocks. Actually, the second participant was always following a script provided by Milgram. In one version of the study, the volunteer 'teacher' and the 'learner' were placed in separate rooms, connected only by a PA system. The teacher sat in front of a shock generator with a range from 15 to 450 volts. For each mistake the learner made on the learning task, as previously scripted by Milgram, the teacher was instructed to increase the voltage of the shock by a 15-volt increment, while the experimenter looked on. If the teacher expressed a desire to stop the experiment, the experimenter would use one of four scripted verbal prods, such as 'It is important that you continue with the task'.

Imagine this situation: The teacher begins to hear the learner grunt as the voltage reaches 75V and above. At 120V, the student screams that the shock is becoming painful—'Get me out of here, please'. At 300V, he is clearly in agony, screaming his refusal to answer. (The responses by the learner were pre-recorded and played on a tape recorder for the benefit of the 'teacher'.) At 330V and above, the student falls silent, supposedly the victim of a heart attack. How far did the participants go as 'teachers'? Of the 40 subjects who took part in one study, 26 (65 per cent) continued until they reached the top level on the shock scale; 5 subjects halted the experiment at 300V after several bouts of intense screaming by the 'learner'; and the rest halted the experiment between 315V and 375V.

We should note that most participants went on hesitantly. In fact, most pleaded with the experimenter to stop the task and check on the learner, and many continued only with extreme reluctance. However, a full 65 per cent completed the experiment, with only a few short prompts from the lab-coated, scientific-looking experimenter. Milgram argued that his studies showed how easily authority—here the authority of science, not of government or military leaders—can get people who accept that authority to hurt others.

Sociological Perspectives

The Structural-Functionalist Perspective

As we have said repeatedly, structural functionalists believe that most elements in society exist to serve some purpose. War and terrorism are no different from this standpoint. If these activities did not somehow further the progress and development of humanity, then people would presumably reject them. Equally, wars may occur because groups or societies do not know how to resolve their conflicts peacefully. They lack the institutions, values, leadership, and resources to bring peace. By this reckoning, war results from the breakdown of peace. Wars may even arise because military institutions and activities hold great importance within the society and culture.

Once in motion, a large-scale conflict increases social cohesion and group identity. Internal squabbles between political parties, ethnic communities, special interest groups, and so on are put aside, at least temporarily, as the entire nation bands together to defeat a common enemy. Only when this common enemy is no longer a threat to national well-being do the internal conflicts resume. Sometimes the solidarity between allies generated through the defence of shared interests lasts for a while even after the war is over.

A second consequence of war is the economic benefit that comes from the fact that industry and business must support the war effort. Canadian participation in World War II led to increased employment and production, helping to end the economic downturn of the Great Depression. After the war, North Americans rode the economic momentum through the next several decades, experiencing prosperity and growth in all aspects of society.

Canadians, the strongest trading partner of the United States, also enjoyed an economic boom during and after the war: the gross national product (GNP) doubled, industry developed exponentially, and consumer spending rose with the baby boom generation (Girvan, 2000). Losers of the war, particularly Germany and Japan, suffered significant setbacks to their economies for many years after the conflict ended.

Wars also lead to scientific and technological innovations that benefit society in peacetime. Military research on laser-based defence systems paved the way for the development of laser surgery; experimentation with nuclear weaponry allowed for the widespread use of nuclear power stations; the airline industry's technological innovations were made possible largely through the work of military defence departments; much of the weaponry used by today's police forces was perfected and first used by military personnel; and the Internet was a result of research sponsored by the US armed services as a possible emergency communications network in case of nuclear war. In this sense, innovations in weaponry are social innovations as well as engineering feats.

This raises the question of whether the bloodiness of warfare in recent decades—indeed, in the twentieth century more generally—is ascribable to an increased bloodthirstiness—a motivation to inflict maximum harm—or merely to an increased ease of inflicting maximum harm. On the one hand, the Nazi Holocaust required few technological innovations. Mainly, it was a feat of social engineering: to kill so many civilians in so few years required tremendous organization and dedication. On the other hand, the enormous harm perpetrated by Americans in Vietnam and since—through aerial bombing and other forms of long-distance attack—demonstrates the ability to inflict maximum harm without much risk or effort that modern technology has made possible. In general, the twentieth century has taught that people will use the most extreme weapons they can devise in the interests of winning a war.

Conflict Theory

Conflict theorists state that wars are struggles between opposing groups over power, limited resources, or ideological domination, taken to their logical, violent conclusions. Just as social classes may battle one another for economic position within a society, so nation-states and interest groups within the society may go to war with one another. The difference is that they routinely use weapons and kill one another.

Conflict theory also stresses the ways in which war benefits some groups—most notably, corporations, politicians, and the military—but not others. The *military-industrial complex*, a term first introduced by US president Dwight D. Eisenhower in 1961, refers to the close relationship between the military and the private defence industry. Corporations contracted by the Pentagon to design, develop, and manufacture weapons and military technology are guaranteed profits even if they overrun their budgets. It is, therefore, in the interest of these companies to ensure that global conflicts and threats to national security continue to occur so that they can operate the highly profitable war machine. Also, as Cynthia Enloe observes, 'government officials enhance the status, resources, and authority of the military to protect the interests of private enterprises at home and overseas' (1987: 527).

Industrialists, politicians, middlemen, and black marketeers, among others, make enormous fortunes from war and weapons of war. This has a considerable effect on the class structure of society. According to one estimate, governments throughout the world were collectively spending $1 trillion per year, or approximately $2 million (US) per minute, to finance various military efforts by the end of the 1980s (Brown, Flavin, and Kane, 1992). These costs included the salaries of military personnel, research into and development of weapons and combat technology, the purchase and manufacture of artillery and wartime machinery, and veterans' benefits. (See Table 11.1.)

Symbolic Interactionism

Symbolic interactionists examine the ways in which cultures socialize people to attitudes toward war and conflict. Adult members of society encourage aggression and the solving of conflicts with physical force as early as childhood, mostly in boys.

Symbolic interactionists also study the language and labels of war. Accordingly, propaganda techniques are employed by the government, the businesses most interested in warfare (for example, munitions manufacturers), the military, and 'patriotic organizations' (such as veterans' groups) to cast the conflict in terms of a 'justified war' against 'evil' terrorism. The media play an important role in the spin-doctoring of this message. In times of war, leaders use a special language to legitimize combat and reduce the emotional impact of the deaths that will follow. Soldiers on both sides are not 'murder victims', they are 'casualties'. They refer to the unplanned but 'unavoidable' killing of innocent civilians as 'collateral damage'. Nuclear missiles are not weapons of mass destruction, they are 'peacekeepers'.

Governments often stress the importance of military preparedness as vital to national prosperity. US president George W. Bush, for example, promoted an as-yet-unproven missile defence system as a critical component of US security, without which the world's only superpower and the country with the mightiest military force in the history of humanity would be nakedly vulnerable to outside attacks. The criticism that such a weapon was costly, unproven, and likely to provoke war preparations by other nations was ignored in a nation roused for revenge through war.

The Feminist Perspective

Masculinity and militarism have had a close relationship over time and across cultures, so that the 'meanings attached to masculinity appear to be so firmly linked to compliance with military roles that it is often impossible to disentangle the two' (Enloe, 1987: 531). The association

TABLE 11.1
The 15 Top Military Spenders, 1998–2001: Spending in Billions of US Dollars

Rank[a] 2001 (2000)	Country	1998	1999	2000	2001	Share of world military expenditure (%)
1 (1)	USA	274.3	275.1	285.7	281.4	36
2 (2)	Russia (PPP)[b]	[30.6]	[35.9]	[40.3]	[43.9]	[6]
3 (3)	France	40.0	40.4	39.9	40.0	5
4 (4)	Japan	37.7	37.8	38.1	38.5	5
5 (5)	UK	37.2	36.8	37.3	37.0	5
6 (6)	Germany	33.1	33.8	33.1	32.4	4
7 (8)	China	[19.0]	[21.1]	[23.1]	[27.0]	[3]
8 (9)	Saudi Arabia	20.8	17.9	20.5	[26.6]	[3]
9 (7)	Italy	23.5	24.4	26.0	24.7	3
10 (10)	Brazil	11.0	10.1	10.7	14.1	2
11 (11)	India	9.4	10.7	11.8	12.9	2
12 (13)	South Korea	9.7	9.4	10.0	10.2	1
13 (14)	Israel	8.5	8.5	9.0	9.1	1
14 (12)	Turkey	8.8	9.7	9.4	8.9	1
15 (15)	Spain	7.5	7.7	8.0	8.0	1
Sub-total					614.7	80
World total		719	728	757	772	100.0

[a] The rank order of countries differs with the base year and the method of conversion to dollars. The base year should ideally be the same as the year of comparison, while this table is based on military expenditure figures in constant (1998) prices and exchange rates because of the lack of PPP data for Russia for 2001.

[b] Conversion to dollars is made by use of the market exchange rate for most countries. The main exception in this table is Russian military expenditure, which is converted by use of the PPP conversion factor. If the market exchange rate is used for Russia, its military expenditure in 2001 amounts to $12.7 billion at constant (1998) prices and exchange rates. Figures are in US$ b., at constant 1998 prices and exchange rates. Figures in italics are percentages. Figures do not always add up to totals because of the conventions of rounding.

SOURCE: Stockholm International Peace Research Institute, *SIPRI Yearbook 2002*, Appendix 6A (Tables 6A.1 and 6A.3), available at <www.sipri.se>, accessed 31 January 2003; the SIPRI database on military expenditure.

between masculinity and militarism begins in childhood socialization. For example, in Western culture, boys wage make-believe wars with GI Joe figurines, while girls are much more likely to play with dolls and act out domestic routines such as baking and child rearing.

With only a few exceptions through the history of Western culture, it has been primarily men who have fought wars. This is due in part to women's smaller physical stature, to the nature of warfare (which has traditionally involved much face-to-face, close range, physical combat), and to men's greater tendency toward aggression and

violence. Some say that a protective chivalry or paternalistic sexism toward the 'lesser sex' is involved, too, in men's largely exclusive role in warfare; men try to protect women, they argue.

This may be true to some extent. However, note the point made by Dr Mary Edwards Walker, a US Civil War surgeon and the only woman to receive the US Congressional Medal of Honor. She argued, 'You are not our protectors. ... If you were, who would there be to protect us from?' (cited in Snyder, 1962: 83).

Entrenched in secrecy, and regarded as men, women soldiers in the Civil War were sometimes

BOX 11.3
Fashions in Masculinity

Go to the movies, turn on the television, pick up a magazine—just about anywhere you look these days, you're likely to find proof: manly men are making a comeback in American culture. Whether it's a film like 'Gladiator', or even a recent New York Times Magazine article in which the (male) author extolled the virtues of regular synthetic testosterone shots—traditional masculine values and role models are enjoying a resurgence.

It's been widely noted by critics, for example, that in 'Gladiator', the hero, played by Russell Crowe, longs to leave the battlefield to return to his wife and child back on the family farm.

'Women have changed a lot in the past 30 years, and men have noticed this, and they're being forced to change, and they can't figure out how', says Mariah Burton Nelson, a former professional basketball player and author of The Stronger Women Get, The More Men Love Football.

'I would like to see men redefine what strong means', Ms. Nelson says. 'And for strong to include being compassionate and honest and wise instead of resorting to physical strength, or military strength, which don't seem very imaginative.'

Other critics warn that the he-man model doesn't offer much in the way of substance to young boys. William Pollack, a psychiatrist whose new book, Real Boys' Voices, comes out next month, says the he-man is 'an impossible test of masculinity'. The problem, he says, isn't so much that boys see aggression and violence in the media; it's that violent acts are usually shown without consequences and that aggression is seldom channeled into the service of a higher cause or some kind of social justice.

Pollack and other observers argue that a different type of male model is needed today. Pollack says he'd love to see a movie version of Homer's classic ancient poem, The Iliad. It's a story with plenty of violence and male swaggering, but to an end: The narcissistic hero finally weeps with his enemies, mourning the senseless loss and destruction of war. 'It's a message that involves aggression', he says, 'but it's a positive one.'

SOURCE: Sara Terry, 'Image: The Manly Man Makes a Comeback', *Telegram* (St. John's), 30 May 2000, final edition, 15.

revealed as women, by accident or casualty. Some startling histories of these military women were current in the gossip of army life. Those revealed to be women were immediately discharged—sometimes honourably, sometimes not—by the generals (all males, of course). However, many others remained undetected throughout the conflict. Some even received pensions for their military service following the war.

As the twentieth century progressed and feminist groups gained some political clout, opportunities became available for women in the military. Currently, women can serve in most ranks and divisions of the militaries in North America; in Canada, all combat units are open to women except for submarines.

Another important aspect of gender in war concerns the innocent civilians of a wartorn region, many of whom are women. Despite prohibitions outlined in the Geneva Conventions, rape, assault, and enforced prostitution of women has continued to occur in armed conflicts. For example, in the years of World War II, the Japanese military forced up to 200,000 young women into prostitution as 'comfort women' for military personnel, with many eventually dying from sexually transmitted diseases and torture. During the recent conflicts in Bosnia-Herzegovina and Rwanda, and almost certainly in most other hostile actions as well, roving bands of soldiers raped, beat, and even killed women (Amnesty International, 1995).

War has had other consequences for women beyond those already mentioned. For one, during major wars women have been mobilized into the workforce, both into the military and as civilians, to replace the men recruited for war. During World War II, this meant the opening up of new job opportunities for women, who had up to then been limited to a narrow range of traditionally female jobs. Now they found themselves working in 'essential' industries such as engineering, metals, chemical, vehicles, transport, energy, and shipbuilding (Summerfield, 2000).

Women who entered the military in wartime were generally enthusiastic about the experiences they had there (Campbell, 1990). True, they were thought by some to be promiscuous. They may in fact have been more sexually active in the military than they would have been had they remained in civilian society. Away from home, often for the first time, these young women were less visible and less restrained than they would have been in the front parlour with a boyfriend from next door. This may have been viewed as a problem at the time (Summerfield and Crockett, 1992), but in retrospect, sexual experimentation was not a bad thing. It would not blossom fully until the 1960s.

Finally, women were also active in professional sports during wartime. With the deterioration of male-dominated sports, women's professional sports—for example, major-league baseball—expanded dramatically. The All-American Girls Professional Baseball League began in 1943 and lasted until 1954. During the war, not only did women take on the responsibilities of work and play, they also volunteered their time in military bases and 'kept the home fires burning'. This kind of activity, at work and in sports, gave support to later demands by the women's movement for equal treatment of men and women at work, at play, and at home—and also helped them to gain the franchise in 1917 and 1918.

As we have noted so often during the course of this book, all of the major sociological approaches have something to offer in interpreting social problems. So, for example, in relation to war, consider the effects of Canada's War Measures Act on Canadian race relations (and vice versa). The War Measures Act was originally legislated in 1914 in relation to anxieties connected with World War I. This legislation was used during two world wars and, in particular, was used to justify the unjust treatment of Japanese Canadians during and after World War II. Using this Act, Japanese Canadians were uprooted from their homes, were detained, and had their properties confiscated; some were even deported (Kage, 2002).

A structural functionalist would note that the imposition of the War Measures Act after the bombing of Pearl Harbor on 7 December 1941 served to rally (non-Japanese) Canadians around patriotic slogans and shared perceptions of internal and external danger. Fearing for their safety and well-being, Canadians united against the Japanese and against Japanese Canadians. At the same time, the singling out of Japanese Canadians and the deprivation of their property and rights suited some Canadians even more than others. Non-Japanese Canadians on the West Coast had felt threatened by the presence of the Japanese community for decades owing to a scarcity of jobs. The enactment of the War Measures Act, as conflict theorists would have it, gave these non-Japanese Canadians more opportunities to access limited resources.

Finally, a symbolic interactionist would note that the war, and the War Measures Act, helped to justify derogatory and racially hostile views that already existed. In short, it made racism acceptable in Canada. Moreover, it blamed the Japanese Canadians for racially hostile sentiments that they had played no part in creating.

Social Consequences of War

The two most socially consequential facts about warfare are, first, that it kills many people and, second, that it costs a lot of money. The rise in casualty rates in modern warfare is in part due to the larger scale of conflict. Besides the economic price that war exacts on society, another consequence is that, for many people, the disruption of hostile combat shatters morale.

Although it is true that countries or groups internal to them who emerge as the victors undergo a general improvement in spirits, for many people war will always be a gruelling and haunting experience. For instance, many Vietnam veterans returned to the United States disillusioned, unable to understand their purpose in the conflict and the lack of sympathy from fellow Americans upon their return.

Increasingly, throughout the century, wars saw the use of child soldiers. Though the United Nations Convention on the Rights of the Child states that children under the age of 15 are not to be used as soldiers, children were used as soldiers as recently as the Rwandan War (c. 1994–6). Human Rights Watch estimates that approximately 250,000 child soldiers were used in more than 30 wars around the world (n.d.: 88). This is not counting the large numbers of children who have enlisted themselves in civil wars, as part of liberation armies in Ireland, Palestine, and elsewhere.

This use of children in warfare has been promoted, unwittingly, by technological innovation—specifically, by the development and manufacture of lightweight automatic weapons. These weapons are light enough for a young child to carry and are relatively easy to use (Human Rights Watch, n.d.: 91). Since more people are able to handle these weapons properly, armies are able to grow faster.

War affects not only those who fight in them, but also civilians, even those who are relatively sheltered from the physical horrors of combat. The Lost Generation and the Beat Generation provide good illustrations of the effects of global warfare on social cohesion. The term *Lost Generation* was coined in conversation by Gertrude Stein, a member of the expatriate American circle in 1920s Paris, in reference to the group of American and British citizens who had rejected the traditional conventions of their homelands for the more appealing lifestyle of the Left Bank.

Just as World War I shattered the world view of the Lost Generation, so too did World War II for those who came of age in the early late 1930s and early 1940s. The Beat Generation, as they came to be called, were just as out of love with the post–World War II lifestyle as the Lost Generation was with that of the post–World War I era. However, unlike their predecessors, the Beats were raised not in an optimistic, flourishing environment like that of the pre– and post–World War I years, but in the crushing melancholy of the Great Depression.

Health Consequences of War

One estimate is that military conflicts in the twentieth century have led to the deaths of over 100 million soldiers and civilians—more than the total number of casualties in all previous wars in human history combined (Porter, 1994). Other estimates vary according to whether we include the deaths stemming from war-related famine and disease. Michael Renner (1993b) calculates that 75 per cent of all military deaths since the reign of Julius Caesar have taken place in the 1900s. Thus, Hobsbawm's characterization of the twentieth century as the 'age of total war' (1994) is not far off the truth.

The rise in casualty rates of modern warfare is due in part to the larger scale of the conflicts. With more countries involved and more troops sent into battle, mounting death tolls are inevitable. As well, as we said earlier, sophisticated weaponry can kill more people and destroy a greater area than ever before.

If these numbers seem appalling, they pale in comparison to the possible death tolls mankind would achieve were a full-scale nuclear war to break out. Currently, the nuclear weapons in the major military arsenals are more than 4,000 times as powerful as the atomic bombs dropped on Japan. George Friedman and Meredith Friedman (1996) estimate that a nuclear war today would kill 160 million people instantly. These people would be the lucky ones; another billion would perish in the first few hours because of radiation poisoning, environmental devastation, and massive social chaos. Many hundreds of millions of others would die more slowly.

Exposure to war also increases the risk of health problems and lowers life expectancy. One archival study of World War II veterans who either remained in the United States or served overseas found that combat experience increased the risk of physical decline or death in the 15 years after the war. Military rank and theatre of engagement with the enemy did not affect the trend (Elder, Shanahan, and Clipp, 1997).

Just as deaths are an unavoidable consequence of war, so too are physical and psychological injuries. Overall, the number of military personnel and civilians who are injured or maimed during a war usually exceeds the number of deaths. Indeed, one common military strategy is to maim rather than kill the enemy since it requires more resources to care for the wounded than to discard their bodies. Anti-personnel land mines are particularly suited for this vicious task. They are effective because they are largely undetectable by civilians or enemy troops without proper equipment, do not require a soldier present to 'pull the trigger', and can kill or injure long after the military has abandoned the area and even after the conflict is officially over. Cambodia has been called the 'land of the one-legged men', referring to the more than 30,000 individuals— mostly rural farmers—who have had limbs amputated because of accidentally detonating a concealed mine (Stover and McGrath, 1992).

Many troops from the Gulf War reportedly contracted a disease that has become known as the 'Gulf War syndrome'. As many as 100,000 US soldiers and at least 150 Canadian soldiers have been affected by this mysterious illness, whose symptoms include fatigue, headaches, immune system depression, reproductive problems, and aching joints and muscles (National Gulf War Resource Center, 2001). It is still unclear what are the causes of this illness, how it may be prevented, and what is the cure.

Surviving a war physically unscathed does not guarantee complete well-being. Many veterans of war suffer the slow torture of psychological disorders. Much of the mental health literature on the effects of war focuses on **post-traumatic stress disorder (PTSD)**, which researchers had previously studied under labels such as 'shell shock', 'concentration-camp syndrome', 'survivor syndrome', and 'war neurosis' (Summerfield, 2000).

Although initially considered an expression of cowardice, we now recognize PTSD as a common form of psychological distress produced by a traumatic experience, especially by crime victimization, sexual assault, or military combat. Symptoms include nervousness, sleep disturbances, disruption of concentration, anxiety, depression, irrational fear, and flashbacks triggered by loud noises like thunder or a car's backfiring. Paul Witteman (1991) estimates that 479,000 of the 3.5 million veterans of the Vietnam War suffer from severe PTSD, while another 350,000 have moderate symptoms. Researchers have also linked PTSD to higher rates of drug use and suicide among veterans.

Civilians are also vulnerable to PTSD and other forms of war-related mental illness. The study of this aspect of the health consequences of war is limited. Only within the past few decades have civilian responses to military conflict been the object of some scrutiny. Examining the effects of the Lebanese civil war on citizens, U.S. Yaktin and S. Labban (1992) find that a traumatic war experience was a risk factor for the development of schizophrenia. During the 12 years of the war, schizophrenia diagnoses and admissions in the country increased substantially, particularly in the periods immediately following intense bouts of fighting.

Another study, of the Lebanese conflict, revealed that malingering and general anxiety disorder (GAD) decreased in the general population during the years of combat, but drug abuse, neuroses, and psychotic reactions such as anti-social personality disorders increased overall (Baddoura, 1990). J.R. Walton, R.L. Nuttall, and E.V. Nuttall (1997) found that children born into the Salvadoran civil war suffered psychological consequences, with those who experienced the highest personal-social impact of the conflict having the poorest mental health.

Victims of terrorism are particularly at risk of psychological trauma because of the unexpected and severe nature of the event, and because civilians are usually sheltered from such events. Henk Van der Ploeg and Wim Kleijn investigated the long-term effects of being taken hostage by terrorists in the Netherlands. They found that one-third suffered from PTSD and GAD, and that 12 per cent of the hostages and 11 per cent of their family members still needed professional therapy even nine years after the incident (1989: 160, 163).

A study of the 1974 terrorist attack on the high school in Ma'alot, Israel, also found that the effects of the traumatic experience among adolescents could last into adulthood. Specifically, a face-to-face encounter with terrorism predicts personal and interpersonal difficulties in later life. Survivors also report decreased intimacy with their spouses, more problems with attachment, an erratic employment history, and a higher risk of developing subsequent mental health problems (Desivilya, Gal, and Ayalon, 1996).

Solutions

Military conflict has occurred so consistently throughout human history that it is unlikely that we can propose any practical solution that will overturn centuries of human practice. Of the social problems discussed in this book, war is among the oldest, along with gender inequality. Also, it is an 'ultimate problem' in the sense that unchecked escalation in frustration and hostility generated by other social problems often leads to war and violence. Still, if we cannot eliminate warfare, at least we can develop policies to help reduce conflict and maintain peace. As with other social problems that are unlikely to go away— alcohol and drug abuse, trafficking in sex—the best we can hope to do is carry out a strategy of harm reduction so that the problem has as few social and health consequences as possible.

The Scale of War

To some degree, the shrinking scale of warfare will accomplish this. Whereas in the past wars were often formal and highly coordinated campaigns waged by well-organized military units involving thousands of soldiers and war machinery, wars today are increasingly taking the form of **low-intensity conflicts (LICs)**, which involve a smaller army of guerrillas, terrorists, or civilians. LICs are less-organized campaigns characterized by small-arms combat, bombings, ambushes, assassinations, and massacres. Martin van Creveld (1991) estimates that approximately 120 LICs have been waged since World War II, with the frequency expected only to rise in the future.

Terrorists are often motivated by causes such as the promotion of an ideology, a struggle for the freedom of religious expression, or the desire to overthrow what they view as an oppressive government or authoritarian body. Terrorism is also blind to borders, and can, therefore, be directed at both domestic and transnational targets. As we have seen, improvements in conditions are likely to incite more social movements to form. The activities of these movements will be largely determined by the availability of resources for mobilization. Thus, one means of harm reduction is to limit the global production and sale of arms.

Arms Reduction

The goal of any limitation of arms would be an international agreement on arms reduction. (See Table 11.2 on the need to do this for land mines.) During the 1960s, the United States and Russia were engaged in an international arms race to amass a dominant military arsenal. However, with the availability of nuclear weaponry, any war between countries in possession of a nuclear warhead would clearly result in all sides being decimated. This principle of **mutually assured destruction (MAD)** was what held nations back from all-out war. If starting a war meant losing it, then, theoretically, it would be in nobody's interest to start one.

TABLE 11.2
Stockpiles of Land Mines

Warning: These statistics may be grossly inaccurate because size of the top 3 stockpiles of anti-personnel land mines, those of China, Russia, and Belarus, are unknown. Below are the 10 biggest stockpiles.

	Number of Land Mines
China	110 million
Russia	60–70 million estimated
Belarus	'Millions'[a]
United States	11.3 million
Ukraine	10 million (being destroyed)
Italy	5.5 million (being destroyed)
India	4–5 million estimated
Albania	2.2 million estimated
South Korea	2 million estimated
Sweden	1.7 million (being destroyed)

[a] Belarus has acknowledged 'millions' in stockpile. However, it has estimated cost of destruction at 'tens of millions', which likely means that tens of millions of AP [anti-personnel] mines are in stockpile.

SOURCE: Mary Wareham, 'Antipersonnel Landmine Stockpiles and Their Destruction', in Human Rights Watch, *Antipersonnel Landmine Stockpiles and Their Destruction: Fact Sheet* (Washington, DC: Human Rights Watch, 1999), part 2, 1.

Recently, however, the United States has created a stir among the international community by signalling its intent to abandon the Anti-Ballistic Missile (ABM) Treaty and begin building a defence shield theoretically capable of intercepting enemy missiles in space. Citing the presence of new threats to national security that have emerged since the end of the Cold War, primarily from 'rogue nations' undeterred by the threat of MAD, the United States argued for the need for a new arms treaty that reflects the current state of global hostilities. President George W. Bush has proposed to rehatch the Strategic Defence Initiative (SDI), better known as 'Star Wars', first presented by President Ronald Reagan in the 1980s.

More recently still, on March 19, 2003, the United States embarked upon war against Iraq, with the assistance of only the United Kingdom, Australia, and several dozen small countries (Albania, Ethiopia, and others) that stand in a client–patron relationship to the United States. (The American government called its allies in war 'the willing states', while an unnamed wag has renamed them 'the billing states'.) This declaration of war ran counter to the expressed will of the United Nations, Canada, most of America's main allies and trading partners, and a majority of ordinary people around the world who publicly expressed their opinions. This act has led some to wonder who are actually the rogue nations in the world—the so-called 'axis of evil' (Iraq, Iran, and North Korea, as the American government has said) or the United States itself and its partners in warfare.

Redistributing Economic Resources

Some believe that terrorism and warfare will be reduced, and peace ensured, only by redistributing economic resources more equally among nations. (See Figure 11.4.) We know that disparities in wealth and resources have been and are causes of many wars, past and present. Thus, we can probably reduce conflict through a more equal distribution of resources among rich and poor nations. However, it is unlikely that prosperous nations will easily agree to lower their standards of living at home to benefit less wealthy societies. Although most developed countries contribute part of their total revenue to foreign aid, they also spend a much larger portion on military interests.

Redistributing economic wealth from core nations to peripheral nations does not guarantee that poorer nations will have a better standard of living. There must be proper regulations to ensure that the citizens will benefit from aid monies. Otherwise, politicians and state elites may use the monies to further their own interests (for example, to build mansions for their personal use) at the expense of their citizens.

At the same time, sometimes the money for foreign aid, in the form of loans, is never moved into the peripheral countries because of strings attached to the loans. Often, through such agencies at the World Bank or the International Monetary Fund, core countries instruct peripheral countries how to spend the loan money. For example, a Canadian loan with strings attached might tell farmers in a peripheral country to spend some portion of the loan money purchasing farming equipment from Canadian companies. This ends up stimulating the Canadian economy, but may or may not help the peripheral country that the loan was supposed to help in the first place. In effect, the aid money never leaves the core country. If farmers were allowed to spend the aid money on local businesses, it would help the peripheral country, since their local economy would be stimulated.

FIGURE 11.4
Where Does All the Money Go? Comparing Priorities in Spending, 1997

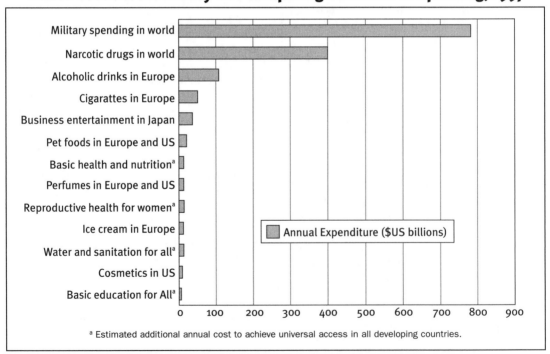

^a Estimated additional annual cost to achieve universal access in all developing countries.

SOURCE: Benjamin Holt, 'Comparing Priorities in Spending: 1997', *Human Development Report 1998*, United Nations Development Program, copyright © 1998 by the United Nations Development Program. Used by permission of Oxford University Press, Inc. available at <www.globalpolicy.org/socecon/tables/priorit2.htm>, accessed 1 February 2003.

International Peacekeeping Bodies

Another harm-reduction and risk-reduction strategy has been to form an international body dedicated to peacekeeping and the prevention of global conflict. The most prominent agency trying to accomplish this task has been the United Nations. UN peacekeepers have been patrolling wartorn regions since 1948, when the UN Truce Supervision Organization was created to observe the ceasefire agreement between Israel and its Middle East neighbours. Peacekeeping troops largely consist of soldiers volunteered by their respective governments to participate in tasks such as monitoring ceasefires, separating hostile forces, and maintaining demilitarized buffer zones.

The need for UN peacekeeping has risen dramatically since the end of the Cold War. In the first 40 years of operation, UN peacekeepers carried out only 13 campaigns. Since 1988, however, 36 operations have been launched. At its peak in 1993, the United Nations deployed more than 80,000 military and civilian personnel across 77 countries. As of May 2002, there were 15 ongoing UN peacekeeping missions in the world, all of which were in Africa, Eastern Europe, the Middle East, and Asia. More than 40,000 personnel from 89 countries were participating at that time in various functions, with annual costs estimated in the $3–$3.5 billion (US) range. Since 1948, 1,674 UN peacekeepers have been killed while on duty (United Nations, 2001). There would likely have been more, and lengthier warfare, without the actions of the United Nations. However, its actions have not been sufficient to largely eliminate war.

These current peacekeeping activities are also results of wars that have occurred during 'the watch' of the United Nations. To this list, we can add the 2003 war between Iraq and the United States, Britain, and others as an unsuccessful attempt by the UN to prevent war.

Concluding Remarks

Some have thought of war as the natural sign of innate aggression. The opposing view is that people are not born to be violent or aggressive but that we learn it. According to this latter explanation, war is a result of social organization and cultural tradition, and a response to cultural symbols.

We could think of the arms race as a symbolic show of power, and also as a means of securing peace through mutual deterrence. However, the negative consequences include the obvious potential for mass destruction and the enormous monetary cost. The resources spent to produce and maintain armaments could instead be allocated to the alleviation of other social problems. This is especially true in Third World countries, where the need for these resources is more prominent.

Terrorism can exist for different reasons. Common forms are revolutionary terrorism, in which rebels wage war on the State, and repressive terrorism, in which the State wages war in an attempt to repress its citizens. Other forms mentioned include transnational terrorism or terrorism by autonomous agents.

In the global economy, there are economic differences at the national level. Superpowers control most of the wealth and resources, which creates a much higher standard of living than in the Third World. Not only do Third World countries have a lower standard of living, but their rapid population growth will also likely worsen the problem. Note, however, that population growth is declining rapidly on every continent of the world, even in Africa, the Middle East, South Asia. and South America, where the rates have been highest. We can foresee that within a generation, the widespread concern will be about labour supply, health care, and support for the aged—just as it is in the economically developed countries today.

War will pose a problem for humanity so long as there are wide inequalities in wealth and power between nations, wide differences in beliefs and interests, and weaknesses in bodies—such as the United Nations—that are charged with keeping the world's peace.

Questions for Critical Thought

1. Think of the some of the war movies you have seen recently (for example, *Saving Private Ryan*, *The Thin Red Line*, or *Black Hawk Down*). How do those movies portray war? Did you leave the theatre with feelings of patriotism or with a sense that war is awful and should be avoided at all costs, or was it a combination of both? Do you feel Hollywood can be realistic in its depictions of war, or will war films always be susceptible to the dramatizations of Hollywood? Finally, what is the responsibility of the film-maker in making war movies, both to war veterans and to the general public?

2. With the proliferation of Internet technology spanning the globe, more of the world's peoples are gaining access to information they never had before. Third World countries are seeing the standard of living of others and are desiring a 'world culture' of homogenized human aspirations. In the 1980 movie *The Gods Must Be Crazy*, an African tribe discovers a Coke bottle and begins to realize all the amenities they lack. What are the implications of this? How will countries that may not be able to afford the Western culture cope with their inability to achieve this potential goal?

3. It is a known fact that girls are usually given Barbies and other dolls as small children and that boys are given GI Joe figures and other war toys. In your opinion, how much do you think toy socialization affects violent and aggressive tendencies in adulthood? Do you prefer a biological approach, with testosterone as the explanatory variable, or is the root cause of aggressiveness in socialization? Where do you fit in this nature-versus-nurture debate? If you think toys and gender differentials in socialization might be to blame, what should we do about it? Is banning action figures and war toys an option for you?

4. Research the Nuremberg trials, which occurred after the Holocaust, in which Nazi officials were tried for their genocidal behaviours during World War II. How do these trials illustrate that war crimes are not to be tolerated? What can we learn from this in order to prevent catastrophic events such as the Holocaust from ever occurring again?

5. The remaining time for survivors of some of the major world wars and conflicts is limited. Do you have friends or close relatives who were in a war? Next time you see them, ask them about their experiences of warfare, such as where they were, how they felt, and who they lost, and try to see the world through their eyes. Research post-traumatic stress disorder (PTSD) further and try to imagine how traumatizing these events were to the individual and how scary PTSD symptoms must be. Keep a journal of your experiences.

Recommended Readings

Rabab Abdulhadi, 'The Palestinian Women's Autonomous Movement: Emergence, Dynamics and Challenges', *Gender and Society*, 12 (1998): 649–73.

This interesting article details the women's movement in Palestine and describes the interaction between femininity, religion, and military uprising.

Cynthia Enloe, *The Morning After: Sexual Politics at the End of the Cold War* (Berkeley: University of California Press, 1993).

Enloe examines international relations and gender issues by looking at the connections between militarism and masculinity. She grounds her ideas in the everyday experiences of women worldwide.

Arturo Escobar, *Encountering Development: The Making and Unmaking of the Third World* (Princeton, NJ: Princeton University Press, 1995).

In his examination of global inequality, Escobar focuses on the many perspectives on Third World development. He argues primarily that powerful nations wish to maintain their dominance over the Third World, not aid it.

Franklin L. Ford, *Political Murder: From Tyrannicide to Terrorism* (Cambridge, MA: Harvard University Press, 1985).

This is a thorough historical analysis of the use of political murder. Ford focuses on 155 specific murders to discern the larger pattern.

Edward S. Herman and Noam Chomsky, *Manufacturing Consent: The Political Economy of the Mass Media*, new edn (New York: Pantheon Books, 2002).

This now-classic text describes the government's use of the media in constructing the apparent consent of the population. Using examples of wars in the Americas, the authors question journalistic integrity as well.

Recommended Web Sites

United Nations

www.un.org

The purposes of the United Nations are to maintain international peace and security; to develop friendly relations among nations; to cooperate in solving international economic, social, cultural, and humanitarian problems and in promoting respect for human rights and fundamental freedoms; and to be a centre for harmonizing the actions of nations in attaining these ends.

Canadian War Museum

www.warmuseum.ca

The Canadian War Museum's Web site represents a living memorial to those men and women who served in Canada's armed forces. It is also a resource base for research and the dissemination of information and expertise on all aspects of the country's military past, from the pre-Contact era to the present. It preserves artifacts of the Canadian military experience and advances Canadian military history.

International Policy Institute for Counter-Terrorism (ICT)

www.ict.org.il

The ICT is a research institute and think tank dedicated to developing innovative public-policy solutions to international terrorism. The ICT applies an integrated, solutions-oriented approach built on a foundation of real-world experience. It provides information, seeks to raise awareness, advises decision makers, and continues to develop research on the issue of counter-terrorism.

References

Ahmad, Aqueil. 2002. 'Terrorism in the Global Society: A Sociologically Neglected Domain?' Paper presented at the annual meeting of the Southern Sociological Society.

Amnesty International. 1995. *Human Rights Are Women's Right*. New York: Amnesty International USA.

Baddoura, C. 1990. 'Mental Health and War in Lebanon'. *Bulletin de l'Academie nationale de medecine*, 174: 583–90.

Badey, Thomas J. 2002. 'The Role of Religion in International Terrorism'. *Sociological Focus*, 35, no. 1: 81–6.

Barber, Benjamin. 1996. *Jihad vs. McWorld*. New York: Times Books.

Benhabib, Seyla. 2002. 'Unholy Wars'. *Constellations*, 9, no. 1: 34–45.

Blackburn, Robin. 2002. 'The Imperial Presidency, the War on Terrorism, and the Revolutions of Modernity'. *Constellations*, 9, no. 1: 3–33.

Boggs, Carl. 2002. 'Overview: Globalization and the New Militarism'. *New Political Science*, 24, no. 1: 9–20.

Brown, Lester R., Christopher Flavin, and Hal Kane. 1992. *Vital Signs 1992: The Trends That Are Shaping Our Future*. Washington, DC: Worldwatch Institute.

Calhoun, Martin L. 1996. 'Cleaning Up the Military's Toxic Legacy'. *USA Today Magazine*, 124: 60–4.

Campbell, D'Ann. 1990. 'Servicewomen of World War II'. *Armed Forces and Society*, 16: 251–70.

Cancian, Francesca M., and James William Gibson. 1990. *Making War, Making Peace: The Social Foundations of Violent Conflict*. Belmont, CA: Wadsworth.

Clough, Patricia Ticineto. 2002. 'Posts Post September 11'. *Cultural Studies—Critical Methodologies*, 2, no. 1: 15–17.

Coupland, Robin M., and David R. Meddings. 1999. 'Mortality Associated with Use of Weapons in Armed Conflicts, Wartime Atrocities, and Civilian Mass Shootings: Literature Review'. *British Medical Journal*, 319: 407–10.

Desivilya, Helena Syna, Reuven Gal, and Ofra Ayalon. 1996. 'Long-term Effects of Trauma in Adolescence: Comparison Between Survivors of a Terrorist Attack and Control Counterparts'. *Anxiety, Stress and Coping*, 9, no. 2: 135–50.

Durkheim, Émile. [1893] 1960. *The Division of Labor in Society*. Glencoe, IL: Free Press.

Eisenstein, Hester. 2002. 'Globalization and the Events of September 11, 2001'. *Socialism and Democracy*, 16, no. 1: 131–6.

Elbaum, Max, and Bob Wing. 2002. 'Some Strategic Implications of September 11'. *Socialism and Democracy*, 16, no. 1: 161–4.

Elder, G.H., Jr, M.J. Shanahan, and E.C. Clipp. 1997. 'Linking Combat and Physical Health: The Legacy of World War II in Men's Lives'. *American Journal of Psychiatry*, 154: 330–6.

Enloe, Cynthia H. 1987. 'Feminists Thinking About War, Militarism, and Peace'. In *Analyzing Gender: A Handbook of Social Science Research*, edited by Beth Hess and Myra Marx Ferree, 526–47. Newbury Park, CA: Sage.

Erickson, Bonnie H. 1981. 'Secret Societies and Social Structure'. *Social Forces*, 60, no. 1: 188–210.

Friedman, George, and Meredith Friedman. 1996. *The Future of War: Power, Technology, and American World Dominance in the 21st Century*. New York: Crown.

Girvan, Susan, ed. 2000. *Canadian Global Almanac 2000*. Toronto: Macmillan Canada.

Harper, Charles L., and Kevin T. Leicht. 2002. *Exploring Social Change: America and the World*. 4th edn. Upper Saddle River, NJ: Prentice Hall.

Held, David. 2002. 'Violence, Law, and Justice in a Global Age'. *Constellations*, 9, no. 1: 74–88.

Hemingway, Ernest. 1926. *The Sun Also Rises*. New York: Simon and Schuster.

Hobsbawm, Eric. 1994. *The Age of Extremes: The Short Twentieth Century 1914–1991*. London: Abacus.

Hudson, Valerie M., and Andrea Den Boer. 2002. 'A Surplus of Men, a Deficit of Peace: Security and Sex Ratios in Asia's Largest States'. *International Security*, 26, no. 4: 5–38.

Human Rights Watch. n.d. 'Stop the Use of Child Soldiers!' Available at <www.hrw.org/campaigns/crp/index.htm>, accessed 17 February 2003.

Huntington, Samuel P. 1996. *The Clash of Civilizations and the Remaking of World Order*. New York: Simon & Schuster.

Kage, Tatsuo. 2002. 'War Measures Act: Japanese Canadian Experience'. Workshop held at a meeting on Immigration and Security, Our Voices, Our Strategies: Asian Canadians Against Racism, June 7–9, University of British Columbia, Vancouver.

Lewis, Bernard. 1990. 'The Roots of Islamic Rage'. *Atlantic Monthly*, September, 47–60.

Malthus, Thomas R. [1798] 1959. *Population: The First Essay*. Ann Arbor: University of Michigan Press.

Michael, John. 2002. 'Intellectuals and the Clash of Cultures'. *Socialism and Democracy*, 16, no. 1: 137–43.

Milgram, Stanley. 1974. *Obedience to Authority*. New York: Harper and Row.

Moore, Barrington. 1967. *Social Origins of Dictatorship and Democracy: Lord and Peasant in the Making of the Modern World*. Boston: Beacon Press.

National Gulf War Resource Center. 2001. '1999 Gulf War Statistics'. Available at <www.ngwrc.org/Facts/index.htm>, accessed 31 July 2001.

Peterson, Jordan B. 1998. 'Individual Motivation for Group Aggression: Psychological, Mythological, and Neuropsychological Perspectives'. In *Personality and Its Transformations: Selected Readings*, edited by Jordan B. Peterson, 1–32. Montreal: P.S. Presse.

Porter, Bruce D. 1994. *War and the Rise of the State: The Military Foundations of Modern Politics*. New York: Free Press.

Rajan, S. Ravi. 2001. 'Democracy, Security, Citizenship'. *Capitalism, Nature, Socialism*, 12, no. 4: 1–2, 170–2.

Renner, Michael. 1993a. *Critical Juncture: The Future of Peacekeeping*. Washington, DC: Worldwatch Institute.

———. 1993b. 'Environmental Dimensions of Disarmament and Conversion'. In *Real Security: Converting the Defense Economy and Building Peace*, edited by Kevin J. Cassidy and Gregory A. Bischak, 88–132. Albany: State University of New York Press.

Rummel, R.J. 1992. 'Megamurders'. *Society*, 29, no. 6: 47–52.

———. 1994. 'Power, Genocide and Mass Murder'. *Journal of Peace Research*, 31: 1–10.

———. 1998. *Statistics of Democide: Genocide and Mass Murder Since 1900*. Piscatway, NJ: Transaction.

Runciman, W.G. 1967. *Relative Deprivation and Social Justice: A Study of Attitudes to Social Inequality in Twentieth-Century England*. London: Routledge & Kegan Paul.

Simon, Jeffrey D. 2001. *Terrorist Trap: America's Experience with Terrorism*. 2nd edn. Bloomington: Indiana University Press.

Snyder, Charles McCool. 1962. *Dr. Mary Walker: The Little Lady in Pants*. New York: Vantage Press.

Starr, Joyce R., and Daniel C. Stoll. 1989. *U.S. Foreign Policy on Water Resources in the Middle East*. Washington, DC: Center for Strategic and International Studies.

Stover, Eric, and Rae McGrath. 1992. 'Calling for an International Ban on a Crippling Scourge—Land Mines'. *Human Rights Watch*, 10, no. 2: 6–7.

Summerfield, Derek. 2000. 'War and Mental Health: A Brief Overview'. *British Medical Journal*, 321: 232–5.

Summerfield, Penny, and Nicole Crockett. 1992. '"You Weren't Taught That with the Welding": Lessons in Sexuality in the Second World War'. *Women's History Review*, 1: 435–54.

Tucker, Robert C. 1978. Introduction, Karl Marx and Friedrich Engels, *The Marx-Engels Reader*. New York: Norton.

United Nations. 1998. *50 Years of United Nations Peacekeeping Operations*. Available at <www.un.org/Depts/dpko/dpko/50web/2.htm>, accessed 31 January 2003.

———. 2001. *United Nations Peacekeeping Operations. (Background Note: July 2001)*. Available at <www.un.org/peace/bnote010101.pdf>, accessed 31 July 2001.

United States. Department of State. 2003. *Patterns of Global Terrorism 2002*. Available at<www.state.gov/s/ct/rls/pgtrpt/2002/> accessed 15 May 2003.

van Creveld, Martin. 1991. *The Transformation of War*. New York: Free Press.

Van der Ploeg, Henk M., and Wim C. Kleijn. 1989. 'Being Held Hostage in the Netherlands: A Study of Long-term Aftereffects'. *Journal of Traumatic Stress*, 2, no. 2: 153–69.

von Clausewitz, Carl. 1993. *On War*. Translated by Michael Howard and Peter Paret. New York: Knopf.

Wallerstein, Immanuel. 1976. *The Modern World-System: Capitalist Agriculture and the Origins of the European World-Economy in the Sixteenth Century*. New York: Academic Press.

Wallis, Victor. 2002. 'A Radical Approach to Justice for 9/11'. *Socialism and Democracy*, 16, no. 1: 156–61.

Walton, J.R., R.L. Nuttall, and E.V. Nuttall. 1997. 'The Impact of War on the Mental Health of Children: A Salvadoran Study'. *Child Abuse and Neglect*, 21: 737–49.

Weber, Max. 1946. *Max Weber: Essays in Sociology*. Translated and edited by H.H. Gerth and C.W. Mills. New York: Oxford University Press.

Witteman, Paul A. 1991. 'Lost in America'. *Time*, 11 February, 76–7.

Wrangham, Richard, and Dale Peterson. 1996. *Demonic Males: Apes and the Origins of Human Violence*. New York: Houghton Mifflin.

Wright, Quincy. 1964. *A Study of War*. Chicago: University of Chicago Press.

Yaktin, U.S., and S. Labban. 1992. 'Traumatic War: Stress and Schizophrenia'. *Journal of Psychosocial Nursing and Mental Health Services*, 30, no. 6: 29–33.

Zimbardo, Philip. 1971. *The Psychological Power and Pathology of Imprisonment*. Statement prepared for the US House of Representatives Committee on the Judiciary, Subcommittee No. 3: Hearings on Prison Reform, San Francisco, 25 October.

Glossary

Collective violence   Often organized by a group of individuals or a social movement, this type of violence is used to promote an agenda or resist an oppressive other.

Globalization   The integration of economic activities by units of private capital on a world scale. Improvements in communication technology have allowed for the proliferation of multinational corporations that organize activity on an international scale. In other words, globalization is the trend of increasing interdependence between the economies and societies of the world.

Ideology   A system of beliefs that explain how society is, or should be; any system of ideas underlying and informing political action. In a Marxist sense, ideological ideas justify and legitimate subordination of one group to another.

Imperialism   The exercise of political and economic control by one state over the territory of another, often by military means. The Third World is often the focus of imperialistic and exploitive activities, stifling its own development and concentrating its resources and labour for the profits of advanced capitalist countries.

Interpersonal violence   Violent interactions occurring between individuals, such as murders, rapes, and domestic and child abuse.

Low-intensity conflicts (LICs)   Conflicts involving smaller armies of guerrillas, terrorists, or civilians. LICs are less-organized campaigns characterized by small-arms combat, bombings, ambushes, assassinations, and massacres.

Mutually assured destruction (MAD)   The fear of destroying one's own people acts as a deterrent to acts of aggression. For example, the detonation of a nuclear warhead could clearly result in all sides being decimated and is often used as a threat rather than as a real option.

Post-traumatic stress disorder (PTSD)   A form of psychological distress produced by a traumatic experience such as crime victimization, sexual assault, or military combat. Symptoms include nervousness, sleep disturbances, disruption of concentration, anxiety, depression, irrational fear, and flashbacks triggered by loud noises like thunder or even a car's backfiring.

Relative deprivation theory   The feelings felt and the judgments reached when an individual or members of a group compare themselves to others more well off. It is not absolute standards that are important in making such judgments, but the relative standards or frame of reference in terms of which people make judgments. These sentiments can be argued as brewing social movements.

Resource mobilization theory Emphasizes the critical role that material resources play in forming social movements. In this perspective, social movements are not founded on hysteria and frustration, but are based on rationality, leadership, and organization.

Social movement Any broad social alliance of people who are associated in seeking to effect or block an aspect of social change within a society. While they may be informally organized, they may in time lead to the formation of formal organizations such as political parties and labour unions. Examples of social movements include political movements, labour movements, the women's movement, ecological movements, and peace movements.

War Violent, usually armed conflict between states or people. This includes armed conflict, undeclared battles, civil conflicts, guerrilla wars, covert operations, and even terrorism. It is often argued that warfare is a culturally influenced phenomenon rather than simply biologically determined (instinctual aggressiveness). This would explain why some countries and cultures are more prone to warfare.

World system theory A conception of the modern social world that views it as comprising one interlinked entity with an international division of labour unregulated by any one political structure. Developed by Immanuel Wallerstein (e.g., 1976), this theory attempts explains the uneven pace of development in the world by looking at the unequal relations between different countries.

Chapter 12

Social Problems in the Future

Chapter Objectives

After reading this chapter the student should understand:
- what 'futures studies' are
- the contributions made by the first systematic futurist, Thomas Malthus
- what past theorists have predicted for our future
- the changing definition of social problems over time
- the trends in social problems that may continue into the future
- the controversy surrounding genetic manipulation
- implications of and the future of cyberspace
- both positive and negative effects of globalization
- the sociology surrounding the rumour
- how contagion leads to the stigmatization and marginalization of some groups

Introduction

This chapter is about predictions and trends, sociology and futures studies, the links between past and future, and how people viewed the future in the past. In this chapter, we wonder what the future will bring. Methodically studying and predicting the future has important practical value. As we shall see, **futures studies** help us think about the future more clearly. Futures researchers track technical innovations, value shifts, geopolitical trends, economic developments, demographic patterns, and other changes. Using these data, they consider possible alternative futures, then use them as part of strategic planning initiatives.

In this chapter, we will examine the ways in which people today think about the future and how people thought about the future in the past. If we are going to think about the future in useful ways, we need to avoid the mistakes people made in the past—today we know the mistakes they made in thinking about the future. If we can avoid their mistakes, we can make better

predictions. By making better predictions, we can prepare better for the future.

This is not to say that we can hope to predict the future perfectly. The bad predictions of the past suggest that we cannot. Moreover, we cannot even hope to prepare perfectly, no matter how good our predictions may be. However, where social organization is concerned, preparing is always better than being taken by surprise. Today, in working to build a better society, we can take advantage of the methods devised by the field of futures studies, which urges us to imagine desired futures and then work toward them.

As we shall see, some social problems of the past will likely persist and new problems will emerge in the future. A future without problems is inconceivable, if only because we humans continue to construct new problems as we go along. A few likely types of problems come to mind fairly rapidly. Like much else in the past hundred years, the problems of the future will probably involve science and technology, travel and communication, war and inter-group conflict. Since we will likely continue to live in a global society, humanity's problems will be (increasingly) global in scope. Though we are an increasingly healthy species, concerns about health will continue to grow. Medical technology will continue to improve, but new illnesses will continue to develop.

Most important, since we are increasingly reliant on information and technology, our problems will be increasingly concerned with information flow, the abuse of technology, and the misfunctioning of technology. **Cyberspace**—the notional location of most of our information in the future—will be the source of new social problems, especially problems of social control and misinformation. **Rumours** and **contagion**, especially where they spread troublesome misinformation, will pose critical problems—even (possibly) creating problems of war and panic.

We end this chapter with a call for modest optimism about the future of humanity and the future of social problems. Like hamsters on treadmills, we might continue to move ahead in absolute terms. However, we will stay more or less where we are in relative terms, since our expectations will rise with our abilities to meet them. Our ability to solve social problems—to improve society in absolute terms—will require better social science. This, in turn, will require a reassessment of what we think sociology can do and of how it should do it. The chapter ends with a call for better measurements of basic social processes.

Past Futures

The future is always before us yet always a day away from being the past. Think how much the world has changed in the last half-century. As we moved out of the shadow of possible all-out nuclear war with the Soviet enemy in the 1950s and 1960s, national concern over military conflict declined. Then people worried increasingly about domestic concerns such as the economy and unemployment, health and aging, and the environment. There has been no 'peace dividend' as far as worrying is concerned. We continue to

imagine, find, and create new social problems.

With better science comes better prediction. As time has progressed and we came nearer to the target, predictions about life in the year 2000 became more accurate. Interestingly, however, the first and most powerful piece of future forecasting was carried out over two centuries ago. The first systematic futurist was Thomas Malthus ([1798] 1959), discussed in chapter 10 on population. His predictions about overpopulation have turned out to be mainly wrong, at least as they apply to the developed world. Malthus failed to foresee the degree to which humans were able to improve food production and limit their birth rates. However, overpopulation, starvation in the developing world, and the depletion of natural resources continue to be serious social problems today. So Malthus was not entirely off base.

Some thinkers in the past imagined something like the current **Information Age**, in which data is available almost immediately over the Internet. Still, many predictions made by futures researchers even as recently as the mid-twentieth century have proven stunningly wrong. These misfires draw attention to an important lesson about futures studies: radical, unpredictable changes in human progress can and will occur. Entire generations of futures forecasters will suddenly look absurd for their lack of insight and moderation.

Having said that, we can venture a few guesses without too much risk. In the future, as society adjusts to the increased role of women in the workforce (see Table 12.1) and to changes in family life, many of today's problems with work and family will likely diminish. However, some things are less likely to change drastically. For example, economic inequality will not disappear. Ethnic and regional differences in thinking will not disappear. Religion itself will not disappear. These are all too firmly rooted in social organization. Put another way, there have never been large or 'complex' societies without these features, so we have no reason to think that there will be in the future.

TABLE 12.1
Median Age at Life Course Events and Years Spent in Life States, Canada, by Birth Cohort

	1841–50	1931–40	1951–60
Median age at event			
1st marriage	26.0	21.1	22.5
1st birth	28.0	22.9	24.5
Last birth	40.0	29.1	26.3
'Empty nest'	60.1	49.1	46.3
Widowhood	59.5	67.2	69.9
Death	64.3	79.4	82.2
Median years spent			
Raising children	32.1	26.2	21.8
Married with no child at home	0	18.1	23.6
In widowhood	4.8	12.2	12.3

SOURCE: Ellen M. Gee, 'The Life Course of Canadian Women: An Historical and Demographic Analysis', *Social Indicators Research*, 18 (1986), Table VI, p. 273 (abridged).

The single biggest influence on societies to emerge in recent years has been the invention of computers. Hundreds of millions of personal computers are in use around the world today. Other important developments have occurred in genetic technology. Never before have humans been able to control the future of their species as much as we can now. Finally, consider the process of **globalization**, discussed in the previous chapter. Globalization seems likely to shrink the world and bring people ever closer together. The future economic and social consequences of this trend are vast and complex.

Thinking About the Future

A recurring theme in this book has been the interconnectedness of social problems. None of the social problems we have discussed stands alone; each is related to other problems. And as we have shown, all have health consequences. What this complexity suggests, in part, is that a change in one area of social life will affect other areas. Another important aspect of the social problems we have discussed is their historical basis. Most problems today are the result of long-standing neglect and simmering conflict.

Consider as an example the current problem of conflictual relations between Quebec and the other provinces in Canada. We can trace this particular conflict back to the early history of relations between the French and English in Canada, three centuries ago. Or consider the problem of race relations between blacks and whites in the United States, which we can trace back 400 years to that country's practice of slavery. Even today, echoes of these earlier periods in Canadian and US history are heard in the relationships between ethnic and racial groups in the two countries. These examples clearly suggest, as do many other social problems, that effective solutions to social problems will often be slow in coming.

At the same time, social problems are dynamic and changeable. For example, as we saw in chapter 2 on alcohol and drug abuse, what people consider an unlawful substance, whose use is therefore a social problem, can shift markedly over time. Cocaine and opium were once considered legitimate medicinal and recreational drugs but now are strictly banned by the criminal justice system. Public officials deemed marijuana use legal, then illegal; today we have tight limits on legal access to marijuana for strictly therapeutic purposes and the prospect of the effective decriminalization of marijuana use. Not all social problems have a long history, however. On the contrary, people are, for various reasons, always creating or constructing new problems.

The dynamic nature of social problems—a result of their relationship with one another and with the past—poses difficulties not only for people actively working to improve social conditions, but also for researchers trying to foresee the social problems of the future. And, as we shall see later in this chapter, the organization of sociological research also makes precise forecasting unlikely if not impossible, though there are ways we can improve that situation. Our goal in thinking about the future is not strictly speaking to foresee the future (this is impossible) but to map out alternative futures. This, ultimately, is what futures studies are about.

What Is Futures Studies?

'Human futures are unpredictable and it is futile to think that past trends will forecast coming patterns' (Gould, 1999: 145). The only exception to this general rule may be that 'technology might offer some opportunity for predicting the future—as science moves through networks of implication, and each discovery suggests a set of subsequent steps. From these data they create scenarios of possible alternative futures, which are then used as contingencies within strategic planning initiatives' ('What Is Future Studies?' 2001). So writes one anonymous futures researcher.

To claim an ability to accurately predict the details of the future would be rash. Nevertheless, it is both practical and possible to make reasonable guesses about the world of tomorrow, for two reasons. The first is that anticipating future events allows people today to prepare better for events in the future. As the global panic (which, fortunately, proved unwarranted) induced by the threat of the Y2K computer bug has shown, a lack of preparation can have strong economic and social consequences. Second, the decisions we make today can shape and alter the future. Defining the world we want can help us to actively work toward it. Occasionally we are successful in that effort.

Wendell Bell, one of the leaders of this field in social research, notes four key assumptions made in futures studies: (1) 'time is continuous, linear, unidirectional and irreversible. Events occur in time before or after other events and the continuum of time defines the past, present and future' (1997: 140); (2) 'not everything that will exist has existed or does exist' (141), meaning that the future will bring novel events, processes, and structures that have no precedent in history; (3) 'futures thinking is essential for human action' (142), referring to the fact that all significant human actions require anticipation and an awareness of a future goal; and (4) 'in making our way in the world, both individually and collectively, the most useful knowledge is "knowledge of the future"' (143–4).

With these assumptions in mind, we will consider some plausible scenarios for the future. Looking back on past efforts to imagine the future is a chastening but invigorating experience.

What Past Experts Predicted About the Future

History has recorded many instances in which highly regarded thinkers made wildly inaccurate guesses about the progress of human society. The Roman engineer Sextus Julius Frontinus, for example, confidently declared in the late first century that 'inventions have long since reached their limit, and I see no hope for further development'. Nor is this form of thinking limited to the pre-modern era. In 1899, Charles Duell, the commissioner of the US Patent Office, seriously considered closing down the Office to save the government money, reasoning, 'everything that can be invented has been invented' (Wilson, 2000: 21).

Any discussion of systematic futures research in the modern sense must start with the work of Thomas Malthus ([1798] 1959). Malthus foresaw population problems in the future based on the premise that populations grow exponentially while food supplies grow additively (see the discussion in chapter 10). He pointed out that any exponential series, however slowly it grows, sooner or later overtakes any arithmetic series, however quickly it grows. Malthus did not anticipate the current dwindling and even negative birth rates in industrialized nations. However, as Malthus predicted, world population, starvation in the developing world, and the depletion of natural resources have become serious problems.

Malthus was not the only thinker to make accurate guesses about the future. In 1888, newspaper columnist David Goodman Croly predicted with remarkable insight that by 2000, 'women throughout the world will enjoy increased opportunities and privileges. Along with this new freedom will come social tolerance of sexual conduct formerly condoned only in men. In addition, because of the availability of jobs, more women will choose not to have children' (cited in Margolis, 2000: 35).

Similarly a British *Daily Mail* writer accurately prophesied in 1928 that by century's end, the prime minister would be female, women would wear trousers and act as power-brokers, the average life expectancy would be 75, and home cooking would be accomplished by a machine that, as described in the late 1920s, sounded much like the modern microwave oven (Margolis, 2000).

Other early writers predicted that by the twenty-first century, 'the U.S. population will have risen to about 330 million [the actual figure is currently around 285 million], and nine out of ten Americans will be living in supercities or their suburbs'. With respect to communications technology,

they wrote, 'cities, like industry, will tend to decentralize; with instant communications, it will no longer be necessary for business enterprises to cluster together' ('The Futurists', 1966: 42). Futurists also anticipated the current Information Age, in which data are available almost immediately over the Internet: 'One thing that they almost all will want is electronic information retrieval: the contents of libraries and other forms of information or education will be stored in a computer and will be instantly obtainable at home by dialing a code' ('The Futurists', 1966: 33).

Still, even as late as the mid-twentieth century, many futures researchers made predictions that were wildly off target. In the 1960s, futures researchers imagined that work would be almost non-existent by the year 2000. They even believed that people at the turn of the millennium would have so much leisure time at their disposal and the need for workers would be so small that people would have to be paid not to work. The logic was simple and, at the time, compelling. Only 40 per cent of the US population worked outside the home in the 1960s. Expecting that figure to decline further as automation increased and production processes became more efficient seemed logical.

Researchers then expected that Americans would nearly eliminate poverty and class inequality by the twenty-first century, and that everyone would live in modest financial comfort. In large part, they relied on technological innovations to bring about such radical social change: with machines fully developed, there would not be enough work to go around for humans. 'Moonlighting will become as socially unacceptable as bigamy', they wrote ('The Futurists', 1966: 33). People would solve the problems of a growing world population, too, through the magic of technology.

Faith in technology has been a staple of the modern world for at least two centuries. Regarding Third World famines, some futurists imagined the following solution: 'Huge fields of kelp and other kinds of seaweed will be tended by undersea "farmers". Frogmen who will live for months at a time in submerged bunkhouses. The protein-rich undersea crop will probably be ground up to produce a dull-tasting cereal that eventually, however, could be regenerated chemically to taste like anything from steak to bourbon' ('The Futurists', 1966: 32). In home economics, an 1950 illustration in *Popular Mechanics* predicted that the 'housewife of 2000' would 'happily be doing her daily housecleaning with a garden hose, since everything would now be made of plastic' (Wilson, 2000: 236). Not only did this picture overestimate a love of polymer furniture at the turn of a new century, it also importantly failed to anticipate the vast changes in views about 'women's work'.

One researcher in the past even predicted that a giant nuclear power station built on Mount Wilson, overlooking Los Angeles, could probably heat the surrounding air and raise it, along with the infamous LA smog layer, safely into the upper stratosphere, while at the same time drawing sea winds and rainfall onto the mainland to irrigate the desert and transform it into arable greenspace ('The Futurists', 1966).

One of the best, and least-known, sets of predictions was made by H.G. Wells shortly after the beginning of the twentieth century. In his book of 'anticipations' about the new century, Wells (1902) correctly predicts that much that occurs in the century would be connected with new marvels of transportation (trains, cars, and airplanes) and communication (the wireless, radio, and telephone). With speedier transportation and communication will come decentralization—for example, the growth of suburbs, long-distance shopping, and more contact over distances for business and pleasure.

It is difficult to predict new technological inventions and their likely social effects. Yet these are easier to predict than changes that are entirely unconnected to technology. Said another way, the effects of people on other people are harder to predict than the effects of machines. Generally, machines that save time or labour or that reduce

the cost of a good or service are quickly adopted by people who can afford it. In recent centuries, this has been true of electricity, telephones, automobiles, and, most recently, computers.

Harder to predict are trends in personal beliefs—in religion or politics, for example. H.G. Wells, who foresaw suburbs and air travel, could not foresee the Nazi Holocaust or the emancipation of women, for example. Without the Holocaust, there would have been no state of Israel. Without the emancipation of women, there would have been no work-family conflict. Until the Berlin Wall had fallen and the Soviet Union had imploded, people could not imagine these things happening.

Our failures to make accurate predictions teach us an important lesson about futures studies, which is that radical, unpredictable changes in human life can occur. When they do, entire generations of future forecasting suddenly look absurd for their lack of insight. While often futures researchers err on the side of wild abandon in their predictions, just as often they err on the side of timidity and lack of imagination. This was the point that Yogi Berra made so eloquently (if unintentionally) when he stated, 'The future ain't what it used to be'. As a species, we are not very good at predicting our future.

Changes in What the Public Sees as Social Problems

What people consider a serious social problem can also change over time, often in response to changes in social, political, and economic conditions. A social problems textbook from 1898, for instance, listed 'Dumping Garbage', 'Over-Production', 'Public Debts and Indirect Taxation', and 'Slavery' among its chapter headings (George, 1898). Another text, published only 18 years later, already indicated concern over some of the harmful social conditions that continue to affect the world today, including 'Unemployment', 'Crime and Punishment', 'The Liquor Problem', 'Poverty', and 'The Conservation of Natural

---

BOX 12.1
Arthur C. Clarke's Predictions for the Twenty-First Century

2002 Clean low-power fuel involving a new energy source, possibly based on cold fusion.

2003 The automobile industry is given five years to replace fossil fuels.

2004 First publicly admitted human clone.

2006 Last coal mine closed.

2009 A city in a third world country is devastated by an atomic bomb explosion.

2009 All nuclear weapons are destroyed.

2010 A new form of space-based energy is adopted.

2010 Despite protests against 'big brother', ubiquitous monitoring eliminates many forms of criminal activity.

2011 Space flights become available for the public.

2013 Prince Harry flies in space.

2015 Complete control of matter at the atomic level is achieved.

2016 All existing currencies are abolished. A universal currency is adopted based on the 'megawatt hour'.

2017 Arthur C. Clarke, on his one hundredth birthday, is a guest on the space orbiter.

2019 There is a meteorite impact on Earth causing devastation over a large area.

2020 Artificial Intelligence reaches human levels. There are now two intelligent species on Earth, one biological and one nonbiological.

2021 The first human landing on Mars is achieved. There is an unpleasant surprise.

2023 Dinosaurs are cloned from fragments of DNA. A dinosaur zoo opens in Florida.

2025 Brain research leads to an understanding of all human senses. Full-immersion virtual reality becomes available. The user puts on a metal helmet and is then able to enter 'new universes'.

2040 A universal replicator based on nanotechnology is now able to create any object from gourmet meals to diamonds. The only thing that has value is information.

2040 The concept of human 'work' is phased out.

2061 Hunter-gatherer societies are recreated.

2061 The return of Halley's comet is visited by humans.

2090 Large-scale burning of fossil fuels is resumed to replace carbon dioxide.

2095 A true 'space drive' is developed. The first humans are sent out to nearby star systems already visited by robots.

2100 History begins.

SOURCE: Raymond Kurzweil and Arthur C. Clarke, 'Arthur C. Clarke Offers His Vision of the Future' (2001), available at <www.kurzweilai.net/meme/frame.html?m=7>, accessed 24 March 2003.

Resources' (Towne, 1916). Obviously, many of these problems are still with us today.

From the time of the Russian Revolution in 1917 onward, Western capitalist societies worried about Soviet communism and the dangers of subversion and war. Soviet communists worried about Western capitalism and the dangers of subversion and war. Between 1917 and 1967, through two world wars and two minor wars (Korea and Vietnam), a global depression, and hunts for traitors in the Soviet Union (in the 1930s) and the United States (in the 1950s), people on both sides waited for the worst—all-out war—to happen. It did not happen, and as the risk of all-out nuclear war with the Russians receded, national concerns over military conflict declined. Growing domestic considerations like the economy and unemployment replaced them. North America rode a technology-driven, record-breaking boom in the marketplace through the 1990s, and at that time crime and other social issues became the main social problems in the eyes of the public.

Since the widely publicized major terrorist events of September 2001, concerns about war and subversion have surfaced again, especially in the United States. In the foreseeable future, we can expect to see high prominence given to terrorism, treason, and national security in the public mind.

Social Problems Trends Projected to the Near Future

Many predictions by today's leading futures researchers will be proven, a century down the road, to have been wrong. Others will have come close to the reality of 2100, and a few may even have hit the bull's eye.

Noted thinker Noam Chomsky is pessimistic about the prospects of futures research: 'The record of prediction in human affairs has not been inspiring, even short-range. The most plausible prediction is that any prediction about serious matters is likely to be off the mark, except by accident' (Chomsky, 1999: 30). However, the goal of futures studies is only partly to paint a picture of what life may be like for subsequent generations. Its more important task is to imagine a desirable alternative future for people to work toward, a future that is actively shaped by the decisions of people living today. With this goal in mind, let us consider the likely future of several different categories of social problems.

Problems of Family and Work

As society adjusts to the increased participation of women in the workforce and to changes in family

Over the last 40 years in particular, women have successfully moved into the workforce, but the ever-present conflict between family and work is a significant burden for many women. We will need to think more creatively about ways of resolving work-family conflicts. (Bruce Ayers/Getty Images)

structure (such as fewer children and higher rates of divorce), some specific social problems we have discussed—for example, balancing family responsibilities with career ambitions and the time constraints of mothers—may be better worked out. We will need to think more creatively about ways of resolving work-family conflicts within the context of marital arrangements that are flexible and constantly changing.

To reduce family conflict, the socialization of men and women will need to continue to change, as will the organization of workplaces. Change in the latter, in particular, may require strong political will by lawmakers to extend pay- and employment-equity legislation to cover more types of workplaces and to develop stronger sanctions against employers who treat their workers unfairly. Change of this kind, however, is complicated by an increasingly tough global market that has the tendency to drive pay and working conditions downward, leaving little room for creative workplace solutions to home problems.

Said another way, capitalists have little motivation to improve working conditions in Canada when they can move the workplace to South America or Asia and pay less for the same work. They do not do so en masse because they need consumers at home who can afford to buy their product.

Problems of Class Inequality

For a variety of reasons, it seems unlikely that social equality will be attained in the foreseeable future. Inequality is firmly entrenched in our society. As well, many of our political and ideological beliefs encourage vastly unequal economic statuses, and economic inequality (like religion, ethnicity, and regionalism) has a long history in our culture. Thus, it would seem unreasonable to work toward the elimination of all social or economic inequality. Given that such inequality exists everywhere and that outside of hunter-gatherer societies it has always existed, a war against inequality seems unlikely to succeed.

Thus, inequality and its associated problems are likely to continue for a long time to come, albeit continuously challenged and modified. As to how much inequality can be changed, the political will of governments or lawmakers to legislate change is central. The legislation of greater equality will meet strong objections from the wealthy, who make out well under the present system. However, taking our lead from futures research, work in the present *can* influence the future, and people who value equality must continue to work hard on such problems.

Problems that remain on the horizon as contributing to class inequality include the rise to power of multinational corporations and the effects of these corporations on Third World labourers. The migration of jobs from North America and Europe to Latin America, Africa, and Asia represents an improvement in the incomes of local Third World people. However, it also spreads sweatshop conditions around the world, creates global dependency on industrial capitalism, and pits Third World labourers against workers in the industrialized world.

Environmental Damage

The destruction of the environment is a growing social problem. Many scientists and theorists believe that unless changes are made today, environmental problems will become more severe and their consequences more intense in the future. Already, the world's temperature has increased, particularly in the 1990s and since. This has led to more frequent droughts and famines in the Third World, higher rates of skin cancer, and more extreme weather conditions throughout the year.

F. Sherwood Rowland, whose early warnings of the effects of CFCs on ozone depletion in 1974 earned him a Nobel Prize in chemistry, hypothesizes that

the global prevalence of smog will rise in the next century because more and more people will use cars. The twenty-first century will therefore begin with three major atmospheric problems firmly entrenched on a global basis: stratospheric ozone depletion, the greenhouse effect from increasing carbon dioxide and other trace gases with accompanying global warming and urban and regional smog. (1999: 209)

Rowland goes on to say, 'My expectation in the coming decades is that the climatic consequences from continued greenhouse gas emissions will be more and more noticeable, and much more ominous' (1999: 209–10).

Technological Haves and Have-Nots

In 1943, Thomas J. Watson, Sr, then chairman of IBM, foresaw a world market for only five computers. His underestimation of the demand for computers is understandable, given that at the time the US military was in the process of building one of the world's first computers, the ENIAC (Electronic Numerical Integrator and Computer). When completed in 1945, that computer cost nearly $500,000 (US) and weighed 30 tonnes. No one foresaw the use of semiconductors for miniaturization. Today, people carry enormously powerful computers in their briefcases or backpacks.

This change is just one dramatic demonstration that technological inventions are almost always initially inaccessible to the average person. Gradually, as demand for the new product becomes evident and production methods become cheaper and more efficient, costs decline to the point where the invention becomes widely available to most, if not all, people. Often supply comes to drive demand for the new technology. (No one 20 years ago would have imagined how much our lives would be controlled by e-mail and voice mail, for example. Yet here we are, working faster and living faster because of these new technologies and the expectation that we will use them.)

Around the world, the benefits of technological innovation are enjoyed first by the most affluent in the most affluent nations. Then, slowly, the new technology spreads to the lower social classes and the rest of the world's population. Thus, the number of personal computers being used in the world today ranges in the hundreds of millions, yet people in poorer societies have few computers per capita. The most advanced machines continue to be available to only a small percentage of privileged buyers.

With computers as with other technologies in the past, those in power steer the spread of technologies in ways that will further improve the quality of their own lives and the lives of others in the privileged social classes. Significant funding is directed at research and development for the latest in technical gadgetry, while technological solutions for poverty and homelessness (for example, affordable housing) remain largely unexplored. As technological development continues, the **digital divide** between the technological haves and have-nots continues to widen. (See Table 12.2.)

One application of technology that will likely gain popularity in the future is the use of **cyberterrorism** and cyberwarfare, particularly by rogue nations and militant groups lacking the military firepower to threaten their adversaries on a traditional battlefield. Specific tactics may include hacking or electronically jamming the enemy's computer and communications systems; using electromagnetic-pulse weaponry to destroy electronic devices; and infecting computer equipment with viruses (World Future Society, 2001).

Genetic Manipulation

Some predictions about the future of humanity hinge on the use of **genetic manipulation** to improve the quality of human life. Already, scientists have mapped out the human genome, the DNA material that contains the genetic instructions that determine hair, eye, and skin colour, height, physical build, predisposition to various diseases, and, possibly, basic personality or temperament.

TABLE 12.2

Internet Use by Household Income, Canada, 1997–2001
(Percentage of Households)

	1997	1998	1999	2000	2001
All households	29.0	35.9	41.8	51.3	60.2
Lowest quartile ($23,000 or less)	12.2	13.1	18.8	23.9	31.6
Second quartile ($23,001 to $39,999)	18.0	23.8	29.2	42.8	51.8
Third quartile ($40,000 to $69,999)	32.3	41.6	48.1	60.6	70.1
Highest quartile ($70,000 and more)	53.5	65.0	71.2	77.9	87.3

SOURCE: Statistics Canada, 'Internet Use Rates, by Location of Access and Household Income' (Cat. no. 56F0004MIE). Available at <www.statcan.ca/english/Pgdb/arts56a.htm>, accessed 2 February 2003.

Many ethicists and researchers are worried about human cloning and the use of embryos made expressly for research purposes. The dominant concern is that without adequate government and institutional guidelines for ethical behaviour in genetic research, humanity risks abusing the new technology in as-yet-unforeseen ways. This concern is justified: over the past century, every powerful technology has been used at one time or another to dominate, terrorize, or obliterate political enemies.

Never before have humans been able to control the future of their species to such a degree. This is a social problem because the manipulation of a person's genetic code not only changes how that individual develops, but can also potentially alter the human gene pool permanently for future generations. So decisions that people make today about the application of genetic research to the general population can have unforeseen effects on future members of the human population. The consequences could extend to the ways in which parents control the sex and racial characteristics of their unborn children, or how genetically altered individuals interact with non-genetically altered people. Health issues may include redefinitions of illness and disability to take into account such characteristics as height, body type, skin colour, and clarity of vision.

Families, Communities, and Governments

As we saw in an earlier chapter, families can be defined in a variety of ways: narrowly, as in the nuclear family (husband, wife, and young children), or broadly, as in the extended family, which includes everyone related by blood, marriage, or adoption. By *family*, we can mean people of common ancestry, those living under one roof, or those having common characteristics or properties.

As sociologist Neena Chappell (2002) points out in a revealing analysis, the essential features of families—their nurturing and supportive roles as well as their socialization functions for the next generation—have remained intact into the twenty-first century and are likely to do so in the foreseeable future. Families remain a basic social institution of society, providing emotional support, identity confirmation, and socialization. In fact, the core family functions have become even more important given recent changes that have tended to reduce the role of government in the economy. New family forms are evolving to permit the continuation of these essential roles under new circumstances.

Even in our individualistic and materialistic Western society, family members care for one another. For example, roughly 75 per cent of the care provided to elderly people in industrialized Western societies comes through informal networks, primarily from family members: spouses

BOX 12.2
Internet Access

Internet use from home took another big jump in 2001, but the rate of growth is easing off, according to the Household Internet Use Survey (HIUS). . . .

Rates of Internet use still varied substantially across family types, and the key factor was the presence of children. Single-family households with unmarried children under the age of 18 had the highest rate of Internet use from any location last year, about 80 per cent. This proportion was double the level of 38 per cent in 1997.

In contrast, about 56 per cent of single-family households in which there were no children used the Internet, up from 27 per cent in 1997.

Regular Internet use increased for all income groups, and the gains during the past five years have been substantial. In 2001, 87 per cent of the one-quarter of households in the highest income bracket used the Internet from one location or another, up from 58 per cent in 1997.

In contrast, only 32 per cent of the one-quarter of households with the lowest income level regularly used the Internet in 2001. Still, this was almost triple the rate of 12 per cent in 1997.

SOURCE: Statistics Canada, 'Household Internet Use Survey', *The Daily*, 25 July 2002. Available at <www.statcan.ca/Daily/English/020725/d020725a.htm>, accessed 2 February 2003.

and children—especially wives and daughters. Despite trends that work against family support—increased proportions of women working for pay, smaller families, increased divorce and remarriage rates, geographical mobility—families overwhelmingly continue to provide care to their members.

To accomplish this, family caregivers give up their own leisure time and sometimes sacrifice jobs and careers. There is no evidence that shows that families are moving away from providing this care. Indeed, societal changes such as globalization and neo-liberalism have strengthened the traditional role of the family. Families continue to offer a refuge from the demands of work life, particularly families facing a variety of difficult economic and political circumstances.

Advanced technology extends the options individuals and families have for becoming involved with one another in spite of distances. While a segment of society now has families and communities at tremendous geographical dis-

tances—we discussed this in chapter 4 in relation to diasporas—many others live their entire lives within narrow geographical confines. The family can become more important in this environment, as a haven from the harsh world.

Globalization makes it possible to help more people, but it also increases the danger that an inequality between citizens will grow. We saw this problem in relation to the digital divide: where computers are concerned, the haves and the have-nots are gaining social and economic benefits at increasingly different rates. More government involvement is needed to ensure strong human and social capital for all Canadians. One critical issue facing governments is how to fight vested interests and create policies that are in the interests of *all* citizens. However, money alone will not be enough; governments need to provide imagination and organization as well. The Commission on the Future of Health Care in Canada (2002)—the Romanow Commission—for example, showed that the health care system requires reorganization, coordination, and a redistribution of funds, not more dollars per se.

Governments also have a role in both national and individual identities, especially during a period of globalization when there is concern that nations' identities become diluted and individual lives become determined by global forces outside of their own and their country's control.

With globalization and the spread of American media, Canadian cultural values and attitudes may be less different from American values and attitudes than they used to be. This need not be interpreted as an Americanization of Canadians. Nonetheless, Canadian culture has always been at risk because of the proximity and the relative size, wealth, and power of our neighbour to the south. A major challenge for Canadian governments is ensuring authentic public participation in order to increase the likelihood that Canadian values will be heard and represented. Ways must be found to capitalize on citizens' increased political skills. To ensure particularly identifying Canadian institutions, such as universal health care, governments must find new ways of working with citizens who are substantially different than in the past.

The Problem of Aging

One thing that can be predicted with reasonable certainty is the continued aging of human populations. Even today there is concern about how a shrinking base of workers will be able to support the growing elderly population in Canada. With aging, the population distribution takes on the shape of an inverted pyramid and the ratio of dependent elderly people to working-age people increases. As we discussed in chapter 8, this aging is the result of continued reductions in fertility and, secondarily, of increased longevity. Whether the younger generations can continue to support an aging population and whether the health care system can cope with demands for better care for everyone remain to be seen.

How society deals with the aging population will determine the future social problems that will be associated with it. Several possibilities present themselves. First, the childbearing population could be encouraged to increase the number of children they produce. This policy would be unlikely to have much effect given continuing declines over the past century, as well as social values (such as individualism) and opportunities (such as urban careers) that work against large family sizes. Second, Canada's immigration laws could be loosened to allow more young immigrants from countries with high fertility. Such a policy, however, would not be likely to win support from Canadians currently in the workforce, who would see it as increasing competition for jobs. Third, a larger fraction of the national budget could be invested in health care. This policy would require either higher taxes (which are unpopular) or reduced spending in other areas, such as education (also unpopular and, in the long run, harmful to the nation's productivity).

Fourth, new ways to raise money might be found—for example, by selling land or water to the United States. However, this policy only works for a short time, as you can sell your inheritance only once. Fifth, through ingenuity or sheer good luck, wonderful new drugs or technologies might be invented; patents for their use would provide long-term wealth to support health care. However, this is not as much a policy as it is a wish. We cannot rely on good fortune. So in the end, it may be necessary for people to lower their health care expectations or pay more of the cost of their own care. This may require the elimination of mandatory retirement so that elderly people can earn enough for their own health care. Governments, for their part, may have to reject demands for further health care improvement out of public funds.

The Uses and Misuses of Information

Of all the changes that will bear on the future of societies, and on the future of social problems, none is likely to have more impact than cyberspace and the information that resides there. In that sense, in shaping social problems of the twenty-first century, nothing will be more real in its effect than virtual reality. This is because in an **information economy** such as ours, information is a major source of wealth and power, and more and more information is coming to reside in cyberspace. (See Figure 12.1 on the scale of the information technology industry in Canada.)

The Rise of Cyberspace

We are now living in what some have called the Information Age. As a species, we have more information about more ideas than at any other time in history. We use this information and exchange it. Information is a commodity, to be bought and sold. Five centuries ago, scholars could decide what was the appropriate body of knowledge within any literate society, be that society Chinese, Western European, or another. It was still possible for someone to imagine becoming an expert—a knowledgeable person—in everything. (People have thought

of the Renaissance scholar Erasmus in these terms, and some would speak of Leonardo da Vinci the same way.) Even 50 years ago, scholars could still distinguish the boundaries of knowledge—what was known and knowable from what was not.

However, today the demarcated body of knowledge is far beyond the reach of a single person, so that we require detailed specialization even within fields (for example, within chemistry, anthropology, or literature). This idea of the demarcated body of knowledge—of what educated people should know—has also been produced by technology of the day, as has the question of 'knowledge ownership'.

Until the invention of the printing press, people did not have an idea of authorship in the modern sense. In Europe, monks spent lifetimes copying ancient manuscripts (many deemed to be the word of God). However, most knowledge or information—information about growing crops, doing blacksmith work, weaving, or any of the other activities that were part of everyday life—was transmitted orally from person to person. The

FIGURE 12.1
Information and Communications Technologies (ICT) Sector Employment Growth, Canada 1995–2000

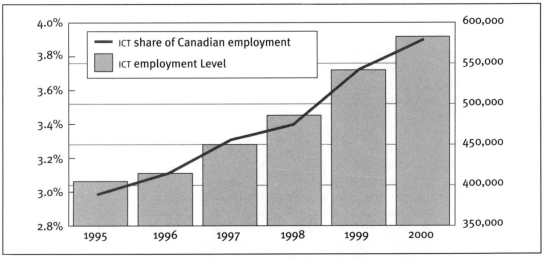

SOURCE: Statistics Canada, *Information and Communications Technology Industry* (Ottawa: Statistics Canada, 2002), available at <www.innovationstrategy.gc.ca/cmb/innovation.nsf/SectoralE/ICTech>, accessed 8 March 2003.

printing press changed this by making possible the rapid copying of what had previously taken months or years. Knowledge was now a thing that people could distribute among strangers, and printers sought material to print. Still, the idea of authorship took several centuries before it gained its modern form (Eisenstein 1979; Rose 1993). With the notion of authorship, or of the ownership of knowledge, came ideas about standards for knowledge. Eventually the standard, in the popular mind, became what was printed.

The ownership of knowledge is important, both for its own sake and for its market value. Increasingly, technology has made the borrowing, stealing, sampling, and reproduction of knowledge possible for everyone, through computers, scanners, photocopiers, fax machines, and, of course, printing presses. The Internet further affects this relationship between consumers, producers, and knowledge, changing the whole way we view information and changing the relations of its production.

Business use of the new technology permits a shift in the location of 'work' to 'home' and allows companies to further spread their functions among many locations, whether these are towns, regions, or countries. The new electronic marketplace is made up of people who have probably never physically met each other but who share beliefs and ideologies, give mutual support, and exchange ideas regularly. The result is a creation of worldwide virtual communities—communities of interest and shared viewpoints that are unhampered by distance or by many social factors (age, race, gender, class) that often keep otherwise similar people from meeting or interacting with one another.

The Internet, unlike other information media, is not centralized and not restricted: anyone who can gain access to a computer and modem can participate. Community nets (or 'freenets') are developing in many towns and cities, often with terminals installed in public libraries, to give access to those who do not have computers at home or work. Pages for specialized groupings—women, African Canadians, bikers, and so on—are rapidly

increasing in number. However, centralization, censorship, and monitoring of the Internet—always possibilities on the horizon—may hinder both access and the spread of ideas among 'alternative' groups and communities. Without vigilance by users, the Internet could go from being an anarchic network of information providers and communicators to a means of surveillance.

The Social Organization of Cyberspace

Not only does the Internet ease information sharing, commerce, and social support, it also allows people to create and try out new identities. The capacity to generate real or virtual identities, in turn, is an essential aspect of postmodern relationships.

The virtual community, mediated by computers and populated by real and constructed identities, provides cybersurfers with a new sense of community. In virtual associations, people may have multiple selves but they share a common goal and common identity. New technologies enable more fluid changes in language use that are largely free of indicators (for example, age, sex, or physical appearance) that limit self-expression. For example, women can experience ungendered interaction for the first time. In turn, this means people in cyberspace can create new social and sexual relationships.

For example, people online can switch genders and, in this way, can disrupt previously held beliefs about gender. Bodily attributes, such as sex or physical attractiveness, are simply irrelevant in cyberspace—at least in principle.

Cyberspace has the potential to blur the distinction between reality and fantasy. However, strange to say, people in cyberspace often behave just the same as ever. For example, many Internet communicators still behave in traditionally gendered and even sexist manners when they have information about the gender of the people with whom they are interacting. Likewise, the 'sexpics' trade over IRC (Internet relay chat) links provides sexual acts and identities that are conventional compared to offline heterosexual norms and (pornographic) representations.

Beyond that, people in cyberspace are just as immature and unkind as they are in real life. Internet relationships are characterized by an increased control of self-information (that is, impression management), short-term and easily forgotten relations, illusions of omnipotence, and avoidance of responsibility and commitment (Gerlander and Takala, 1997).

The ability to depict oneself in a variety of identities and personalities creates a 'zone of confusion' between reality and common-sense notions of the imaginary. There is a danger the Internet promotes emotionally disconnected or superficially erotic contacts. Although anonymity in Internet communication can encourage the development of meaningful personal relationships and allow less powerful users to challenge authority figures, such anonymity also allows malicious communicators to depersonalize others for amusement, and more powerful users to distance themselves from responsibility.

Participants online may experience ambivalent feelings about self-presentation. On the one hand, they may wish for involvement and for a presentation of real, not merely realistic, selves. On the other hand, they may fear self-revelation and lack an ability to trust those whom they contact. The exercise of social control is almost impossible in cyberspace. As a result, online communities develop with more free riders, and problems arise in establishing boundaries and defining membership. Conflicts develop between competing communities, and even among members of the same community. Internet technology, some believe, is resulting in decreased human interaction and community cohesion.

At the same time, the growing influence of cyberspace has resulted in increased power for large corporations and larger power disparities between races, classes, and gender. Commercial, military, and professional contexts are driving virtual technology toward better uses in entertainment and military training. However, few benefits are being seen for the majority of ordinary people. Concentration and commercialization undermine the democratic potential of new communications systems. And outside the Internet, life goes on as it did before. A politics of digital inequality is now surfacing, and questions are arising about the basic conditions of access, capability, and distribution in cyberspace.

At first, the creation of the Internet led to utopian fantasies of citizen empowerment and the revitalization of democracy. Some observers call it the 'Californian ideology'—the belief that the use of new information technologies will create a new democracy that allows everyone free expression in cyberspace. However, dominant economic, social, and political forces in society are struggling, with some success, to capture and regulate the Net. Virtual reality has come to resemble the real world; ordinary, everyday politics have captured cyberspace. Today, every variety of human is found in cyberspace, flogging every type of idea and product. Humanity is no better than before, just more virtual.

The new forms of virtual community, and the technological and cultural resources required for participation in them, are likely to create new forms of stratification and, therefore, barriers to universal access. Given society's social and racial polarization, only some people have access to the new technologies. A reliance on unregulated market forces will create social distance between the 'information rich' and the 'information poor'. Global inequalities of access to information technology mean an increase of Third World disadvantage, reinforcing existing power structures. They must address concerns of territorial sovereignty, unequal access, and guarantees of privacy and security.

What sort of interaction occurs now, and will occur in cyberspace in the future? What kinds of social classes exist there? What sociological ideas should be used to explain this phenomenon? We can probably apply existing knowledge to understand what is going on. Imagine cyberspace as a new frontier in which strangers exchange information and practise impression management on one another in a context rooted in three ways. First, the strangers are themselves the members and products of certain genders, classes, races, and childhood experiences. Second, their interactions are all rooted in a particular historical moment. Whatever they may fantasize, the interactants live at a particular time and place that offers particular opportunities and constraints.

Third, and more specifically, the interests, goals, and technologies of large organizations—chiefly, states and private enterprises—bound their interactions. These organizations have no interest in supporting the creation of a mass democracy based on universal equality. Everything depends on what kind of information people are able to get. And, as we have said, the powerful and wealthy will attempt to control what people know. This issue leads, necessarily, into a discussion of information diffusion and two particular forms of diffusion: rumours and contagion.

Rumour, Contagion, and Moral Panics

In an information society, all social, economic, and political life depends on the quality of the information available. This makes the withholding, piracy, and distortion of information more problematic than ever. In this context, one foreseeable social problem of the future concerns **rumours** and **contagion**, two deviant forms of information flow that can have powerful consequences for societies of the future.

Rumour

In the summer of 1986, during an intense drought, rumours spread through the Dordogne region of France. Allegedly, cloud seeding that was intended to prevent hail and was sponsored by large agricultural enterprises—by Spanish 'tomato barons'—had miscarried, and this had caused the drought. Similar rumours about the Spanish 'tomato barons' had surfaced in 1985 and earlier, during equally severe droughts (Brodu, 1990).

The rumours all contained inaccurate information. While cloud seeding is infamously ineffective at producing rain, there is no evidence that it can prevent rain. Such rumours appeal to people in a time of drought because of popular superstition and the general unreliability of techniques for controlling the weather. Nevertheless, other factors enter in as well. These rumours have a political content that is just barely hidden below the surface. There is a reason the French rumour mongers blamed Spanish 'tomato barons'. After all, the French and Spanish people have been military and economic rivals for over 500 years. Moreover, the alleged wrongdoers were barons—people of wealth and standing. Rumours often contain allegations of wrongdoing by the powerful against the powerless. By studying rumours, we learn something valuable about the organization of society, and also about the organization of people's fantasy lives.

Sociologists view rumours as 'improvised news' (Shibutani, 1966). From this standpoint, rumours are closer to other forms of individual and collective information seeking than they are to dreaming and escapism: a rumour is information provided to solve to an ill-defined problem. In creating a rumour, members of society draw on their limited stock of cognitive resources, but in a purposeful manner. Rumours that convey stereotypes or archetypal images are more likely than other rumours to gain currency in the media and in public discourse and are more resistant to denial. The most 'successful' rumours correspond to what people hope or fear will come true rather than to what has really happened. The power of the rumour is not in its outburst, but in its making visible otherwise invisible relations.

Contagion

Like rumours, popular anxieties can spread rapidly. Often they reflect anxieties about immoral behaviour. For example, during World War I, across Great Britain, young women were seemingly so attracted to men in military uniform that

---

BOX 12.3
Misinformation Contributes to Racism

When the Muslims for Peace and Justice held a conference in Regina this month to discuss what it means to be Muslim in Canada since Sept. 11, 2001, the room was filled with frustration and pessimism.

Keynote speaker Imam Shabir Ally made clear that the frustration stemmed from the understanding that their religion was founded on a desire to bring peace to a troubled world. And the pessimism stemmed from the difficulty Canadian Muslims are having in convincing fellow citizens that peace is still the fundamental value of their religion.

There is little doubt that the Sept. 11 attack on the United States was one of the worst public relations disasters of modern times for the Muslim faith. But the stereotype of Arabs or Muslims as terrorists had already been firmly established in western culture. The image of a Muslim hijacking a plane had become so common that it was a staple of popular media and even comedy.

These popular images bear little resemblance to reality for most of the world's billion Muslims. Nevertheless, they are so ingrained in our mythology that the first action taken when a white-supremacist anarchist blew up a federal building in Oklahoma was to hold any Muslim or Arabic-looking travelers until the culprit could be found.

It's difficult for those of us who don't look Arabic to appreciate how painful it must be to have your government question your loyalty, based on a stereotype. It's doubly painful given that Canada prides itself on its liberal values and multiculturalism.

SOURCE: 'Stereotyping Fatal to Peace', *Saskatoon Star Phoenix*, 17 October 2002.

---

they behaved in what people considered immodest and sexually dangerous ways. People called the outbreak of licentiousness 'khaki fever'. This wartime loss of social control caused public anxiety over young women's social and sexual behaviour. 'Khaki fever' appeared to infect not only the morally lax poor, but even girls from the normally upstanding middle class. Today, we understand that this fear of 'khaki fever' was symptomatic of a change from the secretiveness of the nineteenth century to a more open public display of feminine sexuality in the twentieth century. In turn, the growing openness of sexual display went along with a growing social and sexual independence for women (Woollacott, 1994).

This supposed outbreak of female sexuality illustrates many elements of contagion that need discussion. Most important, with contagion a new behaviour spreads rapidly. People fear that immorality is 'catching', or infecting everyone. The fear is itself contagious, producing what sociologists now call a *moral panic*.

Contagion, like *contact*, comes from the Latin word for 'touching'. It refers to the passing on of something—whether information, behaviour, or disease—by direct contact or touch. In this respect, contagion is merely one form of diffusion. It is also a form of diffusion about which people have old and deep beliefs. The *magical law of contagion*, a traditional belief, holds that properties, both physical and moral, can be transferred through contact, so that some essence passes from source to recipient. Even today, some people act as though they fear that poverty or mental or physical deformity may be catching. This helps to explain the stigmatization and marginalization of some groups.

All forms of diffusion, contagion included, have certain common features. As compared with information that is broadcast, information that is diffused relies on personal connection. For diffusion to occur, a relevant exposure link must connect the people involved. The person receiving it must accept the object of diffusion—for example, a rumour. Having once received the rumour, the recipient continues to have it indefinitely. The same rumour (or other object of diffusion) cannot diffuse twice to same person. These basic features of diffusion are also basic features of contagion, and, like diffusion, contagion is strongly locational. It spreads information spatially, from near the source to farther away. Therefore, the object of contagion shows concentration in space. Over time, the concentrations gradually grow, spread out, and move.

Many view contagion as the unreflective, irrational adoption of a trivial or worthless new behaviour. In this respect, contagion is a dis-

---

BOX 12.4
The Spread of Scientific Misinformation

The 20th century has been the century of the overcooked environmental/health scare. Certainly, news of one impending environmental crisis or another has been a dominant theme of global media coverage, especially in the past 40 years. Many of these stories have more resembled works of the imagination than works of science. Others, while having a basis in fact, have been exaggerated by activist groups with political agendas. The most imaginative and exaggerated of the century's scares follow.

Alar, Apples and Childhood Cancer

The great apple scare of the century was launched on Feb. 26, 1989, when CBS beamed 60 Minutes into the living rooms of 40 million to 50 million people. With a skull and crossbones overlaying a red apple as a backdrop, Ed Bradley alleged that Alar, a chemical sprayed on apples to keep them on the trees longer, presented a high cancer risk to humans, especially young children, which the US Environmental Protection Agency had dangerously underestimated.

Apples and apple products were soon pulled from stores and banned from schools. Many years and millions of dollars in studies later, Alar received a clean bill of health, as it had originally in 1968. Yet by then the damage had already been done to apple growers and to the public's confidence in its food. Today, even scientists sympathetic to environmental causes admit the great apple scare had nothing to do with science.

Climate Change and Greenhouse Gas Warming

Before the Industrial Revolution, the concentration of carbon dioxide in the atmosphere was about 280 parts per million. Today it is above 350 ppm. This rise in carbon dioxide, one of many so-called greenhouse, or heat-trapping, gases in the atmosphere, has led many scientists to predict an era of global warming and climate change, with disastrous consequences, unless we reduce emissions from combustion of fossil fuels.

While the public frequently assumes global warming to be established scientific fact, a large part of the 'evidence' for it comes from computer simulations. For years the computers pegged the estimated average global temperature increase range between 1.5 and 4.5 degrees Celsius, assuming a continued rise in greenhouse gas concentration. More recently, models that include the effects of clouds and deep ocean currents predict an increase half as large.

The measured increase of 0.5 to 1.0 degree Celsius in the average global temperature in the

continued

past century still does not exceed the average noise level of plus or minus 1 degree of natural climate variability. Further, some scientists have argued that much of this increase may be due to heat-island effects created by expanding cities. Climate complexity will no doubt continue to test the limits of science. Much is at stake, both economically and environmentally, in the course of future climate policy.

The cost of these scares, though huge, extends far beyond economics. The hysteria has contributed to a century-long decline in the value we once placed on objectivity, rational thought and human creativity. Yet there is a silver lining, too. These stories have led the media to increase reporting of science generally, a trend that will no doubt enhance the public's scientific literacy, and our ability to judge.

SOURCE: Michael LeGault, 'The Century of Science Scares', *National Post*, 30 December 1999, national edition, C7.

paraging view of diffusion and innovation, associated with mass or popular rather than elite behaviour. Unlike much other innovative behaviour, contagious behaviours are supposedly impulsive (not rational), possibly destructive (not adaptive), ambiguous (not predictable), and group-driven (not fitted to individual needs). In this view, contagion relies on what we might call a snowball effect. A mass or crowd of undifferentiated, irrational actors collects through contagion and then behaves in mindless ways.

Thus, contagion is a form of diffusion that produces group activity that is disapproved of. This is largely how people viewed 'khaki fever' at the time. Like a contagious disease—measles or the common cold—a contagious behaviour follows special rules. First, it requires the simultaneous actions of multiple senders in order to build up a critical mass of influence on the receiver. Second, receivers vary in their openness to the message; some are not merely indifferent, they actively resist it. This not only prevents their adoption of the information, but may even discourage the information sender from making further attempts. Senders are likely to stop their efforts after a certain time. The message 'dies out'—that is, loses its currency—or the sender becomes discouraged and does not attempt to send the message. Said another way, people stop trying to change other people's behaviour when they feel they have made themselves look like idiots.

Some flow processes—epidemics, protest movements, popular fads, high divorce rates—only happen if a few people become involved and remain involved. If the new information or behaviour does not catch on, the spread will decline and die out. Epidemics are most common in populations in which uninfected people have a high average vulnerability and a frequent rate of contact with infected (or information-bearing) individuals.

What is remarkable about collective behaviour is that different people with different motives may generate the same behaviour. Moral panics arise when people come to believe in the existence of a threat from new forms of deviance. However, irrationality is not essential or primary to collective behaviour; outsiders often wrongly assume it. For example, ordinary people respond effectively when people in authority fail to do so. Formal organizations and government often fail to mobilize as quickly as expected because of flaws in emergency response planning. Typically, communication deficiencies, not motivational deficiencies, undermine response efficiency and lead to coordination problems.

There are good sociological (that is, organizational) reasons for seemingly irrational behaviour. Take the crowd crush at Hillsborough Stadium in Sheffield, England, in 1989. A belief that gaining access to the soccer game being played there was both possible and desirable motivated this crush, despite a shortage of space and tickets. Structural conduciveness was created through media hype, poor distribution of tickets, and a market differentiated between ticket-holders and non-ticket-holders. Uncertainty about the possibility of gaining access to the match contributed to the general belief that access could be gained by force. Media hype, poor organization, and peers all pushed toward action. Poor police and stadium security weakened the social control (Lewis and Kelsey, 1994).

Another explanation of the coincidence of irrationality and catastrophe is not that normal people become beastly, but that beastly people come to appear normal. At the outbreak of wars, for example, psychopaths and other social outcasts are able to shift attention away from their personal problems and express politically violent emotions against internal and external enemies. Likewise, disasters and emergencies of other kinds are likely to bring the beasts out of the woodwork without turning normal people into beasts.

Contagion, then, is a process of diffusion that is especially important to sociologists, particularly in an information society, because it addresses the question of how individuals link together and eventually form large groups capable of collective action. Out of pairs—through aggregation—come networks, movements, parties, and other large organizations. Central to this transformation is the flow of information, which we have been calling *diffusion*, and the aggregative process that is contagion. Like other forms of diffusion, contagion passes information through networks of personal contact, although important information may also pass by means of broadcast.

This change, like others we have discussed, often passes through stable networks of personal relations. As we have seen, wrong information, in the form of stereotypes and rumours, can produce a great deal of social harm. It is our job as educated people to learn the difference between facts and fantasies. It is our job as sociologists to learn how to understand and, if possible, control the creation of fantasy. If we fail to do so, the information society will become a misinformation society, and moral panics will be more common than not. Eventually, all information will lose credibility.

The Need for Modest Optimism

It would be appropriate to end this book on a note of optimism that we will eventually be able to foresee and solve our social problems better than we can today. What are the chances that we will be able to do this in future, and what do we need to do as sociologists to make this possible?

The answer to this question becomes clearer when we consider our knowledge, or lack thereof, in relation to the basic social processes that underlie social problems. Consider, for example, our understanding of the flows—diffusion, migration, mobility, renewal (or turnover), for example—that are the basis of all social organization. We know that these flows have certain common elements: source, length, volume, rate. They move through channels and, as such, are subject to flooding and damming.

We know that flow processes are locational changes over time. Sometimes they are processes of change *in* the social system, and sometimes they are so great that they bring about processes of change *of* the social system. We know that flows are both markers and makers of social structure. In effect, what we call *social structure* is merely frozen change—flow processes caught a moment of time.

Time is the backdrop for studying both change and structure. This fact means that as sociologists, we need to have a clear understanding of what we mean by *correlation*, *causation*, and *theory*. Time is of the essence in any social theory. To study flows in time is to study all of the central issues in social science. But what do we actually know about the timetable of everyday flows? We must end this book by confessing that we know very little about the everyday processes that make up the large processes and structures that we call *social problems*.

Here are some things sociologists will, eventually, have to find out:

How long it takes for
- a rumour to pass through a town
- a fad or fashion to die out
- migrant families to assimilate
- a person to find a mate
- a chat room to form in cyberspace
- a jury to decide a murder case

What the half-life is of
- a job search
- a spy network
- a household

What the age structure (or life expectancy, or average age) is of
- 100 Web sites in cyberspace
- 100 social support networks in Quebec
- 100 best-selling books in English

Here are some more difficult, but somewhat easier, problems to which we need to find the answers:

Under what conditions it will take half as much time as usual for
- a rumour to pass through a town
- a fad or fashion to die out
- a secret to be exposed

What the optimal length of time is for
- a person to find a mate
- a chat room to form in cyberspace
- a jury to decide a murder case

How we might speed up
- the completion of a job search
- the discovery of a spy network
- the building of a social support network

How we can double the rate of renewal of
- the Canadian system of beliefs
- the 100 best-selling books in English
- information technology used in British Columbia

To answer these questions, sociologists will need to go about 'normal' science in a different way. We have to start doing this, and sociology will come around to this point of view in due course. Finding the answers to these hard and easier questions will take general agreement on research strategies and research priorities.

So, as to whether we will eventually be able to foresee and solve our social problems better than we can today, the chances are good in the foreseeable future. We know what we need to do as sociologists to make this possible, and all that remains is the doing of it.

In the introduction to this book, introducing social problems, we noted that sociology has historically been a moral discipline. Sociologists who study social problems often think of themselves as engaged in a moral enterprise whose goal is to improve human societies through social change. Seven value preferences guide their enquiries: life over death, health over sickness, knowing over not knowing, cooperation over conflict, freedom of movement over physical restraint, self-determination over direction by others, and freedom of expression over censorship (Alvarez, 2001).

We have demonstrated in this book that sociology—social science more generally, and systematic research most generally of all—has made progress in each of these areas. We know more than we did a decade or a century ago. Our progress is slow and we forget some of what we knew as we move forward, so our progress is lurching, unsteady, and uncertain. Modern societies, it turns out, are not as liberating as people living 200 or 500 years ago expected they would be. Leonardo da Vinci, Erasmus, John Stuart Mill, and Voltaire would be surprised and not necessarily pleased with many of the things to see in an average Canadian city today. Some changes would seem like a parody of their hopes and aspirations.

Yet the dream of human betterment through science and knowledge remains. Although some claim that we are a postmodern society, a majority

Progress, or real solutions for social problems, is often painstakingly slow. Modern societies are not as liberating as the classic social thinkers anticipated 200 years ago. By focusing on the ties that bond people rather than perceived differences, Canadian society can truly evolve. One example is the broadening concept of family to include gay marriages. (Donald Weber)

of people still look to science and technology for entertainment, comfort, safety, and reduced drudgery at work and home. Though religious fundamentalism prevails in some parts of the world, giving people there a needed sense of identity and hope for their own future, religion in the West is post-biblical. Unlike the writers of the Old Testament, we do not believe that disaster—a fall from grace and banishment from Eden—is an inevitable result of knowledge. We believe that knowledge is generally better than ignorance and that more people knowing the truth is better than fewer—only priests and gods—knowing the truth.

Fear and ignorance, as we have seen in our discussions of diffusion, are the context within which lies and errors spread. They support stigma, stereotyping, discrimination, vilification, and warfare. There are many sources of fear, not least the deprivation and violence that flow from

vast social inequality. It is difficult, therefore, to do much about fear by writing or reading a book. Ignorance, however, is something we *can* address, and begin to remedy, by spreading information. Freedom of expression is not only a good in itself, one of our seven guiding values; it is also a means to achieving the other six.

This book has not presented the answers or solutions to our most pressing social problems, but it has succeeded in asking many of the most pertinent questions and in giving some indication of where the relevant research is headed. Much more needs to be done, as we have seen. The readers of this book are prime candidates for doing this needed work. We hope that you are inspired, not turned off, by the importance of the work before us. Given the hopes of humanity, we have no choice but to make the effort.

Concluding Remarks

Knowledge is, to some extent, empowering. As we have seen, wrong information, in the form of stereotypes and rumours, can produce a great deal of social harm. It is our job as educated people to learn the difference between facts and fantasies. It is our job as sociologists to learn how to understand and, if possible, control the creation of fantasy, in the belief that understanding public issues is better than not understanding them. Armed with a greater understanding of the social problems we face, we can pursue solutions through both individual and collective actions. Individual solutions are often easier to achieve, but in the end collective solutions are the only road to long-lasting changes.

As this book has shown, there are a few master problems—in particular, inequality and exclusion, ignorance and misinformation—and they play out in many combinations and historical variations. Our future as a species will depend on our ability to understand and moderate the more harmful versions of these problems. Cyberspace in particular offers us a variety of exciting, challenging, and dangerous opportunities: to create virtual communities that have no visible location, to participate in world events almost instantaneously, and to observe human life in every part of the world. Cyberspace reduces the constraints of space and time to nearly zero. In doing so, it plunges us mere mortals into a larger, faster-moving frog pond than any we have ever known before. Can we handle the challenge?

As with all technological advancement in the last two centuries, the development of cyberspace makes it more likely that we can build a better mousetrap *and* a better gas chamber; we can cure our deadly diseases *and* create new ones; we can tell each other more truths *and* more lies—more quickly (and persuasively) than ever before. How we will survive this ordeal by information remains to be seen.

Nothing shows more clearly than cyberspace the opportunities and dangers that face humanity when new information technology produces 'new societies' without tradition or regulation. Nothing shows more clearly than futures studies the desire of humanity to imagine and, through imagination, to control the future.

Questions for Critical Thought

1. Can you think of a social problem (one not in the text) that will not likely be solved in the near future? Why will this be so? Can you think of one that will not be an issue in the near future? Why will it not be?
2. Future predictions are often used to determine several possible alternative futures. What are some alternative futures regarding the social issues surrounding environmental damage?
3. How has the advent of the Internet affected your life? Do you find that you have more or less information available? Is this information easier or harder to locate? Has its quality gone up or down?
4. The rate at which information spreads is related to its content. Consider the daily newspaper versus tabloids, for example; how many people know the reasons for the conflict in the Middle East compared with who's dating whom in Hollywood? Can you think of any other current examples?
5. Knowing how rumours and contagions spread, what are some ideas on ways we can counteract or slow down this flow?

Recommended Readings

Daphna Birenbaum-Carmeli, Yoram S. Carmeli, and Rina Cohen, 'Our First "IVF Baby": Israel and Canada's Press Coverage of Procreative Technology', *International Journal of Sociology and Social Policy*, 20, no. 7 (2000): 1–38.

This article compares the Israeli and Canadian response to IVF technologies. Using the news coverage in each country, the authors cite the difference in the two nations' cultures as an explanation of their differing levels of enthusiasm regarding IVF technology.

Neena L. Chappell and Margaret J. Penning, 'Sociology of Aging in Canada: Issues for the Millennium', *Canadian Journal on Aging*, 20, suppl. (2001): 82–110.

As Canada's population ages, one critical question is how Canadian society can cope with the new strains on our health care system and family relations.

Crystale Purvis Cooper and Darcie Yukimua, 'Science Writers' Reactions to a Medical "Breakthrough" Story', *Social Science and Medicine*, 54 (2002): 1887–96.

After a *New York Times* story boosted the hopes of cancer patients, 60 science writers from the United States, Canada, and Great Britain posted e-mail messages to the discussion list of the National Association of Science Writers over a period of 12 days in a discussion on the issue of news coverage of medical 'breakthroughs'. The article analyzes these messages and finds suggestions for the future news coverage.

Jim Dator, 'Futures Studies and Sustainable Community Development', paper presented at the First World Futures-Creating Seminar, Renewing Community as Sustainable Global Village, August 1993, Goshiki-cho, Japan; available at <www.soc.hawaii.edu/future/dator.html>.

One of the creators of educational television in Ontario (TVOntario), Jim Dator went on to found the Hawaii Research Center for Futures Studies (at the University of Hawaii) and served as president of the World Futures Studies Federation. His long list of books and papers includes recent works on environmental and sustainability issues.

Johan Galtung and Sohail Inayatullah, *Macrohistory and Macrohistorians: Perspectives on Individual, Social, and Civilizational Change* (Westport, CT: Praeger, 1997).

The essays in this volume focus on historians—from Ibn Khaldhun to Oswald Spengler and from Piritim Sorokin to Arnold Toynbee—who have helped shape our way of conceiving of ourselves.

Sohail Inayatullah and Susan Leggett, eds, *Transforming Communication: Technology, Sustainability and Future Generation* (Westport, CT: Praeger, 2002).

The contributors argue that to create sustainable futures, new ways must be found to make communication inclusive, participatory, and mindful of future generations.

Richard Slaughter, 'A New Framework for Environmental Scanning', *Foresight: The Journal of Futures Studies, Strategic Thinking and Policy*, 1, no 5 (1999); available at <http://members.ams.chello.nl/f.visser3/wilber/slaughter2.html>.

Current president of the World Futures Studies Federation, director and foundation professor of foresight at the Australian Foresight Institute (at Swinburne University), Slaughter has been primarily interested in questions of methodology: that is, how we can know the future, and how we can shape it.

Recommended Web Sites

Environment Canada

www.ec.gc.ca

This government Web site offers information on current environmental issues in Canada and abroad. There are links to various programs for Canadians that can help with the environment.

Greenpeace

www.greenpeace.ca

Greenpeace is an activist organization that operates to preserve the earth's natural environment. Along with causes Greenpeace works on, this Web site has information about current environmental issues and discussion of their effects in the future.

NASA
www.nasa.gov

The National Aeronautics and Space Administration, in addition to space exploration, also researches a wide variety of up-and-coming technologies.

World Health Organization
www.who.int

The World Health Organization is the health agency of the United Nations. It sets out to achieve the highest level of health for people around the world.

The site contains information about current and future health issues around the world.

World Bank
www.worldbank.org

A supporter of globalization, the World Bank helps poor developing countries fight poverty and establish economic stability and growth. The World Bank Web site has readings, statistics, and general information about globalization.

References

Alvarez, Rodolfo. 2001. 'The Social Problem as an Enterprise: Values as a Defining Factor'. *Social Problems*, 48: 3–10.

Bell, Wendell. 1997. *Foundations of Futures Studies: Human Science for a New Era*. Vol. 1. *History, Purposes, and Knowledge*. New Brunswick, NJ: Transaction.

Brodu, Jean-Louis. 1990. 'A Rumor of Drought'. *Communications*, 52: 85–97.

Chappell, Neena. 2002. 'Home and Families in the Future'. Paper presented at the World Congress of the International Sociological Association, Brisbane, Australia.

Chomsky, Noam. 1999. 'Language Design'. In *Predictions*, edited by Sian Griffiths, 30–2. New York: Oxford University Press.

Commission on the Future of Health Care in Canada. 2002. *Building on Values: The Future of Health Care in Canada: Final Report*. Ottawa: Health Canada.

Eisenstein, Elizabeth L. 1979. *The Printing Press as an Agent of Change: Communications and Cultural Transformations in Early Modern Europe*. 2 vols. Cambridge, UK: Cambridge University Press.

'The Futurists: Looking Toward A.D. 2000'. 1966. *Time*, 25 February, 32–3.

George, Henry. 1898. *Social Problems*. New York: Doubleday and McClure.

Gerlander, Maija, and Eeva Takala. 1997. 'Relating Electronically: Interpersonality in the Net'. *Nordicom Review*, 18, no. 2: 77–81.

Gould, Stephen Jay. 1999. 'Unpredictable Patterns'. In *Predictions*, edited by Sian Griffiths, 145–6. New York: Oxford University Press.

Lewis, Jerry M., and Michael L. Kelsey. 1994. 'The Crowd Crush at Hillsborough: The Collective Behavior of an Entertainment Crush'. In *Disasters, Collective Behavior, and Social Organization*, edited by Russell R. Dynes and Kathleen J. Tierney, 190–206. Newark: University of Delaware Press.

Malthus, Thomas R. [1798] 1959. *Population: The First Essay*. Ann Arbor: University of Michigan Press.

Margolis, Jonathan. 2000. *A Brief History of Tomorrow: The Future, Past and Present*. London: Bloomsbury.

Rose, Mark. 1993. *Authors and Owners: The Invention of Copyright*. Cambridge, MA: Harvard University Press.

Rowland, F. Sherwood. 1999. 'Sequestration'. In *Predictions*, edited by Sian Griffiths, 208–11. New York: Oxford University Press.

Shibutani, Tamotsu. 1966. *Improvised News: A Sociological Study of Rumor*. Indianapolis, IN: Bobbs-Merrill, 1966.

Towne, Ezra Thayer. 1916. *Social Problems: A Study of Present Day Social Conditions*. New York: Macmillan.

Wells, H.G. 1902. *Anticipations of the Reaction of Mechanical and Scientific Progress upon Human Life and Thought*. New York: Harper.

'What Is Futures Studies?' 2001. University of Houston–Clear Lake. Available at <www.cl.uh.edu/futureweb/futdef.html>, accessed 2 February 2003.

Wilson, David A. 2000. *The History of the Future*. Toronto: McArthur and Company.

Woollacott, Angela. 1994. ' "Khaki Fever" and Its Control: Gender, Class, Age and Sexual Morality on the British Homefront in the First World War'. *Journal of Contemporary History*, 29: 325–47.

World Future Society. 2001. 'Forecasts'. Available at <www.wfs.org/forecasts.htm>, accessed 22 August 2001.

Glossary

Contagion A passing on of something, be it information, behaviour, or disease, by direct contact or touch.

Cyberspace The abstract location where information is said to be exchanged in the Information Age.

Cyberterrorism A means of attack that relies not on physical damage, but on crippling the enemy's technology and communications infrastructure.

Digital divide The separation between those who have access to technology ('haves') and those who do not ('have-nots').

Futures studies The area of sociology that is concerned with the forecasting of possible future scenarios in order to prepare for and shape what may come.

Genetic manipulation The altering of genes to produce a more desirable physical makeup.

Globalization Denationalization of local politic, markets, and legal systems leading to the formation of a global economy.

Information Age A historical time in which information of all forms is quickly and easily accessible via the Internet and computers.

Information economy An economy in which information in treated like any other commodity and can be bought, sold, traded, and so on.

Rumour A type of information diffusion in which the content is not pure misinformation but is conceived for a purpose with limited reliability.

Appendix

The Sociological Study of Social Problems

Although few students reading this book will pursue a career in social science research, all readers will benefit from understanding the processes by which such research is conducted. Without such an understanding, they cannot hope to decode the information provided in newspapers, magazines, and television. Often social science findings are reported in the media in such a way as to produce the most attention-grabbing headlines. To remain well informed, then, it is necessary to look beyond the results as filtered and presented by the media and interest groups and to understand the research as it was originally conducted by the investigators. The following, then, is a brief overview of the ways in which sociological research on social problems is performed.

Stages of a Research Study

The first step in conducting a research study of any kind, sociological or otherwise, is to come up with a research question: 'What do I want to investigate?'

Sometimes the topic of study is derived from the researcher's personal interests or life experience. For instance, a sociologist whose parents divorced when he or she was still a child may want to explore the factors that contribute to an increased risk of marital separation, or the effects of divorce and custodial battles on the mental health of young people. Other researchers are motivated by a desire to enhance the collective understanding of human nature or to improve the social environment around them. They may seek the answers to questions such as 'What is the most effective way to dispense emergency treatment and resources to victims of a natural disaster?' or 'How do a patient's race and ethnicity

affect the quality and quantity of treatment in an inner-city medical clinic?' Still others are contracted by government ministries or private companies to answer a specific question, the answer to which has important consequences for policy making.

Regardless of their content, the best research questions are specific enough that they can be answered by a well-designed study generating a manageable amount of data over a reasonable period of time, but also broad enough that the results have some significance and applicability to the real world.

Having formulated a research question, the investigator's next step is to review the literature, that is, the published material that documents what is already known about the topic. A review of past research not only helps narrow a researcher's own research project, but also provides ideas about how to conduct the study.

Once the researcher has a good understanding of the current state of research in the topic of interest, she or he may formulate a *hypothesis*, an educated guess about how one or more variables affect others. *Variables* are any measurable events, characteristics, or properties that have the capacity to change in value or quality.

In any scientific study, variables must be operationally defined; that is, it must be made clear how variables will be described and measured by the investigator. For instance, the term *family* may refer to immediate family members (that is, father, mother, and their biological and adoptive children) or it may also include extended relatives (aunts, uncles, grandparents, nephews, nieces, and so on) depending on the researcher's topic or research problem. Similarly, some characteristics may be subjectively defined by different research subjects. Thus, it is necessary to formulate a standard definition of what is meant by a term before a study is conducted. 'Patriotism', for example, might be measured by subjects' responses to the question

'How important is your nationality to your overall sense of self-identity?' or by the amount of knowledge that they possess about their country of residence.

Hypotheses are statements about how a *dependent variable (DV)*—the variable of interest that the researcher is attempting to explain—is affected by an *independent variable (IV)*—the variable that the researcher believes will explain the changes to the dependent variable. In a study of the effects of marital separation on the mental well-being of children, the IV might be types of family background; the DV is the children's mental health. In many sociological studies, several IVs are measured and assessed against one or more DVs, an indication of both the complexity of the subject material and the research task that the sociologists face.

Types of Research Methods

Once the researcher has formulated a research question and derived a hypothesis, the next step is to actually perform the study and collect data to analyze. The majority of sociological research is conducted using one of four research methods or some combination of them.

Experiments

When most people think of scientific experiments, they envision a researcher in a white lab coat, surrounded by test tubes and Bunsen burners in a laboratory. In truth, experiments are much more varied than what the stereotype might suggest; they include any procedure that involves the manipulation of the IVs and the observation of the effects on the DVs.

To ensure that the experimental manipulation was indeed the cause of the changes observed in the DV, such studies are often carried out using several groups of subjects, some of which receive the experimental treatment(s)—that is, the IVs—and a *control group* comprising similar individuals who do not receive the treat-

ment. The latter may receive a *placebo*, an inert substance or procedure that mimics the effects of receiving a treatment but none of the effects of the treatment itself. Thus, any variance between the DVs measured among the experimental and control groups can be attributed to the only factor that differed between them—the type of IV treatment(s) they received.

The primary strength of the experimental method is that it provides good evidence for a causal relationship between IVs and DVs. Unfortunately, experiments can only be performed with small groups in artificial laboratory settings, and only where other factors can be held constant while the IV is being manipulated. Thus, this research approach has two weaknesses: first, it is difficult to generalize experimental findings beyond the lab to the larger population in natural settings, and, second, the experimental method can only be applied to a small percentage of research studies that lend themselves to highly controlled study conditions.

Surveys, Interviews, and Questionnaires

Surveys, which elicit information from subjects through a series of questions, are probably the most popular method of data collection among social scientists. However, because it would be impossible and tedious to administer a survey to every single member of the population of interest (for example, children of divorce, single mothers, Canadians), most survey research is performed using a sample of those being studied. In order for the results to be generalizable beyond the small group who actually complete the study, great efforts must be made to ensure that the sample is representative of the entire population—that is, that it is a *representative sample*. Thus, to arrive at a representative sample of, say, Canadians, a researcher would have to ensure that the proportions of men, women, age groups, racial and ethnic groups, religious groups, socioeconomic classes, and regions in the survey accurately reflect their proportions in the real world.

After a representative sample is selected, the researcher can choose to either interview each subject or provide the subjects with pre-constructed questionnaires. Interviews are advantageous for several reasons. One is that interviewers can clarify questions for subjects and pose follow-up questions to elicit further information. As a result, interviews are particularly suited to studies in which a significant amount of detailed knowledge is required. Another benefit of the interview method is that the researcher can study groups that are typically inaccessible using other forms of data collection. For example, Thomas Plate's study of the advantages and disadvantages of a career in the criminal underworld (1975) was performed almost exclusively through informal interviews; it would have been more difficult to elicit the same data had he been restricted to administering pencil-and-paper questionnaires to the burglars and hit men who comprised his subjects.

However, because interviews are based on face-to-face interaction between the interviewer and the interviewee, some drawbacks are also present. The most significant is the lack of anonymity afforded to the subject, a concern that becomes especially important when the topic is of a sensitive, threatening, or embarrassing nature, as in studies of drug use, economic resources, sexual abuse, or sexual orientation and sexual behaviour. Many subjects may therefore choose not to participate, while others may censor or alter their responses or even lie to reflect socially desirable habits. A second disadvantage of interviews is the cost that comes with paying trained interviewers to perform the time-consuming work. The time constraint also means that only a small sample of subjects can be interviewed; the results may therefore not be generalizable to the larger population.

Precisely for these reasons, many social scientists opt instead to gather information about their study populations by means of formalized questionnaires. The main advantages of questionnaires correspond to the weaknesses of interviews. Questionnaires are cheaply, easily, and quickly administered to a large number of people. Also, questionnaires can be completed anonymously and in privacy, increasing the likelihood of receiving a frank and honest set of data.

Field Research

A third method of data collection, *field research*, involves observing and studying a target population in its natural setting. Rather than having the subjects come to them, researchers who use this approach go to their subjects. Field research is performed in many settings, including schools, prisons, large corporations, small neighbourhoods, tribal communities, and among the homeless. The obvious benefit of this research method is that the behaviours, values, rituals, customs, beliefs, symbols, and emotions observed are more genuine, in that they are the result neither of manipulation of other variables (as is often the case with experiments) nor of artificial and blunt probing (as is often the case with surveys).

The two general types of field research, participant and non-participant observation, each have their own particular advantages and disadvantages. *Participant observation*, as its name suggests, has the researcher collecting information about the group he or she is studying while participating in their social activities. The main benefit of this approach is the wealth of insight that can be harnessed from an 'inside' look at the population of interest. Since the researcher is actively participating in the local customs, habits, rituals, and norms, she or he can often pick up on the nuances of the culture that might otherwise go unnoticed.

As well, researchers conducting field research must be wary of inadvertently altering their subjects' behaviour merely because of their own presence and status as strangers. By integrating themselves into the group and gaining the trust of their subjects, participant observers minimize the effects of their intrusion into a foreign culture. However, because they become so fully immersed in the practices and beliefs of the host population, these researchers run the risk of losing objectivity and constructing a biased interpretation of observed events. As well, as with in-depth interviews, the small sample size of participant observation may preclude any generalization of findings.

Participant observation offers an insider's perspective. Non-participant observation, in contrast, is the practice of viewing and studying a group from an outsider's perspective, without any significant direct interaction between researcher and subject. This method is desirable if information about a specific group is required but any direct contact would likely disrupt the natural flow of activity and prejudice any resulting observations. In additional to the drawbacks that non-participant research shares with participant observation—potential for researcher bias, small sample size—a further disadvantage is the loss of insight that comes from direct interaction with subjects.

Secondary Data Research and Analysis

In addition to the methods described above, which result in *primary data*—information accumulated at first hand and specifically for a given study by probing a representative sample of subjects—social scientists occasionally analyze *secondary data*—information that has already been gathered by another researcher or organization, or that exists in historical documents and official records.

The main benefit of secondary data analysis is that it can be performed without disturbing the subjects who originally provided the source material. As well, it can be used in cases in which the subjects refuse to participate or are unavailable for interview (for example, subjects in a historical sociological study who are now deceased). For these reasons, another name for this method is *unobtrusive research*. The primary drawback is that because the data was collected by a separate agency or researcher, often for an unrelated purpose, the information may not be entirely complete, accurate, or in accordance with the present researcher's specific needs.

Concluding Remarks

Today, there is no single model of analysis in social science, but rather a set of more or less closely related approaches for exploring data and the links between macro and micro levels of reality.

In his fascinating book *Once Upon a Number* (1998), the great popularizer of mathematics John Allen Paulos points out some differences and similarities between stories and statistics. Statistics, typically, address generalities: the characteristics of large populations and large trends, for example. These generalities are so large that we can scarcely hope to picture individuals who personify them. Largely for this reason, statistics often leave people cold; nonetheless, they capture the 'truth' about a population because they are usually based on an unbiased sampling of that population. They are about people just like us, yet they fail to move us. Maybe this is part of the reason people are so willing to believe that statistics are easily manipulated into telling us great lies.

By contrast, the best stories are particular, not general; they sketch particular people caught in particular dramas at a particular time and place. Despite their particularity, stories often capture our interest in a way that statistics do not. Stories also tell 'truths' about the human condition. In the end, every population is just the sum and the product of the unique stories that make it up. Clearly, statistics and stories are just two sides of the same coin, the forest and the trees respectively. Both are true, and both speak to different parts of our need to know the truth.

And just as statistics have a mathematical logic, so too do stories. They have logical structures in the same sense that pieces of music (for example, sonatas and symphonies) do. Good authors (and good composers) know these standard forms and genres of exposition. Their skilful manipulation is largely the reason why people respond to them emotionally, as they often do. It is unclear whether these forms are, in some sense, essential and universal—whether, for example, every successful love story (or sonata) will necessarily have the same structure, wherever and whenever it is written—or whether they all merely reflect particular features of a time, culture, or civilization. In either event, successful stories are no more random than the social statistics describing a crime rate or a population of families. There is order in good writing just as there is in society itself.

These points are important for two reasons. First, they affirm the essential compatibility of statistical analysis and storytelling, quantitative and qualitative analysis, 'scientific' and 'interpretive' approaches to reality. More than ever, social scientists in every discipline recognize the need to bring these approaches together in their respective research enterprises. We rely on all of these skills and insights in discussing social problems in this book. Second, like statistics and stories, people's lives reflect both public issues and personal troubles—the duality that C. Wright Mills (1959) stressed in defining 'the sociological imagination'. There is no good sociological analysis of social problems without recognizing this duality.

References

Mills, C. Wright. 1959. *The Sociological Imagination*. London: Oxford University Press.

Paulos, John Allen. 1998. *Once upon a Number: The Hidden Mathematical Logic of Stories*. New York: Basic Books.

Plate, Thomas Gordon. 1975. *Crime Pays! An Inside Look at Burglars, Car Thieves, Loan Sharks, Hit Men, Fences, and Other Professionals in Crime*. New York: Simon & Schuster.

Index